Praise for *The Nightingale's Song*

"[A] significant contribution to our understanding of recent political and military history. More than that, it is a fascinating chronicle of the human element behind all history, a story of ambition and sacrifice and how good men can go bad and not-so-good men can skate away. . . . Mr. Timberg writes like the former Marine he is. That's not to say he doesn't write well; only that he can be brutally frank, wielding his pen like a K-bar combat knife."

—Nicholas Proffitt, *The New York Times Book Review*

"A tough and fascinating study of war, heroism, politics, and the American psyche at a profound cultural divide . . . *The Nightingale's Song* cannily differentiates its five main characters, whose portraits have a novelistic fascination."

—Lance Morrow, *Time*

"This is an amazing piece of work that could make you cry over descriptions of bravery so bold and so big that you wonder how our country deserves such men who step up to the plate in time of trouble. . . . It is about the war in Vietnam. It is about politics. It is about character. It is about the soul of a nation. . . . This is a stunning book."

—Mike Barnicle, *The Boston Globe*

"If you want to read a terrific book about courage and cowardice, honor and betrayal, suffering and death, and the indomitability of the human spirit, get *The Nightingale's Song* by Robert Timberg, a Naval Academy graduate and Marine veteran of Vietnam as well as a superb reporter. It will help you understand why the unhealed wounds of the Vietnam War still pain and divide this American nation and shadow American politics. . . . Robert Timberg explains brilliantly the price paid by those who went, by those who didn't, and by the nation's leadership that failed them."

—Mark Shields, *The Washington Post*

"Historians eager to explain Iran-Contra in terms of hubris and secrecy of the Reagan White House will be startled by this dramatic volume by a former Marine, Annapolis graduate, and current *Baltimore Sun* reporter. . . . With novelistic skillfulness, Timberg weaves the lives of these men from their days at the Academy, through the Vietnam War, and into the tapestry of the eighties. . . . One need not agree with all of Timberg's judgments to find *The Nightingale's Song* both a gripping story and an important contribution to the literature on the Iran-Contra affair. More important, it is an absorbing meditation on the America of the past three decades. When these five men graduated from Annapolis, the last thing anyone would have imagined is that their lives would follow the tortuous paths that Timberg traces. Just as tales at the company level often show more about a battle than the grand, official versions, this book might well be assigned by college teachers as a poignant complement to the history of the era."

—Michael Beschloss, *The Washington Monthly*

"[A] thunderclap of a book . . . Feel the need to at least get a grip on what went so terribly wrong and how? Then head off to the bookstore and lay your money down.

By the time you finish this broadside across America's last forty years, you will understand. Oh, brother, will you understand . . . [D]eserves to become an instant classic."

—Harry Crumpacker, *The Tampa Tribune and Times*

"Timberg gives the reader remarkable insights into the Navy, Iran-Contra, the Reagan White House, and those of Timberg's generation who served in Vietnam in what Reagan called a "noble cause."

—Peter Braestrup, *Nieman Reports*

"The five lives that form the narrative of Robert Timberg's *The Nightingale's Song* would be interesting and well worth reading about individually. Collectively, however, they become something greater than the sum of their parts. They take the reader on an odyssey across some of the hardest terrain of recent American history. . . . The stories of these five men are the story of the great cultural and political fault line of the last three decades, of wounds that will not heal. The stories have been woven into a single narrative that is as seductive and compelling as the best epic novel. This is a book that will last, one that people will be turning to a century from now when they try to make sense of these times."

—Geoffrey Norman, *American Way*

"A sprawling, passionate account of the Vietnam and postwar journeys of Annapolis graduates John Poindexter, Robert McFarlane, Oliver North, John McCain, and James Webb . . . Timberg uses the stories of five men and the transformation of the Naval Academy to chronicle America's loss of innocent faith in itself and the consequences of that loss for a generation."

—*Kirkus Reviews*

"In the growing library of Vietnam literature, much has been written about disillusioned infantrymen, arrogant policymakers, isolated generals, civilian war victims, and the resulting loss of American innocence and national confidence. Missing from that library has been an unheralded cohort—those dedicated, maybe even naive, men who grew up in a muscular postwar America, made careers in uniform fighting for it, and begged and connived to go fight, and unlike brother warriors over two centuries, returned to a society that reviled their sacrifice. . . . Timberg has filled that void with graceful prose and exhaustive reporting. His compelling account of five fellow Annapolis grads . . . is a perceptive, passionate, and more readable companion to Halberstam's much-heralded *The Best and the Brightest*."

—John Kolbe, *The Phoenix Gazette*

"Timberg devises an original theme: The nation's best warriors, stung by the lessons of Vietnam in the 1960s and 1970s, excessively applied their new resolve about American leadership to the 1980s. He uses revealing anecdotes and access to the principals and their peers to weave a mesmerizing tale. . . . He is a seamless storyteller. The fractious potential of describing thirty years in the lives of five men already fully scrutinized by media and prosecutors is avoided with a revealing, conversational account of their experiences and thinking. As a former Marine and now an honored journalist, he has the credibility needed to make his points and criticisms thud with truth."

—Stephen Bell, *The Buffalo News*

"Timberg has done a masterful job by connecting the experiences of these individuals in a way that reflects, as Timberg puts it, the walking wounded of the Vietnam generation. . . . His abiding anger and frustration animate this provocative book."

—Alan Miller, *San Diego Union-Tribune*

"Some years ago pollster and social philosopher Daniel Yankelovich described American attitudes toward Vietnam as an 'undigested lump.' If you think it's since been digested, read Robert Timberg's truly wonderful new book, *The Nightingale's Song*. When you're finished you won't doubt that there is still smoldering anger among many of the nine million Americans who served in the miliary during Vietnam."

—Ben Wattenberg, author of *Values Matter Most*

"Curiously absent from the painful media rehashing of Vietnam occasioned by Robert McNamara's recent memoir was one significant viewpoint: that of the members of the sixties generation who believed in America, who sought careers in fighting its wars, and who believed then and now that support for South Vietnam was right morally and geopolitically. Timberg has written a remarkable book about five such men. . . . They all strove to get into the war, and were all deeply frustrated by the paralyzing restrictions placed on them by the McNamara Pentagon, by the command bureaucracy, and by the military leaders that Mr. Timberg calls 'terminally inept.' . . . Timberg has done a remarkable job of biography. His research is thorough and his approach sympathetic (although not always sympathetic to his subjects). . . . What emerges is an engaging drama of five very different men, complex and talented, whose personal lives intertwine. Each has been enormously shaped by great events, and each has in turn helped to shape the history of our time."

—John Lehman, *The Wall Street Journal*

"*The Nightingale's Song* is a rich collection of gripping and insightful stories."

—Myron A. Marty, *St. Louis Post-Dispatch*

"The product—part biography, part combat leadership instructional, part history, part political science primer—is a captivating work, which I could not put down. Timberg has written a subtle masterpiece."

—Maj. Michael E. McBride, *Marine Corps Gazette*

"Combat changes men. Vietnam was no exception, but its effects on those of us who were there have been puzzling. Robert Timberg does a masterful job of deciphering the consequences of the war on the lives of five key figures of this decade."

—Walter E. Boomer (General, USMC, Ret.)

"Robert Timberg's *The Nightingale's Song* belongs high on the list of memorable literature of the Vietnam War—a book riveting, provocative, and pungent. It is not, nor is it intended to be, a history of the Vietnam War and postwar era, but it polishes facets of that hard stone to brilliance. . . . This is a book of power and dignity, perceptive and painful."

—Woody West, *The Washington Times*

"Part Greek tragedy, part psychodrama, and part political thriller, the book is virtually impossible to put down. Timberg covers childhood traumas of the five men, furnishes a primer on Iran-Contra, and tells hair-raising stories from Annapolis to Vietnam to Central America. But the book is not just about the Naval Academy or Vietnam or Ronald Reagan or Iran-Contra. It is truly about much broader themes, such as the father-son relationship, the meaning of honor, the place of ambition, courage of all kinds, the pain of intergenerational conflict, and, finally, personal renewal and healing. The narrative is a kind of case study, a jumping-off point for an appreciation of more transcendent issues."

—John L. Dailey, *The Virginian-Pilot*

"Part sociobiography, part war memoirs, part investigative reporting, part military and intelligence anecdotes, part psychological study, part Washington political insider commentary, *The Nightingale's Song* is a trail-blazing feat of empathetic, epochal journalism written with a transcendent authority that Halberstam calls "almost hypnotic."

—Scott Disher, *Books in Canada*

"This tale is difficult to categorize but wonderful to read. It is a biography, history, commentary, and Greek tragedy of the five major players in the Iran-Contra affair. However, this book is no more about Iran-Contra than *Moby Dick* is about whaling. The real themes of this morality tale are the twin towers of ambition and Vietnam and their impact on a generation of Americans."

James Stavridis, *Naval War College Review*

"A seamless and stunning retrospective . . . Beyond the Iran-Contra debacle, this book also illuminates a broad segment of America's post-Vietnam political life. . . . Real-life drama, particularly when played out against a backdrop of the highest levels of government, is infinitely more spellbinding than any novel."

—Lowe Bibby, Associated Press

"*The Nightingale's Song* is a most important book dealing with the central figures in the Iran-Contra controversy. . . . The book is a must-read for all Naval Academy alumni, and for all with even the slightest interest in the inner workings of our government. . . . I, for one, couldn't put it down."

—D. E. Church, *Shipmate*

THE
NIGHTINGALE'S
SONG

ROBERT TIMBERG

A TOUCHSTONE BOOK
PUBLISHED BY SIMON & SCHUSTER

TOUCHSTONE
Rockefeller Center
1230 Avenue of the Americas
New York, NY 10020

Copyright © 1995 by Robert Timberg

First Touchstone Edition 1996

TOUCHSTONE and colophon are registered trademarks
of Simon & Schuster Inc.

Designed by Levavi & Levavi

Manufactured in the United States of America

9   10   8

Library of Congress Cataloging-in-Publication Data
Timberg, Robert.
The nightingale's song / Robert Timberg.
p.   cm.
Includes bibliographical references and index.
1. United States—Foreign relations—1981–1989.   2. Iran-Contra
Affair, 1985–1990.   3. United States Naval Academy—Biography.
4. Vietnamese Conflict, 1961–1975—Influence.   I. Title.
E876.T55   1995
327.73—dc20   95-3446
CIP

ISBN 0-684-80301-1
0-684-82673-9 (Pbk.)

The author is grateful for permission to reprint the following:

"American Pie"
Words and Music by Don McLean
© 1971, 1972 Music Corporation of America, a division of MCA, Inc., and Benny
Bird Music. All Rights Controlled and Administered by Music Corporation of
America, a division of MCA, Inc.

"Laws of the Navy" by Ronald Hopwood, from Laws of the Navy and Other Poems, John
Murray (Publishers) Ltd.

"Lost in the Flood" by Bruce Springsteen, 1973, ASCAP

To my wife,
Kelley Andrews,
and to the memory of my mother and father,
Rosemarie Sinnott Timberg (1912–1994) and
Sammy Timberg (1903–1992)

CONTENTS

Book III. The Nightingale's Song

Shattered mirror stare,
Picasso split face,
missing puzzle eye
mannequin's white hands,
horrible hacked head,
jut from camouflage
clothing, unattached.
Still flinching at the shot
that followed death's hit,
his voice echoes
in his pallbearers'
ears as they needlessly
rush him to the waiting
helicopter.
But his dangling arm
grabs some barbed wire
and he pulls them all
down with him, determined
to make them look at
Death.

—"So Much for Immortality," LIEUTENANT COLONEL
RICHARD C. SCHULZE, USMC, Commanding Officer, Third
Battalion, Ninth Marines, Republic of South Vietnam,
June 18, 1969

PROLOGUE

Like much of the rest of the country, Oliver North's old Annapolis and Marine Corps buddies clustered around their television sets in July 1987 for his six days of gripping, in-your-face testimony before the Iran-Contra congressional committees. Several later mentioned a brief exchange between North and House counsel John Nields that was easy to miss if your ears weren't tuned to the right pitch. Nields, his longish hair brushing his shirt collar, referred North to a document.

"That is a chronology that bears the date and time, November 17, 1986, two thousand—which I take is 8:00 P.M.," said Nields.

"Twenty hundred," corrected North.

"I'm sorry, twenty hundred," said Nields.

"Military time," deadpanned North.

Some of North's friends said they laughed like hell, that it was as if Ollie had tipped the table and Nields's carefully prepared case had slid crashing to the floor like so many elegant place settings. It hadn't, of course. What they heard was a generation cracking along a fault line that first appeared two decades earlier and haunted American society ever since.

As a midshipman, Oliver North had narrowly defeated his classmate James Webb in an emotionally charged championship boxing match that they still talk about at Annapolis today. In the years that followed, Webb attained a measure of fame as a novelist while North toiled in the obscurity of the armed forces. But two decades later, North galloped out of the West Wing of the White House to supplant Webb as the best-known member of the Naval Academy Class of 1968. That happened on November 25, 1986, when Ed Meese, Ronald Reagan's attorney general, walked into the White House pressroom and fingered North as the mastermind of what quickly became known as the Iran-Contra affair. At the time, Webb was about to step down after three years as assistant secretary of defense for reserve affairs, an important if not very visible Pentagon post. Like North, Webb had been a highly decorated Marine infantry officer in Vietnam. Webb's fame, though, rested on his writing, not his government service. His first novel, *Fields of Fire*, a widely acclaimed best-seller published in 1978, was an unapologetic tale of a Marine rifle platoon in Vietnam during a few bloody months in 1969. He had since written two more well-received novels, been twice nominated for the Pulitzer Prize, and won an Emmy reporting from Beirut in 1983 for the "Mac-Neil/Lehrer NewsHour." Along the way, he had become the kickass troubadour for a generation of combat veterans for whom reconciliation will invariably be a concept proclaimed by others, always prematurely.

A few weeks after Ollie North became a household name, Jim Webb's retirement plans were shelved when President Reagan named him Secretary of the Navy. Suddenly he was at a potentially critical juncture in the embattled North's chain of command. In military parlance, he was now the reviewing authority for whatever the Navy, of which the Marine Corps is a part, might have in store for North. "Anything that happens to Ollie comes to my desk," Webb sourly told acquaintances. The coolness, it seemed, was mutual. A fellow Marine remembers that when he mentioned to North back in 1983 that Jim Webb had just been sworn in as an assistant defense secretary North abruptly changed the subject.

I was then the White House correspondent for the *Baltimore Sun*. But as it happened, my background was similar to Webb's and North's—Naval Academy, the Marine Corps, Vietnam—and in those early days of Iran-Contra, I picked up a familiar and troubling aroma. Others saw greed, naked ambition, abuse of authority, a breathtaking disdain for Congress and the federal bureaucracy. I saw those things, too, but what I smelled was cordite, burning shitters, the disinfectant odor of hospitals. And somehow, it seemed, the Academy was mixed up in this, too. North's immediate superiors on the National Security Council staff, Robert McFarlane and John Poindexter, were Annapolis men, McFarlane a Marine as well. As the bizarre tale unfolded, blossoming into the gravest constitutional crisis in a decade, I kept picking up echoes of Vietnam and an ever more insistent refrain— Ollie, Bud, and John. I remember thinking that perhaps Iran-Contra was at least in part the bill for Vietnam finally coming due. Although Webb had absolutely no role in Iran-Contra, I put him in the mix because it seemed that the anger and bitterness that infuse his novels might help explain North and the others. I searched his books for clues and found a piece of the puzzle in *Fields of Fire*. Pinned down in a rice paddy, the Webb-like platoon commander, Robert E. Lee

Hodges, Jr., reacts bitterly to orders from those he sees as living a life of ease in the rear:

Fuck 'em. Just fuck 'em. Fuck everybody who doesn't come out here and do this.

At about this time, I met John McCain, a newly elected U.S. senator and an Annapolis classmate of Poindexter. McCain had had the worst war of all, five and a half years in North Vietnamese prison camps, but somehow had moved beyond it. He seemed to fit into the larger story that was struggling to take shape in my mind, though at first I was not sure how.

The five major characters in this book display vast differences in personality and style, but some remarkably similar strains as well. In a way, though none would be comfortable with this characterization, they are secret sharers, men whose experiences at Annapolis and during the Vietnam War and its aftermath illuminate a generation, or a portion of a generation—those who went. Each in his own way stands as a flesh-and-blood repository of that generation's anguish and sense of betrayal. Whatever they later became—hero, hotdog, hustler, or zealot—they were for a time among the best and the brightest this nation had to offer. And in their formative years—at Annapolis and during the Vietnam era—they shared a seemingly unassailable certainty. They believed in America.

So did Ronald Reagan, who made many things possible.

In the fall of 1980, a few weeks before election day, my newspaper job took me to Carter campaign headquarters in Austin, where I hoped to get a sense of how the presidential race was taking shape in Texas, a crucial battleground state. Talking with Carter political aides, still a cocky bunch at that point, I noticed some news clippings tacked to the wall, an irreverent mishmash, like "Far Side" cartoons slapped on the refrigerator door.

The articles on display related to the Reagan campaign, selected to demonstrate the essential looniness of the GOP standard-bearer. The one I remember was about a speech he had given a few days earlier. The headline, as I recall, was "Reagan Calls Vietnam 'Noble Cause.' " One of the Carter guys smirked as he gestured toward it, as if to say, Can you believe this antediluvian horseshit?

I had long since moved beyond thinking of Vietnam as a noble cause, or so I thought. Nobility was not the word that sprang to mind in light of the costly misjudgments and tawdry machinations of the men who got us into the war, then found themselves stumped for a way to get us out.

I was thus surprised to find myself seeing red when Reagan's remark met with ridicule, not just by the Carter aides in Austin but by press colleagues who dismissed it with superior grins and smug put-downs, the newsroom equivalent of boos and hisses.

Years later, as McFarlane's, North's, and Poindexter's necks were being fitted for the noose, that scene in Austin came back to me, made me wonder whether the attitude I encountered there had played any role in driving them to do the things they supposedly had done. I had a strong but vague sense that it had, but I was having trouble putting it together.

Barbara Feldon did it for me. One day in 1987, as Iran-Contra was at its height, old Agent 99, Maxwell Smart's trusty sidekick, spoke at a Labor Department symposium in Washington. Appearing in her capacity as president of the Screen Actors Guild, she told a little story.

"Did you know," she asked, "that a nightingale will never sing its song if it doesn't hear it first?" If it hears robins and wrens, she said, it will never croak a note. "But the moment it hears any part of a nightingale's song, it bursts into this extraordinary music, sophisti-cated, elaborate music, as though it had known it all the time.

"And, of course, it had."

She explained that scientists had learned that the nightingale has a template in its brain that contains all the notes for the music, but that the bird cannot sing unless its song is first triggered by the song of another nightingale.

Feldon's speech had nothing to do with Iran-Contra. However, the tale of the nightingale, it seemed to me, harmonized perfectly with the burgeoning scandal. I began to think of McFarlane, North, and Poin-dexter in their pre–White House years as akin to young nightingales, voices caught in their throats, awaiting the song of another nightin-gale. And, on finally hearing the melody, responding with a vigor and enthusiasm that resulted in several notable achievements, but perhaps Iran-Contra as well.

The "noble cause" speech was part of the song that attracted Mc-Farlane, North, and Poindexter to Reagan. Not that he or the three Naval Academy men who would soon be working for him did not know by then that incompetence, cynicism, and double-dealing had gone into America's failed commitment to South Vietnam. What Rea-gan was saying, and more important, what McFarlane, North, Poin-dexter, and men like them were hearing, was that when they or their fellow soldiers headed off to war they did so believing that the cause was just, indeed, in its way, noble.

They were also hearing Reagan say that even if the mission was later tarnished beyond redemption, that in a distant land under the most brutal of circumstances their friends and comrades, in some cases they themselves, had often acted with a raw courage that by any measure qualified as noble.

Reagan was not a newcomer to the issue. In his unsuccessful 1976 presidential campaign, he had repeatedly declared, to what Reagan biographer Lou Cannon remembers as rafter-shaking applause, "Let us tell those who fought in that war that we will never again ask young men to fight and possibly die in a war our government is afraid to win." By 1980, he had distilled it to its essence: "No more Vietnams."

The Nightingale's Song, as rendered by Ronald Reagan, did more than attempt to recast Vietnam as a noble cause. Throughout that 1980 campaign and well into his presidency Reagan regularly portrayed servicemen not as persons to be feared and reviled—ticking time bombs, baby-killers, and the like—but as men to whom the nation should be grateful, worthy of respect and admiration. To the men of the armed forces, he had a single, unvarying theme: I appreciate what you have done. The whole nation does. Wear your uniforms with pride.

McFarlane, North, and Poindexter, of course, were not nightingales waiting to sing for the first time. At the Academy and for a time thereafter, their voices had been lusty and full-throated, their pride a seemingly immutable part of them. But their vocal cords had been stunned into silence during the Vietnam era by the hostility and ridicule heaped on them by their own countrymen.

Jim Webb had not been silenced. He had said his piece on Vietnam in *Fields of Fire*, but his message—similar to Reagan's, though earthier and more complex—was given resonance by Reagan, according Webb a stature that would carry him to the upper reaches of government during the 1980s.

John McCain had been silent by choice. Vietnam, he knew, could kill dreams as surely as it had once killed men. Best not to monkey with it. Use it when you can, learn from it, but don't get too close to it.

For him, the Nightingale's Song performed different roles. At first it served as his overture, priming the audience for his entrance onto the national political stage. After that it became his theme, a tune that greeted his every appearance without his ever having to sing a note, though occasionally, when it suited his purposes, he did.

In curious ways, the Nightingale's Song played into the lives of all five men. For McFarlane, North, and Poindexter, it gave them back their voices. For Webb and McCain, it provided mood music. The problem was, the first three confused the singer with the song. The song was sweet. The singer, in many important ways, was a fraud.

*   *   *

I started research for this book convinced that a closer look at Iran-Contra, using the lives of McFarlane, Poindexter, and North as back-lighting, would result in a different picture, possibly ennobling, surely less purposely sinister. As for Webb and McCain, their role was not to be a minor or peripheral one, nor is it. I conceived of their lives as illuminating not just the Iran-Contra figures, but that portion of the generation to which they all belonged. That was my plan: to use all five men as metaphors for the emotions, motivations, and beliefs of a legion of well-meaning but ill-starred warriors.

Along the way, I discovered that living, breathing human beings resist transformation into symbols, that they demand their own humanity, for better or worse. In the end, I granted it to them, reluctantly, and not before having to own up to some things about myself I would have preferred to remain dormant, as they had for a quarter century.

Vietnam had left its mark on me, too, but I resolved long ago to put the war behind me. Without quite realizing what I was doing, but not completely oblivious to it, either, I had unplugged myself from old networks, notably Naval Academy and Marine friends. I felt no hostility, in fact the opposite; I just didn't want to talk about it.

Then came Iran-Contra. My reaction to the early disclosures in late 1986 was that I knew more about what had transpired than I knew I knew, as North would later say of Ronald Reagan. Not the details but the motivations, the things that would drive men like North, McFarlane, and Poindexter to act as it seemed they had.

I had another response back then, though it took me a long time to recognize it for what it was. I knew, or thought I knew, what these men had lived through, just as I knew that many of their detractors had employed the vilest forms of subterfuge to avoid those same experiences. Thus, while I did not like what North, McFarlane, and Poindexter purportedly had done, I disliked their accusers even more. That included everyone who fell into that category: prosecutors, investigators, members of Congress, other reporters. I wasn't inclined to line up with North, McFarlane, and Poindexter, but the self-righteousness of their critics gradually became intolerable to me. It was as if my past, a past I was determined to keep at bay, was equally intent on reclaiming me.

For the next year, I was on the Iran-Contra beat for the *Sun*. Journalistically, it was a productive time. But the more I learned about the scandal, the more I needed to understand why it had happened. I became convinced that Vietnam and its aftermath lay at the heart of the matter, that absent Vietnam there would have been no Iran-

Contra. But what interested me most was not the scandal itself, but the generational divide that it had laid bare.

In the summer of 1988 I took a leave of absence from the *Sun* to research and write this book. Looking back now, having had more than my share of what Scott Fitzgerald called "riotous excursions with privileged glimpses into the human heart," I see the impact of Vietnam more clearly. My original belief—that unresolved anger and bitterness over the war had played a part in Iran-Contra and other affairs of my generation—was borne out. But I discovered other elements that had to be taken into account. They included, in some instances, a staggering degree of personal ambition and questions of emotional stability. In the case of all five principal figures, their formative, pre-Annapolis years exerted a powerful influence and would have done so even if there had not been a Vietnam War.

There was something else. As a reporter, I had established a number of rules for myself. One was to always pay attention to little red flags, those mental warnings that tell you a story is about to veer out of control. One popped up in an interview with Jim Webb. In an aside, he said, "I'm not sure I'm as angry as you want me to be." The reappraisal forced by his remark caused me to question my role, and eventually acknowledge that I had a stake in this that went beyond professional achievement.

I should have known those things going in. But as I began work, emotions disrupted my judgment. I set out to use all five men to say things I had long submerged, but now needed to say and still didn't want to say myself. Their lives would become my voice, a tidy package in concept, in reality anything but.

It hardly needs saying that this book did not turn out precisely as I expected. In the end, it gets messy, in some ways as messy as the war that spawned it.

BOOK ONE

IHTFP

INTRODUCTION

We're a group of people who are being trained to fight. We're not businessmen. We deal in stress. We deal in intense catharsis. We don't deal in sales.

—REAR ADMIRAL HOWARD W. HABERMEYER, JR., '64,
Commandant of Midshipmen, 1987–89

One day not long ago Jim Webb and another Annapolis graduate of similar vintage were reminiscing about their Academy days. After several rounds of sea stories, Academy slang for tall tales, Webb said, "You know, I hated that fucking place."

His friend laughed. "Yeah, I hated that fucking place, too."

The words affirmed their kinship. As midshipmen, they had uttered the same phrase with minor variations many times, at reveille, in the Mess Hall, racing back from a date cut short by the expiration of liberty.

Over the years, the phrase "I hate this fucking place" has become the equivalent of a secret handshake between Annapolis men. It's so common the actual words are superfluous. Usually you just say IHTFP.

Midshipmen mean it when they say it, if only for the moment. Old grads like Webb routinely fall back on it when nostalgia threatens to smother the enormous complexity of their feelings for a place where they had once been young and whole.

Midshipmen reach for lofty phrases to describe the Academy to outsiders. Among themselves they rely on the wisdom of inspired forebears. Thus, within the Yard, the Academy has been known at various times as:

- the only place in the world where they take away the basic rights of man and give them back to you one by one as privileges;

- an institution where you get a $50,000* education shoved up your ass a nickel at a time;
- a four-year breaststroke through a pool of shit.

Let it also be said that the Academy is a place of tradition, pride, and honor that over the years has turned out many of the nation's finest and most heroic combat leaders, among them Admirals Dewey, Nimitz, Halsey, King, Leahy, Burke, Spruance, and Mitscher.

Since the Academy was established in 1845, seventy-two graduates have been awarded the Congressional Medal of Honor, the nation's highest award for gallantry, eighteen of them posthumously. Members of fifty-four Annapolis classes, all the way back to 1892, served in World War II. Six percent were killed in action. They received twenty-seven Medals of Honor, fourteen of them posthumously. Annapolis men won three more Medals of Honor in Korea. During the Vietnam War, 122 Academy graduates were killed in action and James B. Stockdale, '47, received the Medal of Honor for heroism while a prisoner of war with John McCain.

Though much remains the same, dramatic changes have occurred at the Academy over the past twenty-five years. This is how the molding of future combat leaders worked when McCain, John Poindexter, Bud McFarlane, Jim Webb, and Oliver North were serving their apprenticeships.

Then as now, the process started in early summer with the arrival of the incoming class and the beginning of Plebe Year, a trial by ordeal with roots in the Crusades. Its purpose was to weed out freshmen who were not up to the rigors of military life and the challenges of command. Fred Fagan, '64, a retired Marine colonel, explained how he ran plebes as an upperclassman: "I tried to give 'em more than they could handle and see if they could handle it."

The system was untidy, often sophomoric, always vulnerable to abuse. Some good men quit; nearly everyone considered it at least once. The price was high: your youth, at times it seemed your soul, for a slogan—duty, honor, country. That was hard to remember when you were scrambling around on all fours, a jockstrap over your face, running Greyhound Races.

Then as now, a pocket-sized handbook called *Reef Points* was the plebe's bible. It contained nearly three hundred pages of naval lore that new midshipmen were required to master. When an upperclass-

---

*The figure has escalated over the years. In 1994 it was nearly $200,000.

man asked a plebe how long he'd been in the Navy, the plebe was expected to fire back the appropriate passage from *Reef Points*:

All me bloomin' life, sir! Me mother was a mermaid, me father was King Neptune. I was born on the crest of a wave and rocked in the cradle of the deep. Seaweed and barnacles are me clothes. Every tooth in me head is a marlinspike; the hair on me head is hemp. Every bone in me body is a spar, and when I spits, I spits tar! I'se hard, I is, I am, I are!

Reef Points also contained, then and now, a four-page poem called "The Laws of the Navy," by Admiral R. A. Hopwood of the Royal Navy. Plebes had to memorize it. The last stanza, a troubling one in retrospect, goes like this:

> Now these are the laws of the Navy
> And many and varied are they
> But the hull and the deck and the keel
> And the truck of the law is—OBEY.

About the time they cut off your hair—in other words an hour or so after reporting to the Academy—you received a small pamphlet entitled "A Message to Garcia," the inspirational retelling of a Spanish-American War tale of dubious authenticity. In 1898 President McKinley ordered a young naval lieutenant named Rowan to deliver a letter to a Cuban general named Garcia. Without further discussion, so the story goes, Rowan set off on his mission. A month later, having journeyed to Cuba, he disappeared into the jungle, traversed the country by foot, and delivered McKinley's missive. If the details of the parable grew hazy in later years, the theme never did. You don't piss and moan and talk the job to death. You just do it and report back when it's done.

For most new midshipmen, the transition from civilian to military life was brutally abrupt. They quickly learned that they had ventured into a curious subculture whose inhabitants lived by a rigid set of rules and conversed in a language all their own. Floors were decks; walls, bulkheads; stairs, ladders; bathrooms, heads; beds, racks. That was all standard Navy lingo, but the plebes also had to master Academy slang. Seniors were first classmen, or firsties; juniors were second classmen, or segundos; sophomores were third classmen, or youngsters. Freshmen were fourth classmen, or plebes. An Irish pennant was an unseamanlike, dangling loose end of a line or piece of clothing, usually a thread on your uniform. A sandblower was a short guy, a drag a date, a draghouse a place in town where a drag might stay on an Academy weekend. A brick was a homely drag, to bilge was to flunk a course or make someone else look bad. "Never bilge a classmate" may be the most enduring of the Academy's unwritten rules, though it didn't apply to matters of honor. In other words, you were neither expected nor permitted to affirm a classmate's lie or to cover up his cheating or stealing.

The word "grease" had many variations. As a noun, it meant your aptitude for the service, more simply leadership ability. Your grease grade revealed how your superiors and your peers rated you as a leader. You were said to have good grease or bad grease. Grease could be misleading. Often it depended on the degree to which you bought into the system, an attribute that could lead to disaster later in life. John Poindexter had great grease. Bud McFarlane, Jim Webb, and Ollie North had good grease. John McCain had terrible grease. Greasy denoted a midshipman overly concerned with his grease, an apple polisher whose ambition was more naked than most. Greasy midshipmen normally did well early on, but eventually fell of their own weight. You might fake who you were and what you were outside the Yard, but there were few secrets within its walled confines.

The jargon only added to the new midshipman's confusion. A few weeks earlier, he may have been a hot-shot member of his high school senior class, possibly a free-spirited college student or footloose enlisted Marine or sailor. Now he was the lowest of the low, and not just because that's how *Reef Points* defined plebe. The system that blotted up his every waking second seemed intent on crushing his last shred of individuality in order to transform him into something else, a name, a number, another hapless face in the crowd.

He learned the first day the six verbal responses acceptable to his seniors: Yes, sir; No, sir; Aye, aye, sir; I'll find out, sir; No excuse, sir; or the right answer to any question put to him. Even more quickly he was introduced to bracing up, the exaggerated position of attention achieved by forcing his chin toward the back of his neck to form double, triple, quadruple chins. He braced up everywhere in Bancroft Hall except in his room, which he typically shared with one, two, or three other frazzled newcomers, even there when an upperclassman or commissioned officer entered. Venturing outside his cubicle, he tucked in his chin and double-timed through the corridors, obsequiously plastering himself to the bulkhead to make way for his betters. In the Mess Hall, braced up on the forward two inches of his chair, he ate a square meal, his fork rising vertically from the plate, horizontally to the mouth, then back to the plate by the same route. If his deportment displeased an upperclassman, he might be told to shove out. That meant to remain braced as if seated, but without even the lip of the chair for support.

At odd hours his seniors dispatched him on whimsical missions to the farthest reaches of Bancroft Hall, the cavernous midshipman dormitory that housed the entire Brigade within its central structure and six (later eight) contiguous wings. That meant some long, wearying jaunts. As every plebe knew, courtesy of *Reef Points*, the Hall in those days contained 3.6 miles of corridor. (The subsequent expansion occasioned a minor variant in the riddle to which Bancroft Hall is the answer: What has eight wings, 360 heads, and sucks?)

Uniform races required changing from one uniform to another in, say, two minutes, then changing back again, and again, sometimes curled up in a wooden foot locker. To add spice, there were other games—Swimming to Baltimore, Carrier Quals, Sweating a Penny to the Bulkhead, Sitting on the Green Bench, and the always popular Greyhound Races.

Plebes enjoyed one advantage during the summer. There were more than a thousand of them compared to the small, elite corps of upperclassmen and junior officers selected to train them. Their numerical edge came to an abrupt end after Labor Day when the rest of the Brigade returned from leave and summer training. Suddenly the plebes were outnumbered nearly three to one and every upperclassman, it seemed, wanted a piece of them.

Once the academic year commenced, the ability to juggle the conflicting demands of upperclassmen and instructors determined who survived and who didn't. It was easy to see that later. Going through it, all you knew was that you were alone, as alone as you'd ever been in your life, and no one seemed to care whether you made it or not. If anything, the upperclass seemed intent on driving you out. Their ridiculous and demeaning demands consumed every free moment. When they weren't hazing you physically, they were ordering you to find the answers to mindless questions that left no time to study for class.

Your instructors, meanwhile, studiously oblivious to the antics in the Hall, were giving written quizzes each day, more challenging exams called P-works every other week. They were no more interested in your excuses than the second classman who turned beet-red and shoved you out when you told him your four classes between breakfast and noon meal left no time to find out the name of the lead elephant in Hannibal's caravan when the Carthaginians crossed the Alps to invade Italy.

Despite your best efforts, life was fast becoming a descent into madness. Nothing pleased the upperclass. Wrong answers incited abuse, right answers more questions. In class you were barely passing. You were angry, scared, confused, lost. No one was looking out for you except perhaps your classmates and they had big problems of their own. By now the idea of quitting had crossed your mind, but the thought of going home and confessing to family and friends that you couldn't take it kept you stumbling through another day. One day an upperclassman braced you against the bulkhead, tuned his voice so low you could barely hear him, and snarled, Face it, boy, you got no balls, turn in your chit, go home to Mommy. And, Christ, by then you wanted to. No matter what you came from, squalor, familial dysfunction, nothing could be worse than this. You didn't know who you were, why you were at Annapolis. All you knew was that the guy with the stabbing whisper was right, you didn't have it.

By now you wanted out for sure, the only question how to ease the sting of quitting. Lying in your rack after lights out, you tried to concoct a story that your buddies back home would buy. Hey, the place was just infantile bullshit, man, I wasn't learning a goddamn thing. Hell, yes, I could take it, but I didn't need that crap.

Maybe you didn't. As you polished your breakout story, though, you noticed something. You were still there. And as you edged closer and closer to resigning, you began asking yourself some hard questions, harder even than the one about Hannibal's goddamned elephant. This was the hardest: even if I can explain away quitting to my friends and family, will I ever be able to explain it to myself?

Suspended between quitting and staying, you hung on a few more days, trying to balance the unrelieved craziness in the Hall and the relentless demands in the classroom, realizing you could bring it all to an end with a stroke of the pen. But you also started thinking about the upperclass, the third classman who winked at you when a firstie was shoving you out, as if to say, Hey, I understand, I'm just a few months removed from all this shit myself. We all understand, you know. We've all been through it.

You always knew that, but as you dangled between leaving and staying, it began to mean more. All these guys, so crisp and squared away, so seemingly indifferent to your fate, they had all been through it, braced up, shoved out, sweating pennies, chewed out by assholes.

Your sense of self-preservation now abandoned you. The world outside the Yard lost meaning, the sole reality Bancroft Hall, and making it there. The decision out of the way, you reached deep down and found you had something left. The next time a sneering upperclassman growled, Turn in your chit, maggot, you bellowed back at him, Not a fucking chance, sir!

Eventually, June Week arrived. You joined the throng storming Herndon Monument, a tall, pyramidal granite monument across from the Chapel. The firsties had slathered grease all over it to deny you a handhold. Laughing and cursing, starched white uniforms stained beyond repair, you and your cohorts scrambled onto one another's shoulders, ascending by fits and starts, finally placing a hat atop the pinnacle. Plebe Year was over, you'd made it through, and, wonder of wonders, you were not a different person after all. But you were not the same, either.

Today, plebe indoctrination is kinder and gentler, if still no fun. The old system lasted as long as it did partly because of tradition, but also because generations of Annapolis men looked back on it as a crucial experience in the formation of their characters, a time for discovering that when the stakes were high, they could play over their heads.

During your four years at Annapolis you came to understand that more was expected of you than of other young men. Since the first anguishing days of plebe summer you had been trained to shoulder a daunting responsibility, leading other men in combat, bravely, wisely, and with minimum loss of life.

They told you that in lectures, but you learned it by osmosis. On the way to class you passed an officer, noticed his ribbons, recognized the Purple Heart, Silver Star, perhaps the Navy Cross. The monuments in the Yard usually blended into the landscape, but when you took time to read the inscriptions you experienced a chill and wondered if you would measure up if your time ever came. You felt certain at such moments that it would.

The Academy reinforced your love of country. It was not blind affection, and certainly not an overweening patriotism. You knew the United States had its faults, serious ones, none so serious as the institutional racism that had stained the nation since before its birth. But you also felt an optimism that the country could come to grips with its problems if given a chance. That was your job, to give it a chance. You were to be its protector, and that seemed like a worthwhile way for a man to spend his life.

There was something else, best approached indirectly. Three decades ago, a firstie named Ron Benigo, on hearing a friend accuse another midshipman of insufferable grandstanding, laughed and said, "Come on, we're all applause seekers, you know." It was a curious comment coming from Benigo, the most modest of men despite standing fourteenth in a class of over nine hundred. The friend, suspecting he would not like the answer, did not ask him what he meant.

Some years later, after Benigo had won a Purple Heart and Silver Star as a Marine in Vietnam, then embarked on a successful business career, the same friend recalled the applause-seeker line and asked him to explain it.

"I think I meant to say that our prime motivation for suffering through all that USNA put us through was the prospect of glory," he said in a letter. "I believe most of us felt that we would one day be tested in some form of combat—after all, WW2 and Korea were not that long ago and our relations with the Soviets were being severely tested—and if you really looked at what a professional warrior could hope for in his career, it was just that test. After all, one doesn't get one's name in *Reef Points* by being the best darn administrator in the Naval Service. It takes great deeds in the face of overwhelming odds to implant your name indelibly in the minds of all the plebes yet to scale the Herndon.

"Perhaps some of us entered USNA thinking that it would lead to just a job, but after the intensity of the plebe experience, I believe we survivors had more going for us than the prospect of twenty-years-and-out to a nice second career selling life insurance to the next generation of junior officers. I believe we had visions of being someday at that critical moment when what we did would change the course of history."

CHAPTER ONE

HALOS AND HORNS

In June 1954 more than twelve hundred young men in varying states of anxiety assembled in Annapolis, took an oath to support and defend the Constitution of the United States, and transformed themselves into the Naval Academy Class of 1958. Among the uneasy novitiates that day were John Marlan Poindexter and John Sidney McCain III. Four years later, the Class of '58 had been whittled down by 25 percent. Of the 899 survivors, Poindexter, a small-town banker's son from landlocked Indiana, stood number one in the class. As a senior, he wore the six stripes of the brigade commander, the top leadership post at Annapolis. McCain, the scion of one of the most illustrious families in the annals of the Navy, stood 894, fifth from the bottom. He never smelled a stripe.

The two Johns had little in common beyond their first names, McCain rowdy, raunchy, a classic underachiever ambivalent about his presence at Annapolis; Poindexter cool, contained, a young man at the top of his game who knew from the start that he belonged at the Academy. In neighboring Bancroft Hall companies, they were neither friends nor enemies. They moved along paths that rarely intersected, Poindexter walking on water, McCain scraping the ocean floor, a bottom feeder, at least academically.

There was one important similarity. Both McCain and Poindexter were leaders in the class, the former in a manic, intuitive, highly idiosyncratic way, the latter in a cerebral, understated manner that was no less forceful for its subtlety. As the Academy was fully capable of accommodating both leadership styles, they might easily have found themselves competing for top positions within the Brigade. But little else was equal. "John Poindexter was the sort of guy with a halo around his head," said classmate Bill Hemingway. "McCain was the one with the horns." Hemingway was Poindexter's roommate, but not even McCain would contest the point.

*   *   *

John McCain always knew he was going to Annapolis, knew it with such unshakable finality that he never really thought twice about it, at least not seriously. It was part of the air he breathed, the ether through which he moved, the single immutable element in his life. He was the grandson of Admiral John Sidney "Slew" McCain, '06, a high-strung, irascible old sea dog who fought the Japanese with Bull Halsey from Guadalcanal to Tokyo Bay, watched them surrender on the deck of the battleship *Missouri,* then dropped dead four days later. The *New York Times* reported his death on its front page.

The Annapolis tradition continued with John's father, John Sidney McCain, Jr., '31, called Jack, at times Junior, a salty World War II submarine skipper climbing steadily toward flag rank himself. He was known for his trademark cigar, promotion of seapower, and devilish reply when asked how he could tell his wife, a college homecoming queen, and her twin sister apart. "That's their problem," he harrumphed.

Though resigned to Annapolis, John was not happy about it and at times seemed intent on sabotaging his chances for admission. Rebellious by nature, he viewed rules and regulations through a highly personal prism, as challenges to his wit and ingenuity. At Episcopal High School, a private boarding school for boys in Alexandria, Virginia, those qualities emerged with a vengeance.

He was known as Punk, alternatively as Nasty, in another variation, McNasty. He cultivated the image. The Episcopal yearbook pictures him in a trench coat, collar up, cigarette dangling Bogart-style from his lips. That pose, if hardly the impression Episcopal hoped to project, at least had a world-weary panache to it. Generally, though, he mocked the school's dress code by wearing blue jeans with his coat and tie and otherwise affecting a screw-you raffishness. He would later describe himself in those days as a rebel without a cause, a James Dean type, though it's just as easy to imagine him as Holden Caulfield, red hunting hat askew, railing about phonies, sneaking cigarettes, driving old Ackley-kid crazy.

One of his few friends, Malcolm Matheson, remembered him fondly as "a hard-rock kind of guy, a tough, mean little fucker." One time he was hauled into juvenile court after he leaned from the window of a friend's car to berate two older girls with the words "Shove it up your ass" when they ridiculed his awkward pickup attempts.

He dealt with the inevitability of Annapolis like a man loath to take the painful actions necessary to break an unhappy engagement. Rather than telling his parents what he really thought—screw Annapolis, the place sucks—he put himself in a variety of compromising situations, seemingly hoping that the word would filter back so they would take the initiative, leaving him guilt-ridden but free to attend the school of his choice, which meant just about anywhere else.

McCain never went so far in his peccadilloes, however, as to subvert his birthright. He was defiant and flouted the rules, but given his pedigree it would have taken the hand of God to transform his childish pranks and boyish transgressions into something serious enough to bar him from Annapolis. And God, it seems, was otherwise occupied or knew something about McCain that McCain didn't. And so, on an early summer's day in 1954, in a car driven by his father, John journeyed to Annapolis, raised his right hand, and marched joylessly into his future.

To his surprise, he enjoyed plebe summer, thriving on the physical activity and drill. To Ron Thunman, the newly commissioned ensign in charge of his summer company, McCain displayed a dynamic quality, a scrappiness, that revealed itself most clearly in the plebe summer boxing smokers. Unschooled as a boxer, McCain would charge to the center of the ring and throw punches until someone went down. That summer it was always the other guy. He won all his fights by knockouts or TKOs.

His fortunes took a downward turn when the upper three classes returned in September. The least docile of plebes, he refused to accept the notion that someone could demean and degrade him simply because he had been at Annapolis two or three years longer. As he saw it, a lot of guys who had never done anything in their lives suddenly had the power to make his life miserable. "It was bullshit, and I resented the hell out of it," he later said.

As at Episcopal, he reacted by challenging the system, quickly piling up demerits. Shoes unshined, late for formation, talking in ranks, room in disorder, gear improperly stowed. Academically, he spent time, not a lot, on the courses he liked—English, history, and government—ignoring the rest, about 75 percent of the curriculum.

He treated the system throughout his four years like a hostile organism, something to beat back, keep at bay, as if any compromise meant surrendering a part of himself that he might never retrieve. John McCain at Annapolis, however, was not the John McCain of Episcopal days. He shed the punk image and became one of the most popular midshipmen in his class, if one of the least conventional.

He proved to be a natural leader, his magnetic personality making him the unofficial trail boss for a lusty band of carousers and partygoers known as the Bad Bunch. "People kind of gravitated to him," said Chuck Larson. "They would respond to his lead. They pretty much cared about his approval and they cared about what he thought." Larson, an ex-officio member of the Bad Bunch, was McCain's closest friend at the Academy and for some years after. They were known as the Odd Couple, McCain short, scrappy, the consummate screwup, Larson the model midshipman, tall, handsome, smooth, bright. They shared a sense of the absurd and an eye for the ladies. Larson, though, was cautious. Of course, he had more to be cautious about. McCain didn't know what the word meant. As one classmate put it, being on liberty with John McCain was like being in a train wreck.

Even so, his classmates clustered around him, followed his lead, a modern-day Pied Piper decked out in Navy blue. "Whatever John would suggest that we do, whether it was at the Academy or on liberty, I tended to follow," said classmate Jack Dittrick. "And I don't think I was alone in that. I've talked with other classmates and we all marvel at how much control John had over what we did."

He lived on the edge, which only added to his popularity. Even if you held back a bit, followed him so far and no further like Chuck Larson, it was still a hell of a ride.

One night McCain led the Bad Bunch over the wall to a watermen's bar on a small creek outside Annapolis. The place was little more than a screened-in shack with sawdust on the floor and an electric shuffle-board machine in the corner. Its appeal lay in a feature close to the heart of real estate agents and thirsty midshipmen alike: location. The bar was situated about an eighth of a mile beyond the seven-mile limit, within which midshipmen could not be served alcohol. The catch was that midshipmen on liberty were not permitted to wander beyond the seven-mile limit.

Two dozen midshipmen were drinking alongside the bar's usual clientele of fishermen and crabbers when the Shore Patrol burst through the door. "Nobody move," shouted the officer in charge, triggering a mad dash for freedom. Midshipmen crashed through the mesh screens that passed for walls and scurried into the surrounding woods, tearing their clothes, losing their caps. Some reversed field, hid in boats tied to the dock across from the bar. Others huddled in ditches or behind fences. McCain and a couple of buddies were sprinting down a road when a car slowed alongside them. "Get in," said the driver, laughing like crazy. He turned out to be a recent Academy graduate showing his girlfriend one of his old haunts. After dropping McCain and his friends in Annapolis, he returned to the bar and picked up another carload of mids. Everyone made it back one way or the other, hitching rides, scooting over the wall, slipping into Bancroft through any open window they could find.

No one ever had to give John Poindexter a midnight ride back to Annapolis. Bucking the system was not his style. "John lived a complete life at the Academy," said classmate Whit Swain. "He had everything he wanted. He didn't have to go over the wall. He didn't need that challenge. He didn't need to escape from anything."

Poindexter was comfortable with the system from the start. He took his share of abuse as a fourth classman, but seldom became rattled, swiftly establishing his credentials as a big-timer. Less adroit plebes groused that upperclassmen seemed almost respectful when hazing him. On those rare occasions when they turned on him, the reaction of his classmates was curious. He must be something special if they're working him over like that, they marveled, as if unable to imagine him doing anything wrong.

In truth, he rarely did. Ellen Poindexter, with affection and a trace of awe, says of her son, "John was never a little boy. He was born an old man." Her comment recalled political adman Roger Ailes's description of the young Richard Nixon as the kid who carried a briefcase to school and never let anyone copy his homework. But that wasn't John Poindexter. Growing up, he was bright, orderly, and competent, friendly and fun-loving as well. He was also well-liked, a notable achievement for a kid lacking athletic prowess to temper the teenage curse of superior intelligence. His classmates nicknamed him Brain, but affirmed his popularity by electing him King of the Fall Festival, the annual harvest celebration at his tiny high school in Odon, a southwest Indiana town described by Knight-Ridder correspondent Ellen Warren as a no-stoplight rural cliché.

Marlan and Ellen Poindexter, with just a year of college between them, encouraged John and their three younger children to high academic achievement. They also provided a supportive environment in which the abilities of their offspring bloomed. But John, the oldest, was a self-starter, destined for a life of consummate excellence, if not dazzling brilliance, from the day he was born in 1936.

Another ingredient in his personality contributed to his success. From childhood on, at least until he reached the White House, he recognized his limits and resisted the temptation to reach beyond them. "I don't do things I don't do well," he once confided to an acquaintance.

John was an avid Boy Scout, winning induction into the select Order of the Arrow, a scouting fraternity that stresses character, fortitude, and self-reliance. He and his rogue cousin Dickie Ray Poindexter were in the same Scout troop, but viewed their responsibilities to the younger boys in sharply different ways. "My idea was when you brought Tenderfoots in we'd take their pants off and paint their dicks with Mercurochrome," said Dickie Ray. "John's attitude was to sit them down and teach them how to go through the Boy Scout manual and how a Scout is trustworthy, loyal, thrifty, brave, clean, and reverent."

There were few surface similarities between Marlan Poindexter, a hard-driving, at times abrasive small-town banker, and his oldest son, an engaging kid who made everything he did look easy and displayed no special interest in material wealth, then or later. Their differences, however, obscured significant likenesses. Both had well-defined career paths laid out for them—Marlan in the family funeral home business, John in banking—but each chose to strike off in new, unfamiliar directions. They also shared a quiet self-assurance, as if sensing in themselves a special quality destined to bring success if they just trusted their instincts.

Marlan prospered as a banker because he never forgot the marketing skills he developed years earlier peddling Kirby and Regina vacuum cleaners door-to-door. Even so, business would never have mushroomed as it did in the 1950s if not for Marlan's genius in recognizing opportunity in the opening of the sprawling naval weapons facility in nearby Crane.

Tightfisted with his homegrown customers, Marlan cultivated the men and women stationed at Crane, setting up check-cashing booths on the base on payday, offering free checking services, most importantly providing servicemen, especially officers, with easy loan approval, often solely on their signatures. "Marlan learned early on that when you do business with the Navy, the Navy makes you pay your bills, especially if you're a career officer," said his nephew, Dickie Ray.

By the early 1960s, ads for his bank having followed John to Annapolis, the elder Poindexter was on a first-name basis with naval officers all over the world, for whom the phrase "banking with Marlan" had come to mean unstinting personal service. They'd call the little bank at the corner of Spring and Main, tell Marlan they needed a loan, and he'd okay it over the phone. If they ran short of funds some months, Marlan told them not to worry, he'd transfer money into their accounts, comfortable in the knowledge that their allotment checks would arrive in a few days. "Thanks," he'd write on their deposit slips. "Glad to see you're in Naples." Military families driving through Indiana sometimes made a sidetrip to Odon just to meet Marlan face-to-face.

John began talking about the Naval Academy during his junior year in high school. He had never seen the ocean, but tales of the seafaring life spun by such writers as C. S. Forester and Jack London had fired his imagination. Coming of age in a world of winter wheat and small-town ambitions, he was a closet romantic, a latter-day Horatio Hornblower craving adventure, as susceptible to the tug of the sea as a politician to the charm of a big-bucks campaign contributor.

At Annapolis, he started winning honors early. As a plebe, his company took first place in the yearlong brigade competition. He was picked to hold the bouquet of flowers for the color girl as she transferred the American, Navy, and Academy flags to the winning unit in the Color Parade ceremony during June Week.

At the Academy and for years after, he maintained a friendly rivalry with McCain's pal Chuck Larson. Larson was smart, earning an enviable academic standing even if he was not quite in Poindexter's league as a scholar. A slim six foot two, Larson was a charismatic leader, his Scandinavian good looks, outgoing personality, effortless charm, and mild taste for mischief appealing to midshipmen and Academy officers alike. "You looked at Chuck and you saw him as lettering in lacrosse and football and baseball and being number one academically, even though he wasn't any of those things," said Whit Swain. "He had this absolutely magnificent façade, whereas John didn't have any façade."

No one was surprised when Larson was named brigade commander at the beginning of senior year, leading the fall set of stripers in a series of glamorous events, the Wednesday afternoon parades on Worden Field and march-ons at football games at a time when Navy teams were national powers. Poindexter's selection to succeed Larson during the winter was less predictable. His high academic standing, clean conduct record, and squared-away demeanor merited a respectable number of stripes, probably four on the regimental or brigade staff. But brigade commander? The six-striper? "To me, John had zero command presence, as opposed to Larson, who really did," said Harry McConnell, an 18th Company classmate. Said another, Bill Bauer, "I wouldn't have put John on top as a leader."

Those closer to Poindexter had no trouble understanding the choice. If he did not have Larson's golden good looks, he was tall, slightly over six feet, trim, with fine military bearing. His pleasant, youthful features had a vaguely Oriental cast to them. For a time, he was called Babyface, but as he matured and became a presence within Bancroft Hall the nickname was rendered ludicrous. Roommate Bill Hemingway, later a Marine infantry officer who served three tours in Vietnam, remembered Poindexter as having "a real quiet, subtle kind of charisma," the kind not obvious at a distance.

"He was everybody's friend," said Hemingway. "If you had a problem with a class, he was there to help you. He did a lot of that. People admired and respected that because he was so selfless. That's what was so unique, he was so selfless." Bob Caldwell, another roommate, said he wouldn't have graduated if it hadn't been for Poindexter. "I'd read his notes before a quiz," he said. "If John put a blue square around a formula, I'd memorize that sucker."

For all his intellectual prowess, he was not a grind. "He was smart and diligent, but he was not ridiculous," said Hemingway. "He didn't read books with a flashlight after lights out. He didn't have to. He'd read something once and he understood it." Caldwell agreed, adding, "He was just smarter than we were."

It helped that Poindexter had a special skill, one that he regularly employed at the Academy and throughout his life: an exceptional ability to concentrate, to focus completely on what he was doing, shifting effortlessly back and forth between tasks, as if his mind were wired to a toggle switch.

He tended to follow the rules, but occasionally ignored them. In those days, plebes were not allowed to have radios. Poindexter took a toilet-paper roll, wound some copper wire around it, and fashioned a makeshift crystal set for the room. As a senior, he qualified as a yawl captain. On weekends he was not above swinging his sailboat into some small Chesapeake Bay cove and, contrary to regulations, taking on a case of beer for himself, his crew, and their dates.

From time to time he was the butt of his roommates' pranks. They once ground up the rubber soles of some old shoes and stuffed it in the bowl of his pipe. He complained about the odor of the tobacco, but smoked it anyway. At an exam, he opened the case of his Rude star-finder, a circular navigational aid used for celestial navigation, only to find that it had been replaced by a 45 rpm record of Little Richard's "Long Tall Sally."

To Whit Swain, Poindexter's leadership ability was entwined with a taste for power barely noticed by others. "John is a power junkie," said Swain. "Maybe junkie is too strong a word. But I think John likes power, and he knows how to use it and he knows how to get it."

Swain was a friend of Poindexter, but he wasn't as close to him as Larson, Hemingway, Caldwell, and a few others. From the middle distance, though, Swain may have picked up the elusive elements that defined Poindexter as a leader.

At its heart was Poindexter's intellect, which he took pains not to flash, but which could still be intimidating. "John was so sure of his intellectual capability that he knew that the decision he arrived at was correct," said Swain. "So when he approached you with 'Let's do it this way,' he was so sure of himself without being overbearing that you just automatically did it. You just bought it."

It was not charisma as the word is usually understood, but something akin to it. Up close, Poindexter could be an enveloping presence, a cherubic gray eminence, the kind of guy who had thought through a problem and crafted a solution before anyone else realized that a problem existed. Swain remembers a familiar pattern to their exchanges.

"Now, Whit, this is the way we're going to do it."

"Well, John . . ."

"Now, Whit . . ."

"Okay, all right."

Swain said no one else could talk to him like that. It did not seem patronizing coming from Poindexter, more like a dose of common sense gently administered by a favorite uncle who had only your best interests at heart.

Even so, Poindexter seemed to be everywhere, and that sometimes grated. Anybody who tried to stake out some turf, an area of interest in which he could be number one, invariably found that Poindexter had already been there or was coming up fast on the rail. As Swain put it, "He moved ahead of other people in any arena that they contested with him." How? "He was always right," said Swain. "It drives you mad when somebody's always right. It infuriates you. You just don't stand a chance against people like that."

Years later, in a discussion of Eastern religions, Swain was introduced to the concept of *mana*. He decided that it explained much of Poindexter's understated forcefulness. *Mana*, as Swain understood it, was an attribute of chiefs and gods that accounted for their power and good fortune. A man possessing *mana* rarely even moved. He simply lifted his finger and underlings raced to do his bidding. "John didn't move much," said Swain. "John would sit in his room and things would happen around him."

Swain's understanding of *mana* was admittedly incomplete. Carl F. Walters, Jr., a professor of religion at St. Andrew's Presbyterian College in North Carolina, put it all together. "Think of it as The Force," he said. To Whit Swain, John Poindexter was Obi-Wan Kenobi as a young man.

*   *   *

For all his notoriety as the instigator of madcap escapades, John McCain had less flashy qualities that became part of his Annapolis persona. He could not be intimidated, he said what he thought, and he stood his ground. Frank Gamboa, who roomed with him for three years, can tell dozens of stories about McCain, most of them hilarious, but he usually starts with this one:

Early in their sophomore year, McCain and Gamboa were dining in the Mess Hall one Saturday, a day when midshipmen did not have to sit at assigned tables. Barely more than plebes, they were feeling their way, treading lightly, hoping to get through the meal unnoticed. There were also some plebes and juniors at the table, which was presided over by a senior nobody knew. The first classman's mood was dark, his manner unpleasant. During the meal he became angry with the Filipino steward serving the table. The plebes and juniors, sensing trouble, ate quickly and left. In a serious breach of protocol, the firstie began dressing down the steward, as if he were a plebe. The steward, anxious to please, grew flustered under the sustained abuse.

Glancing nervously at McCain, Gamboa saw him grinding his teeth.

"Hey, mister, why don't you pick on someone your own size?" McCain finally blurted out.

"What did you say?" the firstie snapped.

"I don't think it's fair for you to pick on that steward," McCain shot back. "He's doing the best he can. You're picking on him. That's what I said."

"What's your name, mister?" snarled the firstie, the usual preamble for placing a subordinate on report.

"Midshipman McCain, third class," said McCain, eyes blazing. "What's yours?"

Furious, but seemingly aware that he was on shaky ground, the firstie grabbed his cap and retreated from the Mess Hall, never to be heard from again.

Looking back, Gamboa said the incident epitomized McCain's intolerance for anyone lording rank or social position over others. McCain, he said, was probably the only guy in the company who would have reacted as he did, then and there, when it counted. "Give me a couple of weeks to think about it, and I might have been that brave," said Gamboa.

McCain had an advantage shared by few of his classmates. He knew the Academy was not the real Navy. Senators, congressmen, admirals, and generals were frequent visitors to his parents' home in Washington, where his father held several senior Pentagon posts, so the ire of an upperclassman did not buckle his knees. Some felt his family background accorded him special status, that so long as he kept his hijinks within reasonable bounds he could get away with just about anything.

Had McCain relied on that, which he and others said he never did, he might have quickly reverted to civilian life. His grandfather had been dead for nearly ten years when he entered the Academy. His father, though a rising star in the Navy, was still a captain at the time. Navy captains command aircraft carriers and battleships, but they do not swing enough weight to finesse their kids through Annapolis. McCain's younger brother, Joe, in fact, bilged out as a plebe in 1961, three years after John graduated. By then, Jack McCain was a rear admiral. John McCain, moreover, made every effort to downplay his father's rank. Ron Thunman said he never learned of McCain's lineage till long after plebe summer even though as his company officer he had daily contact with him for two solid months.

Like many Annapolis men, McCain felt ambivalent about the Academy. "I hated the place, but I didn't mind going there," he once said. On the plus side, the uniform helped him get dates, not that he needed much assistance. Most weekends he could be seen escorting beautiful women, each more dazzling than the one who preceded her. Roommate Jack Dittrick used to tag along, hoping for a discard. "Women were just drawn to him," said Dittrick, even today amazed by the response McCain evoked in females. "What is it about him?" he once asked a woman friend. "Jack," she said, "the guy just plain has sex appeal. Don't ask me to explain it." Back then midshipmen had a more ribald way to describe the impact McCain and men like him had on women: when they walked into a room, so it was said, you could hear the skivvies drop.

Despite his woeful class standing, McCain was smart, quick, and thoughtful, if not intellectual. So how did he wind up scraping bottom at the Academy? For one thing, class standing was not solely a function of academic performance. A grease grade, relating to conduct and leadership, was also cranked in, and those factors dealt McCain's standing a severe body blow. He piled up an astonishing number of demerits, though always just below the threshold that meant dismissal. The leadership issue was more complicated. Whatever your talents, you cannot routinely thumb your nose at the Academy and expect the system to reward you. Personal appearance, for example, was an important element in the leadership grade. Outsiders may think that all midshipmen look shipshape in their uniforms, but within Bancroft Hall there are sharp divisions. Do shoes gleam from spit-shining? Has a toothbrush been run around the soles to scrape off the mud? Do brass belt buckles have a mirror finish? Does the collar stay known as a spiffy sit out of sight under the collar? Is the dimple in the tie dead center? Do any extraneous creases show up below the knot? Are shirts tucked correctly in back, with equal widths of overlap on each side? Are uniforms free of all lint and Irish pennants? There is more, much, much more, and in that game McCain was a real loser. "I don't want to say seedy, but he was just not your squared-away midshipman," said Frank Gamboa. "He just didn't put any effort into it. I just don't think he gave a shit." Said Jack Dittrick, "Nobody was as sloppy as John."

Academically, he survived because he had a gift for cramming and friends willing to tutor him. He wasn't confused by the course material, he simply didn't want to spend time on subjects that bored him. Many evenings he would drop in on classmate Ron Fisher seeking enlightenment on such matters as Ohm's Law, inductive impedance, covalent compounds, entropy, Bernoulli's principle, and differential equations. His needs were simple, said Fisher: "He only wanted to know enough to get by." Fisher, who stood twenty-ninth in the class, was amazed that McCain picked up the key points of a lesson in a matter of minutes. Fisher never resented the intrusions, in fact, enjoyed them. After a while, though, he began to think of himself as a drug dealer and McCain as an addict coming around for his daily fix.

In his senior year, McCain and a classmate, Ted Smedberg, were waiting outside the Officers Club for their fathers to emerge. Smedberg, the son of Rear Admiral William R. Smedberg III, the Academy superintendent, was in his fifth year at Annapolis, repeating a year because of academic problems. Departing the club, Admiral Smedberg said to Captain McCain, "There stand my two biggest disappointments as superintendent of the Naval Academy."

In the fall of his sophomore year, as a member of the varsity debating team, John Poindexter went to the University of Vermont for a weekend tournament. He would later joke that the timekeeper, a perky Vermont freshman named Linda Goodwin, gave him extra time that weekend. She did, though she swears not on the debating clock. They spent most of the off-hours together, in the company of Poindexter's Annapolis teammates. Going to lunch, she found herself with a military escort, John on one side of her, another midshipman on the other side, and two more in step behind her.

Linda was the daughter of an army colonel. Like Poindexter, she was a product of Indiana, in her case the big city of Indianapolis. Years later, she would be ordained an Episcopal priest, but she was the same at fifty as she was when Poindexter met her in Burlington—smart, saucy, opinionated, and occasionally raunchy—the ideal sidekick for the reserved Poindexter.

For Linda, it was love at first sight. It may have been for John, too, but his life was complicated. When she asked about the picture he carried in his cap of high school sweetheart Laura Russell, he replied, "Oh, just an old friend," a line worthy of John McCain. "He may have been smarter than most midshipmen," Linda would later say, "but he was still a midshipman."

At Thanksgiving, Linda went down to Washington where her father was stationed. On impulse, she called John. He invited her to Annapolis and they picked up where they had left off in Burlington. He took her to the Christmas Hop. A few days later, she drove him to the airport and kissed him good-bye as he boarded his plane back to Indiana for Christmas leave. He returned after the holidays pinned to Laura Russell.

Linda was hurt, furious, and humiliated. John had never mentioned that he was seriously dating someone back home, let alone that he and Laura had talked about marriage, which they had. She fired off an angry letter calling him a snowman, a term that back then had nothing to do with drugs and everything to do with double-dealing. In the time-honored Navy tradition, Poindexter proudly tacked the letter to his door so his pals could decorate it with midshipman wit at its most crass and insensitive.

The distance between John and Laura, however, eventually took its toll. At college in Muncie, Laura had already met the man she would later marry. Shortly after June Week 1955 she broke up with Poindexter.

Linda was spending that summer with her family in Washington. One day she got a letter from Poindexter. He apologized for the shoddy treatment, said he would be passing through Washington on his return from summer cruise, and wondered if they could get together. Hmm, thought Linda, this guy wants a girl with a car for a couple of days.

She decided to ignore the letter. He called two days later and her resolve crumbled. She not only agreed to go out with him, she arranged a date for his roommate, Bill Hemingway, then chauffeured everyone around in her family's aqua and white '55 Pontiac convertible, nicknamed The Man Trap when Linda was behind the wheel. They went dancing on the roof of the old Roger Smith Hotel, then motored over to Hains Point on the Potomac, in those days one of the city's steamier makeout spots.

Linda transferred to the University of Maryland that fall, partly because it was less expensive than Vermont, mostly to be closer to John. He pinned her after the Notre Dame game and they were engaged at the Ring Dance the following June Week.

By senior year, Poindexter was dating Linda every weekend as well as on Wednesday afternoons, when first classmen had three hours of liberty. At one point he told her he was thinking of easing off on his studies—taking a light strain, in Navy jargon—so that he could relax and enjoy his final year. He might drop to second, third, maybe even fourth in the class, he said, but so what? Fine, said Linda, but don't forget Ike will be giving out the diplomas. You'd be first in line.

So much for the light strain.

In June 1957, John McCain sailed off on first class cruise aboard a destroyer. Late in the month, the ship docked in Rio for a nine-day port call. He and a few friends rented an apartment and set up an Annapolis-style snake ranch ashore. The next four days were a blur, involving liquor, women, and nightclubs, everything except sleep, as Rio embraced McCain and his pals in its many charms, X-rated and otherwise.

The four-day spree over, a bone-weary McCain was dragging himself back to the dock when he ran into Chuck Larson, whose cruise ship was berthed nearby. Larson told him that a Brazilian fashion designer had taken a liking to the midshipmen contingent in Rio. He was going to take everyone up to Sugarloaf that afternoon and throw a party for them in the evening. Models were mentioned. "That sounds great, but I'm just too tired," said McCain. "I'm just beat. I couldn't stay awake." McCain hung tough. In other words, it took Larson two or three more minutes to talk him into joining the group.

Before long, the fashion designer's four-car caravan pulled up to the pier. The midshipmen piled in, then headed off for a day of sightseeing in the mountains. Later, the designer took them to his luxury apartment, which was spacious enough for the small band he had hired for the occasion and a makeshift dance floor.

At about eight, the models began to arrive. Bedazzled but hardly becalmed, the midshipmen began pairing off. All but the bedraggled McCain, beyond exhaustion, totally wrung out from his four-day debauch. As his friends swayed to soft Latin rhythms, he chatted with the designer, an engaging but undemanding conversationalist.

At about nine-thirty, McCain stuck out his hand and said to his host, "Look, I'm going to go back to the ship. Thanks for the hospitality."

"No, no," the designer said, "there's a very beautiful girl I want you to meet."

McCain agreed to hang around a little longer. Around midnight, his deteriorating condition got the better of his curiosity.

"I have to go," he said.

"No, no," said the designer, "just a few more minutes."

McCain was insistent. "I've got to go."

The door opened and the most beautiful woman McCain had ever seen walked in. Recalling that moment through the mist of three decades, he remembered that the band and everything else seemed to stop as Elena (not her real name), slim and blond, made her entrance. The designer escorted her over.

"How are you?" she said, offering her hand.

"Fine," said McCain, coming alive.

The next five days were a merry-go-round of parties, receptions, and dinners, each more lavish than the last, interspersed with long walks on the beach. Elena, he learned, was one of Brazil's most famous and successful fashion models. She lived with her aunt and a coterie of servants in a penthouse apartment atop one of Rio's tallest buildings. In one direction, they could see Sugarloaf, from another Corcovado, from a third the sparkling waters of the bay stretched out below them. What they could not see, because of the aunt and the servants, was each other alone.

On the final day in port, five minutes before the ship was to depart, Elena's Mercedes sports car roared up to the pier, butterfly doors popped open, and McCain leaped out to the cheers and catcalls of the midshipmen lining the rail of the destroyer. As the ship got under way, Elena stood on the pier, waving her handkerchief, dabbing her eyes.

McCain dashed home to Washington after cruise, repacked his bags, and caught a military flight back to Rio where he and Elena resumed the gay social whirl. There were more parties and dances, more romantic walks on the beach. Every time McCain looked at a newspaper or magazine, he saw Elena's picture. For all the excitement, though, they were never really by themselves.

Throughout the fall, McCain and Elena corresponded furiously. Sometimes she would send telegrams, at other times a wide-eyed plebe would summon McCain to the phone to take a long-distance call from Brazil. Elena's picture appeared in the Christmas issue of *The Log*, the Academy's humor magazine, the knockout among knockouts adorning a page bearing the caption "So Nice to Come Home to . . ."

McCain flew down to Rio during Christmas leave. Because of military aircraft schedules, he had only four days. At first, he and Elena picked up where they had left off the previous summer. But on the third day, they sat on the beach for hours trying to come to grips with their differing obligations and desires. She was not prepared to move to the States and become an ensign's wife. He was not willing, or even able by law, to abandon his career and move to Brazil.

The following night, McCain's last in Rio, the designer who brought them together had scheduled a farewell party for McCain. He and Elena planned to go to dinner first. He arrived at her apartment about eight, knocked on the door, and readied himself to be greeted by the aunt or one of the servants. No one answered his knock. He tried the door, found it unlocked, and let himself in.

"I'll be right out," Elena called from the bedroom.

McCain wandered onto the terrace. The moon was glinting off the bay. A bottle of champagne was chilling in a bucket of ice. When Elena joined him a few minutes later, she was not, McCain would later say, dressed for dinner.

The next morning, McCain raced to the airport to catch his plane. Elena did not go with him. He never saw her again.

Even though he lived it, or something like it, McCain recounts his romance with Elena these days as if it were a dream. In some ways it was. But it wasn't just his dream. With minor variations, it was a dream of all but the most inert midshipmen. Duty, honor, country, sure, those things were important, indeed, for most, compelling. For all that, the chance of someday being swept away and ravished by a beautiful woman in some exotic locale has always been an unspoken part of the deal. Annapolis men, at least in the days when they were aspiring to the Academy and during their years there, before they started fretting about career paths, before the Vietnam War bloodied their futures, before they resigned themselves to being cast as warmongers, dullards, or dreary pillars of society, were good at a lot of things, but probably nothing so much as stumbling blissfully, all boyish innocence, as if the devil made them do it, into what Catholics charmingly call the occasion of sin. McCain's fling with Elena, though rare, was not all that rare. Things like that happened often enough to keep that goofy dream alive.

On Sunday, January 12, 1958, John Poindexter's picture appeared on the front page of the *Washington Post*. He would show up there many times years later, but on this occasion there was no hint of the dark days to come. He and Chuck Larson were smiling and shaking hands before an American flag. The caption read, "Naval Academy Leadership Changes." The text explained that Larson was passing on command of the Brigade of Midshipmen to Poindexter, the new six-striper.

To Poindexter, his selection as brigade commander meant more than standing first in the class. As a plebe, it seemed as if the six-striper outranked everyone, even the admirals, and it was hard for him to imagine reaching that pinnacle himself. Over the years, though, he knew he was in the running and that this was his game, as important to him as football, baseball, or basketball to someone else. "His goal was to be the best," said roommate Bill Hemingway. He pursued that goal without false modesty, but also without arrogance. Said another roommate, Bob Caldwell, "John was a nice guy who finished first." Whit Swain saw more complexity to his ascension. "He gravitated toward poles of power because it interested him, it was food and drink to him, it was what he wanted to do."

Poindexter's tenure as brigade commander coincided with the Dark Ages, that dispiriting period between the end of the Christmas holidays and spring leave. Chuck Larson had football games and parades; Poindexter had administrative duties. There were some compensations. After Sunday church services Poindexter would meet Linda outside the chapel and escort her over to the Superintendent's Residence where they would join Rear Admiral Smedberg in greeting a variety of distinguished visitors.

There was also the promise of better things to come. In the spring, the fall and winter stripers would be combined. The spring stripers would lead the brigade in a new round of parades and through June Week and graduation. As the Dark Ages drew to a close, midshipmen debated the merits of the only two conceivable choices for spring set brigade commander, Poindexter and Larson.

It was up to Admiral Smedberg, who conferred on the selection with his number two, Captain Al Shinn, the commandant of midshipmen. Shinn favored Poindexter. I've got a problem with Larson, the commandant said, I think he goes over the wall. Did you ever catch him? Smedberg asked Shinn. No, the commandant replied. Grinned Smedberg, I think maybe he's our kind of guy.

Larson reclaimed his six stripes. Poindexter was named deputy brigade commander, a five-striper. He was disappointed, Linda more so, but they took the decision gracefully. He and Larson roomed together for the remainder of their senior year and became good friends. One spring day they escorted a visiting Spanish midshipman around the Academy grounds, a young man named Juan Carlos, now the king of

Spain. By then their classmates were engaged in a new debate. Who would make admiral first, Chuck or John?

Near the end of the final semester, Poindexter's English class was asked to write an autobiographical essay along the lines of the novel it had just read, *A Portrait of the Artist as a Young Man.* Poindexter, in his paper, ascribed his success at Annapolis to being "at the right place at the right time with the right answer." Some excerpts:

... Being a good plebe was easy for me. I kept out of trouble and usually did exactly as I was told. For the next three years the same pattern was followed with amazing results. I stand very near the head of my class academically and was the senior midshipman officer during a portion of my last year. What brought about these results?

First, order and organization are my guiding principles. I can not stand confusion. This is probably the primary reason the naval service has appealed to me. Second, I learned some time ago how to apply myself. When studying had to be done, it was done, but never have I studied extremely hard. When the weekends came, the books were forgotten, and entertainment reigned supreme. Third, I have a fairly good memory and can remember facts without too much effort; although I would rather learn the theory behind the fact and then work for the fact from there. Fourth, I have always taken the part of the leader. Even as a plebe without a recognized position, I was always asked for help and advice by my classmates. I try to tactfully take the initiative and organize the group to get the work accomplished. These four facts have simply been the winning combination.

... There is a certain satisfaction in leading men. I suppose it gives one a sense of power. This leadership plays a large part in the naval officer's career. A good officer must be a good leader. I believe I am a good leader.

... My ambition is to climb to the very top. My goals are high, but, with God willing, I feel that by applying myself to the tasks before me almost anything can be accomplished. This is a rather optimistic point of view. I could be wrong, but I doubt it.

The Class of 1958 was the first to graduate from the new field house and the last to receive genuine sheepskin diplomas. President Eisenhower presented them personally to the one hundred or so midshipmen graduating with distinction. John Poindexter, the number-one man in the class, received his diploma first. "Congratulations, I hope it won't be too much of a burden for you," said Ike as he shook Poindexter's hand. John McCain, lost in the sea of white that was the rest of the class, looked on impassively, clapped politely.

At a ceremony two days earlier, Poindexter had received six awards, two for finishing at the top of his class, the rest spread across the fields of electrical engineering, electronics, and navigation. No one else came close to matching his total.

The *Indianapolis Times*, noting that the Hoosier State had always been well represented at the highest echelons of the Navy, applauded Poindexter's achievements in an editorial headlined, "Another Cornfield Admiral?" Graduating at the top of his class did not guarantee Poindexter flag rank, the paper said, "but it is a lustrous honor . . . and something in which his home state can take pride."

John in dress whites and Linda in a gown of Chantilly lace were married under crossed swords at the chapel two days after graduation. McCain hung around Annapolis long enough to usher at several weddings, then dashed off to Europe to meet his newest flame, a tobacco heiress. A few days earlier, he had received a short telegram: "Congratulations on your graduation. I'll always love you. Elena."

Three decades later, in 1989, as John Poindexter was preparing for his trial on Iran-Contra charges, John McCain got a letter from Senator Sam Nunn, chairman of the Armed Services Committee. The Georgia Democrat informed McCain that he was naming him to the Naval Academy's Board of Visitors, which oversees the operation of the school. Jack Dittrick couldn't contain himself when he heard the news and immediately called his old roommate in Washington.

"Jack," laughed McCain, "it just goes to show that if you live long enough anything is possible."

CHAPTER TWO

IMAGINATION IS FUNNY

Bud McFarlane, studying at his desk in Bancroft Hall, abruptly set aside his book. Bob Drozd, his roommate, looked up, saw McFarlane gazing past him. Suddenly McFarlane's torso started swaying, reeling left and right in elongated circles. His hands were in motion, too, here, there, back and forth, stopping for an instant, then resuming their crisp, rhythmic movements. After about a minute and a half, he relaxed, retrieved his book, and went on reading.

What was that all about? asked Drozd.

Visualization, replied McFarlane.

It was, he explained, a technique he had picked up to prepare for gymnastics matches. The idea was to picture himself performing his side horse routine flawlessly in hopes that he could duplicate what he had seen in his mind's eye during actual competition.

Drozd was impressed, as he often was by McFarlane, now thinks his friend may have been ahead of his time. These days, lots of athletes do it—tennis players, golfers, field goal kickers, pitchers. For McFarlane, though, visualization was more than a trick to improve his athletic performance. From his earliest days at Annapolis, he had visualized his life unfolding in ways that would be rewarding to him and of service to others. On his worst day, though, he never imagined it the way it turned out, that when his time came he would be feeding lines to an actor who once played straight man to a chimp.

On McFarlane's first day at Annapolis, his father dropped him off at Gate 3 and hurried back to Washington, passing up the afternoon swearing-in ceremony for the Class of 1959. That disappointment aside, Bud was thrilled to be at the Academy, a place where the words duty, honor, country came alive for him in the form of men he was soon passing every day in the Yard. The superintendent, Rear Admiral Smedberg, '26, held the Distinguished Service Medal, Silver Star, five Legions of Merit, and the Bronze Star. Captain Eugene Fluckey, '35, one of the academic department heads, held the Congressional Medal of Honor and four Navy Crosses. Captain Slade Cutter, '35, another department head, wore four Navy Crosses, two Silver Stars, and a Bronze Star (though he was best known for booting the field goal that beat Army 3–0 in 1934 for Navy's first victory over the cadets in thirteen years). All relatively junior officers when World War II broke out, they had manned the ships, planes, and submarines that had bested the German navy and the mighty Japanese fleet.

McFarlane's plebe summer roommate, an enlisted Marine before entering the Academy, taught him to spit-shine shoes and other arcane grooming skills that facilitated a squared-away appearance. McFarlane rolled with the hazing, viewing the various indignities heaped on him and his fellow plebes as part of the time-honored process that had produced so many of the men he admired. He spent hours in the library looking up answers to the obscure, frequently ridiculous questions posed by upperclassmen, his answers invariably better and more complete than those of other plebes.

Like John Poindexter, who was a year ahead of him, he embraced the system. "I could see that here were a set of rules and if you obeyed the rules and worked hard you would win," he said. It was, as he saw it, a meritocracy that worked, and one in which he could prosper. Down the road, he envisioned himself a jet pilot like his brother, Bill, who had preceded him to Annapolis by ten years and returned from the Korean War, his chest emblazoned with ribbons.

He soon gained confidence that he could handle anything the upperclass demanded of him. Once he overreached. Braced up in the Mess Hall, he listened indignantly as four football players, all juniors, jokingly insisted that the plebe class was a bunch of pussies. Unbidden, feeling his oats, he announced that the Class of '59 could clean their clocks any day of the week. Oh, yeah, said one of the football players, why don't you come around to our room after chow. Bring as many guys as you want.

The beetle-browed McFarlane figured the odds were with him. He mustered the forty or so 14th Company plebes a deck above the jock room. The raiding party moved out single file, braced up, squaring corners, McFarlane walking point. He planned to lead his troops down the ladder, then sprint the final fifty yards to the room, bursting through the door and throwing the football players into the shower. As they marched through the corridor, though, teams of upperclassmen, alerted to the raid, quietly picked off nearly all the other plebes, individually and in groups. At the foot of the ladder, McFarlane boomed, "All right, everybody double time, here we go!" He crashed into the room, screaming and shouting threats.

"We're going to clean house!" yelled McFarlane.

"You're going to shit," said a burly second classman, calmly seated at his desk, his three roommates equally at ease beside him.

Spinning around, McFarlane saw that his legions had been decimated. He now faced four very big upperclassmen with a single plebe for backup. As he hastily reviewed his options, a hand grasped his collar and lifted him off his feet. Dancing on air, he was deposited in the shower, there to receive an ice-cold drenching. He fled the room amid howls of laughter as his lone partner-in-crime was suffering the same fate.

Later, McFarlane figured he had gotten off easy. His dignity had been bruised and he had gotten a cold shower, no great shakes for a plebe. And he was grateful that the footballers, their menacing appearance aside, were happy-go-lucky guys. The other upperclassmen in his company were much the same, with the exception of one McFarlane considered a "totalitarian son of a bitch." During June Week, to silent cheers, Bud and some other plebes hauled him out of bed at five-thirty in the morning, carried him triumphantly across Tecumseh Court, and dumped him in the Severn River, which runs along the Academy grounds.

With no prior experience, McFarlane tried out for the plebe gymnastics team. It seemed like a sport at which little guys like him could excel. After a rocky start, he did.

"It was one of the stupidest investments of time I ever made in my life," he said, "but I was absorbed in gymnastics at the Academy. And part of it, I think, was because I'd never been an athlete, but I knew I had a gift. I did track [in high school], but I was not fast. But I knew my basic coordination was superior and so I said, 'You've got to find a way to demonstrate some athletic excellence.' And I decided gym was it. I just said, 'You're going to do this. You're going to be a varsity guy.' "

At first he tried the flying rings. They were fun until he attempted a double flyaway and landed on his head. Looking for something closer to sea level, he settled on the side horse and soon mastered it. He won his varsity letter three years running and took third place in the event at the eastern regional gymnastics championships as a senior.

As his first June Week rolled around, he looked back on a successful plebe year. He had done well enough in academics, though his performance in technical courses—those relating to boilers, turbines, pumps, and other forms of naval hardware—would hamper his class standing all four years. For McFarlane, though, his leadership grade was the key, and he stood first in grease among the plebes in his company both semesters.

That, after all, was what mattered. As his father had repeatedly told him, he was a McFarlane, born to lead.

For a solid hour, the father scolded his son, lashing him with his polished lawyer's voice as the boy's three older sisters and new stepmother cringed at the severity of the reprimand.

"Careless!" the father roared. "You can never expect to grow up to a position of leadership if this is the kind of presence of mind that you have. You're going to end up like the dumb kids in your class, and you won't be admired, and you won't succeed in life, and you'll just be a failure."

The boy stolidly accepted the abuse, as if it were his due, occasionally murmuring, "Yes, Dad," but offering no excuses. He was, as he was the first to admit, guilty. It wasn't as if someone else had left his new wool shirt at the park, the misdeed that inspired his father's anger.

The oldest child, Mary, a gentle girl not normally inclined to challenge her father, tried to intercede for her little brother. Rudely brushed aside, she burst into tears and raced from the room.

"You are a McFarlane!" the father thundered at the boy, resuming his tirade. "You're not just an ordinary person. You're somebody with a superior mind and intellect."

On and on it went, the themes of the rebuke unvarying. You have been blessed. Much is expected of you. You are failing to meet those expectations.

That encounter, which took place when Bud was eight, was typical of his relationship with his father, William Doddridge McFarlane, a populist Democrat elected to Congress from north-central Texas in 1932 as voters swept Franklin Delano Roosevelt into the White House.

The elder McFarlane was a vigorous man in his prime when his fifth child and second son, Robert Carl McFarlane, nicknamed Buddy, was born July 12, 1937. But his world would soon be shattered.

In April 1938, Alma McFarlane, lovely and vivacious, set her morning paper aside, took little Buddy in her arms and started up the stairs of the family's Georgetown home. Suddenly she cried out, handed the infant to the housekeeper, and collapsed. Moments later she was dead. She was thirty-seven.

The family had just returned to Washington after Alma's funeral in Texas when Buddy became gravely ill, apparently pneumonia complicated by mastoiditis. After several weeks in the hospital, he went into a sharp and seemingly terminal decline, only to be rescued by a massive blood transfusion provided by his uncle, Robert Norton McFarlane, the first of three generations of McFarlanes to attend Annapolis.

In the wake of his wife's death, William McFarlane found himself fighting for his political life against fellow Democrat Ed Gossett, whose spirited challenge he had barely turned back two years earlier. Two weeks before the July primary, on a cross-country whistle-stop tour, FDR rumbled into Wichita Falls, the district's commercial center, aboard a ten-coach train to lend support to the embattled McFarlane. The President's appearance was enough to force a runoff election a month later but not enough to win it for McFarlane. In the space of five months, McFarlane had lost his wife, been stripped of his congressional seat, and narrowly escaped having to bury a son.

Before his wife's death, William McFarlane had been proud, driven, at times messianic, but he frequently displayed a softer side. Most evenings, as Alma sat at the piano, he gathered his children around and crooned the popular songs of the day in a rich, full tenor. Now, at times, his behavior bordered on monstrous.

Untutored in child rearing, he tried to raise his kids as their mother would have, but he had neither her warmth nor common sense. Well-meaning but baffled, he relied on discipline, sternly meting out punishment. Daughter Barbara at four still wet the bed. He beat her with a hairbrush, sometimes breaking it on her small bottom. He whipped Buddy with a belt or tree switch until the boy entered first grade.

And always, at the dinner table, a constant refrain: You are a chosen person. You have a responsibility to lead. If you don't become a leader at the highest levels of our society, you will have failed.

In the process, he managed to imbue his children with a deep sense of public service, but the message was mixed. Bud kept listening for his father to say public service meant helping people. Instead, the elder McFarlane equated it with popularity and the admiration of others.

Those long-ago conversations bled into McFarlane's life, leaving him vulnerable to intimidation and to a disquieting, at times unseemly haste to accept blame when things went wrong. Nor did he challenge authority, at least not often, and rarely head-on.

He carried something else into adulthood, the belief that a man must be accountable for his actions, that grave failure, personal or otherwise, has a crystalline purity that defies temporizing, demands retribution, and requires a suitable act of atonement.

Along with four hundred other freshly minted sophomores, Bud went to sea for the first time in the summer of 1956 aboard the battleship *New Jersey,* an aging man-of-war. On a port call in Oslo, the midshipmen were guests of honor at a party hosted by the American embassy, which had recruited, as McFarlane remembers it, "about four hundred of the most attractive Norwegian young women that God ever made." As the party wound down, he and another midshipman, Walt Szczypinski, were befriended by two fetching women. Ever loyal, McFarlane asked his date to help him pick out a sweater for his girlfriend of the past year, Jonda Riley. That done, the women took McFarlane and Szczypinski to a restaurant midway up the side of Holmenkollen, the mountain overlooking the city and its harbor. Dining on the balcony, light-headed from aquavit, inhaling the fresh Scandinavian air, the midshipmen and their dates beheld a breathtaking sight on display below them. Two American battleships, two cruisers, and a dozen destroyers floated at their moorings, all their lights ablaze, the electric glow of the flotilla blending with the dying rays of the sun to create a scene of unforgettable brilliance.

For McFarlane, that evening became frozen in time, the naval power of the United States at its zenith, the ships commanded by men of proven courage and skill, the air alive with romance and promise. "I remember sitting up there on the side of that hill at this restaurant with Walt and these young women and feeling so lucky to be part of this country, with all this immense power," he later said.

He never saw his date again, but he still remembers her name: "Guri Horn, dots over the O," precise as always. His old Youngster Cruise ship was to loom larger in his life. Twenty-seven years later, in 1983, the New Jersey broke the horizon off the coast of Lebanon at a crucial moment in cease-fire negotiations in which he was a major participant. Once again, the old battlewagon symbolized American naval power, and, to McFarlane, the prospect that such power could be employed to restore peace to a war-ravaged land. A few weeks later, though, that hope was drenched in blood.

Bud McFarlane was too good to be true as far as Bob Drozd was concerned. Drozd, the product of Catholic schools, remembered that he and his friends back in Newark paid attention to the priests and nuns because there was literally hell to pay if they didn't. McFarlane was different. His exemplary conduct and personal decency did not seem to depend on the fear of temporal punishment or eternal damnation. "They didn't have to teach him anything," said Drozd, who roomed with McFarlane junior and senior years. "He was just a good person."

On Fridays midshipmen routinely tried to persuade someone else to make the long trek to the Bancroft Hall tailor shop to retrieve the freshly cleaned blue dress uniforms worn for Saturday inspections. Picking up uniforms was not a big deal, just a recurring red ass. More often than not, Drozd and his pals would be engaged in mutual cajoling when McFarlane materialized in the corridor, struggling under the weight of a half dozen or more heavy wool garments. "Here's yours," he'd say, handing Drozd his uniform. "Here's yours," he'd tell another friend, barely pausing to acknowledge the thank-yous that swam in his wake. There were other unexpected kindnesses. Drozd marveled at McFarlane's generosity of spirit, for a time worried that something was lacking in his own makeup. "Why can't you be that way?" he asked himself more than once. After a while, he decided he was okay, it was just that McFarlane was better.

McFarlane seemed the perfect midshipman—unflappable, self-contained, at ease with the system, a wise and willing counselor to his friends. "He always aligned himself with the system," said Drozd. "His orientation was to serve and to dedicate himself, never to compound problems."

But there was something missing, or so submerged that it rarely broke through the tight control he seemed determined to maintain—a sense of humor. "Certain things came very difficult to him," said Drozd. "As a matter of fact, smiling came difficult to him. I think he was criticized in his grease on a couple of occasions because he apparently had no fun side to his personality. And yet it was just like a lot of other emotions. He kept them down, he wouldn't let them show on the surface."

Drozd discovered something else about McFarlane that struck him as odd. On the phone, meeting someone for the first time, or in formal settings, his voice dropped several octaves so that he seemed to be speaking in pronouncements. Drozd, one of the first to notice the quirk, called it McFarlane's centurion voice.

"Somebody must have said to him at one point or another, There is no person who is successful that has a high, strident voice," said Drozd. At first he thought McFarlane got it from a Dale Carnegie self-help book. On further reflection he decided it was a legacy of McFarlane's father.

The elder McFarlane, by then a Justice Department lawyer in Washington, would sometimes take his son and Drozd to lunch on Capitol Hill. Drozd enjoyed the outings, but recalls thinking how old the father seemed, almost as if he were Bud's grandfather. He found him prejudiced, especially toward American Indians, even though at the time he was assigned to Indian affairs cases. "His remarks about Indians astounded me," said Drozd. "He had almost no use for them at all." However bigoted the father's views, Drozd considered him a warm person until he noticed he was warm in the same way with everyone he met. Around that time Drozd realized he had never seen him hug his son.

Singing in the Chapel Choir, which he joined soon after arriving at Annapolis, was part of McFarlane's evolving spirituality. As a youth, he had been relatively unmoved by church and Sunday school. At Annapolis, he began questioning his life and its direction, at times his very existence. Why am I here? he asked himself. Not just at the Naval Academy, but here on earth? He concluded that, with the world made up of very unequal beings, the more gifted such as he had an obligation to help the others. But how?

At first, he decided that he should undertake whatever chore was most needed by mankind. That led him to think about practicing medicine in the Third World, perhaps teaching starving natives in Africa how to raise crops. But he knew he would not be much good at such tasks. Soon he was considering a religious vocation.

"I began to think, If you're going to best serve God you ought to be a minister," he said, "because those who have a deep conviction about God and, in my case, Christianity and the basic tenets of Resurrection and eternal life have an obligation to spread the Gospel, literally."

He was well into the first semester of his junior year by then. If he was going to enter the ministry he would have to act quickly since by law he could not resign from the Academy once the current term ended. Confused, he consulted one of the Academy chaplains, Lieutenant Commander Bob Trett, a former naval aviator. Trett explained that he should not view the ministry, missionary work, or other church-related professions as the highest callings. He told McFarlane to look at the church as a family that could be served in many ways. The criterion should be, What do you enjoy doing that can be used to help others?

The talks with Trett helped, providing him with some guidelines for evaluating possible career changes. But the idea of entering the ministry still gripped him, developing into a full-blown religious crisis shortly before Christmas. In his room, in great emotional turmoil, he grew feverish, felt faint, and headed for sick bay. Soon he was in the hospital. After a battery of tests, his doctor delivered the verdict: flu.

"Is that all?" he asked.

"Yes, it is," the doctor replied.

His brother, Bill, who was stationed in Washington, visited him at the hospital. "I've got to figure out what to do with my life," Bud told him. "I'm thinking about the ministry and leaving the Academy." Bill, whose wife was dying of cancer at the time, was unsympathetic. "That's a bunch of crap," he said. "Study hard, get good grades and graduate, and shut up about this stuff."

He went home for Christmas, determined to discuss the matter with his father. After hearing Bud out, his father echoed his brother. "Look, you're going to be a naval officer, so study hard, graduate, learn your Navy skills," he said. "That's your job, that's your profession." Bud pressed his father to engage on the issue, but got more of the same. So he dropped it.

Unwilling to challenge his father directly, he returned to Annapolis after Christmas still floundering. He met with Trett a few more times, as well as Earl Ninow, a sympathetic Navy doctor. Finally, he decided to stay at the Academy, persuading himself that he could be both a great fighter pilot and a good man. But he took lessons from the experience, some of them devastating.

"It was clear that Dad believed that when you had a problem you should solve it," he said. "Every person who aspires to be a leader must be self-contained, that to show uncertainty or vulnerability is a weakness. And even to seek advice is evidence that you don't know something, and you should never do that. It is a weakness."

He bought it all.

"I felt from then on in my professional life that leaders lead. They decide, for better or for worse, and move out, and if you can't do that you shouldn't lead. . . . So that flaw, really, to believe that you have all the answers or that if you don't you can't afford to say so, pretty much dominated the way I lived."

The spiritual crisis more or less behind him, he completed the remainder of his junior year successfully, gave Jonda a miniature of his class ring during June Week 1958 to formalize their engagement, then sailed off on his first class cruise aboard the carrier *Essex*.

The *Essex* was part of the American Sixth Fleet patrolling the Mediterranean. Arab nationalism, ignited by the mercurial Egyptian leader Gamal Abdel Nasser, was flaring across the Middle East that summer, much as Khomeini-style Islamic fundamentalism would inflame the region two decades later. In Lebanon, sectarian violence had erupted.

Aboard the *Essex*, McFarlane went about the business of learning the skills of a junior officer, standing watches under instruction on the bridge and in the Combat Information Center. One night in Athens, he and a friend had a few drinks, grew weary, and returned to the ship hours before liberty expired. Earlier that day, July 14, a military coup had toppled King Faisal II, the twenty-three-year-old pro-British monarch of Iraq, whom Arab nationalists denounced as a Western lackey. He and his family were killed and the king's body dragged through the streets of Baghdad. In Beirut, fighting for his political life, President Camille Chamoun ascribed the assassinations to Nasserites and their Soviet backers, an arguable claim. He further insisted that the killings had unleashed forces that could topple his government within forty-eight hours unless American troops came to his aid. In Washington, President Eisenhower decided to act, dispatching the Sixth Fleet, with its embarked contingent of Marines, to Lebanon at flank speed. McFarlane was barely back aboard ship when the *Essex* weighed anchor for Lebanon. Much of the liberty party, including many officers, were left ashore.

Two thousand Marines in full battle dress, supported by aircraft from the *Essex*, swarmed across the beach south of Beirut on the afternoon of July 15, the unopposed landings scattering sunbathers and teenage soda-pop vendors.

Aboard the *Essex*, midshipmen were plucked from their apprentice roles to take up the slack for officers stranded in Athens. McFarlane, who had turned twenty a few days earlier, suddenly found himself a full-fledged watch officer in CIC, the ship's operational nerve center, overseeing the activities of more than a dozen enlisted men as they peered at glowing radarscopes, tracking the movements of the scores of vessels and aircraft crisscrossing the area.

As he left his stateroom on that first morning off Lebanon, a bustle of activity on the hangar deck caught his attention. Marine sentries had cordoned off a squadron of Navy blue AD Skyraiders, large, lumbering, propeller-driven aircraft that looked like refugees from the golden age of flight amid the sleek, high-performance jet squadrons embarked on the *Essex*. Inside a circle of no-nonsense Marines, ammo handlers were gingerly loading oval-shaped bombs onto the aircraft, attaching them along the centerline, one to a plane, so that they hung like pilotfish below the fuselage. Drawing closer, McFarlane asked an officer what was going on. "Special weapons," the officer replied, using a standard euphemism that McFarlane well understood.

What the hell is going on here? a thunderstruck McFarlane wondered. Why are we arming all these old clunkers with nukes? The officer explained that the fleet's operation order contained a contingency plan for a nuclear attack on the Soviet Union. As for the Skyraiders, their aesthetic shortcomings aside, they had greater range than the jets. The doomsday planning reflected American fears that the Soviets, seeing the United States preoccupied with Lebanon, might move militarily elsewhere, perhaps Berlin or North Korea. Because the Soviets acted with restraint, no planes armed with nuclear weapons were launched. For young Midshipman McFarlane, though, just weeks away from the fun and games of June Week, the vintage Skyraiders and their chilling payload left an impression he would never forget.

A quarter century later, that apocalyptic vision was no less vivid. By then he was in the White House, determined to devote most of his time and energy to reducing the threat of nuclear holocaust. He did, but while he was looking the other way Lebanon creeped up on him again, as did a few other things.

To all outward appearances, McFarlane enjoyed a productive senior year. He wore the four stripes of the brigade administrative officer in the fall and commanded his midshipman company in the spring. Despite difficulties with some of the dreary technical courses, he would graduate relatively high in the class, 108 out of 798.

That fall, the six-striper, Shorty Wilson, was relieved and demoted to the rank and file, the only known instance in which a brigade commander has been shorn of his stripes. A young Annapolis woman had infiltrated Bancroft Hall by masquerading as a midshipman. Wilson was not involved, but he learned of the stunt and failed to report it. The search for a new brigade commander was confined to a dozen midshipmen. McFarlane was in the hunt, though he knew there was little likelihood of making a jump from four to six stripes. He didn't. After the selection was made, however, his company officer told him he had greatly impressed the commandant of midshipmen, who wanted him to know that he had been on the short list of candidates to succeed Wilson. That recognition, from a superior he respected, was almost as good as commanding the brigade.

His personal life was falling into place, too. He and Jonda, nicknamed Jonny, were to be married right after June Week. There had been one major disappointment. His eyes had weakened, ending any hope of flying jets. On service selection night, he chose the Marine Corps because it seemed to offer earlier opportunities for command than the Navy.

At graduation, the Secretary of the Navy, William B. Franke, distributed diplomas to the 107 midshipmen graduating with distinction, an honor McFarlane missed by one place in class standing. The unfortunate Shorty Wilson was one of the elite, his classmates greeting his appearance on stage with a thunderous ovation, by far the loudest for any of the graduates.

A week or so earlier, McFarlane and Bob Drozd were lying in their racks after lights out.

"You know," said McFarlane, "if you were to do the hard thing instead of the easy thing you probably should dedicate yourself to something more altruistic."

Drozd was astonished by the statement, felt it related to McFarlane's decision the previous year to forgo the ministry and remain at the Academy. He was tempted to tell his roommate to lighten up. They were coming to the end of four tough years. In a matter of days, they would be commissioned, which meant moving into the profession for which they had rigorously prepared themselves. They were on the verge of actually enjoying life. Now was the time to raise a little hell, not stare at the ceiling and worry about roads not taken. But Drozd said nothing. What's hounding him? Drozd wondered. Who are these ghosts that are still haunting him? Hasn't he satisfied them yet?

CHAPTER THREE

SHOWDOWN

The family patriarch, Oliver Laurence North, a small, dignified man who sported a thin mustache and refused to eat in restaurants without tablecloths, emigrated from England in 1907. He settled first in Upper Darby, Pennsylvania, then moved to the Hudson Valley town of Philmont in 1927. An expert in textiles, he soon became manager of one of the town's largest mills. His son, Oliver Clay North, known as Clay, graduated from the University of Pennsylvania's prestigious Wharton School of Finance, then joined his father in Philmont, working side by side with him in the mill they opened during the Depression.

Clay joined the Army in November 1941, a few weeks before Pearl Harbor. Not long after, he married Ann Clancy, a tall, slim woman of aristocratic bearing who held a teaching degree from Oswego State College on the banks of Lake Ontario. He returned to Philmont in 1945 wearing both the Silver and Bronze Stars, having distinguished himself in the Battle of the Bulge. Decked out in his uniform and medals, he led the town's homecoming parade down Main Street. The Norths brought with them two sons: a baby, Jack, born earlier the same year, and their oldest, Oliver Laurence, born October 7, 1943, at Fort Sam Houston in San Antonio. Everyone called him Larry, as family and some close friends still do today.

In Philmont, population 1,600, kids used to leap off the railroad bridge into the churning waters of Agawamuck Creek. Larry was never the first to jump.

"Sometimes we had to throw him off," laughed Dale Rowe, an old friend.

As befits a blue-collar town down on its luck for decades, Philmont had its share of tough guys. Larry was not one of them. Smaller than most, he did not look for fights. At times, he ran from them.

At tiny Ockawamick High School, the rugged male that he came to personify tested his manhood on the gridiron. But Larry did not go out for football. He ran track and cross-country instead.

Nearly three decades later, his old girlfriend conceded that the small clique to which he belonged seemed a little different. She searched for a word, settled on one, but held back because she still felt protective after all those years. Finally, hesitantly, she whispered it.

Nerds.

"I think that's how people looked at them," said Lynore White Carnes. "They weren't your glamour boys. They were the sort of boys who grow up into interesting men."

And so he did. More than interesting. A legend in his own time. During his formative years in Philmont, though, the Oliver North the world knows today—tough, daring, a man with a mission and the judgment of a wedge of cheddar cheese—could barely be glimpsed. In Philmont he was neither hotshot nor zealot. Like most of his friends, he was a nice kid going nowhere.

Even so, there were clues. Track and cross-country meant grueling practices and little glamour. No star, Larry North made up in determination what he lacked in talent. "He had guts to spare," said Russ Robertson, who coached both teams. "He pushed and pushed."

During basketball season, North was the team's scorekeeper, a humble supporting role. In taking it on, though, he fortified his reputation as the kid to see when there was a job, rotten or otherwise, that needed doing. "He'd do anything he was asked," said Dale Rowe. "He was always a team guy. If you had any job to be done and you couldn't find anyone else that wanted to do it, you'd give it to Larry. No matter how menial it was or how important it was, he would do the job." In Philmont, it was Ask Larry. At the White House, Call Ollie.

In class North was an above-average student, though he never made the honor roll. Most of his teachers liked him because he was friendly, outgoing, and volunteered a lot, which led some classmates to view him as a brownnose. "If he was absent you always knew it," said Bob Bowes, who taught North world history. "He was the type of kid who would tackle questions most kids wouldn't, even if he was wrong." That was fine with Bowes. "A wrong answer is better than nothing," he said, unwittingly endorsing a penchant for improvisation that would bedevil the nation a quarter century later.

Larry North was a young man in search of direction in 1963 as he approached the end of his senior year in high school. He was one of only three seniors to win a New York State Regents scholarship, which was based on a standardized competitive examination. He was accepted at Notre Dame and Holy Cross, but neither came up with scholarship money and the Regents grant could only be used in-state. He settled on Brockport State Teachers College, a small school near Rochester with a solid, if unspectacular, reputation.

As a freshman, he learned about the Platoon Leaders Course, a Marine Corps program to recruit junior officers. Participants spent six weeks for two summers at the Marine base at Quantico, Virginia. Successful candidates were commissioned second lieutenants upon graduation. Larry spent the following summer at Quantico, going through the officer candidate version of boot camp under the tutelage of a remorseless crew of drill instructors. He loved it. In the fall, he returned to Brockport for his sophomore year and began efforts to get into Annapolis. He was not in the initial group selected, but a few weeks before the new class reported an appointment materialized. For two years he had been marking time. Now he was racing for daylight.

Like John Poindexter, Ollie North came from somewhere, a nice street in small-town America. His classmate, Jim Webb, came from everywhere.

Trailing along behind his father, a rock-ribbed Air Force officer, James Henry Webb, Jr., grew up on a numbing succession of dusty, rundown military bases in the South, Southwest, Midwest, and West. Born February 9, 1946, in St. Joseph, Missouri, he had attended a dozen schools, at times three in one year, by the time he graduated from high school.

In the streets and schoolyards of his youth, during the Vietnam War and later in Washington's power centers, fighting has always been part of Jim Webb's life. He is, as those who know him readily attest, a warrior, the descendant of warriors, an American samurai for whom the ultimate test is combat.

He started early. When he was four, his father, a veteran of World War II and the Berlin Airlift, would clench his fist and hold it out.

Are you tough?

Yes, I'm tough.

Then hit my fist.

Jimmy swung, crushing the knuckles of his tiny hand.

Is that as hard as you can hit? Hit it again.

The boy swung again. Same result.

Are you tough?

Yes, I'm tough.

Then hit it again.

He swung again. By now he was sobbing.

Come on, come on, you're tough. Hit my fist.

The elder Webb had a gentler side, an unrealized artistic strain, alloyed at times with whimsy. He played the trumpet in his high school band, occasionally pulls it out of the closet today. And he loved poetry, encouraging Jimmy, his brother, and two sisters to recite verse at the dinner table, "Gunga Din," the rest of Kipling, Tennyson, Frost.

He also inspired a devotion at times indistinguishable from hero worship. When Jimmy was four, the shortage of family housing forced his wife and kids to live in St. Joe while he bunked in a BOQ nearly four hundred miles away at Scott Air Base in Illinois, his duty station. Driving narrow two-lane roads, he made it home nearly every weekend. One wintry afternoon, Jimmy was in the tub when he realized his father had left to return to base. Naked and wet, he raced outside, frantically searching for him, screaming, refusing to go back into the house, taking ill as a result of the incident.

In his rough-hewn way, the elder Webb gave his son many things, some directly, more often through his bearing, his toughness, his self-discipline. "He brags that he's responsible for my success because at every single decision point in my life he's given me advice that I have ignored," said Webb. But, he added, his father passed on more than bad advice. "I have my dad's ability to run through a wall. He taught me a lot about leadership. He taught me how to fight."

At fourteen, Jimmy began boxing under the lights at tournaments and smokers throughout the Midwest. By the time he finished high school, he had fought thirty, maybe forty times. He loved the scene, rapping with the other boxers, taking on all comers, rednecks like himself, blacks, Indians, whomever they threw in the ring with him. One time his younger brother, Gary, asked why he liked boxing so much. "Because it's just you and the other guy and all that smoke."

As he neared the end of high school, Jim Webb had a secret. He knew he was good for something. Sure he screwed off in class, but he had aced every standardized test he ever took. What did that mean, though? What did you do with it? He was a voracious reader, and he wrote well. Did those things mean anything? He had no idea what civilians did. Should he go to college? Could he even get in? If so, what should he study? He went to his father for advice. He was no help. He didn't know what civilians did, either.

Around that time he overheard his mother and father talking about him. The gist of the conversation was that he seemed determined to be a bum. It scared him, caused him to think seriously about his future.

He decided he wanted to go to college. Prospects were not encouraging. Money was scarce, his grades mediocre. Then a solution beckoned, an obvious one in retrospect. He decided he wanted a career in the military and applied for a Navy ROTC scholarship, which offered a free ride for four years. On paper he didn't have a chance, but his facility with standardized tests helped. There were three finalists from his school for one scholarship—the valedictorian, the salutatorian, and Webb. Webb got it. He had his choice of several colleges, chose the University of Southern California, for the weather.

He did well in class, even better on the drill field. In the spring of his freshman year he was named the outstanding cadet in his NROTC unit. He also received a nomination to the Naval Academy and eagerly accepted it. He finally knew where he belonged, in the Marine Corps, by way of Annapolis.

The night before he graduated from high school in May 1963, he stayed up late and wrote a poem.

> I want to go back, I want to go back,
> Go back to a day left behind,
> Forgotten in life's rush to the grave.
> Go back to a crisp, cutting autumn day,
> With burning leaves and winter's promise in the air.
> I want to go back to a day when nothing happened,
> A day spent lolling in the grass,
> When "the nothings" were my greatest worry,
> And "the somethings" were for the Other World,
> The world of the cannibals known as adults.
>
> I want to go back—
> I'm a fool.
> I'll be very old when I return,
> When once again a nothing will mean something,
> When a day will be spent lying, and thinking, and smelling.
> But then I will envy my cannibal sons,
> And think only of my man eating days,
> When I could brag of sending someone back,
> Back to lie, and think, and smell.
>
> I do not want to be a cannibal,
> But I will learn to like the meat,
> I will learn to live for the kill, and the advance,
> And I won't want the "good life,"
> I won't want to go back.

When Ollie North entered the Naval Academy in June 1963, his life began to weave itself together. He was no longer a dangling man, going through the motions at Brockport because there was no alternative that excited his enormous, if unfocused, enthusiasms. He now had a direction that incorporated his talents, personality, and interests.

With a summer at Quantico behind him, he was better prepared than most for the plebe summer madness. Two years older than the majority of his classmates, he had achieved the physical maturity he lacked in high school. He should have eased right in. He didn't. Briefly abandoning the deference to seniors that has always been his trademark, he made it hard for himself.

"He was a cocky son of a gun," said Walt Teichgraber, North's squad leader that summer. "He was the type of guy who was generally squared away, generally knew his stuff and always looked good, but he had this damned cockiness about him that really pissed the upperclassmen off. You'd have him around for a come-around or something, give him push-ups or shove out or whatever the hell it was, he'd just get this damn smirk on his face that just drove you crazy, like I've seen worse than this, you guys can't do anything to me. I don't know what the hell he was thinking at the time, but, boy, he really teed people off to the point where he was one of those guys that was sort of singled out, you know, let's get him the hell out of here."

The history and tradition that quickly engulf the new plebe were punctuated that August when President Kennedy choppered to Annapolis to mark the torpedoing of his patrol boat, PT-109, in the Pacific twenty years earlier. "You will have the chance in the next ten, twenty, and thirty years," he told the plebes, "to serve the cause of freedom and your country all over the globe, to hold positions of the highest responsibility, to recognize that upon your good judgment in many cases may well rest not only the well-being of the men with whom you serve, but also in a very real sense the security of your country."

His tone was conversational, one sailor to another. He concluded with a joke familiar to most Navy men. It involved an admiral whose career had far outpaced those of his contemporaries. One day he suffered a heart attack. A yeoman who had been with him from the beginning remembered that each morning the admiral would open his safe, pull out a piece of paper, glance at it, then return it to the safe. I've got to see that paper, the yeoman said to himself. Opening the safe, he found the paper. It read, port—left, starboard—right.

Laughing, the President added, "If you can remember that, your careers are assured." In fact, at least one member of the audience would have been better off remembering what Kennedy had said about good judgment.

North was insulated from the worst travails of plebe year. A member of the freshman cross-country team, he dined with other runners at separate training tables in the Mess Hall, where the food was better and there was little if any hazing.

At Christmas he went home to Philmont and resumed a warm if slow-moving romance with his hometown sweetheart, Lynore White. They had known each other all through high school, but hadn't begun dating until after he graduated, a year ahead of her. Lynore was blond, slim, and bright, the class salutatorian. By that Christmas, as North celebrated his first six months at Annapolis, she was halfway through her sophomore year at Smith.

In February, over the four-day Washington's Birthday weekend, North decided to visit his brother, Jack, at Niagara University in western New York State. Five other midshipmen were going in the same direction, so they decided to drive up together. A heavy snow was falling as they began the journey north after their last class on Thursday. Tommy Parker, a plebe from Brockport, was at the wheel of the Chevy II rental car. Outside Harrisburg, a state police cruiser stopped them for speeding. The cop saw the six uniformed midshipmen jammed into the car and let them go with a warning.

The snow let up as they turned onto Route 15 outside of Harrisburg, but negotiating the dark two-lane road was tricky for the sleepy midshipmen as they moved through the mountains of central Pennsylvania. After a stop in Williamsport to let one rider off, Bobby Wagner took over the wheel. Drowsy, Wagner urged the mid riding shotgun to keep him awake. They crossed the border into New York, skirted Corning, and were approaching the town of Painted Post when disaster struck. At about 2:00 A.M., with everyone else asleep, Wagner nodded off. As he did so, the car sideswiped a farm vehicle, then plowed head-on into an oncoming tractor-trailer. Wagner was killed instantly. The other four midshipmen sustained injuries of varying severity. North suffered head, back, and knee injuries, along with a broken nose, jaw, and leg. Parker received a concussion that deprived him of his memory for three weeks. Billy Joe Mullins broke his back and was paralyzed from the waist down. The fifth passenger, Mike Cathey, received burns, a broken pelvis, and a broken arm.

The survivors were rushed to the hospital in Corning, a small facility barely capable of handling an accident of that magnitude. When Herkie Warner, a friend of North's from Brockport, drove down the next day, he found Ollie and two of the other mids lying on gurneys on an enclosed porch. Through battered lips, North said, "I'll beat this."

A day or so later, a local high school senior, Jack Holly, stopped by the hospital. Holly, the son of the doctor who first treated the accident victims, was thinking about the Academy and looking for advice. North, though clearly in pain, was friendly and upbeat and welcomed the youngster's questions. He gave Holly the pros and cons, made sure he understood Annapolis was not for everyone.

Their conditions stabilized, the injured midshipmen were transferred to Bethesda Naval Hospital near Washington, then to a smaller hospital on the Academy grounds. It soon became evident that North could not rejoin his class. To remain at Annapolis, he would have to repeat his freshman year, joining the incoming Class of 1968 in the summer, assuming his recuperation remained on course.

In the spring, the Navy shipped North home to Philmont to continue his recovery. He mounted a Herculean effort to strengthen his right knee. By early summer, he was again being treated at Bethesda Naval Hospital. On a visit, Lynore White, who had not seen him since Christmas, was shocked at how badly he had been hurt. His nose, slim and regular before the accident, was now, as she remembers it, "smooshed in and pushed to the side" pending the plastic surgery that would correct some of the damage. He took weekend liberty from the hospital and drove Lynore to Annapolis, where they toured the Yard on foot. North seemed to enjoy showing her around, but his knees, scarred, encased in metal braces, made walking difficult. Later, they drove to Washington and walked some more. North never complained, acted like he wasn't even hurt.

In August 1964, two weeks before plebe summer ended for the Class of '68, North reported to Bancroft Hall. He had graduated from high school three years earlier and had two full years of college and most of another under his belt. Now he was about to begin a third freshman year, a member of the same class as Jack Holly, the doctor's kid from Corning, and Jim Webb.

Tommy Parker, one of the other accident victims, ran into North that first day back, was amazed to find him as enthusiastic as ever, maybe more so. Parker was turning back, too, but unlike North he had entered the Academy right out of high school. So many years and he's still a plebe, thought Parker, marveling at his friend's tenacity.

Though he had been around the military all his life, Jim Webb never set eyes on a service academy until the day he reported to Annapolis in late June 1964. He flew to Washington a few days early, staying with friends and taking in the sights. One afternoon he wandered through

Arlington Cemetery with its dizzying rows of graves and simple, chalk-white markers. A few years later, as opposition to the Vietnam War intensified and cries of "Yankee, go home" became commonplace, Webb pulled out one of the snapshots he took that day, tacked it to the bulletin board in his room, and scrawled under it, "These Yankees can't go home."

He bought a new suit and spit-shined his shoes to a mirror finish for his swearing-in. As his friends drove him through the gate, he said to himself, "I'm going to die for the Naval Academy. This is really it." On arrival, the new recruits were herded through lines to pick up uniforms, skivvies, athletic gear, toilet articles, everything a new midshipman might need if he showed up naked and empty-handed. There was little fanfare at first. People seemed to be whispering, as if loud voices would alert demonic forces to their presence. A Marine lieutenant flipped through Webb's personal data forms, saw that he had listed thirty-three separate home addresses, muttered, "I can't believe this."

Struggling under the weight of his suitcase, typewriter, and newly issued gear, Webb pushed through a set of double doors in Bancroft when a balled fist slammed into his chest. "Get over there," growled the second classman behind the fist, gesturing toward a dismal group of plebes. Webb was stunned. "Are you allowed to hit us?" he asked in a tone of disbelief. Turning to another second classman, the Fist said, "Hey, we've got a wise-ass over here." Webb quickly brought more grief on himself. "Those are pretty good-looking shoes," said the Fist. "Did you go to prep school?" Replied Webb, proudly, "No, sir. I was in a ROTC unit." Big mistake. Paying special attention to the kid with ROTC roots, the Fist and his cohorts ordered the plebes to race back and forth through the passageways, up the ladders to the next deck, down some more passageways. Then they ran them down to the barber shop, where they had their heads shaved.

Bits of hair now clung to Webb's neck and back. His new suit was ruined, the fabric mottled by white salt stains where he had sweated through it. In Dahlgren Hall, the cavernous armory where the plebes were to take the oath of office, the humidity settled on them like a pernicious vapor. As proud parents lined the catwalk above them, thirteen hundred young men listened to warm welcoming remarks from Academy authorities. They were, they were told, the cream of America's youth. Mothers fanned themselves with their programs as their sons passed out below. Webb was struck by the thought that there were two Naval Academies, "two fucking worlds," as he later put it: the real world behind the massive doors of Bancroft Hall and the ceremonial world that outsiders saw. Watching teary mothers wave handkerchiefs at their kids, he thought of his own family three thousand miles away in California, felt miserable and alone. As he and his classmates took the oath, it seemed as if he could hear a giant umbilical cord snap.

Stowing his gear in his room, he decided to make a tick mark on his blotter each time he thought of turning in his chit. That night, as he prepared for bed, he saw that he already had a dozen ticks. Just before lights out, the Fist chewed him out for marking up his blotter. In his rack, in the steamy darkness, he sobbed soundlessly. Not because of the rough first day and the prospect of many more to come. He knew he could handle that. He cried because he knew that no matter what happened it was not in him to quit and that he would probably be an old man before he knew if any of it made sense. He cried for a long time that night. As he would later write, he cried away his youth.

Boxing helped him get his bearings. One day he was being hazed by a Marine Corps–bound second classman, Chuck Warner. In a couple of hours, Webb was going to take on a bruiser nicknamed "Louie, Louie" in a plebe summer boxing smoker. Warner asked Webb if he was going to win the bout. "Yes, sir," Webb replied. "Bet your ass?" said Warner, meaning if Webb lost the second classman could "take his ass" by whacking it with the large world atlas issued to all midshipmen. "Yes, sir!" Webb replied. "Okay, Webb, your ass against mine," said the segundo. "Louie, Louie," it was later discovered, broke Webb's jaw in the first round, but Webb rallied and won the fight. Warner was waiting for him when he returned to his room. Webb braced up and sounded off. "I'll give you a choice, Webb," the second classman said. "My ass or my spoon." Spooning, or shaking hands with a plebe, meant that an upperclassman not only would never haze the plebe again, but that he would be his friend, often his protector. At that stage in plebe year, spooning was nearly unheard of and much to be desired. Warner extended his hand. "What'll it be, Webb, my ass or my spoon?" he asked. "I want your ass, sir," replied Webb, reaching for the atlas.

Webb had a tough plebe year and made it even tougher because he was, and is, congenitally incapable of playing dumb or backing down. "I told him, Jesus Christ, act humble," recalled George Webb, his first classman, the senior responsible for helping him navigate the reefs and shoals of plebe year. The firstie—no relation—quickly learned he had asked the impossible of Webb.

Shortly after the Brigade returned in September, four seniors who lived down the hall from Webb decided to break the unflappable baby-faced plebe. They told him to report to their room, then ordered him to rig three M-1 rifles, that is, to brace up with the rifles, combined weight about thirty pounds, resting on his outstretched arms. After several minutes Webb's arms started to drop. The firsties removed one of the rifles. Then another. Then the third. Then they ordered him to rig seven books. Then six. Each time his arms gave out he had to start over with one fewer book. Near the end of the grueling half-hour session, he was told to rig a pencil, finally a toothpick. As he strained to hold up the sliver of wood, the firsties clustered around him, peppering him with questions, musing that pain was irrelevant, telling him to quit and go home. Hotshit Webb can't even rig a goddamned toothpick, the firsties laughed.

At evening meal, Webb managed to anger the same first classmen. Ordering him back in their room, they took turns paddling him with a cricket bat, a prohibited practice. Two steps, then *Whack!* Each time a blow landed, Webb would holler, "Beat Army, sir!" or "Harder, sir!" Does it hurt, Webb? "No, sir!" The situation was getting out of hand. Even the firsties seemed to know they had gone too far, but no one would back down. "All you have to do is say it hurts," one of them said. "Harder, sir!" yelled Webb. Finally, someone broke the paddle on him. "Get out of here, Webb," he said. "Aye, aye, sir!" Webb shouted, racing out the door. Back in his own room, he ran into the closet so his roommates couldn't see him, pulled a laundry bag over his head, and cried for fifteen minutes. Looking back, he says he drew great strength from the experience. He had been tested and had survived. He displayed no bitterness, but twenty years later, when he was Secretary of the Navy, he rattled off the names of the four seniors without a moment's hesitation, as if he were reading from a list.

By late winter of his sophomore year, North was in the Academy hospital again. His right knee was badly swollen, his depression intense. On the ward, he told three first classmen that the knee had gotten so bad he was thinking of dropping out of the Academy. The authorities were already talking about having him turn back again, a prospect he dreaded. The firsties—Helmuts Feifs, Michael Wunsch, and Quentin Larsen—all planned to enter the Marine Corps. They liked North and did their best to persuade him to remain at the Academy. Feifs, who had knee problems of his own, felt confident that he would get a Marine commission and insisted that North would, too, probably without turning back. Wunsch made North his special project, taking considerable time over the next week trying to lift his spirits. One evening, after a long session with North, a beaming

Wunsch rejoined Feifs and Larsen. "The kid is going to stay," he said.

As North was fighting despondency, a grizzled Marine major came by to see the firsties. North, who joined the group, complained that even if he got his commission on time, the war in Vietnam—begun the year before—would be over before he had a chance to see action. "Don't worry, Ollie," the major said. "You'll get to go. You may even get to go twice. This fucker is going to go on forever." Thus did Ollie North meet Bill Corson.

Corson's life bears some resemblance to North's, but commands a sweep that makes North look like the underachieving son of a celebrated father. He has been a Marine (World War II, Korea, Vietnam), spy ("Asia—that's all anybody needs to know—as far west as Pakistan"), college professor (University of Miami, Howard University), and author. Some years ago he told *Washington Post* reporter Shelby Coffey III that in 1953 he carried the fuse for the first hydrogen bomb in the trunk of his car from Port Chicago to Oakland, California.

Corson's Marine Corps career was marked by mystery, indirection, and, at times, insubordination. Outside Marine circles, he is best known as the author of a book entitled *The Betrayal*, published five days after he retired in 1968. Corson himself labeled it "an act of heresy." The book is an unsparing indictment of the Vietnam War effort and just about everyone of note connected to it, Americans and South Vietnamese alike. The charges range from deception through stupidity and ignorance to outright corruption.

Corson arrived at the Academy in September 1964 as an instructor. His course in guerrilla warfare quickly became a midshipman favorite. His teaching methods were unconventional. He had books imported from mainland China, including three volumes of Mao's writing. To Corson, the lesson was clear: if you can't outlast the guerrilla, don't get in the game.

In addition to a nimble mind, a challenging intellect, and pronouncements that bordered on the outrageous, Corson was personally approachable. Midshipmen clustered around him, especially budding Marines like Wunsch and North, though not Jim Webb, who was never quite sure what to make of Corson. He defined his role as preparing his charges for combat leadership in Vietnam.

"Vietnam is the most ambiguous battle situation you will ever find if you spend a hundred years in the military," he told them. "Up is down and down is up, and young men will increasingly die if you don't understand that." He also offered personal advice, urging his midshipmen to delay the wedding until after Vietnam because daily television reports from the front would brutalize their wives. Corson's dictum: "Don't put the woman you love through that shit. Screw her if you want to, but don't marry her."

Ollie North and Bill Corson forged a friendship at Annapolis that lasted nearly twenty years. They had a falling out in the mid-1980s when Corson became suspicious of some of the men he would see with North, then a White House aide. Despite the rift, Corson worried about his old student and tried to warn him. Late at night, Corson's wife would tell him to get off the phone and come to bed. "I'm trying to straighten Oliver out," he would reply. There were hours of conversation, but for all the verbiage, Corson's message to North was simplicity itself: you're playing with bad guys, they're going to fuck you.

Jim Webb had a problem. His problem was Ollie North. It was March 1967 and North stood between Webb and the 145-pound Brigade boxing championship he had coveted for nearly three years. Despite his limp, North had battled his way into the finals. Webb knew he could beat him, but strange things had been happening in the days leading up to the fight. Other boxers came up to tell him that North had a steel plate in his head, which was not true but who the hell knew with North. Somebody even said, Jimmy, you hit Ollie in the head, you're gonna kill him. Webb sort of knew it was bullshit, except one day Denny Dilley, a classy boxer with a punch like a butterfly kiss, decked North with a jab in a sparring session, giving him a mild concussion.

Suddenly Webb noticed that the coach, Emerson Smith, had changed his training routine. He usually worked with the whole team, leaving individual instruction to his assistants. Now, every day, he was in the ring drilling North on techniques to use against southpaws like Webb. The coach is teaching him how to fight *me*, thought Webb, darkly. He's teaching him how to beat *me*!

Coach Smith, a warm and gentle man, later pleaded innocent to the charge of favoritism. As it happened, he had an Ollie North problem, too. He knew North's medical history, refused to even let him into the ring until he brought written permission from his surgeon. And, like Webb, he saw what Denny Dilley had done to him. "Denny Dilley can't fight his way out of a paper bag and he hits Oliver and drops him," the coach would later say. "I thought Oliver was going to get killed."

Webb didn't buy any of it. One day, shortly before the fight, the coach finished tutoring North and climbed through the ropes. Webb was standing beside the ring, hands on his hips, glaring.

"What about me, Coach?" he said. "What are you going to teach me about Ollie?"

Smith put his arm around Webb. "Jimmy, this is just a protective measure," he said. "You're ready. I'm just trying to get the bout even."

A young plebe, Fred Peck, watched events unfold. Webb and North, both juniors, epitomized all he hoped to be—a squared-away midshipman, a leader in his class, and, eventually, a Marine. He liked them both, but concluded they didn't much like each other. Both were intense, though neither was above grab-assing at practice. But never with each other. He sensed a rivalry between them, one that seemed destined to endure beyond Annapolis, as if they had been singled out for lifelong competition. To Peck, impressionable, in the throes of youthful hero worship, the Webb-North fight looked like more than a boxing match between two top midshipmen. It looked like a showdown.

On fight night, contrary to Coach Smith's words, Webb was not ready. He found himself in a classic no-win situation. If he beat North everyone would say, Way to go, champ, you beat a cripple. If he lost, humiliation. As Webb well realized, a crucial point was neglected in that equation. Whatever his handicaps, real or trumped up, North had fought and won enough times to get to the championship match. He was no pushover even if Webb had been at the top of his game, which he was not. Missing was the fighting edge, the remorseless determination that a fighter like Webb needed to take into the ring.

Years later, when Webb and North became prominent, the fight took on mythic proportions, as if the entire Brigade had talked of little else in the days preceding it. In reality, the fight was important to the two combatants, their friends, and members of the Academy's boxing brotherhood. For most midshipmen, it was just another bout on a night that everyone looked forward to because it offered a diversion from the Dark Ages. Which is not to say the evening wasn't colorful and exciting. In those days the boxing finals provided a rare public glimpse of the Brigade as it really was, an assemblage of would-be warriors who viewed physical courage as a standard against which they fully expected to be measured. Plebes painted elaborate banners heralding the finalists from their companies. The atmosphere was raucous, the mood bloodthirsty. The noise level compared to that at an Army-Navy game, confined to an enclosed space.

As Webb climbed through the ropes, his best friend, Vic Reston, barely recognized him, could tell from his expression he was not mentally prepared. North, by contrast, looked animated, ready to go. The Brigade was in a frenzy, the plebes, briefly unchained, screamed for blood as the fighters were introduced. The fighters wore the Navy colors, Webb in blue, North in gold.

North was all over Webb at the bell, throwing him off balance with an aggressive, swarming attack. Ollie was clumsy, stiff-legged, but thanks to Coach Smith not without sophistication. Webb packed a wicked left hook, but North kept circling away from it, just as the coach had instructed him. North had also learned that if he crowded Webb he just might be able to smother the stinging right jabs. All this the coach had taught him.

Webb's heart was not in it, but he was good enough to hold North off and land some blows. He was giving North a lesson in footwork, coolly slipping punches as North charged forward. But Vic Reston, at ringside, realized that his friend was not counterpunching, which was what he did best. Instead he'd slip a punch, then dance away. He was making North look awkward, but North knew aggressiveness counted. As the fight wore on, North, according to Reston, started muttering through his mouthpiece at Webb, trying to obscure his own clumsiness by making it appear that Webb was afraid of him. Each time Webb stylishly ducked under one of his lunging punches, Reston could hear North say, Come on, man, let's fight, stop running away.

The crowd roared as the third round ended. A great fight. No one knew who won. Then the announcement. All the cards agreed. First round, North ten points, Webb nine points. Second round, even. Third round, North ten points, Webb nine points. The winner by unanimous decision, Oliver North.

The next day, Webb confronted Coach Smith. "He jumped on me," the coach recalled. "He lambasted me. I walked off. He was probably the only midshipman I had words with in twenty-seven years."

Webb does not remember North talking to him in the ring and North denies it. Any lingering bitterness might have long since faded had it not been for an alleged incident the following fall at the first pep rally of the new football season. Webb was standing with his fiancée, Barbara DuCote, and his company officer, a Marine captain just back from Vietnam named Andy Ennis, when North strolled up sporting his varsity sweater. Patting the large blue and gold "N" adorning it, complete with tiny boxing gloves imbedded in the center, he said to Webb, Hey, how do you like this, what do you think? Webb looked at him, then turned away, as if North were just a bad dream, a fragment of underdone potato, as if he weren't there.

That's Webb's version, according to those who have heard his story. Barbara (DuCote) Samorajczyk, now Webb's ex-wife, also recalled the incident. North said it never happened. "That's totally foreign to my way of dealing with anybody," he said. "I wouldn't do something like that."

A packet of letters greeted Webb in Annapolis when he returned from first class cruise in September 1967. One was from Chuck Warner, who as an upperclassman bet his ass against Webb's on the "Louie, Louie" fight, then became a close and valued friend. Warner, a Marine, was recuperating on Guam from a chest wound, but said he would soon be returning to Vietnam. Glad you're okay, Webb scribbled back, keep your head down, write when you can.

With the Class of 1968 taking over the Academy's leadership posts, Webb was named brigade administrative officer, a four-striper position. His duties were relatively light, though they included one somber element. His in-box was the first stop for reports of Annapolis men killed in Vietnam.

Soon after classes resumed, Webb made his daily visit to the Main Office to pick up official correspondence. Walking back to his room, he saw that the mail included three death notices. He didn't know the first two KIAs. The third name turned him to stone. Charles W. F. Warner, '66. Warner had gone back in-country and taken another round in the chest. In a nearby room, Glen Campbell was singing "By the Time I Get to Phoenix." Webb used to love the song. Since that day, he has gotten sick every time he's heard it.

In the midst of the urban riots that followed Martin Luther King, Jr.'s, assassination in April 1968, a woman on her way to visit North in Annapolis called him from the bus station in downtown Washington. She said she was stranded, that there was burning and looting all around. A frantic North explained the situation to Academy authorities, who provided him with an official Navy car and a .45-caliber pistol. He tore down Route 50 and entered Washington on New York Avenue, but before he could reach the bus station a crowd of angry black men swarmed into the street, forcing him to stop. Jacking a round into the chamber of the .45, he swung open the door and leveled the pistol. The crowd parted, and North drove off and rescued the girl. Afterward, he told the story to Fred Peck and others, though some recalled North saying he was on his way to the Library of Congress to research a paper. "It's a great story," laughed Peck years later. "I don't know if it's true or not."

With North at the Academy, as in later years, that was often the case. His stories were frequently larger than life, bearing all the earmarks of tall tales despite the earnest delivery—eyebrows tented, blue eyes glistening, sincerity etched into his rugged yet boyish features, about the way he looked on the stand at the Iran-Contra hearings.

North's years at Annapolis were replete with dark foreshadowing, at least when viewed from a certain angle. Change the angle, though, and the new perspective offered a more rosy view, less to be alarmed about, much to be admired.

At times he seemed to lapse into caricature. His relations with women often took on a painful correctness. One classmate saw him as a master of phony gallantry, reacting to the off-color remark uttered in mixed company with an offended "Hey, I don't want to hear that kind of talk around here."

From Academy days on, North had a way of making his juniors idolize him and his superiors immensely grateful that he worked for them. North's peers were never quite sure what to make of him, then or now. Even many of those who liked him were vaguely troubled by him, as if they didn't know what he would do next. "Peers cut through all the bullshit," said a classmate in his company. "And with Ollie it was either love him or dislike him. I can't say there was any middle ground." Said another classmate, "A lot of guys thought Ollie was full of crap. But you can't hate him. You can disapprove of him, but you can't hate him." Roommate John Sinclair recalled something a friend said on Graduation Day 1968: "Ollie's going to be in the news twenty years from now. He's either going to do something great or he's going to fall on his nose." About five years earlier, Hal Foster, a high school classmate of Jim Webb's, had described Webb in similar terms. But by 1968 the echo was faint. By then, nobody was saying things like that about Webb.

At the Academy, as elsewhere, Ollie North could always draw a crowd. He was flamboyant and mercurial; everyone always knew he was around. Father Jake Laboon, the Catholic chaplain, could tell when North entered a room even if his back was turned. "He was like an elephant walking in," said the priest. "He made his presence felt."

Webb wasn't Catholic, but Father Laboon knew him as well, at the Academy and later. He described the two men differently. "Jim is a much deeper thinker," he said. "He doesn't show his emotions as easily as Ollie does. I wouldn't say he is unemotional, but Jim is very reserved."

And Ollie?

"Ollie," said the priest, pausing, smiling. "Ollie is champagne."

In the spring of his senior year, Webb made a final run at the Brigade boxing title that had eluded him for three years. It was his last chance to win his letter, the coveted Navy "N" that North had supposedly patted so triumphantly at the pep rally the previous fall. Webb dropped down a weight class this time, hoping to enhance his chances. Not that he was worried about North. North wasn't boxing that year. He was helping Emerson Smith coach the team. And on the night of the Brigade championships, he was working the corner of Webb's opponent, Tommy Hayes.

Webb battered Hayes in the first two rounds and continued to pound him in the third. He could taste victory even though he was angry at Hayes for hitting on the break. With less than a minute left, Hayes took another questionable shot as the fighters came out of a clinch. Webb dropped his hands and glared at him. Hayes couldn't believe Webb was leaving himself defenseless and uncorked a vicious right, staggering Webb and dropping him to a knee.

Rising quickly, Webb shifted his glare to the referee, who was administering the mandatory eight count. Enraged, oblivious to the count, Webb forgot the ref was waiting for him to bring his hands back up into a fighting position, signaling his ability to go on. Suddenly the ref waved his hands above his head, stopping the fight and declaring Hayes the winner by technical knockout.

Webb went crazy, screaming at the ref as North pumped the hand of Tommy Hayes, no less surprised than Webb at the abrupt shift in fortunes. Later, under the ring, Hayes offered Webb his hand. Webb walked away.

Fifteen years later, in a novel about Annapolis, Webb wrote of a fight in which the protagonist, Wild Bill Fogarty, loses a controversial TKO in much the same way. Afterward Fogarty says, "It will piss me off till the day I die." No one who knows Webb doubts the author's voice in his character's words, least of all Tommy Hayes. Hayes was working in the Pentagon in 1984 when Webb was named an assistant secretary of defense. By then a Navy commander, Hayes suspected Webb had never quite put the fight behind him and thought it might be politic to drop by and clear the air with his new boss. Hey, come on, don't worry, said Webb, that was a long time ago. They shook hands, but Hayes walked out rolling his eyes.

It didn't help matters that ever since publication of the Annapolis novel, Webb had been getting occasional reports that Ollie North was claiming that he, not Hayes, was the model for the boxer who beat Webb's fictional alter ego.

At the Academy, North took over as 7th Company commander. His knees still threatened his chances for a Marine commission. "I can't tell you the moxie, the guts, the pain he endured," said his friend John Sinclair. Twice a week, a limping North would lead his troops to the lush Worden Field greensward for dress parades. But just at the lip of the parade grounds, somewhere between "Company, left turn, HUH!" and the "Company, right turn, HUH!" that would take him onto the field in front of officers with a voice in his future, North would grit his teeth and the limp would disappear. Sword unsheathed, marching proudly before his company as it passed in review, so close now to those same officers that they could detect even the slightest grimace, a stonefaced North would snap the hilt of his sword to his chin, then whip it down to his hip as he bellowed loud, clear, and perhaps a little defiantly, "Company—eyes—HHRIGHT!"

Standing watch one night, Rich Petrino, the brigade commander, came upon North in the corridors of Bancroft Hall after lights out. North said he was searching for his medical records so he could remove information that he thought might hamper his chances of getting in the Marines. Petrino did not report the incident, but nearly two decades later, after the Iran-Contra scandal had broken, he told the story in a *Los Angeles Times* op-ed piece. North's defenders were infuriated by Petrino's article, felt he had done the unpardonable, bilged a classmate. North flatly denied the incident. Even so, many of those same classmates believed North had done something along the lines of what he allegedly told Petrino he wanted to do, if not that night then some other time. No one condemned him for it, either. Several, in fact, pointed to the incident as an example of both North's unpredictability and determination. Jack Holly, the kid from Corning, now a Marine colonel, carried the argument a step further. You've got to remember what it was like in those days, said Holly. For a lot of first classmen, a knee injury would have been the million-dollar wound. They take their Naval Academy diploma, head off to grad school, never spend a day in the service. Let alone in Vietnam. Think about that. Ollie's doing this so he can go to Vietnam.

As Webb and North struggled to surmount timeless rites of passage at Annapolis, events that would define a generation were encroaching on their world. The Class of 1968 entered the Academy in late June 1964. Though Vietnam would become an issue in that year's presidential campaign, for many Americans it was still a speck on the horizon, about like Nicaragua in 1981 when Ronald Reagan took office. Things changed fast for Webb, North, and their classmates. The Tonkin Gulf incident, LBJ's pretext for starting the massive United States buildup in Vietnam, occurred in August of their plebe summer.

In the winter of their first class year, the Tet Offensive took place. Widely misconstrued at the time as a major American battlefield defeat, it marked the beginning of the end of American involvement in Southeast Asia. But the protracted fade to black took another seven years.

During the four years '68 was at the Academy, the social fabric of the nation was shredded and rewoven in a way that Webb and North barely recognized. Watts burned during the summer of 1965. In April 1968, King was assassinated and more American cities went up in flames. A few months later, as Annapolis was aglow with the glitter of June Week, Robert Kennedy was gunned down in Los Angeles. Through it all the antiwar movement was in full flower and high dudgeon. Lyndon Johnson bowed to its pressure in March and announced he would not seek reelection, the victim/perpetrator of a discredited war that North and Webb were just getting ready to fight. Then there was the music. Few had heard of the Beatles in June 1963 when North entered the Academy the first time. A year later, when Webb arrived and North limped back, they just wanted to hold our hand. By 1968, Sgt. Pepper a year behind them, they wanted to do it in the road.

The Board went up in the stately marble Rotunda of Bancroft Hall during '68's plebe year. From a distance it was just a freestanding bulletin board with pictures of midshipmen on it. At first glance, it looked like the football team.

"All of a sudden, Vietnam jumped out at us," said Kendall Pease, a classmate of North and Webb. "Maybe not the first three or four pictures, but suddenly there was someone you knew. The Board was always there. It was the shadow in the woods, the fog that crept over the Academy until it blanketed everybody." The pictures were senior photos from the Lucky Bag, the Academy yearbook. "It wasn't like somebody you hadn't seen in two or three years, who maybe had grown a mustache or something, or aged a bit. It was the picture of him the last time you saw him. And he was dead." By the time Webb and North graduated, The Board had grown to three boards and women dating prospective Marines and Navy pilots would not go near it.

Tet dramatically increased the number of pictures on The Board. The battle was still raging the week first classmen officially selected their branch of service. "There's half a dozen guys I know whose girlfriends and families talked them out of going Marine Corps because of the way The Board filled up that week," said Mark Treanor, a senior who took the Marine option. Webb was the Marine whip for his battalion. Going into service selection, he had twenty-two confirmed Marines. Only eleven signed up. One of North's former roommates backed out on service selection night. His fiancée, he said, was dead-set against it. For the first time ever, Annapolis was unable to meet its Marine quota.

BOOK TWO

FIELDS OF FIRE

INTRODUCTION

Mark went to Canada. Goodrich went to Vietnam. Everybody else went to grad school.

—JAMES WEBB, *Fields of Fire*

WASHINGTON—President Johnson has nominated Secretary of Defense Robert S. McNamara as the new president of the World Bank.

—*New York Times*, November 27, 1967

John Kennedy primed the pump. On a bitter-cold day in January 1961, he proclaimed the United States and its citizens willing to "pay any price, bear any burden, meet any hardship" to advance the cause of freedom around the world.

Cheers greeted the declaration. For that moment the youthful, vibrant new President embodied the far-flung, seemingly limitless ideals of the nation that had chosen him as its leader.

Kennedy was wrong, of course, assuming as he did that the generation then moving toward its majority would be like those that had preceded it, including his own, men and women who could imagine something to die for.

The Brigade of Midshipmen, toes numb, lips cracked, fingers frozen on the stocks of rifles, marched in the inaugural parade. Approaching the reviewing stand, the midshipmen executed a crisp eyes left, unaware that the pledge spoken minutes earlier by their new Commander-in-Chief had unleashed forces that would soon thin their ranks and reshape their world.

Kennedy was dead less than three years later, but the legacy of that pledge, the Vietnam War, bruised American society like nothing else in this century. The nation split over the war, as did the generation that has now come of age. Those who opposed the war forged a movement that eventually led to the withdrawal of American troops from Vietnam and created a counterculture that dominated much of the life of the nation in the late sixties and early seventies. By the mid-1970s, unscarred by Vietnam combat, these former antiwar activists had moved into the mainstream of American life, assuming positions of stature in politics, government, education, law, finance, and the arts. By then many were serving in Congress. In January 1993 the first of their number moved into the Oval Office.

For those who served in Vietnam, the war and its aftermath ushered in troubled times. Unlike veterans of other wars, they came home to hostility, contempt, ridicule, at best indifference. Their experiences were at first disorienting, then alienating. As they saw it, they had fought bravely against a resilient and implacable foe, innocently trusting the leadership of the nation that had sent them off to war. Many saw comrades killed and wounded. Thousands came home maimed themselves.

They reacted in different ways. The stereotype became the so-called ticking time bomb, the vet who dashes to the roof of a building in some sleepy southwestern town and guns down a dozen people with a sniper rifle. Others, emotionally shattered by the war, found little meaning to their lives in the confusing aftermath of the conflict. Some became derelicts, street people, drains on society. Still others turned against the war, hurling their medals at the steps of the Capitol. For most, anger, bitterness, and distrust of the institutions of the nation for which they had fought became the prevailing emotions.

John McCain, Bud McFarlane, Jim Webb, Oliver North, and, to a lesser extent, John Poindexter belong to still another group, probably the largest, the one that "went to ground," as Harold G. Moore and Joseph L. Galloway have written, waiting patiently for America to "come to its senses."

No less angry, bitter, and confused, these men were, above all, survivors. However painful their individual wartime experiences, they knew they had to put Vietnam in a safe place, let it scab over and get on with their lives. And so they did. Before long, they were working side by side with men and women who had opposed the war, with others who avoided military service by jiggering their college schedules, marital status, or health histories.

They were not immune to the occasional dark thought. They noticed, for example, that the antiwar movement lost much of its vigor when draft calls slackened and the white, middle-class kids who had been its center of gravity no longer felt threatened. They noticed, as well, that the officials who had maneuvered the nation into the war, then managed to lose it through arrogance, deceit, and incompetence, were making a slick escape, like Robert McNamara, exiled to the World Bank. For a time, though, they were able to ship such thoughts off to the same safe place where they kept other, more brutal Vietnam memories.

For some of these men, though, no place was safe enough. You couldn't tell by looking at them, probably not even by talking to many of them, but they were the walking wounded of the Vietnam generation. And down the road, there would be hell to pay.

The numbers were always important, especially body counts. Since you controlled only the patch of ground you stood on, and since the ground was probably worthless anyway, the body count became the measure of success on the battlefield. There was no Monte Cassino in Vietnam or Mount Suribachi, either, places you took and held, then jumped off from on the way to some new objective closer to the heart of the enemy, whether it was Rome, Berlin, or Tokyo. In Vietnam, the enemy's heart was in Hanoi, and that was off-limits, at least to ground troops, so you settled for any hill or ridgeline or ville or stand of elephant grass where you thought enemy troops might be lurking. Then you attacked. If you were right, they fired back. When it was over, you counted the bodies, theirs and yours, though only theirs went into the body count. The brass cared deeply about the body count. Sometimes they'd send you out to count bodies after a battle even though this meant exposing yourself and your men to further casualties. Such orders led to the coining of the term REMF, an atonal acronym popular with the troops that stood for rear echelon mother fucker.

Other numbers were important, too. Kill ratios, sorties flown, bomb tonnage dropped, all figures regularly trotted out to show we were winning the war. Since the numbers lied, over the years they passed into well-deserved oblivion. When it was all over, though, some numbers surfaced that told a fascinating tale, one that had the added virtue of being true. A sampling of the more important statistics:

- About 27 million men came of draft age between 1964 and 1973, roughly the decade of the Vietnam War. Of that number, 11 million entered the service either as draftees or volunteers. More than 2 million served in the war zone.
- Of those who went to Vietnam, 58,000 died. Another 270,000 were wounded, 21,000 of whom were disabled in some manner. Five thousand lost one or more limbs.
- Sixteen million, or 60 percent, of the 27 million draft-age men escaped military service by a variety of legal and illegal means. *Sixteen million.*

The numbers were compiled by Lawrence M. Baskir and William

A. Strauss for their 1978 book, *Chance and Circumstance*, an authoritative account of how millions of able-bodied young Americans outmaneuvered the Selective Service System and left the fighting and dying to others.

"Through an elaborate structure of deferments, exemptions, legal technicalities, and noncombat military alternatives, the draft rewarded those who manipulated the system to their advantage," say Baskir and Strauss. All it took was "background, wit, or money."

For those with such attributes, a network of draft counselors, attorneys, physicians, and other professionals was available to champion their cause. "By the late 1960s, the only real challenge left to the draft was to find the right advice in time," the authors say.

How did they do it? First, there were college deferments, undergraduate and, until 1968, graduate as well. For part of the Vietnam era, married men and, later, married men with children were deferred, giving rise to practices known as "marrying out" and "babying out." You could gain a hardship deferment if you were the sole support of a widowed mother, or younger sisters and brothers. You didn't even have to be poor to qualify. Actor George Hamilton was excused because, Baskir and Strauss say, his mother lived in his Hollywood mansion and relied on his $200,000 annual salary for support.

Preinduction and induction physicals were standard vehicles for avoiding the draft. Young men, often armed with letters from sympathetic doctors, feigned every conceivable malady to win the coveted 4-F deferment. They starved themselves for weeks so they could report for their physicals underweight. Others stuffed themselves and showed up overweight. Some cut off their own fingers (or prevailed upon a friend to do the deed), claimed psychological problems—often severe depression complete with suicidal tendencies—or homosexuality.

Still others introduced alien substances such as amphetamines into their systems, though a common substance often did just as well. Baskir and Strauss quote a Milwaukee draft counselor as saying, apparently without irony, "The long-term casualties are unbelievable. I know someone who ate six dozen eggs and got an exemption for excessive albumin. Now, for as long as he lives, he has to maintain the lie that he is allergic to eggs."

Grad school deferments were terminated in 1968, so many young men flocked to divinity schools. David Stockman survived the war in this manner, later becoming Ronald Reagan's budget director and spearheading an effort to scale back military pensions and other benefits. Some who dodged the draft emerged in the 1980s as champions of the Reagan administration's tough-talking foreign policy, loudly endorsing a confrontational stance with the Soviet Union, aid to the Nicaraguan guerrillas, and military ventures into Lebanon, Grenada, and the Persian Gulf. They came to be known as chicken hawks, men whose testosterone gland abruptly began pumping after age twenty-six, when they were no longer vulnerable to the draft.

The National Guard, traditionally undermanned in peacetime, became the preferred haven for many men who feared both being stigmatized as draft dodgers (an unnecessary concern as it turned out) and a horizontal, flag-bedecked homecoming. Say Baskir and Strauss, "At the end of 1968, with the draft still in full force, the Army National Guard had a waiting list of 100,000. After two years of shrinking draft calls, that waiting list vanished. Six months later, the Guard found itself forty-five thousand men under strength." Dan Quayle is the best-known Vietnam-era militiaman. He supported the war but cushioned himself against its more unpalatable aspects by writing press releases in the Indiana Guard.

Baskir and Strauss handle the 16 million gently, concurring with a *Washington Post* editorial that called the war "a generation-wide catastrophe," a phrase that sticks in the craw, as if the young man doomed to a life of politely declining egg dishes equates to the veteran with an itch where his leg used to be. The authors suggest, moreover, that a great many men who did serve during the Vietnam era would have availed themselves of the smorgasbord of deferments had they only been sophisticated enough or rich enough to take advantage of them. They may be right. A 1971 Harris poll found that most Americans believed those who went to Vietnam were "suckers, having to risk their lives in the wrong war, in the wrong place, at the wrong time."

Interestingly, according to Jim Webb, an unpublished 1980 Harris poll determined that veterans in the main were proud of their Vietnam service and would serve again if the occasion arose. This result cut severely against the grain of popular perceptions, as if there might well be a few million men out there who hadn't gotten the word.

Many, it seemed, even wanted to serve, not because they thought it would be a great adventure, though that was certainly the case for some, but because with their nation at war they felt an obligation to do so. Looking back, especially in light of the numbers served up by Baskir and Strauss, it seems a quaint notion.

World War II, the myth as well as the reality, was probably responsible, both for those who went and those who didn't. The Vietnam generation grew up on tales of sacrifice and heroism, of long lines in front of recruiting stations the day after Pearl Harbor, of a terrible burden equally shared. The movies of the day romanticized war, or so it was said. Thus, when Sergeant Stryker, the John Wayne character, is killed in *Sands of Iwo Jima*, he takes a clean shot in the back rather than being graphically shredded à la *Platoon* or *Full Metal Jacket*. But even back then young men weren't so dumb. They knew dead was dead, and they knew it could happen to them.

That was a sobering thought and provoked different reactions. Author James Fallows quotes a friend, a former Rhodes Scholar who became a corporate lawyer, as saying, "There are certain people who can do more good in a lifetime in politics or academics or medicine than by getting killed in a trench."

Certain other people, some reasonably bright and promising in their own right, could not imagine staying home while members of their generation risked their lives fighting a war. Once their buddies started getting killed and maimed, when they themselves were forced to contemplate a future sightless, with a limb or two missing, or in a wheelchair, feelings such as rage, resentment, and disbelief took root. Try as they might, they could not get it through their heads that those who avoided serving did so because of higher morality, greater love for their fellow man, or a sudden attack of religion on the Stockman model.

The generational schism broadened with the blossoming of the antiwar movement and the counterculture that accompanied it. Ultimately, those who opposed the war prevailed, but along the way they made a strategic error. They did not attempt to make common cause with their peers in uniform. Instead, they portrayed the men fighting the war with contempt, spitting on them, calling them fascists and baby-killers, as if by a simple act of labeling they could transform them into beings different from and less worthy than themselves, with less reason to live.

Paul Goodwin, Ollie North's company commander in Vietnam, experienced a variation on that theme. Goodwin was tough and profane, a tiger in combat. At home he was a soft-spoken if occasionally prickly southern gentleman. On recruiting duty in Kansas City in the early 1970s, he was living among civilians for the first time in a decade. As he and his neighbors grew friendly, Goodwin was confused by the way they related to him, as if they needed to see him as an anomaly, the exception that proved the rule. It drove him crazy. "This is a horrible war and our troops are doing terrible things over there," his neighbors would say, "but we know you're not like that, Paul." Sputtering, Goodwin would reply, "I am them. I am typical. I am what the Marine Corps is all about."

From where men like Goodwin stood, a different picture was taking shape. The protesters and draft dodgers seemed to be of the privileged class, more prosperous, better educated, predominantly white. The press and many politicians appeared to be cheering them on. Was it possible that they really were smarter, more aware, and as courageous in their own way as the men in Vietnam?

Rightly or wrongly, those questions were answered no, no, and no, but it took a while because it wasn't an easy call. Some antiwar activists won grudging respect, the ones willing to go to jail rather than accept induction. A U.S. prison may not have been quite as perilous as the Vietnam outback but both were Indian country and everyone knew it. For all the chants of "Hell, no, we won't go," however, few were willing to put themselves on the line as had their jailed comrades. They played the deferment game instead, manipulating their college schedules, accelerating their marriage plans, running off to Canada (which was decidedly not Indian country) or Sweden (ditto), and otherwise avoiding and evading.

For many who served in Vietnam, the crucial question became, Could I have done any of those things and still lived with myself? Those who answered in the negative would never see America and many members of their own generation the same way again, especially as they watched their old tormentors and fellow travelers prosper in the aftermath of the war.

"What it does is dislocate loyalty," said Bob Bedingfield, a Navy chaplain with Ollie North's battalion in Vietnam. "It says that I can never believe the system again. That's now part of the means by which I interpret the world I live in."

Milt Copulos, a friend of Jim Webb, spent three and a half years in the hospital and received the last rites seven times as a result of his Vietnam service. He put it this way: "There's a wall ten miles high and fifty miles thick between those of us who went and those who didn't, and that wall is never going to come down."

CHAPTER FOUR

FIRE AT SEA

A fter a European fling with the tobacco heiress, John McCain reported to flight school at Pensacola in August 1958. As at Annapolis, he was brash and immature, at times reckless, a man who turned a night on the town into a test of survival skills. His life revolved around the beach, his new Corvette, the coupe du jour for fledgling jet jockeys, and women, the flashier the better. He dated everyone from schoolteachers to the strippers at Trader John's, the fabled airdale raunch bar, often returning to base just in time to change clothes and drag himself out to the flight line.

Graduation transformed neither his style nor his low tolerance for authority. One night he was playing shuffleboard at the Officers Club. His nondescript outfit included cowboy boots and a chewed-up crew-neck sweater. A cigarette dangled from his lips as an irate commander stormed over. "Ensign McCain, your appearance is a disgrace," said the officer, four grades his senior. "What do you think your grandfather would say?" Squinting through the smoke, McCain replied, "Frankly, Commander, I don't think he'd give a rat's ass."

He learned to fly at Pensacola, though his performance was below par, at best good enough to get by. He liked flying, but didn't love it. What he loved was the kick-the-tire, start-the-fire, scarf-in-the-wind life of a naval aviator. There was an added attraction. Flying was something his father, a submariner, had never done, and he wanted to be seen, for better or worse and at almost all costs, as his own man, not Jack McCain's kid.

He and Chuck Larson roomed and partied together at a series of flight schools over the next two and a half years, Larson the calm if fun-loving eye of the hurricane, McCain the hurricane itself. At advanced flight training at Corpus Christi, they took adjoining rooms in the BOQ, moved the beds into one room, turned the other into an all-purpose party room, stag bar, and penny ante gambling den. The decor was early landfill, artfully set off by empty beer cans, dirty clothes, and cigarette butts.

One Saturday morning, as McCain was practicing landings, his engine quit and his plane plunged into Corpus Christi Bay. Knocked unconscious by the impact, he came to as the plane settled to the bottom. Cracking the canopy against the weight of the water, he squeezed out and fought his way to the surface, where he was raced to the dispensary. His back ached, but X-rays showed no serious injuries. Laughing off advice that he spend the night in sick bay, he hurriedly returned to the BOQ, popped some painkillers, and climbed into bed, hoping to recuperate in time to keep a brush with death from ruining an otherwise promising weekend.

Jack McCain, meanwhile, learned of the accident and dispatched an admiral friend stationed nearby to check on his son's condition. Larson was shaving amid the debris of the previous night's poker session when he was startled by a loud knock. Strolling to the door, straight razor in hand, he heard a second knock, more insistent than the first. "Hey, hold your horses, dammit," he said. "There's a guy trying to sleep in here." Nonplussed, he swung the door open, saw the admiral, snapped to attention, nearly sliced off his eyebrow trying to salute. Thanks to grit and codeine, McCain was on his feet for Saturday night. The following weekend, though, the entire BOQ stood a white-glove inspection.

McCain was an adequate pilot, but he had no patience for studying dry aviation manuals. Instead, he would spend two or three hours each afternoon, whatever time he had between the end of the day's classes and the commencement of happy hour, reading history. At Corpus, he worked his way through all three volumes of Gibbon's *Decline and Fall of the Roman Empire*. When Larson asked why, he said his father had urged him to do so, told him it was the kind of thing a naval officer should know about.

A change, subtle at first, came over McCain during a series of deployments to the Mediterranean between 1960 and 1964. To the unpracticed eye, it looked suspiciously like maturity. Those who knew him better passed it off as an extended hangover. In time, though, even the cynics had to concede he was taking his job more seriously. He liked flying off a carrier, enjoyed being at sea, and seemed to flourish when assigned additional duties. He volunteered to stand bridge watches, eventually qualifying as officer of the deck underway, which meant he was considered capable of maneuvering the ship at sea. Rather than bridling at the confinement of long cruises, he seemed to be thriving, in part because he liked it, but also because he was cut off from the temptations that awaited him on the beach.

To the relief of McCain watchers everywhere, these early glimmers of maturity did not signal a radical transformation. His professional growth, though reasonably steady, had its troubled moments. Flying too low over the Iberian Peninsula, he took out some power lines, which led to a spate of newspaper stories in which he was predictably identified as the son of an admiral. The tale has gotten better with age. These days they talk about the day McCain turned the lights out in Spain.

He continued to play hard on liberty, drinking, gambling, and otherwise availing himself of the charms of the Mediterranean littoral. In 1964 he was back in Pensacola, a short tour notable for the beginning of his romance with Carol Shepp. The two had known each other at Annapolis, where Carol dated a classmate of McCain, whom she later married. By 1964 she was the divorced mother of two. She and McCain met again while she was visiting a friend and renewed an old flirtation that quickly became serious.

Carol, a slim five foot eight, had been a model in her hometown of Philadelphia, where she was again living. Warm, vivacious, and fun-loving, she was a more polished, slightly less electrified distaff version of John McCain. By the time he was transferred to Meridian, Mississippi, as a flight instructor a few months later he was flying up to Philadelphia nearly every weekend to visit her.

Meridian was, to McCain's mind, the "crummiest place in America," but he enjoyed instructing, becoming a better pilot by teaching others to fly. The days were long, usually three training flights a day, not counting preflight briefings and the debriefings once back on the ground. His fitness reports by now were looking very good and he was named instructor of the month.

Off-duty, he and his bachelor cronies brought sleepy Meridian to life. A benighted plan for base beautification became the vehicle for their efforts. The plan called for creating a series of man-made lakes, bulldozers digging the holes, nature providing the water in the form of rainfall. Lake Helen, named for the base commander's wife, was dredged behind the BOQ. More swamp than lake, it soon became a festering depression of standing water, mosquito larvae, and pond scum. Before long Lake Helen was renamed Lake Fester. The tiny island in the middle, a decorator touch about the size of a large room, was dubbed Key Fess.

The Key Fess Yacht Club inevitably followed, complete with membership cards, club officers, and a single vessel, a leaky old rowboat christened *The Fighting Lady*. McCain was named vice commodore. All hands turned out in yachting dress—blue jackets, white trousers, white shoes, white cap—to celebrate the launching of the club. Lights adorned the five hapless trees sprouting against all odds on Key Fess. The commodore, a boozy Marine captain, struck a Washington-crossing-the-Delaware pose aboard *The Fighting Lady* as he and several other tipsy partygoers shoved off on a ceremonial journey to the island. Overbooked, the boat sank a few yards from shore. The scramble to safety resulted in a broken wrist, a few torn ligaments, and some mild trampling of passengers. Evacuation of the wounded barely interrupted the revelry.

Key Fess Yacht Club parties quickly became the focal point of social activities on the base. There was a Roman toga party in which the Officers Club was stripped of furniture and filled with mattresses lugged in from the BOQ. At a Roaring Twenties party, a gilded bathtub was filled with a daunting mixture of French brandy and champagne. Rock bands were brought in from Memphis. The parties became magnets for local women, few of them debutantes. And the word was spreading. When McCain was elected commodore, pilots flew in from as far away as the West Coast for his change-of-command gala. There were flags, banners, side boys, hundreds of people crowding the shore, Richard Rodgers's rousing score for the documentary series "Victory at Sea" blaring from loudspeakers. For the invocation, a Marine serving as chaplain read from *Catch-22*, Joseph Heller's antiwar classic.

By then, McCain had become a one-woman man, logging his flying time on weekend trips to Philadelphia to see Carol and inviting her down for the best parties. In July 1965 they were married at the Philadelphia home of Carol's friends Connie and Sam Bookbinder, the reception catered by the family's seafood restaurant, Bookbinder's, a city landmark. The transformation from playboy to family man was a smooth one. He was twenty-eight and ready to settle down. He loved Carol's children, Doug, five, and Andy, three, who were fun and well-behaved. A year later he adopted them. Rather than settling into domesticity, he and Carol remained fixtures on the party circuit. In a rare concession to his new status, he resigned as commodore of Key Fess, explaining that only a bachelor could uphold the club's high standard of inspired lunacy.

That fall, he flew a trainer solo to Philadelphia for the Army-Navy game. Flying back by way of Norfolk, he had just begun his descent over unpopulated tidal terrain when the engine died. "I've got a flameout," he radioed. He went through the standard relight procedures three times. At one thousand feet, he ejected, landing on the deserted beach moments before the plane slammed into a clump of trees. A chopper picked him up fifteen minutes later. His injuries were minor. The Navy classified it as a "routine ejection." McCain figured that was about right. As he later said of the incident, it wasn't as if he had collided with another plane, or been shot down.

In September 1966, Carol gave birth to a daughter, Sydney. Soon after, John was transferred to Jacksonville and assigned to a squadron slated for Vietnam in mid-1967. He had pulled strings in Meridian to get there sooner, but to no avail. He deployed in the spring, aboard the carrier *Forrestal*, expecting to be home in less than a year.

Carol, who had never been to Europe, decided to move there with the children until John returned. She flew to London, where Jack and Roberta McCain were stationed, then set off with her three kids on a driving tour through West Germany, Denmark, Holland, and Belgium. Her destination was Garmisch, which had an American school for the boys.

July 29, 1967. On the flight deck of the *Forrestal*, McCain climbed into the cockpit of his A-4 Skyhawk. Two years into the war, he was finally where he wanted to be, on Yankee Station, about sixty miles from the coast of North Vietnam in the South China Sea. He was there for a number of reasons, including the professional. No naval aviator was going to climb the career ladder unless he flew combat missions in Vietnam. More compelling, if less discussed, was the excitement, the exhilaration, even the fear. Unlike ground pounders, for whom the shit never ceased, McCain and other carrier-based combat pilots flew missions that rarely lasted more than an hour from takeoff to landing, sixty minutes of gut-wrenching, scrotum-shrinking frenzy. Then they were back in the ready room, cooling out with their buddies, telling war stories, lying about women.

McCain's A-4 and the other Skyhawks, the *Forrestal*'s attack aircraft, were wingtip to wingtip on the port side of the flight deck, angled toward the bow. They were armed with five-hundred- and one-thousand-pound bombs. To extend their flying range, their bellies were fitted with detachable two-hundred-gallon fuel tanks containing highly combustible aviation gas.

On the starboard side, across from the A-4s, angled forward as well, were the fighters, the F-4 Phantoms that flew cover as the Skyhawks delivered their deadly payloads. The F-4s were armed with air-to-ground Zuni rockets for flak suppression and air-to-air Sparrow rockets should they encounter North Vietnamese MiGs.

In preparation for launching aircraft, the carrier's massive prow swung slowly into the wind. The sea was choppy, but the crew hardly noticed, the carrier slicing through the water like a European touring car gliding along the Autobahn.

Strapped into the cockpit, McCain watched a little yellow cart connect up to his A-4. The cart, which pilots called the Huffer, blew air into his engine, turning the blades. McCain hit the igniter. As his engine roared to life, he went through his preflight checks, then passed his flight helmet down to a crewman so he could wipe the visor. It was a ritual, born of concern. McCain never felt he could see clearly through the thick plastic shield.

Across the way, an F-4 had just hooked up to an external power generator that would jump-start its engine. Unknown to the pilot, a small wire called a pigtail was attached to one of his Zuni rockets. For safety reasons, the pigtails, which carry the electrical charge that fire the rockets, were not supposed to be plugged in until just before launch. His engine started, the pilot pressed the button that switched his aircraft from external to internal power, a routine procedure. This time, though, the switch-over sent a bolt of stray voltage through the errant pigtail, igniting the Zuni.

McCain never saw it coming. He had just snapped the cockpit shut when the Zuni punched through his exterior fuel tank. A tremendous jolt shook his plane, bouncing him around the cockpit as two hundred gallons of highly flammable aviation gas streamed onto the flight deck. Billowing black smoke engulfed him. Below, a lake of burning fuel had formed, its edges lapping eagerly across the flight deck. Shutting down the engine, he heard the two one-thousand-pound bombs hooked to his wings clank to the deck. He freed himself from his safety harness, scrambled from the cockpit onto the nose of the A-4, then crawled hand-over-hand along the lancelike refueling probe jutting from the nose of his aircraft.

As he did so, a voice, tense but controlled, with a vaguely southwestern twang, came cross the ship's intercom, alerting thousands of confused crewmen below decks that they were about to be hurled into every sailor's worst nightmare, a fire at sea.

"Fahr, fahr, fahr—fahr on the flight deck, fahr on the flight deck. All hands, man your battle stations. All hands, man your battle stations."

Dangling above the burning fuel, McCain knew he had no options. He dropped into the fire and rolled rapidly through the blaze till he cleared it. Slapping at his flight suit with gloved hands, he put out the flames while sprinting to the far side of the flight deck. Fighting to keep his composure, he saw a handful of men near the edge of the fire aiming a hose at the growing conflagration. A chief petty officer, armed only with a portable fire extinguisher, rushed toward the burning planes, his common sense overwhelmed by concern for the trapped pilots. Through the smoke, McCain saw the pilot of the A-4 next to his trying to escape the same way he had. As the pilot rolled through the flames, McCain started toward him. He had only taken a step or two when the first bomb cooked off.

Red-hot shards of jagged metal screamed across the flight deck. A fiery rain pelted the terrorized crew. McCain was blown backward, tiny bits of shrapnel embedded in his thighs and chest. A larger piece of metal slammed into his radio, which hung across his chest. Struggling to his feet, he looked onto a scene of mind-numbing carnage. Arms and legs tumbled through the air. A body with no head came to rest on the deck near him. The pilot he had been trying to help was dead. The men with the hose, dead. The chief with the fire extinguisher, dead. The crewman who wiped his visor, dead.

Planes exploded on deck. The heat triggered ejection seats, some still manned, blowing them into the burning ether. More bombs cooked off, as did more Zuni rockets, the latter shooting across the flight deck into the flames, as if intent on striking down the inferno touched off by their murderous sibling. Bomb after bomb ignited, rocking the ship, tearing ragged holes in the three-and-a-half-inch-thick reinforced steel flight deck. Burning fuel spilled through the openings onto the hangar deck below. The fire roared on, angry, vengeful, drowning out the cries for help, the shrieks of pain, the final prayers.

Forklifts shoved planes into the sea. Crewmen rolled bombs over the side. A shaken McCain went below. On the hangar deck, to which the fire had spread, someone was trying to unload bombs from a flight elevator before the flames reached them. McCain pitched in. The job done, he staggered into the ready room.

His fellow pilots were in shock. Incredibly, a video camera mounted on the carrier's superstructure was still running, carrying eerily silent real-time images. As the ship's crew battled the fire, McCain and his squadron mates watched the macabre drama unfold on closed-circuit television.

Realizing he was bleeding, McCain went down to sick bay. Crewmen, many little more than kids, lay stretched out before him, stripped naked, horribly burned, in mortal agony. Someone called "Mr. McCain." Following the voice, he moved beside a young man charred beyond recognition. He asked about a chief petty officer in the squadron. "I just saw him, he's fine," said McCain. "Thank God he's okay," said the crewman. Then he died. McCain left sick bay, his wounds untreated.

In the first five minutes after the Zuni ripped through McCain's fuel tank, nine major explosions rocked the *Forrestal*. The fire on the flight deck was brought under control that same afternoon. The fires below raged till the following evening. At one point, the skipper considered abandoning ship. When it was all over, 134 men were dead or missing, hundreds more injured. The damage to the ship was put at $72 million, not counting aircraft destroyed.

In the wake of the fire, the *Forrestal* limped to the Philippines to prepare for an inglorious return to the States and a couple of years in the yard for repairs. In port, McCain and others in his squadron were assembled. An officer explained that the *Oriskany*, another carrier on Yankee Station, had been losing pilots and was looking for volunteers to fill the ranks. McCain signed up.

He did not believe in predestination, but his experiences on the *Forrestal*, flying back from the Army-Navy game, and at the bottom of Corpus Christi Bay made him wonder if he had been spared for a reason. God, with whom he maintained a cordial if casual relationship, seemed reluctant to kill him, in fact, appeared to have plans for him. And so He did. For a long time, though, they weren't very nice plans.

The *Oriskany* was coming off the line for a few weeks, so McCain took leave, hopscotching to Hawaii, then to the mainland and on to London, where his father, by now a full admiral, was Commander-in-Chief, U.S. Naval Forces, Europe—CINCUSNAVEUR in Navy parlance. Carol was still touring the continent with the kids when McCain's mother, Roberta, reached her with news of the fire and John's imminent arrival. After a family reunion, John, Carol, and the children headed for Cannes, where a hotel was offering a free vacation to crew members from the *Forrestal*, in happier days a frequent caller to the ports of the French Riviera.

During the day, John and Carol took the kids to see the sights. After dinner, they enjoyed the nightlife. At the Palm Beach Casino, Carol got a whiff of her husband's past.

"Name, monsieur?" asked the majordomo, obviously new to the job.

"McCain, John McCain," came the Bond-like reply.

Carol remembers heads snapping up, eyes misting over, a small crowd of casino employees closing around them. Clearly, John had been there before, and just as clearly he had not been a piker.

John's orders to the *Oriskany* were delayed. Unsure of his status, the family returned to the Jacksonville area and rented a house in nearby Orange Park belonging to the parents of a woman whose husband, Bill Lawrence, was a prisoner of war in Hanoi.

Chuck Larson and his wife, Sally, stopped by in September. Larson saw changes in his old running mate. He limited himself to a single highball before dinner, by itself worthy of notice. After the meal, McCain took Larson aside. "I'm concerned," said McCain. "I may have to get out of the Navy." Surprised, Larson asked why. McCain explained that his past had become a burden. A lieutenant commander now, he considered himself a seasoned, competent naval officer, but whenever he joined a new outfit he was dismayed to find that his reputation for mayhem preceded him.

"I'm serious about the Navy," he said. "If I can't get people to take me seriously, maybe I'll have to try something else."

A few days later, his orders to the *Oriskany* came through. He said so long to Carol and the kids, told them to expect him back by early summer.

CHAPTER FIVE

MUSIC BINGO, DUMMY MATH, AND GAMMA RAYS

They liked John Poindexter so much at Annapolis they didn't want to let him go. A month after he and Linda left on a Lake Placid honeymoon, he was back for summer duty, training the new plebe class. A newly commissioned ensign, he was welcomed warmly into the fraternity of naval officers that only weeks before seemed obsessed with the errant speck of lint on his blues or the barely perceptible smudge on his belt buckle. It was a marvelous and liberating time, not quite the real Navy but his first extended taste of life outside Bancroft Hall in four years. There were parties nearly every night, pleasure cruises on the Chesapeake, relaxed weekend barbecues across the bay on Maryland's Eastern Shore. At one party an admiring, slightly tipsy commander sloshed champagne into Linda's white mesh shoe, threw his head back, and raised the leaky vessel to his lips. It was an elegant if ludicrous gesture that left him drenched in bubbly, typical of that freewheeling, exhilarating summer of 1958 in Annapolis.

John's stellar class standing paid unexpected dividends. In July he was summoned to New York to audition for a television game show called "Music Bingo," a summer replacement for "The Jane Wyman Theater," a dramatic series hosted by the ex-wife of a fading actor turned corporate huckster. Big-money quiz shows ruled the prime-time ratings. "The $64,000 Question," with its trademark isolation booth, started the parade, followed in short order by "The $64,000 Challenge" and "Twenty-one," on which contestants could win $100,000. "Music Bingo," more modest in its prize money, relied on the patter of emcee Johnny Gilbert and popular songs rendered by the Harry Salter Orchestra.

The gimmicky format involved two contestants, male and female, an electronic gameboard, and an array of bells, buzzers, free squares, and magic melodies. Sneaker-clad contestants were poised behind a white line. On recognizing a tune, they raced across the stage, jerked a rope that sounded a bell, and shouted the name.

At the audition, Poindexter and a crowd of other hopefuls listened to a selection of songs and recorded the titles of those they knew. John was not a music buff, but military men were popular contestants in those days and he made the cut. A few weeks later, he was back in New York, onstage in dress khakis and sneakers, his opponent a slim, beguiling young woman. He remembers her as Astrid, an aspiring dancer. For a time, he held his own, charging to the rope, yanking it, blurting out the answers. After several rounds the game was even, the next song the tie-breaker. He heard it, knew it, couldn't think of the name. Clang! "Jealousy," chirped Astrid, identifying the monster Frankie Laine hit of a few years earlier.

Poindexter was not happy. Music wasn't his strong suit, so he didn't expect to break the bank. And, as he would later confess, he was mildly distracted by his winsome opponent. But to miss on "Jealousy"! They had played it at the audition and he had known it then. But he didn't let it bother him long. He and Linda had gotten an all-expense-paid trip to New York, so why complain?

Before the year was out, the quiz show scandal broke, big winners like Columbia University instructor Charles Van Doren exposed as cheats and liars. As the scandal unfolded, John thought back over his experience. At the time, the audition seemed a simple test of his ability to recall the names of popular songs. Now, on reflection, he realized that by the end of the two-hour tryout the "Music Bingo" team could easily have compiled a pretty full catalog of songs he knew. And many of those songs were played during the show. He wondered if the show had been rigged, possibly for his benefit.

"Music Bingo" was never implicated in the scandal, but investigators probing the big-money games learned that the rigging had its roots in screening procedures similar to the one Poindexter had undergone. By the time of Van Doren and company, the manipulation ranged from the outrageous to the microscopic, everything from giving contestants the answers to prescribing the number of times they mopped their brows.

Not that the audition did Poindexter any good. The man who would later be scolded in print for his heavy reliance on such phrases as "I don't recall" and "I don't recollect" at the Iran-Contra hearings could not even remember the name of a song he had correctly identified a few weeks earlier.

There was this as well: if his suspicions were correct, he had unwittingly flirted with scandal and escaped without a scratch. Three decades later, after a scintillating and unblemished career as a naval officer, he crossed paths with scandal again, this time paying a terrible price. In terms of gravity, there was no comparison between the two episodes. For Poindexter, however, there was an important similarity. In each instance, he never suspected that something shady might be going on. Never had a clue.

The summer behind him, Poindexter went to sea, shipping out on a destroyer berthed in Norfolk. The tour of duty was to be a short one. At Annapolis he had been one of five midshipmen selected to launch the Navy's new Burke Scholar program, named after the sitting Chief of Naval Operations, the legendary Arleigh "Thirty-One Knot" Burke. The program was a reaction to Sputnik, which convinced the Navy to groom officers to speak the language of the scientists and engineers who would shape the future of the service. After a year at sea, selectees would have four years to pursue a doctorate in a technological field at any university they could get into.

At a briefing in Washington, the civilian in charge asked the new scholars which schools they hoped to attend. Poindexter said he planned to study nuclear physics at the California Institute of Technology in Pasadena, one of the nation's most elite universities. The official shook his head: "You'll never make it. I doubt that they will admit you and if they do, you'll never be able to keep up." Poindexter smiled blandly, said nothing, decided Caltech sounded just right.

Poindexter had no compelling desire to study physics. Annapolis had only sharpened his desire to go to sea, and he envisioned a long career as a black-shoe sailor. Like his benefactor, Arleigh Burke, he looked to cap that career at the top of his profession, as Chief of Naval Operations.

Not that he wasn't excited. All his life he had been curious about how things worked, whether it was a radio, a ship, or an atom. Earning a doctorate would be the toughest intellectual challenge of his life, by itself sufficient motivation for a man like Poindexter. He also knew that an achievement of that caliber would elevate him still further above his peers, stamp him as special, damn near unique. Above all, that was what drove him to apply for the Burke program, its value as a credential. Men like Chuck Larson and John McCain dazzled with good looks, charm, and charisma. John Poindexter was different. He dawned on people. Inevitably his bosses noticed that he seemed superior to other officers and checked his background. High school valedictorian, uh huh, brigade commander at Annapolis, uh-huh, number-one man in the class, uh-huh, uh-huh, Ph.D., nuclear physics, Caltech. Whoa!

At that point, though, the odds were against Caltech ever becoming a résumé item. At Annapolis Poindexter had taken a one-year introductory physics course and two years of math. Credible applicants to any respectable doctoral program, let alone Caltech's, usually had at least twice as many courses in those subjects under their belts, most many more. Unfazed, Poindexter mailed his application to Pasadena in early fall, confident things would break his way, if only because they always had.

At sea he was undergoing a bracing, at times perilous initiation into shipboard life. His ship, the *Holder*, a small destroyer of World War II vintage, was part of a task force engaged in developing the next generation of antisubmarine warfare tactics. The venture had both technical and creative elements, which pleased Poindexter. And the sea was the laboratory, which made it even better.

The *Holder* and her sister ships operated in the North Atlantic, turbulent in the best of times, icy and vengeful in winter. The bridge was enclosed, but small and confining, with only portholes for visibility. Deck officers had little choice but to stand their watches on the gray metal catwalk surrounding the bridge, exposed to the elements and the sea itself. As winter took hold, Poindexter outfitted himself in two pairs of socks, shoes, rubber boots, long underwear, heavy pants, and foul-weather gear. At times he could barely climb the ladder to the bridge. In rough weather, freezing rain and powerful whitecaps pounded the ship, the spray like buckshot against the bare skin of his face. But that was trifling compared to those storms that sent solid sheets of water, green water as sailors call it, slamming into the ship and the men on the catwalk struggling to keep the vessel on course. During one storm, Poindexter watched in mute disbelief as wind and rain and fierce seas peeled the flight deck of a nearby carrier back on itself. Fellow officers, aware that the Burke program would soon pluck him from the ship and deposit him in sunny southern California, took turns teasing him about his impending deliverance. Quipped one officer, "John says his prayers every night: Our Father, Who art in Heaven, Arleigh be Thy Name."

In late fall, Poindexter received a call from Carl Anderson, who identified himself as a member of the physics faculty at Caltech. We've received your application, said Anderson, but there's no way you can do graduate work with your math background. There's one possibility. We'll admit you as a special student on the condition that you take a year of advanced math before starting work on your doctorate. That means being away from the Navy for five years instead of four, assuming you make it through. I think I can arrange for the extra year if you're agreeable.

Poindexter thought about it. Special student. Dummy math. He said he'd do it. Fine, said Anderson, see you next fall.

Helpful guy, thought Poindexter, unaware that he had just conversed with the first of several Nobel Prize winners with whom he would soon be rubbing shoulders.

As John began classes at Caltech, Linda enrolled at Southern Cal for her senior year, having left school to get married. He took the car, pleading a lack of public transportation in Pasadena. She traveled by bus and streetcar to the campus in downtown L.A. She became pregnant almost immediately, gave birth to the first of their five sons less than a week after receiving her degree. "I graduated magna cum child," she told friends.

John was having problems. Caltech's version of dummy math, classical mechanics, began several levels above where he had left off at Annapolis. This meant he had to play catch-up just to reach the threshold of knowledge necessary for a course the school considered remedial.

First trimester he got a D, a grade previously known to him only by rumor. Typically, he didn't panic. "Just give me a book and I'll figure it out," he once told a friend, "it" meaning anything. Early in the term he stacked up the books he had to master alongside his desk. The pile rose fully three feet, rank ordered by degree of difficulty, what he knew on top, what he needed to know underneath. Then he threw the mental toggle switch, tuning out the world for the next eight months. The second trimester he raised his grade to C, finished the year with a B, earning admission to graduate standing.

In his second year he began working under Rudolf Mössbauer, a physicist on leave from his teaching post in Munich, then engaged in groundbreaking research on the absorption of gamma rays. Mössbauer at thirty-two had already developed what came to be known as the "Mössbauer effect," which for the first time allowed scientists to prove one of Einstein's fundamental hypotheses—that gravity can change the frequency of a light beam.

One morning that fall, Poindexter hurried to school early, joining a handful of other students in the physics lab. As Mössbauer strolled in, they broke into applause. Corks popped, champagne bubbled up the sides of glass laboratory beakers, and the small gathering toasted the young West German, named hours before a corecipient of the 1961 Nobel Prize in Physics.

Mössbauer, who became Poindexter's primary thesis adviser, remembered him as a very good student, if not a gifted one. "He was not brilliant in the sense that he was foaming with new ideas," said Mössbauer. "For the thesis he had, that was not really necessary. It was more a thesis where I needed a guy to be very careful, really sticking to all details. He had to do an enormous amount of calculations which were difficult to perform and he was absolutely reliable in doing them. I had complete confidence. In fact, he was the most orderly person I had in my Caltech experience."

If Poindexter had any strong political views in those days, no one noticed. Mössbauer, another professor, Felix Boehm, and a handful of students that included Poindexter often lunched together at a campus eatery nicknamed the Greasy Spoon. Political discussions were commonplace at the table, always with a liberal flavor. Poindexter listened with interest, puffed on his pipe, said little. His nonparticipation was not interpreted as indignation, only that he felt out of his element.

That interpretation seems correct. Poindexter spent five years at Caltech, from September 1959 to June 1964, a period that spanned the election of John Kennedy, the Bay of Pigs, the construction of the Berlin Wall, the Cuban Missile Crisis, JFK's assassination, and the deepening, if still barely visible, American involvement in Vietnam. Only the missile crisis made a strong impression. For a few days, until tensions eased, he thought he might have to drop out of school and report for duty.

As in the past, he was even-tempered, good-natured, and open, with no ragged edge to his personality. If an experiment went awry, he might utter a mild expletive, "something between fudge and crap," according to his friend, Herb Henrikson. Caltech's sandaled, long-haired, prehippie undergrads seemed to amuse, not annoy him. At home, incessantly busy with academic demands, he might shout to Linda, "Can't you keep that kid quiet?," but she gave birth to three sons in Pasadena so he must have occasionally taken a break from his studies.

Caltech challenged him intellectually as nothing before. After classical mechanics, however, he encountered no serious problems until his final year. At that point, he could no longer dodge the requirement that he demonstrate a working knowledge of two foreign languages, neither of them the Spanish he studied at Annapolis.

He chose French and German. Lacking the background to pass tests in either one or the time to take courses, he decided to translate a technical research paper in each language, an option that presupposed some proficiency in the languages involved. Existing translations and knowledgeable friends were off-limits.

Both research papers, eighty pages each, dealt with the Mössbauer effect, which meant he knew the physics. Beyond that he was a blank slate. Again he turned to books. Armed with a dictionary and grammar, he completed the French paper in a week, the German in three weeks, putting the finishing touches on his thesis along the way.

He successfully defended his thesis in the spring of 1964 before a blue-ribbon panel that included two Nobel laureates, Mössbauer and Carl Anderson, and a third professor, Richard Feynman, who would win the prize the next year.

A number of his predecessors and successors as national security adviser held doctoral degrees—all, predictably, with a foreign affairs flavor. Their theses:

Walt Whitman Rostow, "British Trade Fluctuations, 1868 to 1892."

Henry A. Kissinger, "A World Restored: Metternich, Castlereagh and the Restoration of Peace."

Zbigniew Brzezinski, "The Permanent Purge and Soviet Totalitarianism."

Brent Scowcroft, "Congress and Foreign Policy: An Examination of Congressional Attitudes Toward the Foreign Aid Programs to Spain and Yugoslavia."

Anthony Lake, "Caution and Concern: The Making of American Policy Toward South Africa, 1946–1971."

As for John Poindexter, his thesis was entitled, "Electronic Shielding by Closed Shells in Thulium Compounds."

Near the end of his time at Caltech, he received a call from Claire Gumz, a civilian in the Bureau of Naval Personnel who had been virtually his sole contact with the Navy since his arrival in Pasadena. She told him that Admiral Hyman Rickover, the imperious father of the nuclear Navy, was demanding the service records of officers who might qualify for the nuclear power program and drafting those he wanted whether they liked it or not. Are you interested? she asked. No, Claire, I'm really not, said Poindexter. I've been in graduate school for five years. It's time I got back to sea. Said Gumz, That's what I thought you'd say. I'll withhold your record. Poindexter never knew precisely what that meant, imagined Gumz with his service record on her desk, casually slipping it into a drawer when Rickover's men came calling.

Poindexter's brother, Chris, who was two years behind him at Annapolis, was swept up in the Rickover draft and bullied into the program. In true Poindexter fashion, Chris stood first in nuclear power school, but he resented Rickover's heavy-handedness and resigned from the Navy a few years later. He went on to build the Calvert Cliffs nuclear power plant for the Baltimore Gas and Electric Company. Today he is chairman of the board. Chris and John would later joke that Rickover went trolling for a Poindexter, but landed the wrong one.

With five years at Caltech behind him and a Ph.D. in physics in his pocket, Poindexter was ordered to boiler school. It seemed ridiculous, but he needed the training to prepare for a tour as chief engineer of the *Pratt*, a Norfolk-based guided-missile frigate, a large, heavily armed destroyer. The three-month course didn't begin until September, so he was moved to San Diego, where the school was to be held, and assigned temporary duty on the *Preble*, a ship similar to the one to which he would soon be going.

The first reports on what came to be known as the Tonkin Gulf incidents reached him as he was eating lunch in the *Preble*'s wardroom. It was the first time he had thought seriously about Vietnam, and he was ready to ship out if needed. But the Navy stuck to its plan, sent him to school, then back to Norfolk and the *Pratt*. "Vietnam was not in the East Coast lexicon in those days," he would later say.

By then he was a full lieutenant, having never gone to sea as a lieutenant junior grade, but his return to the black-shoe Navy was swift and seamless, as if he'd been ashore five weeks instead of five years. As chief engineer, he held the most responsible position on the ship after the captain and executive officer. If the chief engineer doesn't perform, toilets don't flush, showers don't work, guns don't turn, and the ship doesn't sail. Many engineering officers begin to think their first names have been changed to Goddammit, because the captain is always shouting, "Goddammit, Mr. So-and-So, what the hell's wrong with my ship?" The *Pratt*, moreover, had a superheated 1200 psi boiler that generated twice the energy of the power plants on older destroyers. Working with superheated steam was a major challenge. Even minor impurities in the water could build up deposits and cause pipes to rupture, a major catastrophe almost certain to entail loss of life and cut short the career of the officer in charge. But no tragedies occurred on Poindexter's watch and his career moved ahead at flank speed.

He spent nearly two years aboard the *Pratt*, operating in the Atlantic and the Mediterranean. He was having the time of his life when the ship received a message ordering him to Washington to interview for a job in OSD. He had no idea what the acronym meant.

"It means the Office of the Secretary of Defense," said the *Preble*'s skipper.

McNamara's shop. John Poindexter was about to become a Whiz Kid.

CHAPTER SIX

WELCOME TO THE GALLANT MARINES

Bud McFarlane and Jonny Riley were married on June 7, 1959, passing up the Academy chapel in favor of the Chevy Chase Presbyterian Church, in suburban Washington, where they first met as teenagers. Bud had graduated and pinned on the gold bars of a Marine second lieutenant four days earlier. Jonny received her diploma from Penn State the day before the wedding. Honeymooning in Nassau, Bud experienced a newfound sense of freedom, happily squiring his bride around the island in the peppy red MG he rented.

In July he reported to Quantico to begin seven months of training at the Basic School, the officer equivalent of boot camp. Distracted by his elegant new wife, possibly by ongoing if fading concerns about his choice of vocation, he turned in a disappointing performance.

McFarlane could always find shortcomings in himself barely detectable by others. This time his superiors shared his concern. He ranked 154 out of 355 in his class and was graded just slightly above average on his fitness report. His record was so ordinary that he was denied his choice of the infantry as his military occupational specialty and assigned instead to the artillery.

Chagrined, he requested reassignment to the infantry. He was turned down and sent to artillery school at Quantico. Again he performed only adequately, standing twenty-six out of forty-four. More bad news awaited him at Camp Lejeune, North Carolina, home of the Second Marine Division. He hoped for assignment to the division's artillery regiment, which moved with and directly supported the infantry. Instead, he was sent to the Second Field Artillery Group, a lumbering heavy weapons unit that operated independently of the division because its guns could not be lifted by helicopter. McFarlane's career, so filled with promise a year earlier, seemed to be foundering.

He was in the last place an ambitious, energetic young officer wanted to be, that nether world scorned by legions of soldiers: back in the rear with the gear.

His frustration did not last long. Assigned to a 155-millimeter how-itzer battery, he soon won command of a platoon, a captain's billet in that unit. As he settled into his first command, his life took on a fresh complexion. There was hardware involved, but at least he was leading troops. He became intrigued by the diversity of the artillery officer's duties—tactics, training, fire control, keeping trucks running and guns operating. Twice a week he took his troops to the field, training them in the essential elements of the artilleryman's job—shoot, move, communicate.

Leadership in the Marine Corps can be summarized in three sen-tences from *Reef Points*. Take care of your men. See that each under-stands his duties. Exact instant obedience. Living up to that first commandment was a full-time job for platoon leaders, who dealt most directly with the troops, some still teenagers, many others just slightly older. Their personal problems were often intractable. The younger ones were easy prey to charlatans and their own youthful appetites. Married men often encountered financial difficulties, especially in those days when enlisted salaries permitted a barely marginal exis-tence. McFarlane did not insulate himself from their troubles, consid-ered them a test of his resourcefulness, a measure of his leadership. If the gunnery sergeant said he was sending a problem-plagued Marine to the chaplain, McFarlane would usually reply, That's okay, Gunny, send him to me.

In one instance, a young lance corporal and his wife were expecting twins. They lived in a small trailer. His monthly salary was about $160 and he was drowning in debt. McFarlane became his financial adviser and teacher, explaining how a budget worked and helping the couple set one up. He took them to Navy Relief to find cribs, clothes, carriages, and diapers, then directed them to public agencies that might ease the money crunch.

That was not an isolated instance. He tutored troops in algebra and other subjects so they could pass high school equivalency tests, coun-seled men on their drinking or marital problems. His efforts were more than exercises in leadership. He was trying to live up to the belief, spawned in childhood and reinforced at Annapolis, that he had an obligation to help others, whatever their station. In later years, he was seen by many as tightly controlled and dispassionate, a view that obscured the fact that throughout his life, whatever his other failings, he has been a man of uncommon personal decency.

*   *   *

McFarlane came to life professionally at Lejeune, excellent to out-standing fitness reports soon overshadowing his lackluster record at Quantico.

"This young officer became an artillery platoon commander in min-imum time," wrote one of his superiors in August 1960. "He achieved this by energetic devotion to duty, and industry; together with a keen mind, a continual program of self-improvement and an active seeking of responsibility." In January 1961, another senior Marine wrote, "This is one of the finest young officers in the command." Six months later, his battery commander said, "He has a zest for tackling hard problems and thrives on responsibility. . . . His growth potential is unlimited."

In the spring of 1962, he was transferred to the Army Artillery and Missile School at Fort Sill, Oklahoma. Along with thirty other Marine officers and scores of Army men, he served as an instructor at the school, an assignment that moved him onto the fast track for promo-tions. Before taking up his teaching duties, he attended the field artil-lery officer orientation course, placing number one in a class of fifty-two. As an instructor, he was assigned to teach gunnery, the most sought-after subject at the school, a clear sign that he was considered among the elite. His fitness reports reflected his growing stature. "An officer whose quick mind and sound judgment places him in that small group which can be judged a truly outstanding officer," wrote the head of the gunnery division in the fall of 1963. "He is a leader of the future. . . . He should be advanced in rank ahead of his contem-poraries." The following year, the new gunnery chief was equally impressed, calling McFarlane "an officer of such outstanding qualifi-cations that he is set apart from his contemporaries."

On completion of his tour in early 1964, he was awarded the Army Commendation Medal, the first in an impressive array of personal decorations that would come his way over the years. The citation read: "Not only did he exhibit an all-encompassing knowledge of field artillery gunnery, but he also displayed a unique ability to impart this knowledge to his students from all parts of the world in classes that were marked by flawless presentations."

A captain now, he was dispatched on a long-overdue hardship tour. Thirteen months on Okinawa, a mountainous island in the North Pacific known to Marines as The Rock. Off-limits to wives and chil-dren.

Settling Jonny, who was pregnant, and two-year-old Laurie in a garden apartment near her parents' home in suburban Washington, McFarlane shipped out for Okinawa and the Third Marine Division. He was assigned a major's billet, command of Foxtrot Battery, Second Battalion, Twelfth Marines. Denied the gentle diversions of family life, Marines on Okinawa trained hard, trudging into the boondocks for weeks at a time. But McFarlane was to spend little time on the island.

A few months after he arrived, the curious events of August 1964 that became known as the Tonkin Gulf incidents took place in the waters off South Vietnam. As a flurry of frenzied messages pierced the ether between Washington and the South China Sea, the Marines on Okinawa were ordered to mount out.

Foxtrot Battery put to sea in direct support of an infantry unit, the Third Battalion, Ninth Marines, 3/9 for short. For the next two months the Marines, armed to the teeth, steamed in circles without seeing action or a liberty port. To forestall discipline problems, McFarlane reverted to type, again becoming an instructor, perhaps his natural calling. He taught his men—the cooks, bakers, drivers, and medics as well as the gunners—the same artillery course he had taught captains and lieutenants at Fort Sill.

In September Jonny wrote to say that multiple births were a possibility. She wasn't due till November so McFarlane figured he had plenty of time to get used to the idea. Three nights later, the ship's captain awakened him with a message. Jonny had delivered twins. Scott weighed in at five pounds, Melissa at four and a half.

In early October, the Marine detachment returned, unbloodied, to Okinawa. In January 1965, however, as the situation in South Vietnam worsened, 3/9 and its supporting units, including Foxtrot Battery, embarked once more. McFarlane's troops were on the *Vancouver*, a new ship with automated loading and unloading equipment. In early February, they put into Subic Bay, in the Philippines. They were getting ready for a pig roast after a long day on the artillery range when they received top-secret orders. Mount out. Destination: the South China Sea.

The mount-out had been triggered by an attack on a small American base near Pleiku, in South Vietnam's Central Highlands. Vietcong guerrillas, using mortars and automatic weapons, killed eight American military advisers, wounded more than a hundred others, and destroyed ten U.S. aircraft on the ground. President Johnson responded quickly. Jets from the carrier *Ranger* bombed a North Vietnamese army base sixty miles north of the Seventeenth Parallel, which divided North and South Vietnam. More air strikes followed.

As the VC attacks intensified, Johnson on March 2 authorized Rolling Thunder, a program of bombing that would continue for the next three years. Officials huddled to devise a plan to protect the American airbase at Danang, the launching site for the stepped-up aerial campaign. On February 22 Johnson ordered the landing of two Marine infantry battalions, along with supporting units, to provide security. H-hour was set for 0600, March 8, 1965.

The landing was unopposed. As the troops splashed ashore in full battle dress, young Vietnamese women greeted them with garlands of flowers and a poster: "Welcome to the Gallant Marines." The reception left some Marines feeling foolish, but the absence of hostile fire probably precluded a disaster that day. Half the Navy's landing craft were inoperable. Some troops had to be ferried ashore in lifeboats. On the *Vancouver,* said McFarlane, the high-tech equipment began breaking down after the first hour, causing a major delay in the offloading of his guns and vehicles.

However confused the circumstances, on setting foot on the beach McFarlane achieved the status of historical footnote, having led the first Marine artillery battery into South Vietnam as part of a modest landing force of 3,500 troops. That number would mushroom to nearly 200,000 by the end of 1965, eventually to more than half a million. Though individual military advisers had been there for years, the landing marked the first time American ground troops had been deployed to South Vietnam as self-contained operational units.

"The Marine deployment was one of the crucial decisions of the war," wrote Stanley Karnow in *Vietnam: A History,* an acclaimed 1983 chronicle of the war and its roots, "yet it hardly stirred a ripple, either in Congress or in the American press, largely because Johnson had skillfully presented it as simply a short-term expedient."

McFarlane's life would intersect with the war twice more over the next decade, but now he was about to veer off in a dramatically different direction. At Annapolis he had applied for a George Olmsted Scholarship, a program under which officers with five years of active duty under their belts were given two years off to study at foreign colleges and universities. On Okinawa he learned that he had been selected. Thrilled by the news, he gained admission to the Graduate Institute of International Studies in Geneva as a student of international relations. He was to report there at the end of his tour, now almost over.

His troops, though, were dug in west of the airstrip at Danang. They had seen little action so far, but his instincts told him the calm would not last long. He also knew, having spent two years at Fort Sill, that he was one of the most qualified artillery officers in the Marine Corps. He belonged in Vietnam, he decided, not Geneva. He applied to extend his tour, knowing that in all likelihood he would lose his scholarship. The request was denied. He left after little more than a month in South Vietnam, wondering if he would ever see the place again, figuring he probably would.

CHAPTER SEVEN

THE CROWN PRINCE

As John McCain walked out of the pilots' ready room on October 26, 1967, the *Oriskany*'s strike operations officer, Lew Chatham, said, "You'd better be careful. We're probably going to lose someone on this one." Pushing past Chatham, an old friend, McCain shot back, "You don't have to worry about me, Lew."

McCain was charged up. He had been on the *Oriskany* for about a month, having transferred from the fire-ravaged *Forrestal*. The day before he had taken out three MiG fighters sitting nonchalantly on the apron at the Phuc Yen airfield outside Hanoi. Until then, Phuc Yen had been an LBJ-ordained sanctuary for the Soviet-supplied MiGs, which the Americans were permitted to engage in the air but not on the ground. The attack signaled a major escalation of the air war. About time, as far as McCain was concerned. He had flown over the harbor at Haiphong several times while Soviet ships unloaded tons of war matériel, watching as it was trucked away for use against American ground troops, unable to do a thing about it because of the restrictive rules of engagement. Now the rules seemed to be changing. McCain's A-4E Skyhawk was part of a twenty-plane mission getting ready to hit the power plant in Hanoi, another target previously off-limits.

LBJ's forbearance during the two and a half years since the first American ground units landed at Danang had given the North Vietnamese time to beef up the air defenses around their key cities, Hanoi and Haiphong. Hanoi was now more heavily defended against air attack than any city in history. McCain was about to learn what that meant.

Closing on the target, he weaved through airbursts and hurtled past SAM missiles that looked like airborne telephone poles. His instrument panel lit up, telling him a SAM had locked onto his aircraft. He punched out some chaff to confuse the missile's guidance system, then rolled in and released his bombs. He was pulling out of his dive when a SAM took off his right wing, sending his plane into a violent downward spiral.

Plunging toward the ground at about four hundred knots, he reached up with both hands and pulled the face curtain. The canopy blew off as small internal rockets shot him skyward, still in his seat, arms flailing wildly from the plane's uncontrolled gyrations. His right knee was broken, probably from smashing into the instrument panel on ejection. He also broke both arms, apparently when he hit the outside air.

Knocked out on ejection, he regained consciousness as he hit the tepid water of a small lake in the center of Hanoi. He sank to the muddy bottom, about fifteen feet down, then kicked back up gasping for air.

As he sank again, he tried to manipulate the toggles of his life vest to inflate it, but discovered that his arms were useless. He pushed up from the bottom a second time, but couldn't make it to the top. Fighting to hold his breath, he managed to pull the toggle with his teeth, the vest inflated, and he bobbed to the surface.

He floated around for a minute or two before some soldiers swam out and pulled him into shore. An angry crowd of several hundred Vietnamese had gathered, all seemingly armed. Stripped down to his skivvies, he was kicked and spat on, then bayoneted in the left ankle and left groin. Suddenly the pain from the injuries he incurred on ejection, muted until then, flared through his body. He raised his head, was stunned to see that his right calf was nearly perpendicular to his knee, in an unnatural direction.

As he surveyed the damage, an onlooker slammed a rifle butt down on his shoulder, smashing it. Other Vietnamese responded differently. A man yelled at the crowd to leave him alone. A woman held a cup of tea to his lips as photographers took propaganda pictures. Then uniformed soldiers threw him in the back of a truck for the short ride to Hoa Lo prison, North Vietnam's main penitentiary.

John Hubbell, in his sweeping chronicle of the Vietnam prisoner of war experience, *P.O.W.*, would later write, "No American reached Hoa Lo in worse physical condition than McCain."

At the prison, christened the Hanoi Hilton by its American inmates, McCain was placed on a stretcher on the floor of a cell. After his wounds were bandaged, he was told he would receive no further medical treatment until he agreed to provide military information.

For the next few days he lapsed in and out of consciousness. He was fed small amounts of water and food by a guard. He kept the water down, but vomited the food. His captors, demanding military information, told him that as a war criminal he was not protected by international covenants governing the treatment of prisoners of war. He responded as he had been trained, with name, rank, serial number, and date of birth. Infuriated, his interrogators kicked him and pounded him with their fists.

"That just knocked me out, so the interrogations were fairly short," recalled McCain, as if he had somehow outfoxed the North Vietnamese by getting them to beat him senseless.

Denied medication to blunt the pain, he knew after a few days that he had played out his hand. A guard came in, pulled the blanket off him, exposing his lower body. His knee was the size, shape, and color of a football. He realized he was in shock when it seemed that he could look through his skin and see the blood pooling in his knee. The illusion brought back a terrifying memory. When he was a flight instructor, another pilot injured himself in a similar manner, by cracking his knee upon ejection. The knee had swelled the same way. The pilot had gone into shock as blood drained into the joint. Then he died.

"Look, if you take me to the hospital, then I'll give you the information you want," he told his interrogator, hoping he could put him off once his wounds were treated.

The camp doctor was summoned. He took McCain's pulse, shook his head, and whispered something to the interrogator.

"Are you going to take me to the hospital?" asked McCain.

"No. It's too late," said the interrogator.

"Look, take me to the hospital and I'll be okay," pleaded McCain.

"It's too late, it's too late," the interrogator replied as he and the doctor walked out.

In shock, panicked, aware that he had been left to die, McCain lay alone in the cell for the next several hours. Then the door opened, and a camp official he came to know as the Bug walked in.

"Your father is a big admiral," said the Bug.

"Yes, my father is an admiral," McCain replied, confirming the

Bug's suspicions that his countrymen had bagged a most valuable prisoner.

"Now we take you to the hospital," said the Bug.

McCain passed out as he was being transported to the primitive medical facility. He woke up in a room infested with mosquitoes and roaches. Rats scurried over a floor covered with a half inch of water, a byproduct of the rainy season then in progress. But McCain was not complaining. He was snug in a metal frame bed, tubes of glucose and blood pouring into his arms.

In London, Jack and Roberta McCain were dressing for a dinner at the Iranian ambassador's residence when the hot line flashed. An admiral at the Pentagon reported that two planes had been shot down over Hanoi. John was flying one of them. No survivors had been spotted.

Jack passed the news on to Roberta. They talked about it, their faith in John's resilience battling their desire not to delude themselves. "What about the dinner?" asked Roberta. Said Jack, "We're going to go and we're going to keep our mouths shut."

Returning home, they received a call from Admiral Thomas Moorer, the Chief of Naval Operations. "We don't think there are any survivors," he said.

In Florida, Carol had already received official notification when Jack and Roberta phoned to pass on what they had heard via the old-boy network.

"Carol, I think Johnny's dead," said Roberta, her voice hollow, devastated. "I think we'd better just accept it."

"I don't think we have to," said Jack.

Said Carol, "I don't intend to. It's not possible."

On October 28, the *New York Times* reported John's downing in a front-page story by Saigon correspondent R. W. Apple, Jr. The headline read, "Adm. McCain's Son, *Forrestal* Survivor, Is Missing in Raid."

After two weeks in the hospital, McCain was shifted to another part of the building where a doctor attempted to set his right arm, broken in three places. He passed out several times during the ninety-minute procedure, performed without anesthesia. The doctor tried repeatedly to manipulate the two floating bones into place, only to have one or the other slip out of alignment. Frustrated, he gave up and slapped on a plaster cast that ran from McCain's waist to his neck. The arm, still unset, jutted forlornly from his body like a television antenna after a windstorm. No effort was made to set his left arm.

The cast still wet, he was moved to a bright, reasonably clean room.

An hour later he was visited by a dapper North Vietnamese known as the Cat, the commander of all POW camps in Hanoi. Earlier in the day McCain had been told that a visiting Frenchman wanted to stop by to see him and perhaps take a message back to his family. Fine, said McCain, anxious to let Carol and his parents know he was alive. Now the Cat told him that the Frenchman was a television correspondent who planned to film their conversation.

"I don't want to be filmed," said McCain.

"You need two operations and if you don't talk to him, then we will take your chest cast off and you won't get any operations," the Cat retorted. "You will say you're grateful to the Vietnamese people, and that you're sorry for your crimes."

McCain said he wouldn't do it.

The Frenchman, François Chalais, arrived with two cameramen. He questioned McCain for several minutes. On film, shown soon after on CBS Television, McCain looked drugged and fearful, though he answered Chalais's questions cogently. He later ascribed his appearance to fatigue and pain resulting from the abortive bone-setting procedure. Off-camera, the Cat prompted him to say that he was grateful for the humane treatment he had received and to demand an end to the war. He refused. When the Cat pressed the point, Chalais stepped in: "I think what he told me is sufficient." He then asked McCain if he had a message for his family. McCain said he loved them and that he was getting well. The Cat again insisted that he say that he hoped the war would be over soon so he could go home. He wouldn't do it. Chalais came to his rescue once more, saying he was satisfied. As a parting question, Chalais asked him about the prison food. "Well, it's okay, but it's not Paris," said McCain, the elemental wise-ass strain surfacing briefly.

Once the cameras had departed, he was returned to his old, roach-infested room, where interrogators made frequent visits. Incensed by his refusal to cooperate, they resorted to brutality, slapping and punching him. Once they hit him on his right arm, causing him to emit a bloodcurdling scream. They backed off, as if wary of the hospital authorities. McCain decided that officials at the hospital, if not especially competent, were at least protective of him while under their care. After that, he let loose a loud scream of pain whenever the interrogators became too physical.

For the rest of his hospital stay he was never bathed, never cleaned, never shaved, although his knee was operated on. He was told he needed more surgery on the knee but that he wouldn't get it because of his "bad attitude." American doctors later told him the North Vietnamese had simply cut all the ligaments and cartilage, which meant for nearly his entire time in prison he had only 5 to 10 percent flexion in his knee.

Even with medical care, such as it was, and the apparent desire of his captors to keep him alive, McCain was fading. One night an official came in and said, "The doctors say that you don't get better, that you get worse." McCain replied, "You need to put me with some Americans, because I'm not going to get better here." The following night, he was blindfolded and taken by truck from the Hilton to a prison on the outskirts of Hanoi nicknamed the Plantation.

Bud Day, an Air Force pilot, wasn't in much better shape than McCain. After his capture in August 1967, Day was kept in a small underground bunker for several days. He escaped, and struck out for the South. After an epic journey that lasted about two weeks, he was recaptured less than a mile from an American military base, the *whop, whop, whop* of U.S. Army choppers clearly audible as he was led back into a captivity that would last another five and a half years. His dash for freedom would eventually win him the Congressional Medal of Honor, one of only two POWs so honored, but the short-term result was public interrogation and torture.

His arms virtually useless after being hung on torture ropes for three hours, he was thrown in a prison called the Zoo, where his roommate, a fellow Air Force major named Norris Overly, began nursing him back to health.

In late December 1967, the Bug, upbeat, told Day that he was small potatoes, a nothing, that the North Vietnamese didn't care about him. He explained that they had just captured two full colonels. "And," said the Bug with a self-satisfied smirk, "we've got the Crown Prince."

The Crown Prince? Day didn't break the code until the next afternoon, when he and Overly were moved to the Plantation. Then he remembered Hanoi radio a few weeks earlier boasting about the capture of "air pirate McCain, son of Admiral McCain." Now it made sense. Jack McCain had lectured to Day's class at the Armed Forces Staff College in 1963. Day hoped he would get a chance to meet the admiral's son. Outside his cell, he heard a commotion. The door opened and a prisoner strapped to a board was set down on the floor.

"I've seen some dead that looked at least as good as John," Day would later say. McCain weighed less than one hundred pounds. His hair, flecked with gray since high school, was nearly snow-white. Clots of food clung to his face, neck, hair, and beard. His cheeks were sunken, his neck chickenlike, his legs atrophied. His knee bore a fresh surgical slash, his ankle an angry scar from the bayonet wound. The body cast added to his deathly appearance. He seemed to have shriveled up inside it. His right arm, little more than skin and bone, protruded like a stick. But it was McCain's eyes that riveted Day.

"His eyes, I'll never forget, were just burning bright. They were bug-eyed like you see in those pictures of the guys from the Jewish concentration camps. His eyes were real pop-eyed like that. I said, 'The gooks have dumped this guy on us so they can blame us for killing him,' because I didn't think he was going to live out the day."

Suddenly McCain was talking. His voice was weak, little more than a whisper, but Day and Overly were the first Americans he had seen in two months and he had a lot to tell and much he wanted to know. The discussion began in late afternoon and kept going until the early hours of the morning. McCain talked compulsively. He wanted to know about the prison camps, how they were run, what other Americans were being held and where.

At first, Day thought of Overly and himself as gently ushering McCain toward the death they both felt was imminent, as if they were priests performing last rites.

"As the day went on, though, I started to get the feeling that if we could get a little grits into him and feed him and get him cleaned up and the infection didn't get him, he was probably going to make it," said Day. "And that surprised me. That just flabbergasted me because I had given him up.

"I can remember thinking that night, My God, this guy's got a lot of heart. You've been involved in sports and games and things where people kind of rise to an occasion and that was him. He was rising. And if he hadn't been, he'd have been dead. If he had not had that will to live and that determination, he'd have been dead."

At about three in the morning, in mid-sentence, with Norris Overly massaging his leg, McCain fell asleep. To Bud Day, it was as if God had just switched off the light.

Bud Day helped, but it was Norris Overly who put John McCain together again. First he poured the little water allotted him onto a towel and scrubbed McCain's face, though Day recalled that "the crud and the scuzz were so thick on him that it really didn't help much." Soon Overly was massaging McCain's leg at least two hours a day. He also fed McCain all his meals, leaning him against the wall in his body cast, and helped him relieve himself.

"Overly had to get him up and sit him on the john," said Day. "The john was one of these paint buckets, just a big old metal bucket all rusted up. He would sit him on this thing and get him on there and wipe him. You know, he couldn't do the first thing for himself."

By the second or third day, Overly managed to soften up the encrusted filth on McCain's face so that he could scrape it off and shave him. That seemed to boost his spirits. McCain's leg, which had become infected, responded to soap and water. Before long Overly had him on his feet. By early January 1968, he could walk by himself for a few minutes at a time.

Treatment at the Plantation was not overly harsh. At times Day suspected the Vietnamese were trying to curry favor with McCain and, to a lesser extent, Overly. One day an officer asked McCain if he wanted anything special to eat. He said, no, he would eat what everyone else ate. Day concluded that the Plantation was a camp for prisoners the Vietnamese considered candidates for a rumored early-release program. McCain seemed tailor-made for the role. Shipping a senior admiral's son home could harm the morale of other, less well-connected POWs and American fighting men in general. Unknown to McCain, Day, and Overly at the time, Jack McCain had just been named commander-in-chief of all U.S. military forces in the Pacific, including Vietnam, CINCPAC for short, which stood to intensify the propaganda advantage. But the younger McCain would not play along.

"What they were looking for from John was some kind of sign that he was reliable," said Day. "But he didn't give them any kind of a clue that he would help them in any way."

Norris Overly was a different story. One evening he told McCain and Day that the Vietnamese might send him home. "I don't think that's the right thing to do," said Day. Said McCain, "I wouldn't even consider any kind of a release. They'll have to drag me out of here." The only reason to release him, he said, would be to embarrass his father, and he wasn't going to let that happen.

Day and McCain were not indulging in machismo. The Code of Conduct for American Fighting Men, developed by the armed forces after the Korean War, governed the actions of prisoners of war. Key provisions included a prohibition on accepting parole or special favors from the enemy, a requirement that reasonable efforts be made to escape, and, by extension, that any releases prior to the end of hostilities be in order of capture, that is, first in, first out. By early 1968, more than three hundred Americans were in North Vietnamese prison camps, dating back to Navy Lieutenant (jg) Everett Alvarez, Jr., shot down on August 5, 1964. With certain exceptions, accepting a release under any other conditions was tantamount to breaking faith with fellow prisoners.

The next day Overly was moved out. McCain and Day heard on the grapevine that he and two other prisoners were being prepped for release. On the morning he left, Overly—outfitted in a cheap blue suit—stopped back to see his ex-cellmates. "What did it cost you?" asked Day. He meant the release, not the suit. "Nothing, not a thing, didn't do a thing," said Overly. Neither Day nor McCain pressed the point. Overly and two others—Air Force Captain John Black and Navy Ensign David Matheny—left later that day, February 16, the first participants of what the prisoners left behind dubbed the Fink Release Program. Five years later, when McCain was freed with the rest of the POWs, Overly called him. They spoke briefly. They have not talked since.

McCain and Day lived together for another month and a half after Overly left. They would struggle arm in arm out to the bathing area or to get their food. As they did so, two other prisoners, Jack Van Loan and Read Mecleary, would tease them, gallows humor tailored to the POW experience: "Hire the handicapped, they're fun to watch." They got along well, with one brief falling out. One day they killed upwards of four hundred mosquitoes, smashing them against the wall of their cell. They thought they had set a new prison record only to learn that two other POWs were claiming a one-day kill count of over a thousand. Their jubilation soured, angry words were exchanged.

Day was ten years older, but McCain was the more worldly, regaling his cellmate with tales of youthful carousing and womanizing. He was also more politically sophisticated, having kept his ear to the wall when his parents entertained senators, congressmen, and other bigwigs at their Capitol Hill home. Day said McCain helped him understand how Washington really worked, with emphasis on the human dimension. "I had no idea that the whole damn Kennedy family was banging Marilyn Monroe and those sorts of things," said Day.

They talked about politics and the homefront, stimulated by propaganda broadcasts piped into their cells from six in the morning till nine at night. These reports laid great stress on the antiwar movement and political unrest at home.

"Dr. Spock, Dave Dellinger, every wacko that had ever come down the pike and hated the country was on gook radio telling you how bad the United States was and how great Communism was," said Day. "We would talk about the fact that there was no punishment that would adequately deal with these kinds of scuzz that are eating your country, taking all the benefits, and then tearing it apart from the inside."

Vietnamese interrogators encouraged the POWs to repudiate LBJ. In general, they refused to do so, viewing it as unpatriotic and a violation of the Code of Conduct. Privately, Day, McCain, and many others felt Johnson had abandoned them. But one emerging American political figure intrigued Day and McCain: the new governor of California, then completing his first year in office. "We talked about Ronald Reagan being President back in 1967," said Day. "We talked about it frequently."

One day Jack Van Loan peered through a peephole in his cell door and saw a crowd of North Vietnamese dignitaries trudging through the courtyard toward the cell that McCain and Day shared. Nodding sagely, they entered the cubicle. A few minutes later Van Loan heard McCain cut loose with a string of obscenities that knifed through the silence of the cellblock.

"It was some of the most colorful profanity that you would ever hope to hear," said Van Loan. "He was calling them every name in the book, and telling them that he was not going home early, that he wasn't going to ask for amnesty and not to ask him that again and to get out and, furthermore, screw you and the horse you rode in on. John was just shrieking at them.

"Those guys came tumbling back out of there, I mean, they were backing up and John was just fighting back as best he knew how. They came out of there like tumbleweeds. I was laughing and crying at the same time. They would have lugged him out of there that day and let him go. And here's a guy that's all crippled up, all busted up, and he doesn't know if he's going to live to the next day and he literally blew them out of there with a verbal assault. You can't imagine the example John set for the rest of the camp by doing that."

As the spring of 1968 approached, McCain proudly showed one of his interrogators how well he was getting around with the ancient pair of wooden crutches he had been using. That night, guards removed Bud Day from the cell, leaving McCain by himself. He was alone for the next two years.

CHAPTER EIGHT

THE BLOODY FILTER

Vietnam behind him, Bud McFarlane arrived in Geneva in August 1965 to claim his Olmsted Scholarship. A city of cautious diplomats and secretive bankers, Geneva became his refuge, a place to forget the roar of jets, the throaty *ka-boom* of artillery pieces, the menacing snap of small-arms fire. At least for a while.

Unbearded but sporting sideburns, he was just another student at the Graduate Institute of International Studies, trudging to class, matching wits with his professors, marveling at the complexity of a world painted neither Navy blue nor Marine green, but ever-changing shades of gray.

In Vietnam the American military buildup was gaining momentum. Certain he was going back, he might have treated the two-year hiatus in Geneva as a preemptive R and R. Instead, he attacked his studies with a ferocity rarely displayed before. International law, global economics, power and politics, each course became part of a savory intellectual feast he could not devour quickly enough.

Geneva redefined McFarlane, fostering his transformation from tactician to strategist. He later thought of his time there as a second chance, a fresh opportunity to redeem the high promise that his father had proclaimed his birthright. Until Geneva, he had followed a path blazed by others, his brother, uncle, the institutional needs of Annapolis and the Marine Corps. Now, in a pink lakeside château presided over by scholars of international repute, the disparate elements of his personality—Marine, truth-seeker, unfrocked priest—gradually stitched themselves together.

His grades bordered on the spectacular. He finished with a 5.75 average on a 6.0 scale, earning his master's degree in three semesters, using the remaining time to complete resident work for a doctorate. Intellectually aroused as never before, he had finally found a uniform that fit, one with a perfect crease and no Irish pennants. He emerged a big-picture man, a budding Kissinger in combat boots, at least by his own lights.

The professor who influenced him most was Louis J. Halle, an American. Halle was a prolific author, respected strategic thinker, and onetime State Department colleague of Dean Acheson and George Kennan. He favored the containment of Communism, but questioned the will of the United States to take a stand against the Communists and sustain it, as it was attempting to do in Vietnam.

His doubts about Vietnam, as McFarlane read them, related to the mood on the homefront. How long would Americans support a war when they had not been persuaded that their own survival was at stake? Had the United States ever engaged in large-scale military action without a concrete threat to Americans? For Americans to support extended military intervention, Halle asserted, the battleground had to be someplace they at least had heard of. Germany and Japan met that test; Vietnam did not.

As he neared the end of his time in Geneva, McFarlane grew eager to return to that obscure battlefield. The antiwar movement was gathering strength at home and across Europe, but he remained a staunch, at times strident supporter of the war. The cause, he believed, was just. He was equally confident the war could be won. But Halle's questions jarred him, triggering doubts about Lyndon Johnson's ability to inspire Americans to make the necessary sacrifices and feeding his concerns about the battlefield consequences of failed presidential leadership.

Halle also argued that deterrence was the product of two factors, military power and the will to use it. As a result, if you had the power but lacked the will you had nothing since any quantity, no matter how great, multiplied by zero was zero. It was a lesson that many never learned, one McFarlane never forgot.

He requested Vietnam duty after Geneva. The Marines were happy to comply, shipping him back in September 1967, the start of the monsoon season. He rejoined his old outfit, the Second Battalion, Twelfth Marines, then providing artillery support for the Ninth Marines, an infantry regiment operating south of the DMZ in the area known as Leatherneck Square.

As a senior captain, he hoped to command a battery again. Instead, he was assigned as fire support coordinator, planning artillery barrages, naval gunfire from ships offshore (including the battleship *New Jersey*, his old midshipman cruise ship), close air support, and the Arc-light strikes of Air Force B-52 bombers from Guam. The job was crucial, but he had little chance for John Wayne–style heroics, most of his work taking place in a heavily sandbagged command bunker.

He might have played it safe, confining his activities to the relatively secure command post at Dong Ha, where the mess hall served hot meals and the Officers Club poured cold drinks. But he felt detached from the fighting, a technician among warriors, the absence of grave personal risk robbing his efforts of meaning, at least in his own mind.

Vietnam by then was awash in American blood. More than ten thousand Americans had already died, hundreds more were dying every week, many no more than a mile or two from his position. In October he ran into an old friend and Annapolis classmate, Jack Phillips.

"He was commanding a company in combat, the ultimate challenge for a Marine officer," said McFarlane. "He was fit, strong, knowledgeable, a paragon of what our institutions from the Academy to the U.S. Marine Corps are supposed to produce. Two days later, literally, he took an RPG [rocket-propelled grenade] round in the chest and was destroyed."

After that, McFarlane found the isolation of the CP intolerable. He started going into the field nearly every day so he could meet the infantry leaders, walk the ground with them, explain what he did, how he did it, how he could do it for them. Squatting beside a weary rifle platoon leader and grumpy platoon sergeant, he'd break out his cigarettes and teach a quick refresher course on the use of supporting arms.

Look, I can do a lot for you, he told them, but I can do a better job if you help me. See that crater. That's from enemy artillery, right? Okay, it's not round, is it, it's oblong. So when you're taking incoming, if you can get me a back bearing along the long axis, I can find those fuckers and take them out. Oh, yeah, I need to know if it's a steep crater or a shallow crater. But that's it. Give me those two things and I will make your life a hell of a lot easier.

He was in a foxhole, conferring with a young lieutenant, an artillery forward observer, when he found the war.

"Lieutenant, we're about to get hit," the FO's radio operator said.

"Captain, there's not enough room for all of us in this hole," said the lieutenant, pointing McFarlane to a less exposed position on the reverse slope of a small rise.

As McFarlane hunkered down, mortars began tearing up the terrain in front of him. The lieutenant, standing in his hole, exposed to shrapnel and small-arms fire, called in mortars and artillery, shouting commands, hollering encouragement. McFarlane admired the lieutenant's cool professionalism, felt useless himself. He decided to scramble over to the next company's position to see if he could help out there.

He was sliding past the lieutenant's hole when a mortar round landed right behind him. "It scared the shit out of me," he recalled. "I'd never been that close to an explosion, ever. The spray just took out all the trees and bushes and lower growth in the area. But I wasn't hit. I was in enough of a depression to where it all went over me."

Struggling to regain his composure, he heard the radio operator shouting, "Corpsman, corpsman, the lieutenant's hit." McFarlane crawled back, dropped into the hole, and manhandled the wounded officer behind a small incline. Turning the lieutenant over, he saw that shrapnel had torn away half his face and part of his neck. He kept trying to talk, but all that came out were watery gurgles. He was, McFarlane realized, drowning in his own blood. Cradling the lieutenant in his arms, he whispered soothing words, like you do to a kid when he stubs his toe, knowing he'll get over it in a minute or two.

A sudden storm drenched the two men, the rain pelting the ooze that had once been the lieutenant's face. Desperately trying to speak, he finally forced some words through the blood puddling in his throat.

"God bless Mother and . . . Mother and Daddy . . . and Ruth . . . oh, God." Something like that. It was hard to tell.

Then he died. A moment later, a sniper round tore into his head.

McFarlane saw dispiriting contradictions all around him. He admired the gritty personal courage of the young Marines and soldiers he met, both officer and enlisted. Yet the greatest industrial power on earth seemed incapable of supplying them with boots for months at a time. In the field, the troops broke up ammo boxes for wood to reinforce their primitive bunkers. He had been in-country just a couple of weeks when a four-man fire team was wiped out because their ammo box bunker caved in during a monsoon, burying them alive. Back at the Dong Ha CP, meanwhile, lumber was stacked up as far as the eye could see, earmarked for construction of the classic McNamara pipe dream, an electronic fence that was supposed to signal the presence of enemy troops moving south. The war was being run by people with very little understanding of warfare, McFarlane concluded, men who gave greater priority to their high-tech contraptions than to the kids rolling snake eyes out in Indian country.

He was promoted to major, but the advancement did little to dull his unease. Angered by the unfathomable supply problems, beset by a vague sense of guilt because he was not routinely putting his life on the line, he became an advocate for the troops. If he couldn't fight alongside them, he reasoned, he could at least bitch on their behalf. On one occasion, he was introduced to a visiting three-star. "Glad to meet you, General," he said. "By the way, sir, the troops don't have any boots."

He was not impressed by the senior military leadership. In late fall, William Westmoreland flew up from his headquarters in Saigon. Con Thien, not far from Dong Ha, had been taking casualties for weeks, and the plight of the embattled defenders was making headlines back home. Huddling with Colonel Richard B. Smith, CO of the Ninth Marines, and his staff officers, Westmoreland said to McFarlane, Major, you will shoot fifty TOTs (pronounced tee-oh-tees) every night. We've got to get on top of the problem up here.

During a TOT, or time on target, all available artillery units swing their guns toward a designated target and cut loose with everything they have. It's the artillery equivalent of Coney Island on the Fourth of July, as pilots in old World War II movies always seem to describe their bombing runs.

McFarlane was dismayed by Westmoreland's order. A TOT was reserved for a target that you could count on being in a certain spot at a certain time. The target also had to be worth all the attention since the artillery was forced to forgo other fire missions for the duration of the TOT. That meant an ambushed patrol or a rifle company taking fire couldn't count on artillery support until the TOT had been completed.

General, said McFarlane, if I had fifty good targets I'd love to fire fifty TOTs a night. But I haven't had fifty good targets since I got here two months ago. So pulling all my guns off other missions every night to fire fifty TOTs doesn't make sense.

Major, said Westmoreland, you don't seem to understand. I've been in the Army a long time and I know what you can do to an enemy with fifty TOTs a night.

No, you don't, General, said McFarlane. We don't know where the enemy is. On those few occasions when we do, it may be a squad, at most a platoon. And usually only during the day when someone sees them from the air. At night we don't know where they are. I can't devote all these batteries to shooting at points on the ground with no confidence that there is anything there. The price is that other kinds of fire won't get done. This is not wise, General. I can't do that.

Well, Major, said Westmoreland, I guess we'd better find somebody who can.

Stepping in, Colonel Smith said, Don't worry about it, General. We'll take care of it.

When Westmoreland left, Smith turned to McFarlane. That wasn't very smart, snapped the colonel. What do you want me to do? asked McFarlane, furious. Shoot the fifty TOTs, said Smith.

The Tet Offensive of 1968 began on January 31. Some seventy thousand Communist troops broke the lunar New Year cease-fire that they themselves had declared to launch a series of carefully coordinated attacks that, according to Stanley Karnow, "exploded around the country like a string of firecrackers." More than a hundred cities and towns, Saigon included, reeled under the assault. At Dong Ha, McFarlane struggled to coordinate the fire of nine artillery batteries scattered across the countryside, six more than a regimental fire support coordinator usually had to handle. Infantry commanders screamed in one ear, artillery commanders hollered in the other. Cam Lo, just west of Dong Ha, was under assault, as was a position to the north called C-2. Dong Ha was taking incoming as well, but McFarlane was reasonably safe in the command bunker.

At Cam Lo, the American adviser, an Army major whom McFarlane had befriended, pulled the villagers into the fortified compound and was mounting a spirited defense. The initial attack came from the west, the second from the south. During the first five hours the village force—Marines and Popular Force irregulars—beat back a half dozen assaults. During a lull in the fighting, a Marine manning a .50-caliber machine gun reported that he could no longer see because enemy dead were stacked up so high in front of his position. About 2:00 A.M., a North Vietnamese force slipped around to the east and broke through the village's defenses, broke into the command bunker, and killed the major. But still the village held.

McFarlane, tied to the action by radio in Dong Ha, was desperately trying to line up batteries to provide artillery support for Cam Lo and C-2. "You'd sit there in the CP and listen to these poor guys out there," he said, "and you could just feel the mounting scale of death and violence."

Cam Lo survived, but just barely. McFarlane made it over there a day and a half after the battle. "I remember there being a long line of green body bags for soldiers and Marines and then there was another line of body bags for civilians and PFs who were part of the garrison. But spirits were beginning to come back. They understood they had not been beaten."

Tet has been viewed as a turning point in public support for the war at home. The press widely reported it as an American defeat, focusing on the breaching of the U.S. embassy compound in Saigon by nineteen

Vietcong commandos, an audacious attack that reduced the embassy to chaos for the six and a half hours it took to secure the grounds. Lost in the rush to judgment was the fact that the North Vietnamese and their Vietcong allies were unable to hold a single village, town, or city that they had attacked.

The fiercest battle raged in the city of Hue, which the Communists seized from its somnolent South Vietnamese defenders with a lightninglike three-pronged attack. Marines reclaimed the city after twenty-six days of brutal house-to-house fighting. Barely noticed at the time was what Karnow terms "the worst bloodbath" of the war, the systematic butchering in Hue of no fewer than three thousand South Vietnamese civilians by the Vietcong. Also lost in the uproar was the failure of the South Vietnamese population to heed North Vietnam's call for a popular nationwide revolt.

When the Tet Offensive ended, the U.S. command reported that two thousand American and four thousand South Vietnamese soldiers had been killed. The enemy death toll was put at a staggering fifty thousand, an estimate that Karnow, no apologist for the war, calls plausible. In a classic understatement, Tran Do, a senior architect of the campaign, told Karnow years later, "In all honesty, we didn't achieve our main objective, which was to spur uprisings throughout the south. Still, we inflicted heavy casualties on the Americans and their puppets, and that was a big gain for us. As for making an impact in the United States, it had not been our intention—but it turned out to be a fortunate result."

So it had. The Americans and South Vietnamese may have prevailed on the battlefield, but Tet and the reporting of it dealt the war effort a severe body blow. Walter Cronkite, the nation's most trusted journalist, returned from the battlefield in late February to predict that it seemed "more certain than ever that the bloody experience in Vietnam is to end in a stalemate." Film of the embattled U.S. embassy was played and replayed, file footage for the ages, the all-purpose backdrop for gloomy journalistic prognostications.

Ex-Marine Peter Braestrup, who covered the war for the *Washington Post*, would later write in his 1977 two-volume work, *Big Story*, that "crisis journalism" had rarely "veered so widely from reality." But Braestrup's provocative and minutely researched brand of revisionist journalism was still years off. By late March 1968, LBJ divined his fate in the flickering images on the TV screen. He declared an unconditional bombing halt, called for peace talks, and announced that he would not run for reelection.

The reporting of Tet confused and angered McFarlane. To his

mind, and to the minds of many American officers on the scene, the North Vietnamese and their Vietcong allies had badly overreached and been dealt a devastating battlefield defeat. Somehow, though, largely through the magic of television, that defeat had been transformed into a stunning victory for the enemy. He was appalled when he met Jonny in Hawaii in April for five days of R and R. The papers were filled with pessimistic appraisals of the military effort, opinion polls showing diminished public tolerance for the war, and accounts of massive antiwar demonstrations at home.

What the hell is going on here? he asked himself.

Many servicemen were asking the same question. Bitter and frustrated, they felt their countrymen had turned against them. McFarlane shared their rage, but his anger was tempered by a number of complicating factors. The military had fed the press bogus information for years, so perhaps the reluctance of reporters to buy seemingly overblown U.S. victory claims after Tet was understandable. The drop in public support was not entirely without justification, either. Despite the rosy predictions issuing from the lips of everyone from the President on down, the war was now three years old, with no end in sight. In truth, McFarlane himself considered the senior military leadership terminally inept. And Louis Halle's pointed queries had come back to haunt him.

McFarlane was not the typical soldier. Geneva had provided him with a broader strategic framework for viewing events than the majority of men who served in Vietnam. But he was not a disinterested scholar, either, removed from the fray, bemused by the blunders. He was there, on the ground, picking up the pieces. More than anything else, he was a Marine, and as with most soldiers of his generation his memories of Vietnam would always be refracted through a filter smeared with the blood of friends and comrades. As he later put it, men in uniform "expect more of the country, of the Congress, of the press, of Americans generally, when lives are at stake."

CHAPTER NINE

DO YOU WANT
TO GO HOME?

As the weeks in solitary stretched into months, John McCain was indefatigable in trying to make contact with other Americans, routinely defying the edict against communicating with other prisoners. Fellow POWs remember him in those days as an ungainly scarecrow suspended from crutches, loudly taunting his jailers as he limped past on his way to interrogation sessions.

"Fuck you," he yelled at the guards as they hurried him along, aware that other prisoners could see him and were loving every minute of it. "Fuck you, you goddamned slant-eyed cocksuckers."

His antagonism had a macabre looniness to it, like the game but overmatched Black Knight in the movie *Monty Python and the Holy Grail*. Squirming in the dirt, all four limbs lopped off, the Knight shouts after his departing adversary, "Oh, oh, I see. Running away, eh. You yellow bastard!"

Fighting back, even as an exercise in impotence, did a lot for McCain. It got him through the night, kept him sane, helped him maintain his self-respect. Physically, he knew he'd be a wreck if he ever got out of prison, probably crippled. But he was determined to emerge from his incarceration as Salinger's Sergeant X hoped to survive World War II, with all his f-a-c-u-l-t-i-e-s intact.

His Vietnamese guards were willing participants in his self-help program. They responded to his insults by knocking him down, flinging him against the wall, or punching him in the head. Despite the pummelings, McCain suspected he was getting special treatment. The guards seemed under orders to go easy on him unless he grossly violated the rules, at which point they were free to hammer him. Even then they kept their brutality within limits. It was a fine distinction. The Prick, as McCain named his major tormentor, might kick him as he lay on the floor of his cell, but he noticed the jailer never kicked him in his bad right leg. And though the Prick sometimes booted him in the head, he stayed away from his face. McCain knew he was escaping the Prick's full fury; he just didn't know why.

In June 1968, around the time Jim Webb and Ollie North were graduating from Annapolis, McCain learned the reason. By then, he had been undergoing interrogation for months. The sessions fell into a predictable pattern. He refused to cooperate. The North Vietnamese told him he would be tried for war crimes and never go home.

One night the pattern abruptly changed. He was summoned to an unfamiliar room. It had soft chairs and a glass coffee table supported on each end by marble elephants. Usually he was interrogated in a bare cell with a stool for the prisoner and a chair and desk for the questioner.

Major Bai, known to the prisoners as the Cat, was waiting for McCain. As commander of the Hanoi prison system, he orchestrated the effort to break the spirit of American prisoners, by co-opting them if possible, with torture when necessary. A second Vietnamese, known as the Rabbit, stood by to serve as translator.

Cookies, a pot of tea, and cigarettes were on the table. McCain helped himself as the Cat began speaking through the translator. To McCain, the conversation had a rambling quality. They talked of McCain's father, other members of his family, the war. Two hours went by. McCain, puzzled, couldn't figure out what the Cat was up to.

Then the Cat mentioned that Norris Overly and the other two freed prisoners had been welcomed home as heroes.

"That's interesting," said McCain, unimpressed.

"Do you want to be released?" said the Cat.

McCain, momentarily speechless, fought to keep his composure. "Frankly, I don't know," he finally said. "I don't know."

"You go back and think about it," said the Cat.

In his cell, he tapped on the wall, raising his neighbor, Bob Craner. Craner listened to McCain's tale, then told him to take the release. McCain said he didn't think it was right to do so. They went back and forth without resolving the question.

McCain faced a dilemma. He was trying to adhere to the POW interpretation of the Code of Conduct that said prisoners could accept release only in order of capture. That meant Everett Alvarez and a lot of others should go home before he did. But the Code, as construed by the prisoners in North Vietnam, provided an exception for the seriously sick and injured, saying they should receive priority. The exception was driving McCain crazy. He was in wretched physical condition. Crippled, emaciated from months of dysentery, he doubted he could last another year in captivity.

Three nights later, the Cat sent for him again. Same pleasant room, more hours of aimless conversation. Finally, from the Cat, "Do you want to go home?" McCain: "No."

He explained the Code of Conduct and said Alvarez should be the first to go. The Cat said the Code did not apply to war criminals. Then he announced that Lyndon Johnson had ordered him home. That got the Cat nowhere, so he took out a letter from Carol to McCain. She said she wished he had been one of the three prisoners who had come home. Until then, none of her letters had reached him. He took his wife's sentiments for what they were, an expression of love, not an exhortation to break faith with his comrades.

The Cat told him that the doctors said he couldn't survive much longer unless he returned to the States for treatment. That unsettled him since he had been agonizing over the same issue himself. But the assertion rang false. He hadn't seen a physician in months.

"Guess they're keeping in touch with my case by long distance," he said.

"Do you want to go home?"

"No."

Three days later, July 3, the Cat again summoned McCain, this time to one of the regular interrogation rooms. The Cat and the Rabbit sat at a table, McCain on a low stool in front of them. The Cat fumbled nervously with a fountain pen.

"The officer wants to know your final answer," said the Rabbit.

"My final answer is the same," said McCain. "It's no. I cannot accept this offer."

"That is your final answer?"

"That is my final answer."

The Cat, incensed, all traces of civility gone, crushed the pen in his hand, splattering the room with ink.

"They taught you too well," he said in perfect English. "They taught you too well."

Rising brusquely, knocking over his chair, he stormed out of the room, slamming the door behind him.

McCain and the Rabbit stared at each other. "Now, McCain, it will be very bad for you," said the Rabbit.

Shit, thought McCain.

For the next few days, he lived in terror, trembling at each sound in the corridor, knowing beyond question that his refusal to accept a release meant the good times were over. But nothing happened. A sense of relief began to take hold. He didn't trust it.

He was right. A week later he was braced in a stark room before Slopehead, the camp commander. Ten guards were standing by, including McCain's old pal, the Prick.

Slopehead told McCain he was a "black criminal" who had broken all the camp regulations. He must confess his crimes. McCain said he wouldn't.

"Why are you so disrespectful of guards?" asked Slopehead.

"Because the guards treat me like an animal," snapped McCain.

The Prick gleefully led the charge as the guards, at Slopehead's command, drove fists and knees and boots into McCain. Amid laughter and muttered oaths, he was slammed from one guard to another, bounced from wall to wall, knocked down, kicked, dragged to his feet, knocked back down, punched again and again in the face. When the beating was over, he lay on the floor, bloody, arms and legs throbbing, ribs cracked, several teeth broken off at the gumline.

"Are you ready to confess your crimes?" asked Slopehead.

"No."

The ropes came next. McCain had never been in torture ropes, but he had heard about them from Bud Day and others. He was moved to another cell where his arms, battered, broken, and bruised in one way or another since the day he was shot down, were lashed behind his back, then cinched tightly together to intensify the pain. He was left on a stool. Throughout the night, guards came in, asked him if he was ready to confess, then smashed their fists into him when he told them no.

The next several days fell into a harrowing routine. The ropes came off in the morning. Beatings were administered throughout the day, usually by one guard, sometimes two. On occasion two guards would hold him up while a third hammered him senseless. At night, the ropes were reapplied.

After a couple of days, he got some water. He was also given a bucket so he could relieve himself. Often he was so battered he could barely crawl to the bucket. Still plagued by dysentery, he often regained consciousness to find himself lying in his own waste. During one beating, staggered by a fist to the face, he slumped to the floor, smashing his left arm into the bucket, breaking it again. But he was back in torture ropes that night.

Each time the guards came in, they asked if he was ready to confess. After about a week, he knew he could not hold out any longer. Years later he would write, "I had learned what we all learned over there: Every man has a breaking point. I had reached mine."

Guards moved him to a separate building and set him to work on a confession. Like Americans before him, he tried to write in generalities, working in misspellings, grammatical errors, stilted phrases, and Communist jargon—constantly referring to Ho Chi Minh as "beloved and respected leader"—anything to make clear that it was a forced confession. He and an interrogator wrote and rewrote for about twelve hours. He was told to say that he bombed a school. He refused, and made the refusal stick. The final draft was written by the interrogator. In it, McCain said, "I am a black criminal and I have performed deeds of an air pirate. I almost died, and the Vietnamese people saved my life, thanks to the doctors. . . ." Aching and exhausted, he signed it.

Back in a cell, cut off from Bob Craner and other Americans, McCain told himself that he had held out as long as he was capable, longer than most men. But he could find no solace in excuses. No matter how he tried to sugarcoat his actions, he could not avoid the conclusion that he had dishonored his country, his family, and himself, betrayed his comrades, and besmirched the flag.

The cockiness was gone, replaced by a suffocating despair. He looked at the louvered cell window high above his head, then at the small stool in the room. He took off his dark blue prison shirt, rolled it like a rope, draped one end over his shoulder near his neck, began feeding the other end through the louvers . . .

A guard burst into the room, pulling McCain away from the window. The guard then administered another beating. For the next few days he was watched day and night.

"I don't know whether I would have actually gone through with it or not," said McCain as he sat in his Senate office two decades later. "I have no idea. I kind of doubt it."

But it could have happened?

"It could have."

He did not know at the time of his aborted suicide attempt that virtually every American who refused to cooperate with the North Vietnamese, including those widely viewed as the most courageous—Bud Day; Jim Stockdale, who disfigured himself by battering his face with a stool rather than make a public confession; Jeremiah Denton, who spelled out t-o-r-t-u-r-e in Morse code by batting his eyes at a television camera—had all been broken, often more than once. Now he knows, but it doesn't make any difference.

"I still believe that I failed," he said.

The words came slowly, as if his father and grandfather were in the room, measuring him, not pleased with what they were seeing. "I'm convinced that I did the best that I could, but the best that I could wasn't good enough."

* * *

As John McCain flirted with suicide, Jack McCain was two thousand miles away in Hawaii assuming command of the Pacific Theater. As CINCPAC, he was now the senior military man in the operational area that included Vietnam.

Flying to his new headquarters in Honolulu, he and Roberta picked up Carol in Jacksonville so she could attend the change-of-command ceremony. It was held in Pearl Harbor, aboard the *Oriskany*, the carrier John was flying off when he was shot down.

Those who knew Jack McCain during those years said he never brought up John's plight. When others did, he diplomatically changed the subject. But they also recall that he spent every Christmas for three years running with the Marines on the DMZ so he could be closer to his son.

During the dark and brutal days following McCain's refusal to accept early release, Charlie Plumb and Kay Russell were in a cell about twenty yards from him. They didn't know who their mystery neighbor was, but they could tell he was in sorry shape. Day after day they saw rags thrown out the cell door. Before the camp dogs got to the rags, Plumb and Russell could see they were covered with blood, pus, and scabs. They tried various ways to contact the unknown prisoner, but received no response. Plumb finally got a chance to walk past the cell. As he did so, he whistled a few bars of "Anchors Aweigh."

Toooot Toot Toot Toot
Toot-toot
Toot Toot Toot Toot.
After a second or two, there came a feeble response.
Toooot Toot Toot Toot
Toot-toot.

Plumb and Russell now knew their neighbor was a Navy man, but they still could not figure out who he was. One day, in addition to the rags, a pile of hair, human hair, much of it brilliant white human hair, was piled outside the cell.

"There's only one guy in the world with phosphorescent hair," said Plumb.

"John McCain must be down," replied Russell.

News traveled slowly in prison. By then, McCain had been a captive for nearly ten months.

CHAPTER TEN

THE CHERRY BOY

Bill Corson, the crusty Marine guerrilla warfare instructor, was right: the war waited for Ollie North. But he wasn't taking any chances. He headed straight to Quantico after his June 1968 graduation from Annapolis, passing up the thirty days leave he had coming to him. He gained a competitive edge, joining a Basic School class virtually bereft of Academy graduates, in theory the cream of the crop, the vast majority of whom would not arrive for another month. A few classmates saw that as the real reason for his haste in reporting to Quantico. True or not, he excelled.

"I liked his act," said Mike Flynn, a captain on the Basic School staff. "I just liked the way the lad stood there, looked you in the eye, and said, 'Yes, sir' and 'No, sir' with conviction."

Impressing instructors with his maturity, organizational ability, and military bearing, he was quickly assigned a leadership position in his student company. "When the new lieutenants first came in, somebody said, Hey, here's a kid out of the Academy who looks like he's got his shit in one bag, let's use him," said Flynn.

So they did, using him in the best sense, encouraging him to test his leadership skills and to display initiative. But always within limits, under adult supervision, with due consideration to his weaknesses. "He wasn't the sharpest kid in the class," said Flynn. "He was no mental giant. He was all attitude, perseverance, and desire."

At Quantico, North was romancing a Swedish woman. His friends were impressed, her style and good looks a perfect match for his flamboyance. If he didn't marry her, he seemed likely to wed someone equally glamorous.

Basic School was almost over when North announced he was getting married. The Scandinavian beauty was history. His choice was Frances Elizabeth Stuart, sales manager for a suburban Washington department store chain. Some North friends were surprised. Betsy, as she was known, was nice, not captivating.

Years later, Betsy North told the story of their courtship and marriage to *Life* magazine. A Penn State graduate, she had just moved to the Washington area when a friend suggested a blind date with her cousin Oliver North, a senior at Annapolis. Betsy was not interested. Previous blind dates had not turned out well and she figured a midshipman would be too young for her anyway. She had a change of heart when the friend showed her North's picture.

"He's good-looking," she said. "You can give him my number." After several tries, North got through to her and they dated for the first time in March 1968.

"He had a fancy car—a real pretty dark green Shelby Cobra," Betsy told *Life* in 1987. "I acted impressed. We had a lovely elegant dinner. I don't believe in love at first sight. I really thought he was nice and I suppose he thought I was. We went back to my apartment and my roommate said, 'That's the one, Betsy.' "

North, it seems, was not so sure. His romance with the Swedish woman carried into his early months at Quantico, acquaintances said, even though he writes in his autobiography that by June Week he and Betsy "had already started discussing our future."

Midway through the five-month Basic School program, North proposed. "I remember when he gave me my engagement ring," said Betsy, continuing her story in *Life*. "I had always wanted a Naval Academy 'miniature'—an exact replica of his ring. One night he arrived for a date with one rose. He just handed it to me without saying anything, and I just happened to notice the miniature on one of the leaves. I was very excited."

Minor discrepancies aside, North's account mirrors Betsy's. Both give the courtship a fairy-tale gloss, neither mentioning the Swedish woman. They also neglect another issue. Said a Quantico classmate, "The reason they got married was Betsy was pregnant."

On that point, North said in a 1993 interview, "I'm telling you that we've been happily married for twenty-five years. And there are some things that ought to remain private between a husband and a wife." Betsy declined to be interviewed.

Oliver North and Elizabeth Stuart were married at the chapel in Quantico on November 13, 1968. By then, Basic School was over. North was an honor graduate, finishing twenty-one out of 374, though Jim Webb would later outdo him, standing at the very top of his Quantico class a few months later.

As the year drew to a close, North shipped out to Vietnam. Two decades later, *Time* senior writer Lance Morrow recalled those days in a haunting essay.

"Nineteen sixty-eight," he wrote, "was a knife blade that severed past from future, Then from Now: the Then of triumphant postwar American power, the Then of the nation's illusions of innocence and virtue, from the more complicated Now that began when the U.S. saw it was losing a war it should not have been fighting in the first place, when the huge tribe of the young revolted against the nation's elders and authority, and when the nation finished killing its heroes."

Arriving in South Vietnam in December, North was assigned to the Third Marine Division, taking up duties as a rifle platoon commander in the rocky, battle-scarred northern tier of the country. The area was heavily contested. North Vietnamese Army units, well-trained and equipped, regularly slipped across the DMZ to attack the Marines. When the tactical situation was not to their liking, they ducked back into the safety of North Vietnam, knowing the Americans were forbidden to pursue them.

North took over the second platoon of Kilo Company, Third Battalion, Third Marines. He quickly acquired a nickname, Blue. It came from the color code for compass points used by radio operators: north was blue. His troops called themselves Blue's Bastards.

He paid attention to the little things that can make a difference in combat, personally inspecting each of his men before leading them into the bush. Canteens full. Helmets buckled. Ammunition properly packed. Because of the heat, many Marines sliced the protective plates out of their flak jackets. He insisted they be worn as issued. Think of yourselves as knights, he told his troops. These jackets are your armor.

According to one of his men, Randy Herrod, North initiated a precombat ritual, a no-holds-barred football game played in helmets and flak jackets, the ball a wad of socks pounded into the shape of a pigskin.

"The blocks and tackles were bone-jarring, and you'd clobber your closest friend if he stood in the way of a touchdown," Herrod later wrote. "This is the way Lieutenant North wanted us to play."

Knowing that combat leadership required an unblurred line of authority between superior and subordinate, North was close to his men, but not their buddy. Herrod remembers falling asleep during a break on patrol only to be roused by a whack on the helmet that set his head ringing. Glaring down at him, North said, "Don't you ever go to sleep when we're on patrol. Not ever. You understand." Groggily, Herrod replied, "Yes, sir." Added North, "Never."

The platoon, under North's leadership, distinguished itself. "They never backed down," said Don Moore, a fellow platoon commander. "They always went back for a second and third licking. His troops have a right to be proud. If they got pushed off the hill, they went back until the job was done."

As for North, Moore remembers him as having a runner's build, a "skeleton with steel cables" for muscles. He still had a pronounced limp from the car accident five years earlier, but it didn't seem to matter. "As far as endurance, as far as ability to take the heat, incredible, the guy could go forever," said Moore. "I'd hate to go on a forced march with him because the sucker could run."

Moore recalled something else about North, the ability to focus on his assigned mission to the exclusion of everything else: "You know, wh-o-o-o-sh, we're not talking tunnel vision, we're talking needle-point vision, he was bore-sighted."

Father Jake Laboon, the regimental chaplain, had known North at the Academy, as he had Jim Webb, by then with the First Marine Division farther south in Quang Nam province. "Everybody knew who Ollie North and Jim Webb were, even when they were just second lieutenants," said Laboon. "In the Third Marine Division, the word was that Ollie was the best platoon commander. In the First Marine Division, it was that Jim was the best. They all talked about them, they talked about both of them."

Chuck Krulak, a captain who commanded another company in the battalion, knew North well and became one of his closest friends. "He was a charismatic leader," said Krulak. "His people loved him, he was tactically sound, and he was, for the most part, fearless. He looked out for his people and they responded to that."

But Krulak said Laboon went too far in calling North the best platoon leader in the division. "There were a lot of good lieutenants," Krulak insisted. Far from diminishing North, Krulak was paying tribute to the extraordinarily high caliber of Marine junior officers—captains and lieutenants—who served as company and platoon commanders in Vietnam. North was a thoroughbred, but in a very fast field, a point to which anyone who served with John Ripley, Fred Fagan, Ron Benigo, Jim Webb, Mike Wunsch, Jim Messer, Chuck Krulak, and scores of others will readily attest.

Bob Bedingfield, a combat-savvy battalion chaplain, admired North, but with reservations. "The guy I knew in the bush was a very able guy, probably one of the select young Marine officers I've known. He was fearless, reckless as well. One of the great concerns we always had was being able to make sure that he understood precisely what had to be done. Given an open space, he would fill it; he, like nature, abhorred a vacuum."

Even in combat, North had a flair for the dramatic. One night he discovered that his platoon had stumbled into a North Vietnamese Army base camp. As yet undetected by the enemy, North sketched the situation for his company commander, Captain Paul Goodwin, in whispers over the radio. "How close are they?" asked Goodwin. "Close," murmured North. "How close?" demanded Goodwin, hackles rising. "Here, I'll let you talk to them," replied North. Goodwin backed off.

Paul Goodwin got his first glimpse of Oliver North in March 1969 as he was being briefed at battalion headquarters prior to taking over Kilo Company.

"There's one of your platoon commanders," said the ops officer, nodding toward the young second lieutenant at the far end of the CP. "He's awfully good, but he's a little bit of a hotdog."

Goodwin glanced over. The lieutenant needed a haircut, sported a bushy, Pancho Villa mustache, and carried a nonregulation Swedish submachine gun. Goodwin did not introduce himself.

Goodwin spent two days looking over the company before taking command. He did not like what he saw. The departing skipper wore a red bandanna around his neck and was known to the troops as the Organ Grinder. Goodwin had no intention of earning himself a cuddly nickname. As he put it, "I wasn't going to be a fucking Organ Grinder." The platoon leaders impressed him even less. North's hair was the longest and his mustache the most obnoxious, but the others weren't much better. Man, he said to himself, are you guys in for a shock.

Finally he called the platoon leaders together. "This place is a fucking disgrace," he told them. "It's now 0830. At 1000 I want everybody back here clean-shaven, with a haircut, and then you're going to be allowed to talk to me."

Goodwin was neither a martinet nor a fool. A trim six foot one, with deep-set, riveting blue eyes, he was confident of his ability and as tough as they come. On his first tour, he commanded both a platoon and company in the First Reconnaissance Battalion. This time around he would earn a Silver Star, a Legion of Merit, and two Bronze Stars.

He wasted no time in molding Kilo Company to his personal specifications. I want you to shave, he told his lieutenants. I want you to have haircuts. Not because we're going to make you pretty, but because to me personal appearance is an extension of discipline. You cut your hair because I said cut your hair. You shave your mustaches because I don't like them. It doesn't have to make any sense, just do it. I want you to get used to doing what I say, when I say it, just because I say it. One day it's going to save your ass. This is not a debating society. I'm in charge and you execute my orders.

One more thing, he said. I'm not interested in excuses. Excuses are like assholes. Everybody has one.

Each evening after chow Goodwin called his lieutenants together. As they gathered around, he pulled out a flask and poured a shot of Jim Beam into their tin canteen cups. A cigar clamped in his teeth, he graded their performance and reviewed plans of action for various combat situations. Ambushes. Listening posts. Day and night patrols. Breaches of the perimeter. Calling in artillery. Air support. He quizzed his lieutenants incessantly. What do you do if you're getting overrun? Goddamned right, hot rod, you throw your red star cluster, go to ground, and kill everything that moves on top of it.

North occasionally irritated Bill Haskell at these evening sitdowns. Slim, quiet, unimpressive in repose, Haskell was the most aggressive of Kilo's three platoon commanders. Nobody was better at sniffing out the enemy and initiating action. "I smell gook," Haskell would whisper into the radio, his talented nostrils picking up the distinctive scent of the enemy, the food they ate, the cigarettes they smoked, the aroma of danger. He loved it when his platoon was ordered to walk point, stationing himself with the lead fire team. He drew the line at one thing. He refused to volunteer his platoon for combat missions because it conflicted with his overriding goal in Vietnam, keeping as many of his men alive as he could. North, by contrast, "would volunteer to do anything," said Haskell.

"The captain would mention something and Ollie would say, 'Yes, we'll do it.' His platoon. I wanted to do it, but I absolutely would not volunteer my platoon for anything. If I could do it myself, sure, I'd love to." He did not think of North as kissing ass. His complaint was more convoluted: if North hadn't volunteered, Goodwin would have to pick a platoon for the mission, giving Haskell an equal chance at the action he craved while relieving him of guilt if any of his men were killed or wounded.

North flourished under Goodwin's rough-and-tumble leadership. "I don't know what he would have been without Paul," said Haskell. "Paul was a very good leader. And if Ollie was good, which he certainly was, a good part of his strength in being a platoon leader was the fact that he got very good instructions from Paul. Paul was very precise. He told you exactly what to do and how to do it and when to do it."

By his own admission, Goodwin was harder on North than he was on his other lieutenants. For a time North simply did not measure up to Goodwin's demanding standards. On one company operation, North's platoon was on the point, but advancing too slowly to suit Goodwin. He prodded North.

"Stop pissing around, I want to get to the top of that hill before it gets dark."

Said North, "We're moving as fast as we should be moving."

"That's not fast enough," the company commander fired back.

Goodwin finally lost his patience. "Stop your mob!" he radioed North, ordering Haskell's troops to bypass North's platoon and take up the point. North was humiliated, as Goodwin knew he would be. "I was disgusted with him," Goodwin later said. "I think that he thought there was no way he could please me."

Goodwin's view of North soon changed. On May 25 Kilo Company was operating in the hills near the DMZ when it came under withering machine-gun fire. The lead unit, Haskell's platoon, was shredded by the initial burst. "I got a bunch of people down and these fuckers are all over me," Haskell radioed back to Goodwin. Then the radio went dead. When it came back up, Haskell's radio operator was screaming hysterically: "My actual's down, my actual's down. God, he's bleeding. Skipper, we're getting overrun." In the calmest voice he could summon, Goodwin replied, "We're coming." To his own radio operator, he said, "Call Blue. Get him up here." North came running. Goodwin grabbed him, told him Haskell had been hit. "Get your people and get on line and let's go get them," said Goodwin.

Maneuvering his troops through Haskell's bloodied ranks, North led them into assault after assault, repeatedly exposing himself to hostile fire. "Up he went, dragging kids and kicking them," said Goodwin. Recalled Ernie Tuten, one of North's machine-gunners, "He was hollering and raising hell with us. Every time we did what he told us, the damn fire coming at us would decrease. You know when a guy knows what he's doing. It took eight to ten hours to take that damn hill, and he was in control the whole time. It was an unbelievable thing. . . . We knew Oliver North wasn't trying to cover his sweet little ass. He put his ass on the line just like the rest of us, and that's what we respected most about him."

Haskell suffered a severe head wound and the loss of his right eye. He won a Bronze Star to go with the Silver Star he had been awarded previously. North received the Silver Star. He also won the confidence of Paul Goodwin. A few months later, when it came time for Goodwin to choose a godfather for his son, he selected North.

"I said, this is the guy I'd like my son to be like," explained Goodwin. "When I asked him for 100 percent, he gave me 110. And when

I was tough on him, he didn't buckle. And I was real tough on him. He just said, 'I'll show you' and kept coming at me.''

Kilo Company was in a defensive perimeter in the early-morning hours of July 28 when North, alerted to enemy movement outside his lines, climbed onto a tank to confer with the commander of the armored unit. Peering through a starlight scope, he saw a half dozen NVA troops about fifty yards away. Moments later, a rocket-propelled grenade slammed into the tank, spraying the company commander's chest and neck with shrapnel, killing him. The blast blew North from the vehicle.

From his fighting hole a few yards away, Randy Herrod saw North crumple to the ground unconscious, his flak jacket shredded, legs, buttocks, and neck pockmarked with shrapnel, bullets whizzing around him. Detecting a quiver of movement in North's body, Herrod scrambled from his hole, grabbed his platoon leader's arm, shielded him with his body, and dragged him to safety.

Minutes later, North's head cleared, though he could hear nothing, the blast having punctured both eardrums. "Keep firing," he shouted at Herrod as he clambered out of the hole. The next time Herrod looked back, North was down on one knee, hollering into a field phone, in full view of the oncoming enemy.

"If you were charging a hill, you'd never want a better target," Herrod would later write. "But he didn't appear to be bothered by the fact that bullets were bouncing off the tank next to him like heavy hail. I had watched him under fire before, but never at such close range. He was the kind of battlefield commander you saw in old movies—calm, oblivious to danger, concerned only with the problem at hand, which was saving his platoon from being overrun and blown to bits. And he went about the task with such cool concentration you'd think he was standing in a telephone booth on Main Street.''

As North was directing fire, an incoming round blew him into the air for the second time in half an hour. Herrod again left the safety of his fighting hole to pull North to cover. Regaining his senses, North returned to action, calling in the air support that finally forced the NVA to break off the attack.

The battle lasted about three hours. Several tanks were knocked out, but the company held, thanks in large part to Herrod, who poured devastating machine-gun fire on the enemy. "He saved the perimeter that night," said Paul Goodwin, a man not easily moved to compliments. Herrod had also risked his life twice to save North's. North put him in for the Navy Cross.

There was a darker subtext to that firefight. Back in Washington,

Helmuts Feifs and another Marine out of the class of 1966, Roger Charles, stopped by to see Bill Corson. They had good news. Their classmate, Mike Wunsch, whose hospital counseling three years earlier had helped persuade Ollie North to stay at Annapolis, was within days of completing his tour in Vietnam, where he commanded a tank company. He had orders to return to the Academy to teach Chinese. Plans for a welcome-home party were under way. "Shut your fucking mouths," snapped Corson. "Don't talk about Mike until he's home." His visitors felt as if they had been punched in the gut, but they understood. Of the many midshipmen who had clustered around Corson back at Annapolis, he felt closest to Wunsch, whom he thought of as his intellectual heir, almost a son. Twenty-four hours later Wunsch was dead. He was the armor commander killed by the RPG round that blasted North from the tank in the first moments of battle.

Feifs, who had helped Wunsch buck up North's spirits at Annapolis, Corson, and others close to Wunsch have never forgotten that North's platoon was responsible for perimeter security that night, including the security in front of Wunsch's tanks. Feifs, for one, has often wondered darkly how enemy troops managed to move undetected so close to friendly lines, fifty yards from Wunsch by North's own account, if North's troops were alert and doing their jobs.

Paul Goodwin and Chuck Krulak were like big brothers to North. Lieutenant Colonel Dick Schulze, the battalion commander, may have been the authentic surrogate father in a long line of prospects stretching as far back as coaches Russ Robertson and Emerson Smith, as far forward as Bud McFarlane, CIA director Bill Casey, even Ronald Reagan.

A lean six foot four, Schulze was to all outward appearances a recruiting poster Marine. Otherwise he defied the stereotype. Gentle, soft-spoken, and introspective, he spent his free time writing graceful combat poetry. His poems, many written in Vietnam, represent his reflections on the war and its aftermath. Some are angry, others whimsical; all ring true.

As a combat Marine, Schulze cast a long shadow. He came back from Vietnam with a Silver Star and two Legions of Merit, along with a host of other decorations. Before he retired as a major general in 1981, he had, according to his friend Colonel John Scharfen, inspired a generation of young Marine officers, becoming a touchstone of fearless integrity and uncommon if understated leadership.

Of all the lieutenants in his battalion, Schulze was most fond of

North, whose youthful enthusiasm and disarming freshness superiors invariably found irresistible.

"Old Schulze really liked North," said Krulak. "North was very much an idealist from the word go, very much people-oriented. Not naïve, but kind of cherry. He was a cherry. He had gone through a lot at the Naval Academy. You know all of those stories. But even though he had done all of that, he was still a cherry boy."

A cherry boy?

"Yes. And because of that you had to like the guy. And I liked him and Goodwin liked him and Schulze liked him, because you could see there was so much talent there. He was—like a football coach would say of a player—he was very trainable and teachable. He was like a sponge."

Schulze never lost touch with North and the other officers in his battalion. "If you served in Vietnam with Schulze," said Chaplain Bob Bedingfield, "you were always his."

After months in the field, the battalion choppered to Cua Viet on the South China Sea for a few days of in-country R and R. For the Marines, it was a rare opportunity to relax, get some hot chow, splash around in the surf, drink to excess. North was not immune. Don Moore snapped a picture of him passed out on the beach, later sent it to his parents. "I thought you weren't allowed to take pictures of dead Americans," Moore's folks wrote back.

The enlisted men, in a variation on the busman's holiday, set up a boxing tournament, pounding each other to mush. The two survivors then egged Eric Bowen, the lieutenant who took over Haskell's platoon, into climbing in the ring with them. Bowen, a high school and college football player, stood six foot four and weighed 225 pounds. He quickly flattened both men. North was watching and, like the other onlookers, swilling beer. "Come on, Eric," he said, "let's you and I box now." Bowen did not know North had been a boxing champion at Annapolis. Looking him over, Bowen figured him at five foot ten, 175 pounds max. I'm going to murder this little shit, he thought.

"We put the gloves on," said Bowen. "We danced around about ten seconds and I was gone. He cold-cocked me. I did not know what hit me. Bam, bam, bam. He knocked me out. Cold. Thump."

Cua Viet was not all fun and games. The battalion formed in ranks for a memorial service. Nearly a dozen rifles, helmets, and pairs of boots sat on the sand near Kilo Company in silent salute to Marines lost over the previous few weeks. A lone bugler played taps. Paul Goodwin, in front of his troops but with his back to them, was panic-stricken. Tears were streaming down his cheeks. In a matter of moments he would have to do an about-face and dismiss the company. He could not imagine letting his men see him crying. He had no choice. On cue, he spun around, eyes red, face blotched, only to see his private anguish mirrored in the stricken faces of Oliver North and every other man in his outfit.

North came to see the world through the same bloody filter as Bud McFarlane. In North's case, though, it was often his own blood and the blood of men under his command that colored the view. Paul Goodwin said North was wounded at least five times, none life-threatening but any two sufficiently serious to get him pulled out of the field had he reported them in a timely manner. One day Goodwin spotted him wearing a long-sleeved utility blouse beneath his flak jacket instead of the usual green T-shirt. He grabbed North's arm as he tended to do when conferring with his lieutenants. Wincing, North fell to his knees. Goodwin ordered him to strip to the waist, discovered angry red streaks running the length of a severely swollen arm. North had picked up a small piece of shrapnel and ignored it. When blood poisoning set in, he persuaded the corpsman to secretly medicate him with penicillin. Goodwin exploded when he heard the story and immediately medevacked him. It was nearly two weeks before the doctors judged him fit to return to duty.

As for his troops, North dutifully checked their camouflage, shook their canteens, and did all the other little things to increase the odds of survival. But it was never enough. Randy Herrod, in his book, *Blue's Bastards,* described the aftermath of one two-hour mortar attack atop a little piece of heaven overlooking the DMZ called Mutter's Ridge: "There were guys with arms and legs torn away, feet missing, guts hanging out. And the corpsmen cleaned them up and stuffed them in bags, the way you'd gather up spilled garbage—quickly, mechanically, without looking at what you were doing or risking a deep breath."

At about that same time, back in the States, the enlightened elite of North's generation was celebrating itself in a three-day orgy of rock music, sex, and drugs called Woodstock, named for a hamlet in upstate New York about thirty miles from his hometown of Philmont.

But war is hell, right? At least North could see the sacrifice leading somewhere. Sure, right back up Mutter's Ridge for the fifth or sixth time, in easy range of the big guns nestled in the sanctuary of North Vietnam, barely three miles away across the DMZ. North thought he had a better idea, and so did a lot of others. "He believed if we put the entire ThirdMarDiv on line we could march to Hanoi," said Don Moore. "His idea was, Okay, you want a war, guys? We'll see you in Hanoi in thirty days."

North's zeal to supply the Nicaraguan Contras years later, even after Congress restricted American aid, had its roots in Vietnam. "The supply situation was atrocious," said Moore. "We were stripping the bodies of our wounded and dead to get canteens, to get boots and ponchos. In a firefight, you'd hear, 'Corpsman! Corpsman!' then, 'Dibs on the canteen, dibs on the boots.' When you're talking about Ollie North and the Contras you're talking about Ollie North and Mutter's Ridge. He knew what it was like not to have beans, boots, Band-Aids, and bullets."

Chuck Krulak was the son of a general and destined to become one himself. His prep school classmate, novelist John Irving, author of *The World According to Garp*, calls him "my hero." During his first Vietnam tour his father, Victor H. Krulak, was Commanding General, Fleet Marine Force, Pacific, the senior Marine in the Pacific Theater. Victor Krulak had been known since Academy days as the Brute, a jocular reference to his slight stature, but a tribute as well to his commanding personality. His son shared those characteristics. By the time he had completed two tours in Vietnam, Chuck Krulak held the Silver Star, three Bronze Stars, and two Purple Hearts.

After he was wounded the second time, in the summer of 1969, Krulak was assigned to division headquarters and put in charge of the Combat Operations Center. Not long after, North was pulled out of the field for similar reasons. Krulak arranged for him to be assigned to COC as a watch officer and his unofficial deputy.

Seven mornings a week, Krulak climbed the stage of a cavernous Butler building at Dong Ha and briefed the division commander, Major General William K. Jones, and the thirty or so senior officers on his staff. At first, North assisted Krulak in preparing the briefings. After a time, Krulak decided to let him troop the boards himself, was amazed by North's performance. Only a second lieutenant, he seemed totally at ease addressing an assemblage composed of officers far senior to him, many of them generals and colonels. "This guy had an unbelievable talent for putting together and presenting briefings," said Krulak.

About two months after North and Krulak teamed up, Jones assigned them to brief Lieutenant General Melvin Zais, who commanded the Army's XXIV Corps, which had taken operational control of elements of Jones's Third Marine Division.

Krulak and North were wary of the assignment. Army men and Marines rarely blend easily. At times, it seems, they don't even speak the same language. Moreover, Zais was rubbed raw, having come under sustained criticism in June from Congress and the press for his direction of the assault on what came to be known as Hamburger Hill, a bloody monthlong engagement in which the Americans suffered forty-six dead and over four hundred wounded. "Senseless and irresponsible," said the critics. One of his strongest detractors was Senator Edward Kennedy, who a few weeks after delivering his commentary on Zais zigged when he should have zagged approaching a small bridge on Martha's Vineyard.

At the briefing, General Zais witnessed a superbly choreographed team that knew the material cold and presented it with style and wit. North stole the show. "It was a good briefing and it wasn't because I was doing the briefing," said Krulak. "It was like Huntley-Brinkley and he was Brinkley and I was Huntley. And when Brinkley was talking, I'll tell you, I was listening."

The briefing, begun in rigid formality, went so well that the mood lightened considerably as Krulak and North neared the end of their presentation. Finally, one of the Marine staff officers, addressing Zais, expressed sympathy for the criticism he had received back home over Hamburger Hill, "particularly from Teddy Kennedy."

Zais held up his hand. "Let me tell you something," said the general. "At least I evacuated my dead and wounded."

North and Krulak were shocked. Said Krulak, "I'm not kidding you, Ollie and I almost fell off the stage."

CHAPTER ELEVEN

THE NATURAL

Oh, but it was glory in them fields! Fields of fire, boy! They walked right into that cannon, all those Yankee guns and the guns ripped at them, all the smoke and fire and cannister and case shot, and they never lost a step!

—JAMES WEBB, *Fields of Fire*

Jim Webb married Barb DuCote in the chapel after graduation, then remained at Annapolis for the summer, one of a handful of newly commissioned Marines selected to train the new plebes. At summer's end, he was off to Quantico and the Basic School, emerging five months later as the honor graduate, the top man in the class, standing first in military skills and second in leadership.

The majority of second lieutenants at Quantico expected to be shipped to Vietnam once the course ended, though most seemed unruffled by the dangers awaiting them. One day the captain in charge of Webb's student platoon decided his men needed a reality check. As the captain knew, a sense of invulnerability can be an asset in combat; carried too far it can lead to rash decisions and reckless actions. How many of you guys are going infantry? he asked his young hardchargers. As Webb's hand and a lot of others shot up, the captain informed them that 85 percent were destined to become casualties. That got their attention, but not for long. They quickly transformed the grim statistic into the raw material of black humor, massaging it, rubbing down its sharp edges, neutralizing the terror.

An aging mustang colonel finally got through to them. Near the end of the course, he assembled the lieutenants selected for the infantry. "I fought in World War II, Korea, and Vietnam," he said, "and this is the hardest war the Marine Corps has ever fought."

He told them a story, a cautionary tale: "When I got to Korea I was a seasoned combat infantryman from World War II. I was a new lieutenant. I was taking a patrol out and we hit a Chinese unit up on a ridge. It was a perfect envelopment. I split my platoon in half. I set up a base of fire. I sent my platoon sergeant with a squad through the trees to envelop these guys. I sent fifteen men into the trees and fifteen men died."

He paused, letting his words do their work, then continued: "Why do you think I'm telling you this? Because I don't care how good you think you are. You're going to come back with skeletons in your closet. You're going to come back with memories that are going to follow you around the rest of your life. And if you aren't tough enough to handle it, get out of here now."

Webb had orders to the First Marine Division. He and Barb drove across country, stopping off to see relatives en route to San Francisco, where he was to begin the first leg of the journey that would eventually deposit him in Vietnam. They spent a week with his grandmother in Riverside, California. During the visit torrential rains caved in a portion of the roof above the kitchen, a natural-enough occurrence, but Webb sensed that Granny Hodges was mortified, as if she had somehow lost face. Webb climbed out on the roof and patched it with tarpaper. His grandmother was grateful, but she remained unsettled right up till the time he left.

He spent five days on Okinawa, the major Marine transshipment point, waiting for a flight to Danang. It was March 1969, more than a year after the Tet Offensive. In Paris peace talks were under way, lending some credence to the notion that the war was winding down. But that was wishful thinking. On the ground in Vietnam, an average of 440 Americans were dying every week, about the same number lost in the entire Persian Gulf War.

Webb and the other replacements finally boarded a Continental Airlines jet for the midnight flight to Vietnam, four months after Ollie North had made the same trip. Expecting a lumbering military transport, he found the air-conditioned comfort of the passenger cabin and the polished civility of the flight crew disorienting. "Well, gentlemen, have a good war," said the attractive German stewardess as the aircraft touched down in Danang.

The heat hit him like a blast of bad breath as he stepped from the plane. By the time he reported to First Marine Division headquarters his uniform was soaked through. On arriving he was told to read and sign a copy of the rules of engagement. The document ran seven pages. Some of it made sense, but a lot of it seemed an exercise in politics, micromanagement, and preemptive ass covering, a script for fighting a war without pissing anybody off.

The division's area of operations was displayed on a military map pitted with red dots, each marking a location where one or more Marines had been killed or wounded. Some sections of the map were flecked with dots. In other sections, the dots bled together, so that they looked like large red smears. Webb was assigned to the Fifth Marine Regiment, which meant he was going to big smear country.

That evening he was as filthy as he had ever been in his life, just from the heat and the humidity and the dust. He did what he could to freshen up, throwing away his skivvies in disgust, little suspecting he was cleaner at that moment than he would be for most of the next year. The following day he was shipped to An Hoa, headquarters of the Fifth Marines, linking up with a friend from Basic School, Ken Rosser, a slow-talking Georgian. Rosser had arrived the day before, an old salt compared to Webb. "Ken, what's going on?" asked Webb as artillery fire erupted nearby. Rosser looked up from the letter he was writing. "Well," he drawled, "boom-swish means they're going out, swish-boom means they're coming in."

Webb was supposed to spend five days in An Hoa undergoing field indoctrination. He had one day. Delta Company, out in the Arizona Valley, was hurting. The troops called it Dying Delta. Mike Wyly, the company commander, had taken over a few days earlier and needed help. Learning Webb was in An Hoa, he radioed headquarters: this guy was the honor grad at Basic School. Screw indoctrination. Get his ass out here.

Lance Corporal Mac McDowell was relaxing with a few other battle-weary Marines when the resupply chopper settled itself on Henderson Hill and disgorged its cargo of replacement troops. The new men charged down the tailgate amid a spray of dust and stinging pebbles. McDowell, his thousand-yard stare firmly in place, focused on one of them, the only officer aboard. "Get a load of the teeny-bopper lieutenant," he muttered to his fellow grunts. Pushing his luck, he snapped out "Boot!" as the young officer trotted by. The lieutenant stopped, spun around, and marched over to McDowell.

"Do you know who I am?" asked the officer, pinning him with what McDowell later described as a look that could crack rock.

"No, but it doesn't matter," shrugged McDowell, meeting the laserlike glare with a wise-guy smirk.

"I happen to be Lieutenant James H. Webb, Jr. You can call me lieutenant or you can call me sir."

His voice like a filleting knife, Webb lectured McDowell on the fundamentals of military courtesy.

"You got that?" said Webb as he finished.

"Yes, sir," said McDowell, mildly cowed but furious. Another ass-hole second lieutenant, he grumbled under his breath.

Later, Webb introduced himself to the rest of the men who would make up his first command, the third platoon of Delta Company, First Battalion, Fifth Marines. It was like an audition for a fragging. "Now this is the way it's going to be," he said. "Anything you say to me I will believe. If you tell me the sky is brown, I will believe it." He paused. "If I ever find out you lied to me, you're dead meat."

That evening, he led a squad on patrol. Before long the squad stumbled into a larger North Vietnamese unit. Both sides opened up, the Marines coming under wilting .50-caliber machine-gun fire. At his CP on Henderson Hill company commander Wyly watched red and green tracers rip through the valley below. He had met Webb only hours earlier. There goes my Naval Academy lieutenant, he said to himself, I'll never see him again.

Webb, in the field, summoned his radio operator. Straining to read his map in the darkness, he called in mortar fire, then artillery, finally air support, routing the enemy. On the company net, he reported to Wyly: Delta Six, this is Delta Three Actual. No friendly casualties. Over.

Cool as a cucumber, marveled Wyly, like he's been doing it all his life.

A masterful performance by a green second lieutenant and the troops were impressed. The following night he did an encore. The next day, one of his Marines said, "Hey, don't get hurt, man." Webb had been wearing a gold second lieutenant's bar on his flak jacket. The glinting metal made him an irresistible target for snipers, but he looked young and he wanted to make sure the troops knew who he was. A few days later he awoke to find that someone had painted over the bar with black enamel, dulling the glare. The troops, it seemed, knew who he was and had decided he was a keeper.

For the next year, Webb's life was defined by an expanse of cratered rice paddies, hostile villages, decades-old fighting holes, and splintered trees known as the An Hoa Basin. Surrounded by mountains except to the northeast, the basin was cut by two rivers, the Vu Gia, which flowed generally eastward, and the Thu Bon, which traced a northeasterly course. They came together just west of Liberty Bridge. The Fifth Marines CP at An Hoa lay east of the Thu Bon. The Marines nicknamed it Little Dien Bien Phu because the mountains that soared above it to the south and east lent an air of vulnerability that reminded the historians among them of the doomed French fortress of an earlier war. On the far side of the river, running from the Vu Gia in the north to the mountains in the south and west, was the region the Americans called the Arizona Valley.

The Arizona was infested by VC, who trooped down from the mountains to attack the Marines and melted back into them when the odds were not to their liking. They found sanctuary in the villages of the Arizona, whose inhabitants looked on balefully as Marines tripped booby traps, then professed ignorance that such devices had been planted so close to their hooches. Like Go Noi Island to the northeast, another area that would be well watered by the blood of Webb's troops, the Arizona was less a place for large-scale operations than the setting for what the military high command, and thus the press, took to calling isolated incidents.

Isolated incidents. Nickel-and-dime shit. The booby trap that in a split second radically altered the course of a life yet to be lived. The ambush whose fury lasted only a minute or two, less time than it took to brush your teeth, long enough to make teeth useful only for purposes of identification. The indifferent sliver of flying metal that killed or maimed anyone unlucky enough to cross its flight path. "The victims were selected so randomly," Webb later wrote. "You could be 100 percent right and still be 100 percent dead."

Whether in the paddies of the Arizona or the elephant grass of Go Noi Island, land mines and booby traps were a fixture, the great leveler, the stuff that lent drama to the daily accretion of isolated incidents. In *Fields of Fire*, one of Webb's characters comes across an old ammo box and idly picks it up.

He straightened, the lid of the ammo box in hand, and—disappeared. At one moment he was stooping, grinning caustically to Cat Man, and in the next there was a violent rending of the earth, a belch of smoke and dust that sprayed half the platoon, the equivalent of a large artillery round impacting underneath him as the pressure-release detonator set off the booby trap. He did a full flip in the air. His rifle spun off in the distance, a black baton. He landed where he had stood grinning to them only a half-second before, but now he was a scorched, decapitated ash heap that reminded them all of how very close they stayed to death, even on a boring day.

Combat came naturally to Webb. Over the years he had given himself a tutorial in warfare, reading about strategy, tactics, and leadership, poring over battle maps, trying to figure out why generals through the ages deployed their forces as they did. Despite a mild concern about how he would perform when the bullets began flying, he felt fully prepared to lead troops when he took over his platoon. That confidence was quickly ratified on the battlefield, so much so that tales of his exploits became a fixture on the Bullshit Freq, the outlaw radio frequency used by the troops for extracurricular conversations with their buddies in other units.

His military skills resulted from more than books and maps. Like an athlete, he relied on his instincts. He knew the school solution for any situation, and usually employed it, but he also knew when to throw the book out the window. He came to think of his mind as a computer programmed for war, sorting out the chaos of the battlefield to provide him with a continuously updated readout of rapidly changing combat conditions. Healthy piles of fresh excrement on the outskirts of a village set off alarms. Somebody in that ville is eating well, and it sure in hell isn't anyone who lives there. Wading through a rice paddy, he scanned the terrain, his brain spewing out the best course of action should his platoon take small-arms fire from the paddy dike dead ahead or the treeline to the right or come under mortar attack from damn near anyplace. Where to take cover, how to set up his fields of fire, when to go into the assault, what supporting arms—mortars, artillery, air cover—were available to him.

He never questioned his courage after his first taste of combat, but he knew courage was not enough. The lives of his men depended on his ability not simply to act bravely, but to make wise decisions, often under conditions of complete pandemonium. It was fine for generals and scholars to talk of the fog of war and other gauzy abstractions to explain away battlefield mistakes, but Webb and young officers like him who breathed that fog every day knew that no words would help if a miscalculation on their part cost a man his life. *I sent fifteen men into the trees and fifteen men died.* And as good as Webb was, his men started dying.

James Ward, slim and bespectacled, known to everyone as Snake, was one of Webb's most talented squad leaders. Cool and resourceful in combat, Snake was Webb without the college education and the Academy polish. Webb admired his bush smarts, liked his gentleness and easy rapport with the kids in the villages. He came to think of Snake as both a bleeding heart and the bravest man he ever knew. He encouraged him to apply for officer training. Snake was not interested, even when Webb pressed him to reconsider.

The issue became moot in early May as Snake neared the end of his tour. Caught in a vicious cross-fire, partially blinded by grenade fragments, he hoisted a wounded Marine onto his narrow shoulders and was carrying him to safety when a burst of machine-gun fire tore his midsection apart, his lifeless body falling at Webb's feet.

Mac McGarvey, called Little Mac to distinguish him from Big Mac McDowell, became a combination alter ego and little brother to Webb. He was Webb's radio operator for about two months, not long in real time but a lifetime in the bush. During that period the platoon had fifty-six men killed or wounded, the grisly alchemy of war turning replacements into statistics overnight. Snake, Dombrowski, the other McDowell, Cooper, Mount, Welch, McKinnon, McCart, Baker, Shepherd, Tucker, Jonesy, Lyles, Paison, Soper, McNamara, the first four dead, the others casualties. Webb carefully shielded his emotions from the troops, but the relentless butchering was taking a fearsome toll on him. One night he and McGarvey huddled under a poncho and talked about a lot of things—family, friends, faith in God, and how they'd react if they were seriously wounded.

"Could you handle it, Mac?" asked Webb.

"Yeah," said McGarvey.

The next day, someone tripped a booby trap and McGarvey's arm was sheared off by a piece of shrapnel that looked like a meat cleaver flying toward him. As the corpsman tied off McGarvey's stump, Webb kneeled over him, tears etching grooves in his dirt-encrusted face.

"Knock that shit off, sir, it's only an arm," said McGarvey.

The corpsman, for reasons that must have made sense at the time, wrapped McGarvey's severed arm in a T-shirt and placed it on the poncho with him as the medevac helicopter prepared to lift off.

"Maybe he thought they could put it back on," said McGarvey, mystified to this day. "I remember trying to pick it up. I held on to it all the time I was on the chopper, hoping it was a nightmare."

Squad leader Tom Martin was Webb's confidant, the man to whom he confessed his doubts during those dark days in the late spring of 1969 when he came to believe that no matter what he did, few of his troops were destined for a normal rotation home. Martin, soft-spoken and introspective, had waived his student deferment and enlisted while an undergraduate at Vanderbilt. Webb thought of him as nothing less than a treasure, his anchor when the incessant grinding up of his men threatened to send him spinning out of control. Which made it all the harder when a bullet clipped Martin's spinal cord, paralyzing him from the waist down. That happened the week before McGarvey lost his arm.

The antiwar movement was of little interest for Webb in those days.

He did not recognize the strength and depth of it. As a platoon leader in the bush, he did not have much time for reflection or intellectual musings. There was also a credibility problem. In the America in which Jim Webb grew up, it was inconceivable that the nation could be at war and tens of thousands of men his own age might connive to avoid it, knowing all the while that other young men of similar promise and equally lofty dreams risked living out their futures in darkness, in a wheelchair, or in the next minute.

Webb's medals attest to his bravery and composure in combat. He is cited time and again for rallying his men under fire, capturing VC single-handedly, and pulling wounded troops to safety. "I never did so much award writing as I did for Jim Webb on that tour," said company commander Mike Wyly. It became routine for one of Webb's troops to wander up to Wyly and say, "Skipper, the lieutenant earned another medal last night."

Webb and Mac McDowell were clearing a string of spiderholes when a VC popped out of one, a grin on his face, a grenade in his hand. Webb killed him with his .45, but not before the VC released the grenade, which began rolling toward McDowell. Webb pushed McDowell to the ground, then threw himself between his comrade and the exploding grenade, sustaining serious fragmentation wounds that left him with a limp much like Ollie North's. "He saved my life," said McDowell of Webb. "He just totally shielded me." That incident capped a sequence of feats that earned Webb the Navy Cross, second only to the Medal of Honor among the nation's awards for valor in battle.

Right from the start he took time to sit down with his men, singly and in groups, to find out who they were, what they were thinking, how to motivate them. He urged them to come to him with personal problems, promised to fix them if they could be fixed. He also encouraged them to ask questions, to offer tactical advice, even to suggest a course at odds with his plan of action. More than once they sniffed out trouble before he did.

He did not hesitate to question orders himself. On one occasion, his platoon was dispatched to bail out an infantry company that had taken heavy casualties. The company commander, a captain, was preparing to assault into a clump of trees hiding the enemy that had decimated his unit. He told Webb to set up his platoon in an open rice paddy about two hundred meters from the trees and provide covering fire while he maneuvered his men into position to attack.

Webb balked. His platoon had been in action almost constantly for days. Now he was being told to establish a position out in the open within easy range of a treeline infested with well-equipped NVA regulars. At two hundred meters they would be sitting ducks for small arms, rockets, and anything else cached in the woods. Webb told the captain of his concerns and suggested a more defensible position, farther from the trees but close enough to bring effective fire on the enemy with his M-60 machine guns. As he saw it, he could still accomplish the mission but his troops would be less vulnerable.

"I'm giving you a direct order," said the captain, unmoved by Webb's reasoning.

"You're not my company commander, sir," said Webb, a defiant retort that came perilously close to direct disobedience of an order, a general court-martial offense.

Another captain joined them. Webb appealed to him. He seemed sympathetic to Webb's plight, but reluctant to side with a lieutenant against another captain. Webb felt like a fourteen-year-old as the two older men talked past him, decided he was a grown-up, too. "I'm not going to do it," he said, rousting his platoon and leading it out to the position that made sense to him. In the battle that followed, his machine-gunners killed eight NVA. He never heard another thing about his refusal to follow orders.

Webb later explained that challenging his superiors had value even when it did not cause them to change course: "To me it was like a safety valve. I wanted to make sure these people were thinking before they sent us off to do something weird."

Webb was promoted to first lieutenant in September 1969. Three days later he was given command of Delta Company, a captain's billet. At twenty-three, he was commanding 170 men. He wondered how many were older than he was. He polled the troops. Only four were older, all career NCOs, lifers. The rest were mostly eighteen-, nineteen-, and twenty-year-old kids.

The survey triggered a realization so obvious and logical in retrospect that he was amazed he had not hit on it before. Civilians fight wars. The professional military holds the terrain until wars begin and then civilians fight the wars. He did not focus on the 1960s variant of that proposition, that is, some do, some don't. Nor did it cross his mind that his troops were little more than overgrown boys. "I didn't have that sense then," he said. "I figured eighteen, nineteen was plenty old and plenty tough when I was twenty-three."

The killing and maiming of his men continued. Dale Wilson, a good ol' boy from North Carolina, was due to go home in eleven days when he became a statistic. He was the victim of a booby trap, an American artillery shell recycled by the VC, peerless combat ecologists. "I thought I'd been hit by napalm because there was smoke coming off me," said Wilson. "The sun was in my eyes, so I tried to cover my eyes with my right hand, and my hand fell off in my face." He came out of his morphine stupor about seven that night. "I realized I had lost more than I thought," he said. He meant his right arm and both legs. He was nineteen, plenty old, plenty tough.

By the time Webb left for home he had added the Silver Star, two Bronze Stars, and a host of other decorations to his Navy Cross. He had also collected two Purple Hearts, testaments to wounds that threatened to end his promising Marine Corps career. He had taken shrapnel in his left knee, left arm, the back of his head, and his right kidney. The biggest problem was his knee, the one hit by grenade fragments when he threw himself in front of McDowell. Evacuated to the rear, he had gone back into the field prematurely because he was afraid he'd lose his platoon and wind up in a staff job. First the knee joint, then the surrounding bone tissue became infected. On occasion it split open, oozing green and yellow pus. One morning he squatted down to make coffee and the wound burst open. A clot of pus and dead skin the size of a tennis ball blew out of his knee. He had the battalion surgeon clean it up and give him a shot of penicillin, then returned to his platoon.

Approaching the end of his tour, he dreamed of the Freedom Bird, the fabled aircraft that would fly him back to the World, as the troops referred to anyplace other than Vietnam. Instead, he went home by ship, drafted to ride herd on thirty-two grunts who had also completed their time in-country.

From the moment he stepped on board nothing went right. At first, the ship's captain wasn't going to give the Marines sheets. "What happened to your sleeping bags?" he asked. Webb laughed: "I haven't seen a sleeping bag since Quantico." To make matters worse, the senior Marine on the ship insisted on holding white-glove inspections of the troop spaces. He also demanded high-and-tights, the standard Marine haircut. Webb was furious. The men were mostly draftees, scheduled for discharge almost as soon as they docked. They had fought hard, done their duty. As thanks, they were being given a ration of Marine green chicken shit.

That wasn't the worst of it. The ship had full-time barbers who cut the crew's hair free of charge, but the captain decreed that the Marines had to pay for the haircuts they didn't want to begin with. Webb kept his cool. I'll tell you what, he said to the skipper, the barbershop is mine from the time your barbers knock off work until the next morning. He cut hair all the way across the Pacific.

By then, Webb had turned twenty-four and been deep-selected—meaning ahead of his peers—for captain. He had orders to Quantico. Barb met him shortly after he debarked and they drove across country. On the way, they stopped in Riverside to see Granny Hodges. She was standing at the sink doing dishes when they walked in. "Well, we got that fixed," she said, never greeting them directly, just pointing to the ceiling Webb had patched more than a year earlier. "You can't even tell anything happened to it."

The same could not be said of Jim Webb. Something had happened and people could tell. He was never happy-go-lucky, but friends from Annapolis remember a youthful Tom Sawyer–like quality that would break through back in Academy days. Whatever it was, it did not make it through the war. "Vietnam changed Jim a great deal," said Glenn Boggs, an Academy roommate who went into the Navy. "I remember talking to him after Vietnam and telling my wife he had had some terrible experiences in combat and it had changed him in a way I'd never understand." Some say his marriage to Barb was a casualty of the war, too. "Jim came back and Barbara didn't recognize him," said Jake Laboon, the chaplain. Nearly twenty years later, Webb insisted that his Vietnam tour was a normal one, nothing much out of the ordinary. But he also said, "I was probably older when I was twenty-four than I am right now."

> Then General Lee himself come out to meet them. They all said he was crying, riding on his white horse from group to group, that white beard of his just soaked with tears. Told them he was sorry. Told them they were God's bravest creatures, that they'd earned a glory spot in heaven. Told them it was himself who lost the battle. That's the kind of man our General Lee was, son. That's why you and your daddy both were named for General Lee. He was a man of honor and he cried the day three Hodges died on the glory field.
>
> —*Fields of Fire*

CHAPTER TWELVE

TRUSTING THE SYSTEM

When Robert McNamara left the Ford Motor Company in January 1961 to become John Kennedy's Secretary of Defense, he installed in the Pentagon a cadre of young technocrats cast in his own image, "men of mathematical precision," as David Halberstam described them. Recruited from private industry, the finest research universities, and cutting-edge think tanks like the Rand Corporation, they were to be the weapon by which McNamara would lay siege to the Pentagon, subdue the generals and admirals, drag the old warhorses kicking and screaming into the twentieth century.

Their ranks included defense intellectuals eager to test their theories in the real world, bottom-line economists unmoved by tradition or sentiment, and the cream of the new managerial class, driven by numbers and statistics, at ease with computers, flow charts, and decision trees. Inevitably, they came to be known as the Whiz Kids, the same sobriquet that had attached itself to McNamara and the kiddie corps of analysts who came out of the Army Air Corps bureaucracy after World War II to take over the management of Ford.

Layered throughout the upper echelons of the Pentagon bureaucracy, they congregated most noticeably in the Systems Analysis shop under the brilliant Alain Enthoven, Rhodes Scholar, holder of degrees from Stanford, Oxford, and MIT, so many degrees that it seemed niggling to mention that he and many of the other civilian hotshots had never actually been in the armed forces, let alone heard a round fired in anger. To remedy that shortcoming, they tapped the services for their brightest, best-educated young officers, men like John Poindexter, independent minds, not toadies to their superiors in the military chain of command.

Poindexter worked in the manpower directorate of the Systems Analysis operation where he continued to accumulate admirers. Thor Hanson, a Rhodes Scholar, later a three-star admiral, was one: "I always thought he was going to go a long way. He was just head and shoulders above the others." A civilian boss, Harvey Safeer, agreed: "I had him pegged for flag rank even then. He was one of those guys, you tell him what the assignment is and that's it. He was probably one of the brightest guys I dealt with. I'm no dummy myself, and I think he had me beaten hands down."

By the time Poindexter arrived in the summer of 1966, the novelty of the Whiz Kids had worn off, along with much of the early luster. Vietnam played a big part. McNamara explained the war in terms of numbers—body counts, bombs dropped, decreases in infiltration—did so with the kind of statistical invincibility that had become his hallmark. When reports from the battlefield did not support the sanguine picture McNamara had painted, when, in fact, people started to say the secretary had just made up the numbers, the reputation of the Whiz Kids suffered, too.

Enthoven and his crew had little if anything to do with cooking the numbers or, for that matter, Vietnam. They were pricing out bigger issues, a conventional land war in Europe, a nuclear exchange between the superpowers, figuring out how to avoid a nationwide recession when Vietnam was over and the boys came home, which they figured would be soon. Mark Hill, a Navy captain who worked for Enthoven, couldn't believe how little thought the civilian Whiz Kids gave to the war, the real war, the one the United States was fighting *at that very moment*. It's not touching them, Hill told an old admiral. They come in, do their jobs, go home, go to sleep. Replied the admiral, Remember, Mark, their friends are not over there.

Curiously, Vietnam did not seem to touch John Poindexter all that much, either, at least not directly. Fresh from his tour on the *Pratt*, he made another seamless transition, this time from chief engineer on a guided-missile frigate to Whiz Kid in the Office of the Secretary of Defense. He was angered by the antiwar protests, not because he supported the war, but out of a vague sense that the high moral tone of the demonstrators masked cowardice. He was also annoyed that the young, unbloodied civilians at the Pentagon treated senior military officers, men he respected, like errand boys and worse. Still, it was a measure of Poindexter's ability to focus on the job at hand that a war then convulsing the nation rolled right past him, nicking him here and there, but not tearing him apart, as it did so many others.

Poindexter would later say that Vietnam "didn't have much impact" on him, that he viewed it as "just another mission to be performed." He was, moreover, not all that enthusiastic about the mission, though he generally favored it, and even less enthralled with the manner in which it was being executed. LBJ's guns-and-butter policy didn't make sense, he decided. Moreover, political considerations denied the military the tools and the freedom to pursue the war effectively. And the micromanagement of the battlefield by Johnson and McNamara was proving a disaster, perhaps the most enduring lesson of the war that Poindexter carried with him into the Reagan White House. He and Linda came to the conclusion that in the absence of a national will to win, the United States was better off out of Vietnam. "It just seemed like a rathole that we were determined to destroy people in," said Linda.

Poindexter, amazingly, was insulated from the war at the Pentagon. The operating forces of the Navy consisted of three main branches: surface line, that is, the black-shoe Navy of which he was a part; the submariners; and aviators like John McCain. The airdales had to fly combat missions in Vietnam if they hoped to advance, but there was no need for surface types or submariners to have their ticket punched there. But within the Systems Analysis office there was an atmosphere, akin to secondhand smoke, that infiltrated Poindexter's value system, if not immediately, then down the line.

Mark Hill, whose desk was next to Poindexter's, felt it most keenly and was outspoken in his frustration. Hill was there in mid-1965, when Johnson was priming the nation and the Pentagon for the American entry into the war. Like most military men, he anticipated a full-scale buildup, complete with a mobilization of the reserves. Instead, when Johnson finally divulged what he was up to, he increased monthly draft calls from seventeen thousand to thirty-five thousand, but he did not call up the reserves. To Hill, Johnson was signaling to Hanoi a lack of American resolve. Hearing Johnson's speech, Hill said to a friend, "We've just lost the war, because Ho Chi Minh can count."

The Whiz Kids made the mistake early on of antagonizing the military professionals. Some of it was unavoidable. The military was resistant to change, making bruised feelings inevitable. But some of the officers in Systems Analysis, and all of those at the higher echelons of the Pentagon, were decorated veterans of World War II and Korea, men of substance and stature within the military fraternity. Whatever their bureaucratic shortcomings, they had served their nation well in times of dire need. Suddenly, economists and defense intellectuals in their twenties and early thirties who had never worn any uniform besides a prep school blazer were treating them like corporals. At times the arrogance was breathtaking. One young civilian routinely took over a three-star general's chair when he went to his office to confer with him.

Poindexter, laboring quietly away, noticed such things, the imperious slights, the casual demeaning of the uniform, the stunning presumption on the part of the civilians that they knew how to fight a war better than men who had spent their lives trying to master the complexities of combat. He later said, "The civilians seemed to have the view that everything the services did was all screwed up."

But that was mild stuff in the context of the times. He did not leave the Pentagon with grudges or obvious scars, just some perceptions filed for future reference. He did depart with many friends, notably Hill, who years later as a retired rear admiral would head the defense fund that raised money to help him pay his legal costs in the aftermath of Iran-Contra. No one thought of him as a budding zealot. When the Iran-Contra scandal broke, Harvey Safeer couldn't believe it. "I really had to look closely and ask myself if this was the same guy who worked for me. I would not have associated the two."

At Caltech, the Poindexters had been the conservatives among liberals. They discovered in Washington that they were much more liberal than their military friends, and many of the civilian ones, too. "We were probably just mavericks," said Linda. "Whatever everybody else was, we weren't." In 1960 they voted for Richard Nixon. Eight years later, they turned their backs on Nixon and cast their ballots for Hubert Humphrey. By then a peace symbol dangled from Linda's neck.

Their liberal sentiments extended not just to the war, but to the other great issue of the day, civil rights. At first it was an intellectual commitment to the idea of equal opportunity. The King assassination in April 1968, however, spurred Linda to become personally involved. Following the postassassination riots in Washington, she brought food to St. Stephen and The Incarnation Episcopal Church in the inner city. In preparation for the Poor People's March that began a month later, she spent time at the church and at the headquarters of the sponsoring organization, the Southern Christian Leadership Conference, compiling mailing lists, addressing envelopes, registering marchers as they arrived, then helping them to get settled.

Mother's Day 1968 fell in the midst of premarch activities. Linda was torn between family and lending a hand downtown. "It's your day," said John. "Do what you want to do. I'll watch the kids." Thanks, she said, climbing in her car. Friends complained that the Mall was being destroyed by the encampment of poor blacks known as Resurrection City. Oh, come off it, she snapped.

*   *   *

His first Washington tour behind him, Poindexter reported for duty aboard the *Lawrence*, fifth in the line of vessels named for Captain James Lawrence, whose dying words, "Don't give up the ship," became the Navy's battle cry. The *Lawrence*, a swift, highly maneuverable guided-missile destroyer berthed in Norfolk, was skippered by Commander Dan Costello, a friend of Poindexter's from his earlier tour on the *Pratt*. Poindexter was the executive officer, the second-ranking officer on the ship, as he was when Commander Dick Murphy replaced Costello several months later.

The new skipper took an immediate liking to Poindexter, was amazed to discover that he was a superb shiphandler despite substantially less time at sea than most line officers of comparable grade. Murphy also noticed that Poindexter, though proper and dignified, related easily to junior officers and enlisted men. He was handy, too. During a routine overhaul, Murphy and Poindexter decided to install TV sets in the crew's compartments. The two officers were having coffee when an electronics technician reported a seemingly intractable problem in hooking up the sets. Poindexter turned over a napkin, sketched out a complex wiring diagram, said something Murphy didn't understand about impedence and splitters, then handed the napkin to the technician. End of problem.

In early 1971, while aboard the *Lawrence*, Poindexter was called to the White House to interview for the post of naval aide to the President, a position then held by his old classmate and rival Chuck Larson. Larson had strongly promoted Poindexter as his replacement, but he wasn't selected. Afterward, Larson asked his boss, a retired Air Force general, why he rejected Poindexter. "He's too intelligent for the job," the general replied. At first Larson was amused by the response, then wondered what it said about him. The rejection didn't seem to bother Poindexter, who saw the post as lacking substance and weighted down with social responsibilities.

That spring John Chafee, the Secretary of the Navy, was in Norfolk for a change-of-command ceremony. He was accompanied by his naval aide, Captain Thor Hanson, who had been one of Poindexter's senior colleagues in the Systems Analysis office. Coming down the gangway from the carrier on which the ceremony was held, Hanson spotted Poindexter on the deck of the *Lawrence*, tied up on the other side of the pier. He suggested to Chafee that they go aboard for a short visit. Murphy was not around, so Poindexter squired the secretary around the ship.

You could use a guy like that, Hanson told Chafee on the way back to Washington. Chafee agreed. Not long after, Poindexter received orders to the Pentagon as the secretary's administrative assistant.

Dick Murphy sent him on his way with a fitness report that said, "Lieutenant Commander Poindexter is the most outstanding officer I have met in the naval service." Years later, Murphy bristled at the suggestion that he had overstated the case. "The *Lawrence* was my third command," he said. "I had seen a lot of officers. He was the best."

The Secretary of the Navy's personal staff is reserved for water walkers, men being groomed for bigger things. During Poindexter's three years as administrative assistant, 1971–74, an aura of predestination hovered over the staff, along with a hefty dose of foreshadowing. Thor Hanson had followed future CIA director Stansfield Turner as naval aide and eventually retired as a vice admiral. Hanson, in turn, was succeeded by ex–Whiz Kid Carl Trost, later Chief of Naval Operations, thanks in part to Poindexter. The Marine aide was Dick Schulze, Ollie North's old battalion commander, a future general destined to play an even larger role in North's life in the years ahead. Herb Hetu, the public affairs officer, had worked for Jack McCain, John McCain's father, and would later work for Turner at the CIA. During the Reagan years he handled public affairs for a number of high-visibility presidential boards and commissions, notably the Tower Commission, which investigated the Iran-Contra affair. Steve Pfeiffer, a speechwriter and Rhodes Scholar who worked for Hetu, left the Navy for law school, joined a high-powered Washington law firm that later supplied Poindexter's Iran-Contra defense team. A junior member of the secretary's staff, working under Poindexter, was a young Marine captain named Jim Webb.

Poindexter served as administrative assistant to three Navy Secretaries, Chafee, John Warner, and J. William Middendorf. All three held him in high regard. "He was excellent," said Chafee. "You had a lot of confidence in him. You knew he'd do it right." Warner considered him an "absolute model naval officer." Middendorf awarded him the Legion of Merit. Everyone in the office trusted his judgment; none picked up a whiff of high-handedness or zealotry.

As administrative assistant, Poindexter oversaw the handling of every piece of paper that went into or came out of the secretary's office. Most of the documents were classified, many highly sensitive, all routed through an archaic system of paper shuffling that cost time and money. On his own initiative, Poindexter streamlined and computerized the office, supervising the writing of all the programs, writing some of them himself. "He brought the Navy's secretariat into the modern age," said Thor Hanson.

During John Warner's tenure as SecNav, Poindexter was visited by an officer on the staff of Admiral Elmo Zumwalt, the CNO. Warner and Zumwalt did not get along, and the officer told Poindexter that Zumwalt expected to be kept informed of the secretary's activities. Poindexter wondered if Zumwalt had ordered the approach or if the officer, who was senior to him, was simply free-lancing, trying to establish his own pipeline into the secretary's office. Not that it mattered.

Forget it, said Poindexter, I work for the secretary. I'm nobody's spy.

He and Linda remained troubled by Vietnam. One day Bob Caldwell, his former Academy roommate, dropped in to say hello, mentioning that he had noticed a McGovern bumper sticker on Poindexter's car in the Pentagon parking lot. What's that all about? he asked. Caldwell remembered Poindexter brushing off the question. Linda later said Caldwell probably was thinking of the "I Have a Dream" sticker they had on their car about that time, but conceded the possibility that Caldwell was right. John, meanwhile, had taken to wearing sideburns that curled up slightly at the bottom. Colleagues teased him about his "Caltech hairdo."

He got his first taste of politics in the job, and he didn't like it. He wasn't alone. Hanson, a Democrat with strong liberal leanings, admitted to Chafee after about six months as naval aide that he had developed "almost a hatred of Congress." For both Poindexter and Hanson, the issue was not Vietnam but base closings. Politicians who demanded cuts in the defense budget invariably undermined their credibility when it came to shutting down military installations in their own states or congressional districts.

Poindexter couldn't tolerate such reactions on the part of senators and congressmen, began to view them as hypocrites. As he saw it, you either needed a facility or you didn't. If you didn't, close it. He may have been sophisticated about the nucleus of an atom, but he began and ended the SecNav job with a knowledge of the American system of government little advanced beyond the level of high school civics. The importance of the trade-offs and compromises that grease the wheels of government eluded him. He would later say, "I think elected officials should be statesmen, and they aren't. They have the privilege of knowing a lot more than the general public, so they have a responsibility, which most of them shirk, of performing a leadership role. . . . By and large, they take the easy way out. They don't make the hard decisions." Whatever else may be said of Poindexter, no one ever accused him of dodging the hard decisions.

He went back to sea in the fall of 1974, this time as the commanding officer of the *England*, a guided-missile frigate upgraded during his tour to a guided-missile cruiser. It was a captain's billet and he was a commander, but Admiral Zumwalt, the CNO, was experimenting with giving a few handpicked younger officers—the Mod Squad, as they came to be known—greater leadership opportunities.

The captain of a ship at sea may be the last of the world's absolute monarchs. His authority is unquestioned, his power unrivaled. Equally undiluted is his responsibility. He can delegate authority, never responsibility. If things go well, he gets the credit. If they go poorly, he takes the blame. An unsuccessful tour as commanding officer severely limits his career, an accident at sea—no matter how unavoidable—effectively ends it.

Poindexter assumed command of the *England* in Subic Bay. The next day the ship put to sea. A day or so later, he came down with a bad case of the flu. The corpsman served up the school solution—a handful of green pills, lots of fluids, and bed rest. Poindexter's second-in-command, executive officer Will King, shook his head, smiled to himself. It was, King knew, hard enough for a commanding officer to leave the bridge in the best of times, let alone a brand-new skipper in his first week at sea, flu or no flu.

Poindexter took the corpsman's advice, retiring to his cabin for the next two days. King was flabbergasted. At first he figured he was witnessing a monumental display of coolness. Later, he decided it was not that at all, that what he was seeing in Poindexter was a true believer, a man who took it on faith that the Navy had provided him with a crew fully capable of performing any and all the tasks expected of it, up to and including operating the ship in the event of the death or disability of its captain.

Other incidents hammered home the point. Steaming toward the Gulf of Tonkin, the fleet commander summoned all captains to his flagship for an operational briefing. The timing was bad as the briefing coincided with an unusually complicated underway replenishment. The *England* was to simultaneously take on supplies from a ship steaming alongside and a fleet of helicopters hovering overhead. Under the circumstances Poindexter might easily have begged off the briefing and sent King in his place. Instead, he exchanged salutes with his XO and climbed aboard a chopper, displaying more confidence in King than King had in himself. "It scared the shit out of me, quite frankly," said King. But he carried out the replenishment without a hitch, came away from the experience with new confidence in his abilities as a shiphandler. Even so, he wondered if he would have taken the same chance had he been the skipper.

During tactical exercises, King discovered that Poindexter was himself a shiphandler without peer. Nothing seemed to catch him by surprise because, King concluded, he had thought through every possible eventuality, worked out the responses, and stored them away in his mind until he needed them. Even when reacting to the evasive movements of another vessel, he did so with such assurance that it seemed he knew in advance how the other ship planned to maneuver.

Poindexter's duties, as he viewed them, included training his junior officers for greater responsibilities. To his mind, that meant not just letting them perform the conventional tasks, but the more tense, demanding ones as well. He gave advice without seeming to interfere in the duties of his subordinates. When they sought his counsel, he discussed problems with them, pointed them in the right direction, but rarely said do this or do that.

On one occasion, he did, narrowly averting disaster, but even then he did so with such restraint that few detected his involvement.

The *England* was taking on fuel from an oiler cruising in tandem with her on the port side. Poindexter was on the bridge, listening, watching, but allowing one of his subordinates to conn the ship. The replenishment was proceeding smoothly until the *England* nosed slightly ahead of the oiler, caught the wind from port, and started to swing to starboard, away from the oiler. The officer of the deck noticed the swing and ordered the helmsman to apply left rudder to correct it. The OD failed, however, to give the helmsman a new course to steer, in this case the one the ship had been on before the wind took her.

The rudder still over, the *England* began swinging back to the left, past the old course, toward the oiler. With a coolness that surprised even him in retrospect, Poindexter quietly told the OD to order the helmsman to check the swing and come back to the old course. The helmsman did so, but a ship is not a car, sensitive to the slightest movement of the steering wheel. Even with the helm thrown back to the right, the prow of the *England* continued to swing left, closing the distance between herself and the oiler.

For a few agonizing seconds a collision seemed inevitable. With no more than a foot between the two vessels, the *England* answered the helm, stopping her swing and moving right, out of danger.

On that day in 1974, one foot was all that separated John Poindexter from civilian life. Ultimately, his naval career did end prematurely, and some of the reasons were evident from his tour as commanding officer of the *England*. He was, above all, a man who trusted the system, the time-honored system of winnowing in and winnowing out employed by the armed services. With rare exceptions, a man was not promoted unless he had earned it, was not entrusted with a job unless he had shown himself over a long period of testing that he was capable of performing it. If the Navy decided Will King was good enough to serve as executive officer on a ship of the line, Poindexter assumed it to be so. By the same token, if the Marine Corps decided Ollie North belonged in the White House, it never occurred to Poindexter to doubt it. For John Poindexter, the system worked. Until it didn't.

CHAPTER THIRTEEN

'TIS THE SEASON TO BE JOLLY

Christmas Eve, 1968. Hanoi.
   "You are going to a church service," a guard told John McCain.

McCain had been in solitary since Bud Day was removed from his cell nine months earlier. He was fifteen months into his captivity, deathly pale, eyes sunken, arms twisted, "as though he had suffered polio," according to author John Hubbell.

He hobbled into a spacious room gaily decorated with flowers. About fifty POWs were seated on benches, spaces between them to discourage conversation. An aging Vietnamese clergyman presided at a makeshift altar. A small choir of Americans was singing seasonal hymns. A noisy pack of photographers jostled for position at the rear and sides of the room. Movie cameras rolled, flashbulbs popped.

McCain decided to ruin the picture. Acting as if he owned the place, he smiled and waved at other prisoners. "No talking, no talking," warned the guard as he escorted him to his seat.

"Fuck that," said McCain. Turning to the nearest American, he said, "Hey, pal, my name's John McCain. What's yours?"

"McCain, stop talking," cooed a smiling guard called Soft Soap Fairy, aware that he was on-camera.

"Fuck you," said McCain, louder than before. "This is fucking bullshit. This is terrible. This isn't Christmas. This is a propaganda show."

McCain hastily briefed his new friend. "I refused to go home. I was tortured for it. They broke my rib and rebroke my arm. . . ."

"No talking!"

"Fuck you!" said McCain, momentarily interrupting his briefing. Resuming, he said, "Our senior ranking officer is—"

"No talking!" said the Prick, who had rushed to a spot just outside camera range to try to control his favorite prisoner.

"Fu-u-u-u-ck you, you son of a bitch!" shouted McCain, hoisting a one-finger salute whenever a camera pointed in his direction.

Returned to his cell, he awaited the retribution of his jailers. Nothing happened that night or the following day. It was, after all, Christmas. The next day the anticipated pounding materialized, like a present delayed in the mail.

Christmas Eve, 1969. Hanoi.

Christmas carols over the loudspeaker, every other song "I'll Be Home for Christmas," the Dinah Shore version. McCain, still in solitary, was squatting in his cell when the door swung open. The Cat entered.

McCain was wary. A year and a half earlier the Cat had unleashed his goons when McCain refused to take early release. This time the Cat was in a reflective, seemingly sentimental mood, as if he wanted nothing more than conversation.

He showed McCain the small diamond embedded in his tie clip. McCain, the gracious host, complimented him on it. "Yes," said the Cat, "I received this from my father, and my grandfather before him had this tie clip." He pulled out a cigarette case, told McCain it was made from the fuselage of an Air Force Thud bomber.

"I know you miss your family," said the Cat.

"Well, I miss them, but I think this war is going to last for a very long time," replied McCain.

"Yes, you are right," said the Cat. "That's why you should have accepted my offer."

"Someday you'll understand why I could never accept that offer," said McCain.

"I may understand more than you think," said the Cat.

The conversation meandered here and there for about an hour, long enough for McCain to smoke a dozen of the Cat's cigarettes. The Cat reminisced about his family, the war, this one against the Americans and the previous one against the French, where he had been, what he had done. He asked about Christmas and how it was celebrated in America, explained Tet to McCain, what it meant, the customs surrounding it.

McCain concluded that the Cat had no hidden agenda, that this was just a time-out, akin to the brief fraternization between German and Allied troops during the first Christmas of World War I.

The Cat got up to go.

"Merry Christmas," he said.

"Thank you," said McCain.

Christmas Eve, 1969. Philadelphia.

Carol and the children were spending the holidays, the third without John, at her parents' home. At one point, she burst into tears in front of the kids.

"You don't let us cry, so you're not allowed to cry, either," said Andy.

"Okay, you're right," said Carol.

After dinner she decided to drop off some presents at her friends the Bookbinders. The task completed, she started home. It was snowing and the roads were icy. She turned onto a lonely country road. Approaching an intersection, she misjudged the stopping distance, hit the brakes, skidded, and rammed into a telephone pole.

She was thrown from the car into the snow. Alone, in unbearable pain, she went into shock. Sometime later, police responding to a routine report of an abandoned vehicle found her unconscious body by the side of the road.

At Bryn Mawr Hospital, physicians pumped blood into her. "If you can hear us, wiggle your fingers," a doctor said. She did, or thought she did, until she heard the doctor say, "If you can hear us, blink your eyes."

She passed in and out of consciousness for the next day or so. She overheard doctors discussing whether or not to amputate her left leg. Terrified, she tried to scream, No, don't do that, I'll be fine. But it was several days before she could speak.

When her condition was stabilized, the doctors put her in the picture. Both legs were smashed, her pelvis and arm broken. Internal injuries included a ruptured spleen. She was told she might never walk again, but amputation was ruled out.

She spent the next six months in the hospital, undergoing a series of operations. She made friends with a doctor and his wife. After several months, they brought her to their home for the afternoon, all eighty pounds of her, complete with cast, braces, wheelchair, and catheter.

Over the next two years she had twenty-three operations. By the time the surgeons finished with her, she was five foot four, four inches shorter than before the accident. She was confined to a wheelchair, one leg in a cast, the other in a brace.

Back in Jacksonville, she began physical therapy twice a day at the naval hospital. The operations continued, but by late in the year the cast was off and she could get around on crutches.

Soon after the accident, the doctors had said they would try to get word to John about her injuries. No, she said, he's got enough problems, I don't want to tell him.

And she never did.

Christmas, 1970. Hanoi.

Guards transferred McCain from his remote one-man cell into a section of the Hilton called Camp Unity. They put him in a large room with fifty other Americans, among them Bud Day. McCain couldn't believe his good fortune. It was the perfect Christmas present. In the thirty-three months since he and Day were separated in March 1968, he had spent thirty-one months in solitary.

CHAPTER FOURTEEN

STRANGER IN A
STRANGE LAND

An enviable combat record behind him, Jim Webb looked ahead to a long career in the Marine Corps when he returned from Vietnam in March 1970. Two years later he was a civilian, having failed to reckon with some souvenirs from the war—the shrapnel lodged in his head, back, kidney, left arm, and left leg. The big problem was his infected left knee, the one that kept blowing open in Vietnam. From October 1970 until April 1972, when he knew it was all over, he was in a cast, in the hospital, or taking physical therapy.

He did not go easily. Assigned to the staff of Officer Candidate School at Quantico, he worked eighty-hour weeks when he wasn't in the hospital, guiding two platoons through the ten-week program, the second with his leg in a cast from ankle to hip. He skipped the runs, but did everything else, day and night patrols, helicopter insertions and extractions, combat assaults. When he saw a kid screwing off, he threw his cane at him.

His knee was not getting better. The infection moved from the soft tissue of the joint into the bone, the beginning of osteomyelitis. The Marine Corps wanted to medically retire him in April 1971. He talked the doctors into giving him one more year to clear up the infection, but it was getting harder to ignore the signals his body was sending. It was a disquieting time. Since the Academy, even before, he had defined himself as a Marine, essentially a physical person. Now his body was letting him down, threatening a radical alteration in the only future he had ever conceived for himself.

In June 1971 he was reassigned to a less taxing post in the Pentagon on the staff of Navy Secretary John Chafee. The White House funneled queries or complaints about the Marine Corps to his section. Some came from members of Congress, others from parents of recruits upset about the rigors of boot camp. He drafted the responses, occasionally for President Nixon, more frequently for the secretary. He liked the job, but thought of himself as the stateside equivalent of a REMF. Less than a week after reporting in, he called his monitor and pleaded for a transfer. "You've got to get me out of here," he said. The monitor just laughed.

Webb had only occasional dealings with John Poindexter, the secretary's administrative assistant, but became close friends with Dick Schulze, the senior Marine aide. Not all of Schulze's friends were Webb's friends. One day Schulze called him to his office. Ollie North was sitting there. Schulze thought the two Annapolis classmates might like to say hello. They did, said hello. Schulze asked Webb if he wanted to join them for lunch. Said Webb, Wish I could, Colonel, eating at my desk today, lots on my plate.

Whatever the drawbacks of the Pentagon job, he rediscovered writing, which he had enjoyed in high school and college. Soon he was publishing articles in professional journals.

His second Bronze Star completed its course through the bureaucracy during this period. Poindexter told him that Secretary Chafee planned to award the medal personally at a ceremony in his office. Horrified, Webb said, Sir, I really don't want this to be a big deal. Nobody who will be there knows what the medal means to me. It's personal. I'd just as soon not do this. Well, Captain, said Poindexter, I guess I'm just going to have to order you to do it. At the ceremony Poindexter read the citation.

Webb fought retirement to the end, but by April 1972 he had run out the string. His final option was a limited-duty billet, which meant he could never again hope to lead troops in the field, that he would be nothing more than a supporting player in an organization dominated by infantry officers. He turned it down. If nothing else, the fight with Ollie North had taught him he was incapable of operating well at half speed.

But what next? He had no idea. Schulze sensed his uncertainty. "What do you want to do?" asked the colonel. "I want to serve my country," he replied. "I don't know how civilians do that, but that's what I'd like to do."

Schulze had a friend, a retired Marine colonel named Bill Holmberg, a Navy Cross winner in Korea, at the newly created Environmental Protection Agency. "How about the environment?" asked Schulze. Webb loved the outdoors, had hunted and fished all his life. By early July he was at EPA, working on environmental impact statements.

Four days later, he walked into Holmberg's office. I'm not cut out to be a bureaucrat, he said. Frankly, I'm not sure what I'm cut out for, but it's not this. Holmberg had called in more than a few chits for Webb, but he liked him and kept his temper in check. What do you really want to do? he asked. Said Webb, I want to go to law school, except it's too late to apply. No one wants to talk to me. I haven't even taken the law boards.

Holmberg picked up the phone, dialed a number. "Howard, I've got a guy I want you to meet. He's interested in going to law school." Replacing the phone, Holmberg turned to Webb. "Go to the Metropolitan Club for lunch today," he said. "Just stand there. A guy is going to walk in. He looks like a former Marine. His name is Westwood."

At noon Webb stood in the lobby of the Metropolitan Club, an exclusive preserve of capital power brokers and old Washington money. A man in his sixties approached him. "You Jim Webb?" he asked. "I'm Howard Westwood." It proved to be one of the most fortuitous meetings of Webb's life.

Westwood came by his leatherneck looks honestly. He had been an established Washington lawyer of thirty-four when the Japanese bombed Pearl Harbor. He enlisted in the Marines, went through boot camp, and spent the war at Parris Island as a DI. In private practice, he had drafted and lobbied through Congress the Civil Aeronautics Act of 1938, effectively creating a monopoly over air travel for the eighteen airlines then existing. By the time Webb met him he was a senior partner at Covington and Burling, Washington's premier law firm.

Over lunch Westwood questioned Webb about his background, goals, motivations. When the session ended, Webb felt as if he had been turned inside out. He marveled at the force of Westwood's mind, a type of power he had previously discounted.

The next day he stopped by Westwood's office with the résumé he had been asked to prepare. Westwood paused at the list of decorations. "You are a hero, boy," the lawyer said. Webb was stunned. No one had ever said anything like that to him before. "I'm not," he replied. "We really don't have any."

Said Westwood, "Where do you want to go to law school?"

Thanks to Westwood, Georgetown and the University of Virginia agreed to interview him. With virtually no preparation, he took the law boards, scoring in the ninety-seventh percentile. Both schools accepted him. He chose Georgetown because it offered night courses and Barb was thinking of entering law school the following year. This way he could take care of their infant daughter, Amy, when Barb was at school.

He liked what he saw as his class assembled in late August 1972 for its first orientation lecture. Lots of guys in utilities, jungle boots, Sam Browne belts. He felt a little foolish, all the other vets decked out in their old bush gear, him in a sports shirt, pressed slacks, and polished shoes, camouflaged as a preppie. It felt good, though, knowing he wouldn't be the only ex-grunt in the class.

Suddenly someone leaped onto the stage, a man maybe three years older than Webb, by then twenty-six. At first Webb was startled. The man, introducing himself as a law professor, sported a pageboy haircut, handlebar mustache, glasses that seemed to grow out of his head, boots, tight trousers. After a few moments, Webb relaxed. It was, he realized, a classic attention-getter. In a minute, the guy is going to pull off the wig and false mustache and show us what a real law professor looks like.

In his first half hour as a law student, Webb had already made two mistakes. The first involved his khaki-clad classmates. They had been outfitted by the local Army-Navy surplus store, not Uncle Sam. He was the only Vietnam veteran in a class of 125. The second mistake related to what he assumed was the professor's wig and phony mustache.

It was a time for misjudgments. He had spent nearly his entire life in a military environment. Now he was struggling to find his way in the unfamiliar world of civilians. As he later explained it, "I'm a first-year law student still trying to figure out what civilians eat for dinner."

He learned. Some of the lessons were humorous. One day in the cafeteria a couple of classmates were teasing him about spreading mayonnaise on his pastrami sandwich. "What's it to you?" he fired back. "You're not even Italian."

Other lessons were not funny at all. On a rainy night early in the term, he paused outside the law library to shake the water from his bush hat. A young woman, like him a first-year student, was doing the same to her umbrella.

"You were in Vietnam," she said, her inflection making the statement a question.

"Yes," replied Webb.

"I've never met anyone who was in Vietnam before."

As it turned out, she didn't even know anybody who had been drafted. How can that be, wondered Webb, taken aback. He did some mental arithmetic, figured the woman had graduated from high school in 1968, the year of the highest draft calls of the war. What's going on here? he asked himself.

In those days, Jim Webb was a bit of a cherry boy, too.

He did not enter law school with a chip on his shoulder. Howard Westwood had dispatched him with an admonition: "Go in there and learn from these people. They've had different experiences. Listen to them. Talk to them." He did, spending as much time that first year talking and listening to his classmates as he did studying law. At times the process was painful. In moving almost overnight from the Marine Corps to Georgetown, he had crossed untutored into an alien culture. He got along with the majority of his fellow students, most of whom seemed indifferent to the war and his part in it or mildly curious about his experiences. But he had a number of storied clashes with the school's sizable antiwar clique, which included professors as well as students. Even with the less militant and doctrinaire, discussions about Vietnam started from the premise that the war was at best a mistake, more probably an evil undertaking. He counted it a victory to win an acknowledgment, however grudging, that the NVA and VC might, just might, be pretty bad people themselves, not the gallant peasant-saints many of his classmates thought them to be. In those days he wasn't all that certain where he himself stood on the war, which made life doubly difficult.

Struggling to work through his confusion, he continued to talk, listen, and learn. One of his classmates, a Quaker, was an outspoken opponent of the war. But he had spent two years in Vietnam working in an orphanage, which gave him standing with Webb. The two men discussed the war for hours, arguing and rearguing their positions, both gaining insight.

Sometimes, like anyone feeling his way in an unfamiliar culture, he stumbled. In the student union, someone said he had read that there were 200,000 refugees in Vietnam. "Two hundred thousand?" laughed Webb. "Hell, we probably made half of them in one operation." A woman nearby went pale, got up, and walked off, obviously shaken. Learning that members of her family had been refugees during the Hitler years, Webb found her and apologized.

Through the fits and starts of that first year, he had a formidable anchor, a Philadelphia kid named Leo Kennedy, who became his closest friend at Georgetown. Kennedy had gone through Quantico, intent on becoming a platoon leader in Vietnam, only to have the American role shut down before he got there. Unmoved at the prospect of three years as a grunt lieutenant in the peacetime military, he accepted the offer of the Marines to send him to law school on the condition that he practice in the Corps for a few years after he graduated.

Kennedy was smart, fun-loving, and impulsive. More important, he refused to let Webb take himself too seriously, perhaps the best favor any of Webb's friends can do for him.

Webb, let's go to the basketball game tonight.

I don't know, Leo, let me think about it.

Hey, Webb, if I asked you if you wanted to go to the head, you'd set up a decision tree. Come on, man, let's go.

He also forced Webb to use his brain. A news item on the car radio would set Kennedy off. He'd take a side of the issue he knew to be opposite Webb's, argue it like crazy, then switch and argue the reverse if Webb conceded a point.

As Kennedy got to know Webb better, he told him he was a Hemingwayesque character.

Ever read Hemingway, Webb?

Yeah, some, at the Academy.

Read it all.

Webb came to view the majority of his fellow students as the most miserable, neurotic, and obsessive collection of individuals he had ever met. He'd look for reading assignments in books at the library only to find the assigned pages cut out, as if to deny them to others. In class he watched with bemusement, then irritation as classmates questioned or challenged a professor, decided the process was an elevated form of ass-kissing. For all the rebellious, antiestablishment manners of their classmates, Webb and Kennedy decided that most were frauds. These guys show up here in hippie headbands and walk out in three-piece suits, the two friends laughed. They even came up with a game about Georgetown law students. They called it Who's Going to Sell Out Next?

Webb insisted that Georgetown was not hell for him, but his criminal law class that first year came perilously close. The professor was Heathcote Wales, last seen in what Webb took to be a wig and false mustache. Wales, part of the antiwar set, often dreamed up vignettes to explain points of law, at times giving the characters the names of his students. The initial question on the first-term final was about search and seizure. It involved a Marine sergeant named Webb who attempts to ship home pieces of jade in the dead bodies of two Marines from his platoon. Webb would later say that he felt like he had been shot as he read the question. "All those broken bodies and nights in the rain, for what? To be laughed at?" he said. Immobilized for a full fifteen minutes, he thought about walking out of the exam, but stayed and finished it.

That night, he went through some of the bleakest hours of his life, repeatedly bursting into tears as he tried to study for the other finals. Two days later, he confronted Wales in his office. "I just want you to know it wasn't funny," he told the professor. "I went over to Vietnam with sixty-seven lieutenants, twenty-two died, and it wasn't funny."

However painful, something valuable came of the experience. "I decided then and there never to take any shit on that again," he said, meaning his Vietnam service.

The first year ended with many students taking summer jobs in air-conditioned law offices on Wall Street, K Street, or similar venues. Some traveled around Europe. Leo Kennedy worked at a logging camp in Maine. Webb went to Micronesia and greeted friends he never knew and never would.

Webb's passion for the Pacific had been sparked during an earlier summer, when as a fifteen-year-old grocery clerk he read James Michener's *Hawaii* between customers. His fascination intensified at Annapolis, where he studied the epic World War II naval battles in the Pacific. As a Marine, such storied tropical islands as Guadalcanal, Tarawa, Kwajalein, Saipan, Guam, Peleliu, and Iwo Jima exerted the primal tug of an ancestral home.

His trip in the summer of 1973 had its roots in an article he had written for the *U.S. Naval Institute Proceedings* a year and a half earlier, while still at the Pentagon. He argued that Guam, a U.S. trust territory, might be the perfect fallback position for the Pacific fleet if, as seemed likely, the Vietnam War ended in defeat and the Philippines continued to protest the massive American military installations there.

Guam was not so sure a beefed-up naval presence would be a blessing. The article triggered a nervous editorial in the Guam-based *Pacific Daily News* that began on the front page and completely filled an inside page. The editorial called Webb's piece a trial balloon floated by the Pentagon. His research was so comprehensive, the paper said, that he must have been fed his information by military planners secretly covetous of the island and its deep, protected anchorage.

The work was all his, but the reaction intrigued him. He decided he wanted to see the Marianas, the chain of Micronesian islands of which Guam was the largest. With two hundred dollars in his pocket, he hitchhiked across the Pacific, flying space-available on military aircraft, a privilege of retired servicemen.

He found that his article had conferred on him minor celebrity status, facilitating access to legislators and other dignitaries with whom he exchanged views on the future of Micronesia. Kinship as much as curiosity, however, had drawn Webb to the region. On Guam and two of the other islands, Saipan and Tinian, Marines had engaged in some of the bloodiest fighting of World War II. He felt compelled to pay tribute to the 5,487 Americans killed and the 21,189 wounded in those battles. After several days on Guam, he flew to Saipan, about one hundred miles to the north, the island of greatest carnage, and commenced a bewildering journey into the past. He later wrote:

> I can still taste the mix of warm rain and my tears as I stood on top of a Japanese pillbox on the invasion beach of Saipan in 1973, staring out into the emerald lagoon and distant reef from whence came two divisions of American Marines, 29 years and two wars before. I had arrived on the island on the anniversary of the invasion, which took place two years before my birth, and found it still littered with the artifacts of war: rusted hulks from landing craft, pillboxes buried to their firing apertures in sand, thick jungles filled with weapons and helmets and dud artillery rounds.
>
> In the lagoon itself, two American tanks sat forever frozen in the attack, clanking war machines that had become tombs for youths making their way onto the beaches of this unknown, isolated spit of coral. The young Marines in the tanks, as well as 3,400 other Americans over the space of three weeks, had given the ultimate, irretrievable gift to the culture that nurtured them.
>
> Later, sitting in a hotel restaurant filled with Japanese tourists, I wondered whether the events of the ensuing years could justify their deaths. How would I have explained to them on June 15, 1944, that within a generation the very nation they died helping to defeat, whose soldiers aimed the artillery piece that shot them dead, would economically dominate their battleground and graveyard under the protection of our own military? How would they have reacted if I could have predicted for them that their metal coffin would become a conversation piece for the children of their defeated enemy? "History," wrote T. S. Eliot, "has many cunning passages, contrived corridors and issues." And the unimaginable becomes unexplainable.

His thoughts returned to Vietnam. If the meaning of the Marine deaths on Saipan seemed blurred, how much more fleeting were the fresher sacrifices of the Arizona Valley and Go Noi Island destined to become? He had spent untold hours insisting to his troops that their service counted for something. Now, staring out at the lagoon, surrounded by Japanese on holiday, he thought of McGarvey, Tom Martin, Dale Wilson, Snake, the others. A storm of emotions swirled in his mind, leaving him light-headed. Alone and on foot, he set off to explore the island, looking for other killing fields, struggling with timeless questions that suddenly demanded answers.

Moving away from the beach, he plunged into dense, matted jungle. The brush was so thick in places that he could make headway only by crawling along trails blazed by wild pigs, sweeping brilliant blue spiders as large as crabs from his path with a palm frond. He literally tripped over the detritus of war, an unopened tin of C-ration coffee, the heel of a boot, a Japanese canteen, unexploded rocket rounds protruding from the ground, uncleared nearly thirty years later.

He worked his way around to Marpi Point, Saipan's northern tip, the rock face looming above it studded with star-shaped fractures where naval guns had pounded the island's Japanese defenders. From that very cliff, he knew, hundreds of frightened Japanese civilians had leaped to their deaths rather than face an uncertain fate at the hands of the victorious Americans.

At the base of the hill he saw tanks heeled over, blown open, planes smashed, scarred by fire. And caves, scores of them, the redoubts from which the Japanese ripped apart the advancing Marines only to be sealed inside by demolition teams when they refused all calls to surrender. He came upon the last command post of Lieutenant General Yoshitsugu Saito, commander of the thirty-two-thousand-man Japanese force, tracing the general's steps to the small cave where he committed *hara-kiri* when he realized the battle was lost.

Scrambling up the ridge, he saw a small opening near the top of one of the caves. He tried to enlarge the aperture so he could crawl through, but had to give up. After eight hours in the bush, he was parched, woozy, and out of water, his electrolytes wildly out of balance. He knew there was a dirt road not far away, but he didn't know how to get to it. Drenched in sweat, he worked his way on his stomach down a pig trail to the edge of the ridge, but it was a thirty-foot drop, a perilous leap even for someone with two good legs.

He crawled back up the trail, the steamy jungle continuing to leach fluids from his body. I'm going to die up here, he thought, and nobody is going to find me for years. He struggled along the ridge. He found a way down, if only he could negotiate two separate ten-foot drops.

Tree branches hung over the ridge. Clinging to them, he lowered himself onto the first face. Halfway to the bottom, a flight of angry hornets swarmed over him, stinging his face. As he slid awkwardly the rest of the way down, his watch popped off his wrist. Searching the ledge for the timepiece, he plunged his hand into a colony of fire ants.

Dehydrated, clothes shredded, his face bruised and swollen, he made it down to the road, caught a ride back to civilization about an hour later.

He returned to the Marianas the following summer, this time with Barb and two-year-old Amy, and in relatively grand fashion. He had turned his conversations and experiences of the previous year into a small book, which had impressed Guamanian officials. They hired him for three months to study U.S. military facilities on the island and the implications of possible base expansion in the region. Again he combed the islands. As on the earlier trip, the images overwhelmed him.

One day he found an enormous cave. The Marines had sealed it in 1944, but it had later blown open, probably when trapped gases exploded. Pickaxes lined one wall, grenades another. Bottles and jars rested on a shelf built into a third wall, along with stoppered medicine vials, rice dishes, a soap dish, here and there a boot, scraps of uniforms. Human bones were scattered everywhere, but no intact skeletons; the wild pigs, iguanas, and other animals that roamed the island had long since seen to that.

He heard water dripping in a smaller cave connected to the larger one. Crawling in, he saw a shaft of light shining through the rocky ceiling. The hole opened onto the ridge above. Squirming and wiggling, he managed to get his head through the opening. A Marine helmet rested no more than two feet away, rusted and covered with bright green moss. He worked his arm out and reached for the helmet. As he touched it, the helmet disintegrated, turning to dust under his hand.

In the years ahead, in various capacities, he would return to the Marianas, and visit Marine battlegrounds on Guadalcanal, Iwo Jima, and Okinawa as well. On those occasions, his sympathies were invariably with the Marines, but in the end it was the enemy from that long-ago war that helped him make sense of it.

Saipan provided part of the answer. Monuments to the Japanese war dead were a familiar sight on the island, some erected at a cost of several million dollars by private citizens. At the base of Suicide Cliff, groups of Japanese sifted through the dirt for flecks of bone so they could give ancestors and friends a proper burial. Shinto prayer sticks dedicated to fallen warriors were strewn at intersections, so dense in number they looked like clumps of weeds. By contrast, the sole memorial to the American presence was a small cross with a helmet on top, erected in the early 1950s. It stood untended in front of the local Toyota dealership.

Eventually, he tried to sort out his confusion by writing about it. "There is strength to be gained from remembering," he began.

The Japanese, I think, groped with this question from the other end of the dilemma: how could a nation beaten on the battlefield find meaning and momentum in the events of its defeat, while at the same time renouncing war? The answer, predictably for their culture, lay in their war dead. The Japanese renounced war but embraced their warriors. It was as if each death involved a transfer of energy, the soul of the soldier feeding into the soul of the nation, until the very enormity of Japan's defeat became itself the fuel for its post-war emergence.

Years later, when asked why he started writing, Webb cited an Auden poem, "In Memory of W. B. Yeats," singling out the line "mad Dublin hurt you into poetry." The Georgetown Law Center was Webb's Dublin. Rejected by the Marine Corps, the institution on which he had planned to build his life, he felt invisible as the war was debated and condemned around him by what he came to view as a pampered, unbloodied elite.

At first he was puzzled. He didn't agree, but he viewed opposition to the war as a legitimate philosophical position. What he couldn't comprehend was the degree to which many of his classmates and their friends identified with and promoted the cause of the Vietcong and North Vietnamese. The brandishing of Vietcong flags, the chants of "Ho-Ho-Ho-Chi-Minh, The-NLF-Are-Gonna-Win." All this while the VC and NVA were killing and maiming other young Americans.

More perplexing was the sense that his antiwar classmates not only opposed the war but reviled, truly reviled, the men who fought it. He decided their actions were too personal to solely reflect a political position, but he could not figure out why. One day, out of an accumulation of conversations and encounters, the mist cleared and he understood it. And the more he understood, the angrier he got.

First came the notion of class, triggered by the chance encounter with the woman on the library steps. Unlike World War II, Vietnam had not been fought by all segments of American society. The World War II model of the Ivy League lieutenant leading a platoon of farmers, drugstore cowboys, and street kids had been altered, drastically and at great cost. Lacking more desirable material, the Army made a youthful misfit named William Calley a lieutenant, gave him a platoon, and the rest, tragically, is history.

"I think the people who went to those schools—Harvard, MIT, whatever—are collectively responsible for William Calley," said

Webb. The reason: they never showed up, so the Army took Calley instead.

Webb decided the hostility of many of his antiwar schoolmates was an expression of suppressed guilt. By arguing that the war was illegal and immoral, that all American soldiers did was shoot civilians, torch hooches, and do dope, they were trying to get themselves off the hook for their own actions. Employing the tortured logic of the time, they succeeded in imputing to themselves the virtues of courage and integrity even if to less sensitive souls like Webb they seemed singularly lacking in those qualities.

Webb delivered his remorseless judgment in his third novel, *A Country Such As This*, a flawed work that nevertheless contains some of his most passionate writing. The scene is the October 1967 march on the Pentagon.

> The students, the people of books and pep clubs and prom committees, who had from their childhood feared the simple power and brutality of the blue collar kids, the red-necks, the bowling alley kings, the hot-rodding, ducktailed greasers who once mocked their studies and their lack of manliness, who might attack them over the tiniest issue of honor, now found their scourges trapped as a result of those same aggressive instincts. The boys whose sense of danger and action had lured them into the Army instead of college wore their uniforms like straitjackets, becoming quiet, enduring objects, repositories for the insults of those they could have squashed in a microsecond if the odds were fair.
>
> So the students unloaded on the soldiers, cursing them, daring them, under the accepted guise of hating Army, Pentagon and War. The insults issued, and the soldiers did not move. Tomatoes and bottles smacked into them, and the soldiers did not move. Girls undid their blouses, dangling firm inviting breasts over tightly gripped rifles, and the soldiers did not move. Students spat on them, grew more hateful, megaphones telling them they were dupes, fools, *fuckheads*, that their war was sinful, immoral, *genocidal*, and the soldiers did not move.

His contempt did not extend to all who opposed the war. He expressed ungrudging respect for those willing to go to jail for their beliefs, in contrast to those who evaded or avoided the draft or fled the country. As he later wrote, "Thoreau went to prison, not to Canada."

Looking back on Georgetown, Webb seemed to view it as a valuable experience, in its way akin to plebe year at Annapolis.

"I'm a combative person, I know I am, and the greatest thing about law school was I learned to fight with my brain," he said. "I clarified something to myself. No matter how much you want to live in the white man's world, you either live by what you believe in or you die."

His matriculation had spanned three of the most tumultuous years in the nation's history. The Watergate break-in, June 17, 1972, two months before he began classes. Agnew's resignation, October 10, 1973. Nixon's resignation, August 9, 1974. The Nixon pardon, September 8, 1974. The fall of Saigon, April 30, 1975, deepening the decline in America's prestige abroad and the sense of despair at home.

Like so many other veterans, he saw the American pullout not only in terms of lost comrades but as the betrayal of. an ally as well. In *A Country Such As This*, one of Webb's characters, a former POW named Lesczynski, exclaims, "No, I'll *never* get used to it. It's the most deplorable thing this country has ever done." Glued to the television screen on the final day, Lesczynski reflects Webb's judgment of the retreat: "There was a weakness in his country, in its leaders or maybe its system, that had botched this thing badly, called on citizens to sacrifice and then rebuked their efforts, fading again and again in the clutch."

Webb, like his fictional POW, was repulsed by the images barreling across the screen at him. South Vietnamese clamoring at the gates of the embassy, American helicopters tumbling from the decks of carriers, the tanks of the victorious enemy rolling into Saigon. Grabbing his books, he drove to school to study for his last set of exams, just days off. He arrived to find students gathered in animated clumps. outside the law library, redeemed, intact, to Webb's eye secretly exchanging high fives. He spotted his Quaker friend, the one who had spent two years in Vietnam, one of the few members of the class he respected.

"Are you really happy about this?" asked Webb.

"Yes, I am," replied his classmate.

"You make me want to puke," said Webb.

CHAPTER FIFTEEN

THE REASONABLE AND HONEST WAR CRIMINAL

Ollie North had been home about three months when he read a shocking battlefield dispatch. A Marine patrol had allegedly gone on a murderous shooting spree in the village of Son Thang (4) near Danang on the evening of February 19, 1970. The patrol leader and another Marine were charged with the premeditated murder of sixteen Vietnamese civilians—five women and eleven children. Two other patrol members faced sixteen counts of unpremeditated murder. Disgust welled up in North as he read the report. By his own account he nearly fainted when he came to the name of the patrol leader and apparent chief culprit.

Randy Herrod, his old machine-gunner, one of the best of Blue's Bastards.

North could not believe Herrod was guilty. He had trained Herrod. North-trained men did not commit atrocities. He viewed the crime of which Herrod was accused as the act of a coward, the last word he would apply to the man he had recommended for the Navy Cross.

"But even if Herrod had acted wrongly, which I doubted, I still wanted to help him," North later wrote. "Randy Herrod had saved my life, and you don't forget something like that."

He contacted Herrod's civilian attorneys, described Herrod as a brave and courageous Marine, and said he would return to Vietnam to testify if they thought it would help.

The defense team was in no position to turn down any offers of assistance. The Son Thang (4) incident was the Marine Corps version of the My Lai massacre, which had come to light only a few months earlier. Anxious to avoid the appearance of a cover-up, the Marines quickly made the charges public and began court-martial proceedings. Command interest swirled about the case, so much so that the military lawyer assigned to defend Herrod, Captain Robert C. Williams, cried foul. He was quoted in the *Pacific Stars and Stripes* as saying the case was being controlled by higher headquarters to make sure that "the Marine Corps is not going to get caught up like the Army did, covering up My Lai."

Drawing on precious leave time and some of his own money, North made his way by commercial airlines and space-available military flights back to Vietnam, aware that his efforts were not likely to endear him to his superiors.

"Betsy wasn't exactly thrilled, either," he says in his 1991 autobiography, *Under Fire.* "For one thing, she was now pregnant with our second child. For another, the prospect of her husband returning to the war at his own expense, and using his leave time to do it—all this did not strike her as a particularly brilliant course of action. We had been married a year and a half, and I had already spent two-thirds of that time in Vietnam."

North arrived in Danang as the court-martial was about to get under way. Herrod's prospects were not bright. One member of his patrol had been acquitted, but two others had been found guilty. Said Harry Palmer, Jr., one of the civilian lawyers who assisted in Herrod's defense, "They had already convicted two of three and our guy was the leader of the patrol."

North was to be a character witness. As usual, he went the extra mile. The defense team, headed by two state senators from Herrod's home state of Oklahoma, told North they did not think their client could get a fair trial in Danang. North undertook an informal survey of the Marine officers in the compound from which the court's panel was to be chosen, chatting them up at the Officers Club and mess hall. The results bore out the fears of the lawyers—all but one of the thirty or so officers with whom North spoke thought Herrod was guilty. The attorneys entered the survey in pretrial proceedings, arguing for a change in venue. The motion failed, but the results became part of the record, available for use on appeal in the event that Herrod was convicted, which Herrod and his lawyers fully expected.

North helped in other, more important ways. Challenge anyone assigned to the court who is not a combat Marine, he counseled the attorneys. Only men who have been under fire can appreciate the situation in which Herrod found himself that night. The lawyers took the advice, rejecting prospective jurors until they fashioned a court composed of seven combat-decorated Marines.

Herrod's lawyers were influential men back in Oklahoma, but their political clout at home meant little in Danang. They complained to

North that their request to tour the tiny three-hooch ville where the killings occurred had been turned down, purportedly because of the danger involved. That meant they had to rely on Herrod's dim recollections and descriptions of the scene provided them by the prosecution. North solved that problem, talking some Marines into sending a patrol out to the ville and letting him tag along. He returned with a detailed sketch map of the site, complete with the location of hooches, dimensions, distances, directions, and terrain features.

He brought back other information valuable to the defense. He discovered that the bodies of the sixteen victims had remained unburied for two days, raising questions about the failure of Marine officials to conduct autopsies. The defense called this a suspicious oversight in view of Herrod's claim that the civilians had been caught in a crossfire between his men and enemy troops whose very existence the prosecution questioned.

North also learned that there had been at least one Vietcong in the village on the night of the shootings despite the prosecution's contention that there were no men present. Armed with the results of North's reconnaissance, Herrod's lawyers elicited a telling admission from a prosecution witness, a Vietnamese woman whose daughter was one of the sixteen victims—her daughter had been spending the night with a VC soldier.

When his time came to testify, North put on the kind of performance the nation would see seventeen years later when he faced John Nields, the chief House counsel of the congressional Iran-Contra committees. Chin up, feet flat on the floor, hands on his knees, he was, said Harry Palmer, "two right angles." Said Denzil Garrison, a trial lawyer for more than thirty-five years, "He was the most believable witness I've ever seen."

North described for the court how Herrod had saved his life and that he had put him in for the Navy Cross, information the prosecution had until that point succeeded in keeping out of evidence. His case damaged, the prosecutor tried to soften the impact of North's testimony. "He was like a bear cub playing with his you know what," said attorney Garrison. "He was worse than Nields." Thanks in part to North's appearance and his behind-the-scenes efforts, Herrod was acquitted of all charges. "We walked the patrol leader," said Garrison, still seemingly amazed by the verdict.

Jim Webb had little sympathy for Herrod or for North's spirited defense of him, but in 1971 he was drawn into the case, too. At the time, he was in the Secretary of the Navy's office, fighting to beat back retirement. His job included reviewing criminal cases and he was struck by the story of a young Marine named Sam Green. Green was one of the two members of the five-man Herrod patrol to be convicted. He received fifteen concurrent five-year prison terms for unpremeditated murder, the prosecution having successfully portrayed him as an aider and abetter in the atrocity.

Webb saw incredible injustice at play. Herrod, the patrol leader and a veteran of more than five months in-country, had been found not guilty even though he admitted giving the order to shoot and acknowledged blasting away with an M-79 grenade launcher loaded with buckshot. Green, an eighteen-year-old inner-city black with eleven days in Vietnam at the time of the shootings, had been convicted even though no testimony was presented that he actually killed anyone. Green, moreover, was of marginal intellect; there was evidence that he could not spell his own middle name. He had been in trouble as a civilian, but he received extremely high ratings in boot camp, 4.6 in both proficiency and conduct out of a possible 5.0. It appeared that Green joined the Marines in hopes of moving beyond his youthful transgressions and making something of himself.

The case continued to bedevil Webb after he entered Georgetown law school in the summer of 1972. He wanted to help Green, but wasn't sure what he could do. By this time Green's sentence had been reduced and he'd been released from prison, but he remained distraught over the conviction. During the Christmas holidays, Webb set up shop in the office of a Navy legal officer and went through the thousands of pages of pleadings and testimony in the Green trial.

Eventually he produced an article for the Georgetown law review, entitled "The Sad Conviction of Sam Green: The Case for the Reasonable and Honest War Criminal." As portrayed by Webb, Green was a scared kid barely off the plane who found himself in hostile and threatening surroundings. Because of his youth and inexperience in combat, he had reason to believe that he was expected to participate in the shootings. Moreover, he was under the command of a seasoned patrol leader, Herrod.

Having served in the same locale, Webb was able to describe from firsthand knowledge the difficulty in distinguishing friend from foe, particularly at night. Like North, Webb understood the importance of having combat Marines on the court, arguing that Green was effectively denied a trial by a jury of his peers in that not one of the five jury members was an infantryman.

The article won the law school's prestigious Horan Competition, a significant honor for a first-year law student. But he wasn't finished with the case. He joined forces, *pro bono*, with James Chiara, a lawyer from Cleveland, Green's hometown, to try to get the conviction overturned in a civilian court. He wrote the twenty-two-thousand-word brief used in the appeal. Contrasting Herrod and Green, he wrote, "If there was no guilt on the part of the person who ordered, how could there, by any stretch of judicial imagination, be guilt on the part of the person who obeyed?" The judge, William K. Thomas of the Northern District of Ohio, denied the motion, saying he could not find sufficient constitutional error to void the conviction. Later, though, the judge wrote to the Secretary of the Navy, J. William Middendorf, saying that clemency might best serve the interests of justice. "Given the apparent inconsistency and injustice of the Green conviction and the Herrod acquittal . . . it seems manifestly unfair that PFC Green should bear the continuing stigma and disability of a dishonorable discharge in addition to the sentence already served," the judge said. The secretary declined to act. Webb was depressed by the Navy's response, Green more so. About two weeks later, in August 1975, Webb received a telegram from Chiara:

TRAGIC CONCLUSION SAM GREEN DESTROYED HIMSELF.

Webb got the news that night in Lakeland, Florida, where he and his four-year-old daughter, Amy, were visiting his parents. He had never met Green, spoken to him only once by phone, but he had committed himself to clearing his name. Green's death had come less than four months after the fall of Saigon, for Webb a transcendent event that continued to torment him. He felt helpless, his sense of futility laced with outrage, a potentially explosive mixture. Isn't any of this ever going to come out right? he asked himself. The next morning he piled Amy into the car and headed north, turning off when he saw a sign for a lake. For the next three days he and Amy camped out as he struggled to regain his bearings. It rained the whole time.

Back home in Arlington, he called Green's mother, Roberta Green, and learned that her son had shot himself. She also read Webb the suicide note. As Webb remembered it, the letter said: *What could I do? What was I supposed to do? This was an accident. Nobody'll ever make me understand. They give you orders and then they still throw you into prison.*

Green was dead, but Webb couldn't let the case go. He and Chiara filed an appeal with the Board for the Correction of Naval Records asking that Green's dishonorable discharge be upgraded to honorable. Webb personally argued the case before the board. In December 1978, eight years after the shootings and three years after Green's suicide, Webb wrote to Mrs. Green: "At last, Sam's name is

U.S. NAVAL ACADEMY

(U.S. Naval Academy photos)

Class of 1958

John Marlan Poindexter

John Sidney McCain III

Class of 1959

Robert C. McFarlane

Class of 1968

James Henry Webb, Jr.

Oliver Laurence North

John Poindexter, the brigade commander, as he appeared in *The Log*, the Academy magazine, in 1958. (U.S. Naval Academy photo)

John Poindexter, the number one man in the Class of 1958, receives his diploma from President Eisenhower. "Congratulations, I hope it won't be too much of a burden for you," said Ike of Poindexter's lofty class standing. (U.S. Naval Academy photo)

Jim Webb and Ollie North square off for the 147-pound brigade boxing championship in March 1967. North won the close match by unanimous decision. (U.S. Naval Academy photo)

Jim Webb as a twenty-three-year-old second lieutenant on Go Noi Island in the spring of 1969, more than a year after the Tet Offensive, which dramatically diminished public support for the Vietnam War. At the time, Webb commanded the Third Platoon, Delta Company, First Battalion, Fifth Marines.

John McCain in the hospital in Hanoi shortly after he was shot down in October 1967.
(CBS News Archives)

President Nixon greets Lieutenant Commander John McCain at a May 1973 White House reception for former POWs.
(UPI/Bettmann Newsphotos)

President Reagan surprises national security adviser Bud McFarlane (left) and his deputy, John Poindexter (second from left), by bringing a cake to the White House Situation Room for a joint birthday celebration in July 1984. Chief of staff James Baker, later Secretary of State under George Bush, follows the President. McFarlane was born in July, Poindexter in August. (White House photo)

Bud McFarlane addresses the White House press corps on December 4, 1986, after President Reagan's announcement that McFarlane has resigned as national security adviser and will be replaced by his deputy, John Poindexter. "Will we ever see you again?" reporters shout to the publicity-shy Poindexter. "Maybe," he replies.

(Reuters/Bettmann Newsphotos)

Less than two weeks after the revelation that profits from the secret Iranian arms sales had been diverted to the Nicaraguan Contras, Oliver North was called to testify before the House Foreign Affairs Committee. On December 9, 1986, he was sworn in; however, he invoked his Fifth Amendment right against self-incrimination. The following July, testifying with a grant of immunity, he put Congress on trial. (UPI/Bettmann Newsphotos)

Navy Secretary Jim Webb visits an American military cemetery in Manila in July 1987. "There is strength to be gained from remembering," he had written a few years earlier. (U.S. Navy photo)

Oliver North, retired from the Marine Corps, talks to an audience in Highland Heights, Ohio, about the importance of family and the dangers of drugs on May 11, 1989, a week after being found guilty on three of twelve counts stemming from the Iran-Contra scandal. (UPI/Bettmann Newsphotos)

Senator John McCain, who stood fifth from the bottom of his Annapolis class in 1958, congratulates a graduating midshipman after delivering the commencement address at the Naval Academy in May 1993. (U.S. Naval Academy photo)

Vietnam veterans Jim Webb (left) and Senator Bob Kerrey of Nebraska (right) denounce Republican senatorial candidate Oliver North in front of the Iwo Jima memorial in Arlington, boosting the reelection hopes of incumbent Democratic Senator (and Vietnam-era Marine officer) Charles Robb of Virginia (at podium). (AP/Wide World Photos)

Oliver North in Richmond, Virginia, on election night, November 8, 1994, as he concedes to Charles Robb, but broadly hints that he will return to the political wars again. (AP/Wide World Photos)

cleared." He explained that her son's discharge had been upgraded to a general discharge. Though less meritorious than an honorable discharge, a general discharge is conferred "under honorable conditions." The board denied restoration of rank, back pay, or benefits, including burial expenses.

"This is small solace, I know," wrote Webb. "I only regret we were unable to do more for him sooner."

A few days later, Webb received a Christmas card and a note from Mrs. Green: "My son Samuel Jr. is happy in heaven and grave about this."

CHAPTER SIXTEEN

LONG TALL SALLY

Among the American prisoners in North Vietnam, the appetite for knowledge was insatiable, not merely as a diversion but as an intellectual stimulant, a device to keep their minds from going to seed.

Orson Swindle, a tall, rangy Marine fighter pilot out of Georgia Tech, mastered six thousand words of German, thanks to a prison friend. Jim Warner, a Marine flyer who later worked in the Reagan White House, learned integral and differential calculus from his fellow inmates, then wrote a calculus textbook on sheets of cigarette paper. One day Jim Stockdale received a message from Bob Shumaker, relayed by finger code by Nels Tanner: "If you get stuck alone, remember that e to the x is equal to the sum, from n equals one to n equals infinity, of the expression x to the n minus one, over n minus one, factorially."

The POWs had one mental exercise in common. They committed to memory the name of every prisoner they knew of, which eventually included almost all of the nearly six hundred aviators in captivity. This mind game was serious business. Suspicious of Vietnamese claims that they had made public an accurate prisoner list, the Americans wanted to be ready for any opportunity to smuggle out a complete roster. Instead of counting sheep, John McCain dozed off reciting names to himself.

At Camp Unity, McCain and Swindle joined forces to teach a course in English and American literature. Their lectures had a Classic Comics flavor, but they prepared as rigorously as college professors. The course included the works of Fielding, Melville, Kipling, Conrad, Hemingway, Fitzgerald, and Maugham. McCain, on his own, taught a social studies class. Never one to underplay his hand, he called it The History of the World from the Beginning.

There were less academic pursuits. McCain and Swindle pooled their knowledge of movies to entertain the troops, telling the story and doing bits and pieces of dialogue. The shows became an evening ritual, Monday Night at the Movies, Tuesday Night at the Movies, and so on. The regulars would arrive early, squat down in front, lay out a stash of cigarettes, their own and those they were able to scrounge from nonsmokers, and wait for the performance to begin. Whatever the other drawbacks, at least you could smoke at the movies in Hanoi.

"I did over a hundred movies, some of which I'd never seen," said McCain. A favorite was One-Eyed Jacks, in part because it contained a popular all-purpose epithet, "scum-sucking pig," which many POWs deemed dead-solid perfect for LBJ and various antiwar figures.

In early 1971, the prisoners at Camp Unity defied the North Vietnamese and held a church service, then staged a near-riot when three of their leaders were marched off in irons. Once it was over, Bud Day, the ringleader, and his partners in crime, McCain among them, were shipped off to Skid Row, a punishment camp.

The living conditions, rather than the behavior of the guards, accounted for the camp's reputation. The rooms were tiny, about six feet by three feet, the food terrible, the sanitation even worse. Jaundice and dysentery were rampant. Several prisoners came down with hepatitis. "Really bad," said McCain. "I mean, there were turds floating around in the well."

McCain and the rest of the Skid Row crew were returned to the more commodious Camp Unity in November 1971. McCain spent most of his remaining imprisonment there, though he was moved for a time to a small camp near the Chinese border called Dogpatch and spent the weeks before his release back at the Plantation.

The prisoners coasted through the last year or so of their captivity. The guards were generally tolerant, the food improved, and the men rallied physically. Two years before, McCain weighed 105 pounds, was covered with boils, and suffered from dysentery. Now he was fit enough to work out daily. Soon he was doing forty-five push-ups and a couple of hundred sit-ups, more than he could do before he was shot down.

Normal human needs, submerged by years of physical deprivation, reasserted themselves. Men talked warmly about their families and how much they missed them. McCain dreamily told his friends about his wife, the sleek ex-model, "Long Tall Sally," as he affectionately referred to Carol.

Orson Swindle remembered the John McCain of this period: "He looked sort of funny when he talked to you. He just couldn't move his arms very much, nothing above his shoulders. Yet the rascal was over there doing push-ups. They were a funny sort of push-ups, sort of tilted. And he would run in place. We occupied a lot of our time with exercises and he was stiff-legged, bouncing as best he could running in place. And an absolute chain-smoker. I've seen John have two or three cigarettes lighted at the same time."

Some things never change. Despite the dismal conditions, most of the POWs took pains to maintain a soldierly appearance. After washing their shirts and trousers, they stretched them out on the stone floor, using the flat of the hand to press out the wrinkles and iron in sharp military creases. Once the garments had dried, the men carefully folded and stored them under their bedding. Not McCain. He tied knots in the legs of a pair of trousers, then jammed the rest of his clothes down into them, as if he were stuffing a scarecrow. Swindle, echoing McCain's Annapolis roommates, told him he was the sloppiest man he had ever met.

Richard Nixon resumed sustained bombing of North Vietnam in April 1972, three and a half years after LBJ declared a bombing halt. The POWs were overjoyed by Nixon's action.

"We knew at the time that unless something very forceful was done that we were never going to get out of there," McCain later said. "We were fully aware that the only way we were ever going to get out was for our government to turn the screws on Vietnam. So we were very happy. We were cheering and hollering."

It was Nixon's decision, but Jack McCain, as CINCPAC, actually issued the orders that dispatched the bombers to the skies over Hanoi, in effect directing the bombardment of the city where his son was held captive.

Jack hid the strain well, though not from his wife, Roberta. She remembered that after John was shot down her husband would retire to his study for an hour every morning and night, get down on his knees and read his Bible. "He was," she said, "in agony."

Nixon suspended the bombing when the Paris Peace Talks appeared on the verge of a breakthrough in the fall of 1972. But the talks broke down, and in mid-December Nixon resumed heavy air attacks on Hanoi, Haiphong, and other major North Vietnamese cities by B-52s based on Guam. Though no B-52s flew on Christmas Day, the attacks became known as the Christmas Bombing and ignited a fresh storm of controversy at home.

There was little second-guessing among the guests at the Hanoi Hilton when the bombs began to fall about an hour after dark on December 18. Though the closest landed thousands of yards away, the explosions shook the ground of the prison compound and caused plaster to fall from the ceilings. The prisoners cheered, and cries of "Let's hear it for President Nixon!" swept the cellblocks.

At first the North Vietnamese had a large stockpile of SAMs on hand, capable of knocking down a B-52 at thirty thousand feet. When they scored a hit, the explosion lit the sky, the aircraft plunging to earth like a gigantic flare in free fall. But as the bombardment continued day after deadly day, the SAM supply dwindled.

"The bombers kept coming, and we kept cheering," Jim Stockdale would later write. "Guards who were normally enraged by loud talk, guards who normally thrust their bayoneted rifles through the bars and screamed at us if we dared shout during air raids, could be seen silently cowering in the lee of the prison walls, their faces ashen in the light reflected from the fiery skies above."

In Stockdale's view, the North Vietnamese could hardly find comfort in a burning B-52 tumbling from the sky.

"For the North Vietnamese to see that and the bomber stream continuing to roll right on like old man river was a message in itself—proof that all that separated Hanoi from doomsday was American forbearance, an American national order to keep the bombs out on the hard military targets. We prisoners knew this was the end of North Vietnamese resistance, and the North Vietnamese knew it, too."

Nixon halted the bombing on December 30. Formal negotiations resumed in Paris on January 8, 1973. On January 23, the President announced that an agreement had been reached to end direct American involvement in the war. The provisions called for the accord to be read to all the prisoners. They were formed in ranks for the ceremony. On orders from their superiors in the prisoner chain of command, they displayed no emotion when the section providing for their staged release was read. The cease-fire went into effect January 28.

Henry Kissinger, the chief American negotiator, later told McCain that when he was in Hanoi to sign the treaty documents the North Vietnamese said he could take one man back to Washington with him: John McCain. Kissinger said he refused the offer. McCain thanked him.

The initial group of prisoners was flown out of Hanoi on February 12, 1973. In line with the "first in, first out" rule, they were led to the plane by Everett Alvarez, in captivity since August 1964. Jim Stockdale and Jeremiah Denton followed close behind.

McCain, slated to leave with the third group, was moved back to the Plantation on January 20. He and his comrades were fitted for trousers, shirts, windbreakers, and shoes. The guards left them alone, the food got better, but time dragged despite card games, sex talks, and the occasional flare-up.

Playing bridge, Orson Swindle and his partner trounced McCain and his partner.

"I was just teasing the hell out of John," said Swindle. "And he got mad with me and he got all puffed up because he hates to lose. . . . He had this peg leg of his, he's limping and everything. He's just fuming. And this goes on for a couple of days. He wouldn't even speak to me."

A few nights later guards called off the names of several prisoners, including Swindle's, and told them to roll up their gear. They were going home. McCain, stricken, rushed over to Swindle, told him he was his best friend, apologized for being a shit.

"Don't even talk to me, you little shrimp," said Swindle, cutting him no slack.

Swindle was released on March 4. A few days later he found himself in a hospital bed in Jacksonville, not far from where Carol was living in Orange Park.

"I want to see Carol McCain," he told his doctors. To prepare her for the shock of seeing John, he explained.

"He'd been hurt and it showed," Swindle later said. "I just wanted to tell her that John's okay. His mind is great. He's a little broken up, but the therapy is going to cure that."

The next day, he was told that Carol was on her way to see him. He climbed out of bed to greet her, peered down the long corridor, spotted her as she came through a set of double doors. From the deep dip in her gait he could see she was severely crippled. He was stunned, knew John had no idea anything had happened to her.

"God," he said to himself, "how much do we have to endure?"

*　*　*

A day or so before he was released on March 14, McCain was summoned by a team of North Vietnamese officials. He noticed a tape recorder in the room.

"The doctors have been asking about your condition," said one of the officials.

"That's interesting," replied McCain.

"You know, the doctors that operated on you," the official said.

"Oh, yes," said McCain.

"We wonder if you would like to say a word of thanks to the doctors for the operation on your leg," the official continued.

"Well, not exactly," said McCain, "but I'm extremely curious since I haven't seen the assholes for five years why they should have their curiosity aroused at this point."

McCain and the official stared at each other.

"I know they've been awfully busy," said McCain, a ball-buster to the end.

On receiving the news that John was free and had landed in the Philippines, Carol called the kids into the house, which she had filled in her husband's absence with all sorts of animals—dogs, cats, birds, fish, gerbils.

"Your daddy is coming home," she said. "He is out. They cannot get him anymore."

Andy and Doug cheered. Sydney, who was six, looked puzzled.

"Where will he sleep?" she asked.

"He will sleep in my bed, with me," replied Carol.

Sydney thought that over for a few seconds.

"And what will we feed him?" she asked.

CHAPTER SEVENTEEN

THE WATER WALKER

There's something happenin' here,
What it is ain't exactly clear.

—BUFFALO SPRINGFIELD, 1967

After two tours in Vietnam, Chuck Krulak was back at Annapolis in the fall of 1972 as a company officer, overseeing 150
rambunctious midshipmen. He liked the job, but Headquarters had
handed him an additional duty that was driving him berserk. He was
put in charge of recruitment, making sure that the Marine Corps secured its full complement of graduating seniors the following June.
Throughout most of its history, the Academy had rarely if ever failed
to meet its Marine quota. That changed with the Class of 1968, Jim
Webb and Ollie North's class, the first one ever to fall short of the
prescribed goal. The succeeding three classes, spooked by continuing
hostilities in Vietnam and the unblinking smiles of friends on The
Board, also missed the mark. Headquarters told Krulak to reverse the
trend, in the process increasing the quota by about forty.

Krulak was desperate for a good idea. Then one hit him. He placed
a call to a friend in Quantico and explained his plan. A few weeks
later, hundreds of midshipmen jammed Mitscher Auditorium after
evening meal. Krulak had invited men from all four classes with even
a remote interest in taking their commissions in the Marine Corps,
promising a presentation that would be worth their time. There was
the usual after-dinner banter as the mids trooped in, much of it directed at the more committed Marine prospects by buddies lured to
the event solely by its amusement potential. Marines might be sailors
who had failed to evolve, but they always put on a good show.

The lights dimmed, quieting the crowd. Only the curtain over the
darkened stage remained illuminated. Martial music, quickly identi-

fied as the theme from the film *Patton*, began to drift through the hall. Anticipation gripped the audience. As the music swelled, the curtain parted, revealing a second curtain bearing an enormous American flag. The midshipmen burst into applause.

A solitary figure stood before the Stars and Stripes, a trim Marine captain at rigid attention, medals dripping from his chest. His immaculate dress blues were set off by his white gloves and white barracks cap. An elegant, scarlet-lined boat cloak draped his shoulders. Those nearest the stage recognized him immediately and yelled out his name. Soon the shouts were coming from all parts of the auditorium.

Hey, it's North! Okay, Ollie! *A-ru-gah! A-ru-gah!*

Few who saw North's performance that night have forgotten it. For the next forty-five minutes, marching up and down the stage in the glare of the flag, he held the midshipmen spellbound. Never glancing at a note, he described what it meant to be a Marine officer, the rigors and the rewards. He spoke of the challenge of leading men in combat, of making snap decisions in life-or-death situations. He laid heavy emphasis on the special responsibility borne by officers entrusted with the lives of brave young men. Unlike Patton (or Patton as interpreted by actor George C. Scott), he did not beat his chest or recount his own considerable battlefield exploits. Even so, a few Marine officers in attendance, themselves decorated Vietnam veterans, were troubled by the Patton analogy, with its undercurrent of impetuous leadership and borderline lunacy. They were also uncomfortable with the romanticized, guts-and-glory portrait of Marine life that North conjured up for the midshipmen.

Afterward, midshipmen departed the auditorium quietly, wary of gushing over North and opening themselves to ridicule from friends who, unlikely as it seemed, may have been unmoved by the occasion. A month later, on service selection night, first classmen filed into Smoke Hall only to see North standing at a relaxed parade rest at the Marine sign-up table, waiting to welcome his new comrades into the Corps. The Marines not only made their quota; for the first time in years they had a waiting list.

The midshipmen in attendance that night had not been at the Academy when North was an undergraduate. They recognized him from his occasional stints as celebrity referee at the brigade boxing smokers staged by Coach Emerson Smith, and from Quantico, where he ran second classmen through one-week training stints in the summer. He was magnetic in both roles. At the fights, the boxers often seemed secondary to North's roaming presence in the ring. He separated them with theatrical scowls, warned them with overblown gestures, drenched them with concern when hurt. At Quantico, he was the midshipmen's friend and taskmaster. He gave every midshipman his home phone number, urged them to call if they had a problem. He told them he expected a lot from them. He delivered, too, turning a week of heat, dust, and swamp gas into a time to remember. Lee Johnson, '73, recalled an outdoor lecture in which North staged an armored version of the car chase from the movie *Bullitt*. As he was speaking, the mids picked up a low rumbling in the distance. North ignored the noise, even as it grew louder. Suddenly two heavy tanks roared over the berm behind him, hung in the air as if suspended from skyhooks, then slammed to earth and screamed to a halt before the wide-eyed midshipmen.

North achieved stardom at Quantico, not because he was so highly decorated—the place was awash with heroes—but because he made the sexiest course there, patrolling, even more exciting. For three years, from late 1969 through early 1973, hundreds of boot lieutenants relished his antics as he taught them the rudiments of pooping and snooping. He crashed through doors, fired off blank rounds in the classroom, booby-trapped outdoor lecture sites, rappelled from choppers, crawled up behind fellow instructors (they were in on the stunt) in bush hat, camouflage paint, and tree branches, ambushed them, searched their bodies, dragged them off the stage, and took over their classes. Sometimes North's special effects included a K-bar knife clamped in his teeth. "We looked forward to his classes, couldn't wait," said John Sattler, '71. "And he never let us down. Never." He was more than an entertainer. The stunts had a purpose, serving as a point of departure for the lecture to come. For many students, North became a role model. "As a young lieutenant, if I could have been any officer in the world, that's who I wanted to be," said Sattler.

Even as North went about making himself into the embodiment of the Marine Corps officer, he was having grave doubts about his chosen profession. They came to a head in 1973. Thanks to Dick Schulze, and a cameo appearance by Texas billionaire Ross Perot, he resolved them.

North, as related in his autobiography, *Under Fire*, had joined the Marine Corps with plans to become a pilot, but had selected the infantry because he feared the war would be over before he finished flight school. He never gave up on the idea of flying, though, and applied for flight training while teaching at Quantico, only to learn the age limit for new pilots had been lowered, making him ineligible.

Disappointed, he began looking for opportunities in civilian life, was intrigued by a Dallas firm, Electronic Data Systems, founded by

Perot, a 1953 Annapolis graduate. EDS was one of the hottest new companies in the burgeoning computer service field and Perot was hiring Academy graduates in battalion strength, especially Vietnam veterans. It was, North decided, the closest thing he would find to a military environment outside the military. He submitted his resignation to Headquarters Marine Corps and applied to EDS.

A few days later, he received a call from Schulze, then working for the Secretary of the Navy. "We hate to lose you, but I understand you're interested in EDS," North quotes Schulze as saying. "Ross Perot is coming in next week to have lunch with the secretary, and I'd like you to join us." North, relieved that Schulze had not tried to talk him into rescinding his resignation, said he'd be there.

After lunch, the secretary having departed, Schulze sat quietly by as Perot launched into an eloquent thirty-minute lecture on why the Corps needed men like North. According to North, he touched all the bases, the value of serving your country, patriotism, mom, apple pie, the works.

Concluding his pitch, Perot said, "Well, what are you going to do?"

"I guess I'm staying," replied North, sheepishly.

"Good," said Perot. "If that's the way you feel . . ." He turned to Schulze, who handed him North's resignation letter. Passing it on to North, Perot said, "Why don't you just tear this up?"

A great story, drawn directly from North's autobiography. The question is, Is it true?

Schulze died in 1983. Sally Schulze, his widow, said her husband never mentioned lunching with or even meeting Perot during the time he worked for the Secretary of the Navy or after. Perot was already a national figure by the early 1970s, in part because of the success of his firm, more so because of his efforts to assist Vietnam POWs. Had her husband lunched with Perot, Sally Schulze said, he almost certainly would have told her about it. He always recounted events of more than passing interest when he came home at night.

Chuck Krulak, then and now one of North's closest friends, said North never talked to him about going to flight school or submitting his resignation even though they were in frequent contact during that period.

"Never heard a thing about wanting to be an aviator, never heard anything about his desire to retire," said Krulak. "That's completely news to me. . . . If he was thinking about getting out, my gosh, he really covered it [up] in all my discussions with him and Paul Goodwin never mentioned it to me and Dutch Schulze never mentioned that Ollie was thinking about getting out. That's not saying he didn't. He just really kept it, obviously kept it pretty close hold."

Perot does not remember any of it and questions the accuracy of the story. "I have no recollection of this at all," he said in a 1993 interview. "First time I remember meeting Ollie North was when he was on the National Security Council." That was nearly ten years later. Perot also said he never met Schulze and does not recall ever having lunch with any sitting Secretary of the Navy.

"The facts are Ollie has a very active imagination," said Perot. "See, Ollie believes this stuff. . . . He lives in this fantasy world and that's his problem, not mine."

North's view of the contradiction? "I point out that those of us who remember things differently aren't doing anything but remembering things differently."

In Vietnam North earned the respect of subordinates, peers, and superiors alike. At Quantico, however, a pattern took shape that would trail him throughout his Marine Corps career, including his years in the White House. To men under him, he was the perfect officer. To his bosses, the fair-haired boy. To his peers, a talented but flawed Marine, at times a horse's ass. A few held him in open contempt.

Some of the disdain may be chalked up to professional jealousy. Like Jim Webb, he had been promoted to captain ahead of his class. And wherever he served, he became first among equals, as much a water walker in his way as John Poindexter. But Poindexter rarely stirred resentment. North often did. From Quantico on, he managed to transform himself into one of the more unpopular men in the Marine Corps, at least among officers of similar rank.

There were exceptions. Some of his peers thought the world of him. Among superiors, his champions tended to be men who counted, like Dick Schulze and Chuck Krulak, officers in positions to advance his career because they themselves were moving steadily up the ladder.

For some of his detractors, the antics at Basic School rankled. The stunts were in line with time-honored Quantico tradition, wake-up calls concocted to induce student lieutenants, weary from the demanding daily regimen, to pay attention to the lesson. But North, in the opinion of many, went overboard. "Too much flash," said one fellow instructor. "The word hotdog fits him. A hotdog is a guy who moves before he thinks." By itself, the hotdogging did not explain the hostility of his peers, but it formed the backdrop for deeper concerns.

At Basic School, North established his reputation as a workaholic, often sleeping on the floor of his office rather than making the fifteen-minute drive home to Betsy and the kids. Some admired his dedication. Others were suspicious, viewed his late-night stints as a device to make it look as if he were working harder than everyone else. "To work twenty-four hours a day just to make people say, 'My God, look how dedicated this man is,' is bullshit," said a Marine who served with North at the Basic School.

Another strain began to declare itself at Quantico, one that threatened to adulterate the carefully concocted North persona. Accurately or not, he left some compatriots with the belief that he had lost his desire to lead troops, that he saw command positions as potentially damaging to his career. A commanding officer in many ways is at the mercy of his troops. That was especially true in the 1970s, when anti-military sentiment was high and racial and drug problems pervaded the services. For that reason, so it was said, North preferred operating on his own, a lone gunslinger, rather than taking on responsibility for other men, any one of whom might create an incident that reflected poorly on him. Fairly or not, such criticism was fed by the fact that he spent his entire three years at the Basic School teaching patrolling, rather than splitting his time between instructing and leading a platoon of student lieutenants, as did most of his peers.

There was a revealing dustup during his time at Quantico. North was invited to a Mess Night hosted by Annapolis midshipmen planning to enter the Marine Corps. Mess Nights are proper occasions, at least until the after-dinner speeches conclude and the fun and games begin. It was during this latter period that Don Price, then a major stationed at the Academy, noticed North chewing out a midshipman. North, it seemed, had queried the young man about his reasons for joining the Marines and found the responses lacking in ardor. Price, a grade North's senior, told him to lay off. North bristled and continued to upbraid the midshipman. Price ordered North into the men's room, hoping to cool him down. For a few minutes they were eyeball to eyeball, North with a cigar stub clenched in his teeth, Paul Goodwin incarnate. There was some shoving, but no blows. Others quickly separated them.

"It didn't diminish my respect for him," said Price. "It wasn't the first time guys peed on each other's legs at a Mess Night. But I did see another dimension to him, that he could be surly and defiant."

After attending Amphibious Warfare School and a shorter course on nuclear and chemical weapons at Quantico, North was assigned to the Third Marine Division on Okinawa, a tour that kept him overseas nearly all of 1974. On Okinawa, patterns that had begun to emerge at the Basic School crystallized, at least in the eyes of his critics.

During a night training exercise, North commanded the aggressor forces. After midnight he moved two tanks onto the high ground overlooking the friendly battalion command post. Suspecting that security was lax, he ordered his tank commanders to put their vehicles in neutral and let them roll down the slope in the pitch darkness. Firing up the engines near the bottom of the hill, the tanks roared into the encampment. The flustered battalion commander looked outside his operations tent into the muzzle of a tank-mounted ninety-millimeter cannon no more than ten feet away. The North-led aggressors had pulled off an incredible coup, capturing the CP, the battalion commander, and his entire staff.

North had been daring, audacious, and, to Colonel Dave Haughey, grossly irresponsible. "Those tanks could easily have rolled right over somebody," said Haughey, a captain like North at the time and an umpire for the exercise. "If this had been a real battle, what Ollie North did in that particular case was great. However, since this was a training exercise and you've got two sixty-ton monsters coming down a hill and it's in the hours of darkness, it was terribly, terribly dangerous. Combat is one thing; training is something else." Haughey confronted North afterward. North's response: "Hey, nobody got hurt, did they?" Recalling the incident years later, Haughey said, "There's not enough mustard in the world for that hotdog."

The sense that North was wary of command continued to gain currency on Okinawa. The majority of infantry captains led rifle companies for most of their tours. North spent nearly his entire time as officer in charge of the Northern Training Area.

The NTA was rugged mountainous terrain more than thirty miles by dirt road from any other base. "In addition to the challenge and responsibility that I craved, I now had the chance to do all the exciting things the Marine Corps depicts in its recruiting posters—and without getting killed in the process," North writes in *Under Fire*. "We conducted mountain-warfare training, ran jungle-warfare tactics, taught amphibious nighttime raids in rubber boats launched from ships and submarines, rappeled from helicopters, and parachuted with Army and Marine reconnaissance units. We taught survival skills to pilots and air crews, ate snakes and other jungle delights just to impress the new arrivals, and had an absolutely glorious time. It was exhausting and occasionally dangerous, but it was also the most fun I ever had as a Marine."

It was also a long way from commanding troops. By his own account, North's small, tight-knit team of instructors at NTA was handpicked, consisting of former drill instructors and junior officers he had trained himself at Quantico.

Jim Jones, then a captain, now a major general, was a company commander when North ran NTA. Jones wanted a rifle company and he got it, but he remembers it as perhaps his most difficult time in the

Corps. There were racial problems, drugs, and residual antiwar sentiments. On Okinawa in those days, said Jones, anybody who wanted a rifle company could get one.

"It's generally accepted that Ollie carved out the jobs he wanted—high-visibility, low-risk, high-reward possibilities," said Jones. "The NTA was kind of a plum, but it was a low-risk job. The commanding general liked it, wanted things to go well, but it was easy to make things go well. In 1974 what was very tough to do was lead a rifle company." North flatly denies trying to avoid command.

In fact, North did take over a rifle company in the final month of his tour, recruited for the job—he says in *Under Fire*—by the new battalion commander, Lieutenant Colonel Chuck Hester. Jones and others saw it as North getting his ticket punched, nothing more. "Anybody who served over there will tell you that," said Jones. "That was Ollie North."

A bad rap? Perhaps. North, in his book, says he requested an extension of his tour when he took over the company, which was on alert for possible deployment to Vietnam, where the situation was deteriorating. He withdrew the request after Betsy threatened divorce and his battalion commander urged him to go home.

"It's not worth it," North quotes Lieutenant Colonel Hester as telling him. "You care about these guys, and I appreciate that, but nobody else does. The politicians in Washington have thrown away the lives of so many young men. They don't care if your family gets ruined, or your kids grow up without you. The war is over anyway; it's only a question of when the shooting stops. Your giving your life over there won't change a thing. Go home to your family."

A poignant recital, made all the more dramatic by North's noting that "within days" of his departure Hester and the battalion deployed to rescue the crew of the *Mayaguez*, an American merchant ship seized by Cambodian gunboats in the Gulf of Thailand. "Instead of being with them," wrote North, "I was sitting alone in Virginia with what appeared to be an unsalvageable marriage and two children whom I couldn't even see on Christmas." It remained for another Annapolis Marine, Roger Charles, '67, to point out in a review of North's book that the *Mayaguez* rescue mission took place not within days of North's return home in December 1974 but the following May, a full five months later.

Another element seems off-center. North says in *Under Fire* that Lieutenant Colonel Hester asked him when he was due to rotate back to the States just a week before he was scheduled to do so. That means Hester recruited him as a company commander without bothering to check his rotation tour date, a surprising oversight. The RTD is one of the first items on a battalion commander's check list when survey-ing the officer pool. The reason? You don't want to give a man a company if he is getting ready to go home, as North was, especially a company on combat alert. On the other hand, if you thought a return to Vietnam was unlikely, as it most assuredly was in late 1974, and you wanted to help a guy get his ticket punched as a company com-mander . . .

In fact, Hester said in a November 1994 interview that he did not recruit North as a company commander and denied the lengthy quote attributed to him in North's book. North, said Hester, had already relinquished command of the company and departed Oki-nawa when he took over the battalion. Hester recalled that North later served under him at Headquarters Marine Corps where they worked well together. Hester said he thought it likely that some se-nior officer had encouraged North to go home. But it had not been Hester. North, in an interview, reiterated his contention that Hester recruited him.

Then there was this. A few months after his return to the States, North was at a farewell party for Roy Carter, an Annapolis classmate deploying to Okinawa. Recalling their conversation, Carter said, "He was not hesitant about saying—and I'm sure I'm not the only one he said it to—that he didn't want certain responsibilities because they would hurt his career."

Carter had been a big admirer of North's, but he was beginning to see him differently. "Ollie had changed," said Carter. "He wanted to be Commandant of the Marine Corps and he was not hesitant at all about saying it. . . . I thought he had become a zealot, a zealot toward his personal ambition and his career."

In December 1974 Ollie North almost wrecked his Marine Corps career, and he did it without the help of unruly, recalcitrant, or doped-up troops. Dick Schulze weighed in to salvage the situation, though how far he went on North's behalf remains in dispute, as do other aspects of the murky episode.

There is general agreement that the "Dear Larry" letter that North received from Betsy near the end of his tour on Okinawa set in motion the events that followed. It came after he informed her that he had taken command of a company and planned to extend his tour.

As North described it in his autobiography, Betsy said she had fi-nally realized that the Marine Corps was more important to him than she and the children. She told him to stay on Okinawa and "do what-ever it is you need to do." She had had enough. She wanted a divorce and enclosed the name of her lawyer.

North's first reaction was to agree with her assessment of the relationship. "I believed what I was doing really *was* more important than my family. I was worrying about the two hundred and ten Marines whose lives I was responsible for, not to mention the fate of the free world. Betsy would just have to wait."

In retrospect, he conceded that his wife was justifiably angered by his workaholic ways; he had been neglecting his family for years. Others, without disputing that element, said there was more to it: they claimed that Betsy, ignored too long, had found someone else. Few blamed her.

Returning stateside in mid-December with orders to the Corps's most prestigious post, the Marine Barracks in Washington, North learned to his amazement that Betsy was serious about the divorce. "I meant what I wrote in that letter," he quotes her as telling him on the phone. "I'm sorry, but if you want to see the kids, call my lawyer." The lawyer was out of town for the holidays. His secretary told North to call back in January.

He took a room at the BOQ in Quantico, physically ill and emotionally strung out. He had come down with a bad case of bronchitis before leaving Okinawa. On the trip home he was coughing up blood and had blood in his urine. Now he was on antibiotics, but the medicine was not helping.

"I was hurt, angry, and confused," he writes. "Physically, I was in miserable shape with a terrible cough that wouldn't go away, no desire to eat, and for the first time in my life, an inability to sleep. For years I had exercised every single day, but now I could barely drag myself out of bed. Today, I can look back on that period and recognize the full-blown symptoms of depression. Back then, I wouldn't have admitted it even if I had recognized it. *Real* men didn't have that kind of problem—and I knew I was a real man."

To this point, the story is not in dispute, at least not so that it matters. What happened next is very much in dispute.

According to North, he was driving up Interstate 95 from Quantico to visit his old friend from Vietnam, Bill Haskell, when he started coughing so violently he nearly ran off the road. Realizing he needed medical attention quickly, he reported to the Quantico dispensary only to find Dick Schulze, then the commanding officer of the Basic School, waiting to take a physical.

"Blue? You look terrible," said Schulze, using North's nickname from Vietnam. "What's the matter?" North was in tears. Schulze told the doctor to look him over. After a complete physical, the doctor said, "You're a wreck. You've probably got parasites, you're anemic, and you have fluid in one of your lungs. I'm putting you in the hospital today."

Schulze drove North to Bethesda Naval Hospital, where he was admitted, presumably for the physical ailments enumerated by the doctor. For the next several days he languished in the hospital, reading any book he could get his hands on, watching daytime TV, fixating on the bad news from Vietnam. He was not getting better and Christmas was approaching.

"And yet I refused to admit that I was depressed," he writes. "I knew I was angry at Betsy, and I was convinced that all of this was her fault. On top of that, the war I had fought in and trained for, and trained so many others to fight, was ending all wrong. I was in trouble, but I didn't know it."

After a few days, he says, Schulze told him that he had conferred with the doctors, who told him that North needed psychiatric help. Schulze said he agreed. North exploded at him. *"I'm fine. There's nothing wrong with me! I am very calm! I don't need that kind of help!"* (North's italics.)

Schulze persisted and eventually North, grudgingly, took his advice.

"Now this was something *really* new," he writes. "I don't know what I expected: drugs, electroshock therapy, straitjackets, padded cells. But there was none of that. Instead, I was put on a regimen of 'milieu therapy'—hours of group discussions and one-on-one sessions with a battery of doctors. I hated it. It was humiliating even to be there. I kept looking around and asking myself, *Who are these people, and why am I here?"*

North's description of the near breakup of his marriage and how he and Betsy survived as a couple is one of the most dramatic sections in his book. In short, North says the therapy at Bethesda helped to an extent, but that marriage-counseling sessions with a Quantico chaplain were the key to saving the marriage.

"The recovery process took time," North writes. "It began the moment I turned around on Interstate 95 on that bleak December day, and it required the help of several people. There were ups and downs along the way, but by the time Saigon fell at the end of April, I was able to watch it on television with Betsy. I cried unashamedly, and Betsy had her arm around me. She understood."

That is the sanitized version, much of which is probably true. Where it seems to veer from reality is in North's explanation of how he wound up in the hospital and the seriousness of his condition.

There is no doubt that Schulze played a role, for the most part a kindly, wise, and sympathetic one. But accounts of how he became involved vary radically from North's.

Sally Schulze, Schulze's widow, said her husband told her the following story when he came home from work later that same day.

North was in the waiting room of the Quantico dispensary when Schulze arrived on an unrelated matter. "What's the matter?" Schulze asked. "You look terrible." North said he was upset, was trying to see a psychiatrist, and was distraught at being forced to wait.

Schulze, alarmed, went to find the psychiatrist. When he returned to the waiting room with the doctor North had vanished. They raced out to the parking lot to look for him.

"They found him in his car, sitting in his car, threatening suicide," said Mrs. Schulze. She could not recall the details of what was said. She did remember her husband telling her that North was holding a pistol in his lap, she believes a .45, as he talked of suicide.

"So they got an ambulance and took him to Bethesda," said Mrs. Schulze.

Schulze told the same story to a fellow Marine officer, a close friend of North.

"Ollie was in a car ready to do it," said the friend. Did he have a weapon? "Yes. And that's when he went to the hospital."

The friend said that Schulze managed to calm North down, then arranged for him to enter Bethesda.

"Schulze saved his life, literally," said the friend, who told the story on the condition that he not be identified by name. "He was suicidal. . . . It was just a miracle."

With North safely in Bethesda, Schulze ran down friends from the old battalion—Paul Goodwin and Chuck Krulak, both still Marines, Richmond O'Neill, another platoon leader, then a civilian in Houston, others wherever he could find them—and urged them to call and cheer up their old comrade.

Schulze softened the story the next day when he told it to North's classmate, Roy Carter, while keeping it graphic enough that Carter understood the situation was serious.

Carter, who was stationed at Basic School, said Schulze came up to him and asked how well he knew North. Carter replied that he knew him well. "Well, I found him wandering around the PX in a daze yesterday," said Schulze, who then informed Carter that North was at Bethesda and could benefit from seeing friends.

Carter, who had not yet begun to sour on North, visited him a day or so later. North talked about the incredible pressure he had been under on Okinawa. According to Carter, he also used a phrase he did not use in his book: "He said, 'I think I had a nervous breakdown.' "

North, in a December 1993 interview, denied there had been a weapon involved in the events immediately preceding his hospitalization. Asked if he had ever considered himself suicidal, he replied, "There are things between my wife and I that are going to remain private until the day I die, all right, and that's the way they're going to stay." *Under Fire*, he maintained, was "absolutely accurate."

There was more. Schulze, out of loyalty, affection, or the Oriental belief that by saving a man's life you somehow take responsibility for it, went way out on a professional limb for North.

"Schulze subsequently insured that this incident did not reflect badly on him," confided a North friend, who said it would have been "a monstrous stain" on North's career.

Precisely what Schulze did is not clear, though there is little doubt that he did something. Various published accounts have said that Schulze purged North's records of any reference to his hospitalization. But there is another possibility, one more in keeping with Schulze's reputation for integrity.

According to the North friend, the more likely scenario is that Schulze spoke to the right people, dissuading them from making any written report on the episode that might find its way into North's service record, formally known as his Officer's Qualification Record, or OQR, the file normally considered by promotion boards.

In other words, Schulze probably never pulled anything from North's OQR; he simply threw himself in front of anything relating to the illness headed in that direction.

North and Betsy, in any event, were reconciled. Not long after, he was deep-selected for major. Once again, the water walker was traipsing the waves.

CHAPTER EIGHTEEN

ADULT EDUCATION

B ud McFarlane spent the final six months of his second Vietnam tour as the operations officer of an artillery battalion, an extraordinarily busy time. Near the end he was smoking three packs of cigarettes a day and getting by on four hours of sleep. He lost weight, too, easily twenty-five pounds. But he never felt sluggish, thought of himself as enormously efficient, a perception borne out by his fitness reports.

Back in the States by the fall of 1968, he spent the next three years as a staffer at Headquarters Marine Corps, housed in a dismal set of buildings adjacent to the Pentagon known as the Navy Annex. At first he worked for a general who was trying to promote an amphibious landing on the coast of North Vietnam. McFarlane thought it was a fine idea, as did many battlefield veterans who had long since concluded that the price of the Johnson-McNamara "measured response" strategy was too high and now wanted to take the fight onto the enemy's home turf.

He was reassigned the following spring, first as the Marines' Latin American desk officer, a year later to a similar billet with responsibility for the Middle East and South Asia. In both jobs, he spent most of his time reviewing contingency plans for U.S. military action in the countries under his purview. As always, he did the job efficiently and without complaint, but found the contingency planning process alternately laughable and deceitful, a ploy by which the services sought to justify bigger budgets and an expansion of forces.

He also detected a tacit understanding among the four services by which each branch carved out a piece of the action, whether it made tactical sense or not. Planning documents invariably called for what amounted to the war movie fiction of ethnically diverse fire teams writ large, the Army, Navy, Air Force, and Marines preempting the roles of the Irishman, Jew, WASP, and optional fourth guy. "And I didn't have enough guts to stand up ever and say, This is a crock," recalled McFarlane. "I didn't make waves. I just did the contingency plans."

Misgivings aside, his diligence continued to catch the eyes of his superiors. As a junior major, he was elevated in the fall of 1970 to the NATO desk, normally a senior lieutenant colonel's billet. NATO planning had an exhilarating if fearsome sweep to it, running the gamut from border skirmishes to nuclear war. For the first time, he was a player, if a small one, in matters of grand strategy and alliance politics. He thought of the job as a first step onto the global stage that he had seen as his destiny since Geneva.

At Headquarters, he also developed a bitter attitude toward the antiwar movement. For the most part, he saw its members as "long-haired, tie-dyed assholes" using words like peace and love to obscure cowardice. He wondered how the same nation that had produced his own generation—one that in the main did not question concepts such as duty, honor, country—could turn out people like that only a few years later.

Over the years, the armed forces had been well represented in the ranks of White House Fellows by, among others, Chuck Larson. But never by a Marine. In 1971 the program got two, both majors, Bud McFarlane and John Grinalds.

Grinalds graduated near the top of his West Point class in 1959, the same year McFarlane finished Annapolis. He took his commission in the Marine Corps, an unusual but permissible step in those days. After Basic School, he attended Oxford on a Rhodes Scholarship. During two tours in Vietnam, he accumulated an impressive array of personal decorations, led by the Silver Star and two Bronze Stars. As White House Fellows, he and McFarlane became fast friends, building an enduring relationship. Grinalds would soon prove an influential figure in the life of a young Marine officer then stationed at Quantico named Oliver North.

Then as now, only a handful of Fellows actually worked in the White House. Most were farmed out to various executive branch departments and agencies. Slated for Agriculture, McFarlane finagled a job in the White House legislative office, the President's lobbying arm, housed in the East Wing.

"I was overwhelmed with this sense of being privileged to work there and challenged to measure up and in awe of the presidency and totally deferential to the office," he said. "At the beginning I never expected to see the President. I thought that surely I was too low a station in life to aspire to actually see the presidential deity, but that I could justify my existence only by traditional kinds of hard work and imagination. And so I decided my best course was just to come earlier, stay later, work harder in my little niche and stay out of sight and don't make trouble."

He got an education at the White House, a valuable one, though it was no more uplifting than his stint at Marine Headquarters. The legislative office was staffed by a corps of lobbyists whose job was to power Richard Nixon's bills through Congress while beating back the ones the President opposed. Their weapons included wheedling, cajoling, and arm-twisting of a nature McFarlane's congressman father never told him about. The stakes were high. Nixon had an ambitious package of domestic measures on Capitol Hill. Amid escalating antiwar sentiment, the President was also fighting a rearguard action against legislation to end or severely limit continued American involvement in Vietnam.

McFarlane was losing his illusions about Congress, too. He knew that senators and congressmen were advocates for their states and districts, but he went to the White House believing that the foremost concern of lawmakers was the good of the nation, the well-being of all Americans. He discovered that he had it backward. If it was good for the First District of Illinois or the Eighth District of Pennsylvania, then it was good for the U.S.A. If not, not. Tobacco subsidies, a textile bill, a new aircraft carrier, Christ, even war and peace. At least that's how he read it.

He had orders to the Armed Forces Staff College after the White House, but they were scrapped when William Timmons, his boss, was promoted in the summer of 1972 and moved to the West Wing, taking McFarlane with him. In contrast to McFarlane's disenchantment with Congress, his regard for the President rivaled the awe in which plebes at Annapolis held first classmen. In truth, he had never even seen Richard Nixon in the flesh. If he had, he said, "I think I would have braced up . . . and hit a bulkhead."

The West Wing, the White House power center, was a new world. McFarlane occupied a small cubicle adjacent to Timmons's suite, down the hall from the Oval Office. He saw Nixon often, though they had no personal relationship in those days, and exchanged pleasantries with Kissinger, the national security adviser, and his deputy, Alexander Haig. On paper, Timmons was the President's senior legislative adviser, but with Nixon's reelection campaign in full swing he was devoting more of his time to politics, leaving the routine office chores to McFarlane.

The Watergate break-in occurred in June, but it would be months before it mushroomed into a full-blown political scandal. McFarlane, an innocent in mufti, saw little likelihood Watergate would reach Nixon and tended to discount its impact on the administration.

Timmons, meanwhile, was distracted by a separate controversy relating to the 1972 Republican National Convention. McFarlane was never touched by what came to be known as the ITT scandal, but what he glimpsed on the margins was a revelation.

"I began in Timmons's office to meet . . . the groupies and the professional pol handlers and advance men, convention mongers," he said. "And for the first time in my life began to understand it is a pretty sleazy bunch of people."

In June 1973, McFarlane was marking time in a dreary wood frame building next to Arlington Cemetery. He had completed his White House fellowship six months earlier, but rave reviews from 1600 Pennsylvania Avenue had elicited only yawns from his superiors at Marine Headquarters. Without explanation, they bumped him off the fast track, assigning him to a backwater of the Corps known as the Education Branch. In dark moments, he suspected that he was being punished for enjoying his White House duty too much. To Marines, the things that count are mud and blood and leading troops in combat; fondness for less gritty pursuits bespeaks a character flaw.

Deliverance was only a phone call away. The man on the other end of the line was Brent Scowcroft, deputy to Henry Kissinger, President Nixon's national security adviser. Calling from San Clemente, Scowcroft told McFarlane that his boss was in the market for a new military aide. Do you want to interview for the job? asked Scowcroft. Yes, sir, I do, replied McFarlane.

The thirty-six-year-old major was amazed to find a four-engine Air Force Jetstar standing by at Andrews Air Force Base to ferry him to California. At the Western White House, as Nixon's San Clemente retreat was known, Scowcroft asked McFarlane a few questions, explained the job, then sent him off to see Kissinger.

On the way, he trooped a line of offices that left him slack-jawed. First, Richard Nixon's. Then the field headquarters of Alexander Haig, the White House chief of staff. At the end, commanding a panoramic view of the Pacific, Kissinger's office.

"Before I even got in the office I was kind of just blown away," McFarlane later said. "God, it was just kind of an edifice of power that was well beyond anything I had ever been exposed to."

Kissinger, wearing a tie despite the informality of the beachfront locale, did not look up or otherwise greet him. Instead, he paged silently through McFarlane's file. Kissinger, McFarlane knew, was distressed about losing Jonathan Howe, the able Navy commander who had been his military aide for the past four years.

Kissinger reviewed McFarlane's papers for what seemed a full half hour. At last, in his measured German accent, Kissinger said, "You know, I don't think it's possible for anyone to replace Jon Howe, a man of enormous talent and intellect." Thanks a lot, thought McFarlane, reading the remark as a commentary on his own credentials.

"Are you willing to work like crazy for no reward whatsoever?" asked Kissinger. "You know, I'm not in the business of hiring self-promoters."

There was no pretense at dialogue. Kissinger spoke in pronouncements. McFarlane responded to each with what he later termed "some obsequious acknowledgment," meaning Yes, sir, I understand that, sir, I'll do my best, sir.

Drained by the interview, McFarlane reported back to Scowcroft. "How'd it go?" asked Scowcroft.

"He didn't say anything positive," murmured the dejected McFarlane.

"Did he say anything negative?"

"No, sir."

"Then you're in. He never says anything positive."

To McFarlane, it was the chance of a lifetime.

"I was finally getting into what had become an obsession after I left Geneva," he said. "I knew that someday I was going to be able to work in shaping U.S. foreign policy and this seemed to me to be the ultimate opportunity for learning and maybe even contributing to it as a young officer. And I was just thrilled. I don't know when I've ever been as genuinely excited as I was when I was hired there. I really felt blessed, that there was a purpose in this, that I was really a chosen person to have such good fortune."

As if to ratify his high expectations, he managed to hitch a ride back to Washington aboard a plane with "United States of America" emblazoned on its fuselage—one of the presidential jets.

On paper the military aide to the national security adviser is an exalted horse holder. Jonathan Howe, Annapolis '57, with a doctorate from the Fletcher School of Law and Diplomacy at Tufts, expanded the position far beyond its job description. By the time McFarlane returned from his brief exile to succeed him in July 1973, Howe was the NSC's de facto chief of staff. The two men overlapped for six months, then Howe left to command a destroyer.

The deepening Watergate scandal aside, those first six months provided a fresh learning experience for McFarlane, a fly on the wall at a fascinating time, the period surrounding the October 1973 Arab-Israeli War. As the crisis unfolded, he sat at rapt attention as the National Security Council, led by Nixon and Kissinger, sorted through intelligence reports and plotted the American response.

As in any crisis, there were more questions than answers. What's happening on the ground? Can we get more information? What can we do diplomatically? Militarily? How will our adversaries react? What about our friends? As the NSC swung into action, McFarlane discovered the bleak reality of crisis management, that leaders must make tough decisions on the basis of incomplete, at times suspect information.

He was anything but a bystander in another major foreign policy episode. On orders from Kissinger, Jonathan Howe, then McFarlane, as the latter revealed in his 1994 autobiography, *Special Trust,* passed highly sensitive intelligence information on Soviet capabilities to the Chinese. The information included American assessments of Soviet military dispositions and readiness, not just of nuclear forces, but the positioning of conventional units along the Chinese border and at sea. In exchange, McFarlane says in his book, the Chinese "gave us access to invaluable sites for intelligence gathering on the Soviet Union that were not available anywhere else in the world."

The exchanges, about which McFarlane assumed the Soviets soon learned, had to cause "enormous ambiguity" in the minds of Kremlin leaders. If the United States was sharing intelligence with the Chinese, the next step might well be military cooperation. In McFarlane's estimation, the Soviets now had to fear "facing not one rival military giant, but two."

McFarlane asserts that the predicament in which Moscow found itself proved enormously draining economically and contributed ultimately to the collapse of the Soviet empire and the end of the Cold War. However, had Congress known about the exchanges, he further theorizes, they would have been immediately curtailed or ended.

"Kissinger took a risk and clearly withheld information from Congress," said McFarlane, with an obvious eye to intelligence-sharing activities during the Iran-Contra affair. "Yet in doing so, he undeniably nurtured a relationship of profound importance to our security. The Nixon-Kissinger strategy to outflank the Soviet Union by engaging the country on its southern border was a historic stroke of geopolitical wisdom, and one with extremely valuable returns for all Americans."

On the homefront, Watergate was drawing blood. A siege mentality gripped the White House staff. Few were immune. As far back as 1969, Kissinger, supposedly alarmed by leaks to the press that he felt endangered national security, had approved FBI wiretaps on the home and office phones of certain reporters and some of his own NSC aides. McFarlane now found himself plugged into the prevailing paranoia, forced to review wiretap transcripts for security leaks, a chore he despised.

But he had an even more dispiriting duty, one that all but completed the education of a man who had never purposely strayed beyond his Boy Scout roots. Kissinger, nothing if not a survivor, had all his calls monitored, taped, and transcribed, including those with the President. At Kissinger's direction, McFarlane became an official eavesdropper, a silent witness to his boss's most sensitive conversations.

There was a lot to hear in the months leading up to Nixon's August 1974 resignation. The President, drunk, profane, his manner alternately pathetic and arrogant, often turned for solace to his chief foreign policy adviser, sometimes issued orders so bizarre that Kissinger, by then both national security adviser and Secretary of State, had no alternative but to ignore them.

The Nixon presidency was perched on a scaffold of its own devising, soon to plunge through the trapdoor into an infamy of historic proportions.

McFarlane watched the Vietnam War hurtling toward its conclusion, never imagining that he would end up playing a minor supporting role in the humiliating final act of a conflict that had ground up so much of his generation.

By then, the spring of 1975, Nixon was gone, having surrendered his office the previous August. McFarlane liked working for Gerald Ford, the new President.

"Ford had this kind of innocent freshness about him . . . that at once worried you and inspired you," he said. "He would come out with these very basic questions that made you kind of shudder and say, 'God, you've got to know that.' . . . But then he would turn right around and work hard, read everything in the book, and perform in a session with a foreign head of state extremely well."

Any chance that Ford could rejuvenate the American commitment to the South Vietnamese was lost a month after he took office when he pardoned Nixon, outraging the public and undercutting his moral authority. By early 1975, when the North Vietnamese launched their final offensive, the South Vietnamese Army did not have the firepower to repel them. The Ford administration begged the newly installed Watergate Congress for a $700 million supplemental appropriation to mobilize fresh South Vietnamese units but the legislators balked. On April 23, Ford, speaking at Tulane University, referred to Vietnam as "a war that is finished."

Not quite. On April 29, as North Vietnamese rockets bombarded the Saigon airport, Ambassador Graham Martin ordered the emergency evacuation of Americans and South Vietnamese facing imprisonment and worse at the hands of enemy troops poised on the outskirts of the city.

The next day and a half ranks with the most ignominious episodes in the history of the nation. Panic gripped Saigon. Television pictures shot by intrepid, die-hard cameramen showed Americans and South Vietnamese on the roof of the U.S. embassy clambering helter-skelter aboard helicopters while other Vietnamese clung to the skids as the choppers lifted off. Mobs of Vietnamese desperately tried to scale the wall of the embassy grounds in hopes of finding a safe haven or joining the general exodus.

From his chancery office, the sixty-three-year-old Martin, racked by pneumonia, directed the evacuation. Over the previous two weeks, he had resisted White House urgings that he set the evacuation plan in motion, believing to the end that the situation could be salvaged.

As the White House screamed for details on the progress of the evacuation, McFarlane was in his West Wing cubbyhole adjacent to Kissinger's office, monitoring message traffic among Martin, the Pentagon, and State. From noon Washington time on April 29 until it was over, he was passing information on the progress of the evacuation to Kissinger and, through him, to President Ford.

At times, he talked directly to Martin. The ambassador, determined to save as many Vietnamese as possible, had taken it upon himself to expand the airlift. At first he told Washington he had to get six hundred Americans out of the embassy. Soon, though, McFarlane saw a loaves-and-fishes operation taking shape. After several waves of choppers had lifted off, Martin radioed that he still had six hundred and fifty people left.

"Look," McFarlane remembered Kissinger saying, "tell him from me, the Secretary of State, that I understand the pathos and personal anguish that he must be going through, but his President has decided that we must evacuate all Americans immediately and that Americans must be given priority and to bring this thing to a close as quickly as possible."

McFarlane passed the directive on to Martin, who acknowledged it, but continued to shepherd more Vietnamese aboard the choppers. McFarlane transmitted similar messages throughout the day. As darkness fell in Washington he was still getting reports of fresh waves of choppers lifting off from the embassy roof.

An anguishing night for McFarlane. He saw his experiences as bookends for the entire Vietnam tragedy. Memories stabbed at him. He remembered that March day in 1965 when his artillery battery landed at Danang. *Welcome to the Gallant Marines.* Hopes had been high then, the American commitment seemingly unshakable. Until independence is guaranteed, declared LBJ a month after the Marines arrived, "there is no human power that is capable of forcing us from Vietnam." Now, by a quirk of fate, McFarlane was holding an open line to the man feebly clutching the remnants of that pledge. Kissinger, usually brusque with subordinates, seemed to sense his aide's emotions. "He was more gentle than I've ever seen him that night," said McFarlane.

Finally, Ford and Kissinger told McFarlane to order Martin onto the next helicopter. Throughout the day, adhering to protocol and his own sense of propriety, McFarlane had addressed Martin as Mr. Ambassador. By now, though, they had been through a lot together. As Martin renewed his demand for more time, McFarlane cut him off. "Graham," he said, "you have your orders." Martin got the message. Clasping the folded American flag that had flown over the embassy in better times, he boarded a chopper.

"Mr. Secretary," said McFarlane to Kissinger, "Graham Martin just lifted off."

Shortly before midnight, a weary McFarlane headed home. As he turned the day's events over in his mind, his first thought was that the United States, in throwing in the towel, had crippled its credibility as a reliable ally.

"That lasted about a nanosecond," he recalled. "What pushed it out of my brain was all the dead people."

CHAPTER NINETEEN

A TUTORIAL WITH
THE GREATS

B y August 1973, when Jim Webb returned for his second year at Georgetown, the United States had retired to the sidelines in Vietnam, its role reduced to arms supplier and increasingly lifeless cheerleader. The last group of POWs had come home on April 1, two days after the departure of the remaining American combat units. It was a troubling time for Webb on many levels, including the personal. His marriage, outwardly stable, had become strained. Aside from his daughter, Amy, the one unalloyed good in his life was his impetuous classmate, Leo Kennedy, the Marine who missed the war and decided to become a lawyer. But early in the term, Leo was killed in a bizarre accident.

When Kennedy died, his family gave Webb some bullets he had found years before at Gettysburg. Webb still keeps them with him, moving them from office to office, along with his other treasures, sand from Iwo Jima, a medicine vial from the big cave on Saipan, the notebook his great-grandfather carried while riding with Confederate cavalryman Nathan Bedford Forrest. Kennedy's most enduring bequest to his friend, however, was the frequent exhortation that he read Hemingway.

Webb finally did. By the end of that semester, he had worked his way through everything Hemingway had published, partly as a gesture to Kennedy's memory, mostly because the loss of his friend and the sere aftertaste of the Wales exam had made law classes barely palatable.

He started with *A Moveable Feast*, Hemingway's sketches of his life as a young writer in Paris in the 1920s. He also read the story "Soldier's Home," about a Marine returning too late from World War I, when "the greeting of heroes was over." He found it simple and moving. "I can write that," said Webb.

One Saturday morning he tried, filling page after page of yellow legal paper with a tale of his own. He read it over, knew it was terrible. How did Hemingway do it? he asked himself, how could writing something so simple be so hard? Despite his initial failure, the excitement that had gripped him as he scribbled away convinced him he was on to something.

He resisted books on writing. Instead, he kept reading, but in a new way, not as a passive receptacle of the author's words, but as a student of his craftsmanship. How does Hemingway infuse a few words with such power? Why does he set a scene as he does, mentioning some things, ignoring others? He moved on to Faulkner and Steinbeck, subjecting their works to the same scrutiny, trying to understand how they did what they did, the force of their prose. He began to experiment, employing the techniques he had gleaned from his unwitting mentors. He would later say, "I learned to write by conducting a tutorial with the greats."

In *A Moveable Feast*, Hemingway expresses admiration for the French Impressionists, saying he learned much about writing by studying Cézanne. Webb enjoyed Hemingway, but occasionally found him hard to take. The comment about Cézanne struck him as "typical Hemingway bullshit." Webb often said, half-jokingly, that painting was invented because we didn't have cameras; now we have cameras, so why paint?

He followed Hemingway's lead anyway. He began roaming the National Gallery of Art on Thursday afternoons, when he had no classes, always ending his tours with the Impressionists. One day, browsing among these latest recruits to his tutorial, his eyes settled on a landscape. He was reminded of a favorite passage, the first paragraph of *A Farewell to Arms*, in which Hemingway contrasts the pebbles and rocks in a swiftly flowing stream with a column of troops kicking up dust as they march to the front. If Hemingway had been a painter, Webb told himself, he would have painted that. He crossed the room to study the picture more closely. It was a Cézanne.

In Constitutional Law, the class was debating the War Powers Act of 1973, then before Congress. The discussion had deteriorated into an antiwar free-for-all. Genocidal, racist, the well-worn laundry list, ticked off with the usual high passion and moral arrogance. Webb, a purposeful noncombatant, sat in the rear of the lecture hall reading Hemingway.

The rhetorical piling on continued. What's missing in all this is the human face, Webb decided. Scanning the room, he put a silent question to his classmates: What if I took you or you or you and put you in a grunt squad for five months? What would you be saying now? Not this, he told himself, definitely not this. Laying his book aside, he turned to a fresh page in his legal pad and started a short story about the homecoming of an aimless Harvard undergrad named Will Goodrich who joins the Marines in the belief that he is destined for the Marine Band. Instead, he winds up as a rifleman in Vietnam. *I'll tell you what it did to me,* the story began.

The sentence didn't survive, but Goodrich had staying power. With no advance, no publisher, and little more than anger, pride, and ego to sustain him, Webb settled in to compose, in his words, "an enduring piece of great literature." As the second semester commenced in January 1974, he was writing days, nights, and weekends. "I didn't know what I was doing, really," he said. "It's like the old Irish saying: How do you get over a wall you can't climb? Just throw your hat on the other side." He threw his hat with a flourish, announcing to one and all that he was writing a novel.

He aspired to depict the war as he knew it, a conflict in which young men, some just months removed from the high school gridiron, the local bowling alley, or the steamy back seat of the family car, faced ethical dilemmas, made moral judgments, at times horrible ones, and struggled to survive into adulthood. He labored to capture the confusion of a battlefield on which lines were not neatly drawn, when the friend by day became the enemy at night, where all the soldier usually knew was that, as Webb put it, "someone generally over there just tried to take my head off."

He liked to think he was writing for the young rifleman, wanted him to say as he put the book down, this is real, this is what it was like, the way it smelled, how I felt. He also wanted to impart dignity to the rifleman's service without enmeshing him in the tangled politics of the war. The grunt wasn't his only target. He wanted his law school classmates, and the segment of his generation they represented, to read it as well. He wasn't looking to be their friend, but he wanted them to read the book.

By term's end, he had written eighty thousand words. The novel had begun to take shape, although it would go through seven drafts over the next three years before it was finally accepted for publication. In late spring he took the unfinished manuscript to Lois O'Neill, an editor at Praeger, which had published his earlier book on Micronesia. She singled out a passage in which Hodges, a young Marine lieutenant preparing to leave his hardscrabble Kentucky town for Vietnam, sifts through a mildewed footlocker containing the musty uniform, Purple Heart, and other personal effects of his father, killed in World War II, four months before his birth. "If you can write like this, you're a real writer," said O'Neill.

Buoyed by her praise, unfazed by her reservations, he worked to complete the novel. His second summer in the Marianas intervened, but he returned with a sheaf of notes two inches thick, character sketches, scraps of dialogue, plot revisions. He had been writing in longhand, but he picked up a smashed typewriter free at a damaged-goods sale, unbent the space bar, jury-rigged a handle onto the carriage.

By the second semester of his third and final year at Georgetown he was so far along he cut back on his course load to devote more time to the novel, requiring him to take a last class during the summer of 1975. He did not bother to send out résumés to law firms or other institutions that might be looking to employ young lawyers. He had punched through to a part of himself largely untapped for nearly a decade, and was fully committed to becoming a novelist.

Tom Martin, his friend and onetime squad leader, came up from Nashville that summer, then as now using a wheelchair. Webb was working on his fourth draft. Martin asked to read some of it. "I can't believe this," he said. "Nobody's going to believe it except the people who were there. Show me more."

When he finished, Martin asked, "What are you going to do with this?" Said Webb, "I don't have the slightest idea." Martin knew a newspaper columnist and author, Ed Syers, in Texas. Martin persuaded him to read the manuscript. Syers liked it and sent it to an editor he knew in New York named Ted Purdy.

By then, Purdy was in his seventies and retired. But for decades he had been a major force in New York publishing circles, having closed out his career as editor-in-chief at Putnam. His discoveries included Leon Uris, an ex-leatherneck who wrote *Exodus* and *Trinity*, but who is best known to generations of Marines for his first novel, the World War II epic *Battle Cry*.

One Sunday morning that fall Webb was arguing with Barb, an increasingly frequent occurrence, when the phone rang. It was Purdy. "This is the finest combat writing I've ever read," he told Webb. He said he wanted to work with him on the book. They arranged to meet in Washington a few days later.

Purdy arrived with a long, handwritten critique of the manuscript, enthusiastic about its strong points, unsparing of its faults. The major problem lay in the portrayal of Will Goodrich, the pivotal character, with whom Webb had struggled from the start. The two men closeted themselves for six hours in Purdy's room at the Sheraton Carlton Hotel on K Street. They would spend many such days together. Purdy never told Webb how to handle a character or a scene. Instead, he explained in a professorial manner what worked, what didn't, and pressed Webb to explain what he was trying to do in passage after passage. "This novel is going to grow inside of you," Purdy said. "It is going to last. Don't give up on it."

Over the next year, the book was rejected by a dozen publishers. Webb, cheered on by Purdy, never lost hope. By the summer of 1977, having taken a job on Capitol Hill, he decided it was time to take the D.C. bar exam. Most fledgling lawyers take an intense six-week course to prepare for the test, some withdrawing from the world for that entire period. Webb bought the books for the course and took Friday and Monday off so he would have four consecutive days to study for a Tuesday exam.

By Monday afternoon, he was weary, his brain about to shut down, when a letter slid through the mail slot. It contained a copy of a two-page memorandum on Webb's manuscript from John Kirk, editor-in-chief at Prentice-Hall. Kirk was not sold on the book, but he was clearly interested. The major novels of previous wars, he said in the memo, had gone against the grain of the "accepted pieties" of the day. He mentioned Erich Maria Remarque's *All Quiet on the Western Front*, and *The Naked and the Dead*, the Norman Mailer opus. Webb's book, Kirk said, seemed intent on striking a similarly unpopular stance.

Webb could barely control his excitement. Kirk was the first editor who understood what he was trying to do. Screw the bar exam, said Webb, hauling a six-pack from the refrigerator. He passed the test anyway. A few weeks later, he was summoned to New York for lunch at the Harvard Club with Kirk, a naval aviator of Korean War vintage. Kirk was enthusiastic, but he had a problem. Again it was Goodrich. By this time, Goodrich had gone through several incarnations, as had the crucial section in which he returns to Cambridge from Vietnam with his leg blown off. I think you're missing an opportunity here, said Kirk. Goodrich is the one character who brings the message home. We need to hear more from him. Grinned Webb, Do you want the fifty-six-page version, the thirty-six-page version, the twenty-five-page version, or the three-page version? Kirk explained more fully. Webb got the picture. Back home, he went to his files, retrieved the twenty-five-page version, and shipped it to New York.

John Herrington was a young assistant DA in Ventura County, California, when he first heard of Jim Webb. It was 1978 and Webb was just another unheralded author plugging a book, background noise on the car radio as Herrington and a buddy chatted their way across San Francisco's Bay Bridge on the way to a boxing match.

"Oh, Mr. Webb, Jane Fonda is going to be in San Rafael this weekend," the talk show host said as he wrapped up the interview. "Are you going to catch her?" The question met with dead silence, the kind of silence you notice on the radio. Finally Webb replied, "Jane Fonda can kiss my ass. I wouldn't go across the street to watch her slit her wrist." Herrington, a former Marine twice turned down for Vietnam duty because of a college shoulder injury, turned to his friend and said, "I've got to read that book."

Years later, as Ronald Reagan's White House personnel chief, Herrington would recruit Webb into the administration as an Assistant Secretary of Defense, then promote him vigorously for Secretary of the Navy.

Fields of Fire, as it finally emerged in the fall of 1978, was a morality play performed by a ragtag company of players in camouflage paint. Under Webb's direction, they deliver a gripping, no-holds-barred depiction of the war as experienced by young foot soldiers in Vietnam. Keeping the politics of the war offstage, Webb challenges the reader to engage in the actions of his characters, dusting each scene with ambiguity, offering no pat answers. Some reviewers compared the book to *The Naked and the Dead*, others to *Heart of Darkness*, still others to James Jones's *The Thin Red Line*. The bloodlines traced most directly to *Lord of the Flies*, William Golding's dark tale of boys marooned on an island, slowly losing their connection to civilized behavior. Webb describes the Arizona Valley, where much of the action takes place, as "a veritable island." The climactic combat sequence races to its brutal conclusion on Go Noi Island. And the longer the troops remain on these islands, the meaner they get.

Through it all, Webb weaves a theme of abandonment. "Shit, Lieutenant, you'd hardly know there was a war on," says the platoon sergeant.

"It's in the papers, and college kids run around screaming about it instead of doing panty raids or whatever they were running around doing before, but that's it. Airplane drivers still drive their airplanes. Businessmen still run their businesses. College kids still go to college. It's like nothing really happened, except to other people. It isn't *touching* anybody except us."

The Marines in *Fields of Fire* would be no more at home on a recruiting poster than they are crawling through the paddies of the Arizona. Other than Hodges, the platoon leader, they do not dream heroic dreams or fight for anything beyond the survival of themselves and their friends. They are not in Vietnam to save the world for democracy. Most are simply unlucky. They do not come from privileged homes so they never knew they could beat the draft. Not that many of them would have chosen that course had they known about it. They are throwbacks to earlier days, when young men joined the service because they understood, however vaguely, that it was expected of them, especially in wartime, consciousness-raising not yet having trickled down to the poor and uneducated, both black and white, the ones who fought and died in Vietnam. Webb portrays them with controlled affection, rarely allowing sentiment to blind him to their occasionally deplorable excesses. He establishes the tone on the first page, quoting the words of an anonymous general to correspondent Arthur Hadley:

"And who are the young men we are asking to go into action against such solid odds? You've met them. You know. They are the best we have. But they are not McNamara's sons, or Bundy's. I doubt they're yours. And they know they're at the end of the pipeline. That no one cares. They know."

The lieutenant, Hodges, most resembles his creator. Hodges is pure warrior, the last in his line to troop off to war, the battle in his blood. Webb describes Hodges's forebears as "glorying in the fight like unmuzzled sentry dogs, bred to it, for the benefit of the ravishers who owned and determined the reasons."

Snake, a nineteen-year-old squad leader, resembles the similarly nicknamed James Ward, a member of Webb's platoon killed in Vietnam. An urban tough, the fictional Snake matures and blossoms on the battlefield, finds a home in the Marine Corps. On the street, you ignore him or give him a wide berth. In the bush, you depend on him, follow his lead, trust his judgment, confide in him.

Goodrich is Snake's opposite number. A bright but indifferent student at Harvard, he shares the antiwar attitudes of his Ivy League peers and the law school students who inspired Webb to write the novel. He is the most complex character, the sensitive and alienated outsider who serves as the moral fulcrum upon which the book turns thematically. He is in the squad, but not of it. He does not like his squad mates and they do not like him, dubbing him Senator because of his genteel background. He whines and complains. At one point his action, or lack of it, smacks of cowardice, and a man dies. He hates Snake, yet craves his approval.

Goodrich embodies the ambiguities built into the novel. In a brutal action sequence, he witnesses an atrocity. Snake and three other Marines shoot a Vietnamese couple they suspect of taking part in the execution of two comrades. Goodrich reports the crime to headquarters. While the investigation proceeds behind the scenes, Goodrich blunders on the battlefield, costing himself a leg and another man his life. Snake rescues him from certain death, carrying him to safety across a field raked by machine-gun fire. As Snake drops the delirious Goodrich at Hodges's feet, bullets rip through his torso, his death mirroring the demise of his real-life namesake.

Returning to Cambridge, Goodrich remains confused and troubled by his time in Vietnam, much like the disoriented doughboy in "Soldier's Home." He does not romanticize his experiences or his Marine comrades, but his judgment of them has softened. When it counted, he admits to himself, they were better than he was.

For all the book's virtues, none surpasses Webb's sense of place. The dialogue is crisp and true, the narrative lean, often chilling.

> The god of night pulled his shade across the sky, unleashing all his demons as the gray set in. The platoon moved quickly down the sawgrass trail, racing him, hurrying to beat the black. The black belonged to those others, the night god's children, who frolicked, even murdered under the romance of starbright. Night for the platoon was hiding time, time to dig deep holes and wait in fear for the loneliest of deaths, the impersonal shattering projectile that would just as soon kill a tree or air as man.

The *Washington Post* hailed *Fields of Fire* with a rare front-page review in its trendsetting Style section, coupling the highly favorable critique with a long, colorful profile of Webb. Reviewer Marc Leepson said Webb had at least matched Tim O'Brien's achievement in *Going After Cacciato*, the standard against which Vietnam war fiction was then being judged. *Newsweek* called *Fields* a "stunner." Said reviewer Richard Boeth, "In swift, flexible prose that does everything he asks of it—including a whiff of hilarious farce, just to show he can—Webb gives us an extraordinary range of acutely observed people, not one a stereotype, and as many different ways of looking at that miserable war." *Time* followed three weeks later with another glowing report, placing *Fields* among the best fiction the war had produced. In the *Houston Post*, Harold Scarlett wrote that "few writers since [Stephen] Crane have portrayed men at war with such a ring of steely truth."

Webb did not get rich on the book. The *New York Times*, whose Sunday *Book Review* has the greatest impact on sales, was in the midst of a strike and did not review it. Some critics were put off by Goodrich. Webb could live with the criticism. Along with *Cacciato* and a handful of other Vietnam novels, *Fields of Fire* has endured. A decade after publication, Pulitzer Prize–winning columnist Jimmy Breslin said the book "stands as the most impressive work of fiction done on Vietnam." Against daunting odds, Webb had scaled the wall and retrieved his hat.

CHAPTER TWENTY

REENTRY

Free at last, a smiling John McCain hobbled down the steps of an Air Force C-141 at Clark Air Base in the Philippines on March 14, 1973. He was greeted at the foot of the ramp by Admiral Noel Gayler, who had relieved his father as CINCPAC the previous year. The *New York Times* ran a picture of his descent from the plane on its front page the next day, attesting to his celebrity status among the returning POWs.

A team of debriefers was standing by to break the news of Carol's injuries. Before they could do so, a well-meaning officer, unaware that John knew nothing of his wife's injuries, said, "Carol's been doing fine since her accident."

Later in the day, after he had been put in the picture, he called Carol in Jacksonville.

"There's something I've got to tell you," she said.

"I already know," said John.

"What do you know?" asked Carol.

"I know you had an accident."

"John, it was really bad. You might be upset when you see me."

"Well, you know, I don't look so good myself. It's fine."

At Clark, he was poked and prodded by doctors and fitted with a false tooth, easing his snaggle-toothed appearance. When not closeted with doctors, he read hungrily, trying to fill in the five-and-a-half-year gap in his life. He already knew about the bad things that had happened since he was shot down in October 1967—the Kennedy and King assassinations and Watergate, news his captors were only too eager to provide. He had learned indirectly of the 1969 moon landing, the camp loudspeakers having blared out a 1972 campaign speech in which George McGovern said Nixon could put a man on the moon but he couldn't put an end to the war. Beyond that, he was pretty much in the dark.

After a few days at Clark, he was flown home to Jacksonville. Appropriately enough, he got there on a holiday, St. Patrick's Day. For years Carol and the kids had lived from one holiday to the next. Maybe he'll be home by the Fourth of July, or Thanksgiving, or Groundhog Day, she would say, breaking time into more easily digestible chunks for the children. He was on crutches when he arrived, as were Carol and fourteen-year-old Doug, who had broken a leg playing soccer. The *Jacksonville Times-Union and Journal* headlined its story of the homecoming, "No Limps in Joy of McCain Family Reunion." Carol laughed when she saw it: "I thought, of course, we would live happily ever after."

Carol rented a small beachhouse at South Ponte Vedra, about forty-five minutes from their Orange Park home, so that she and John could have some time alone. She gently questioned him about prison. At first he did not want to talk about it. Finally, he said, "Do you really want to know what happened?" Said Carol, "I really do." Over the next few days he told her all of it.

"What didn't you buy while I was in Vietnam that you'd really like to have?" he asked her one day. Without hesitation, she replied, "A house at the beach." A few days later, on a walk along the oceanfront, they stopped in front of a small cinderblock bungalow. Beaming, John said, "I just bought it."

In the years to come, they would add a bedroom with a large fireplace and a porch, then a deck. On a visit, POW friend Bob Craner helped John build a railing to make it easier for Carol to get over the dunes to the beach. Carol thought of the beachhouse as heaven, the nicest present she had ever received. Eight years later, she sold it, unable to imagine ever setting foot in it again.

Unlike most Vietnam veterans, McCain and the other POWs were welcomed home as heroes. To many Americans they were. To others they symbolized the national catharsis that effectively marked the end of the nation's participation in the Vietnam War. There were parades in their honor, speeches lauding their gallantry, a visit to the White House. In a memorable UPI photo, McCain is seen in dress whites, awkwardly draped over his crutches, a spectral stick figure shaking hands with the President, Richard Nixon.

As in Hanoi, McCain at home was one of the best-known prisoners. In May, two months after his return, he wrote an article on his imprisonment for *U.S. News & World Report*. The magazine devoted thirteen pages to the piece, entitled, "Inside Story: How the POWs Fought Back." It ran with a sidebar, "Three Generations of a Famous Navy Family," with pictures of his father and grandfather.

McCain ended his article by saying, in words that hinted at the politician to come, "I had a lot of time to think over there, and came to the conclusion that one of the most important things in life—along with a man's family—is to make some contribution to his country."

The tone of the article was significant, too. There was anger toward his captors, but he seemed remarkably free of bitterness toward those of his countrymen who had opposed the war. Unlike many other returning POWs, he did not get apoplectic over the dramatic changes in social mores, either.

"Now that I'm back, I find a lot of hand-wringing about this country," he wrote. "I don't buy that. I think America today is a better country than the one I left nearly six years ago."

His homecoming was different from Jim Webb's, Ollie North's, or Bud McFarlane's. He led parades, gave dozens of speeches, received scores of letters from young people, many containing POW bracelets bearing his name that the senders had worn during his captivity. He called the outpouring of goodwill toward him and the other ex-prisoners "staggering, and a little embarrassing."

The public adulation did not fully explain his measured reaction to American society of the 1970s. He was, probably without realizing it, in the process of reinventing himself. Though the irreverent, fun-loving aspect of his personality remained intact, he was older and more mature. As his heroism in prison became more widely known, he began to move beyond the long shadows cast by his father and grandfather and his own zany reputation. Most important, he recognized himself as a survivor and wondered anew what that meant. Prison could now be added to the crash into Corpus Christi Bay, the fiery holocaust on the *Forrestal*, the last-second ejection over the Eastern Shore, the power lines in Spain. God, it seemed, was keeping him around for a reason.

The Lord's plan, whatever it was, did not appear to include remaining in the Navy. Both his arms, objects of sustained abuse in prison, were in wretched condition. He could raise neither above shoulder level. One shoulder socket had been smashed beyond repair by a rifle butt. The major problem, though, was his right knee, which he could bend at most five degrees.

After the short interlude with Carol at the beach, he entered the naval hospital in Jacksonville. The doctors decided to leave most of his injuries alone. Too much time had passed; little could be done about them. He had two operations on his knee, removing scar tissue and otherwise trying to free up the joint. At the end of his hospitalization, which lasted about three months, he was able to bend it ten degrees. Like Jim Webb a year earlier, he was facing retirement for medical reasons. In the case of McCain and the other returning POWs, however, the Navy was careful not to be seen as rushing men who had endured so much into premature retirement.

For McCain it was not enough to stay in the Navy. He wanted to fly again. The doctors told him to forget it, that flying was out of the question, but—as with Ollie North at Annapolis—he was determined to prove them wrong even if he had no idea how he was going to do it.

The answer came in a phone call he received that summer. By then he was a student at the National War College at Fort McNair, in southwest Washington.

You don't know me, said Diane Rauch, but I'm a physical therapist and I want to help you.

McCain had been taking physical therapy at Bethesda Naval Hospital, but the trek from his home in Alexandria to Fort McNair and the hospital north of Washington was taking a toll. Moreover, he did not see himself benefiting much from the treatment, which the doctors said would provide only twenty-five degrees of flexion at best. Diane said she could do better and suggested he talk to her other patients, including Sonny Jurgensen, the Washington Redskins quarterback, whom she had treated for a shoulder injury. McCain was impressed, but there was a problem. The Navy would not pay for a private therapist when it had a facility of its own in the area providing a similar service.

I know, said Diane, I'll do it free. I'd consider it an honor.

She did more than that. When she learned another member of the family was in bad shape, she told her partner, Barbara Devine, who volunteered to treat Carol free of charge as well.

Over the next year, Diane worked on John's frozen knee for two hours a day twice a week. She called her procedure manipulation/mobilization. McCain called it the pain method. After he had spent a half hour in the whirlpool, Diane braced her shoulder behind his knee and slowly tried to bend it. He never screamed, just said, "That's it, honey," when her efforts became unbearable. After a few minutes, she repeated the process, bending the knee a dozen times a session. She was a hard taskmaster, but she relaxed one of her standing rules for him: he was the only person she ever let smoke in the whirlpool.

Progress was slow, the pain excruciating, ten on a scale of ten, according to Diane. On good days, he gained two degrees of new flexion. Sometimes a week or more went by with nothing to show for it. But by the end of eight months, he could bend his knee a full ninety degrees.

The McCains repaid the favor. Diane was separated from her husband, a Navy admiral, so they introduced her to a POW friend, Bill Lawrence. Of all the men he knew in prison, McCain most admired Lawrence. At Annapolis he had been captain of the football team and brigade commander. In Vietnam he was a quiet presence, the man everyone leaned on when times were bad. Returning home after nearly six years, he learned that his wife had divorced him and remarried. Diane Rauch and Bill Lawrence were married in August 1974. Four years later he became superintendent of the Naval Academy, where he had a stormy tenure, thanks in part to Jim Webb.

Near the end of his time at the War College, determined to regain flying status, McCain went to Pensacola for a medical screening. He demanded that the doctors strictly adhere to the detailed list of physical parameters, not simply look him over and decide on the basis of what their eyes told them that he could not fly again. He could bend his knee ninety degrees, the minimum requirement for pilots. Some of his other ailments did not seem to be listed at all, probably because it stood to reason that no one so afflicted could hope to pilot a plane. Somehow, he was cleared to fly. He later joked that he probably wouldn't have been able to get his arm up high enough to pull the curtain if he ever had to bail out again.

At the War College, John McCain decided to find out what historical forces had combined to land him in a North Vietnamese prison. Like

Jim Webb, he designed a personal tutorial, not with the masters of art and literature but on Vietnam. For the next year, he read whatever he could find about Vietnamese society, politics, and the wars, the one the Americans were just finishing as well as the French debacle that preceded it.

He read the classics, Bernard Fall's *Street Without Joy* and *Hell in a Very Small Place*, Graham Greene's *The Quiet American*, everything on Dien Bien Phu.

He also looked closely at American decision-making, as described in David Halberstam's landmark chronicle *The Best and the Brightest* and in the supersecret government documents known as the Pentagon Papers, leaked to the press in 1971 by Daniel Ellsberg, a Pentagon official who ardently supported the war early on but later had a change of heart.

McCain never turned against the war or apologized for his part in it. Nor did he portray himself as a pawn in the grip of forces beyond his control. "Nobody made me fly over Vietnam," he said publicly on more than one occasion. "Nobody drafts you into doing those kinds of things. That's what I was trained to do and that's what I wanted to do."

Some of his judgments were harsh, but he confined them mostly to the power structure. Political and military leaders had grossly underestimated the will and resiliency of the enemy. Senior military men had been delinquent in other ways. Most if not all recognized that the strategy employed was not merely flawed but doomed to failure. "The military leadership wouldn't stand up and be counted," he said. As far as he was concerned, the top generals and admirals should have resigned in protest, preferably en masse, his father included.

As for members of the antiwar movement, he did not buy their reasoning, but he endorsed their right to demonstrate against government policy. "The freedom they were exercising was what I was fighting for," he said.

He even took a live-and-let-live attitude toward draft dodgers. "They have to judge whether they conducted their lives in the best fashion, not me," he said. "God knows I've made enough mistakes in my life and did enough things wrong and continue to do enough things wrong without being a judge of others."

To the extent he admitted any anger, it was toward a system that put the burden of service on the poor and the powerless, then through mismanagement, duplicity, and political cowardice allowed nearly sixty thousand young men to die for vaporous national goals: "Those who were better off economically did not carry out their obligations, so we forced the Hispanic, the ghetto black and the Appalachian white to fight and die. That to me was the greatest crime and injustice of the Vietnam War."

The year at the War College helped McCain come to terms with Vietnam. At the end of his tutorial, he felt he understood enough about the war to set it aside and move on. He was determined not to become a professional POW, partly because it was not his nature, mostly because it meant living in the past, which did not interest him. "I don't talk about prison because it bores the shit out of me," he once said.

As much as any POW, McCain transformed his prison experience into a positive force in his life, one from which he drew strength and, eventually, power, but which by an awesome act of will he refused to dwell on. "Just as I profited from my first year at the Naval Academy, which I didn't enjoy, I profited from my time in prison, which I didn't enjoy." At times, it came back to haunt him. Usually, though, what he felt came out in small ways, often in an eruption of temper out of all proportion to the provocation.

"You either go in one of two directions," he later said. "Either you go forward, and try to rebuild your life—not just the material part, but the spiritual part, too—or you look back in anger. If you look back in anger, it can be not only nonproductive, but self-destructive."

He added, "It's all been part of my life, but it was just a part of my life, and it's over."

There was one exception, the confession tortured out of him during his first year in prison. "It's the only blemish," he said. "It's something I'll never get over."

John McCain's relationship with Ronald Reagan began in the spring of 1973, about two months after his release. He and Carol were in Los Angeles, where McCain was waiting to testify against Daniel Ellsberg, under indictment for passing the Pentagon Papers to the press. McCain had found the documents riveting, basing some of his strongest judgments about the war on their contents. But he considered Ellsberg's disclosure of the papers an act of unspeakable treachery and readily agreed when prosecutors asked if he would describe for the jury how the enemy could have used the information against Americans.

He never testified. A report in late April linking the Nixon White House to the 1971 burglary of the office of Ellsberg's psychiatrist was followed in early May by the government's admission that it had failed to provide all its wiretap information to Ellsberg's lawyers. On

May 11 the judge dismissed all charges, saying government misconduct had "incurably infected the prosecution."

Freed from trial duties, the McCains flew up to San Francisco where Ross Perot was hosting a gala homecoming weekend for POWs at the Fairmont Hotel.

Nancy Reynolds, a special assistant to Governor Reagan, was in the hotel lounge with a group of ex-prisoners and their wives when someone at the table, as if spotting a movie star, shouted, "There's Johnny McCain."

McCain was on crutches; Carol had crutches and a wheelchair. Even so, Reynolds had never met a happier, jauntier, more delightful couple. "It was like meeting two people you know you'll never forget," she said. McCain struck her as a natural celebrity: "He walks into a room and it's *bing, bing, bing* and everybody's sort of dazzled."

Reynolds was not at the Perot party by chance. From the late 1960s on, Ronald and Nancy Reagan had taken a personal interest in the POWs. Reynolds served as staff liaison with the families. At one picnic in their honor, a young boy, Todd Hansen, said to the governor, "Will you bring my daddy home?" Reagan was speechless until Todd asked a follow-up question that got him off the hook: "Will you take me to the bathroom?"

The Reagans' concern for the POWs seemed genuine. "I can't wait to get my arms around each of those men," Nancy Reagan sobbed as the first group touched down on American soil. The Reagans hosted a total of four parties for the men and their families, two in Sacramento, two in L.A., Mrs. Reagan planning all the details herself, down to the place settings. At one party, a POW gave her the tin cup and spoon he had used in prison. She burst into tears on the receiving line.

Back in the office after the Perot weekend, Reynolds told the Reagans, "You have to meet the McCains." She arranged for the two couples to get together a few days later when both would be in Los Angeles.

The governor, singing the praises of California wine, ceremonially uncorked a bottle of Wente Brothers Gray Riesling as John and Carol arrived at the Reagan home in Pacific Palisades. Even with Reagan and his wife doing all they could to put them at ease, the McCains were uncomfortable at first, not quite sure what they were doing there.

When everyone was settled, the Reagans began peppering John with questions about prison. For the next two hours, they led him through a chronology of his experiences. "They wanted to hear every detail," said Carol. John fretted over wearing out his welcome, but each time he made overtures to leave, the Reagans said, "No, no, stay right where you are."

"Did you ever want to kill yourself?" asked Reagan, a piercing question of the type he would rarely ask as President.

"Sure, but that's easy," said McCain, shading the truth. "That gives you a way out if you kill yourself."

The McCains became favorites of Reagan and his California crowd. They all knew John had suffered terribly, but he made it hard for them to feel sorry for him. When pressed to talk about prison, he spoke about the heroism of others or transformed the Hanoi Hilton into an updated version of *Stalag 17*, a bunch of wild and crazy guys outsmarting a crew of bumbling, if sadistic, jailers.

A favorite story concerned a prisoner who built himself a motorcycle only he could see. When he finished, he took it out each day for a spin around the courtyard. At times it broke down and he would have to repair it. Give me a wrench, he would demand of the guards, give me a screwdriver. Crazy, crazy, the guards would say, shaking their heads. One day, though, he hit a curve too sharply, taking a nasty spill. Racing over, the guards assisted him to his feet, picked up the motorcycle, and helped him remount.

In 1974, his last year as governor, Reagan invited McCain to speak at the annual prayer breakfast in Sacramento. "Nancy cries when we send out the laundry," said Reagan in his introduction, "so I want to tell you, she'll never make it through listening to a talk by our next guest, Commander John McCain."

Never glancing at a note, McCain told a prison parable, of being in solitary, a hole in the ground, unbearable heat, suicidal thoughts intensifying. By chance he discovered some scratchings on the wall, the words of a previous inmate: "I believe in God, the Father Almighty."

Reagan was right. Mrs. Reagan had the Kleenex out within five minutes. She wasn't alone. "There must have been three hundred or four hundred people, maybe more than that, all these people sobbing," said Nancy Reynolds. "Not just sniffling. Ronald Reagan was sitting up there bawling.

"We were all dazzled," she continued. "He was a natural speaker, a natural storyteller. He was attractive. He was very funny." In short, as she was beginning to realize, a natural politician.

For McCain, Reagan was the real thing, a politician who stood for something, who insisted the men who fought in Vietnam were deserving of honor. Equally important, he declared that a nation should never send its sons to die in a war it was unwilling to win.

"He loved him, he loved Ronald Reagan," said Carol. "He was music to John's ears."

In November 1974, twenty months after his release from prison, McCain accepted an invitation from the South Vietnamese government to join an American VIP contingent visiting Saigon. Having completed his studies at Fort McNair, he was intrigued at the prospect of seeing the country with a more educated eye.

The old colonial capital seemed frozen in time. The restaurants were still magnificent and the shops continued to do a brisk trade. The sweeping veranda of the Hotel Continental, symbolic of a century of French rule, remained a pleasant and sophisticated gathering place for afternoon cocktails, assuming you could ignore the muffled reports of artillery fire in the distance.

He met with South Vietnamese officials and found their brave talk hollow. Any real hope South Vietnam had for sustaining itself was about to end as the newly elected congressional class of 1974, dominated by antiwar Democrats, readied itself to severely scale back American aid. The situation, he believed, had been preordained by the failure of the Paris peace accords to require the withdrawal of North Vietnamese troops from the south. To his mind, Nixon and Kissinger had done their best to keep faith with the American commitment, but under intense domestic pressure had agreed to terms that guaranteed a North Vietnamese victory.

Before departing, he spoke at the South Vietnamese war college. He offered words of encouragement that he did not feel, though he was not certain, based on his brief stay, that things were as bad as they seemed. Hang in there, he told the assemblage. Had he trusted his instincts, he might have been tempted to offer different advice, that is, You can't count on us, run for your lives.

A few months later, as North Vietnamese forces poured across the DMZ, he knew his instincts had been right, that the United States had ceased to be a reliable ally.

"These weren't guys in black pajamas," he said. "It was a conventional invasion of the South while our Congress cut the aid and cut and cut again."

In the fall of 1974, McCain was transferred to Jacksonville as the executive officer of Replacement Air Group 174, the long-sought flying billet at last a reality. A few months later, he assumed command of the RAG, which trained pilots and crews for carrier deployments. The assignment was controversial, some calling it favoritism, a sop to the famous son of a famous father and grandfather, since he had not first commanded a squadron, the usual career path. McCain ignored the howls. He had been given his chance and intended to make the most of it. He did. At the end of his tour the RAG received a Meritorious Unit Citation, its first ever.

At the change-of-command ceremony, Jack McCain, retired but still wielding his big cigar, shared the dais with his son, as did Roberta. Bud Day was there, too. An old family friend, Admiral Ike Kidd, spoke. Kidd's father had died at Pearl Harbor, where he won the Medal of Honor. In Kidd's remarks, he evoked echoes of the past, praising Jack's service, and Slew's before that. As for John, the admiral said he had earned himself a place of honor alongside his father and grandfather. Carl Smith, a friend and fellow officer, later said he never saw McCain so moved as on that day.

There was a dark side to the Jacksonville tour. The storybook marriage that had survived separation, pain, and prison began to fray. Off-duty, usually on routine cross-country flights to Yuma and El Centro, John started carousing and running around with women. To make matters worse, some of the women with whom he was linked by rumor were his subordinates. In some ways, the rumors were an extension of the John McCain stories that had swirled in his wake since Academy days—some true, some with an element of truth, others patently absurd. Asked about them, he admitted to having a series of dalliances during this period, but flatly denied any with females, officer or enlisted, under his command.

Though officially frowned upon, romantic relationships between officers of different grades are not uncommon and for the most part free of a superior-subordinate element. Many have led to marriage. But fraternization between officers and enlisted persons is considered over the line, not because of caste discrimination, but because the color of authority is too vivid, almost impossible to soften.

At the time the rumors were so widespread that, true or not, they became part of the McCain persona, impossible not to take note of. What is true is that a number of POWs, in those first few years after their release, often acted erratically, their lives pockmarked by drastic mood swings and uncharacteristic behavior before achieving a more mellow equilibrium.

More troubling, sad beyond words, was the failure of the marriage. If there was one couple that deserved to make it, it was John and Carol McCain. They endured nearly six years of unspeakable trauma with courage and grace. In the end it was not enough. They won the war but lost the peace. Hemingway writes of people becoming stronger at the broken places, which is a heartening thought, and sometimes true. All too often, though, it belongs in the file that Jim Webb labeled typical Hemingway bullshit.

John and Carol would not discuss the breakup of their marriage in any detail. McCain spoke vaguely of time having taken its toll. "I had changed, she had changed," he said. "People who have been apart that much change." He added, "I think she has reason to be bitter." Carol was less vague, but equally terse: "The breakup of our marriage was not caused by my accident or Vietnam or any of those things. I don't know that it might not have happened if John had never been gone. I attribute it more to John turning forty and wanting to be twenty-five again than I do to anything else."

The conventional view is that John came home not to the Long Tall Sally of his overheated prison imaginings but to a real woman—older, shorter, crippled—and before long began to stray. No doubt it was more complicated. Like most marriages that fail, theirs was a drama that involved two people who themselves could only make educated guesses about what went right and what went wrong.

Carol was mistaken on one point. Vietnam did play a part, perhaps not the major part, but more than a walk-on. McCain was no different from most veterans of that war. As he went through life, Vietnam kept scrambling onstage and chewing up the scenery no matter how often he thought he had written it out of the script.

CHAPTER TWENTY-ONE

A CHANGE OF HEART

In the spring of 1976, Admiral James L. Holloway III had a tough decision to make. That was not unusual. Over the course of a thirty-four-year naval career, the mantle of command had settled on him many times, and he had always been comfortable with it, as he was now, in his final and most prized post, Chief of Naval Operations.

On this occasion the decision was a personal one. It did not involve global strategy or matters of state, though it carried important professional implications. Entering his final two years as the nation's senior sailor, he had to choose a new executive assistant, the man who would be his closest aide, in many ways his alter ego.

The decision, as Holloway well knew, would be crucial both to him and the man he selected. Over the previous four years he had been blessed with two stellar executive assistants, Navy captains whose service to him had burnished their prospects for flag rank. The first, Bobby Ray Inman, would eventually gain promotion to vice admiral, become deputy director of the CIA under Bill Casey, then Bill Clinton's nominee for Secretary of Defense until he shocked the nation by announcing he didn't want the job. The second of Holloway's EAs, Powell Carter, would go on to four stars and command the Atlantic Fleet.

The CNO's executive assistant holds the Navy's premier captain's billet, his in-service clout usually greater than that of his counterpart in the Secretary of the Navy's office. The secretary is an administrator, outside the operational chain of command, a political appointee with often little to recommend him for the post besides dutiful service to his presidential patron. The CNO, by contrast, runs the Navy, sits on the Joint Chiefs of Staff, can make or break careers. When any of the world's trouble spots flare, it is the CNO, not the secretary, who normally advises the President on the employment of naval and Marine forces. It is said, with amusement and no small degree of cynicism, that Navy secretaries fall in love with their EAs. After years in the flabby civilian world, so the reasoning goes, the secretaries are overwhelmed by the crisp demeanor and unflagging energy of their chief aides, viewing them as a breed apart, the best the Navy has to offer. In fact, they are a special breed, men who have distinguished themselves over nearly two decades of service. But they are not the best the Navy has to offer. The Navy reserves the best for the CNO.

Holloway knew neither of the men he was considering for the job. Both, of course, had superb records. Captain Frank Kelso was a submariner, a large, craggy man of accomplishment and enormous promise. His credentials included a number of important duty assignments, among them command of two nuclear-powered submarines. After interviewing the candidates, however, the CNO decided to pass on Kelso and go with the second man, a line officer who had been a couple of years behind Kelso at Annapolis, had less command experience, but who seemed, for Holloway, a better fit.

A few weeks later, John Poindexter reported for his third tour of duty at the Pentagon.

Holloway never regretted his choice, considered Poindexter close to perfect, "a guy whose loyalty and judgment were second to none." Some viewed the relationship as transcending the professional, as if Holloway saw in the trim, scholarly, slightly balding Poindexter a surrogate for the college-age son lost in an auto accident a dozen years earlier. As for Poindexter, he discovered in Holloway qualities he had found lacking in his earlier tours in Washington, deemed him a man of principle, nothing less than a statesman. Years later, Linda Poindexter would say, "Admiral Holloway's opinion probably matters more to John than almost any man I can think of." She also remembered the glow that lit her husband's bland features when Holloway casually referred to Poindexter as his best friend.

Like John McCain, Jim Holloway sprang from illustrious Navy roots, though he had less trouble coming to terms with his legacy. His father, nicknamed Lord Jim because of his aristocratic bearing, had been a full admiral. The son, "young Jimmy" as older members of the naval community persisted in calling him, was less austere, more approachable, a sailor's sailor. On the road to CNO, he touched all the bases, including skipper of the Navy's first nuclear-powered carrier and commander of the Seventh Fleet. When he put on his fourth star, he and his father joined Slew and Jack McCain as the only fathers and sons to make full admiral in U.S. Navy history.

Seated outside the CNO's door, Poindexter found himself a few steps removed from the desk at which he hoped to cap his own naval career. That goal dated back to his midshipman days. *My ambition is to climb to the very top*, he had written in his senior essay at the Academy eighteen years earlier. To Linda, his only true confidante, he had reasserted that intention at odd moments over the years, though with more precision: *I want to be the CNO*. He could not expect to fulfill his ambition for another decade, but the new job ratified his belief that he was being groomed for greater responsibilities and in due course would be among the select few in the running for the coveted post.

Poindexter's ambition, though focused, had no raw edges to it. He had positioned himself for advancement honestly, by committing himself to excellence in every job assigned him. In his reserved and dignified way, he, too, was a sailor's sailor, happier at sea than behind a desk. He had sought none of the flashy shore billets that marked him for bigger things, invariably requesting sea duty when asked his preference for future assignments. But he had fallen captive to his own reputation. "He was doing well on the sea duty side, he was doing well on the Pentagon side, everybody wanted him," said Vice Admiral Staser Holcomb, a more senior ex–Whiz Kid also working at the Pentagon.

For all its prestige, the EA job was studded with pitfalls. As guardian of the gate, Poindexter was the man through whom two-, three-, and four-star admirals had to pass before seeing Holloway. Often they asked his guidance before entering the CNO's office, using him as a sounding board. What's the chief's mood today? What's his thinking about such and such? How do you think he'll react to this idea? At times he had to turn the admirals away or diplomatically warn them they were about to make fools of themselves. It was a delicate job, perhaps the most nerve-racking shore billet a captain could hold. He could not allow Holloway's time to be frittered away, but neither could he afford to antagonize men who would be around for years after Holloway retired.

If he felt the stress, and it is difficult to imagine that he didn't, he never showed it. Colleagues from those days remember him working well into the night, puffing contentedly on his pipe, a man at peace with himself. "He was never ruffled, just Mister Cool, a real pro," said Vice Admiral Holcomb. "I said at the time that if I ever become CNO, this is the guy I want outside my door."

In addition to controlling access to Holloway, Poindexter screened all documents—message traffic, readiness reports, contingency plans, intelligence estimates—addressed to the CNO. Some never made it to Holloway, or were kicked back for reworking since the CNO expected his EA to handle matters that did not require his personal attention and to ensure the thoroughness of material that came to him. That gave Poindexter considerable power, but he never abused it. "That was the marvelous thing about him, he just had this exquisite feel for how far he should go," said Holloway. "He didn't load me up with details. He took care of the details . . . but always reserved for me the decisions that should be made by me."

Some observers looked on Holloway's tenure as CNO as a period of consolidation, a time to heal the wounds of Vietnam and bring the Navy to a steadier course after the reforms of his predecessor, Elmo Zumwalt, whose trademark Z-grams touched everything from hair length to race relations. From the CNO's office, the view was different. With antimilitary sentiment rampant in the aftermath of Vietnam, the Navy had fallen from about a thousand ships at the height of the war to less than five hundred, lower than before Pearl Harbor.

Said Holloway, "John and I were fighting like hell to keep the Navy together."

John and I. An interesting pairing on the part of Holloway, one that cemented the widely held view that the two men were as much a team as officers of such disparate ranks could be. "They just went click, click, click," said Will King, the erstwhile *England* executive officer whom Poindexter recruited as the CNO's administrative assistant. Holloway was the team member on the firing line, but when he returned angry and frustrated from a White House meeting or another dispiriting session on the Hill, Poindexter shared his fury.

Holloway saw himself under sustained attack by Congress. It was as if members viewed senior military leaders as the prime culprits in the Vietnam debacle. He was accused of squandering the nation's money to feather the Navy's nest, of having no higher priority than building large carriers for a bunch of peacock admirals to ride around on. A man of great personal dignity, he felt demeaned, abused, his uniform at times sullied. "I was disillusioned by how meretricious—I don't use that word often, but it's associated with whoring—many members of the Congress were," said Holloway. "They pretended they were going in to ask questions to determine the facts, but the truth of the matter was, they were going in to ask questions to discredit and embarrass." Did Poindexter share that view? "I'm absolutely convinced he did," said Holloway. "He couldn't have helped but be disillusioned by the political side."

Congress wasn't the only problem. Gerald Ford had been supportive of the Navy as President, beating back some of the deeper congressional cuts, but the election of Academy man Jimmy Carter in November 1976 redrew the battle lines.

Holloway respected Harold Brown, Carter's Secretary of Defense, but he did not consider Brown or his closest aides friends of the Navy. Said Holloway, "All the things we had successfully fought against in the past were resurrected: 'Let's build small, cheap carriers. Let's build small, cheap airplanes. Let's build conventionally powered submarines.'" In a lighter moment, Holloway joked that before long he expected someone to suggest running subs on hydrogen peroxide.

There were few light moments. Holloway considered the Navy greatly underfunded. In the aftermath of Vietnam, he said, operational readiness was suffering because of a lack of spare parts. The skilled enlisted men who kept the ships running were being leached from the service, some lured away by better-paying jobs in private industry, others simply throwing in the towel, their pride damaged beyond repair by shortages that made it nearly impossible for them to do their jobs. To save money, lengthier sea tours were instituted, creating morale and marital problems for officers and enlisted men alike, aggravating the personnel drain.

One day Holloway came storming back into the office after another frustrating encounter, either on Capitol Hill or the White House, Poindexter can't remember where. "I wonder why anybody would want to be CNO," Holloway sputtered. Poindexter thought about his boss's words, and the job he himself had long looked on as the capstone of his career. The CNO's power was far more limited than he ever imagined. The chief spent most of his time in a defensive perimeter, circling the ships, not initiating action. Perhaps worst of all, he had to deal on a daily basis with politicians, whether in the White House, the Pentagon, or on the Hill. About that time he told Linda, "I've decided I don't want to be CNO anymore."

On completing his tour as Admiral Holloway's executive assistant in July 1978, John Poindexter headed off to San Diego to begin his fifth sea tour, this time as Commander, Destroyer Squadron 31. He relieved Captain Jonathan Howe, whom Bud McFarlane had replaced five years earlier as Henry Kissinger's military aide.

DesRon 31 was a major seagoing command, which meant Poindexter was on course to make rear admiral. Depending on operational requirements, he usually had five to eight destroyers under him, including the *England*, his old ship.

His flagship was the *Elliot*, a Spruance class destroyer, which held symbolic meaning for Poindexter. Admiral Raymond A. Spruance, "the Quiet Warrior," as his biographer, Thomas B. Buell, dubbed him, was as close as Poindexter came to having a hero. A major World War II naval figure, Spruance distinguished himself at the Battle of Midway in June 1942, as Nimitz's chief of staff, and—alternating with the more outgoing and voluble Bull Halsey—as commander of the Fifth Fleet in the Central Pacific in the last two years of the war.

Poindexter never met Spruance, who died in 1969, but knew him by reputation, was temperamentally in tune with him, and thought of him as a role model. Had there been no Iran-Contra scandal, John B. Lundstrom might well have been writing about Poindexter in his introduction to Buell's 1987 biography.

He was a very private person, unemotional and undemonstrative in public. To a great degree he was unconcerned about his image, caring little for "glory" in the conventional sense. His gods were logic and reason. The character of Mr. Spock in the popular science-fiction series

"Star Trek" could easily have been patterned after Spruance. The admiral competed not with others but with his own impossibly high self-expectations, and that is the way he judged his successes and failures. A man who relied on deeds rather than words to make his mark, Spruance seemed oblivious to what posterity would think of him. He did not like to speak publicly, nor did he do much writing if he could avoid it. He authored no wordy, self-justifying memoirs. His achievements, intellect, and integrity were responsible for the great respect accorded him by his peers.

In 1979 Poindexter led the squadron on a seven-month cruise to the Western Pacific, through the Strait of Malacca and into the Indian Ocean where DesRon 31 and a handful of Soviet warships took turns observing each other's underway operations. A week before the squadron pulled into Hong Kong for a six-day port call, Poindexter asked Linda to fly over and meet him there. "Do you want the bad news now or later?" he asked her when she arrived. A typhoon was on the way, he said, the squadron was leaving the next morning. Linda did some quick arithmetic on the cost of her trip and replied, "That puts me in the $1,500-a-night class."

The following year Poindexter was having lunch aboard the *Elliot* with Frank Gamboa, John McCain's old Academy roommate, when he was summoned topside. Linda, in jeans and sweatshirt, was on the pier, hollering at the ship. A concerned Poindexter, unable to make out what she was saying, thought something had happened to one of the five boys. It turned out she was trying to tell him he had been selected for rear admiral. The ship's communications system was down, so the Pentagon had called him at home with the news and passed it on to Linda. He was the second man in his class to make flag rank. Chuck Larson had been selected the previous year.

In September 1980, he reported to Pensacola as the number-two man at the Navy's Education and Training command. Poindexter watchers were surprised. In comparison with his previous shore billets, the assignment seemed commonplace. Some wondered if he had fallen into disfavor. Poindexter saw it as a holding action, a place where he could do some good while waiting for a rear admiral's billet to open up.

On the national scene, Ronald Reagan was challenging Jimmy Carter for the presidency. "I was pretty fed up with Carter because I thought he was a weak person," said Poindexter. "I thought that he had not handled the Soviets very well. In fact, his approach to the Soviets may very well have led them to go into Afghanistan because they thought they could get away with it." He had also been dismayed by Carter's handling of the 1979 oil crisis, "sitting there wringing his hands and wearing a sweater in the Oval Office because the heat was turned down." As for Reagan: "He was saying the right things."

In the spring of 1981, he got a call from James W. "Bud" Nance, an aide to Richard V. Allen, Reagan's national security adviser. Poindexter had met Nance, an Academy graduate and retired rear admiral, at the Pentagon when he was working for Admiral Holloway. Nance told him Allen was going to be in Florida and wanted to talk to him. Poindexter assumed it was about a position in the White House.

Allen told Poindexter he was looking for a military aide. In particular, Allen said he wanted someone to take charge of and reorganize the White House Situation Room. Asked if he was interested, Poindexter said he was. A few weeks later he found out he had gotten the job. He reported to the White House on June 1, 1981. Like Jonathan Howe and Bud McFarlane before him, he would not be a horse holder in the job, at least not for long.

If things had gone differently, he might have become CNO anyway, perhaps chairman of the Joint Chiefs, leading the nation's military to glory in Desert Storm. But Poindexter was right in the decision he made when working for Jim Holloway. CNO was not the job for him because he did not have a political bone in his body. He was a product of two institutions that may be as close as we have in this country to pure meritocracies—the United States Naval Academy and, at least through the rank of captain, the United States Navy. In both he played above the rim, because that was his natural habitat. At a certain point in his career, though, it became important that he understand politics and politicians, and he never did.

He had the chance. As a Whiz Kid, as a senior aide to three Secretaries of the Navy, and during his years with Admiral Holloway, he had incomparable opportunities to find out what drives politicians. By focusing so intently on the job at hand, though, he lost peripheral vision. He accepted the stereotype of the politician, saw virtually all of them as self-important charlatans pandering to any crowd of ten or more people, never bothering to learn about the complexities of their vocation or the dilemmas that confront even the most high-minded.

In some ways, he was simply following the time-honored tradition of the Navy wardroom, which forbids discussion of three topics— women, religion, and politics. But his wardroom days would soon be over. Three years after completing his tour with Holloway, he would be in the White House, taking on a series of posts for which he was superbly qualified in most respects, in one singularly deficient. Two decades earlier, Harvard professor Richard E. Neustadt, a veteran of the Truman White House, published a small volume, *Presidential Power*, that quickly became a classic. Neustadt made the case that the single most potent weapon in a President's arsenal was the power to persuade. With it, he is a leader, without it a glorified clerk.

Poindexter never seemed to understand that, or much else about how American government works, as opposed to the way one might like it to work. Nor did he bother to look for answers. On this matter he was singularly incurious. Moving now toward the most crucial and demanding time of his professional life, he had many things going for him, but one severe handicap. He was like a superbly trained boxer with fine footwork, a great punch, and a glass jaw.

CHAPTER TWENTY-TWO

PUG HENRY

By August 1976, Jonny McFarlane had decided enough was enough. In her husband's three years on the NSC staff he had not taken a day off. Not Christmas, not Thanksgiving, not a single Sunday. He had taken leave twice. The first time, the Yom Kippur War broke out in the Middle East and he was called back to the White House. The second time they rented a house in Rehoboth, a beach resort on the Delaware shore. No sooner had they unpacked the car than the phone rang. A crisis in Cyprus. They lugged the bags back out to the car and returned to Washington. When McFarlane arrived at the White House, Kissinger said, "Bud can't go on leave anymore. Something goes wrong every time."

This time Jonny had made a deal with Brent Scowcroft, now the national security adviser, Kissinger having relinquished his dual role and settled in solely as Secretary of State.

"We're going to Nantucket," Jonny said as Bud woke up that August morning.

He could not believe she was serious. "I am not going to Nantucket," he said. "I'm going to work."

She was serious. So was he. She tried reasoning. "Look, you're exhausted. You can't do your job well in the shape you're in. We need some time together."

"No," he said.

"I've bought the tickets," she said. "I've paid for the lodging. I've arranged for someone to take care of the kids. I've spent a lot of money. We don't have a lot of money."

"Forget it," snapped McFarlane.

She dropped the bombshell.

"I did this because Brent told me to."

"What?" cried a disbelieving McFarlane. "You went to my boss and asked for leave without checking with me?"

He shouted and stomped. In the midst of his tirade, a friend drove up in his new Cadillac, a little black hat on his head. Jonny had arranged for him to chauffeur them to the airport.

"No, go away," Jonny, in tears, told the friend. "It's not going to work. He's crazed."

As the friend departed, McFarlane went into the bathroom and slammed the door on his sobbing wife, ending the discussion.

Or so he thought. He was shaving, trying to concoct an excuse for his wife's behavior when Jonny rapped on the door.

"The general's on the phone," she said.

"What? You called him? Goddammit!"

Composing himself, McFarlane took the phone. "General, I'm sorry," he told Scowcroft. "There's been a mistake here. I'm on my way in."

Jonny had done her homework. Scowcroft told McFarlane he wanted him to go to Nantucket. McFarlane, glaring at Jonny, insisted he didn't need leave, that he was almost out the door and would see him in a few minutes.

Scowcroft wouldn't budge. "You're no good to me right now," he said.

McFarlane would not speak to Jonny as he packed his bags. He drove to the airport in white-knuckled anger. His silence continued as they checked in, boarded the aircraft, and took off.

The plane was small, the ride was bumpy.

Turning to her husband, who sat clench-jawed beside her, Jonny said, "They call this the Provincetown Airline and Screen Door Company."

He stared straight ahead. Slowly, almost imperceptibly, she saw his jaw muscles relax. Then she noticed a slight quiver at the corner of his mouth. A moment later, for the first time since he had awakened that morning, Bud McFarlane smiled.

Bud McFarlane left the White House in January 1977. By then he had compiled a record of being at the scene of the action that another much-traveled Annapolis man, Pug Henry, the fictional naval hero of Herman Wouk's *Winds of War* and *War and Remembrance*, might well envy. McFarlane had made the first landing in Vietnam and participated in the American pullout ten years later. He fought in Tet '68, then worked at Marine Headquarters and the White House as the war effort plunged into the vortex of defeat. He had witnessed, at times all too intimately, Spiro Agnew's resignation in disgrace and the Watergate-driven dissolution of the Nixon presidency. He had traveled with Kissinger to China twice, helping to lay the foundation for a new Sino-American relationship. By his own account, he spent three solid days in 1974—and again the following year—in a private room of the Great Hall of the People passing American intelligence on the Soviet Union to the Chinese.

At the NSC under Nixon and Ford, he seemed a highly competent, if colorless, military bureaucrat. He was rumored to have a keen sense of humor, though he rarely displayed it. He did a terrific Kissinger impersonation, but in those days nearly everybody did good Kissinger. He had a few idiosyncracies. He rode a motorcycle to work until he crashed on Wisconsin Avenue and Scowcroft gave him a White House parking space for his car. He unwittingly amused colleagues by his habit of dropping his voice several octaves in formal settings, a quirk first noted by Bob Drozd, his Academy roommate. Less obvious, because he kept his emotions under such tight rein, was that he loved what he was doing. And he was getting better at it every day.

McFarlane found that he had underestimated Gerald Ford. Just nine months into his unique unelected presidency, flanked by cabinet officers and other aides whose egos matched their considerable intellects, Ford refused to play the passive bystander. He took charge, running the meetings, asking pointed questions, monitoring developments closely. To McFarlane, he personified the engaged President, one prepared to make the hard decisions and unwilling to be immobilized by the absence of consensus among the strong, often conflicting personalities advising him.

That was the good news. The bad news was that McFarlane came away from the experience assuming that was the way Presidents did business.

*   *   *

McFarlane left the White House reluctantly, but with an emerging sense of his own talents. In the early years, around Kissinger, he had been deferential, rarely questioning him, at least not out loud, even though he sometimes felt an alternative course of action made more sense. Kissinger could intimidate him, at least to the extent of throwing him off his game. It was as if he needed a wizard, even an ersatz wizard like Frank Morgan, to provide him with the credentials he felt he needed to level the playing field. That guy isn't smarter than you, Bud, the kindly old charlatan might have smiled, he just has something you don't have—a doctorate from Harvard.

In some ways, the years at the White House evened things up. Moving on to his next duty station, he realized that much of the advice he might have given Kissinger, or that he did give Brent Scowcroft, with whom he felt more at ease, would have been precisely the right thing to do in this or that situation. So, yes, he did want to return to the White House someday, but not as a horse holder. The next time, he told himself, he was "going to propose and to lead and advocate and to be more assertive."

Of all the men he worked with in the White House, he felt closest to Scowcroft, a West Pointer. Scowcroft's slight stature belied his clout. Soft-spoken but firm, he was not afraid to challenge Kissinger and other cabinet officers on policy matters, though he was tactful and pragmatic enough to do so in ways that did not call attention to himself or draw the limelight away from his more image-conscious peers. McFarlane viewed him as the near-perfect national security adviser, determined to provide the President with the often conflicting views of his senior aides—notably the Secretaries of State and Defense—but equally determined to make sure the Chief Executive knew his position, too. In other words, an honest broker with brains and balls.

The relationship between the two men had a big brother–little brother quality to it. Certainly professional respect was blended with personal fondness. In many ways, it was similar to the relationship that McFarlane as national security adviser would enjoy with another hardworking Marine officer, Ollie North. Scowcroft considered Mc-Farlane a superb aide, and often told him so, even though he never quite got the message across. "He did try to resign, more than once, because he thought he was not doing the kind of job for me that he thought I deserved," recalled Scowcroft. "I had a terrible time convincing him how valuable he was to me."

*   *   *

After three and a half years at the NSC, McFarlane's Marine Corps career was far off course. His high-profile White House tours notwithstanding, he had not served in a combat unit since his return from Vietnam in 1968, an almost unforgivable gap of nine years. Bad enough that he had not honed his warrior skills for nearly a decade, but he had spent much of that time cozying up to politicians, a group never popular with Marines, less so in the aftermath of Vietnam. He was tagged a "political Marine," a moniker that can play hell with your career, especially when it has the ring of truth to it.

Any chance he had to recover probably evaporated near the end of his time at the White House. The Marine Corps, impressed despite itself by his performance, not to mention by his high-powered patrons like Scowcroft, seemed willing to forgive and forget if he went to Okinawa for a year without his family. That made sense from a career standpoint, but personal factors intervened. Other than the week in Nantucket, he had not had a day off between June 1973 and January 1977. He was exhausted. He realized that he owed something to Jonny and the kids. He asked Scowcroft to pull some strings to keep him in Washington for the next year. Scowcroft came through, quietly orchestrating an assignment to the National War College, a few miles from the White House. Air Force Colonel Andy Dougherty, who became a close friend at the War College, remembered meeting McFarlane for the first time.

"He was punchy, palpably punchy," said Dougherty. "He was almost in shock."

Like John McCain, McFarlane found the War College the perfect place to decompress. As a senior research fellow, he was expected to read and think and produce a couple of articles. He more than met that standard. Along with two colleagues, he wrote a book on presidential decision-making under crisis conditions. Though it attracted little attention outside professional circles, the book painted a vivid picture of the nation's national security apparatus in action.

He also wrote an article detailing his view of the new geopolitical realities. In slightly more than a nutshell, he constructed a framework against which he would later analyze developments on the international scene. A key element: in a world where the superpowers faced mutual annihilation if they resorted to nuclear weapons, the Kremlin's appetite for expansion was being fed by the actions of surrogates—insurgent forces, terrorist groups, and radical regimes in lesser developed countries.

In light of Vietnam, he wrote, a policy of employing proxies to foment crises and subvert U.S. interests made sense for the Soviets. "Without firing a shot (or being shot at), the Soviet Union has watched while the United States was brought to its knees in a foreign war after an investment of more than $100 billion."

The article was prescient. By extension, McFarlane anticipated the emergence of Khomeini, Qaddafi, Islamic Jihad, the Sandinistas in Nicaragua, individuals and organizations that would reshape the international arena a few years later.

There was no hint of zealotry in the article. Nor did it contain any of the hard-edged anti-Soviet rhetoric that catapulted Ronald Reagan and the conservative New Right movement into the heart of the national political debate in the late 1970s. McFarlane revealed his worldview as very much in the Kissinger mold. He distrusted the Soviets, detecting their hand in various insurgent movements around the world. However, he saw the superpower relationship as one that could be managed successfully through traditional means such as arms control, other forms of diplomacy, economic leverage, and, if necessary, by application of measured amounts of force. That wasn't zealotry; that was garden-variety Cold War dogma.

At the end of his year at the War College, McFarlane was promoted to lieutenant colonel and given orders to Okinawa. He fully expected to command an artillery battalion. Instead he was assigned a staff job with his old outfit, the Twelfth Marines.

A few months into his tour, Headquarters dispatched an assignment officer, known as a monitor, to Okinawa to discuss future duty stations with the lieutenant colonels stationed there. McFarlane hoped for a post in which he might exercise his talent for international relations. No chance, Bud, said the monitor. You've done that. You've got to become well-rounded. We need officers at senior levels who know all about the Corps—logistics, communications, personnel, whatever. You know about geopolitics, fine, great, you don't need to do that anymore. We don't want you to do that anymore.

Not long after, McFarlane requested retirement. For twenty years he had been a good Marine, but in the later stages of his service he had diverged radically from the classic career pattern. The Marine Corps did not fancy itself a breeding ground for foreign policy intellectuals. It was, at its best, an organization of warriors, shock troops, men who prided themselves on being the first to fight. The rest might not be exactly bullshit, but it was not what Marines did. And, McFarlane admitted, most of the time they did what they did exceedingly well. He had to face facts. He wasn't right and the Corps wasn't wrong. It was just time to move on.

*   *   *

Anxious to begin a second career, McFarlane hoped for a job in the Executive Branch, preferably back at the White House. When nothing materialized, he persuaded John Tower, the ranking Republican on the Senate Armed Services Committee, to hire him as a committee analyst.

He reported to work on Capitol Hill in July 1979 with mixed feelings. Senators and congressmen, to his mind, could do little more than obstruct, delay, tinker at the margins of national policy. His youthful view of Congress as an honorable body had suffered severe blows over the past dozen years. Even so, the idea of spending a few years on the Hill made sense to him, if only from the standpoint of knowing your adversary.

A curious thing happened to McFarlane during his year and a half on the Hill. He developed a grudging respect for the institution, if not for many of its inhabitants. Along the way much of the contempt he had felt throughout the war years slowly bled off.

It wasn't an overnight conversion. The first six months were depressing. He was, to his mind, woefully out of the action. "Leadership to me was the guy who set the policy, not the kibitzers," he later said. Up close, most senators and congressmen met his expectations—shallow, petty, vain, and parochial. Like John Poindexter, he bristled as he watched vital national security issues trivialized by a senator or congressman trying to wheedle some special advantage for his state or district.

Gradually, though, he came to the conclusion that Congress, for all its fools, blowhards, and intellectual pipsqueaks, was a precious resource for the nation. It provided a forum for the American people to voice their concerns and judgments loudly enough to compel the attention of the White House. Often, he thought those concerns and judgments superficial and worse. But that did not mean they were to be ignored, or circumvented. If the people disagreed with the President, it was the President's job to win their support. He even made a peace of sorts with the obstructionist qualities of Congress, deciding that its ponderous pace and glaring inefficiencies were not all that bad a check on the power of the executive. He fashioned a whimsically idiosyncratic view, part James Madison, part Woody Allen. This place may be all fucked up, but that's okay, that's the way it's supposed to be. All that means is the system works.

"Wisdom lies in accepting Congress for what it is," he would later say. "I disagreed with virtually every decision the Congress was taking on foreign policy in the 1970s, from Vietnam, the cutoff of aid, to the War Powers Resolution, yet came to accept that, well, if you're going to be an effective public servant, you can't simply refuse to deal with it or things will turn out worse."

As, when he tried to deal the kibitzers out of the action a few years later, things did.

CHAPTER TWENTY-THREE

WOMEN CAN'T FIGHT

The ceremony was winding down. Minutes earlier Jim Webb had received the Veterans Administration's first Vietnam Veteran of the Year award for a variety of activities on behalf of ex-servicemen. As dignitaries and well-wishers began to disperse, he held up his hand: "Wait a minute. I'd like to say something." The crowd regrouped, wary, not sure what to expect. No one was in the mood for another aggrieved veteran's harangue against the war or the fecklessness of his government. But Webb had something else on his mind, the curious, at times bewildering twilight world inhabited by the soldier not simply untroubled by his combat record but proud of it.

"I don't need to elaborate in front of this assemblage about how incredibly difficult it has been for the Vietnam veteran," he began. "His anonymity and lack of positive feedback about himself and his fellow veterans have intensified all the other difficulties he has faced, including those shared with nonveterans. With the exception of a few well-publicized disasters, he is invisible."

In public discourse, continued Webb, the veteran has no voice, those who opposed the war having long since been accorded the role of spokesmen for his generation. His antiwar peers convert their activities into credentials, "much as the veteran of World War II did with his campaign ribbons." By contrast, society seems to view him as an accident waiting to happen. Editorials urge amnesty for those who fled the country, insisting they obeyed "a higher law," leaving unwritten the implication that he responded to something less honorable, even brutish, in choosing to serve.

"To be blunt, we seem to have reached the anomaly where the very institution, and the same newspapers, who only a few years ago called on us to bleed, have now decided we should be ashamed of our scars."

"Well," said Webb, pausing, eyeing his audience, "I'm not ashamed of mine."

The crowd broke into applause. His words had the defiant ring of a manifesto. He had declared that no longer would his generation be represented solely by evaders, avoiders, drug-crazed ex-GIs, and embittered antiwar veterans. He had demanded a voice for the men and women who had fought the war, then returned home unheralded, but with a sense of personal achievement. Above all, he had proclaimed the right of the Vietnam veteran to take pride in his service.

A few weeks after the awards ceremony, the *Washington Post* published a text of Webb's remarks on its op-ed page, under the title "The Invisible Vietnam Veteran." That led to a television appearance in which he assailed the amnesty proposal then being promoted by Jimmy Carter, the Democratic presidential nominee. His performance caught the eye of President Ford's political handlers. Webb, a lifelong if lukewarm Democrat, was soon installed as cochairman of a group called Vietnam Veterans for Ford.

His political conversion had its roots in a phone call in late 1975 from an old Academy roommate, Glenn Boggs, a lawyer in Florida. Many Annapolis men, Boggs included, were climbing aboard the long-shot presidential campaign being mounted by Carter, one of their own. Boggs urged Webb to join the Carter effort. Webb, intrigued, looking for a fresh challenge after three years in the classroom or hunched over a typewriter, tentatively decided he would. First, though, he wanted to check out Carter for himself. He read through news clippings, speeches, and position papers, coming away disillusioned. Carter stood for nothing, he concluded. That kept him from throwing in with the ex–Georgia governor. Carter's subsequent endorsement of pardons for draft resisters was too much, the twisting of the knife. Adrift politically, Webb washed ashore a Republican.

Carter was inaugurated as the nation's thirty-ninth President in January 1977. His first official act was to grant unconditional pardons to draft evaders. By then, Webb was back at the typewriter, reworking *Fields of Fire*. But he had enjoyed the excitement of the campaign and missed the action. A month later, he received a call from Bill Ayres, an ex-congressman who had recruited him for Ford. How would you like to work for the House Veterans Affairs Committee? he asked. I might, replied Webb. In March 1977, he was named assistant minority counsel, the first Vietnam veteran to serve on the committee staff.

Soon after Webb reported to work, Carter's discharge review proposal was sent to Capitol Hill. This was an effort to redress the grievances of veterans who had received something other than honorable discharges—undesirables, unsuitables, and some deserters. Their advocates argued that a President who pardoned men who violated the Selective Service laws should show the same compassion to those who actually went into the service, even if they fouled up once in uniform. Under the Carter plan, their discharges could be upgraded, in many cases qualifying them for veterans' benefits.

Webb was perplexed. His experience with Sam Green had convinced him that a number of veterans—maybe 10 or 15 percent—deserved better discharges than they had received. But he didn't like the philosophy behind the upgrades, which seemed to say, as he put it, that "every son of a bitch who deserted did so for valid reasons." His old radioman, Mac McGarvey, gave the issue a human dimension.

There's a guy back home, McGarvey told Webb. We both went into the Marines. I went to Vietnam. He deserted. I never felt anything toward him at all. I lost my arm. He got a bad conduct discharge. I live with what I did, he lives with what he did. Now you're saying that what he did was okay?

For the next six months, Webb worked day and night to kill the bill. He failed, but the final version of the measure barred deserters from receiving benefits without the personal approval of the VA administrator, a small but symbolic victory.

Like many Vietnam veterans, Dale Wilson put his life together after the war. It was harder for him than most, having lost three limbs, all but his left arm, back in 1969. By the late 1980s, he was a college graduate, a married man with two children, living in a house he had designed himself in Troutman, North Carolina, about thirty miles north of Charlotte.

When Jim Webb called in 1977, however, Wilson found himself facing a dilemma. His old platoon commander, working for the House veterans committee, had prodded the bureaucracy and shaken loose the Silver Star for which he had recommended Wilson eight years earlier. Now Webb wanted to arrange an award ceremony.

Jim, there's something you ought to know, Wilson began. He explained that earlier in the year, when Carter granted amnesty, he had organized a protest demonstration that had received considerable publicity. Summoning some three hundred veterans from North Carolina and surrounding states, he staged a march through the streets of Statesville, the county seat, and nailed the medals he had already received—the Bronze Star, two Purple Hearts, several campaign ribbons—to the walls of an outhouse. The other vets followed suit, one hammering an artificial limb to the structure for good measure. Then they doused the outhouse with gasoline and burned it down. Wilson called it the ultimate political platform: you ask politicians for relief and they give you shit. If the metaphor seemed slightly out of whack, the rage it conveyed was clear. So was Wilson's reaction to Webb's call. Thanks, Jim, but no thanks.

Webb argued, but Wilson wouldn't budge. Think about it, said Webb, I'll get back to you. Wilson was conflicted. Webb was a friend. He had written to Wilson often while he was recuperating from his injuries. A few years earlier, Wilson had driven up to Washington with another disabled veteran. Webb had put them both up at his house for a week. But Wilson truly didn't want the medal. As far as he was concerned, Carter had defiled the service of every man who fought in Vietnam. On top of that, how could he, Wilson, accept a medal now without looking like a hypocrite?

He thought about his father, a working man, someone he loved and admired. He was ailing, heart problems and diabetes taking a fearsome toll. His dad had helped him make his way back into the world after Vietnam, but Wilson would never forget the tears running down the old man's cheeks when he first saw what the war had done to his once strapping young son. He's given me so much. I've never given him anything. He called Webb. Okay, he said, let's do it.

Hundreds turned out in Statesville for Dale Wilson Day. Webb rolled in with McGarvey, Tom Martin, Dale Tucker, and several other members of the old platoon. McGarvey's stump bore a tattoo: CUT ALONG THE DOTTED LINE. Webb had rousted the whole crew. He also arranged for the appearance of the Marine band from Camp Lejeune. A three-star general was on hand to pin the Silver Star on Wilson's chest, again thanks to Webb. Wilson presented the medal to his father. Thirteen days later his father died.

In the fall of 1978, Webb gave a reading from *Fields of Fire* at Annapolis. Afterward, his old English profs came up to praise the work. You ought to be teaching here, said one. Make me an offer, smiled Webb, smitten by the idea. A few weeks later, the Academy offered him a position, writer-in-residence, created with him in mind. He quickly accepted, perhaps too quickly, leaving behind a Hill job he enjoyed and a personal life that had been in turmoil for years.

Separated from Barb, he reported to Annapolis in January, renting a townhouse in the Eastport section of the city. At about that time he had lunch with Jack Limpert, the editor of *Washingtonian* magazine. Limpert thought it was time to take a close journalistic look at the women who had entered the Academy for the first time in 1976. By then they were well into their junior year. You're going to be at Annapolis, said Limpert. Are you interested in writing something? Sure, said Webb.

Like many Annapolis men, Webb had been vaguely troubled in 1975 when Congress mandated the entrance of women into the service academies. Even that low level of concern had passed by the time he arrived at Annapolis to teach nearly four years later. He had, he said, absolutely no point of view. He intended to research the story as any journalist would, by talking to a lot of people, mostly women. He figured he would find some problems, but expected the overall tone of the article to be like those that had preceded it, positive and uplifting.

Women aside, the Academy seemed to have fallen victim to some of the relaxed, go-with-the-flow attitudes of the larger society. Invited to dine in the Mess Hall, he saw none of the constructive pandemonium he remembered, the plebe system a pale imitation of itself, unpleasant but not pressurized, a year to endure rather than survive, a quiz instead of a test, certainly not an ordeal.

He sensed that the Academy, at least the military side of it, was running scared, the legacy of a lost war and a muddleheaded Congress determined to take the rough edges off the armed services. Seeing a void, the long-suffering academic departments had moved to fill it, quietly gaining the upper hand in the age-old tug-of-war between Athens and Sparta.

Had he become another peevish old grad grousing because things weren't the way he remembered them? Could be, he admitted, filing away his concerns pending further evidence. Turning to the article he had promised *Washingtonian*, he commenced a series of interviews with female midshipmen. His first draft was a predictable series of character sketches that did not even address whether or not women belonged at Annapolis. Unhappy with his initial effort, he set up more interviews. One day, because of a mix-up in names, a male midshipman, a junior, reported to his office instead of the female he had asked to see. Since you're here, said Webb, sit down and let's talk. "Sir, what you'd hear from me you'll hear from any guy in our class," said the midshipman. "I'd much rather have been in the last class with balls than the first class with women." With that, he spun around and walked out.

Webb had heard the line before, recognized it as the seemingly jocular lament of the male members of the Class of 1980. He knew there was some male disgruntlement. The men in '79 toyed with inscribing the letters LCWB on their class rings before settling on a more subtle alternative, "Omnes Viri," Latin for "all male." In the rough-and-tumble midshipman milieu such protests seemed mild enough, inside jokes rather than acts of defiance or disparagement. But the kid in his office hadn't been smiling.

Resuming his research, no longer limiting his interviews to women, Webb gradually realized there was a story he hadn't begun to touch. The women were the story, sure, but so were the men. And at the heart of the tale was the very soul of the Academy.

Predictably, he heard complaints of preferential treatment, but in sufficient detail to persuade him that a double standard had taken root. Punishment meted out unequally. The grooming of women for high-striper positions to meet public relations needs. A severe scaling back of plebe indoctrination occasioned by the admission of women. Moreover, contrary to the official Academy line that no serious problems had been introduced by the presence of women, he heard numerous tales of sexual tension and fraternization. One male midshipman, assigned to work for a female midshipman, summed up his conflicting emotions by saying, "Half the time I wanted to kill her and half the time I wanted to fuck her." He learned of a lesbian ring presided over by a female officer on the Academy staff, hushed up by officials. Of female plebes huddling under blankets in the back seat of cars as male upperclassmen, prohibited from dating freshmen, smuggled them out of the Yard for romantic assignations. A female midshipman told Webb of her roommate bragging that she had "knocked off" more than one hundred guys, of sitting at her desk trying to study while the roommate performed oral sex in the closet, of the roommate musing aloud over the "three flavors" of ejaculate.

Keeping the sensational information to himself, he produced a piece that in most ways was a model of restraint. Entitled "Women Can't Fight," it challenged the growing political sentiment for women in combat roles as well as the presence of women at the service academies. "There is a place for women in our military, but not in combat," he wrote.

In a graphic opening passage, he described combat conditions as he and his troops had experienced them in Vietnam. Months without bathing except in muddy communal baths, forced marches laden with seventy pounds of gear, answering calls of nature by straddling a slit trench dug between fighting holes, for security reasons always within sight of other Marines. He told of waking up in the middle of the night to the sounds of one of his machine-gunners stabbing a dead enemy soldier, "emptying his fear and frustration into the corpse's chest."

"We killed and bled and suffered and died in a war that Washington society, which seems to view service in the combat arms as something akin to a commute to the Pentagon, will never comprehend," he wrote.

He argued that Congress, in requiring the service academies to admit women, had diluted their mission, which he saw first and foremost as the training of combat leaders, a role for which he insisted women were monumentally ill-suited. Women were a distraction to the men, he asserted, "poisoning" their preparation for combat command. He recounted the trials of his own plebe year, the testing and the abuse, of crying in the closet after the paddling, with the laundry bag over his head.

"That was the plebe system," he wrote. "It was harsh and cruel. It was designed to produce a man who would be able to be an effective leader in combat, to endure prisoner-of-war camps, to fight this country's wars with skill and tenacity. And it is all but gone."

Some extreme practices, such as those he described, had no place at the Academy, he said. But, he added: "I don't see anything at the Naval Academy anymore that can take a person deep inside himself. I see refinement. I see an overemphasis on academics at the expense of leadership. Harvard and Georgetown and a plethora of other institutions can turn out technicians and intellectuals en masse; only the service academies have been able to turn out combat leaders en masse, and they have stopped doing so."

It was a relentless but generally controlled attack. Occasionally he went too far, as when he described Bancroft Hall, in which some three hundred females were surrounded by four thousand males, as "a horny woman's dream," a line he later regretted. He applauded the advances made by women over the previous decade in business and the professions, said he could imagine a woman President. But it was folly, he argued, to use the armed forces and the service academies, as Congress seemed determined to do, to placate interest groups and as test tubes for social experimentation.

"You might not pick this up in K Street law offices or in the halls of Congress, but once you enter areas of this country where more typical Americans dwell, the areas that provide the men who make up our combat units, it becomes obvious. Inside the truck stops and in the honky-tonks, down on the street and in the coal towns, American men are tough and violent. When they are lured or drafted from their homes and put through the dehumanization of boot camp, then thrown into an operating combat unit, they don't get any nicer, either. And I have never met a woman, including the dozens of female midshipmen I encountered during my recent semester as a professor at the Naval Academy, whom I would trust to provide those men with combat leadership."

The article, which appeared in the November 1979 issue of *Washingtonian*, ignited a firestorm. Women were angry, liberals gasped, Navy and Academy officialdom excoriated Webb. The charge was led from the banks of the Severn by the Academy superintendent, Vice Admiral Bill Lawrence, John McCain's hero and the husband of his physical therapist, the man he considered the most heroic of the POWs. To make matters worse, Lawrence's daughter, Wendy, was a midshipman, destined to stand twelfth among the 966 members of the class of 1981. To Lawrence, Webb was guilty of disloyalty and deceit.

Not long after the article hit the streets, a senior admiral from the Pentagon was a guest in the Mess Hall. Suddenly the place erupted as male midshipmen leaped to their feet and blasted the admiral with their new rallying cry: "Webb was right! Webb was right! Webb was right!"

The wounds never had a chance to heal. During his brief teaching stint at the Academy, Webb began an Annapolis-based second novel that on publication in March 1981 again scorched his alma mater. But it did much more. *A Sense of Honor* breathed life into the Academy, distilling its essence into three hundred pages of crisp prose and crackling dialogue.

Webb took the reader on a guided tour of the Yard, mustering a crew of vivid, robust characters barely recognizable as the polite, housebroken young men beaming vanilla smiles at tourists. His midshipmen were lusty, often profane, some of the Academy's officers fools and petty martinets. All the madness was there: chow calls, come-arounds, uniform races, gross-out contests, the tyranny of the clock that for four years controlled every moment from reveille to lights-out. Bancroft Hall was portrayed as what it is, or perhaps what it was—an incubator for combat leaders, a place where sometimes it's more important to spit-shine your shoes to a blinding gloss than to study for a chemistry exam.

The book surged with power and machismo, brought to critical mass by confining most of the action to Bancroft Hall and compressing it into a six-day period in February 1968. In its rambunctious energy, the novel resembled *West Side Story*, not the movie but the original 1957 stage version, when the walls of New York's Winter Garden Theater could scarcely contain the electricity as switchblades flashed, teenage thugs scaled ten-foot-high chain link fences, and a single gunshot froze the heart of the audience.

A Sense of Honor was a critical success, though it did not sell as well as *Fields of Fire*, at least to the public at large. In Annapolis midshipmen were tripping over each other to buy it. Academy officials, aghast at the book, labored to dampen the demand, performing a series of verbal pratfalls that gave the novel even greater currency, proving in the process that Webb had been overly kind in peopling his novel with a mere handful of bumblers.

Other than Academy officials, few readers managed to miss the message. David Shribman of the *Washington Star* called the book "a lament to the passing of the rigorous stress indoctrination that gave a formidable meaning to the expression 'military academy.' " Carey Winfrey, in the *New York Times*, said Webb's "flawed Academy ultimately emerges . . . as a place where such out-of-fashion concepts as duty, honor, and country can still be evoked without irony." On the op-ed page of the *Washington Post*, R. James Woolsey, former Undersecretary of the Navy, later Bill Clinton's CIA director, said, "The book is no more just about hazing than *Moby Dick* is just about whaling."

The comment Webb treasured most came from Herman Wouk, a World War II ninety-day wonder who put his Navy experience to work in writing *The Caine Mutiny*, *The Winds of War*, and *War and Remembrance*. Said Wouk in a note to Webb, "You have written the Academy a bittersweet Valentine that the Academy will never understand."

Webb already knew the Academy would not understand. He found that out in early 1980, a few months after publication of "Women Can't Fight." Mac McGarvey was in Washington. Webb thought he might enjoy seeing the Academy and dining in the Mess Hall. He called a midshipman friend, asking him to make the arrangements. When Webb and McGarvey entered Bancroft Hall, a forlorn, apologetic mid greeted them. McGarvey's chit had been approved, he said, but not Webb's. McGarvey wanted to leave, but Webb insisted he stay. Then Webb wandered into town and ate alone, beginning a banishment from the Academy that would last for the next four years.

CHAPTER TWENTY-FOUR

GUERRILLA WARFARE

In early 1977, as John McCain was finishing up his command tour in Jacksonville, Admiral Jim Holloway, the Chief of Naval Operations, learned he was slated for a low-profile staff billet. The assignment seemed unimaginative, a waste of talent. McCain's a well-known guy, people like him, the CNO told the Bureau of Naval Personnel, let's put him where he can do us some good. McCain soon had orders to Washington as the number-two man in the Navy's Senate liaison office. Several months later, after his selection for captain, he took over the office.

The Navy, like the other services, maintains liaison offices in the House and Senate. A large part of the job is constituent service, determining, for example, why a sailor from a lawmaker's state or district is being court-martialed or why his wife has not received his allotment check.

Liaison officers also act as go-betweens, facilitating the exchange of information between legislators and the Pentagon. On overseas congressional trips, they serve as escorts, arranging for transportation, lodging, at times even lugging suitcases.

McCain's father, a liaison officer two decades earlier, had greatly expanded the position, becoming a lobbyist in uniform and a presence on the Hill. Most of Jack McCain's successors, however, reverted to the standard role of medal-bedecked attendants, their chief duty the care and feeding of senators and congressmen.

John McCain reversed the trend again, giving new, at times unusual twists to the job, along the way limbering up for the political career he would launch five years later.

Under McCain, the Navy's small liaison office on the first floor of the Russell Senate Office Building became a late-afternoon gathering spot where senators and staffers, usually from the Armed Services and

Foreign Relations committees, would drop in for a drink and the chance to unwind.

The magnet was McCain, a fun-loving, irreverent, mildly impetuous figure whose judgment members trusted on military matters because of the long naval tradition that he embodied and his own well-chronicled experiences.

Though invariably courteous, he was without awe, rarely minced words, kowtowed to no one. For all the Hill's caste consciousness, he was soon moving on an equal footing in a bipartisan circle of junior senators and staffers.

"I never ran across any people in the military liaison offices that were at all like John," said Albert (Pete) Lakeland, a senior Foreign Relations Committee staffer. "In fact, I really didn't even get to know any of the others. They handled baggage and that was it."

His closest friends were two of the younger, more independent senators, Democrat Gary Hart of Colorado and Republican Bill Cohen of Maine.

Hart had managed George McGovern's 1972 antiwar presidential campaign, but it did not become an issue in the friendship between the two men. "Never crossed my mind," said McCain.

In fact, though McCain held Congress in part to blame for the Vietnam debacle, there was no discernible evidence that he nursed a grudge, let alone a corrosive anger on the order of many other veterans.

"John McCain was as easy, as open, and as accepting of the United States Congress, both as an institution and as individuals, as any military officer that I've seen in twenty-five years," said William B. Bader, majority staff director of the Foreign Relations Committee.

McCain did not view lapses in taste and personal behavior as heralding a national Armageddon either, his live-and-let-live attitude in sharp contrast to the grim moralizing of another former POW, Alabama Senator Jeremiah Denton. Bader thought of McCain as emerging from prison as St. Francis of Assisi, Denton as the Grand Inquisitor.

Not all McCain's senatorial friends came from the junior ranks. During four years on the Hill, he developed special relationships with some of the Senate's most powerful figures, most notably Texan John Tower, an ex-Navy man and the ranking Republican on the Armed Services Committee.

"He was very much loved by John Tower," said Jim Jones, the Marine who questioned Oliver North's commitment to command on Okinawa, by then serving under McCain on the Navy liaison staff. "I think that John McCain is the son that John Tower never had."

His popularity was wide and deep, his friendships nonideological. His affection for Tower, a Vietnam hawk, was mirrored by his admiration for Jacob Javits, sponsor of the Vietnam-inspired War Powers Resolution, which sought to limit the ability of Presidents to wage undeclared wars.

"John McCain, as a Navy captain, knew on a personal basis more senators and was more warmly received than virtually any lobbyist I have ever known in this town; they loved to see him," said Jim McGovern, a Navy lieutenant on the liaison staff, later undersecretary of the Air Force.

McCain was much in demand for overseas escort duty, especially by members of the Armed Services and Foreign Relations committees. He was fun to be around, his wit appealing, his natural exuberance infectious. In an Athens taverna, he danced on a table with Senator Joseph Biden's wife, Jill, a red bandanna clenched in his teeth. In Seoul he told Bill Cohen that a seemingly empty room in their hotel was filled with Korean security men. Cohen laughed. McCain dared him to walk in. As Cohen tried to enter, a dour Korean stepped out of the shadows and blocked his path. "Just looking around," said the senator, retreating sheepishly. At the Peking Opera, Cohen marveled at the brilliant costumes, the acrobatic performances, and the enthusiasm of the audience. Said McCain as they departed the theater, "That's the most fun I've had since my last interrogation."

An episode on a flight to China in the spring of 1979 left Bill Bader wondering if there might be more to McCain's appeal than his reputation as an engaging traveling companion. During the trip, no fewer than five senators, all antiwar Democrats, wandered separately to the rear of the plane where McCain was seated and invited him to join them up front. After watching the parade for several hours, the perplexed Bader puzzled it out. The senators, he decided, were making their peace with John McCain.

On the same trip senators and staffers were touring a factory complex outside Shanghai. McCain and Bader, losing interest in the official blather, began wandering around the outbuildings. They poked their heads into one, a primitive infirmary, its metal-frame beds covered with gray blankets, a red stripe running through them. Bader turned to McCain. He was ashen. "John, what is it?" asked Bader. Murmured McCain, "Those were the blankets we had in Vietnam."

Bader had rarely seen that side of McCain. If he talked of prison at all, it was almost always in a joking way, as with the wisecrack to Cohen at the opera. Bader later concluded that his long incarceration, for all its hardships, had lent a different dimension to McCain, made him more than he might otherwise have been.

"I knew two hundred John McCains," said Bader, a Navy bombardier-navigator during the Korean War. "And I still know them. They're vaguely paunchy, overgrown boys. If John McCain had not had this Vietnamese experience, of prison, of solitude, of brutality, he would have just been one more Navy jock."

McCain and Pete Lakeland were in Honolulu, at a CINCPAC reception for a Foreign Relations Committee contingent on its way to China. They were having a drink together when someone tapped Lakeland on the shoulder. He swung around, exchanged a few words. When he turned back, he spotted McCain introducing himself to an attractive young blond woman across the room.

Lakeland was surprised. He knew that McCain, by then separated from Carol, liked women, but casual pickups were not his style. Something clearly was going on. McCain and the woman spent the entire reception together, talking, laughing, an island to themselves. Whenever Lakeland walked toward them, McCain maneuvered his back to him, as if he didn't know him.

The party was closing down when Lakeland finally broke through the invisible barrier McCain had erected around his new acquaintance.

"Hey, John, are you going back to the hotel or what are you doing?" said Lakeland, peeved at his friend.

"Oh, Pete, I want you to meet Cindy Hensley," said McCain. He explained that Cindy was visiting Hawaii from Phoenix with her parents. He added, "We're going out for dinner." Lakeland waited. "You wouldn't like to join us, would you?" asked McCain. "No, no," said Lakeland. "I'll see you. Have a good time."

Walking back to his hotel, Lakeland realized that whatever he had witnessed, it had not been a casual pickup. "John was smitten," he said. "He was instantly, compellingly, attracted to her."

The senatorial contingent left for China the next morning. Throughout the journey, McCain talked about Cindy, insisted she was someone special, became testy when teased about earthy motives. Midway through the trip he called her in Phoenix. She was in the hospital, recuperating from minor knee surgery. Earlier in the day an arrangement of flowers had been delivered to her room, the card signed "John." She thanked him effusively. "It was nothing," he said, "I just wanted you to know I was thinking about you." Two years later, she found out that McCain's only involvement with the flowers had been to take credit for them. They had been sent by another John, an old friend in Tucson.

Over the next year or so, they got together often, in Washington, in Arizona where Cindy lived, in Fort Walton Beach, Florida, where they stayed with an old McCain friend, Jerry Dorminy, the owner of the Hog's Breath Saloon.

At twenty-five, seventeen years McCain's junior, Cindy had the youthful good looks of a beauty queen without the shallowness that goes with the stereotype. Her wide-spaced blue eyes communicated intelligence, her demeanor casual elegance, the product of the best schools and the better southwestern country clubs. She was rich, but not idle rich. When McCain met her she was teaching disabled teen-age children of migrant farm workers, defying superiors who forbade her to make home visits because they were not considered safe.

The family money came from beer. Her father, Jim Hensley, hocked everything he had in 1956 to come up with $10,000 to buy a small Anheuser-Busch distributorship. Two decades later he had turned it into the largest in the country. The Hensleys, said one observer, had "more money than most small countries."

McCain's detractors, and some of his friends, would later say that he saw Cindy as the ultimate target of opportunity and locked on to her with single-minded, even cynical calculation. It was fine that she was young and beautiful, so it was said, but the real attraction was that she was the daughter of a rich, well-connected businessman from a state that seemed to offer opportunities to someone with McCain's emerging political ambitions.

"Absolute bullshit," said Jim McGovern. "One thing I can say about John McCain is, he ain't calculating."

The scenario is hard to take seriously. Was it even remotely possible that the impulsive, hot-blooded McCain who used to take his Navy pay in cash had suddenly been reborn as a gold-digging manipulator, coolly mapping out a marriage of convenience? Even if he contemplated such a union, he had to realize that divorcing Carol, an essential part of his alleged game plan, could easily sidetrack his political career at any point down the line. The courageous, crippled wife cast aside for a wealthy and beautiful younger woman—how understanding were the voters likely to be in a conservative state with a large, politically active, fundamentalist Christian community? Especially when many of his friends, people who knew and liked him, already held the failure of his marriage to Carol against him.

McGovern had a simpler explanation: hormones. That fits. But Cindy may have represented more to McCain.

"I think John very much saw her as reclaiming the life he had lost," said Pete Lakeland. "I think that was the real theme, that Cindy stood for everything he didn't have in prison. This was the sweet, innocent, pure American dream."

It was as if McCain had decided to start life over again. "I think he was determined that his future was not going to be controlled by those five and a half years and his POW experience," said Lakeland. "He saw Cindy as the focus for his regeneration."

As the Navy's emissary to the Senate, McCain was mindful of what he perceived to be the best interests of the service even if, on occasion, those views were not shared by the Carter administration or, officially at least, by the Navy itself. On more than one occasion, he went his own way on issues in which administration policy seemed driven by politics, expediency, ignorance, or some combination of those factors. He knew he was taking risks. He didn't care. After five and a half years in prison he had no intention of meekly falling in line. Too many generals and admirals had done that during Vietnam, ruining their reputations, ill-serving the nation, getting a lot of kids killed.

McCain's reluctance to follow in their footsteps was demonstrated most graphically in the battle between the Carter administration and Congress over an aircraft carrier. Of merely passing interest today, at the time the confrontation between the two branches of government was intense, triggering a presidential veto one year and embarrassing acquiescence the next. McCain's role in all this was a small one, but not all that small and not all that defensible. In his way, he was a double agent, in the main arranging trips, guiding Navy department officials to meetings with senators, on the side waging guerrilla warfare.

The carrier issue flared in 1978 when Jimmy Carter decided the fleet did not need a new supercarrier to replace the *Midway*, an aging flattop built during World War II. The Navy, unhappy with Carter's judgment but having no choice in the matter, went along with the Commander-in-Chief. McCain did not.

For the next two years, McCain, assisted by Jim McGovern, quietly but effectively lobbied for the new carrier in secret defiance of Navy Secretary W. Graham Claytor, for whom he worked, and President Carter.

Retired Rear Admiral Mark Hill, chief lobbyist for the Association of Naval Aviation, the organization that spearheaded the drive to push the carrier through Congress, remembers McCain's activities well.

"John McCain was a stalwart little soldier in that fight," said Hill,

John Poindexter's old friend from Whiz Kid days. "He never wavered. He was supporting the big carrier and he did a lot of stuff behind the back of the Secretary of the Navy. . . . He was gutsy enough to say, Screw my boss."

McCain did not flaunt his opposition to the administration's policy. At first, when senators or staffers asked his opinion, he explained the President's position. If they pressed, he told them that he thought the carrier was badly needed and why.

As time went on, he intensified his efforts, still keeping a low profile. He talked with senators on overseas trips or when they dropped by his office, to their aides, even their friends. Jim McGovern, with McCain's encouragement, wrote a position paper laying out the case for the carrier. No letterhead, no signature, wide distribution.

McCain was also serving as a forward observer for the pro-carrier forces, relaying target data from his perch in the Senate to Mark Hill and like-minded lobbyists about which senators were wavering, where their concerns lay, what arguments might sway them.

"John McCain had his ear to the ground closer than anybody else," said Hill. "He was an absolutely essential nerve center."

Over the objections of President Carter, Congress in 1978 approved $2 billion for a new nuclear carrier. To kill it, an outraged Carter had to veto the omnibus $36 billion defense authorization bill, which contained the funds for the ship.

Congress sustained the veto. "Admiral, we're not going to give up, are we?" McCain asked Hill when the veto override failed. "No way," Hill replied. The following year, with McCain and Hill once more lobbying furiously, Congress again funded the carrier. This time Carter signed the legislation.

McCain saw nothing disloyal in what he and McGovern did: "It wasn't like I said to Jim, Let's overturn the President, let's go do battle with the administration. We both believed the carrier was pretty important. . . . We knew all of the uniformed Navy agreed with us. . . . We didn't ever portray it as anybody's views but our own, but because we had credibility with people, they listened to us."

How did Carter administration officials react? "They didn't even know what hit them," laughed McCain. "It had never happened before and it's never happened since."

McCain's reasons, as he later explained them, included his personal dismay with the state of the post-Vietnam military, which he ascribed primarily to Carter, but to Congress as well. "We had enlisted petty officers with families on food stamps, we had ships that couldn't leave port. The problems were just incredible."

There were other reasons. McCain himself was evolving. He loved working in the Senate, but he was not content with being a bit player, solving constituent problems for senators, running their errands, handling their baggage.

Said McCain: "We [meaning he and McGovern] recognized that you can do that job, be a caseworker, see that Seaman Smith gets his hardship discharge, or you can get involved in issues of substance, and that's what we did."

"The Vietnam experience made me want to be involved more in public service," he said on another occasion, "*and seeing things happen right.*" It was a breathtaking assertion, worthy of Ollie North and John Poindexter after a few years in the White House.

Laboring away in the Senate as a junior captain, McCain knew his Navy career was about over. His annual physicals were not good and he hadn't been slated for a major sea command, the usual stepping-stone to flag rank. He figured he might make rear admiral, but vice admiral, let alone full admiral like his father and grandfather, seemed out of the question.

He began thinking of retirement and life after the Navy. He considered staying in Washington as a civilian lobbyist, probably for a defense contractor, but the prospect didn't interest him. He knew that John Tower wanted him on the Armed Services Committee staff, which was more appealing. Finally, though, he admitted to himself that what he really wanted to do was enter politics.

It was not a new idea. Back in 1976, when he was stationed in Jacksonville, he thought about running for the House, tested the waters, decided the incumbent congressman would be too hard to beat. If the prospect had merely intrigued him then, his time in the Senate had whipped his ambition into a lather.

It was a time of change. His marriage to Carol had been effectively over for some time. After a number of trial separations, they were legally separated in January 1980 and divorced a month later. In May he married Cindy Hensley in Phoenix. Senator Bill Cohen was his best man, another senator, Gary Hart, an usher. The newlyweds honeymooned in Hawaii. A few weeks earlier, they learned each other's real ages, thanks to the local paper, which routinely published marriage-license data. Cindy, worried that John might think she was too young for him, had told him she was three years older than she was. John, fearing the opposite, had shaved four years from his age.

Carol, despondent, in need of diversion, had gone to work as Nancy

Reagan's personal assistant a few months earlier, traveling the campaign trail with the future First Lady throughout the primaries.

Carol's friends in the press corps helped buoy her spirits with black, convoluted humor. On the day John and Cindy were married, reporters on the press bus serenaded her with endless refrains of "Those Wedding Bells Are Breaking Up That Old Gang of Mine." When Reagan made a patriotic speech at the Alamo, asking his audience what had become of the heroes of yesteryear, Lou Cannon of the *Washington Post* slipped up behind her and quipped, "Yeah, Carol, just where is that son of a bitch?"

CHAPTER TWENTY-FIVE

GARLIC IN A CROWDED ELEVATOR

By early 1975, Ollie North was scrambling back onto the fast track. It did not happen overnight. In the aftermath of his hospitalization, his post-Okinawa orders to Washington's Marine Barracks, the showplace of the Corps and home of the commandant, were rescinded.

At the Barracks—known as Eighth and I because of its location—he would have been in the spotlight, his natural element, leading troops in precision drill at the weekly sunset parades, a major tourist attraction that each summer lures Washington's most powerful and influential figures, often the President. At Headquarters Marine Corps, to which he was sent instead, he seemed destined to join legions of other junior officers in lugging charts, fetching coffee, and otherwise sinking into the bureaucratic sludge.

Typically, he confounded the conventional wisdom. Assigned to Manpower, he immersed himself in one of the Corps's most vexing post-Vietnam problems, how to maintain adequate troop levels for its combat units overseas. For most of the previous decade, those units, in Vietnam and later on Okinawa, had been replenished by shipping over individual replacements for a year or more. In the aftermath of Vietnam, these so-called hardship tours were causing severe morale problems, leading to broken families and declining reenlistment rates. For the commandant and his chief lieutenants, few issues had higher priority.

Before long, North had become a strong proponent of and the primary briefing officer for a possible solution to the problem, one that was eventually adopted. He argued for scrapping the system of individual replacements and sending entire units overseas for six-month deployments. "The tours were shorter, morale was higher, unit integrity was far better, and a lot more marriages survived," he later wrote. His efforts earned him another decoration, the Meritorious Service Medal.

North was once more flying high. However, he was again exhibiting disturbing, at times erratic behavior—spending unnecessarily long hours on the job, spinning tales that exaggerated his importance, displaying a fierce personal ambition that seemed excessive even for the highly competitive military milieu.

At around this time he began car-pooling to Headquarters from his home in northern Virginia with three colonels, all later generals. "Had you been a passenger in that car, you would have thought Ollie was already a general and the three colonels were merely window dressing and straight men," said Jerry Hagen, one of the colonels.

North was often late to the designated pickup point. "Most·of the time we would drive to Garrisonville, pull into his driveway, and sound the horn," Hagen said in a 1991 letter, its tone a mixture of fondness and concern.

> Ollie's dog would bark, a light would come on and Ollie would come sprinting for the car in his underwear or sometimes trousers. He would have shirt, perhaps trousers and shoes in one hand, shaving kit, cap and briefcase in the other.
>
> While dressing and dry shaving, Ollie would regale us with stories of the special event that took place the night before and which caused him to oversleep. Usually the event was a special recall back to HQMC to work an important paper for DC/S Manpower, the Asst. Commandant or CMC.
>
> It always amazed me, especially when I was secretary to the General Staff in the office of Chief of Staff, HQMC, that the colonels and generals seemed never to be involved in these "special"–"high-priority" actions, only Ollie. I never doubted that he did go to HQMC at night,

nor that he did work on a paper (at least I don't doubt it too much), but I strongly suspected that his imagination and need for attention greatly colored his version of the event.

. . . In appearance, Ollie epitomized all that is fine about Marines. In terms of dedication, energy and initiative, he was hard to keep up with. Yet he constantly needed attention and recognition. In some ways he was like a puppy who would chase a stick for you until he dropped so long as you gave him a pat and some nice words on a frequent basis.

Ollie enjoyed being close to senior officers. . . . His stories were usually colored by references to his conversations and meetings with General Jaskilka (ACMC) and the DC/S for Manpower. Everyone in HQMC knew Ollie, and insofar as I know, liked Ollie and thought well of him. Many, however, tired of his constant need for attention and recognition.

Ollie also had a timetable for advancement that was considerably faster than that of the Corps and Navy Department. My selection below the zone for lt. colonel and colonel occupied much of his conversation when we were together. Ollie needed the "secret." Of course I had no such secret. I often told Ollie that he would have no problem being promoted. He was smart, had a superior appearance, worked hard, had a fine combat record, and was in a job where he got all the recognition he would ever need. My advice never satisfied Ollie. I don't think he was much concerned with promotion to major. He was already thinking about colonel and above.

There were periods of exhaustion and burnout, said an officer familiar with North in those days, when he would be told not to come to work for a week. As such periods approached, he seemed almost electrified, reacting to jokes that merited at most a smile with roars and guffaws, telling war stories that, according to one officer, were "just so fantastic that they were not realistic."

At Headquarters, North continued to bedevil his peers. Because of his involvement with the troop-level issue, he frequently briefed the most senior generals. Officers of similar grade envied his access. Consciously or not he rubbed their noses in it. In conversations with peers, he made the right sounds, but his eyes flitted here and there, seemingly scanning the terrain for someone more important. At times, acquaintances recall, he would break off in mid-sentence if he spied a colonel or general walking down the hall. He also gained a reputation for pandering to his bosses, telling them what they wanted to hear.

"I think Ollie basically judged you based on what your utility was to what his basic particular ends were," said Jim Jones, who served with North at Headquarters and earlier on Okinawa, as well as with John McCain on Capitol Hill. "I think he was manipulative in that way. That contributes to the peer problem. You can't hide from your peers. I mean, you just can't."

Chuck Krulak, perhaps North's most eloquent defender among those who have known him well over the years, laid much of the peer criticism, then and later, to envy.

"There was a lot of professional jealousy of Ollie North by his contemporaries. And it got worse and worse and worse, because . . . he was good. He was probably not as good as he thought he was, but he was good. He was very articulate, he found himself in good jobs and performed well. He always sought to set himself apart and then make it into something."

Krulak compared North to one of his own Academy classmates, Walt Kesler, like John Poindexter the brigade commander and the number-one man in the class. At Annapolis Kesler established himself as head and shoulders above his classmates, but did so effortlessly and with grace, never generating resentment. In the Class of 1964, there was Kesler and everybody else, a natural order to which all subscribed.

North could play at Kesler's level, even sustain it for long periods of time, said Krulak, but it did not come naturally. "It took twenty-four hours a day, seven days a week. He worked his ass off all the time. There is very little time that Ollie North didn't put 110 percent into what he was doing."

Much of the time, North's superhuman efforts were not necessary, but he was incapable of assigning priorities in his life, a man for whom everything was, as Krulak put it, a "graded requirement."

"Taking a piss was a graded requirement," said Krulak. "There was no time to take your pack off. Life is a graded requirement. He had a lot of graded requirements. But the flip side is he always did well, which pissed people off even more."

There was another element. "He likes to work," said Krulak. "He worked for me a couple of times and he actually got his rocks off working hard. Most people don't, but he did."

Krulak conceded some shortcomings. "I don't think there's any-body who knows Ollie that doesn't think that he has an ego," he said. "And I think his enemies will really expand on that. His friends see it as a chink in his armor."

As for his exaggerations, said Krulak, "Most of his close friends crank in about a 10 percent bullshit factor." The sad part, he said, was that North had no need to overstate his accomplishments. "It just was not necessary," he said. "He was good enough without all that."

Fred Peck, the plebe boxer who idolized upperclassmen North and Webb at Annapolis, came to see North from different angles in ensu-

ing years. He tried in a 1988 letter to explain the conflicting perceptions by subordinates and superiors on the one hand and peers on the
other. "Having been one of the adoring underlings twice, as a midshipman at USNA and as a 2nd Lt at TBS [the Basic School], I can
attest to the power of his persona," wrote Peck. "Then, having risen
to the same rank, major and now lieutenant colonel, I have also experienced the other reaction."

> I have arrived at some conclusions on this duality of impressions about
> one man. Those above and below him see Ollie the performer. He is
> both a performer of deeds, a dynamic man of action who gets things
> done while others flounder around; and he is also a performer in the
> dramatic sense, the showman, the "hotdog" who attracts attention and
> admiration.
>
> Those who find themselves on the same plane with Ollie see the
> shark; the ultimate competitor who makes them feel uneasy. To bor-
> row from Shakespeare, "Yon Cassius has a lean and hungry look. He
> thinks too much. Such men are dangerous." (I'm trusting my memory
> from 11th grade English on that quote, so don't hold me to its complete
> accuracy; but it expresses the sentiment I want very well).
>
> The military is a very competitive field of endeavor. . . . Most of us
> who succeed in it are extremely competitive individuals. The element of
> competition is with us from the very first day, especially in places like
> Annapolis and Quantico where class standing can be so important to
> your future. Certainly all officers realize that they are constantly com-
> peting for fewer and fewer vacancies in the hierarchy of the military's
> leadership pyramid. Only 75% of the captains become majors, 66% of
> the majors make lieutenant colonel, and only 50% of the light colonels
> get those eagles. Then come the real major leagues of competition—
> rising to flag or general officer rank—where only 7 or 8% will be cho-
> sen from those colonels who have survived the vicious winnowing out
> process of the field grade officers.
>
> Even in such a keenly competitive environment, most of us don't
> consciously think about the fact that we are constantly vying with our
> peers to make [it] to the next rung in the ladder. With Oliver Lawrence
> North, that sense of being in direct competition hits you like garlic in a
> crowded elevator. It's right there, in your face, and you can't get away
> from it. And even if you try to ignore it, it lingers with you, like the oily
> smell of that pungent herb that sticks to your clothes and skin.

At Headquarters, North met Major John Grinalds, Bud McFarlane's
friend from their days as White House Fellows. Sitting on the reverse
side of an office partition from Grinalds, North noticed that the major's intellect was highly regarded by more senior officers. "Whenever

there was an important decision to be made, people would ask, 'What does Grinalds think about this?' " recalled North in his autobiography.

North noticed something else. Grinalds kept a Bible on his desk, and from time to time would read it to himself. He was known as a born-again Christian, a term new to North. Even so, writes North, "he was never one to wear his faith on his sleeve." That judgment would later be disputed by a number of other Marine officers, but North said the closest Grinalds ever came to discussing his personal beliefs at Headquarters was to occasionally point to his Bible and say, "You might want to know a little more about this."

In 1978 Grinalds received orders to the Second Marine Division at Camp Lejeune, North Carolina, where he was to command a battalion. North was due for orders as well, and Grinalds invited him along as his operations officer. Both had recently been selected below the zone for promotion, Grinalds to lieutenant colonel, North to major.

Betsy's initial reaction to Lejeune was not encouraging. "Tell me it's only a nightmare," she said as she awoke from a long car ride and looked for the first time on the seedy main street of Jacksonville, the town outside the sprawling base that passed as home for twenty-five thousand Marines. Soon, though, the Norths and their three children came to enjoy Lejeune, especially its fine recreational beach, where they would swim, boil shrimp, and barbecue.

Professionally, North was flourishing. As operations officer for Grinalds's Third Battalion, Eighth Marines, he was responsible for training as well as planning the unit's shipboard deployment to the Mediterranean. Two weeks before they were to embark, an event occurred of transcendent importance to North and endless amusement to others.

Jumping from a tracked vehicle, North aggravated an old back injury that dated to his car accident while at Annapolis. He was on the ground, writhing in pain, when Grinalds rushed up. Writes North in his autobiography:

> He helped me to a sitting position, and knelt down beside me. Placing his hands on my legs, he said, "I'm going to pray for you."
> This wasn't exactly the kind of help I had in mind. I'm lying here in agony and he wants to *pray*? This guy must be nuts.
> Then John Grinalds called out in prayer: "Lord Jesus Christ, You are the Great Physician. Heal this man."
> Suddenly the pain disappeared. Slowly, the feeling came back in my legs. I didn't know what to say beyond a muttered "Thank you."

"Don't thank me," said Grinalds. "Thank your Lord and Savior. *He* is the Great Physician. You have to turn to *Him*." [North's italics.]

North, in his words "profoundly humbled" by the experience, did so. Shepherded by Grinalds, who according to one source baptized North at the beach at Lejeune, the former Roman Catholic altar boy was born again. Soon he and Betsy joined a charismatic branch of the Episcopal Church that included Grinalds and, later, Chuck Krulak.

"I had been raised to know who my Lord and Savior was," writes North. "I knew *about* Him, but I didn't know Him personally. It was like reading about some important world figure, seeing him on television, reading things he had written and said, but never actually meeting him. That, to me, is the clearest way I know of explaining how that relationship has changed. Today, I've met Him and I know Him personally."

There were differing reactions to North's religious conversion. Some thought it did him a world of good.

Don Price, the major who had the run-in with North at the Academy Mess Night five years earlier, was stationed at Twenty-nine Palms, in the California desert, when Grinalds and North brought the battalion out from Lejeune for desert training.

"You could tell that Ollie was really responding to the positive role model of John Grinalds," said Price. "He seemed quieter, more professional, and, I won't say subdued, but more controlled."

Others felt that finding himself on speaking terms with Jesus only enhanced a messianic strain in North that had been struggling to surface for years.

Still others weren't buying his conversion, not then, not now. It is a measure of the good will that North had squandered over the years that some of his peers continued to question his sincerity even after he had been a regular churchgoer and active participant in prayer and Bible study groups for well over a decade. For these men, the miraculous healing at Lejeune was just another example of North currying favor with a superior.

"John Grinalds is a born-again, that's a fairly well-known fact," said classmate and fellow Marine Roy Carter in a typical comment. "And Ollie pandered to him. But Ollie panders to everybody."

North spent two years with the Second Marine Division, a tour that included two six-month deployments to the Mediterranean. In 1980 he was one of twenty Marine officers selected to attend the Command and Staff course at the Naval War College in Newport, Rhode Island, a prized assignment.

North called the year at Newport the one time in his Marine Corps career that he was able to strike the proper balance between personal and professional responsibilities. He worked hard, found the classes stimulating, but he was home for supper by six-thirty and usually had his weekends free. The family explored New England, he and Betsy made it down to New York a couple of times to see Broadway shows, and their fourth child, a daughter, was born.

As a student, he was well-prepared, thoughtful, and articulate, though at times too sure of his views for some of the more veteran instructors. Nathaniel Davis, a well-traveled former ambassador, enjoyed having North in his course on the Soviet Union, but often felt he was not getting through to him.

"I was presenting too many ambiguities, too many shades of gray," said Davis. "I was too skeptical, had seen too many foreign policy failures and had too little faith that resolute action, ideological commitment, and the willingness to smash constraints could turn the world around. My vision of the 'evil empire' was not clear enough for Ollie North."

He also gained a reputation as a "springbutt," a War College expression that describes the student who is constantly popping out of his seat to ask self-promoting, often sycophantic questions of the instructor or guest lecturer.

In the fall of 1980, an officer from the Manpower branch, Lieutenant Colonel Harry Jenkins, visited the War College and met with Marine student officers to discuss their next duty stations.

"It looks like you're going to recruiting duty, Major," Jenkins told North.

"Don't bet on it, sir," replied North.

North's flip response startled Jenkins. As he later told associates, he had never met North before and found his response presumptuous, out of line, and unfathomable. Unless, perhaps, he had friends in high places.

Back at Headquarters, North was penciled in for duty as commanding officer of the Marine recruiting station in New York City, a high-visibility post in which he would have had ample opportunity to shine.

But recruiting duty was a two-edged sword. The pressure to meet the monthly quota of recruits was enormous; failure to do so meant a lot of explaining. Most officers took such assignments with trepidation; few went willingly.

At Headquarters, Vic Taylor, who was in charge of making assignments for his fellow majors, fully expected North to move to New York when his year at the War College concluded in mid-1981. Instead, to Taylor's surprise, he learned that another officer had been tapped for the job.

Perplexed, Taylor set about trying to find another slot for North, decided to send him to the recruit training depot at Parris Island.

No sooner had Taylor made that decision than he received a message from the White House: we need the best major in the Marine Corps.

"Within a couple of seconds, I think of Ollie," recalled Taylor. Not that he considered North the best major in the Corps. He had, as it happened, some of the usual peer concerns about him. But his job was to put the right man in the right place and North seemed like a natural.

"They wanted an easel carrier over there," said Taylor. "And Ollie, quite frankly, would love the heady atmosphere . . . would revel in it."

For years, Taylor has thought of himself as the man who sent Ollie North to the White House. In fact, he may well have been a bit player.

"He got to the White House because of me," said Chuck Krulak, a flat statement, neutrally delivered. He was not boasting. Neither was he admitting an error in judgment. He was setting the record straight, as befits a man who sits behind an embroidered nameplate bearing a single word, "Integrity."

Krulak was working two levels above Taylor in the Office of Personnel Management, along with another old friend of Oliver North, Paul Goodwin. Their boss was Major General Dick Schulze.

Taylor may have initially proposed North, but Krulak said the list of candidates that eventually worked its way up to Schulze for approval did not reflect that. "When the list came up to me, it did not have his name on it," said Krulak, who was Schulze's administrative assistant at the time.

Krulak dutifully delivered the list to Schulze, but with a caveat. "I said, 'Sir, there's one that I think ought to be in there,'" recalled Krulak. "He said, 'Who's that?' I said, 'Ollie.' He said, 'Holy mackerel, you're right.' Basically, he became the pick."

Krulak later explained that he frequently suggested changes to slates of candidates for various posts after they reached his desk. "It was my job to run a sanity check on who the heck came up there," he said. "And the sanity check [for the White House job] said if they're looking for a young, representative, articulate, smart officer, here's one that fills the bill."

The final list sent to the White House may have contained as many as five names, as few as two, no one seems sure. All agreed, though, that the list as approved by Schulze was rank-ordered, North's name on top.

At the time, Krulak knew that seven years earlier North had been hospitalized for emotional problems. Unlike Schulze, he did not know all the details.

Years later, Krulak refused to second-guess himself even though in the interim he had learned more about that troubled period in North's life. As far as Krulak was concerned, North had encountered marital difficulties, suffered some temporary emotional problems, and been returned to duty, not an unusual situation in the aftermath of a war, the Vietnam War in particular.

"Ollie North was not a crazy man," insisted Krulak. As for North's hospitalization: "It was a pimple on a boar's ass."

Judging by North's reaction to the White House assignment, at least as he and some others have described it, he would not have been pleased had he known of the efforts put forth by his friends. North biographer Ben Bradlee, Jr., quotes Robert L. Schweitzer, an NSC official who screened candidates for staff positions, as saying he chose North because he didn't want the job.

"I was the one who could have turned Ollie down," said Schweitzer, a retired Army general. "I didn't want an Ollie North. I made an argument for policy-oriented guys, veterans who were experienced and who had advanced degrees in international relations—people who understood the give and take of policy-making. What endeared Ollie to me was, I asked him did he want to be here. 'No, absolutely not,' he responded. I'd rather have someone who wanted to be a soldier or lead troops than someone who wanted to get into the White House. He was a very humble guy. His honesty and fundamental approach drew me in."

North, in his autobiography, recalls fighting the assignment, even voicing his displeasure to the commandant, General Robert Barrow, as he was about to depart for the White House. Barrow, writes North, was having none of it.

> "Majuh," he said in his long Louisiana drawl, "Ah understand that you'd prefer not to go to the National Security Council."
> "Sir," I replied, "I'll go where I'm sent, of course, but I'd rather return to the fleet."
> "Brotha' North," he said, " 'tisn't like you to whine. Carry out yo' orders."

A postscript. For all his seeming consternation over the White House assignment, North did not register any complaint with Schulze or Krulak when he talked to them before starting the job.

"Absolutely not," said Krulak when asked if North ever told him he did not want to go. "If he didn't want to go, he wouldn't have gone. All he had to say was, 'I don't want to go.' You don't send an individual inside the gates there who doesn't want to go."

Krulak characterized North's self-proclaimed unhappiness as a time-honored ritual, the striking of a macho pose by Marine officers assigned anywhere but to a combat unit.

"That's what being a Marine's all about," said Krulak. "There's a big difference between walking in and making that statement and going to your monitor or to the director of personnel and saying, 'General Schulze, please let this cup pass me by.'"

In other words, North told a lot of people he didn't want to go, but he never mentioned it to Schulze and Krulak, the two people in the best position to keep it from happening.

BOOK THREE

THE NIGHTINGALE'S SONG

INTRODUCTION

Ronald Reagan's optimism and sunny disposition made him the perfect tonic for the gloom and self-conscious handwringing of the Carter years. He looked like a President and acted like one, at least in public. The private Reagan—passive, incurious, often befuddled—was the dirty little secret at the heart of his presidency.

Donald Regan, Reagan's second chief of staff, said it best: no other President of the modern era was so much a presence in the affairs of state without being an actual participant. Transported to the White House in a sedan chair, he was insulated from the nuts and bolts of governing by his own inclinations and the protectiveness of his aides. As a gesture of respect for his predecessors, he never took off his jacket in the Oval Office. Lamentably, he never got down to his shirtsleeves figuratively, either. He was a public President, playing what his biographer Lou Cannon called "the role of a lifetime."

Like any successful actor, he did not lack talent behind the camera. In Michael Deaver, he had an image-meister whose touch bordered on genius, the Busby Berkeley of the national political stage. His crew of speechwriters made music of cant. Could any American with a sense of history remain dry-eyed watching Reagan at Normandy in 1984 as he paid tribute to the men who stormed the cliffs at Ponte du Hoc? That was Reagan at his best, looking the part, hitting his marks, flawlessly reading his lines. But when the mist cleared, insiders noticed the credits. Produced by Michael Deaver. Words by Peggy Noonan, the gifted speechwriter who penned many of the lyrics to the Nightingale's Song.

Reagan was known as the Great Communicator, but that reputation was built on those occasions when he had a script in his hand. At news conferences, he stumbled all over himself, especially when pressed to move beyond canned answers. "Saturday Night Live" once did a press conference skit in which Reagan had a tiny microphone in his ear so that aides behind the scenes could feed him answers. The mike started picking up police calls. Now about Lebanon, our Marines are there because—One Adam Twelve, we have a burglary in progress at . . . because, uh, because . . .

In private he was even worse. He knew what he knew and that's all that he knew. He has been compared to the rudder on the ship of state, which was accurate as far as it went. He had strong views on certain things and those views guided his administration in the areas where they applied. He believed taxes were too high, the budget should be cut, national defense must be strengthened, and the Soviets were a menace. On those four points he was nearly unmovable.

Once, after a news conference, aides took turns telling him he had gone too far in ruling out a tax hike. As he did a slow burn, his spokesman, Larry Speakes, drafted a short statement designed to give him space to maneuver, "wiggle room" as it's known in Washington. Ripping the draft from Speakes's hand, he snatched a pen from his desk so fiercely the inkstand flew across the office. "Here's what I want to say," he fumed. With that he scrawled "No New Taxes" across the page and thrust it back at the wide-eyed aide.

Even in areas of his most deeply held convictions, however, Reagan was often lost once he moved beyond the rhetoric and into the details. His champions would argue that he was a big-picture man, a true Chief Executive, not a slave to minutiae like Jimmy Carter. But to avoid the pitfalls that afflicted his administration, he needed to master more than a few broad strokes.

On arriving in Geneva in 1985 for his first U.S.-Soviet summit, according to Bud McFarlane, he leaned over to George Shultz, his Secretary of State, and said, Now tell me again, George, what's the difference between a ballistic missile and a cruise missile?

And it wasn't just arms control.

Reagan has been called intellectually lazy, but that may overstate the case. The best word is incurious. Each night he would take a pile of papers prepared by his staff up to the family quarters. His aides said at the time that he did his homework religiously, though Cannon says he practiced triage, reading what piqued his interest, ignoring much of the rest. Either way, he was almost totally dependent on his advisers. He read what his staff gave him, met with those his staff thought he should see. There is little evidence that he ever reached out beyond that bubble, called people outside his inner circle to see if they might have a different slant on what he was being spoon-fed.

Francis X. Clines, a veteran *New York Times* reporter, in casual conversation once drew a distinction between Reagan and John Kennedy. Reagan would meet someone and charm them with affability. Kennedy was a charmer, too, but he wanted to know about people, not just who they were but what they knew. By the time Kennedy was finished with them, said Clines, he had cleaned their clocks.

No one ever accused Reagan of cleaning anybody's clock. Not even close. In the congressional Iran-Contra hearings of 1987, Donald Regan, former White House chief of staff, testified to what he called "a battle for the presidential mind," as if Reagan's brain lay in state in the Oval Office, a shivering blob of protoplasm over which his advisers conducted daily high-noon shoot-outs.

One of Reagan's great strengths was the ability to project himself over the television tube as a nice guy. But it was mostly surface affability. not personal warmth. Beyond his wife, he had few if any close friends. Those who seemed to fall into that category were said to be merely the husbands of Mrs. Reagan's friends. As for the men closest to him in the White House—Michael Deaver, Ed Meese, Jim Baker, Bill Clark, Don Regan—he enjoyed their company and treated them with courtesy, but only Regan failed to realize where they stood. They were staff, not the President's buddies.

He also was given to appalling lapses of loyalty. No one served him more faithfully than Michael Deaver, who began working for him soon after he was elected governor of California. Someone once asked Reagan if he thought of Deaver as a son. No, Reagan replied, winking, I think of him as a father. Yet when Deaver resigned from the 1980 campaign to spare his boss an embarrassing internal power struggle, Reagan never bothered to call once to see how he was holding up. Years later, after returning to Reagan's side and brilliantly stage-managing his presidency for four years, Deaver plunged into a morass of alcoholism and legal troubles. Again Reagan was conspicuously silent. A public defense of his old retainer would have been out of line. But the absence of a private, "Hi, pal, how ya doin'?" spoke volumes about Reagan and relationships.

Deaver, who seems not to resent Reagan's indifferent treatment, explained it as "a problem with intimacy," perhaps stemming from childhood. Reagan, he said, could become very emotional about men and women he barely knew or knew not at all. "He can weep about unknown people in lands far away very easily," said Deaver. POWs. The starving masses. Hostages.

Because Reagan was able to charm people, but never fully connect with them, he tended to view his aides as interchangeable parts. Thus in January 1985 when Jim Baker, the White House chief of staff, and Don Regan, the Treasury Secretary, told him they wanted to switch jobs, Reagan said, Fine, sounds good to me.

"Reagan made no inquiries," Regan later wrote. "I did not know what to make of his passivity. . . . He seemed to be absorbing a *fait accompli* rather than making a decision."

The President paid a price for his unblinking acquiescence. Baker, the architect of Reagan's first-term congressional triumphs, made a smooth transition to Treasury. But Regan, a cut-the-crap Wall Street executive and capable Treasury Secretary, proved a ham-handed chief of staff.

If the President's easy agreement to the job switch surprised Regan, he would quickly learn, as others had before him, the closely held reality of the Reagan presidency. Rather than being the strong, decisive leader the public saw, the private Reagan was in many ways a passive, disengaged Chief Executive. Determined to "let Reagan be Reagan," the new chief of staff discovered that there was no there there, that Reagan was in many crucial ways a creature of his staff, its guiding star perhaps, but not its captain.

Then there was the weirdness. "Virtually every major move and decision the Reagans made," Regan wrote in his autobiography, "was cleared in advance with a woman in San Francisco who drew up horoscopes to make certain that the planets were in a favorable alignment for the enterprise."

The influence of Mrs. Reagan's astrologer friend was so pervasive that Regan kept a color-coded calendar on his desk—green for good days, red for bad days, yellow for iffy days—that dictated when the President of the United States could travel, make a speech, or begin negotiations with a foreign power.

With eight years as governor of California behind him, Reagan came to the White House reasonably comfortable with his grasp of domestic issues. Foreign policy was a different matter. Once beyond his view of the Soviet threat, he was on uncertain ground and he knew it. As a result, on many if not all occasions he lacked the confidence to mediate between Caspar Weinberger, his Defense Secretary, and George

Shultz, the Secretary of State. In addition to holding divergent views on most issues, the two cabinet officers despised each other. At times they would erupt in shouting matches at White House meetings, an embarrassed Reagan looking on, incapable of containing the outbursts.

In general, his head tended to side with Shultz, but his heart was usually with Weinberger. Shultz was a new member of the team, a product of the suspect Eastern Establishment rushed into the lineup in 1982 when Alexander Haig faltered. Weinberger went back to 1965 with Reagan, his helmet plastered with battle stars earned in the Reagan cause. George makes sense, the President seemed to say, but if Cap feels so strongly about it, well, you guys work it out.

In *Banana Diplomacy*, Roy Gutman, *Newsday*'s national security correspondent, called it decision-making by the splitting of differences, in effect an abdication of leadership. More often than not, Reagan postponed a decision or merely nodded, leaving some participants believing he had sided with them, others without a clue. Cannon writes that Reagan aides came to resemble "pre-Glasnost Kremlinologists," seeking to divine the President's motives or desires from body language, a nod of the head supposedly signifying agreement, a tightening of the mouth the opposite.

To his credit, Reagan was not afraid to make the tough decisions when his advisers were in agreement on a course of action, even knowing that he alone would have to answer for the consequences. On occasion, notably in his advocacy of a space-based missile defense system, he would go against Shultz and Weinberger, apparently willing to disappoint them equally rather than please one and aggrieve the other. And, of course, he approved the Iranian arms sales over the objections of both men, which begs the question of how vehemently those two worthies actually protested and to what extent they sustained their opposition.

Ronald Reagan, in truth, was anyone you wanted him to be, stone soup made flesh, a vessel into which others contributed both their own expectations of him and many of the ingredients that defined his presidency.

In Reagan's case, the stone flavored the broth. Blending his personal beliefs with the talents of Deaver, Noonan, and others, he portrayed himself as a strong leader determined to renew America at home and restore its standing abroad.

In the process, he praised the service of soldiers, sailors, airmen, and Marines. To the veterans of Vietnam, he had a special message, the essence of the Nightingale's Song. The war was a failure not of your making. We're not going to be spooked by it anymore. I see you as you see yourselves, as men of dedication and proven courage, troops I can count on.

His words hit home. Announcing for reelection in January 1984, he would claim that America was back, standing tall. This time no one laughed. Even his critics recognized it as a politically potent assertion, notwithstanding the avoidable slaughter in Beirut a few months earlier and unrelieved tension in U.S.-Soviet relations. Just how powerful a message was hammered home on election day as voters in forty-nine states cast their ballots, pumped their fists, and shouted Yes!

Eventually the Nightingale's Song grew tinny, more like bubble-gum rock than a call to arms, but that didn't happen until its strains had swept Bud McFarlane, Oliver North, John Poindexter, Jim Webb, and John McCain into national prominence.

When the music died eight years later, only two of the five were still standing, the others ruined men, or so it seemed at the time—betrayed once more, by themselves certainly, but by others as well.

All that lies ahead. For now, let us go back to the early days of the age of Ronald Reagan, when the Nightingale's Song was still so sweet it almost made you cry.

CHAPTER TWENTY-SIX

OLLIE, BUD, AND JOHN

At Annapolis in the 1950s Bud McFarlane knew Major Alexander Haig only by reputation, as the West Point exchange officer who delighted in putting errant midshipmen on report. The two men came to know each other, if not well, in the Nixon White House during the final days of Watergate.

In late 1979, presidential politics drew them closer together. Haig, newly retired from the Army, was testing the waters for a possible White House run the following year. McFarlane was working on the Hill. At the direction of his boss, John Tower, the ranking Republican on the Senate Armed Services Committee, he met with Haig to see if he wanted to testify on the SALT II arms control treaty then awaiting Senate ratification. Haig, still formulating his position on the accord, asked McFarlane for his opinion. On its face, it's not so bad, said McFarlane. The problem is, the Soviets are causing problems in Angola, Ethiopia, and other places around the world, and ratification might make it seem that we don't take that kind of thing seriously. And I think we should. Not long after, Haig testified against SALT II. As he traveled the presidential trail over the next several months, he called McFarlane from time to time to ask his counsel and try out foreign policy ideas on him.

Nominated for Secretary of State by President-elect Reagan in December 1980, Haig recruited McFarlane for his transition team, responsible for surfacing policy ideas and suggesting names for top positions in the department. McFarlane never put himself on any of the slates he sent to Haig. He didn't have to. He had become part of Haig's inner circle and knew a job would materialize.

Haig appointed him State Department counselor, a little-known post with more clout than the name implies, the sixth most senior official in the department, equivalent to an undersecretary. Lacking clearly defined duties, the counselor becomes whatever the secretary wants him to be. Haig defined the job as a combination policy coordinator, confidant, troubleshooter, and personal emissary.

Three and a half years earlier McFarlane had been shuffled off to what he called a "candy-assed staff job" on Okinawa. Now he occupied a coveted seventh-floor office down the hall from the Secretary of State. Looking out at the marble monuments to Washington, Jefferson, and Lincoln, he knew that he had survived his time with the kibitzers and was back in the action. Though he betrayed no hint of excitement, he was exhilarated, revving his engines, poised to fly.

John Poindexter and Oliver North reported to the White House to join Richard Allen's National Security Council staff within two months of each other in 1981. Neither made an immediate impression.

Introducing himself to Roger Fontaine, the head of the NSC's Latin America section, North said through his Alfred E. Neuman grin, "I'm the jarhead Marine around here." Fontaine was put off. Who's this jerk? he wondered.

Veteran Washington correspondent Jeremiah O'Leary, at the time an NSC public affairs officer, took an equally dim view of Poindexter. He reminded O'Leary of "a bank clerk in charge of uncollectible debts."

Both Poindexter, who arrived at the White House in June 1981, and North, who reported in August, were surprised at how antiquated the NSC's facilities and office space were.

Poindexter was crammed into a converted closet in the West Wing basement. North shared a high-ceilinged office with three other NSC staffers in the Old Executive Office Building, a gothic and imposing structure across West Executive Drive from the White House.

Computers had not yet found their way to the Old EOB. Phones were scarce and had to be shared. A rattling Teletype spit out message traffic, which piled up on the floor because the secretaries were too busy to distribute the cables. The building's heating system was so inefficient that some staffers brought portable heaters to work in winter.

There were also safety problems. "One of my colleagues was sitting at his desk when a two-hundred-pound block of plaster fell from the eighteen-foot ceiling and landed on his desk, just missing his chair," writes North in his autobiography.

The conditions reflected the status of the NSC staff, under Richard Allen, during Ronald Reagan's first year in office. As governor of California, Reagan had come to believe in cabinet government, meeting weekly with agency and department heads, in theory to thrash out major decisions. In practice, according to Lou Cannon, it rarely worked that way, key issues often being decided by a handful of close aides who presented their handiwork to the governor for ratification. Nevertheless, Reagan carried his attachment to cabinet government to Washington, which meant downgrading the national security adviser, who was a member of the White House staff, not a cabinet officer.

There was more to it. The President and many of the conservatives close to him were wary of an organizational setup in which the national security adviser might eclipse the Secretary of State, as Kissinger had done under Nixon, in the process ushering in the hated policy of *détente* with the Soviet Union. Richard Allen did not even have direct access to Reagan, reporting to him through Edwin Meese, the President's counselor.

Soon after their arrival, Poindexter and North became part of the NSC team attempting to power the controversial $8.5 billion sale of AWACS aircraft and related equipment to the Saudis through a recalcitrant Senate. This was Reagan's first major foreign policy initiative and the lobbying effort was intense.

North and Poindexter were little more than energetic gofers during the AWACS battle. The key Pentagon figure was Air Force Major General Richard V. Secord. Lobbying for the Saudis was Prince Bandar bin Sultan, son of the Saudi defense minister, later ambassador to the United States. Secord and Bandar. Names to remember.

McFarlane considered Haig well-equipped for the job of Secretary of State, both intellectually and from the standpoint of experience. But, McFarlane came to believe, Haig lacked the political skills for dealing with Congress. Until too late, he also failed to recognize that the Reagan White House was a far different place from the one presided over by Nixon and Ford. In those days, Kissinger had been the administration's chief foreign policy spokesman, first as national security adviser, later as Secretary of State. Haig anticipated playing a similar role under Reagan, so much so that he described himself as the "vicar" of foreign policy. The expression made key White House aides, who already viewed Haig as a self-promoter, even more wary of him.

"What he failed to realize was that he was dealing with a group of people who were really pretty superficial when it came to foreign policy, and therefore couldn't evaluate the merits of what he had to say," said McFarlane, "but instead made judgments on the basis of how it affected Ronald Reagan politically."

Haig's problems aside, McFarlane was blossoming, the grooming process that had begun in Geneva accelerating. He had an impact on policy. His idea for building up the economies of friendly Latin American states became the Caribbean Basin Initiative, an ambitious program of tax breaks, trade incentives, and financial aid announced by the President with much fanfare in February 1982. McFarlane also pressed for a strategic military relationship with Israel, which would have elevated the Jewish state to the status of a full-fledged ally. That idea was moving along steadily until December 1981, when Menachem Begin extended Israeli law into the occupied Golan Heights, a move viewed by the United States as an illegal annexation.

McFarlane's most intoxicating role was the one Haig carved out for him as his personal back-channel operative. "I want you to be the person who is seen to be, and is, in fact, a man that Fahd, Sadat, Zia, and a host of others can call to get something to me promptly," McFarlane quoted Haig as saying. "There has to be someone that is seen to be a channel to me and from me to them." Haig was not being conspiratorial, said McFarlane. Many heads of state distrusted bureaucracies and preferred to deal on a personal basis when sensitive national issues were involved.

Soon McFarlane was circling the globe, flying commercial because it was less conspicuous, his trusted aide, youthful Middle East expert Howard Teicher, at his side. On arrival, he held private tête-à-têtes with foreign ministers, often heads of state—Israel's Begin, Egypt's Anwar Sadat, Saudi Arabia's Crown Prince (soon to be King) Fahd, Pakistan's Mohammad Zia ul-Haq, others.

The trips took him to the Middle East, Western Europe, South Asia, Central Africa, the Far East. Part of his job was to explain the Reagan foreign policy to his hosts, to listen to their security concerns, then determine their views on how the United States could assist them. "It was kind of a get-acquainted but intimate one-on-one kind of honest exchange of views about how we saw the world," he said. "I don't know that there's a lot more that I can talk about."

The parts he couldn't talk about drove some of his colleagues in the foreign policy bureaucracy crazy, especially on the NSC staff. "There was a very deliberate attempt to compartmentalize information, stemming, in part, from McFarlane's naturally secretive outlook on life," said the NSC's Geoffrey Kemp.

Over the objections of the Israelis and their powerful supporters in Washington, the Senate approved the AWACS sale on October 4,

1981, by four votes. Poindexter was now free to turn his attention to the project that had attracted him to the White House in the first place, the upgrading of the Situation Room.

By late 1983, he had not only completed that project but created a $14 million high-tech Crisis Management Center in the Old EOB, complete with computers, video, and the ability to monitor the cable traffic of State, Defense, and the intelligence agencies.

He also took the NSC into the Computer Age. Working with IBM, he arranged for the installation of a computerized system called PROFS—for Professional Office System—which allowed staffers to communicate electronically with one another. It was to be a Pyrrhic accomplishment. In early 1987 a presidential commission investigating the Iran-Contra affair found thousands of notes and messages between Poindexter and North they thought they had destroyed. The "delete" key, it seems, had serious limitations. It cleared the screen, but not the memory in the mainframe computer.

Unlike Poindexter, North had no projects awaiting him in the aftermath of the AWACS battle. At times he would stop by to see his friend Vic Taylor at Headquarters Marine Corps and ask in a frustrated tone, "When are they going to give me something to do?"

By then, Roger Fontaine had revised his opinion of North: "He wasn't a jerk. He was having problems." His biggest problem was that he wanted to work, but everyone seemed to have forgotten he was around. Fontaine, by contrast, was overwhelmed. His area of responsibility extended from Mexico to the tip of South America. He had no assistant. North volunteered to help. Before long they were working Latin America together.

The irony of the arrangement, and others he would find himself in, was not lost on North, who had no Latin American experience. "I was over my head at the NSC, and I knew it," he says in his autobiography. "The problem wasn't my military background, because there were military officers at the White House who certainly belonged there. But most of them had advanced degrees in foreign studies or political science, while the bulk of my experience was in military units and combat training."

In the months that followed, North would find others like Fontaine who needed help. The Latin American account put him in touch with the Nicaraguan Contras and soon afterward the Kissinger Commission, appointed by Reagan at McFarlane's suggestion to recommend policy initiatives in Central America. North also became involved in antiterrorism activities and emergency planning for natural or manmade disasters such as a nuclear attack. By mid-1983, through hard work, personal initiative, and a degree of bureaucratic bullying, he had transformed himself into the NSC's version of the indispensable man.

His attitude, as he once explained to Fontaine, was, "If it means digging latrines, I'll do it." His Marine Corps work habits had not changed, either. As he later put it, "I worked like a dog, right up until the day I was fired."

In September 1981 Ollie North and two other NSC staffers inadvertently discovered $1,000 in cash and three watches in the safe that had belonged to their boss, Richard Allen. They turned the contents over to a security officer. When the dust settled three months later, Allen was out as national security adviser even though a Justice Department investigation cleared him of any wrongdoing. As Allen's replacement, Reagan named William Clark, Haig's number two at State.

Clark had been Reagan's chief of staff in Sacramento, later moving on to the California Supreme Court, but he had no foreign policy training or expertise. That failing made for an awkward entrance onto the diplomatic stage, his Senate confirmation hearings as Deputy Secretary of State deteriorating into an Annapolis-style pop quiz, the worst kind, no multiple choice.

Clark's grasp of international relations had nothing to do with his State Department appointment. He was put in the job because of his supposedly shrewd political instincts and his loyalty to Reagan. It was widely believed that he had been planted at State to ride herd on Haig. True or not, Haig didn't mind. He wanted, in his words, "a guy who can speak Californian."

In a burst of generosity, Haig responded to Clark's appointment as national security adviser by telling him that he could take anyone he wanted over to the White House with him. "I want McFarlane," said Clark. "Good God," said Haig, "that's my right arm."

McFarlane was skiing at Vail with Jonny and the kids when Clark called. It was shortly before midnight on New Year's Eve. He told McFarlane that he had just been named to replace Allen and wanted him as his deputy.

Years later, McFarlane would recall that his first thought on hearing Clark's offer was that it had been too easy, that, as he put it, "the system isn't supposed to work this way." The more he thought about it, he realized the enormity of what lay before him. Because of Clark's limited knowledge of foreign affairs, the substance of policy would likely fall to him. And because of Clark's close relationship to Reagan, as close as the White House troika of Michael Deaver, Edwin Meese, and James Baker, his views would probably be conveyed unadorned directly to the President. As McFarlane saw it, he would be the de facto national security adviser.

"And I hoped so," he said years later. "I was confident and I was ready and I was eager for it. I didn't believe then, I don't believe now, that there was anyone who knew quite as well the agenda of the United States, their interests and how to promote them as I did."

In January 1982 Clark took over as national security adviser, an event that elevated the status of the NSC overnight. His arrival at the White House immediately expanded by one the West Wing power centers previously staked out by Meese, Deaver, and Baker. Clark had direct access to the President, which meant he could walk into the Oval Office any time he pleased.

His closeness to the President paid immediate dividends for NSC staffers. At his behest, many were upgraded in rank and accorded the privilege of dining in the exclusive White House Mess. On a more substantive level, when Poindexter came to him with his idea for a Crisis Management Center, Clark was able to make it happen.

The installation of Clark and his tapping of McFarlane also brought together in the White House the trio of Annapolis graduates and Vietnam-era military men who singly and together would drive the Reagan administration to some of its major foreign policy accomplishments, but in the end almost bring it down.

McFarlane and Poindexter worked well together and complemented each other's strengths. The key to the tripartite relationship was North. He was always there when McFarlane and Poindexter needed him, which turned out to be all too often.

Ollie, Bud, and John, names forever linked, reminiscent of the saddest song of 1968, that knife blade of a year that severed past from future, Then from Now.

Even at State Bud McFarlane had his suspicions about the level of foreign policy expertise at the White House, but it wasn't until he attended his first senior staff meeting with the President in February 1982 that his worst fears were confirmed.

He's not sure who said it, possibly press spokesman Larry Speakes, maybe Mike Deaver, the keeper of the Reagan image, conceivably Dave Gergen, the communications director. Whoever it was, in the course of the meeting he told the President that critics were saying he did not have a coherent foreign policy.

"Well, you don't," cracked an aide.

Unbidden, privately steaming, McFarlane broke the brittle, embarrassed silence: "Yes, you do!"

Heads snapped. The unfamiliar baritone seemed to be coming from a spot behind Vice President Bush and national security adviser Clark, who were seated across the long table from the President.

"It has seven elements," intoned McFarlane. He proceeded to enumerate an elaborate if predictable laundry list involving deterrence, alliances, the Soviets, arms control, and so on.

The recitation complete, someone said, "I think we just got ourselves a foreign policy."

Nobody laughed. If anything, there was a collective sigh of relief. Reagan said nothing. As the meeting broke up, Deaver told McFarlane he had done a terrific job and asked him to write down the seven points on a three-by-five card.

McFarlane couldn't believe it. More than a year in office and the President's top White House advisers seemed surprised to learn not merely the elements of the Reagan foreign policy, but·that such a policy even existed. McFarlane and others at State had been enunciating it for months, publicly and privately. It wasn't a secret, something he had snatched out of the air at the meeting. He later wondered what would have happened if he had added an eighth or ninth or tenth element. Would the President by his silence have implicitly taken them on board, too?

CHAPTER TWENTY-SEVEN

THE CANDIDATE
FROM HANOI

In early 1981, a few months into Ronald Reagan's presidency, Washington political consultant J. Brian Smith got a call from a client, Senator Bill Cohen, asking him to get together with a Navy captain named John McCain and brief him on Arizona politics. Smith, who did not know McCain, was busy and tried to bury the request, but Cohen called back a few days later and pressed him. Smith agreed to meet McCain for lunch.

Avoiding the usual noontime haunts, they met at The Broker, a tasteful Swiss-run restaurant about a mile from the Capitol. As Smith listened skeptically, an animated McCain explained his plan. When he retired from the Navy, he said, he was going to move to Arizona and run for Congress. "What district?" asked Smith. "I haven't figured that out yet," said McCain, as if it were a mere detail. "Well, when are you going to run? In 'eighty-four?" asked Smith. "No, 'eighty-two," said McCain.

"I was astounded," Smith later said. Charmed and entertained as well. To this day he cannot recall ever laughing as much as he did that afternoon. McCain talked nonstop, interrupting himself every five minutes to say, "You think I'm crazy, don't you, Jay?"

McCain had a simple scheme. He would run for the new seat Arizona would get in 1982 because of population growth over the previous decade. He figured the seat would be in the Phoenix area, where he and Cindy were about to move. Smith, who had experience in Arizona politics, was not so sure. His contacts were telling him the seat would probably be carved out of the southern portion of the state, near Tucson. But that was nothing compared to the larger issue, that McCain didn't live in the state, had never lived in the state, yet had the audacity to believe he could be elected to Congress barely a year and a half after taking up residence there.

Jack McCain died on March 22, 1981, aboard a military transport while flying from London to the United States. The Navy contacted Carol when officials couldn't find John. By chance she knew how to reach him, called and gently broke the news. The plane bearing Jack's body had stopped to refuel in Bangor, Maine, so John and Cindy were able to meet the aircraft when it landed at Andrews Air Force Base outside Washington.

John McCain retired around the same time. Before he left Washington, John Lehman, the new Secretary of the Navy, awarded him the Legion of Merit at a private ceremony in his Pentagon office. John Tower hosted a huge farewell reception for McCain in the Senate Caucus Room where Bud McFarlane, John Poindexter, and Ollie North would meet their congressional accusers six years later, a few months after Lehman turned his office over to Jim Webb.

In late March, John and Cindy boarded a plane that would take them to their new home in Arizona. Earlier in the day, Jack McCain had been buried at Arlington Cemetery. After the funeral, John stopped by the Navy offices in Crystal City and turned in his active-duty identification card. He was optimistic as he prepared to depart Washington, but the relinquishing of his ID card coupled with the great sadness surrounding his father's interment dampened the leave-taking. For virtually the first time in this century, he realized, no member of the McCain family wore the uniform of an officer in the United States Navy.

"For God's sake, be very discreet," Jay Smith had admonished McCain as he left for Arizona on the outbound leg of what he hoped would be a round trip back to Washington.

The worst thing you can do, Smith warned his new client, is let people know you plan to run for public office. "It would be viewed as very opportunistic," he said. "Let's face it, it is, but let's not have it viewed that way."

Smith advised McCain to get himself known around the state. He went at it like a full-time job, raising his profile in a remarkably brief period of time. Cindy was his advance man. When she was tied up, he did it himself. "Hi, I'm John McCain," he would greet some home-grown power broker. "I'm new to the state and I'd like to come over and say hello." He became active in the state Republican Party, helping with fund-raising, local campaigns, and phone banks. Service clubs like the Rotary and Kiwanis, always looking for luncheon and dinner speakers, were only too happy to provide a forum for the war hero and Washington insider who had generously volunteered his services. Soon he was speaking twice a week, usually on defense and foreign policy issues. Meanwhile, Cindy's father, beer baron Jim Hensley, gave him a public relations job that took him to conventions around the state where he built up his contacts as he promoted the King of Beers. Smith was amazed by McCain's energy and enthusiasm. We have a secret weapon here, he told himself. Too bad he doesn't have anyplace to run.

Those first nine months in Arizona put McCain's discretion, never his long suit, to a severe test. His time in prison had intensified his natural impatience. He was, in effect, a stealth candidate, racing around auditioning for a job that didn't even exist. To make matters worse, he couldn't tell anyone about it. Instead, he talked in vague terms, coy claptrap. I want to get involved politically, I've been interested in public service all my life.

Smith's sources, meanwhile, turned out to be right: the new congressional district was in Tucson, too far to jump without indelibly branding himself a carpetbagger. The Phoenix-area seats were all held by strong incumbents, among them John Rhodes, a fellow Republican, and Morris Udall, an entrenched and popular Democrat.

In January 1982, Rhodes called a press conference amid rumors that he might announce his retirement. Since he resigned as House minority leader a year earlier, there had been speculation that he might not run again for the First Congressional District seat he had held for three decades. The district fell completely into the Phoenix metropolitan area, and included suburban Tempe, Mesa, and portions of Scottsdale. John McCain lived just outside the district, in central Phoenix, a stone's throw away.

This is how Jay Smith remembers the day John Rhodes announced his retirement from Congress.

Smith is in Washington, on the phone with McCain in Phoenix. McCain has a second phone to his ear, an open line to someone he has sent to the Rhodes press conference. Rhodes says he is stepping down. McCain gets the word, passes it on to Smith. Jubilation. Whoops and cheers career across phone lines from the Salt River to the Potomac. Then, from McCain, Okay, what now?

They discuss plans. Smith hears McCain talking to someone else, realizes Cindy has just walked into the room. "Did you buy it? Did you get it? Did you find it?" Smith overhears McCain ask his wife. Murmuring in the background. McCain, back on the line. "She got it. Great. Yea!"

"What's that?" asks Smith, perplexed.

"We just got a house in the First District."

Jay Smith later called it "the Super Bowl of all campaigns . . . the toughest, the hardest, the most amazing."

One of the most difficult parts, for Smith, was restraining McCain. He wanted to declare his candidacy for the First District seat the same day Rhodes called it quits. "Calm down," said Smith. "This is a long-distance run. It's not a forty-yard dash. There's time."

At Smith's urging, McCain announced the formation of an exploratory committee while he went through the motions of weighing his decision. A time-honored political ploy, the pose created artificial tension—Who is he? What's his story? Will he run?—that McCain milked for weeks of free publicity.

McCain understood the strategy, but he didn't like it, making Smith's life miserable. "He just wanted to go," said Smith. "If he could have found a way to have the election held that week he would have done it."

By the time he declared his candidacy in late March, three other candidates—two state legislators and a politically active veterinarian—had entered the race for the GOP nomination. All were given a good chance to win, McCain next to none. The September 7 GOP primary would decide the nominee, tantamount to election in the solidly Republican district.

With McCain officially in the race, Smith could finally employ his secret weapon, his candidate's immense energy. He launched him on a grueling schedule of door-to-door campaigning, saying, "You want to win? This is what you've got to do." Smith had tried this tactic with other candidates, found their enthusiasm for door-knocking held up only so long as reporters were following them around.

McCain was different. "Let's go hit the bricks, Brad boy," he'd tell his driver, Brad Boland, each morning as he reported to headquarters to pick up the day's voter lists. Through the late spring and summer, when temperatures in the Phoenix area routinely climb above one hundred degrees, he campaigned door-to-door six hours a day, six days a week, personally knocking on twenty thousand Republican doors. By the end of the campaign, he had gone through three pairs of shoes—Cindy had the third pair bronzed—and developed skin cancer, which has since required four minor surgeries.

At first, it was drudgery, the glazed look and the dismissive question, "What are you selling?" He would later joke that he began the campaign with 3 percent name recognition with a 3 percent margin of error. If he felt discouraged, he never let on, showing up each morning, grabbing Brad boy and hitting the bricks. One day he noticed that fewer people were asking him what he was selling. Instead, they brightened and said, "Oh, yeah, John McCain," when they saw him perched on their doorsteps.

Part of his evolution into a plausible candidate was due to the targeting. He may have been new to the area, but so were a lot of others. The population of the district had increased nearly 50 percent between 1970 and 1980. Smith directed him to those areas in which the newcomers were concentrated.

In addition, he raised $313,000 for the primary, more than half of it, $167,000, in loans from himself. The amount wasn't staggering, but it was more than his three better-known rivals had to spend, and it lent credibility to his dark-horse candidacy. More importantly, it permitted him to run a modern, high-tech campaign, complete with slickly produced television commercials.

TV spots for congressional races often look like a cross between used-car commercials and hair-weaving ads, but McCain's, produced by Smith & Harroff, Jay Smith's consulting firm, were several cuts above the norm. They promoted him as "a new leader for Arizona," a man who "knows how Washington works," picturing him at a table with Nancy and Ronald Reagan or standing beside his friend John Tower, the popular Republican senator from Texas. His POW days were recounted, then voters were told "he's come to Arizona to serve again." Though no more substantial than the usual election-year hype, the spots introduced McCain to prospective voters in an upbeat, engaging, and effective way. Soon kids were stopping him on the street, asking for his autograph. Drivers honked. Not everyone knew his name. They recognized him as the guy with the white hair from television, the one who spent all those years in a North Vietnamese jail.

There was something else. During his campaign and now in the White House, Ronald Reagan was changing the way America looked at its servicemen, past and present, including veterans of the nation's longest war, Vietnam. As evidence of the shift in perceptions, a memorial to Vietnam veterans was nearing completion on the Mall in Washington. In the fall, hundreds of thousands of veterans and their families would converge on the nation's capital for the dedication, cheered on by many of their old adversaries in the press and the public at large. For many, the dedication of the memorial would symbolize reconciliation and healing and the long-delayed greeting of heroes. And among that elite fraternity, there were few who swayed to the rhythm of the Nightingale's Song as effortlessly as John McCain. It was as if it had been written for him.

The carpetbagger issue plagued him from the start of his campaign, became the killer question at the candidates' forums to which the four hopefuls dragged themselves two and three nights a week. You've just lived here a year, how can you know Arizona or the district? Aren't you just an opportunist? At first he explained that, having never lived anywhere permanently, he moved to his wife's home state when he retired from the Navy, just as many others had settled in Arizona in recent years. It was a weak response and he knew he was getting beat up.

One night he turned it around. This time his face grew red as he listened to the familiar question.

"Listen, pal," he replied, "I spent twenty-two years in the Navy. My father was in the Navy. My grandfather was in the Navy. We in the military service tend to move a lot. We have to live in all parts of the country, all parts of the world. I wish I could have had the luxury, like you, of growing up and living and spending my entire life in a nice place like the First District of Arizona, but I was doing other things.

"As a matter of fact, when I think about it now, the place I lived longest in my life was Hanoi."

The audience sat for several seconds in shocked silence, then broke into thunderous applause. "The reply was absolutely the most devastating response to a potentially troublesome political issue I've ever heard," said political columnist John Kolbe, of the *Phoenix Gazette*.

With Ronald Reagan's election, Carol McCain became head of the White House Visitors Office, arranging tours and the like. She was working late in her East Wing office one night when she received a phone call from State Senator Jim Mack, one of the other candidates in the First District race. Mack said a friend told him Carol had some "negative material" on her ex-husband that she might be willing to share. Carol was outraged, refused to discuss her marriage with Mack.

"I told him I believe in John McCain," she said in an interview with columnist Kolbe. "He's a good person. I wish him every bit of success. I was appalled Senator Mack would ask such personal questions. I can't imagine a gentleman doing that."

The unmasking of Mack by the *Gazette* was not enough for Jay Smith. We've got to put a stop to this kind of thing, he told McCain. You'd better talk to him. McCain needed little prodding. The next time the candidates got together, he maneuvered Mack away from the others.

As recounted by Smith, McCain said to Mack, "I understand you called my ex-wife. I want you to know that campaign aside, politics aside, you ever do anything like that again, anything against a person in my family, I will personally beat the shit out of you."

McCain was a nervous wreck on election day, the one day in a campaign when the candidate is superfluous. He was in the way, driving campaign staffers crazy as they went about the mechanics of getting out the vote. Go home, go anywhere, Smith told him, just let us do our jobs.

He went to a movie, *Star Wars*, couldn't sit still, got up every ten minutes and paced in the lobby. It was worse that night, as the votes started rolling in, showing him with an early lead. He stayed home until ten, then went down to headquarters. By eleven, the momentum had swung in his direction. The final totals: McCain, 32 percent; Russell, 26 percent; Mack, 22 percent; Carlson-West, 20 percent.

At the victory celebration, he ascribed his win to the months of intensive door-to-door campaigning, told the press he would be out again early the next morning, a statement he later regretted (though he made good on it) because he never got to bed that night.

Those were his public comments. Privately, according to Jay Smith, "He started talking about running for the Senate."

The general election, as expected, was no contest, McCain besting his Democratic opponent, William Hegarty, by thirty-five percentage points. It was a remarkable political story: elected to Congress eighteen months after moving to the state, less than a year after taking up residence in the district. In those moments of victory, had he ever looked back on how far he had come since saying so long to the Prick, the Cat, Soft Soap Fairy, and his other friends in Hanoi?

"No," he replied. "The moment I landed at Clark I started putting the Vietnam experience behind me."

In prison McCain and Orson Swindle discovered that as kids they had both been fans of "Felix the Cat" cartoons. When Felix got in trouble, they laughingly recalled, he would raise his paws and roll his eyes, a picture of innocence. They started doing the same thing when one or the other seemed too full of himself.

Years later, as McCain was moving into his first congressional office, Swindle poked his head in the door. "This is for you," he told the new lawmaker, presenting him with a large Felix doll. "You put this somewhere where you can look at it. And don't you ever forget where you came from and get too big and get too wrapped up in all this crap."

Pointing at Felix, Swindle added, lightly but not too lightly, "This is reality."

CHAPTER TWENTY-EIGHT

SCORPIONS IN A JAR

In September 1979, returning from a monthlong book tour to promote the paperback edition of *Fields of Fire*, Jim Webb moved back to Arlington from Annapolis. As he broke open one of the packing boxes, a letter dropped out. "Dear Jim," it began, "We're so happy you're going to help us." It was signed Jan Scruggs.

Holy shit, thought Webb, I haven't done anything for these guys.

Webb's life had been in flux for months. He was in the midst of a divorce, he and Barb disputing custody of nine-year-old Amy. His teaching stint at Annapolis had not ended happily. He had fallen in love with JoAnn Krukar, a former Army nurse who had served in Vietnam and whom he would marry two years later.

Two months earlier he had met with Scruggs and four other men about a memorial to honor veterans of the Vietnam War. Scruggs and Jack Wheeler had taken the lead in explaining their plan. They wanted to build the monument on the Mall, site of some of the most virulent antiwar demonstrations of the Vietnam era. Inscribed on the memorial were to be the names of all 58,000 men and women who had died in the war. Because emotions still ran high, they said, the memorial itself was to make no statement on the rightness or wrongness of the conflict.

They told Webb they wanted his help. He had standing with veterans and Capitol Hill contacts, especially in the House. Legislation authorizing the memorial was already in the works in the Senate. As Wheeler later put it, Webb's participation would give them and their project "credibility."

Webb quickly took to Wheeler, a West Pointer, Class of 1966, which Webb knew had suffered the heaviest casualties of any Military Academy class. Several times during lunch, Wheeler said, "Now it's *our* turn on the Mall." As the meal concluded, Webb said, "Absolutely, I'll help."

He had then done something completely out of character. He forgot all about it until he discovered the note from Scruggs.

The next morning, he uncrated his IBM Selectric and pounded out a short floor speech for his old boss, Arkansas congressman John Paul Hammerschmidt, the senior Republican on the Veterans Affairs Committee. Scruggs had enclosed the draft Senate bill. Webb clipped it to the speech and phoned John Holden, the committee's minority staff director. "These are good guys," he said. "This is a good bill." Then he jumped in his car and delivered the packet to Capitol Hill. Holden called later the same day to say Hammerschmidt liked the bill and had introduced it that very afternoon.

That night, Webb went over to JoAnn's, switching over his phone so that calls could reach him there. It was late in the evening when the phone rang. Webb picked it up.

"What do you and your fucking Arkansas Republicans think you're doing?" said a disturbed voice.

Webb was dumbfounded.

"I don't know who you are or what you're talking about," he said.

"You just ruined four million dollars' worth of publicity," the caller said.

"What are you talking about?" repeated Webb.

In the course of the brief, angry conversation, Webb realized he was talking to Jack Wheeler, the West Pointer, and that he was being accused of jumping the gun by getting the bill introduced in the House.

"I don't believe this," said Webb, steaming. "You can go fuck yourself, man."

The next day, Scruggs called Hammerschmidt's office, made similar accusations, and said Webb was trying to curry favor with the congressman to get his old job back.

What the hell have I gotten myself into? Webb asked himself.

There had been a breakdown in communication. Scruggs and Wheeler had wanted a bill introduced in the House. But not until they had staged a full-blown press conference to publicize the introduction of the Senate bill a few days before Veterans Day. In fact, no harm was done. The Hammerschmidt measure attracted little press attention and the news conference two weeks later was well-reported.

Relationships, however, had been bruised. Webb and Wheeler patched things up, at least for a time, but Webb couldn't forgive the call by Scruggs to Hammerschmidt. "I'll deal with you," Webb told Wheeler, "but you keep Scruggs away from me."

*   *   *

Jan C. Scruggs, the son of a waitress and a milkman, kept his eye on the ball. An Army enlisted man out of Bowie, Maryland, he had seen heavy fighting in Vietnam, half his infantry company having been killed or wounded during his yearlong tour. He himself was hit by shrapnel from a rocket-propelled grenade in May 1969, leaving him with eleven metal fragments in the knee, an injury not unlike Webb's. After coming home to the Washington area, Scruggs drifted for a while, put himself through college, then got a job with the Labor Department.

In March 1979, he saw *The Deer Hunter*, a film about the war's devastation of a blue-collar Pennsylvania town. He couldn't sleep that night, grisly images of the war assailing him. The next morning he told his wife he was going to build a memorial that listed the names of every single man and woman who had died in Vietnam. In the years ahead, he never swayed from that vision. Though less obviously formidable, he was, in his way, as tough as Webb.

Scruggs announced his plans to reporters in Washington on May 28, 1979, ten years to the day after he was wounded. Wheeler, who had spearheaded a drive to build a small Southeast Asia memorial at West Point, called Scruggs and offered his services after reading that the Memorial Fund had collected only $144.50 in the month since the announcement.

John Parsons Wheeler III was second-generation West Point and, like Webb, the descendant of a long line of soldiers. At their first meeting, Webb got the impression that Wheeler had seen combat in Vietnam. That was not the case.

Nearing graduation in June 1966, nearly one hundred members of Wheeler's class volunteered for Vietnam duty. Wheeler was not among them. Ambivalent about West Point and the military throughout his time at the academy, he chose to attend Harvard Business School for two years after first taking a year's assignment at a Nike Hercules missile base near New York City so he could be near his girlfriend, a ballerina. He finally made it to the war zone in the summer of 1969.

Unlike Webb and Scruggs, who were in-country at the same time but in far more hazardous circumstances, Wheeler fought the war in climate-controlled comfort as a computer specialist in Long Binh, a base about twenty miles northeast of Saigon that author Rick Atkinson, in *The Long Gray Line,* describes as resembling a small American city, complete with swimming pools, movie theaters, and its own Chinese restaurant.

In 1971 Wheeler requested and was granted early release from the Army. He enrolled in Virginia Theological Seminary for a time with thoughts of becoming an Episcopal priest. "My conviction is that most West Pointers in the Army, especially general officers, are morally reprehensible because they blind themselves to much of the evil work that they do," he wrote in his application essay. He left the seminary after a year to enter Yale Law School, graduating with honors in 1975.

Wheeler was earnest and often emotional, at times without apparent rhyme or reason. In a 1990 profile, after quoting Wheeler as saying, "You can understand me by saying that I'm an artist," Ned Martel provided an arresting sketch.

> He certainly fits the stereotype: creative, temperamental, intense to the point of exhaustion. His mind moves so rapidly—from Søren Kierkegaard to Zorba the Greek to the New Testament to Paul Simon's "Graceland"—that his face often contorts with the effort of keeping up. In repeated interviews he swoops into fits of sentimental digression, which he refers to as "psychodrama," breaking into tears often and without apology. He will talk, at length, about intimate details of his life: the breakup of his marriage, a failed engagement to a McDonald's heiress a few years ago, his religious convictions. He has suffered from at least one episode of paralyzing depression.... After the Vietnam Veterans Memorial was completed, Wheeler reports, "My depression was outrageous. It lasted about a thousand years, which means I must be very creative, like Abraham Lincoln." He chuckles, ending with a gasp.

Webb would later say of Wheeler, "I'll never know who he is, but it took me a couple of years just to unravel his basic résumé."

The angry exchanges over the bill introductions behind him, Webb joined forces with Scruggs and Wheeler's organization, the Vietnam Veterans Memorial Fund, to push the legislation through Congress. Back at work on the Hill, he helped set up press conferences for lawmakers, prepared statements for them, and authored "Dear Colleague" letters by which congressmen solicited support and cosponsors for the measure. He also became a member of the fund's National Sponsoring Committee, along with a number of other prominent Americans, which meant his name could be used on fund-raising solicitations.

On July 1, 1980, President Carter signed into law PL96-297, setting aside two acres on the Mall in Constitution Gardens near the Lincoln Memorial for a memorial "in honor and recognition" of Vietnam veterans.

The congressional battle had been reasonably arduous, remnants of the antiwar movement having surfaced to oppose the memorial, but not outrageously so. The country not only seemed ready for a memorial, it apparently wanted one. As far as Webb was concerned, the hard part was over; it was time to move on to other matters.

The following month the fund announced a competition to design the memorial. The cost was underwritten by Ross Perot to the tune of $160,000. At the behest of the Fund, Paul D. Spreiregen, an authority on design competitions, assembled a jury of eight judges, all prominent in the fields of sculpture, architecture, and landscape architecture. Their average age was sixty-five. None had served in Vietnam. The absence of a Vietnam veteran on the panel was purposeful. The fund asserted that the jury might overly defer to the views of someone who had actually experienced the war firsthand even though he might have little aesthetic sense.

In defending that decision and other similarly controversial ones in the stormy months that followed, Scruggs, Wheeler, and other fund officers would insist that time was always of the essence even though the legislation gave them five years to break ground. Their stated concerns included potential opposition from antiwar figures, which never materialized, a perceived desire on the part of many other Americans to forget the war, and the fear that something could go awry in the course of shepherding the winning design through the various commissions and agencies that would have to approve it before construction could begin.

To make their point, Fund officers often cited the proposed Franklin Delano Roosevelt memorial as evidence of what could befall a project that failed to move quickly from conception to completion. In 1958 Congress reserved funds and land on the Mall. A prestigious panel of experts approved the design in 1960, but the choice met with such fierce opposition, led by the Roosevelt family and many members of Congress, that to this day the memorial has not been built.

The fund may have been misreading history. Scruggs, Wheeler, and the others saw the FDR memorial as evidence of the dangers of delay. They might have been better off focusing on the design itself, the element that author Tom Wolfe said actually accounted for the opposition to the Roosevelt memorial.

"The public," wrote Wolfe, "was waiting for some classic FDR . . . Roosevelt with his great leonine head thrown back, his prognathous grin and cigarette holder, his cape with the silk frogging . . . and what the public got was eight enormous upright abstract marble slabs that became known as 'Instant Stonehenge.' "

Scruggs, for his part, acknowledged in a 1993 interview that he had no idea what the FDR design looked like.

Ronald Reagan was inaugurated on January 20, 1981. Webb applied to join the administration and quickly became the leading candidate to head the Veterans Administration. He was wary, however, of the growing power of David Stockman. The new budget director was taking the ax to federal programs all across the board. Webb was already outraged that Vietnam veterans had gotten a second-rate VA bill. He had no intention of leaving the meager benefits that existed to the tender mercies of divinity school stalwart Stockman. He demanded budgetary appeal power beyond Stockman, if necessary to Reagan himself. Denied such authority, he withdrew his name from consideration for the VA post.

Webb had little involvement with the Memorial Fund during the six-month period between the commencement of the design competition and the announcement of the winner. At one point, viewing himself as a friend of the court, he came across a *Texas Monthly* article about a flap in Austin over a Vietnam memorial planned for that city. The local arts council had chosen a design that resembled an egg carton with twenty holes. One hole was black. The other nineteen were white, symbolizing the nineteen men the city had lost in the war. He sent the article to Wheeler with the comment, "We're not going to get an egg carton, are we?"

"And we didn't," he later wrote. "We got a mass grave."

On May 1, 1981, Scruggs, Wheeler, and nine other men and women associated with the Memorial Fund gathered in Hangar No. 3 at Andrews Air Force Base to learn the jury's selection. When Paul Spreiregen unveiled the winning entry, Number 1026, most of those in the small audience were astonished.

The jury had selected a pastel sketch showing a black V-shaped polished granite wall sunk into the ground of the Mall, its arms stretching toward the Lincoln Memorial and the Washington Monument. The 58,000 names were to begin at the apex and move outward in chronological order of date of death.

The artist was Maya Ying Lin, a twenty-one-year-old Yale student who had produced the sketch for an assignment in her funerary architecture class, receiving a B+ for her effort. Maya Lin, of Chinese-American ancestry, claimed no knowledge of the Vietnam War, knew no one who had fought in it, and had never even suffered the loss of a loved one. The design had been a purely intellectual and aesthetic exercise on her part. At the press conference to publicize the winning design five days later, she said, "I wanted to describe a journey—a journey that would make you experience death."

Scruggs did not know what to make of the jury's choice. In his book chronicling the memorial saga, he described his first impressions: "A big bat. A weird-looking thing that could have been from Mars. . . . Maybe a third-grader had entered the competition and won. All the fund's work had gone into making a huge bat for veterans. Maybe it symbolized a boomerang."

The first reaction of Robert Doubek, the fund's key organizer, mirrored that of the opposition waiting in the wings. "It looks like you've given us a memorial to the dead," he told the jury. Replied architect Henry Weese, a panel member, "It can be for the living, too."

According to Rick Atkinson, Wheeler was no less mystified, could not make sense of Spreiregen's explanation of how the wall tied in with the Lincoln Memorial and Washington Monument. But he remained mindful of the unpredictable approval process still ahead. Rising to his feet, he said, "This is a work of genius," and began clapping. Soon the others were clapping as well.

Much of the veterans community did not join in the applause, including Jim Webb. Webb communicated his sentiments to Wheeler, who urged him not to speak out against the design for at least a month. Doing so now, said Wheeler, could destroy the memorial. "Jim, it's the Eiffel Tower," he said in a note to Webb. "The design needs time to understand." He hinted at modifications. Webb agreed to say nothing publicly. Three weeks later, around Memorial Day, Wheeler wrote Webb again, asking him to withhold public comment for "another month or so." Once more Webb agreed. He called Wheeler from time to time during that two-month period, privately passing on to him the hostility of veterans he encountered. He came away from each conversation believing an accommodation was in the offing. He felt no sense of urgency. After all, they had five years to begin construction. Which explains his shock one morning in late July when he read in the newspaper that Maya Lin's design had been approved by the city's unpredictable Fine Arts Commission.

As the news sank in, Webb could not escape the conclusion that Wheeler had sandbagged him. After gaining a promise of silence from Webb, Wheeler had quietly won design approval from the single most influential panel in the entire process, effectively preempting the opposition of Webb and others. Or so it seemed.

Despite the evidence, Webb was still not completely sure that Wheeler was acting in bad faith. In addition, he still wanted a memorial, even

Maya Lin's wall as long as there were changes to soften its bleakness. In September he wrote to the fund, suggesting, at a minimum, the installation of a flag that would be permanently lit. He received no answer, a surprising oversight since he had honored his promise to Wheeler and not stated his views publicly. Also, he was still a member of the National Sponsoring Committee, presumably worthy of a response.

In September the conservative *National Review* labeled the memorial "Orwellian glop." The following month, the controversy within the veterans' community flared into public view. Tom Carhart, a West Point classmate of Wheeler and twice-wounded veteran of ground combat, spoke out against the design at a meeting of the Fine Arts Commission. As television cameras rolled, Carhart called the memorial "a black gash of shame and sorrow, hacked into the national visage that is the Mall." Soon the *New Republic* weighed in, Charles Krauthammer maintaining that the design treated the Vietnam dead "like the victims of some monstrous traffic accident."

The battle had been joined, though the lines were blurred. The American Legion endorsed the design; the Marine Corps League withdrew its support, calling the design "an insult to the memory of those it is intended to memorialize." The press tended to line up with the fund, which through the efforts of Wheeler and Scruggs succeeded in portraying those seeking changes in the design as right-wing Neanderthals. Veteran was pitted against veteran.

"The simple questions of modification now were metaphorical for a national debate on the meaning of the war itself," Webb later wrote. "And we were like scorpions in a jar, with the rest of the country shaking it."

In early November, he decided to write an article about the controversy for the *Washington Post*'s Sunday Outlook section. As a member of the National Sponsoring Committee, he felt duty-bound to inform the fund. He called Wheeler and read the article to him. Wheeler pleaded with him to withdraw the piece, again insisting that it would destroy the memorial and promising to work for design modifications. On the Thursday before his piece was to run, Webb pulled it, figuring the design changes he now fully anticipated outweighed any damage he might be doing to his relationship with the *Post*.

Wheeler had promised Webb he would call within a week. A week passed. Then another. No word from Wheeler. Webb's patience was exhausted. "It became clear that I had again been manipulated toward a short-term gain," he later said.

*   *   *

Wheeler's role in all this was complicated. In truth, he dutifully communicated Webb's views to the fund's board of directors, which he chaired. He also argued forcefully for some of the changes sought by Webb, only to be outvoted by board members, including Scruggs, who wondered at times if Wheeler had thrown in with Webb.

Those concerns had no foundation. It was true, however, that Wheeler decided early on that Webb had to be, in Wheeler's words, "managed," that is, kept from taking his complaints public before the fund had time to marshal support for the design.

"The later Webb went public, the better for us," said Wheeler in a 1994 interview, "because the more time we had to go down the road of convincing the whole country that this was a good thing. The earlier Webb attacked us, the less momentum we would have."

As Wheeler conceded, however, Webb never even threatened to make his misgivings public from the unveiling of the design in May 1981 through early November 1981. At that point Webb wrote the *Washington Post* article, only to withdraw it at Wheeler's request. Throughout that crucial six-month period Webb conveyed his views to Wheeler, seemingly without animosity.

"His manner was not threatening," said Wheeler. "It was matter-of-fact. And he did it with respect. My feeling, however, was that he was a man to be feared because of the power he had and I had to do everything I could to persuade him that the actual design we had should be built. And I dreaded him turning on us."

Wheeler's dread seems more a matter of intuition than anything Webb said or did. On first meeting Webb, Wheeler said, he sensed that he could be "imperious." In addition, after reading *Fields of Fire* and *A Sense of Honor*, Wheeler said he gained insight into Webb's character, creativity, and power—his "emotional charge," as Wheeler described it. "I read his book. I read both of them. So I knew the man," said Wheeler.

Wheeler angrily denied misleading Webb. Asked if he informed Webb that the design was moving toward approval by the Fine Arts Commission, he replied, "Hell, no." But, he asserted, he did not purposely keep that information from Webb.

Though he adamantly objected to the phrase, Wheeler seems to have indulged in preemptive damage control with Webb. He accurately transmitted Webb's views to the board, but invariably left Webb with the impression that changes were likely, which was not true.

Believing modifications were in the offing, Webb held his peace, deprived of a more active voice in the critical approval process by Wheeler's soft words and dubious handholding. Webb, of course, made many of the misunderstandings possible by confining his contact with the board to Wheeler. In any event, Webb's public silence was nearly over.

In late November he wrote to the fund, resigning from the National Sponsoring Committee and demanding that his name be removed from all fund-raising materials. In December a slightly reworked version of the *Post* piece ran on the op-ed page of the *Wall Street Journal.* "At what point," he asked, "does a piece of architecture cease being a memorial to service and instead become a mockery of that service, a wailing wall for future antidraft and antinuclear demonstrators?"

Webb no longer thought of himself as a friend of the court. To his mind, the fund had used his prestige within the veterans community for its own purposes, then discarded him when he dared challenge the board's vision of the memorial. As for Wheeler, Webb decided he was more and less than he seemed to be. On the slimmest of reeds, at least as far as military service was concerned, Wheeler seemed intent on establishing himself as the voice of the Vietnam veteran. For nearly two years Webb had thought of Wheeler as a friend. Now he saw him as a self-promoting adversary in a high-stakes chess game that would decide the manner in which Vietnam veterans were to be honored. Webb brought all his weapons to the table: his lawyer's training, his Washington savvy, and his credibility with veterans.

He started by conceding that Maya Lin's wall was going to be built. The nation's taste mavens, the "mullahs" of modernism, as Tom Wolfe would later characterize them, had already decided that and sold their point of view. The Wall was to be dedicated over Veterans Day weekend of 1982. The question was, What could be done before then to modify the memorial—to transform it from what Webb termed "a nihilistic statement that does not render honor to those who served" to one that did?

His first and most important move involved James Watt. Webb learned that the Interior Secretary had to approve the design before construction could begin. Looking to buy time, Webb marshaled his forces, primarily well-placed veterans of Vietnam and other wars, including members of Congress, to put pressure on Watt. On January 4, 1982, Watt put the memorial on hold.

Watt's action gave Webb and the other opponents a lever, though one likely to have a short shelf life. It was long enough. On January 27, after a rancorous meeting that went on for hours, a compromise was reached. Maya Lin's design would not be changed, but a statue, a revised, improved inscription, and a flag would be added to the site.

The Memorial Fund, in a rare burst of savvy, named Webb and Milton Copulos, both opponents of the original design, and supporters Bill Jayne and Art Mosely, a West Point classmate of Wheeler, to the four-person panel to recommend a sculptor, a statue design, and a location for it. The sculpture panel selected Frederick Hart to design the statue. Hart had placed third in the original design competition, the highest-ranking representational sculptor.

At first a single soldier was envisioned, but Webb's father insisted to him that any statue depicting Vietnam fighting men had to include a black soldier. Webb made his father's argument to the other panel members. They readily agreed and decided that the statue should consist of three servicemen. That night Wheeler phoned Webb. In a voice that recalled their bizarre conversation in October 1979, Wheeler accused Webb of trying to create another Iwo Jima memorial. Webb responded that Wheeler had promised the panel complete independence and threatened to resign if Wheeler didn't back off. Wheeler backed off.

Unlike Maya Lin, Hart was not a blank slate on Vietnam. He was not a veteran, but he had steeped himself in the literature of the war and interviewed scores of soldiers on their experiences. In June 1982, he unveiled a bronze model of his handiwork—three young soldiers, one white, one black, one of ambiguous ethnicity, seemingly returning from patrol or a night in a listening post outside the perimeter. Through its placement, the statue was to interact with the Wall, joined to it through artistic tension, as if the soldiers had just broken through a clearing and unexpectedly come upon it.

The next two years would be filled with acrimony. Webb, estranged from Wheeler and distrustful of Scruggs, used all his influence and ingenuity to gain approval of the statue before the Wall was dedicated, believing the sculpture, whatever its merits, would not pass muster with the Fine Arts Commission once the dedication had taken place. He had reason for concern. Maya Lin accused Hart of "drawing mustaches on other people's portraits." J. Carter Brown, chairman of the commission, called the two designs "as different as opera and country music." Support from the fund seemed lukewarm at best. But Webb managed to push the statue through to approval in October, a month before the gala National Salute to Vietnam Veterans at which the Wall was dedicated.

Years later, in 1993, Scruggs said his harsh view of Webb, at least in the early years of the battle, was based almost totally on information provided by or filtered through Wheeler. By then Scruggs had come to share Webb's belief that Wheeler was a shameless if increasingly pathetic self-promoter. But it was more than that. Scruggs suspected that Wheeler harbored "a Mitty-esque fantasy" about Webb. Like Webb, Wheeler had written a book about Vietnam, one which Scruggs found "incomprehensible." In Scruggs's view, Wheeler was the REMF who wanted to be a warrior, a warrior who was also a good writer. Webb was both. Wheeler was neither.

On Veterans Day 1984 Frederick Hart's statue was dedicated. By then there had been charges and countercharges from opponents and supporters impugning motives, actions, and integrity. Neither side covered itself with glory.

To this day, Webb cannot discuss the ugly saga coolly. "This is the bottom line," he said in 1991, coming as close as he ever does to sputtering. "I put a black man on the Mall and they can kiss my ass."

He did more than that. Today the Wall and the statue seem inseparable, one complementing the other, a place to contemplate the horrible cost of the war while paying tribute to the young men and women, the living as well as the dead, who fought it. The inscription reads:

Our nation honors the courage, sacrifice and devotion to duty and country of its Vietnam veterans.

Without Webb, they would have had a wall. Unadorned, chilling in its starkness, akin to the silent, heather-covered mounds at Bergen-Belsen. Worthy of a similar inscription.

HIER RUHEN 58,000 TOTEN.

CHAPTER TWENTY-NINE

NOBLE CAUSE REDUX

On first meeting the president of Syria, Hafez al-Assad, Bud Mc-Farlane detected an avuncular quality that brought to mind the old character actor Walter Brennan. To retain his focus, McFarlane reminded himself that a year earlier Assad had presided over the massacre of at least ten thousand of his own people in Hama, Syria's fourth-largest city. Walter Brennan, crusty but harmless, did a fast fade.

McFarlane, at President Reagan's direction, had journeyed to Damascus for secret consultations with Assad about Lebanon. The meeting was not going well. Twenty minutes of chitchat was standard practice in Arab countries. Assad's icebreaker that July day in 1983 did not involve the usual pleasantries about family, travel, or weather, but, as McFarlane described it, "cosmic phenomena, the influence of extraterrestrial forces on earthly events."

The Bermuda Triangle, how do you explain that? Assad asked McFarlane.

McFarlane's head was swimming. The twenty-minute mark had long since passed and here he was embroiled in a rambling discussion about the secrets of the universe and extraterrestrial civilizations. Was Assad talking about the supernatural? The occult? Two hours into the conversation, McFarlane had a chilling thought. Is this guy going to get up, slap me on the ass, and thank me for dropping by before we even get around to Lebanon?

Assad finally turned to temporal matters. The meeting lasted another four hours. Through it all, Assad fixed McFarlane with an intent gaze, behind him an enormous painting that portrayed Saladin expelling the Crusaders from the Holy Land. There were no breaks. No rest calls either. McFarlane began to view the dialogue as a test of bladder capacities. I'm not going to go to the head if he doesn't, he remembers telling himself. And he didn't.

When it was over a weary McFarlane decided that two elements of possible promise had emerged in the six hours of talks. First, Assad seemed open to a renewed dialogue with the United States on Lebanon as long as it did not involve Philip Habib, the presidential envoy whom Assad had decreed persona non grata. Second, aware that inducing the occupying armies of Syria and Israel to return home was a primary American policy goal, he proffered a formula, a murky one, for pulling his troops out of Lebanon. Syrian forces would withdraw, said Assad, "in light of Israeli withdrawal." McFarlane pressed him. What does that mean? At the same time? A week later? Whenever you feel like it? Assad refused to clarify his statement. You can be confident we will do the right thing, the fair thing, he said.

Back at the White House, McFarlane briefed the President and senior officials. Assad is willing to talk. In fact, he seems to want to reengage with us. But it won't be easy, and who knows what he's up to. He says he can imagine withdrawing. Whatever that means. Maybe nothing. The Saudis are committed to help. We don't have much leverage, but we have some. The Saudis and their money for starters. Riyal diplomacy, a straight cash deal, buy off Assad. The Marines. Maybe some allied support. Not a lot to go on. Plus we've wasted a lot of time.

National security adviser Bill Clark knew that Habib had been asking to come home for months. He was also aware that McFarlane, frustrated by the infighting between George Shultz and Caspar Weinberger, wanted to leave government, had already offered his resignation. At the very least he wanted out of Washington.

Why don't you succeed Phil? Clark said to McFarlane. Go out there, see what you can do.

And so he did. Like Ollie North and Jim Webb shipping out to Vietnam after the Tet Offensive of 1968, Bud McFarlane in the summer of 1983 readied himself to march off in pursuit of another lost, if arguably noble, cause.

As he prepared to mount the next rung on the Reagan administration's creaky foreign policy ladder, McFarlane was best known, to the extent that he was known at all, as a behind-the-scenes mover and shaker with an apparent passion for anonymity. He broke cover on July 22, 1983, when Reagan named him to replace Habib as his special Middle East envoy.

McFarlane, looking capable and steady, was pictured on the front page of many of the nation's newspapers the next day. The *New York*

Times gave him its Man in the News treatment, Steven R. Weisman writing that McFarlane "has won praise from so many quarters that many people reacted with dismay when they learned he would be moving to another post." Despite an aversion to the limelight, Weisman said, he had emerged in the past year as "one of the most trusted, influential and effective members of Mr. Reagan's foreign policy inner circle." In a light aside, Weisman mentioned McFarlane's near-addiction to ice cream, quoting him as saying, "When it comes time for me to pass on, my kids intend to pass a bowl of vanilla ice cream across my nose to see if I'm really dead."

Nine days later he was in Beirut. What he found was not the Lebanon of TV's madcap Uncle Tonoose or of poet-mystic Kahlil Gibran, whose gossamer verse the flower children of the 1960s wove into their marriage vows at fashionably déclassé backyard weddings. Beirut had become, in author Steven Emerson's memorable phrase, "a theme park for paranoiacs."

By then, hostilities begun in 1975 had reduced much of the city to rubble, its stubbornly resilient people terrorized by murderous bands of armed marauders. These private armies, or militias as they were known, owed their allegiance to a freakish assortment of power-hungry, often corrupt warlords. In *Best Laid Plans*, a chronicle of antiterrorism efforts during the Reagan years, David C. Martin and John Walcott compared the de facto partitioning of Lebanon to the carving up of turf by urban street gangs: "It was the Sharks and the Jets, the Diablos and the Shamrocks, but instead of chains, stilettos and zip guns, they used automatic rifles, mortars and rocket-propelled grenades."

Even on paper, had such a paper existed, Lebanon was a jumble. Since 1943 the country had been governed by an unwritten National Pact that apportioned power among the three major religious groupings. The presidency was reserved for a Maronite Christian. Though Christians were barely 51 percent of the population, their dominance in the parliament was assured by a requirement that the chamber maintain a six-to-five ratio of Christians to Muslims. The prime minister was a Sunni Muslim while the speaker of the parliament was a Shi'ite Muslim.

This bizarre political arrangement, which had been given a semblance of legitimacy by the 1932 census, had long since been rendered obsolete by rapidly changing demographics. By the 1980s, Christians represented at best one-third of the population, Muslims the remaining two-thirds. The Shi'ites, meanwhile, had become the nation's largest religious community even though they remained impoverished and politically impotent.

Viewing the political landscape of Lebanon as divided into three parts—Christian, Sunni, and Shi'a—was misleading. Each community contained wheels within wheels. The Christians included Roman Catholics, Greek Orthodox, Greek Catholics, a sprinkling of Protestants, and the Maronites, who trace their spiritual heritage to a fifth-century Syrian monk. The Maronites, the country's dominant political and economic force since the late nineteenth century, were themselves riven by old rivalries and antagonisms.

The Sunnis and Shi'ites had divisions as well. The latter contained elements that had aligned themselves with Islamic fanatics driven by the fundamentalist teachings and anti-Western pronouncements of Iran's Ayatollah Ruhollah Khomeini. Then there were the Druse, a small, mysterious, and militaristic Islamic sect that had long feuded with the Maronites.

As the various homegrown tribes clamored for a choice table in the Intergalactic Bar that was Lebanon, another group of customers sat off in the corner, brooding over their fate and plotting to better it. The Palestinians looked like trouble, and they were, but for a variety of reasons the enfeebled Lebanese bartender felt compelled to serve them rather than kick them out. They had poured into Lebanon by the tens of thousands following the founding of the Israeli state in 1948, settling in refugee camps that were little more than shantytowns. Before long, they had become a state within a state. Thousands more flocked to Lebanon after their expulsion from Jordan in 1970, among them Yasir Arafat and the leadership of the PLO. Hostile, disenfranchised, often bereft of hope, the Palestinians were united in their hatred for the Israelis and those they saw as Israel's protectors, the Americans.

Like Philip Habib before him, McFarlane, his wife, Jonny, and a small team of aides moved into the American ambassador's residence in the hills of suburban Yarze, near the Lebanese Defense Ministry. His job, as he saw it, was to get Syria and Israel out of Lebanon.

Ten months earlier, after Israel had invaded the country and then been implicated in the massacre at the refugee camps of Sabra and Shatila, McFarlane had championed a bold plan within the administration. He urged an expansion in the size and mission of the existing multinational peacekeeping force—which included French and Italian troops, and later a small British unit, in addition to 1,200 American Marines deployed at the Beirut airport. A beefed-up MNF, he argued, could move into the high ground above the Lebanese capital to enforce a demand that Syria and Israel withdraw.

If his plan was not without risk, his reasoning was logical. Both Syria and Israel had been badly bloodied. Assad's Soviet-supplied military arsenal was bare, his vaunted air force, armored units, and missile emplacements decimated by the Israelis.

Israel had also suffered heavy casualties in Lebanon. More to the point, support for the war at home had fallen off dramatically after Sabra and Shatila. Now was the time, McFarlane argued in the fall of 1982, for the United States to flex its military muscle, preferably in concert with other members of the multinational force, before the Soviets rearmed their Syrian client and the shock of the massacre wore off in Israel.

McFarlane later described his plan more bluntly: "W. C. Fields had a point. You should never kick a man unless he's down. And Syria was down and we should have insisted that they get out."

By the time he arrived in Beirut in late July 1983 the opportunity to muscle Israel and Syria out had long since passed. Now they would have to be persuaded to leave voluntarily.

He knew neither was likely to depart while chaos reigned, creating a power vacuum that the other might be tempted to fill. Confusing the issue was the determination of the Israelis to redeploy south from the Shouf mountains overlooking Beirut. For the time being, that was the last thing he wanted. The Druse, egged on by the Syrians, and the Maronites were already maneuvering for position and no doubt would be at each other's throats as soon as the Israelis left.

For all McFarlane's importunings, President Amin Gemayel resisted any new governmental arrangement that might jeopardize Maronite hegemony. Instead he wanted a replay of 1958, when the Sixth Fleet plied the Mediterranean off Lebanon and some fifteen thousand American troops stormed ashore to help restore the status quo. That's not going to happen, McFarlane told Gemayel and his lieutenants. President Reagan isn't willing to do that. Even if he were, Congress wouldn't let him. The fact is, a Maronite restoration not only wouldn't be stable, it wouldn't be right.

McFarlane's first meeting as special envoy with Assad had some of the elements of their secret discussion in July. It lasted some six hours, beginning once again with two hours of obscurantist small talk. Turning to substance, Assad largely extinguished any hope for a Syrian withdrawal. He objected vigorously when McFarlane referred to Lebanon as a sovereign nation. The Lebanese people are Syria's people,

Assad insisted. We are one people, one geography, one faith, one country.

Afterward, McFarlane tried to persuade himself that Assad was using the classic negotiator's tactic of establishing a tough going-in position.

"But," he said, "the strongest feeling I had was, Goddammit, we really have let these guys rearm and recover enough strength to stiff us. We were right last fall. We should have been kicking this guy in the teeth then, before we let him rearm and get back up to a powerful position. And what the hell was I doing here now after all these months where we've wasted all this political capital? . . . We're dealing with a strong pan-Arab ambitious leader. We have no leverage against him. How in the hell am I supposed to make something out of this?"

Two weeks into the job and he realized the enormity of his undertaking. Gemayel wanted thousands of U.S. troops, not to defend Lebanon, but to maintain the power of the Maronites. Assad and Menachem Begin, Israel's prime minister, had treated him like an errand boy who couldn't deliver. The Saudis and other moderate Arab leaders engaged in some titillating foreplay, but none seemed inclined to pressure Syria to withdraw. About that time, one of Gemayel's advisers, after yet another maddening recital of the party line, confided to him, You know, Bud, it is a hopeless thing that you are trying to do here.

As reality set in, he saw himself as having two choices. The first was to stay on course, encourage the withdrawal of the Israelis and Syrians by restoring some political cohesion to the central government. The second was a variation on the always undervalued do-nothing alternative. Write Lebanon off, try to establish some sort of demilitarized zone between Israeli and Syrian forces, and hope for the best. In some ways, his decision to pursue the first option represented the triumph of hope over experience, as Samuel Johnson said of second marriages. But there was more to it. Poised over the madness in Lebanon was the threat that war between Israel and Syria could break out and escalate into a confrontation between their respective patrons, the United States and the Soviet Union.

Publicly, McFarlane insisted that the Lebanese armed forces would maintain order once Syrian and Israeli troops pulled out. Privately, he didn't believe the LAF would be up to the job for at least a year, probably two. Nor did the Syrians or Israelis, which made it doubly difficult to sell them on the idea of withdrawal.

As a result, he resurrected his proposal of the previous fall. His plan was to move a sizable multinational force consisting of Americans,

French, British, and Italian troops into Lebanon to hasten the Syrian and Israeli withdrawals and to reassure their leaders that the buffer between them was back in place. He asked the ambassadors of the multinational force partners to sound out their respective governments about such an undertaking. The response was lukewarm but not a flat rejection, which was something.

He was also growing apprehensive about the Marines at the airport. If they came under attack, they would be at a disadvantage in terms of the range and firepower of their artillery. Beyond that, he felt the need for a more dramatic display of the American commitment to Lebanon. He directed two of his aides, Howard Teicher and Philip Dur, to put together a list of options. Dur struck on the idea of stationing the newly recommissioned battleship *New Jersey* off the coast. At the least, it would be an imposing presence, a symbol that the United States meant business. If the situation heated up, the ship's sixteen-inch guns could hurl shells the size of a Volkswagen Beetle deep into Syrian-occupied Lebanon. Dur and Teicher typed up their options paper, rolled it up like a scroll, tied a ribbon around it, and presented it to their boss on a silver serving platter borrowed from the ambassador's residence.

McFarlane got the chance to discuss his ideas directly with Reagan in early September. A few days before, two Marines had been killed and fourteen wounded by mortar fire at the airport and Congress was threatening to bring the troops home under the 1973 War Powers Act. McFarlane was summoned to Washington to confer with the President and help rally Capitol Hill support.

On his way to Washington, McFarlane scooped up Howard Teicher in Cyprus. Teicher was making his way to Washington, too, not for a White House meeting, but for Yom Kippur and a reunion with Gayle, his wife of two months. During his five weeks in Lebanon, he had been shot at enough to realize that diplomatic immunity was a sometime thing. Sporadic shelling of the ambassador's residence had set trees and gardens at the compound ablaze. Smoke drifted through the rooms of the building, permeating furniture, rugs, and clothes. He and McFarlane reached Washington in the predawn hours of Saturday, September 3. When Teicher got home, Gayle sniffed his suit. Have you taken up smoking? she asked. Not exactly, he replied.

That morning, McFarlane laid out his plan for a beefed-up multinational force to the President and senior White House aides. The President's response was noncommittal. Said McFarlane: "Whenever you reached kind of a hard place in a conversation like that with the

President, and he basically agreed but didn't know how to cope, he would say, 'Well, it sounds okay to me.' And he'd look around."

After McFarlane's private briefing, Reagan convened a meeting of his senior national security and foreign policy advisers. McFarlane repeated his pitch. Shultz was not enthusiastic. His goal remained implementation of the peace accord between Israel and Lebanon that he had hammered out in May. Nearly everyone else had already pronounced it dead. Weinberger flatly opposed any expansion of the military mission. The Defense Secretary, along with most senior Pentagon officials, were wary of using the Marines for the kind of coercive diplomacy envisioned by McFarlane. Had it been up to Weinberger, he would have pulled the Marines out that day.

The meeting ended inconclusively. Israel had postponed its withdrawal from the Shouf to let McFarlane try to sell his plan. At Reagan's direction, McFarlane called Jerusalem and urged a further delay. The Israelis were fuming. Forget it, they said. Within hours Israeli tanks and other military vehicles were streaming south out of the mountains toward a more defensible position along the Awali River.

The next day the bipartisan leadership of the House and Senate was invited to the White House for a status report on Lebanon. McFarlane, the man on the scene, was in the spotlight. He put the best face on the situation. He said Gemayel was taking tentative steps toward power-sharing but he would never go through with it if the Marines were pulled out. Asked about the safety of the Marines, he conceded that they were vulnerable at the airport and perhaps it was time to think about a different way to use them. No one asked him what he had in mind, nor did he volunteer anything.

The lawmakers appeared impressed by his performance. Leaving the meeting, House Speaker Tip O'Neill (D-Mass.), long dubious about the Marine deployment, seemed inclined to give the President the benefit of the doubt.

McFarlane returned to Beirut with little hope that his expanded MNF proposal would be approved. With the Israeli pull-out, the situation in Lebanon had become, as he saw it, "very near impossible." Incapable of throwing in the towel, he decided that his last chance to salvage his mission was to step up pressure on Gemayel to broaden his government and implement economic reform.

He received help from exotic quarters. Bandar, the Saudi prince who helped push the AWACS sale through Congress, had become, if not an official member of McFarlane's team, an important and engaging adjunct to it. So had the Saudi royal family's favorite construction contractor, Rafiq Hariri, a portly billionaire said to aspire to high political office in his native Lebanon. He came to be known to McFarlane's crew as the Fat Man. Both Bandar and Hariri had a flair for diplomacy and enjoyed credibility in Beirut and Damascus. Bandar, energetic, ebullient, a bear of a man, delighted in discarding his Bedouin robes (or the tailored Savile Row suits he wore in Washington) for a helmet and Marine-issue camouflage utilities. His high-performance brain was constantly churning out ideas. He bombarded McFarlane with so many cables the team nicknamed them Bandar-grams.

As McFarlane struggled to find the key to peace, the situation on the ground continued to deteriorate. On September 6, two days after the Israelis began their withdrawal from the Shouf, a rocket barrage killed two more Marines at the airport. The next day, about 120 rounds landed inside the Marine perimeter. Aircraft from the carrier *Eisenhower* flew the first American reconnaissance missions over Lebanon on September 7. On September 8 the destroyer *Bowen* fired its five-inch guns in support of the Marines.

Much of the hostile firing was coming from the vicinity of the Shouf mountain town of Souk el-Gharb, situated on a ridge commanding Beirut. A major battle between the Druse and the Maronite militia had begun as both sides rushed to take the high ground abandoned by the Israelis. To separate the warring factions, a brigade of the fledgling Lebanese army had been dispatched. Before long, the brigade, trained by the United States, came under fire from forces that McFarlane described as "part Palestinian, part Druse, part Syrian, part Iranian irregulars."

The U.S. ambassador's residence, from where McFarlane and his team were operating, was again taking fire from the Shouf, primarily Souk el-Gharb. For three nights running, 122-millimeter rockets had landed inside the compound. When the rockets came, McFarlane, Jonny, McFarlane's team, Ambassador Robert Dillon, and his wife would hunker under a stairwell. One team member, Geoffrey Kemp, remembers scurrying for cover in helmet and flak jacket only to see McFarlane coolly descending the stairs in his pastel pajamas, as though he were engaged in nothing more perilous than a nocturnal raid on the ambassador's refrigerator.

The intensified fire directed at the Marines and the American diplomatic mission created a dilemma. As McFarlane explained it, "If people shoot at you, they might kill you or the Marines. If you did nothing about it, you would be seen as impotent. And if you did something about it, you might kill innocent people."

Lebanese army intelligence claimed Souk el-Gharb was under attack by twenty-five thousand troops, although Martin and Walcott say in *Best Laid Plans* that there was hard evidence of only twenty-five hundred. Though the details are unclear, there seems little dispute that on the night of Saturday, September 10, a hostile force overwhelmed a company of the Lebanese army brigade and chopped the commander to pieces with axes. The following afternoon, McFarlane conferred with his advisers at the ambassador's residence. He believed it was time for the rules of engagement to be changed to allow the Marines and ships offshore to fire in support of the Lebanese army. According to Martin and Walcott, that opinion was shared by Brigadier General Carl Stiner, an expert in small-unit warfare. Although the Lebanese brigade still held Souk el-Gharb, he warned that another attack could turn into a rout. Stiner was the representative of the Joint Chiefs, a cool, battle-hardened soldier not given to panicky judgments. "If he was worried about a rout, it was time for everyone else to worry about a rout," write Martin and Walcott.

The battle for Souk el-Gharb, and McFarlane's reaction to it, came at a crucial juncture in the history of the American presence in Lebanon. From the residence, McFarlane dictated an "action message" back to Washington. Martin and Walcott reproduced it for the first time. "There is a serious threat of a decisive military defeat which could involve the fall of the Government of Lebanon within twenty-four hours," it began.

McFarlane argued in the cable that the Marines at the airport and American diplomats in the residence were in grave danger unless the rules of engagement were broadened to permit the Marines to mount a defense by returning fire.

In time, the message would be ridiculed in some quarters as Mc-Farlane's "sky-is-falling" cable. He would be faulted for allegedly overstating the threat, relying too heavily on Lebanese military intelligence that he knew to be suspect, and casting the situation in East-West terms that he knew would resonate with Reagan.

The reality of Lebanon in September 1983, moreover, was that the beleaguered Lebanese army was seen by many citizens, and especially the leaders of non-Christian sects, as nothing more than another Maronite militia. Thus, critics have argued, once U.S. forces started shooting, as they finally did about a week later, they forfeited the remnants of their neutrality in the eyes of the non-Christians, making them just another target of opportunity, a most inviting one at that.

In light of what would soon follow, and the blame that some would ascribe to McFarlane, it is important to recall the relationship of the United States to the Lebanese army. From the beginning of American involvement in Lebanon, the creation of a national army had been a goal of U.S. policy, ranking with efforts to encourage the withdrawal of Syria and Israel. Washington had supplied the Lebanese with $290 million worth of military equipment, including sixty-eight new M-48 tanks. For nearly a year, the United States had been training the LAF, as well as running joint patrols and manning checkpoints with the Lebanese. Certainly bombarding Souk el-Gharb from ships offshore represented an escalation, but it was consistent with the U.S. policy of attempting to prop up the central government, which McFarlane's instructions called on him to do.

There was a potentially important, all-but-forgotten episode between September 19, when American guns first fired in support of the Lebanese armed forces at Souk el-Gharb, and the grisly tragedy waiting in the wings.

On September 23, McFarlane traveled to Damascus. He suspected Assad might be reviewing the bidding in light of the new if limited American willingness to take military action against his Lebanese surrogates. For four hours he and the Syrian president talked past each other, accomplishing little. As McFarlane prepared to leave, he played his ace.

"President Reagan feels quite strongly about the importance of reconciliation in Lebanon, of the restoration of Lebanese sovereignty over its entire territory, and the withdrawal of all foreign forces," he said. "As a sign of that commitment, the battleship *New Jersey* will be sent to augment the Sixth Fleet here in the next week."

By then, McFarlane and Bandar had made six trips together to Damascus as McFarlane engaged in intense shuttle diplomacy reminiscent of Henry Kissinger a decade earlier. Now they split up. McFarlane in Beirut pressured Gemayel to call for a cease-fire, which he was reluctant to do because the army for the moment was performing better than expected, thus advancing Maronite interests. In Damascus the dogged and tireless Saudi prince, assisted by Rafiq Hariri, finally persuaded Assad to agree to the truce. On September 25, the day before the *New Jersey* was to arrive off the coast of Lebanon, a cease-fire was announced.

The *New Jersey*. More firepower than all the other vessels in the American flotilla combined. McFarlane was swept back a quarter century to that golden summer of 1956 when he had proudly strolled its decks, fresh from the travails of Plebe Year at Annapolis. Now his old cruise ship was steaming out of the past to redeem the most important mission of his life. For a time it seemed to do just that. "The airport was reopened, and soon more than seventy international flights a day were arriving and departing," write Martin and Walcott, among McFarlane's severest critics. "The American show of force seemed to have worked."

In Beirut there was a round of parties as a festive air took hold among the American diplomats. One night, they even ventured up into the battle-scarred Shouf for dinner at one of Lebanon's most elegant restaurants, newly reopened following the cease-fire. The team felt a sense of relief, at times even giddiness, as if against great odds they had accomplished something that mattered.

At the ambassador's residence, they relaxed with cocktails at poolside. McFarlane, the old gymnast, regaled the gathering with picture-perfect double gainers from the low board. Geoffrey Kemp donned mask and snorkel to retrieve chunks of shrapnel from the bottom of the pool, distributing the pieces to the others as souvenirs.

CHAPTER THIRTY

THE DOUBTERS

The Washington press quickly pegged the new congressman from Arizona as a predictable conservative, thus a reliable vote for the administration. The label didn't bother John McCain. He had known and liked Ronald Reagan for a decade, admired him even longer, never more so than during the first two years of his presidency. McCain's estrangement and divorce from Carol and his remarriage to Cindy had cooled the personal relationship, but politically he and Reagan were on the same wavelength.

There was one major exception. John McCain wasn't buying anything coming out of the White House about Lebanon. To McCain, Lebanon looked too much like a ghost from the past. Not long past. His past.

On September 28, three days after Bud McFarlane had engineered a new cease-fire under the fearsome shadow of the *New Jersey,* the House prepared to vote on a war-powers measure that would permit the President to keep the Marines in Lebanon for another eighteen months. During a seven-hour debate long on references to Vietnam, one of the few congressmen who had been there took the floor.

"The fundamental question is, What is the United States' interest in Lebanon? It is said we are there to keep the peace. I ask, What peace? It is said we are there to aid the government. I ask, What government? It is said we are there to stabilize the region. I ask, How can the U.S. presence stabilize the region?"

Do you really think naval forces off the Lebanese coast are going to so intimidate the Syrians that they engage in meaningful negotiations? he asked his colleagues. For this to occur, he said, echoing Louis Halle's old argument, the Syrians must believe we will use the full military power at our disposal.

"Are we prepared to use this power? I do not think so, nor do I believe the Syrians think so."

He knew a quagmire when he saw it. "The longer we stay in Lebanon, the harder it will be for us to leave," he said. "We will be trapped by the case we make for having our troops there in the first place."

McCain concluded by saying the American presence would not make a difference, that the same things would happen—more factional violence, more innocent civilians killed and wounded—whether the Marines were there or not. "I am not calling for an immediate withdrawal," he said. "What I desire is as rapid a withdrawal as possible."

He cast his vote against the resolution, one of twenty-seven Republicans to defy Reagan. The final tally in the House was 270 to 161. Tip O'Neill led the fight for the White House, bringing 129 other Democrats with him. The Speaker's fears were calmed by a promise from Reagan to seek congressional authorization for any "substantial expansion" in the size or mission of the Marine contingent, which seemed to sound the death knell for McFarlane's grand scheme of an expanded multinational force.

A few weeks later, the liberal *Rolling Stone* magazine, a product of the social and political upheavals of the 1960s, flayed O'Neill and the Democrats who followed his lead in an article entitled "Profiles in Cowardice." But the author, William Greider, tipped his hat to McCain: "In the House of Representatives, a respected veteran of Vietnam . . . chose to remind his colleagues of that war's lessons. . . . It takes enormous courage for an old military man to deliver a message like that."

*   *   *

On Friday evening, October 14, the "MacNeil/Lehrer NewsHour" broadcast a report on the Marines in Lebanon. The correspondent was Jim Webb, whom the show had sent on special assignment because of his dual qualifications as soldier and writer.

There were differences in terrain features, but Webb discerned a sameness between the Arizona Valley and the Marine positions around Beirut International Airport. He called the encampment "a place of red dust and foul air, of heat and, when the shells are not flying, of tedium."

With his curly hair, wire-rimmed glasses, Levi's, and preppy polo shirt, he looked like the standard yuppie reporter. But the troops opened up to him, as if they were talking to a mirror image of themselves, the only journalist who seemed to envy them. In the previous three weeks, four Marines had been killed and many more wounded. "Lots of people would like to make some frontal assaults out there," confided First Lieutenant Andy May, a bespectacled platoon commander whose predecessor, Second Lieutenant Donald G. Losey, Jr., was killed in a rocket attack a few weeks earlier.

Webb focused on Alfa Company, First Battalion, Eighth Marines, as they filled sandbags, cleaned weapons, and scurried through bunkers. "They are infantrymen or, as they call themselves with perverse pride, grunts," he said. "Under the traditions of the Marine Corps, the greatest respect is accorded those who are nearest to danger. It may seem more exciting to fly a helicopter or blast away with an artillery piece but the grunts have always been called the pride of the Corps because they are the ones who stand on the cusp. They take the most casualties. They have the fewest creature comforts. They must answer in their honor to no one."

He smelled something wrong, both with the mission and the disposition of the troops. He reported that the last time Marines came to Lebanon, in 1958, they landed with eight times as many men. Now, with just three rifle companies ashore, he said, "they lack the forces even to pursue an aggressive defense." The "narrow political goals" of the mission, he continued, had put them in "a militarily vulnerable position, defending the low ground."

Beneath their flak jackets and helmets, the troops at the airport were mostly kids, 80 percent under twenty years old. In interviews with them, Webb captured an odd blend of confusion, machismo, commitment, hope, and youthful sweetness.

"I really want to go home," said one young Marine, "but when I leave I want to know that deep down in my heart that four guys that died, they died for a good reason, because something turned out good because of us being here."

Wrapping up the piece, Webb signaled his fear that nothing was going to turn out good.

"There's a small irony in hearing the men of Alfa Company talking about their presence here in Lebanon," he said. "The lowest private seems to understand the value of this American commitment more clearly than most congressmen. In a way it made me feel deeply protective of these men. I and my fellow veterans from Vietnam still feel the pain of having made a greater commitment than the political process was willing to uphold. These men are trusting their very lives to the wisdom of our leaders. Our government's obligation to them, which was too frequently betrayed in Vietnam, is to proceed with a clarity of purpose that matches their own trust and commitment."

Webb's report from Beirut, which lasted barely seven minutes, was awarded an Emmy. It was his first foray into television. He would later say that the lesson of Lebanon was: "Never get involved in a five-sided argument that's been going on for two thousand years."

CHAPTER THIRTY-ONE

THE PRESBYTERIAN CLIMAX

James Watt, the Interior Secretary, put his foot in his mouth for the last time on September 21, 1983, by publicly congratulating himself for fashioning a federal commission of exquisite balance. The panel, he happily proclaimed, consisted of "a black . . . a woman, two Jews and a cripple." The remark provoked outrage and demands for his firing. When damage control efforts faltered, he grudgingly submitted his resignation.

Amid the fallout of a public relations fiasco, William Clark and the James Baker–Michael Deaver team separately saw opportunity. The two White House factions had been feuding almost constantly from the moment Clark moved from State to the NSC twenty-one months earlier. With Watt's departure, Clark, an outdoorsman, saw a way to make a graceful exit, suggesting to Reagan that he take over at Interior. Independently, Baker and Deaver proposed the same thing as the opening gambit in a staff reshuffling scheme they had hatched to restore the more collegial pre-Clark White House relationships. When Reagan agreed, Baker and Deaver moved quickly to cement the once and future power structure.

Unknown to Clark, they sold Reagan on the idea of naming Baker national security adviser and Deaver White House chief of staff. Richard Darman, a Baker aide of shimmering intelligence, devilish wit, and barely relieved smugness, was to be Baker's deputy at the NSC, replacing Bud McFarlane.

On the afternoon of Friday, October 14, Clark was escorting Reagan down to the Situation Room for a National Security Planning Group meeting. The President casually mentioned that later in the day he was going to announce Baker's appointment as national security adviser, with Deaver taking Baker's old job as chief of staff. The press release, Reagan said, had already been written. Clark, stunned, urged Reagan not to announce the changes at the NSPG meeting. Reagan seemed surprised by the vehemence of Clark's reaction.

McFarlane was already in the Situation Room when Clark ushered in Reagan. He could see the President was troubled. Reagan took his seat at one end of the table, Clark at the other end. Baker normally attended NSC meetings and Deaver was free to do so, but for reasons of atmospherics they chose to remain in Baker's office, a tactical blunder. Clark ran through the day's agenda. Here's the issue, Mr. President, here's what you have to decide. He then called on others—Shultz, Weinberger, Ed Meese, CIA director William Casey, UN ambassador Jeane Kirkpatrick—for their views on the matters at hand. But McFarlane, seated behind Clark, noticed something odd. As others talked, Clark was furiously scribbling notes, passing them on to his conservative soulmates Weinberger, Casey, and Meese.

To Clark's relief, Reagan said nothing at the meeting about the staff switches. As the participants filed out of the Situation Room, Clark took the President by the elbow and guided him into his office next door. Meese, Weinberger, and Casey joined them. McFarlane, watching the procession from his small adjoining office, wondered what was going on.

He had an inkling. A few days earlier, Clark had told him that he considered him the best man for the NSC job and asked if he would take it if Reagan offered it. McFarlane replied that he would never decline a request from the President, that he saw himself as qualified, but pointed out that there were others with longer and closer associations with Reagan, far more political clout, and a variety of other qualities that made them superior candidates.

"Well, we'll see," said Clark.

The rump session in Clark's office broke up after about twenty minutes. As Weinberger and Casey went on their way, Clark walked into McFarlane's office and filled him in. First he explained what Baker and Deaver had cooked up. Then he said he told the President that it would be a horrible mistake, that it was contrary to all he stood for and would eliminate the opportunity for leaving the Reagan imprint on world affairs. Casey and Weinberger had reinforced Clark's argument and Reagan agreed to rethink the matter over the weekend at his Camp David retreat.

At some point, possibly during that conversation on Friday, perhaps a day or two earlier, Clark informed McFarlane that he had recommended him to the President as his successor. I believe it will come out that way, Clark added.

As he listened, McFarlane sensed that the promise, indeed the expectation, of a lifetime was about to be consummated. Since childhood, he had seen himself as endowed with qualities of intellect and character that foreshadowed a role at the highest levels of government, a view reinforced over twenty-eight years of service by his elevation to ever more lofty positions of leadership and responsibility.

Outwardly, McFarlane responded to Clark's words by making the necessary, if genuine, genuflections. He was, he told Clark, humbled, flattered, grateful for the trust Clark had placed in him by advancing his name; he pledged to vindicate that trust.

But as he spoke, deep within, obscured as always behind a visage he kept under such tight control that at times his eyes seemed almost dead, a serenity—religious, transcendent, perhaps something else as well—settled on him. "There was," he later said, pausing, sighing, searching for words, "a calm sense of Presbyterian climax."

"This was," he continued, "the fulfillment of what had been intended, what had been predestined and that now was beginning the ultimate challenge, the opportunity for the greatest service to my fellow human beings that I would ever have in my life."

He felt the need to do two things immediately, pray and call Jonny, give her the news. He also thought of his father, whose words, "You are a McFarlane," had echoed through his life. Now, without apology, with the becoming diffidence that was always the flip side of his towering ambition, he could reply, Yes, well, I guess I am. Except that his father had died three years earlier.

The following Monday, after a weekend of heated maneuvering at which McFarlane emerged as everyone's second choice (a distant second choice, according to Reagan biographer Lou Cannon), Clark returned from his daily nine-thirty meeting with the President and told him he had the job. Reagan was going to announce it personally that afternoon.

McFarlane reported to the Oval Office fifteen minutes before he and Reagan were to mount the stage in the White House press briefing room. Up till then, he had neither seen nor spoken to the President.

Sitting there with a President who was about to confer on him one of the most powerful and sensitive posts in the world, McFarlane expected marching orders. He wanted Reagan to say, Bud, here is my agenda, these are my priorities. I want us to establish a framework for stability between us and the Russians. Here are my ideas for doing that. I want to solve the international debt problem. Here are my ideas for doing that. I want to engage Japan in a new strategic partnership. I want to do this, I want to do that. Your job is to squeeze the bureaucracy, make it spit out the new ideas and initiatives that will cause these things to happen.

Reagan said nothing of the kind. As McFarlane recalled it, the President, after greeting him, sat thumbing through index cards from which he was to read the announcement McFarlane had written for him, now and then crossing out a line.

And when Reagan spoke, what he said was, "Well, what time do we go out?" He meant into the briefing room to meet the press.

The cease-fire orchestrated by McFarlane in Lebanon was still in place at twenty-two minutes after six on Sunday morning about a week later when a bearded Muslim, a smile frozen on his face, gunned the engine of his yellow Mercedes-Benz stake-bed truck. Speeding past a wide-eyed sentry who because of orders from his superiors didn't even have a magazine in his rifle, the driver rammed his vehicle, laden with the equivalent of twelve thousand pounds of TNT, into the central lobby of the Marine barracks at the airport. Two hundred and forty-one men died in the explosion, making October 23, 1983, the deadliest day for Marines since they had hit the beach at Iwo Jima nearly forty years earlier.

CHAPTER THIRTY-TWO

PUT 'EM UP, PUT 'EM UP

Let terrorists beware that when the rules of international behavior are violated, our policy will be one of swift and effective retribution.

—RONALD REAGAN, January 27, 1981, welcoming home the
fifty-two Carter-era hostages after 444 days in captivity
in Tehran

By Saturday evening, the night before the tragedy in Lebanon, a relaxed October weekend at Augusta National Golf Course had already taken on an anxious complexion. In the afternoon an armed, seemingly deranged man had commandeered the pro shop, taken seven hostages, and threatened to kill them all unless he met with President Reagan. The Secret Service surrounded the President's foursome—which included George Shultz, Donald Regan, and former senator Nicholas Brady—and rushed them to safety from the sixteenth hole. Two hours later the gunman released his captives and surrendered to authorities, but the incident had sent a chill through the presidential party.

At dinner Nancy Reagan was shaken. The day's events had given fresh currency to the nightmare that had haunted her since the March 1981 assassination attempt on her husband. She tried to make conversation, but her nervous stabs at sociability soon gave way to long, distracted silences.

Bud McFarlane, the new national security adviser, was in Augusta on a working weekend. On the job just six days, he joined Reagan and the others for dinner, but thought of himself as a member of the President's staff, not his golfing buddy.

At about 2:00 A.M. on Sunday, October 23, McFarlane was awakened by the ringing of his secure line. The White House was calling on orders from John Poindexter, whom McFarlane had installed as his deputy. In Washington, Poindexter, Ollie North, and others were putting the finishing touches on a plan to invade the tiny Caribbean nation of Grenada on Tuesday.

The call had nothing to do with Grenada. A truck bomb, the White House told McFarlane, had destroyed the Marine barracks building in Beirut. The casualties were still being counted, but massive loss of life seemed certain.

A troubled weekend had just become a descent into Hell.

McFarlane made his way over the darkened grounds to the Eisenhower cottage, where he was joined by Shultz. Reagan, in pajamas, bathrobe, and open-toed slippers, listened as the two officials passed on the few details they had. It's not confirmed yet, but it looks like two hundred or more fatalities, said McFarlane.

Reagan looked stricken. God, he said, just think of those poor guys, their families. His voice trailed off. He looked away and shook his head. When he turned back, the grief had melted away, replaced by what McFarlane called "an expression of hatred and wish for revenge that I never saw in him before or since."

Those sons of bitches, said Reagan, let's find a way to go after them.

Whatever his other failings, Ronald Reagan always talked a good game.

Within days, American intelligence had identified those behind the attack. The evidence pointed to a previously unknown group, Islamic Jihad, or Holy War, as the perpetrators. Planning and financing had come from Iran. Syria had provided a haven for the training of the terrorists at the Sheik Abdullah Barracks, a former Lebanese army post in the city of Baalbek, in the Bekaa Valley. The evidence might have fallen short in a court of law, but, as authors Martin and Walcott put it, the Reagan administration "knew to a moral, if not a legal, certainty who was responsible for the massacre of the Marines."

Go after it, said Reagan at a meeting of his senior national security aides. He meant the Sheik Abdullah Barracks. Shultz and McFarlane agreed, as did Vice President Bush. Weinberger was not enthusiastic, voicing misgivings about the impact of a retaliatory attack on moderate Arab states, the possibility that those responsible were no longer at the barracks, and related concerns.

At the conclusion of the meeting, McFarlane summed up. As I understand it, Mr. President, you want the Pentagon to commence planning a retaliatory mission. That's right, Reagan replied. McFarlane also received authority from the President to discuss joint action with the French, who had lost fifty-eight men in a similar bombing of the headquarters of their multinational force contingent minutes after the Marines were hit.

At McFarlane's direction, Poindexter and Navy Commander Philip Dur, a Middle East specialist on the NSC staff, initiated discussions for a joint retaliatory raid with the French. They reported back that the French were interested. As both nations had flattops in the Mediterranean, planners concentrated on a raid using carrier-based aircraft.

McFarlane, meanwhile, was swept up in the Grenada invasion, launched on schedule Tuesday morning, two days after the barracks bombing. A weeklong presidential trip to South Korea and Japan, on which he accompanied Reagan, also intervened. Before leaving for the Far East, the President traveled to Camp Lejeune to pay tribute to the servicemen killed and wounded in Beirut and Grenada.

Speaking under a steady rain and leaden skies, Reagan quoted philosopher John Stuart Mill: "War is an ugly thing, but not the ugliest of things. The ugliest is that man who thinks nothing is worth fighting and dying for and lets men better and braver than himself protect him."

The mourners included two hundred family members of dead servicemen and a group of wheelchair-bound Marines wounded in the Beirut bombing. "I do not know why young men die," said Navy chaplain John R. McNamara. "I do not know why we must endure the grief and pain. You would think it would break the heart of God." McFarlane, standing next to Weinberger in the front rank of White House officials, lost his composure, could not stop his tears.

On returning from the Asia trip, according to McFarlane's account, he queried Poindexter on the status of planning for the retaliatory strike with the French. Everything's pretty much ready to go, Poindexter replied, but Cap's worried about it. Wary of Weinberger, McFarlane urged the President to convene his top advisers to thrash out differences. At a White House meeting on November 14, General John Vessey, the chairman of the Joint Chiefs of Staff, told the President the military was prepared to launch an attack. Let's do it, the President said, ordering the attack for the morning of November 16, two days hence. Weinberger agreed, but told Reagan he would monitor the situation for developments that might require a change in plans. Replied Reagan, I can't imagine anything like that. Said Weinberger, Well, I'll keep an eye on it.

To McFarlane, Reagan's statement seemed unequivocal. The President had ordered the military to strike. But he realized that Weinberger had gotten in the last word, perhaps opening the door a crack. McFarlane recalled going back to his office after the meeting, slamming his papers on the desk, and saying, That son of a bitch is going to fuck this up.

Weinberger's version of events is sharply at odds with McFarlane's. In *Fighting for Peace*, Weinberger's memoirs of his seven years as Defense Secretary, he flatly denied having received any orders from the President to launch an attack. He remembered a call early on the morning of November 16 from Charles Hernu, the French defense minister, telling him that French planes were going to attack Syrian positions in about two or three hours. He said he wished Hernu and his pilots good luck, adding, "Unfortunately it is a bit too late for us to join you in this one." In a 1994 interview, he said much the same. General Vessey told author Hedrick Smith that he knew of no planning for a joint raid with the French.

Is it conceivable that McFarlane and Weinberger could have walked out of the same meeting with such different views of what had taken place? Perhaps the confusion, if that's what it was, can be explained in part by considering the makeup and experiences of the two men. McFarlane was steeped in a military tradition that holds that your commanding officer's wish is your command. He did not need a signed presidential document that read "Attack Repeat Attack," though in retrospect he should have demanded one.

Weinberger, by contrast, went back a long way with Ronald Reagan. While it is unthinkable that he would disobey a direct order, he was adept at recognizing or creating wiggle room in presidential pronouncements, especially those he viewed as unwise. Like all the President's oldest and most trusted advisers, Weinberger understood Reagan and was protective of him. If he sensed any uncertainty in Reagan's comments at the November 14 meeting, he might well have felt that none of the President's statements constituted a clear-cut order.

In *Best Laid Plans*, Martin and Walcott sought to unravel the details of the meeting that preceded the air strike that never was. They came away ascribing the confusion to Reagan.

It was not unusual for two of the President's closest advisers to come out of a meeting with completely different impressions of what Reagan had decided. Although he projected the image of a strong leader, Ronald Reagan frequently relied on ambiguity to resolve—or bury—the conflicts within his administration. Never one to master the intricacies of a problem, he was dependent upon his advisers to tell him not only the facts but also what they meant. When his advisers gave him conflicting opinions, when the time came for him to make a complex and truly difficult decision that only the President could make, he frequently failed. The President's involvement in foreign affairs was episodic, anecdotal, impulsive, and rarely decisive. It was no wonder that the staff of the National Security Council later concluded that the best way to serve Reagan was to do the job for him.

Whatever truly occurred, McFarlane, Poindexter, Dur, Howard Teicher, and others on the NSC staff came away believing that Weinberger had sabotaged the retaliatory raid. McFarlane, Dur, and Teicher considered it tantamount to direct defiance of a presidential order. Poindexter's recollections are slightly different.

"There's no doubt in my mind that the President, in Cap and Jack Vessey's presence, approved the cooperation with the French and carrying out a raid when the forces were ready," he said.

As far as Poindexter was concerned, no further direction from the President was necessary. Weinberger could order the raid by issuing the so-called execute order to the fleet at his discretion. Technically, however, he could also withhold issuing the order if he felt the circumstances were not favorable for success. "He did act in a high-handed manner," said Poindexter. "Did he violate a direct presidential order? Probably not, in that there was probably room for him to maneuver, which he took advantage of." And, added Poindexter, "The President was never very clear."

That was the problem with the Nightingale's Song as it gained complexity after Reagan reached the White House. At times the lyrics seemed to enter a scrambler once they issued from Reagan's lips, only to emerge in versions that resonated to the individual tastes of the listening audience. Much like Reagan himself, the Nightingale's Song could be anything you wanted it to be.

Eventually the United States did retaliate, but in a manner so bumbling that all McFarlane's Vietnam-era misgivings about the top echelons of the uniformed military were revived.

Retaliation was sparked by the firing of surface-to-air missiles at U.S. reconnaissance planes flying over Syrian positions in Lebanon. None of the planes was hit, but the President decided, despite the resistance of Weinberger and Vessey, to respond with an air strike. The provocation was small. Everyone knew this was to be a vengeance mission for the killing of Marines.

Plans called for launching aircraft at 11:00 A.M. the next day, December 4. Time over target was set for 11:30. Early that morning, however, the task force commander received orders through the scandalously cumbersome military chain of command to mount the attack at 6:30 A.M., or in about one hour. He was not ready and sought permission to strike as planned. The best he could get was a one-hour delay.

"There followed a mad flail," John Lehman, the Secretary of the Navy, would later write. "Normally the strike crews must begin briefing at least two hours before launch time in order to be prepared properly. Now, neither air wing had sufficient numbers of aircraft loaded nor crews assigned, let alone briefed. Aircrews scrambled to take whichever aircraft were available, and without any time to brief, launched on schedule."

Some planes took off with only two bombs, said Lehman. Others carried payloads more appropriate to hitting targets in Baalbek, for which the crews had been readying themselves. Because of the haste and confusion, radio silence proved impossible to maintain, alerting the Syrians. The targets selected were small and, with perhaps one exception, inconsequential. Worst of all, because of the change in launch time, the attacking aircraft found themselves flying into the fiery glare of the early-morning sun while the Syrian gunners they were searching out awaited them in the shadows.

The only plane carrying a full load of bombs never dropped them. It was hit by a SAM and crashed. Both crewmen ejected. The pilot, Lieutenant Mark Lange, Annapolis '79, bled to death after his Syrian captors failed to apply a tourniquet quickly enough to his severed left leg. The bombardier-navigator, Lieutenant Robert Goodman, a 1978 Academy graduate, was taken prisoner. He was subsequently released to the Reverend Jesse Jackson, causing Lehman to suggest that the survival packets issued to naval aviators should be modified to include a roll of quarters and Jackson's phone number.

The raid was a fiasco. In return for two planes lost, one airman killed, and a second captured, the Americans managed to knock out two gun emplacements and damage a radar installation that was back in business a day later.

"There'll be people licking their balls for a long time after this one," an officer aboard the carrier *Kennedy* told George Wilson of the *Washington Post*. "I wrote my wife that I hang my head in shame for the part I played in this strike."

By early 1984, McFarlane had thrown in with those who felt the time had come to pull the Marines out of Lebanon, if for different reasons. As he saw it, the troops remained vulnerable, were accomplishing little, and seemed likely to accomplish even less. Weinberger's and Vessey's hostility to the mission of the Marines was well-documented and long-standing. Now Jim Baker and Mike Deaver wanted them out as well. Going into a reelection campaign, they did not want Reagan squandering any more of his political capital in what had become a classic no-win situation.

The lone holdout was Shultz, who insisted the United States would lose all credibility in the Middle East if it walked away from a commitment the President had termed in the vital interests of the nation and its allies. Once, at a White House meeting, Shultz turned to Weinberger and said, Cap, why are you buying all this military equipment if you never want to use it?

Reagan's public statements in the days before he ordered the Marine pullout from Lebanon resembled those of a man who has not yet been told what he thinks. In a *Wall Street Journal* interview published Friday, January 3, 1984, he said of House Speaker Tip O'Neill, whose earlier concerns about the deployment had returned, "He may be ready to surrender but I'm not." On Saturday, February 4, in his weekly Saturday radio address, he maintained that efforts to strengthen the Lebanese army were making progress and said the dangers and frustrations in Lebanon were "no reason to turn our backs and to cut and to run." On Monday, February 6, as he participated in a triumphant, flag-waving return to his hometown of Dixon, Illinois, to celebrate his seventy-third birthday, he said in a statement issued by the White House that "the commitment of the United States to the unity, independence, and sovereignty of Lebanon remains firm and unwavering."

The next day, Tuesday, February 7, he ordered the withdrawal of the Marines from Lebanon. It was called a "redeployment" to ships offshore, but no one was fooled. NSC aide Howard Teicher reduced it to an equation: "Redeployment equals failure and retreat with our tail between our legs."

Earlier in the day, Reagan had given a speech on education in Las Vegas, then flown on to California for a few days at his Rancho de Cielo retreat in the hills above Santa Barbara. John Poindexter, traveling with the President, was saddled with the task of reading the withdrawal announcement to the Air Force One press pool on the tarmac at Point Mugu Naval Air Station. By then, Reagan had boarded a chopper and lifted off for the ranch, as if the decision and the ludicrous efforts of his minions to explain his abrupt conversion had nothing to do with him.

The October 1983 bombing of the Marine barracks shredded U.S. policy in Lebanon with the same finality that it visited on most of the four hundred American servicemen sleeping inside the building. By

February of the following year, for all the brave but hollow words mouthed in the interim, the Marines had departed Lebanon, their mission, and McFarlane's, a failure.

Weinberger had made no secret of his reluctance to deploy the Marines or his desire to withdraw them as quickly as possible, wearing his opposition as a badge of honor, the implication being that had his advice been heeded the barracks disaster would have been averted.

General Vessey shared Weinberger's hostility to the deployment, but in retrospect had some second thoughts. "The question that has nagged at me ever since the bombing of the Marines is how much did our opposition to being there affect our performance in ways that may have permitted the bombing," he told Martin and Walcott. "How much did our hopes to get out of there affect our ability to protect ourselves?" In another revealing comment to the same authors, he said, "After the decision was made to go back in [after Sabra and Shatila], then we debated this business of what are we going to do. That was the question we never did get answered to our satisfaction. Perhaps it was our own pigheadedness that kept us from seeing what there was useful to do."

Apprised of Vessey's statements, Poindexter's usual coolness deserted him. "He's damn right," he said. "It was a self-fulfilling prophecy. They didn't want to be in there, they didn't do anything to make it work, and it failed."

McFarlane and Poindexter looked on Weinberger and Vessey as captives of the so-called Vietnam syndrome, a deeply ingrained wariness of deploying American troops without a national consensus supporting such action. McFarlane understood that sentiment and sympathized with it, but felt that Weinberger and Vessey carried it to such extremes that any foreign policy initiative that relied on the threat of military force was likely to fail. Poindexter, who unlike Vessey and McFarlane did not serve in Vietnam, never understood it. Instead, he joined with aides in privately ridiculing Vessey and like-minded military leaders as belonging to a Vietnam Never Again Society. Did it matter? Perhaps. Had Poindexter understood that Vietnam continued to haunt the military in the 1980s no less than it did the larger society, he might well have associated himself with those concerns. In so doing, he could have dampened the fear that the White House, which he represented, was willing to dispatch troops on misconceived and potentially deadly missions. The result might have been a more productive working relationship.

Some critics ascribed much of the blame for the attack on the barracks to McFarlane. The decision to let the Marines fire in support of the Lebanese army at Souk el-Gharb, which McFarlane urged on Reagan, stripped the Americans of their already tattered cloak of neutrality in the eyes of the Druse and other anti-Christian militias, setting the stage for the bombing. Or so it is argued by Walcott and Martin, among others.

Missing is a crucial element. The Druse don't seem to have done it. Nor do any of the other well-established Lebanese factions. According to Martin and Walcott's own account, "Most of the evidence . . . indicated that the government of Iran had directed the bombing while Syria looked the other way." A Pentagon commission headed by retired Admiral Robert L. J. Long investigated the attack and made this further point: "Iranian operatives in Lebanon are in the business of killing Americans. They are in that business whether or not the USMNF trains the LAF or provides indirect fire support to the defenders of Suq-Al-Gharb."

What would have happened had the bombing never occurred? Hard to say. Nothing very good ever seemed to happen in Lebanon. However, the cease-fire, though growing frayed, remained in force at the time of the attack and plans were under way for a conference on political reconciliation at the end of the month. McFarlane still hoped to expand the multinational force and give Lebanon some breathing room. Might he have succeeded in getting the Reagan administration, racked by its own factional conflicts, to go along? Probably not, but who knows?

A few years later, Pat Collins, a Marine officer who was there, said, "Lebanon was a goat fuck." At a certain point, McFarlane probably felt the same way. He went to Lebanon believing that there was a slim chance that Lebanon could be salvaged. That was probably a mistake. But even McFarlane, by then more foreign policy intellectual than soldier, was not immune to the teachings of Annapolis and the Marine Corps. And in that theology, and it is little short of that, it is unheard of to say to your superior, in this case the President of the United States, Sir, you know that thing you asked me to do? Well, I can't do it. Forget that it may be impossible, genuinely impossible; it is equally impossible for a man like McFarlane—or North or Webb or McCain or Poindexter—to say, Mr. President, I couldn't find Garcia, the message didn't get through, return to sender.

Vice Admiral Staser Holcomb was at his wit's end in early 1984 when an old friend, John Poindexter, walked into his London headquarters overlooking Grosvenor Square. As deputy commander of U.S. Naval

Forces in Europe, Holcomb, Annapolis '53, was enmeshed in the serpentine chain of command that traveled from the Pentagon to the Marines in Lebanon, with pit stops in Brussels, Stuttgart, London, and points east. Holcomb was upset and alarmed by a proliferation of mixed messages issuing from the Pentagon and the White House in the weeks following the bombing of the Marine barracks.

"That was a traumatic period because the signals coming out of Washington were confused, worse than confused, it was outrageous," he said. There were on-again, off-again air strikes into Syrian-held territory in Lebanon. One minute he was being told to prepare to launch reconnaissance aircraft over Lebanon, the next minute he received orders to cancel the mission. Sometimes the *New Jersey* was alerted to blast away with its sixteen-inch guns, then the fire mission was put on hold. "These kinds of things had happened countless times by the time John stuck his head in the door," said Holcomb.

Holcomb had known Poindexter for years, since Alain Enthoven's Systems Analysis shop in the 1960s. And because Holcomb thought highly of him and admired his judgment, he was pleased to see the new deputy national security adviser stop by for a cup of coffee.

"John, what in the world is going on?" asked Holcomb. "Why are we getting these different signals?" He explained to his visitor that Weinberger and Vessey were saying one thing while the White House was saying something else.

"It's a terrible problem, isn't it," said Poindexter, puffing on his pipe.

"You've got to straighten it out," said Holcomb. "You're going to tear the military apart trying to respond to all these different instructions."

"We can't work with those two," said Poindexter, meaning Weinberger and Vessey.

Flabbergasted, Holcomb replied, "I can't believe what you're saying to me. If you can't work with them, fire them."

Poindexter blinked at Holcomb through his glasses. "You've got to understand the pressure, the tension we're under," he said. "We just can't work with them."

Holcomb was more alarmed than ever after Poindexter departed. He couldn't believe that relations between the White House and the Pentagon had reached such a state. Or if they had, that nothing could be done to repair the damage. Poindexter seemed to be saying, as Holcomb recalled their conversation, that "bypassing the chain of command was good, proper, acceptable, and the right thing to do."

Holcomb was dismayed. He decided the thin air of the White House had clouded his friend's judgment. Three years later, he was not surprised to see Poindexter, a pipe clenched in his teeth, lashed to the prow of a scandal.

CHAPTER THIRTY-THREE

REMEMBER YAMAMOTO

"You're wrong. She is a phony. But on the other hand you're right. She isn't a phony because she's a *real* phony. She believes all this crap she believes. You can't talk her out of it."

—O. J. Berman on Holly Golightly, in *Breakfast at Tiffany's*,
by TRUMAN CAPOTE

On Monday, October 7, 1985, four young Palestinians armed with automatic weapons seized the Italian cruise ship *Achille Lauro* as it sailed the Mediterranean off the coast of Egypt. The seizure was triggered by a curious steward who discovered the men cleaning their weapons, readying them, it was later learned, for a terrorist operation inside Israel, where the ship was scheduled to dock later in the week. Most of the 750 passengers were ashore, visiting the Pyramids, but the ninety-seven who chose to remain on board were taken hostage. Among them were eighteen Americans, most old or infirm.

On the second day of the takeover, the terrorists shot and killed a sixty-nine-year-old New Yorker, Leon Klinghoffer, then ordered his body dumped from his wheelchair and into the sea. The next day, Wednesday, the hostage holders surrendered to Egyptian authorities on the condition that they and the man from whom they allegedly took their orders, PLO leader Abu Abbas, receive safe passage out of the country. The original mission bungled, Abbas had flown to Cairo to negotiate an end to the crisis. The Egyptian president, Hosni Mubarak, said he was unaware of the Klinghoffer killing when he agreed to the deal.

The United States angrily demanded that Egypt turn over the hijackers and Abbas so they could be tried for murder in an American court. Mubarak said it was too late; Abbas and the four gunmen had already departed Egypt, possibly for Tunisia.

By early Thursday morning, the Americans were fighting mad. Mubarak was lying and they knew it. At the NSC Ollie North had learned from his Israeli contacts in Washington that the hijackers were still in Egypt. Navy Captain James Stark, an NSC staffer working with North, confirmed the report and added a crucial piece of intelligence: the Palestinians were to be flown to freedom that night.

Having discovered the hijackers' plans, Stark, a 1965 Annapolis graduate, crossed the small reception area separating his office from North's.

"Hey, we can intercept these guys," said Stark.

"What do you mean?" asked North.

"Remember Yamamoto?" said Stark.

Admiral Isoroku Yamamoto had planned and executed the 1941 Japanese attack on Pearl Harbor. Two years later, American fighters, alerted to his flight plans, ambushed his aircraft and blew it out of the sky over the Pacific.

"You mean shoot them down?" asked North.

"No, I don't think we want to shoot them down. We can just fly up alongside of them and make them land," said Stark.

Deputy national security adviser John Poindexter later recalled that he was already thinking along the same lines. He had received an earlier intelligence report that the hijackers might still be in Egypt and asked Vice Admiral Arthur Moreau, of the Joint Staff, if the Pentagon was willing to consider military action to seize the terrorists. Moreau said he would discuss it with his superiors.

North now brought the news to Poindexter that the hijackers were indeed in Egypt and suggested intercepting them if they tried to fly out of the country. Poindexter told him to call Moreau with the new, harder information and raise the specific issue of an airborne intercept. Not long after, Moreau called back to say that Admiral William Crowe, who had replaced General Vessey as chairman of the Joint Chiefs, liked the idea.

Having laid the groundwork, Poindexter now needed the President's permission to initiate operational planning. Reagan was in Chicago, speaking to workers at the Sara Lee Bakery, when Poindexter reached McFarlane in the large, aromatic kitchen that was serving as a holding area. We have intelligence that tells us they're still in Egypt, he told McFarlane. We think they're going to fly out. If they do, we may be able to intercept them.

McFarlane passed the information on to Reagan when he finished his speech. He also explained the potential problems, the operational —the chances of intercepting the wrong plane in the crowded night-time sky over the Mediterranean, a refusal by the pilot to land—and the diplomatic—bruised relations with Egypt and other Arab states, possibly with Italy as well since preliminary plans called for forcing the plane down at the American base in Sigonella, Sicily. McFarlane also encouraged the President to consult with the Secretaries of State and Defense.

"Well, good God, they've murdered an American here," said Reagan, according to McFarlane, "so let's get on with it."

McFarlane called Poindexter and told him the President had agreed in principle to the intercept and authorized the Pentagon to begin the military planning process. He also directed him to inform Shultz and Weinberger and encourage them to call the President to voice their views.

Back in Washington, North was tracking the movements of the hijackers through Major General Uri Simhoni, his primary Israeli source, and passing the information on to Moreau at the Pentagon for dissemination to Vice Admiral Frank Kelso's Sixth Fleet in the Mediterranean. Simhoni provided exquisitely detailed information, including the location, takeoff time, and tail number of the EgyptAir 737 aircraft on which the terrorists hoped to make their escape.

At about 4:30 P.M., as Air Force One was arriving back at Andrews Air Force Base, Reagan disregarded Weinberger's warning that the intercept would devastate Egyptian-American relations and ordered the Pentagon to proceed with the plan.

On landing at Andrews, McFarlane separated himself from the presidential party, boarded a small plane, and flew up to New Jersey to keep a dinner date with Richard Nixon at the former President's Saddle River home. McFarlane wanted Nixon's advice on the U.S.-Soviet summit set for the following month in Geneva. Though McFarlane monitored the action through secure communications equipment that traveled with him, his departure left Poindexter as the White House nerve center for the entire period of the intercept and its aftermath, as he had been throughout the four-day crisis. It was an enormous vote of confidence in Poindexter's skill in operational matters, just as it was the best possible evidence of what really mattered to McFarlane. Not arms sales to Iran, which had begun through the Israelis about five weeks earlier, not even the imminent execution of the boldest, most daring stroke yet by the Reagan administration against terrorists. McFarlane was obsessed with orchestrating a successful summit. Everything else was a distraction.

The responsibility rested lightly on Poindexter's shoulders. Throughout the day he had been busy, but confident that he could run the show in McFarlane's absence. Rules of engagement had to be hammered out. Action plans had to be coordinated with State, Defense, and Justice, which had to prepare extradition documents. Last-minute glitches had to be smoothed over. By the time the execute order went out, he was satisfied that he had handled his duties capably and felt sure that Kelso's carrier-based aircraft would carry out the intercept if at all possible.

That evening, as the action Poindexter had set in motion played itself out over the Mediterranean, three White House aides poked their heads into his cramped West Wing cubicle adjacent to McFarlane's splendid corner office. They were amazed to find him sitting at his desk calmly eating a grilled-ham-and-cheese sandwich and enjoying a glass of white wine.

The following morning, the *New York Post* headline read, "Got 'Em." The *New York Daily News* crowed, "We Bag the Bums." McFarlane, who returned from New Jersey immediately after dinner with Nixon, brought Poindexter with him to the regular 9:30 A.M. national security briefing. As they entered the Oval Office, Reagan stood up, brought his right hand to his brow, and said, "Admiral, I salute you." Poindexter thanked the President, but told him the accolades belonged to the Navy. When news of Reagan's extraordinary tribute began to make the rounds, the admiral instructed aides to tell anyone who asked that what the President actually said was "I salute the Navy."

The *Achille Lauro* intercept in most respects showed McFarlane, Poindexter, and North at their best. But there were some troubling aspects to the affair.

The following week, *Newsweek*, relying on unnamed sources, provided its readers with a gripping inside account of the intercept. Only the real insiders, however, knew that the magazine had made some errors. It gave credit for dreaming up the idea to North, not James Stark. Moreover, as the magazine related the story, the episode's memorable signature line, "Remember Yamamoto," was delivered by North to Poindexter rather than by Stark to North. The subsequent exchange between Stark and North came out wrong, too. *Newsweek* had North speaking Stark's lines and Poindexter responding with North's. Stark was not mentioned.

At the time, Stark did not bother to correct the errors. He was not interested in publicity. He didn't mention it to North, either. There seemed no reason. He figured *Newsweek*'s reporters had just screwed up, misunderstood their sources, whoever they were, or erred in writing a very complicated story. As far as he was concerned, North had played a far more important role than he had and deserved enormous credit. "Believe me, he was the one that made it happen," said Stark.

Two years later, during the Iran-Contra hearings, North launched a series of attacks on congressional leakers, saying they endangered national security, citing particularly the *Achille Lauro* episode. North's champions nodded gravely. North's huffy indignation, however, had reporters at *Newsweek* tearing their hair out. The following week, the magazine took an almost unheard-of step. It reported that one of the primary sources for its *Achille Lauro* story, a story that heavily promoted the behind-the-scenes activities of Oliver North, had been none other than North himself.

As for Poindexter, he later said he did not recall any "Remember Yamamoto" exchange with North or anyone else. Moreover, he said he told North that he was already thinking about an intercept when North first broached the idea to him.

In leaking the inside story to *Newsweek*, North had not only taken credit for Stark's idea, but appropriated his words as well. Then he made it appear as though the idea of an intercept was a bolt out of the blue to Poindexter.

Or so it seemed. The possibility still remained that *Newsweek* had gotten the story wrong, mistakenly transposing North for Stark, Poindexter for North. That excuse evaporated in 1991 with the publication of North's autobiography in which he again ascribes the "Remember Yamamoto" line to himself, not Stark. He followed that with a remarkable statement: "The idea that we might try something similar had just occurred to me."

The *Achille Lauro* affair embodied the living contradiction that was and is Oliver North. The idea for the intercept was not his, but no one disputes the centrality of his role in making it happen. His sources, his unflagging energy, and his supercharged brain were virtually indispensable to the successful completion of the mission. And yet, as if that stunning achievement fell short of some insuperable standard existing solely in his own mind, he outrageously and ruthlessly exaggerated his participation.

Stark, who likes North, respects his judgment on tactical matters, and considers him a friend, had a ready explanation. "Ollie might tell you a falsehood or put a spin on a story for a particular reason," he said, "but after he'd done it a couple of times he came to believe it himself. So if you gave him a lie-detector test afterward, he'd pass it. He believes his own stuff."

Achille Lauro was not a unique occurrence. North biographer Ben Bradlee, Jr., among others, recounts the well-traveled story North told admirers in the aftermath of the Grenada invasion in 1983, an action in which he, McFarlane, and Poindexter all played important and productive roles.

As American medical students attending school on the island were being evacuated to the States aboard troop transports, North learned of an appalling foul-up. Officials assigned to fly back with the students and brief them on the reasons for storming the island had missed the planes. North was stunned. He had visions of the students accusing the President of ordering a pointless invasion, their uninformed comments feeding into the controversy already brewing over the assault. North raced up to the White House family quarters to alert Reagan to the possibility of a public relations disaster once the students landed at Charleston, South Carolina, where reporters and television crews were awaiting their return. He found Reagan alone. North related his fears and apologized for the mistake. The President told him to calm down and turned on the television.

Moments later, the first student stepped off the plane, knelt, and kissed the ground. Reagan smiled, put his arms around North, and said, "You see, Ollie, I told you not to worry. You can trust Americans."

It was a great story, classic Reagan, classic North, the sole impediment its lack of veracity. After Iran-Contra broke and the anecdote began to crop up in journalistic profiles of the suddenly famous but barely known Oliver North, White House spokesman Marlin Fitzwater said it never happened. According to Fitzwater, North had never met with Reagan alone, never set foot in the family quarters, and on the day in question had not even seen Reagan. North affirms in his autobiography that he never met with Reagan alone, neither repeating nor explaining the tale of the returning students.

In 1987, the *New York Times* Sunday magazine carried a lengthy piece by Seymour Hersh on the April 1986 American bombing raid on Libya. In it, Hersh recounts another tale that raises questions about North's veracity. Citing unnamed sources to whom North told the story, Hersh reports that in an Oval Office meeting North tried to persuade the President to employ various weapons and resources other than or in addition to conventional bombers. They included the supersecret Stealth bomber, said to be invisible to radar, and conventionally armed Tomahawk cruise missiles. Admiral Crowe, chairman of the Joint Chiefs, argued against North's suggestions and the President sided with Crowe.

At the conclusion of the meeting, according to North's recounting of the tale, Crowe walked up to North, stuck his nose in his face, and warned, "Young man, you'd better watch your step."

Crowe, through an aide, denied the whole thing to Hersh, saying he "did not recall any discussion on substantive matters that he ever had" with North. "Nor does he recall any meetings with North except as a back-bench note-taker" at White House meetings, the aide said.

Poindexter, who was also at the meeting, sided with Crowe in a 1993 interview. North was probably at the meeting, Poindexter said, but he played no role in the discussion. He certainly did not go head-to-head with the Joint Chiefs chairman. If anything, he was precisely as Crowe described him, a back-bench note-taker.

"Ollie was and is pretty flamboyant, but he was smart enough to know when to keep his mouth shut," said Poindexter.

As was often the case with North's stories, this one got even more weird. Retired Rear Admiral Mark Hill, Poindexter's friend, recalled North relating essentially the same tale to him not long after the Libyan raid.

In the version North recounted to Hill, there was an exchange between North and Poindexter after Crowe's warning to North. "According to Ollie," said Hill, "he stood there with John Poindexter and, as everybody broke up, he made some remark to John Poindexter about 'I thought this was a military man' or words to that effect. And John Poindexter says, 'It makes you a little ashamed to wear the uniform sometimes, doesn't it?' "

Poindexter, in the 1993 interview, flatly denied the story. "Never," he said. "If I felt that way [about Crowe], which I didn't, I wouldn't have said that to Ollie. I don't know where [the story came from], but it's a fabrication." Poindexter was not informed that the source was his friend, Hill, who had heard it firsthand from North, of whom Poindexter remains admiring and protective.

The last chapter of *Guts and Glory*, Bradlee's 1988 biography of North, is entitled "Ollie's World." In it, Bradlee recounts page after page of stories, statements, or claims that he says North made to various people while at the NSC that the author calls "either untrue, strongly denied or unconfirmable and thought to be untrue." For those sympathetic to North, the bad news is, Read and weep. The good news is, There is no good news.

A military officer who served with North on the NSC staff said in a

1992 interview, "The problem with Ollie was you just didn't know whether he was telling you the whole truth. Nor had any of the rest of us seen a guy like that. You don't find officers that are habitual liars." Despite the strong words, the officer evinced real warmth for North. Asked about his seemingly contradictory feelings, he replied, "That's what I was going to say. I blurt out that Ollie's an habitual liar, and yet I still say I like the guy. And I do." A day or so later, he called to say he thought he had gone too far in describing North as a "habitual liar." Was he saying North did not lie? No, he said, but he was not comfortable with the word habitual. And, he reiterated, Ollie was a friend.

That interview and the follow-up phone call captured one of the rarest of North's gifts. He could make men who would not utter a gratuitous falsehood if their privates were wired to a field telephone feel disloyal if they even hinted that North sometimes shaded and occasionally obliterated the truth.

Some looked on his cavalier attitude toward the facts as a harmless, at times amusing sidelight to his high-octane personality. Others seemed to view it as a disability for which he bore no responsibility, like a clubfoot. Almost everyone routinely cranked in what Chuck Krulak called a 10 percent bullshit factor. Unfortunately, 10 percent didn't always do it. The precise ratio of fact to fiction in North's assertions was elusive, at times anybody's guess.

It has always been hard to get a fix on Ollie North, never more so than when he was at the NSC. Tom Hayes, his old Academy classmate, once tried to explain the phenomenon. "You can't pin him down," said Hayes. "He's like mercury. Try to put your finger on him and he squirts somewhere else."

There were plenty of negatives. In matters of veracity, his assertions ran the gamut from sea stories—Academy slang for harmless and amusing tall tales—to outright falsehoods. One NSC staffer went so far as to call him delusional.

He was also a fierce bureaucratic infighter, ruthlessly guarding and enlarging his turf, at times barreling over any colleague blocking his path.

Everyone at the NSC knew him as a workaholic. Often his ever-expanding duties demanded it, but not always. As one acquaintance put it, "Ollie could turn a two-hour job into a three-day crisis."

In the eyes of some, he was shameless in currying favor with anyone in a position to advance his career or promote his achievements to those who could. If any of his patrons fell out of favor, so the rap went, he simply dropped them. NSC aide Constantine Menges compared North to the office Romeo flirting at the water cooler with his latest flame while the erstwhile object of his affection sniffles into a Kleenex at a desk in the corner.

He could be ridiculously officious and infuriatingly self-important. Speechwriter Peggy Noonan, in her White House memoir, *What I Saw at the Revolution*, recalled first encountering North at a meeting to drum up support for the Nicaraguan Contras.

> He talked like no one I had ever heard. When he wanted to say he was not responsible for a specific memo, he snapped, "That's not off my disk." A suggested idea was a "notional," and getting something going was "ginning up." . . .
>
> He was standing now, talking about a memo, saying things like, "And don't forget this is in accord conversation Casey-North approximately fifteen hundred this date."
>
> Someone said something about the rebel leader Edèn Pastora. "Don't talk to me about Pastora, I'm not speaking to Pastora," he snapped.
>
> I started to laugh. He looked at me like I was a girl.

But Tom Hayes was right, you couldn't pin down Ollie North. He was a moving target, a shimmering silhouette, with tongues of flame occasionally flaring out to surprise and bewilder. And for a long time, for every negative, there was a countervailing positive, and then some.

The taxpayers may not have liked the result, but they got their money's worth out of North. Read any of the Iran-Contra chronicles. It's as though there were ten of him. One minute he's in Frankfurt, the next in Costa Rica, then on to Tehran or Jerusalem or Tegucigalpa or Beirut or London or squiring Iranians around the White House or telling falsehoods on Capitol Hill or debriefing freed hostages or hitting up old ladies for big bucks at the Hay-Adams Hotel or transferring funds to numbered accounts or working up the cost figures on weapons going to Iran.

And there's more. Jim Stark remembers North coming into work one Monday morning filthy dirty and obviously in pain. What happened? asked Stark. North said he had been in Honduras over the weekend inspecting a Contra camp and fell off a mule going up a mountain.

North's reports on his weekend activities used to leave Bud McFarlane slack-jawed: "I would say to myself occasionally, 'Well, I think about half of this is objectively true and the rest is kind of extrapolation and exaggeration. And yet even if half of it is true, it's impressive.' And usually about half of it was true."

If there was any glamour to be had, North wasn't getting much. He was not invited to state dinners and he didn't troop the cocktail party circuit unless he was trying to raise money for the Contras. Mark Hill sent North and Betsy complimentary tickets to a screening of the film *Top Gun* at the Kennedy Center and the reception afterward in the USAir hangar at National Airport. They attended both, showered Hill with such gratitude that he was left with the feeling that, as perks go, that was about as good as it got for the Norths.

North was always more than the sum of his parts. He could be officious and overbearing, certainly, but when there was a messy job to be done and it had to be done quickly and without complaint, the reaction of his superiors was instinctive: Call Ollie.

"He personified the 'Message to Garcia' mission that they preached at the Academy," McFarlane told Ben Bradlee, Jr. "He didn't ask, 'Where is he?' or 'Who's going to pay my per diem?' or 'What support will I have?' He just turned around and did the job."

Poindexter said much the same: "He was a self-starter. You could give him a job to do and he didn't come back fussing and whining that it was too hard or he didn't know how to do it. He'd just go off and do it."

That may have been part of the problem. North invariably spoke "in a tone of cockeyed reasonableness," as Raymond Chandler described one of his characters. Said an NSC colleague, "Ollie is one of those people who will speak to you with equal energy and conviction and will have a plan mapped out in any area. Some of his ideas and plans will be based on a great deal of knowledge and will be really smart things to do. Others will be based on no knowledge and will be really dumb things to do. But you won't be able to tell the difference by listening to him because they will both sound the same. And unless you had your own knowledge of the area, you'd be convinced by him. . . . He knew Central America pretty well. He didn't know shit about Iran."

Said another NSC staffer, "He didn't ask for a lot of guidance. The problem was, he needed it."

North's can-do attitude explained a lot of his appeal, but not all of it. There was also his personality. He was, at his best, a frothy meringue of charm, flaws, and contradictions, Holly Golightly in Marine green. He was simply fun to be around, exciting, too, a human whirlwind who could sweep up those near him, making them believe, until the groggy morning after, all the crap that he believed. Lacking rank, he traveled on a wink and a nod and a sunny gap-toothed grin, his arrival on the scene—whether a dilapidated office in the Old Executive Office Building or a rugged mountain camp in Honduras—the occasion for celebration. To his colleagues, his appearance meant a good joke, a tall tale, a whacked-out idea or a great one; to the beleaguered Contras, a pat on the back, guns and butter, the promise of a better day.

McFarlane and Poindexter were not so dazzled by North's charisma and can-do heroics that they didn't recognize his faults.

McFarlane recalled an instance when North sent him a report on supply shortages facing the Nicaraguan Contras, claiming to have personally witnessed and evaluated the depth of the problem. He later learned that North was merely repeating the assessment of Contra leader Adolfo Calero.

"Now there may have been times when he did witness it," said McFarlane. "I expect there were. But this particular time he was reporting what Calero had told him, without attributing it to Calero. And that's different. . . . Something I hear from Calero is a little bit different than what my staff has seen firsthand."

McFarlane felt a kinship with North, as if he were a son or younger brother. When North was promoted to lieutenant colonel in October 1983, McFarlane dug out his old Silver Oak Leaves and pinned them on his fellow Marine. But McFarlane said he began to suspect a credibility gap that same year.

"I should have then sat down with him and said, 'This is bullshit.' But I didn't and there's not any excuse for it. The reason that I didn't was I just let other things get in the way and just didn't take time."

McFarlane also noticed that sometimes North would send him memos that undermined his colleagues and exaggerated his own efforts. In response, McFarlane tried to get him to coordinate more with other members of the staff. "But Ollie didn't," said McFarlane. "He liked to operate on his own and take credit on his own, and it was really my fault that I didn't insist more than I did on it."

Poindexter picked up on the same problems as McFarlane—the exaggerations, the need for recognition, the occasional misappropriation of other people's work and ideas. But because North generally performed at such a high level, Poindexter didn't hold it against him.

"If it was a situation where he talked a good game, but didn't play a good game, it would have been an entirely different matter," said Poindexter. "But he talked a good game and played a very good game.

It's just that he tended to elaborate and exaggerate on some aspects of it."

Some NSC staffers believe Poindexter, at least while he was Mc-Farlane's deputy, had the more realistic view of North. It also appears that North, despite fulsome praise for Poindexter in his autobiography, was not always enamored of the admiral.

"Ollie is a born-again Christian that can curse like a sailor," said James Stark. "He would be so pissed at Poindexter because Poindexter had stopped him from getting Bud to do some crazy thing with the Contras and Ollie would say that Poindexter was a traitor. Ollie would be able to make these very emotional arguments to Bud and get Bud to finally cave in and do them. Not all the time, but sometimes. He would say, 'When our grandchildren are fighting the commie hordes coming across the border from Mexico, you'll think back to this moment and will know it was you that didn't have the backbone, Bud, to stand up for your country and do what was right.' . . . He could turn on those emotions. And he could turn them off just like that. It was like an act. But see, Poindexter was not swayed by that. He would look at him and say, 'Oh, Ollie, come on.' "

Stark recalled a day in early 1985 when North stormed into the office suite they shared in the Old EOB, slammed his briefcase down, and said, "I hate this fucking place. That asshole Poindexter is going to screw this country up. Bud won't make a decision. We're abandoning the Contras. And they won't let me do anything."

Deriding his superiors behind their backs apparently was not unusual for North. Constantine Menges, in his 1988 book, *Inside the National Security Council*, says of North's relationship with Poindexter and McFarlane, "Ollie simply manipulated them as best he could and ignored them when necessary. Then, to colleagues like me, he would fulminate about that 'stinking wimp McFarlane—he's always giving in to Shultz.' He would complain bitterly about Poindexter's remoteness and ridicule Poindexter for bringing all of his 'navy yes-men buddies' to the NSC. Everybody lets off steam at times, but I was always startled by the vehemence and cunning with which Ollie attacked colleagues whom, for the moment, he found to be a problem."

Poindexter has never publicly accused North of acting on his own volition, either in Iran-Contra or anything else. But it sometimes seemed that Poindexter felt that way. NSC aide Jacqueline Tillman remembered him saying, "His wings are going to be clipped," when she passed on a report that North had arranged for cash to be passed to some Contra allies on the street outside the White House. Another

NSC staffer recalled a seemingly exasperated Poindexter, who rarely used profanity, saying of North, "He's fucking out of control."

Richard Armitage, Annapolis '67, had a similar exchange. Soon after taking over as national security adviser, Poindexter called Armitage, an assistant secretary of defense and close Weinberger confidant, and asked him to be one of his two deputies. Armitage conferred with Weinberger, then called Poindexter back and politely declined the offer. "Well, Rich, I'm not surprised at your answer," said Poindexter, as Armitage recalled the conversation. "I know you and Cap have a great affection for each other. But, you know, I've got a real problem here. One of my problems is Ollie North. I've got to get him under control."

Said Poindexter, flatly, "I never thought that. He kept me informed." But he also said, in what sounded like a compliment but hinted at something more, that he had come to the conclusion that North was uniquely a product of the Marine Corps, that the Navy simply did not turn out officers like him.

"Ollie was one of a kind in my experience," he said.

> "I like the kid. Everybody does, but there's lots that don't. I do. I sincerely like the kid. I'm sensitive, that's why. You've got to be sensitive to appreciate her: a streak of the poet. But I'll tell you the truth. You can beat your brains out for her, and she'll hand you horseshit on a platter."
>
> —O. J. Berman on Holly Golightly, in *Breakfast at Tiffany's*

CHAPTER THIRTY-FOUR

AN ALIEN PRESENCE

Bud McFarlane, a man with a mission, worked his way up the narrow aisle of Air Force One toward the President's stateroom. It was November 1984, about a week after Ronald Reagan's landslide reelection victory. A few days earlier, through chief of staff Jim Baker, Reagan had asked him to remain as national security adviser in the second term. McFarlane wanted the job, but not at all costs.

After greeting Reagan, he began: "I must tell you, Mr. President, we do not have a team in national security affairs."

Through pursed lips, Reagan replied, "Yes, I know."

McFarlane painted a bleak picture of the administration's foreign policy landscape. Your Secretaries of State and Defense agree on next to nothing, whether it's East-West relations, the Middle East, economic matters, trade, or dealing with terrorism. When a decision goes against one of them, he does all he can to obstruct its implementation.

There is also personal hostility between them, he continued, a constant air of confrontation. "The result," said McFarlane, "is to create paralysis."

There are two ways to deal with the problem, he insisted to the President. Choose one of them, Shultz or Weinberger, and build your foreign policy team around him. Ask the other for his resignation. My choice would be to keep Shultz and fire Weinberger. But even if you choose Weinberger and let Shultz go, you will be better off than you are right now.

There is a second option. If you keep them both, these disputes are going to continue. That means that you will have to take a more active role in making sure your decisions are carried out.

Reagan, according to McFarlane, said Shultz would remain his chief foreign policy adviser. But he was not going to fire Weinberger. He didn't always like his advice, but Cap was a friend.

"So what I want you to do," the President told McFarlane, "is just make it work."

McFarlane wondered if he had missed something. Option one clearly was unacceptable. Had the President responded to option two? Had he agreed to participate more fully in foreign policy matters? No, McFarlane conceded, he gave me a roger, not a wilco. He understands what I'm telling him, but he's not saying he's going to do it.

McFarlane didn't fold. He told the President that a new national security adviser might be able to make the foreign policy apparatus function more productively. He was offering to resign, playing his deuce of clubs as he later described it.

Reagan, according to McFarlane, replied, "Bud, I don't want that. You're about as close to the indispensable man as anyone who's ever worked for me and I don't know what I'd do without you. I would never accept your resignation unless, of course, it were for personal reasons. I can understand when family demands require it. But on no other terms would I ever accept your resignation."

McFarlane was astonished. Reagan's vote of confidence had been forceful, personal, and totally unexpected, tantamount to a laying on of hands. "I didn't think it was a time for words at all except to be grateful," McFarlane later said. His head was spinning as he left Reagan's stateroom. He was vaguely aware that he had failed to move the President. He decided he would try harder. Not to move Reagan. He knew now that was impossible. To make it work.

The Reagans, as was their custom, spent the post-Christmas 1984 holidays at the Palm Springs estate of TV Guide publisher Walter Annenberg. For McFarlane, with Jonny back in Bethesda, it was another working vacation. The Soviets had called for a January meeting of foreign ministers in Geneva that seemed likely to lead to a resumption of arms control talks. On December 31, huddling with Shultz, Weinberger, and the President in the library of the Annenberg residence, McFarlane put the finishing touches on the administration position, finding the elusive middle ground that all the participants could live with.

The work complete, there remained only the Annenbergs' New Year's Eve party, an annual gathering of the Palm Springs elite.

"For some reason I was invited to that party that night," McFarlane later said. "Boy, talk about an alien presence. This is the Annenbergs and Bloomingdales and Robinsons of American Express and Reagans."

If McFarlane felt out of place, he didn't let on. He proved a witty conversationalist, belying his solemn image with a flair on the dance floor. The next day, Nancy Reagan said, "You cut quite a rug last night."

McFarlane later spoke with wonderment about receiving an invitation to the affair. "I was surprised and gratified," he said. "I don't know quite how it happened, but it did."

Learning the Reagans had arranged it, he finally came up with an explanation: "At the end of the day I thought that this was an act of kindness that was not just kindness—that they were saying, 'We approve of you. We respect you.' And that meant a lot to me." It was a comment worthy of actress Sally Field, who set the teeth of a nation on edge with the mawkish refrain, "You like me . . . you like me!" on accepting an Academy Award in 1985.

McFarlane was not surprised to see Shultz and Weinberger at the party. Yet he thought of himself, in his own words, as an "alien presence." The phrase spoke volumes about his sense of himself and the place he felt he occupied in the administration's pecking order.

Would any other national security adviser, even the most obscure, think he didn't belong at such a function? He might feel the guests were not his kind of people, maybe even envy them their money, but "alien presence"? One can imagine Henry Kissinger walking into the same party, looking the place over, then greeting the crowd with something akin to Paul Goodwin's hello to Ollie North and his other platoon leaders back in 1969: I want everybody back here clean-shaven, with a haircut, and then you're going to be allowed to talk to me.

The emotions McFarlane experienced at the Annenberg party were not confined to that affair. At dinner with Richard Nixon during the *Achille Lauro* crisis, the former President uncorked a bottle of Château Lafite-Rothschild.

"I said, 'God, you're not going to waste a bottle of that on me?' Well, I thought that, I didn't say it. I really kind of swooned."

Had he said it, it wouldn't have mattered. Lots of well-adjusted people are prone to silly, self-effacing remarks. The troubling aspect was that he thought it, and thought things like that all the time. It was as if one side of his brain was forever echoing the words of his father, telling him that he was a McFarlane, destined for greatness, while the other side kept whispering that he really wasn't good enough, that he didn't belong at the same party as the big boys, let alone drinking their best wine.

In truth, even as national security adviser to the President of the United States, one of the most powerful positions in the world, Bud McFarlane in certain situations remained as vulnerable to intimidation as he had been working for Henry Kissinger a decade earlier. Or as a child, sitting silently at his father's table.

It never made sense. He was a man of unquestioned physical courage, as he proved during the Vietnam War. And yet some men could bully him, like White House chief of staff Don Regan, or throw him off his game, like Ronald Reagan, as if they carried chunks of kryptonite in their pockets.

McFarlane's deference to Reagan used to drive Mike Deaver crazy. For domestic political purposes, Deaver was intent on softening Reagan's hard-line, confrontational stance toward the Soviet Union. He saw an ally in McFarlane, who firmly believed warmer U.S-Soviet relations were possible.

"The real frustration I had with Bud was that Bud would come into my office and we'd have these long discussions about what ought to happen," said Deaver. "And I could never get him to say it to Ronald

Reagan. . . . I'd say, 'Bud, tell the President that. That's what you're paid for, for God's sake.' "

McFarlane, according to Deaver, invariably had an excuse for not doing so, something along the lines of, "Well, he's the Commander-in-Chief. . . ." Or else he'd drift into Budspeak, the deep voice, the twenty-dollar words, the stultifying monotone that had you licking the roof of your mouth so you didn't crack your skull when your head hit the table.

Said Deaver: "I can remember taking him in almost by the hand and sitting him down and saying to the President, 'Now Bud has just told me something that you've got to hear.' And the President got very interested and Bud would kind of skirt around the whole thing very carefully. And I'd say, 'Goddammit, Bud, tell him the way you told me.'

"I kept saying to Bud, 'You don't realize how much the President respects you, relies on you, seeks your advice. I can't think of anybody in the White House he has a higher regard for.' And that was true. . . . Here was a guy who in Ronald Reagan's mind is a recognized authority. And immediately that kind of a person, particularly if he's a decent man like Bud is, held a lot of power with Ronald Reagan. I could never get that across to Bud."

Regan arrived from Treasury to replace Jim Baker in February 1985 and attempted to take control of what had been a bizarre, trifurcated management system whose sole saving grace was that it had worked rather well. The first-term troika of Baker, Meese, and Deaver, reflecting Reagan's preference for domestic policy, gave McFarlane wide latitude in foreign affairs. Regan, as the new chief of staff, created a hierarchical structure in which all roads to the President ran through him. It was neither sinister nor unreasonable. For McFarlane, it was not all that different from the way he did business under Jim Baker.

But Don Regan was not Jim Baker. Baker was silk, Regan sandpaper. Baker's long, graceful three-pointer broke your heart as it swished through the net. Regan elbowed his way into the low post, smashed you in the mouth as he went up with the ball, then rattled it in off the rim. Baker carried himself with the cool self-assurance of a man born to wealth. He trusted people to do the right thing. Regan, the son of a Boston policeman, used to say that as a young lifeguard he was always on the lookout for the kid peeing in the pool. Baker could have been McFarlane's older brother. Regan was part of Reagan's generation, in his bruising, overbearing manner a lot like McFarlane's father.

They had some nasty run-ins. On two occasions early in Regan's tenure, important overnight developments on the international scene prompted McFarlane to awaken the sleeping President. Both times he neglected to alert the chief of staff. At least once Regan was embarrassed when the President mentioned the occurrence to him and he had to admit he knew nothing about it. McFarlane explained that he assumed that the Situation Room, which had called him, had also called Regan. The first time, McFarlane wrote a letter of apology to Regan. The second time, according to McFarlane, his apology was not enough. Regan lapsed into profanity, saying McFarlane had better get it through his "fucking head" that he worked for Regan.

"Wait a minute, Don," McFarlane recalled saying. "You should have been notified. I should have notified you. And I'm sorry. But I work for the President."

"The hell you do. You work for me."

Regan finally told McFarlane that if he couldn't work under the new system they'd just get someone who could. Said McFarlane, loudly flinging open the door as he exited, "I'll be out of the office by the end of the day." A few minutes later, Regan phoned McFarlane, said that he had been out of line and suggested they put the whole thing behind them. McFarlane agreed to stay on.

Late in the summer a new issue arose that imperiled the uneasy truce between the two men. On Sunday, August 11, *Parade* magazine said in its personality column that "print and broadcast journalism circles" had hushed up gossip about an affair between a married White House official and a White House reporter. No names were mentioned. The magazine added that there was no "conclusive evidence" that the gossip was true.

The item was old and suspect news to most White House insiders, including the press corps, which for weeks had been treated to titillating but uncorroborated reports of an affair between McFarlane and a member of the White House press corps.

McFarlane had known of the rumors as far back as June when his press aide, Karna Small, told him that such tales were circulating through the press room. Small said she thought the source was Regan's staff. The *Parade* blurb turned backroom gossip into a source of humiliation for McFarlane and potential embarrassment to the President, then vacationing at his California ranch.

A few days later, McFarlane and Regan went to lunch at a Mexican restaurant outside Santa Barbara to discuss the matter. Their accounts of the luncheon differ. McFarlane said that he told the chief of staff that not only were the rumors false, but that he had heard they originated with Regan's closest aides. Regan replied, according to McFarlane, that he had "not imagined" that the rumors applied to him and promised to discuss the allegation of rumor-mongering with his staff. Regan, in his autobiography, makes only passing reference to the luncheon, saying he asked McFarlane if there was any truth to the *Parade* item. "He assured me that there was not," Regan wrote. "I dropped the subject, but the gossip persisted."

He had a hand in the gossip, before and after his lunch with Mc-Farlane, according to well-sourced accounts by authors Jane Mayer and Doyle McManus in *Landslide*, a 1988 study of Reagan's second-term failures. Over cocktails on the Sunday the *Parade* item appeared, Regan blurted out, "It's Bud and ———" when his companions asked about the rumors. Not long after, he again lent a gloss of truth to the report at an off-the-record editorial luncheon at *Newsweek*'s Washington bureau. "I've tried to counsel Bud about it . . . but these things happen," he said when asked about the rumors. "You know how these things are." Such reports drifted back to McFarlane, further poisoning the relationship.

There were other points of conflict. Depending on the President, the national security adviser may or may not be a member of the cabinet. Richard Allen and Bill Clark were not, but Reagan had elevated McFarlane to cabinet rank. When he was not invited to a cabinet meeting, he said he asked Regan about it and was told it was for "real" cabinet members. Ed Rollins, the White House political director, recalled the chief of staff, an ex-Marine, informing McFarlane in Reagan's presence that he had made lieutenant colonel in six years while McFarlane had taken nearly twenty years to achieve the same rank. That was true, but Regan served during World War II, when promotions were greatly accelerated. Was Regan taunting McFarlane, attempting to diminish him in the President's eyes? Or was it just good-natured kidding? Neither McFarlane nor Rollins thought Regan's remark was meant in jest.

"I watched the hair literally rise on the back of McFarlane's head," said Rollins. "It was the meanest fucking thing I saw in my whole five years in that White House." Perhaps you had to be there. From a distance, Rollins's characterization seems much too strong, a reflection perhaps of McFarlane's sensitivities at the time and Rollins's undisguised dislike for Regan. For his part, McFarlane, apparently enraged, said nothing to Regan, just let it go. Rollins responded differently when Regan made a similar crack to him. Your problem, Rollins, is that you were never a Marine, said Regan. Rollins, a burly ex-boxer, shot back, Don, I made a career out of beating up Marines.

Differences with Regan aside, 1985 was a year of singular accomplishment for McFarlane. By all accounts, he skillfully managed the TWA hostage crisis in June in which 151 passengers and crew members, 135 of them American, were taken captive by two Arab gunmen whose demands included the release of seven hundred Lebanese Shi'ites from an Israeli prison. The sixteen-day crisis ended as another cost-free victory for terrorism. The Israeli prisoners were freed, the hijackers escaped, and an American, Navy diver Robert Dean Stethem, was murdered, his battered body dumped on the tarmac at Beirut airport. Thanks in large part to McFarlane's adroit efforts, greater bloodshed was avoided and all the other hostages survived the ordeal. His stock rose still higher in October when Poindexter, North, Stark, and others of his subordinates conceived and coordinated the airborne intercept of the *Achille Lauro* hijackers.

For McFarlane, however, 1985 was the Year of the Bear.

Two years earlier he had midwifed the birth of the Strategic Defense Initiative. To McFarlane, if not to Reagan, SDI stood to be "the sting of the century," in theory a futuristic space-based shield against Soviet missiles, in reality a lever to force the Kremlin to severely scale back its nuclear arsenal. The Soviets would do so, McFarlane believed, in recognition of their limited economic resources and their inability to compete with the United States on the high-tech playing field. The previous year, moreover, working alone and in concert with Deaver and George Shultz, he had maneuvered Reagan from a stance of intractable anti-Communism to a point in which improved relations with the Soviet Union seemed possible, assuming the Soviets cooperated.

The ascension of Mikhail Gorbachev, pragmatic and progressive, to the leadership of the Soviet Communist Party in March 1985 offered new promise. A month later both sides agreed in principle to a summit, the first of Reagan's presidency. In early July it was set for November 19–20 in Geneva.

From January, when he accompanied Shultz to Vienna for the U.S.-Soviet ministerial meeting that resulted in the resumption of arms talks, McFarlane devoted virtually all his energy to preparing for the historic gathering. He chaired interdepartmental meetings at which policy was hammered out. He brought in experts to brief Reagan, provided him with a paper a week for twenty-five weeks on all aspects of the Soviet Union, its history, people, culture, essentially a primer on what the President called the Evil Empire. He wrote speeches, mediated disagreements between State and Defense, orchestrated a public diplomacy campaign that sent the President off to Geneva with Congress, the allies, and the American public solidly behind him. He would later say that he felt that he had done the best work of his life during that eleven-month period. Few disagreed.

But something else was going on during the Year of the Bear. Michael Ledeen, an occasional NSC adviser, would say in his 1988 book *Perilous Statecraft* that McFarlane was undergoing a "serious psychological crisis" during 1985. Those closer to him questioned Ledeen's grave diagnosis, but conceded that it was a strange time, that something was troubling McFarlane that could not be blamed on Reagan, Regan, Shultz, Weinberger, fatigue, or the Iranian arms sales, which had started by then.

"It was pretty clear that Bud was having some significant internal turmoil during this period of time," said a colleague. "Now exactly when it started, what caused it, I don't know."

In the past, he had often displayed a refreshing sense of humor. An aide, James Rentschler, remembers him listening to a congressman explain over the phone his reasons for going against the President on a key vote. As the lawmaker droned on, McFarlane held the receiver away from his ear and made bug eyes at it, like Harpo Marx reacting to an attractive woman. Now such flashes of zaniness had become rare. Instead, he seemed unusually curt, quick to anger, frequently gloomy, as if in the throes of an existential depression. One NSC staffer described it as "a downward spiral."

"He just seemed frustrated, unhappy, burdened," said Navy commander Paul Thompson, his military assistant. "I certainly regretted, as did a number of people who were close to him, that we couldn't make him happier, relieve the pressure, stop the ominous feeling that was there. . . . He was internalizing whatever was bothering him, so we couldn't very well figure it out."

In the spring of 1985, McFarlane agreed to speak to a gathering of Boy Scouts and their parents in Montgomery County, Maryland, outside Washington.

"This was a very heavy presentation, a very intense presentation," said Thompson, who accompanied McFarlane to the event. "He kind of went inward. I mean, it was the most substantive set of remarks I'm sure those kids ever heard. He stood up in front of them, no podium, and started right in. And it was a lot like a preacher. Very measured tone, very stream of consciousness. . . . He didn't really look anybody in the eye. He just kind of had that faraway look like he was almost meditating or something. I thought he was overly somber, but that's often the way he was. . . . He could have been talking to himself or he could have been talking to a group of theologians or he could have been, as he was, talking to some Boy Scouts."

On the way home, heading south on Interstate 270, Thompson asked McFarlane about a minor issue that had been left hanging earlier in the day. McFarlane responded with such angry vehemence that to this day Thompson cannot drive down I-270 without remembering the outburst even though he can't remember the issue.

There were other odd occurrences. In May, following a presidential trip to Europe that ended in Lisbon, McFarlane decided to spend the weekend in the Portuguese capital before returning to Washington. Thompson remained behind with him, along with a crew and equipment from the White House Communications Agency so that he could be reached in an emergency. Over that weekend, NSC staffers at the White House received a mildly alarming SOS from Thompson: he did not know where McFarlane was and did not know how to contact him. He had checked out of the hotel, telling Thompson he was going to the seashore. He called in periodically for messages, but he was unreachable except on his own terms for the better part of a day.

Despite his denials, a number of associates believe to this day that he was romantically involved, if not actually having an affair, with a reporter. Rumors also linked him to a White House staffer. Thompson didn't believe any of it, but thought he knew the reason for the gossip.

After work, he said, McFarlane would often meet in his office with one or the other woman to discuss the issues of the day. "He generally enjoyed having them ask him questions," said Thompson. "It would be kind of fun. They both have a sense of humor and they both are kind of quick and they're well-dressed. I think that was his emotional release. It had nothing to do with any sort of physical relationship."

Without question, something was going on. At times it seemed to be tearing him apart.

In mid-October, Bud and Jonny McFarlane invited George Shultz and his wife, Obie, to their small cabin in the Shenandoah Mountains for the weekend. While there, McFarlane told Shultz he planned to resign after the summit, then about a month away. Shultz, said McFarlane, tried to talk him out of it, but he maintained that he held firm then and in the weeks that followed. To members of the NSC staff, however, he seemed racked by indecision regarding his future even as he performed at what most regarded as an extraordinarily high professional level.

Geneva was a success, the initial step in a process that would lead over the next several years to sweeping arms control accords. For the first time, both sides agreed in principle to reduce their nuclear arsenals. In addition, Reagan and Gorbachev agreed to two more meetings, first in Washington, then in Moscow. Most of the pictures of the

American summiteers focused on Reagan, Shultz, and Regan, but close observers knew the important role McFarlane had played. As the meeting concluded, however, reporters had begun querying Karna Small on his possible resignation. On McFarlane's orders, she put them off.

McFarlane's staff, meanwhile, treated him like a conquering hero as he shuttled about Europe briefing allies on the results of the summit. During one flight, Karna Small composed and read a poem of thirty-one stanzas entitled "A Toast to Bud" that ended, inevitably, with the line "This Bud's for you!"

McFarlane caught up with the President a few days later in California, where he and Mrs. Reagan were spending the Thanksgiving holidays. Though he later insisted that he never wavered in his determination to quit after his conversation with Shultz more than a month earlier, his aides back in Washington were picking up mixed signals.

They urged him not to do it. Get some rest, they told him, relax, take a vacation. Don Fortier, a senior aide, sent him a long, scholarly memo about other foreign policy advisers who had battled through bad times and gone on to great achievement. You're making a tremendous contribution, said Fortier, you still can, work through the frustration, other guys have. *Newsweek*, poised to go to press with the first story on his impending resignation, called Karna Small for comment. Over the phone, McFarlane told her, "I haven't decided yet."

The day before returning to Washington the President and his party moved from Santa Barbara to Los Angeles. That evening McFarlane sent his letter of resignation up to the presidential suite at the Century Plaza Hotel. He cited personal reasons. The President accepted it the next morning when the two men met. McFarlane regretted his decision from that moment on.

To this day, no one claims to fully understand why he did it. His after-the-fact explanation sounds logical enough. The Regan relationship was a big factor, he said. So was the continuing hostility between Shultz and Weinberger. After five frenetic years in the administration, he wanted to spend more time with Jonny and their children. He had been in government service for thirty years. It was time to make some money. The summit had been a success. He would be leaving on a high note. Finally, he was exhausted.

It all seemed to fit. In an administration of millionaires, he and Jonny, who had been a high school teacher for years, were scrambling to put their two daughters through blue-chip colleges, Wesleyan and Northwestern (Scott was at Annapolis, a free ride until you graduate and someone starts shooting). Karna Small remembers McFarlane saying that Jonny always had to wear the same dress to state dinners.

As for leaving on a high note, it made sense both in the short and long term. He could get some rest, make some money, and look to the future. He was close to Vice President Bush, who unlike Reagan loved foreign policy and national security issues. It was not hard to imagine a day down the line when a President Bush might well tap a rested, financially secure McFarlane for Secretary of State or Defense.

Still, it never quite fit together.

On the afternoon of December 5, 1985, the Indian Treaty Room in the Old Executive Office Building was jammed as the NSC staff and other White House officials gathered to bid farewell to McFarlane. He began in his familiar monotone, explaining that he had submitted his resignation, saying it had been a difficult decision, lauding his aides for great accomplishments and thanking them for their help. Soon, though, his composure crumbled and he stood before the gathering in tears, unable to continue. Finally, he bolted for the door. Ollie North was standing there. The two men embraced.

"Skipper," said North, "it's not going to be the same ever again."

A few minutes later, in a hushed White House press briefing room, the President, flanked by a solemn, red-eyed McFarlane and a thoroughly composed Poindexter, announced the departure of one Annapolis man and the promotion of the other.

"Will we ever see you again?" a reporter asked Poindexter, known for his low visibility.

"Maybe," the admiral replied from the podium, permitting himself a slight smile.

CHAPTER THIRTY-FIVE

I DON'T HAVE ANY LIFE

When Ronald Reagan endorsed Bud McFarlane's recommendation that John Poindexter succeed him as national security adviser, he wrote across the paper, "Hope it doesn't hurt his future career!"

Reagan's comment, in December 1985, was eerily reminiscent of Dwight Eisenhower's remark nearly three decades earlier when, on congratulating Poindexter for standing first in his Academy class, he said, "I hope it won't be too much of a burden to you."

Poindexter, supremely confident of his abilities, took both remarks in the jocular way in which they were intended. He should have taken Reagan's seriously.

John Poindexter was a mystery, if for most not a terribly intriguing one. He was an admiral in the Navy. For many, that said it all since a growing percentage of those whose opinions count in Washington—congressmen, journalists, assorted kibitzers—had little firsthand experience with things military. The military mind was a known quantity—combative, inflexible, blind to colors other than black and white—and they quickly fit Poindexter to the stereotype.

As national security adviser, he was usually described as a typical military bureaucrat, a reasonably talented if colorless administrator. Discussions of his background invariably focused on his achievements at Annapolis and his high-profile shore billets, as if he had never gone to sea, commanded a ship of the line, or guided a destroyer squadron across the Pacific, earning outstanding performance evaluations on every operational tour.

In truth, the conventional wisdom on Poindexter was not completely off the mark. Ellen Warren of Knight-Ridder aptly compared his visage to a pan of warm milk. But his unremarkable features were misleading. He was not a passive bureaucrat, but rather an active participant in virtually every major foreign policy initiative during the first five years of the Reagan presidency.

There was something else about him that was often missed. He may have lacked the flashy personal magnetism of an Ollie North or a John McCain, but he retained the quality that his old classmate Whit Swain detected back at Annapolis. Swain called it *mana*, someone else The Force. Whatever it was, its major ingredients were in wretchedly short supply in the nation's capital in the 1980s. He was simply a man of enormous personal dignity and inner strength.

As national security adviser, he tried to be an honest broker, if not a disinterested one, much like Brent Scowcroft under Gerald Ford. He made sure the President had the views of his senior cabinet officers, notably the Secretaries of State and Defense. He then weighed in strongly with his own opinions. Whenever possible, he offered his counsel privately, avoiding the limelight so that it did not appear that he was competing with Shultz and Weinberger for the President's favor.

Unlike McFarlane, he was not by nature a compromiser. As the annual congressional battle over Contra aid heated up in 1986, he urged the President to resist a deal with Congress and hold firm to his insistence on a substantial aid package with no strings attached. After Poindexter met with senators on Capitol Hill, one of the Democrats grumped, "The admiral came up here clearly not for a compromise. He's damn the torpedoes, full speed ahead." You got it, thought Poindexter, that was the message. Not long after, Congress passed a $100 million Contra aid package, $70 million of it unrestricted, the largest appropriation ever for the Nicaraguan resistance.

After four and a half years at the White House, he was hardly without credentials when he took over for McFarlane in December 1985. He understood national security affairs and had a coherent vision of global strategy. More than anything else, however, he viewed himself as a manager. Asked to describe his role in any foreign policy episode in which he participated, he invariably replied, "I managed the staff." On one occasion, pressed to elaborate, he said, "My primary responsibility was to keep the staff organized and productive and keep them from killing each other."

It was more complicated than that. In managing the staff, he used his aides to ensure compliance with the President's directives, never more skillfully than in the period leading up to the April 1986 bombing raid on Libya, never less wisely than in the latitude he gave Ollie North at about the same time to handle the Iranian arms sales and the Contra support operation.

He was not, however, a foreign policy specialist. He had no training in the field and little practical experience prior to the White House. But he recognized his limitations and did not consider them a handicap.

"You can always get an expert," he said. "What an organization needs is somebody to lead it, to command it, to manage it. And that's the role I've tried to fill."

In managing the staff, he played favorites. He tended to shut down aides he viewed as self-promoters, ideological purists, or ticket punchers, dealing with them curtly, as if they didn't matter, which drove them crazy. Most of those he felt he could count on, who worked and produced, found him approachable and helpful, warm if not effusive, guiding rather than dictating, always the admiral but often a friend. Ollie North fell into both categories, a self-promoting can-do guy. Sometimes Poindexter shut him down, other times he turned him loose.

In contrast to McFarlane, Poindexter was a low-maintenance employee. He did not doubt his ability or require frequent pats on the back to ratify his sense of self-worth. That temperament allowed him to speak his mind, clearly and forcefully, if not always wisely, without worrying about covering his ass or second-guessing himself. Invade Grenada. Intercept the *Achille Lauro* hijackers. Bomb Libya. When Ollie North said he wanted to use excess funds from the Iranian arms sales to help the Contras, Poindexter didn't hesitate: "I said, 'Okay, go do it.' "

"I was willing to take risks," he later said. "My whole life was not tied up in being national security adviser."

Though he grew more conservative during his years in the White House, Poindexter had no agenda of his own. He did not play bureaucratic games, either, in part because he lacked the skills, in large measure because he had little tolerance for manipulation. To his mind, he was the President's man, the instrument through which Ronald Reagan exerted his will in matters of national security.

"Beyond loyalty to the country, which I put at the top, I'm loyal to who it is I'm working for," he once said. "And if I can't be loyal to them, I shouldn't be there."

He was not a right-wing zealot. His worldview was the standard cold-warrior variety, his position on social issues moderate to liberal. He didn't talk gender equity; he lived it. In 1985 Reagan was resisting intense pressure from Congress to impose economic sanctions on South Africa. Linda, who was studying for the ministry, told him she was going to join friends from church in picketing the South African embassy. She didn't exactly ask his permission, but she let him know she was willing to reconsider her participation if he felt it might prove embarrassing to him. He told her to go ahead. She did, was arrested, handcuffed, put in a paddy wagon, booked, and released. No news organization connected the name Linda Poindexter on the daily arrest record to Ronald Reagan's deputy national security adviser. Knowing Poindexter—more accurately, not knowing him—no one made the connection.

Explained Linda, "John would always say, 'Do what you want to do, go where you want to go, my career can take care of itself.' It was sort of like John lived his life the way he wanted to and I would live mine the way I wanted to and we'd negotiate out the rest."

That was one of Poindexter's problems. He tended to treat men and women of a certain age as grown-ups, which was fine when it came to Linda, often perilous when applied to colleagues at the White House and the upper reaches of the administration.

From school days on, he had approached difficult assignments by saying, Give me a book and I'll figure it out. But no book could tell him or anybody else how to be Ronald Reagan's national security adviser. Even if the book had existed, Poindexter had no time to read it. Henry Kissinger offered him some advice when he complained that the incredible demands of the job made it impossible for him to do the background reading he thought he should. As national security adviser, said Kissinger, you are too busy to create new intellectual capital. You just consume it. That means you are dependent on the members of your staff and you have to get the very best out of them.

Carol McCain was working at the White House when she caught a glimpse of the pressure Poindexter was under even as deputy. She later thought of the encounter as a rare human moment with a man she had thought of as far back as midshipman days as prim and stuffy.

She was lunching in the White House Mess with an old friend, Dick Haase, like Poindexter and John McCain a member of the Class of 1958. Spotting Poindexter, she brought Haase over to say hello. "Dick, you remember John Poindexter, our leader," she said, a joking reference to his days as brigade commander. Poindexter expressed amazement on learning that Haase had kept up with so many members of their class. He said, wistfully, that he and Linda had not done so.

Then, as if the unexpected appearance of two old friends had triggered a despair he had ignored until that moment, he launched into a description of his daily routine. As Carol recalled his words, Poindexter said, "I get up at four-thirty in the morning and I come to work and I'm here by six and I stay here and I leave here at eight-thirty or nine at night and then I go home and Linda's left my dinner in the oven. I don't even see my boys. I get that dinner out of the oven. I eat that dinner and I go to bed, because I get up at four-thirty in the morning."

Carol and Haase exchanged disbelieving looks as Poindexter concluded his unusually emotional monologue: "I don't have any life. I don't see my children. I don't see my wife. I only work."

Poindexter was not a complainer. That may have been the only instance during his time at the White House that he spoke such words outside his own home. But that was the reality of his life; the demands of the job never slackened. Years later, looking back, he said, "The issues are so broad and so many that there weren't enough hours in the day. And they keep coming. They don't stop."

He was at his best in operational situations, such as the *Achille Lauro* crisis or planning the invasion of Grenada. Both those episodes occurred when he was McFarlane's deputy. As national security adviser, working quietly behind the scenes, he deftly engineered an operation that reduced Muammar Qaddafi to a petty annoyance, the status the mercurial Libyan leader has occupied in the years since.

In Poindexter's view, the Soviet Union's appetite for expansion during the 1970s, climaxing with the December 1979 invasion of Afghanistan, had been fed by the failure of the United States under Jimmy Carter to move beyond the Vietnam syndrome and assert American interests overseas. In the 1980s, the job of the Reagan administration was to transmit to the Soviets a series of easily decoded signals that, placed side by side, meant something new and different: America is back.

"Our objective was to build a record," Poindexter later explained. "Nothing big. No single event that was big. We didn't want to do anything that they would view as a vital threat. . . . We wanted to build a record to convince the Soviets that they simply could not win this competition. That it could be a draw, but they weren't going to win."

Economic leverage was part of the package. So was stepped-up counterintelligence and propaganda through such vehicles as Radio Martí, which beamed anti-Castro programming into Cuba. On the military front, there were arms control, Central America, Grenada, Afghanistan, Ethiopia, Angola, and, not least, Libya, the haven of choice for many of the world's most notorious terrorists.

By the mid-1980s the United States had spent more than half a decade enduring humiliation by terrorists. The humbling 444-day Iranian hostage crisis started it all. The process was accelerated by the failure to retaliate effectively for the terrorist bombings in Lebanon. The culprits in the TWA hostage crisis that cost the life of Navy diver Robert Stethem made their point and gained major concessions. Then they disappeared into the slums of Beirut, like a VC hit team going to ground after killing the village chief. The list went on and on. By December 1985, when Poindexter took over as national security adviser, Associated Press newsman Terry Anderson and five other Americans were hostages in Lebanon. America looked helpless, inept, and without gumption, a timid superpower that lacked the will and the fine motor skills to do anything about its ragtag tormentors.

Under Qaddafi, Libya trained terrorists, provided them sanctuary, dispatched them, backed them financially, loudly cheered them on. Qaddafi's hand had been discerned in numerous terrorist episodes and assassination plots. Libya was also a Soviet client-state. To Poindexter, this made Libya a two-fer. A blow struck at Libya would send a message to terrorists everywhere, and to the Soviet Union as well.

Among nations that supported terrorism, Libya was not necessarily the worst offender. Syria and Iran, both of which had been implicated in the Marine barracks bombing, could also make strong claims to the title. But Syria was central to the Middle East peace process and Iran might well hold the key to the release of the American hostages.

That left Libya, which was militarily suspect and had very few friends. The intelligence, though not conclusive, strongly suggested that the Soviet Union would not rush to Libya's aid in the event the Reagan administration decided to move against Qaddafi. That meant the United States probably was not risking a major superpower confrontation when and if an opportunity to strike at Libya presented itself.

There was also Qaddafi himself, erratic, unstable, largely shunned by fellow Arab leaders, blood on his hands. Martin and Walcott describe him as "the moral equivalent of a serial killer on the loose." In short, the perfect villain. "We didn't invent him," said Poindexter. "Qaddafi was an excellent bad guy who deserved to be handled and confronted and put down."

From late 1983 on, Poindexter was the prime mover within the administration for military action against Libya. None of his schemes envisioned the use of American ground troops, though detractors felt that might be the unanticipated result. Invariably his efforts were stymied—by leaks to the press; by opposition from the Pentagon, where most of the leaks seemed to originate; or other, more pressing national concerns. In the summer of 1985, however, following the TWA hostage crisis, Poindexter pushed for a joint military operation with Egypt against Libya, the United States to provide logistical support to the Egyptian army. The Pentagon balked, said six American infantry divisions might be needed if the Egyptians ran into trouble. Typical Weinberger, thought Poindexter, always overstating the military requirements to explain away doing nothing. Weinberger was not alone in his opposition. Nicholas Veliotes, the American ambassador to Egypt, didn't like the idea any more than the Defense Secretary. "Talking to this crowd, and especially John Poindexter, was really something," Veliotes told Martin and Walcott. "He didn't understand. He didn't want to understand. He wanted action."

At about the same time, Poindexter, with McFarlane's blessing, persuaded the President to sign an intelligence finding that committed the United States to ousting Qaddafi. Reagan needed little prodding. For the President, the Libyan strongman had become the personification of evil on the world scene.

Poindexter viewed the finding as a chance to get his operation back on track. Over the Labor Day weekend, he and an aide, Don Fortier, flew to Egypt to consult with Egyptian President Hosni Mubarak, the target of a Libyan assassination attempt several months earlier.

Conferring with Mubarak on the porch of his retreat in Alexandria, Poindexter explained the importance of the finding to the Egyptian president. He encouraged Mubarak to plan military action against Libya. As Poindexter saw it, even if Egypt never actually followed through, the planning process would lend support to anti-Qaddafi dissidents and divert the Libyan strongman from his usual mischief-making. But, as Veliotes had correctly surmised, Poindexter wanted action, not feints or shadow boxing. Should Egypt move against Libya, he told Mubarak, the United States was prepared to provide intelligence and logistical support, including weapons and ammunition. In the event the Egyptian army found itself bogged down in the desert, the United States would provide close air support.

Mubarak listened politely, occasionally interjecting questions, but Poindexter could see that he was not interested in moving against Libya. Old ghosts haunted the discussion. Mubarak questioned the ability of the United States to keep such maneuverings confidential. The year before, according to Martin and Walcott, he had secretly agreed to permit an American nuclear-powered cruiser to transit the Suez Canal—a violation of Egypt's law forbidding nuclear ships to pass through the waterway. The ship had barely cleared the canal when the passage was reported in the American press.

Poindexter also concluded from the conversation that Mubarak did not believe that the United States could be counted on to keep its commitments. It was, said Poindexter, an old story, "the legacy of Vietnam—deserting allies."

Plans for action against Libya moved to the back burner until the end of the year, when post-Christmas terrorist attacks at the Rome and Vienna airports left twenty-five people dead, including five Americans. Natasha Simpson, an eleven-year-old American schoolgirl going home for the holidays, was among the victims. One of the terrorists, North later said, "blasted . . . Natasha Simpson to her knees, deliberately zeroed in and fired an extra burst at her head, just in case." Libya was implicated and action plans were dusted off.

By then Poindexter had become national security adviser. Over the next three months, he was the White House nerve center as the United States turned up the heat on Qaddafi. He mobilized the NSC staff. Don Fortier was the action officer, his key phrase "disproportionate response," a pointed rejection of the Vietnam-era tit-for-tat policy. If Qaddafi jabbed, Poindexter and Fortier wanted the United States to respond with a right cross, a left hook, and an uppercut to the belly. Contrary to some reports, they weren't looking to kill Qaddafi.

Reagan, like Carter before him, had issued an executive order prohibiting assassinations. Legality aside, Poindexter reasoned that Qaddafi could be more dangerous dead than alive, an Arab martyr whose name would live on the lips of terrorists for decades. Better to knock the wind out of him, humiliate him, let his people know the price they were paying for his murderous antics. Libyans themselves might then be emboldened to administer the coup de grâce.

With Reagan aroused by the Rome and Vienna airport massacres, the military began drafting plans for a retaliatory air strike. Poindexter had been through that drill before, saw his job as shepherding the national security bureaucracy beyond contingency planning and dummy bombing runs to an unequivocal execute order.

Bitter experience had taught him that virtually any national security action, military or otherwise, needed the cooperation of the Secretary of Defense. He now moved swiftly to smooth the stormy relations between the Pentagon and the NSC that had prevailed under McFarlane. Tilting toward George Shultz, McFarlane had arranged regular weekly meetings between the Secretary of State and the President. McFarlane, of course, sat in, as did Poindexter when he took over. Aware that Weinberger was miffed that McFarlane had not done the same for him, Poindexter initiated weekly meetings with the President for the Defense Secretary as well.

Setting up the get-togethers was a symbolic gesture on Poindexter's part, an olive branch to Weinberger. "I just thought Bud had created a situation where it was impossible to get any cooperation out of Cap," he said. "It seemed to me that there was good reason why Cap was always very critical and very suspicious of the NSC—he was always very uneasy that we were doing things behind his back."

There was a little more to it. Poindexter knew, as had McFarlane before him, that Weinberger could, and often did, slip in to the Oval Office to press his views, often gaining the crucial last word with the President. By institutionalizing Weinberger's tête-à-têtes with Reagan, Poindexter ensured that he was at least aware of what the secretary was telling the President since, as with the Reagan-Shultz meetings, he was the third man in the room.

Meanwhile, preparations for action against Libya were creating a philosophical conflict for Poindexter. One of his few strong feelings about the Vietnam War was his belief that the White House should not micro-manage the armed forces in carrying out a military mission. But the Lebanon debacle caused him to rethink his position. To his mind, the Pentagon under Weinberger and Vessey had done much to subvert the mission there as well as efforts to retaliate for various terrorist incidents. This time, he decided, the White House, specifically the NSC, had to be more of a player, at least until the execute order went out and the shooting started.

He deployed his staff—Fortier and James Stark, to a lesser extent John Douglass, Vince Cannistraro, Howard Teicher, and Ollie North —to ensure that the President's desire to respond militarily against Libya was transformed into action. Huddling with Pentagon officials, Poindexter's aides discussed and argued over proposed targets and weapons. Stark wanted to use highly accurate cruise missiles called Tomahawks, which could be fired from submarines offshore, reducing the risk of friendly losses. For similar reasons, another aide favored the supersecret Stealth fighter. Admiral William Crowe, who had succeeded Vessey as chairman of the Joint Chiefs, vetoed both out of a concern that one or more of the high-tech, state-of-the-art weapons might fall into the hands of the Libyans and quickly find their way to the Soviets.

Poindexter backed his lieutenants, but he respected Crowe's views and did not suspect him of trying to subvert the mission. "I don't think Bill was as contaminated by the Vietnam experience as Jack Vessey was," said Poindexter.

His team won some arguments, lost others. Poindexter kept his eye on the ball. In some ways it didn't matter if his aides prevailed. Their participation in the planning process had reshaped the debate. The Pentagon, despite resistance from Weinberger, was arguing the details of military action, not digging in its heels to avoid it.

Despite improved relations between the Pentagon and the NSC under Poindexter, Weinberger remained a potential stumbling block. At the time of the airport killings, there was one carrier in the Mediterranean. Weinberger insisted on three as a precondition for striking at Libya. Poindexter thought the secretary was being overly cautious, if not once more trying to preclude action by ratcheting up the force requirements to outlandish levels. But Poindexter kept his suspicions to himself and outwaited Weinberger. By mid-March two more carriers had steamed into the Med. Once the fleet, commanded by Vice Admiral Frank Kelso, was assembled to Weinberger's specifications, it stepped up a series of provocative maneuvers begun in late January. Sooner or later, Poindexter reasoned, Qaddafi would do something dumb.

In late March Qaddafi rose to the bait. First he challenged the Navy, only to have his missile-guidance coastal radar knocked out and two patrol boats armed with antiship missiles destroyed. On April 5 a disco in West Berlin frequented by American servicemen was bombed.

Two American sergeants and a young Turkish woman were killed. Communications intercepts tied the bombing to Libya.

Ten days later, at about 2:00 A.M. on April 15, Air Force F-111 bombers from bases in England and carrier-based aircraft from the Sixth Fleet bombed military and political targets in the Libyan capital of Tripoli and in Benghazi, the nation's second-largest city.

The NSC staff jammed into the Situation Room in the basement of the White House as reports of the raid came in. In his first-floor office, John Poindexter watched the action on CNN. The raid had been far from perfect, but he was pleased by the results. The message had been delivered to Qaddafi and his fellow terrorists, copy to the Kremlin. A short time later, an aide suggested he go down to the Situation Room to congratulate his subordinates. He told them he was proud of them, that they had done a fine job. He had just managed the staff.

The Libyan raid, Poindexter later said, "helped to demonstrate to the Soviet Union and others throughout the world that we were not going to be stepped on, that if provoked we were going to respond with deadly force. I don't think that lesson was lost on the Soviets."

A month after the Libyan raid, Ronald Reagan had to choose a new CNO to replace James Watkins, whose term would soon expire. Normally the choice belongs to the Secretary of the Navy, the President merely rubber-stamping the name he sends forward. Not this time.

The secretary, John Lehman, selected Frank Kelso, a hero of *Achille Lauro* and the attack on Libya. His appointment by the President seemed assured until Poindexter stepped in.

Though highly regarded throughout the Navy, Kelso was still a vice admiral and a relatively junior member of the Navy's upper echelon. Poindexter explained to Reagan that naming Kelso CNO would mean passing over all the Navy's full admirals and many vice admirals, propelling the majority into retirement. As he saw it, the Navy would see its talent pool vastly depleted if Kelso got the job this time around.

Poindexter recommended instead Carl Trost, a full admiral who shared a distinction with the national security adviser. As a midshipman, he had been both the brigade commander and the number-one man in his Annapolis class, the Class of 1953. Though not intimates, Trost and Poindexter were friends, dating back to the early 1970s when both worked at the Pentagon in the Secretary of the Navy's office.

Lehman lobbied intensely for Kelso, even, according to sources, threatening to resign if Reagan disregarded his choice. In the end, the President followed Poindexter's lead and named Trost. In 1976 Jim

Holloway had picked Poindexter over Kelso as his top aide. Now, for the second time in ten years, Poindexter had aced Frank Kelso out of a job.

Lehman was furious. He thought Poindexter had acted out of friendship for Trost. He was wrong.

John Poindexter intervened because he believed in the Navy system of grooming its officers for higher responsibilities before asking them to take on such responsibilities. Ensigns didn't command destroyers. Captains didn't command fleets. There were things to learn at every step along the tortuous path to flag rank and a lot more once you sewed on your first star. Little things like a shift in the wind, the value of cloud cover, a ping in the boiler. Big things like whom you could count on.

Years later, he would contrast the rigors of the Navy system with the way things were done in Washington, lamenting—without a trace of irony—that enormous authority was often conferred on men and women who simply lacked the training and experience to handle their jobs.

Many of Poindexter's subordinates later confessed themselves flabbergasted by his complicity when the Iran-Contra scandal engulfed the NSC. And more than one, as they tried to puzzle it out, came up with the same name.

Don Fortier. The missing man.

"That was key," said Jim Stark. "One of the real ifs of this whole thing is what would have happened had Don Fortier not been sick."

On taking over as national security adviser, Poindexter named Fortier, a highly regarded thirty-eight-year-old NSC staffer, as his principal deputy. Despite his youth, Fortier's appointment was seen as a solid, perhaps inspired choice. Fortier had Capitol Hill experience and enjoyed good relations with the press, precisely the areas in which Poindexter was most vulnerable. Fortier was also cool under pressure and an able manager in his own right, which in theory freed Poindexter for the expanded duties that went with his new post: dealing with the President, the Cabinet, and the larger issues.

Not long after Fortier's promotion, however, he was diagnosed with liver cancer. In May he was unable to report to work. Poindexter moved a safe out to his house and arranged for him to work from home until his condition improved. It never did. He died in August, never returning to the White House. As a result, Poindexter was without a deputy for a full five months, until mid-September. Clark had McFarlane. McFarlane had Poindexter. For a crucial period in his tenure as national security adviser, Poindexter had no one of similar stature.

Poindexter could have, probably should have, found a new deputy. Out of loyalty to Fortier and concern for his morale, he did not. He did not even permit himself to sound out possible replacements because he feared the word would get back to Fortier. But he could not afford his generous and kindly instincts. He needed help. By the time Fortier's replacement arrived in mid-September it was too late. By then much had slipped by Poindexter or failed to gain his full attention. Some ex-members of the NSC staff maintain that Fortier's lengthy absence made possible all that followed, that had he—or someone of comparable standing—been on board, he or she almost certainly would have walked into Poindexter's office and said, Whoa, Admiral, let's take a closer look at this stuff that Ollie's been doing. We're playing with fire here.

During the time Poindexter was McFarlane's deputy, some NSC aides thought he was better than McFarlane at restraining the impulsive North. Once Poindexter took over the top job, though, McFarlane's control of North seemed in retrospect far more skillful, especially with Poindexter hampered by the absence of Fortier.

"Bud kept Ollie on a chain," NSC staffer Jonathan Miller later explained to Jane Mayer and Doyle McManus for their book, *Landslide*. "Don Fortier was another chain. He was Mr. Caution—it drove Ollie nuts. Poindexter let go of that chain. Ollie went from being a good staffer to being almost a megalomaniac."

CHAPTER THIRTY-SIX

THE WHITE TORNADO

John McCain was an interloper, his election to Congress in 1982 an aberration, a prelude to the crushing defeat that awaited him two years down the line. By then real Arizonans—defined by McCain's political rivals as anyone who had lived in the state longer than he had—would rally behind a single candidate and boot him out of office. Or so it was said.

To the consternation of real Arizonans, Republicans and Democrats alike, McCain refused to play along. Instead, he settled on a strategy to solidify his political base, working at it as if the 1982 campaign had never ended.

He promised to return to his congressional district every weekend, a ridiculous pledge entailing a four-thousand-mile round trip. He made good on it, though, racing to catch the last flight to Phoenix late on Thursday, when the House normally completed work, then riding the red-eye back Monday night so he was in his office Tuesday morning, when the legislative week began in earnest. He did it forty-seven weekends that first year, a pace he barely eased in the years that followed.

He was not merely accumulating frequent-flyer miles. The weekends were spent in grueling and frenetic political activity. He marched in parades, met with constituents, spoke to political and service clubs, weighed in on local issues, held town meetings. When possible, he and Cindy reserved Sundays for themselves. To cement his ties to the state, they made a cold-blooded political decision. She would reside in Phoenix, in their new First District home, not Washington.

He was welcomed to Capitol Hill as a celebrity. On his arrival, he was elected president of the GOP freshman class, a largely honorary title but enough to cut him out of the herd. A month in office, he was the subject of a long, admiring profile in the *Washington Times*, entitled "From Hanoi to the House." Though his interests lay in foreign affairs, defense, and national security policy, he took a seat on the House Interior Committee, which handles water, land reclamation, and similar issues close to the heart of Arizona voters. In deference to the state's large retired population, he joined the Select Committee on Aging.

His support for Reagan was genuine and pleased the folks back in Phoenix. He created a mild furor in the district with his September 1983 vote on Lebanon. The criticism lasted a month, until October, when the Marine barracks was bombed and coffin-laden troop transports began the long, mournful journey home.

The base-building strategy paid off. On primary day 1984, he was the only Republican on the ballot. He won the general election against Democrat Harry Braun 78 percent to 22 percent, a landslide. Time to turn his attention to the Senate and the seat that would be up for grabs two years later.

*   *   *

In December 1984, a month after the election, Walter Cronkite invited McCain to join him on a trip to Hanoi where the former CBS News anchorman was to film segments for an April documentary commemorating the tenth anniversary of the end of the Vietnam War. The McCain portions of the nationally televised special were described in the *Arizona Republic* as "a true American hero returning to his prison camp." A politician's dream, if it didn't turn into a private nightmare.

The anticipated benefits were enormous. Though well-known in his congressional district, McCain was less familiar to voters elsewhere in the state whose support he would need if, as expected, he ran for the Senate. The documentary would help remedy that problem. The broadcast would also highlight his war record, which Arizona voters knew only vaguely. It might also attract campaign contributions from donors in and out of the state.

As if the potential payoff wasn't great enough, Hanoi raised the stakes, allowing McCain to hit an even greater jackpot. Miffed by McCain's promise to bring up the issue of Americans missing in action, Vietnamese officials refused to grant him a visa. For nearly two months, Arizona citizens followed the saga of McCain's off-again, on-again return to Hanoi. From the sidelines, political consultant Jay Smith and other McCain aides provided running commentary. "It's a sticky situation," Smith told the *Arizona Republic*. "He was a thorn in their side." Vietnamese officials, Smith added, considered him "a very bad man."

In January, still lacking a visa, McCain took matters into his own hands, flying to Bangkok and linking up with the CBS film crew in the hope that his heavily reported presence there would persuade the Vietnamese to relent and admit him. They didn't, the PR adroitness they employed to such devastating effect during the war deserting them. McCain cooled his heels in Bangkok for four days, then flew home, saying he had to get back for the christening of his daughter Meghan, the first of three children he would have with Cindy.

As McCain was making his way home from halfway around the world, a political adviser, Grant Woods, said, "If I had to orchestrate it, it couldn't have worked out better. He's the first congressman they wouldn't let in."

Woods was wrong. It could have worked out better. And it did. In February the Vietnamese issued the visa and McCain, a four-man film crew, and Walter Cronkite, the most trusted man in America, arrived in Hanoi.

With cameras rolling, the two men strolled along the edge of the lake into which McCain had plunged eighteen years earlier. As curious Vietnamese gathered around, they inspected an elaborate stone monument erected years earlier to celebrate McCain's shoot-down and capture. It depicted a figure resembling the crucified Christ, slumped forward, head bowed, arms stretched skyward as if attached to torture ropes. Cronkite informed the Vietnamese onlookers that his white-haired companion was the man identified on the inscription as "McCan . . . the famous air pirate."

The friendly crowd closed around the two men, pumping McCain's hand and shouting his name. "They felt they were meeting some kind of hero," Cronkite later said. McCain told Cronkite that Hanoi was the only place in the world where he was better known than the famed newsman.

At the former prison the POWs called the Plantation, they had tea with their Vietnamese hosts in a room adjoining a cell in which McCain had been tortured. "He was obviously not comfortable and anxious to get out of there," said Cronkite.

On-camera he was an accomplished tour guide, smoothly conducting Cronkite here and there. In one of his old cells, he explained that the shutters were always kept closed, described how he and Bob Craner communicated through the walls by tap code. Now, though, he seemed less smooth, a bit harried, and when the camera caught his eyes, they looked wider than usual, almost doelike, with highlights that for a split-second betrayed a terror long held at bay. Then the moment passed.

"Honor, Duty, and a War Called Vietnam," as the heavily promoted special was entitled, was thoughtful and moving, the kind of high-quality production for which CBS and Cronkite had long been known. McCain was prominently featured throughout the hour-long broadcast. The opening segment concluded with the stroll along the lake as Cronkite, in a voice-over, said, "It has been almost eighteen years since former Navy pilot John McCain parachuted into that small Hanoi lake. Tonight he will see it again, and the monument the Vietnamese built to commemorate his capture. He also will walk back into the cell where he spent much of his five and a half years as a prisoner of war. Tonight John McCain returns to his battlefield as we return to others in the war America did not win."

It was billed as a battle of titans. Bruce Babbitt, the youthful, enormously popular Democratic governor, versus John McCain, the ambitious, headstrong, and energetic Republican champion with the trademark head of white hair. The prize: the senatorial seat held for the better part of three decades by Barry Goldwater, one of the most influential figures in postwar American politics.

That was the popular perception in the weeks immediately following the 1984 election, but the McCain camp was already maneuvering to smother the high expectations of Arizona's political junkies.

The key to victory, McCain's advisers decided, was to keep Babbitt out of the race. If they could do that, and avoid a primary battle that might splinter the party, McCain could expect to be sworn in as the junior senator from Arizona in January 1987.

"It became the campaign within the campaign to convince Bruce Babbitt not to run for the Senate," said Jay Smith.

Babbitt, though clearly interested in running for Goldwater's seat in 1986, was said to view the Senate as a stepping-stone to something loftier, a presidential bid in 1988 when Ronald Reagan's second term ended. A Senate race made sense for him only if he could avoid a costly, draining campaign. He also needed to win. A loss would doom his presidential aspirations. McCain and his political team embarked on a course to persuade Babbitt that the risk of defeat was simply too great.

They employed various tactics to feed Babbitt's anxieties. To remove any doubts Babbitt might have about the resolve of his prospective rival, McCain and his lieutenants spread the word in political circles that nothing could keep him out of the race, that he saw it as a win-win situation. He would run a spirited campaign and broaden his appeal around the state. If he lost, he would challenge the incumbent Democratic senator, Dennis DeConcini, when he came up for reelection in 1988.

He also intensified the frenetic activity that marked his first term, extending it now all across the state. "John McCain is still driven," wrote Richard de Uriarte in the *Phoenix Gazette*. "No rural hamlet too remote to visit. No fund-raiser he can't attend. No interest group he can't romance. No civic organization he can't address. No social event he won't grace with his Boy Scout earnestness. No constituent meeting he can't fit into his schedule."

Then there was the money. McCain had raised $522,000 for his 1984 congressional campaign, compared to a paltry $2,700 by his opponent, Harry Braun. There seemed little doubt that he could raise millions for a senatorial race, especially with the well-heeled national Republican Party trying to beat back a strong Democratic drive to regain control of the Senate. To Babbitt, this meant he would be facing not only a vigorous and attractive opponent but a well-financed one as well.

By early 1985 any thought Babbitt may have had about using the senatorial race to prep for a 1988 presidential run had been exposed as a pipe dream by the man dubbed by the press "the White Tornado."

On March 18, 1985, Babbitt ended months of speculation by announcing that he would not run for the Senate the following year. He called it a personal decision, the best thing for himself, his wife, and his two young sons. "At this time in my life and our lives, it's not right for us," he said. He denied that McCain had bullied him out of the race.

McCain, in Washington, scrambled the troops as soon as he learned the news, alerting Cindy, who was in town, and Jay Smith. All three converged on National Airport late that afternoon for a flight to Phoenix. He officially declared his candidacy for the Senate the next morning.

To Smith, an election that wouldn't go to the voters for another year and a half had already been decided: "We knew McCain was going to be the next senator if he didn't shoot himself in the foot. He tried to, but even he couldn't do it."

Occasionally John McCain's rat-a-tat style and his bubbling self-confidence grated on people, but they were a minority. Thanks to his natural magnetism, he had made friends easily all his life. Nothing changed when he settled in Arizona. Like Ollie North, he could always draw a crowd. Looking back, though, he might have been better off had he been a late bloomer, a nerd, a geek, anything but a guy used to being the center of attention. That way, when everyone started gathering around, he might have asked himself an important question:

What do all these people want from me?

One of his earliest and closest friends in Phoenix was Darrow "Duke" Tully, the swashbuckling publisher of the *Arizona Republic* and its sister paper, the *Phoenix Gazette*. Of all McCain's friends, Tully seemed to need the least from him, or anyone else for that matter. If anything, the reverse was true. Tully's position made him one of the most powerful men in the state, a peerless ally for an ambitious politician like McCain. "I tell Arizona what to think," Tully was once quoted as saying.

The relationship between Tully and McCain was grounded in their common military backgrounds. Both were war heroes, Tully having compiled a long list of decorations as an Air Force fighter pilot in Korea and Vietnam. Unlike McCain, Tully gloried in his past exploits, regaling acquaintances with tales of his crash-landing in Korea, his hundred combat missions over North Vietnam, filling his home, office, even his bathroom with military memorabilia. A lieutenant colonel in the Air Force Reserve, he often attended social events in uniform, medals adorning his chest, surrounded by senior officers from Arizona's many military bases.

Two days after Christmas 1985, the headline on the *Republic*'s lead story read, "Publisher Tully Quits; Made Up War Record." A day earlier, Tom Collins, a local prosecutor, had shocked the state by revealing that Tully had never been in the Air Force. Tully had lived a delusion for thirty years, conjuring up war stories, awarding himself medals, periodically promoting himself to higher ranks. Though a skilled private pilot, there had been no crash-landing in Korea, no combat missions over North Vietnam, only a bizarre "Mittylike fantasy," as the *Republic* called it.

As Tully's world disintegrated, he was scorned and ridiculed. Bumper stickers appeared saying, "I Flew with the Duke." A local topless-bottomless club promoted "The Duke Tully Memorial War Heroes Party."

McCain was astounded by Tully's sham, but he did not join in the piling on. "He was my friend and he is my friend," said McCain. "Politics does not take precedence over friendship, but that certainly does not mean that I condone what he did. The whole thing smacks of tragedy."

He was right. Beneath the deceit lay a tragic tale of a bookish child growing up in the shadow of an athletic older brother, a Marine lieutenant killed in a midair collision during World War II, and of a grieving father who for the next thirteen years lavished his love on the dead son before finally climbing a tree, looping a rope around his neck, then shooting himself.

McCain said he never suspected that Tully was engaged in an elaborate masquerade, an admission the *Republic* reported under the headline "Tully's Lies Rang True to Combat Flier McCain." The story seemed the ultimate in chutzpah, as if McCain were somehow remiss in failing to unmask the man who had run the paper for seven years in full view of scores of ace reporters and crackerjack editors who never smelled a rat.

As for Tully, he wanted something out of his relationship with McCain and he got it. The friendship reinforced his lies, allowed him to bask in reflected glory. Whatever the root of Tully's problem, Torie

Clarke, a McCain aide, described him accurately, if indelicately, as a jock sniffer.

For McCain, the Tully episode proved little more than an embarrassment. But he had other friends with more concrete needs that would be harder to meet and more difficult to explain. And one of them, a savings-and-loan mogul named Charlie Keating, would soon ask too much.

In May 1985, McCain's sole potential rival for the GOP senatorial nomination, five-term congressman Bob Stump, a Democrat turned Republican, announced he would not enter the race. Stump's decision meant McCain had achieved the twin goals of his campaign strategy a year and a half before the election—no bruising primary fight and no Bruce Babbitt toting the Democratic standard.

Babbitt's decision two months earlier not to run for the Senate shifted the political spotlight to other well-known party members. None seemed eager to take on the carpetbagger. McCain finally got an opponent in October, Richard Kimball, a tall, grim thirty-seven-year-old often described as a Robert Redford look-alike.

Kimball had a respectable political pedigree. A native Arizonan, he was the son of a former state senate majority leader and had served four years in the legislature himself. Unlike McCain, he had a successful statewide campaign under his belt, having been elected to the three-member Corporation Commission, which regulates public utilities. In that post, he had championed consumer causes, demanding that utilities use resources in an efficient manner as a precondition to rate increases.

He was not, by any measure, a political heavyweight. To some, he came across as an odd, occasionally fey personality. In a campaign profile, the *Republic*'s Don Harris reported that when Babbitt named two members to the Corporation Commission to fill unexpired vacancies, leaving Kimball as the lone elected member, the trio was dubbed "two lame ducks and a daffy duck."

In his announcement speech in October, Kimball lambasted Duke Tully, whose ticket to Fantasyland had not yet expired, and portrayed McCain as a pawn in the publisher's power game. The attack gained him some attention, but Tully's fall two months later deprived him of a villain and his campaign was effectively becalmed for the next three months.

Supposedly Kimball was boning up on issues and preparing position papers, but when he unveiled the first in February, *Republic* political columnist Pat Murphy found the fifteen-page document riddled with fractured syntax, aimless phrasing, and misspellings—"barrow" for "borrow," "lisensing" for "licensing," "physical" for "fiscal." Someone penciled in the correct spelling of fiscal before the paper was released, but *Gazette* columnist John Kolbe swore in print that Kimball used the word "physically," as in "We can be physically responsible without abandoning social issues," several times when he interviewed him.

By early 1986 Kimball had regressed from a credible dark-horse candidate to a figure of fun. Murphy concluded that Kimball's missteps were part of a devilishly clever scheme to transform himself into the artless James Stewart character in *Mr. Smith Goes to Washington*. Kolbe, less charitably, diagnosed Kimball's problem as "terminal weirdness."

Kimball shared his name with the David Janssen character in the old TV series "The Fugitive," even using a stick figure of a running man as his logo. The graphic would have been more appropriate for his opponent. McCain, taking nothing for granted, was campaigning as if running against Goldwater rather than trying to succeed him. "I think the worst enemy of any politician is overconfidence," he said. "Remember President Romney and President Muskie?" The press, in state and out, did not share his caution. A *New York Times* op-ed piece in May 1985, entitled "The Changing Faces of Politics in Arizona," focused on McCain, tagging him as the "likely heir" to Goldwater's seat. George Will, in a glowing February 1986 column, said McCain "almost certainly" would win the seat. In May, *Baltimore Sun* syndicated columnists Jack Germond and Jules Witcover said McCain "threatens to become an instant institution in Arizona politics." By May he enjoyed a two-to-one margin in the polls over Kimball. A *Gazette* writer actually urged McCain to ease his frantic pace, saying Arizonans had too much invested in him for him "to drive himself to an early grave."

Meanwhile, nothing seemed to work for Kimball. He lagged behind McCain in the polls and fund-raising. He tried to turn his underfunded, long-shot candidacy into an advantage, declaring he represented the people, not the big corporations, but he remained underfunded and no less a long shot.

As far back as January, however, the *Gazette*'s Kolbe had spotted an unsettling flaw in McCain, his temper, and warned that it could derail his campaign. "It is because McCain's temper flares up so unpredictably, often over such inconsequential trivia, that his friends fear it could jump up and bite him at an inopportune time—such as late October," wrote Kolbe.

This was a variation of Jay Smith's belief that, once Babbitt dropped out, no one could hurt McCain but himself. Both Kolbe and Smith were right. McCain, meanwhile, flew into private rages each time Kolbe mentioned his temper in print. "I don't have a temper," he thundered at staffers as they struggled to keep straight faces. "I just care passionately."

The first issue to slow McCain's progress cropped up in June when Kimball allies unearthed a tape recording of remarks he had made in February to students at the University of Arizona. In a wisecracking style tailored to his youthful audience, he urged the students to register and vote, suggesting they emulate the heavy voting patterns of the elderly if they wanted their voices to be heard. "Most of the people coming here presently are senior citizens moving to Leisure World, I mean Seizure World," he said, drawing some politically incorrect laughs. On a roll, he continued, "I mentioned about Seizure World a few moments ago. . . . The last election in 1984, 97 percent of the people who live there came out to vote. I think the other 3 percent were in intensive care."

Typical McCain wisecracks, neither vicious nor terribly original. Residents of Leisure World, an east Mesa retirement community, had heard worse jokes and probably coined many of them. But there was hell to pay. Democrats jumped on McCain, accusing him of insensitivity toward the elderly. Puffed up with indignation, Kimball pronounced himself offended by the joke. "It leaves me humorless," he said.

McCain had stumbled. He might have quickly righted himself, John Kolbe maintained, by issuing an apology, admitting he had said a dumb thing and moving on. Instead, he kept the issue alive, reacting at length each time anyone said the magic words Seizure World, trotting out his record of support for the elderly and complaining that he had been quoted out of context. "We're hard-pressed to think of a context in which it would sound better," quipped Kolbe.

Finally drawing blood, Kimball moved to exploit the wound. In July, at a convention of public employees, he described McCain as "bought and paid for" by corporate fat cats and labeled his contributor list "a *Who's Who* of high-dollar special interests looking for political protection." Hammering home the charge, he pointed to $100,000 in contributions from defense-related companies and their political action committees, $53,500 from petroleum-related businesses, $43,300 from utilities, and over $50,000 from real estate interests and developers.

Few campaigns are complete without such charges. They are standard, predictable, and legitimate grist for the political mill, especially when one candidate is being outspent four to one by his opponent. What was not predictable was McCain's response. He called a press conference and angrily denounced Kimball for waging "one of the most sloppy and dirty campaigns in Arizona history."

McCain's overblown reactions to Kimball's taunts threatened to throw him off his game. He was beginning to resemble a rabbit-eared rookie unable to ignore the trash talk from the opposing team's dugout. Jay Smith patiently explained the facts of life to him. When you're an underdog, you try to get under the skin of your opponent. So you needle him, make him react to you. If you get lucky, he says something stupid. That's what Kimball's doing to you and you're playing into his hands. McCain nodded in agreement and held his peace—until the next time.

Throughout the summer, Kimball agitated for debates, dared McCain to meet him face-to-face. The McCain team had decided they did not want to debate until mid-October. A radio station tried to set up a debate and pressed McCain for a commitment. "I want to do it, Jay," said McCain, infuriated by Kimball's charges that he was ducking him. "Look, we're not going to let this turkey run the campaign," said Smith. "We'll do it on our terms. When you debate, it is going to be when it's good for us, it's going to be on statewide TV, and we're going to kick his ass." McCain persisted: "I don't want people to think I'm afraid of him." Said Smith, "John, nobody cares."

By mid-September, Kimball had closed to within thirteen percentage points. The McCain camp was worried and looked to the first of three televised debates, scheduled for October 17, to halt Kimball's advance. McCain was tense as the showdown approached. His advisers insisted that all he had to do was look senatorial and avoid a major blunder.

To prepare for the debate, McCain went into seclusion two days beforehand at his cabin in Sedona with aides Jay Smith, Grant Woods, and Wes Gullett. Smith played Kimball, hurling charges willy-nilly at McCain. Seizure World. Bought and paid for. Reagan puppet. PAC-man. Tool of defense contractors. Never saw a weapons system he didn't like. McCain was slow hitting his stride, seemed inarticulate, blocked. By the morning of the debate, though, he felt confident, as if he had broken through a wall.

That afternoon Smith checked out the debate site, a high school auditorium. He immediately sensed a problem. The two candidates were to be positioned in such a way that McCain, a good six inches shorter than the lanky Kimball, would appear even shorter to viewers because of the camera angles. "I don't want John to look like a pygmy," Smith angrily told the producer. The producer suggested placing a riser behind McCain's podium for him to stand on. Smith reluctantly agreed.

The debate began with brief opening statements. Kimball appeared earnest and intent, if somewhat brittle. McCain seemed polished and affable, though from time to time his eyes dropped disconcertingly to his notecards. Once into the questioning, stylistic differences emerged. McCain, fully in control, fielded the questions smoothly, made his points coolly. Kimball, by contrast, grew angrier and more self-righteous by the minute. Instead of Robert Redford, he looked like Alan Alda as Hawkeye Pierce in moments of high dudgeon, but without the offsetting charm and humor. Near the end Kimball almost seemed to be snarling, as if ready to reach through the television screen and grab the throat of any viewer who disagreed with him.

Kimball had openings, but failed to capitalize on them. His responses were long and confusing, fat paragraphs without topic sentences. Though he was neither mean-spirited nor arrogant, everything he said seemed to come out that way. "I understand John's confusion about my Central American policy," he said at one point. "This is the first time he has been allowed to be in my presence in this campaign." Translation: McCain had been dodging him.

Kimball got to McCain once. In an exchange over whether McCain had voted for a weapons system called the Bradley Infantry Fighting Vehicle, Kimball said, "You come in here and you treat people for suckers. You stand on a soapbox to make yourself appear to look taller." McCain's eyes flashed, his only response on camera. Afterward, though, he was furious. "Wanted to kill him," reported Jay Smith.

Kimball devoted most of his closing statement to reasons why voters should reject McCain without offering even a marginally compelling reason why they should elect him. McCain finished up by citing his experience and accomplishments. He then recalled how the terminally ill Lou Gehrig had bowed out of baseball by calling himself "the luckiest man on the face of the earth."

"I feel the same way," said McCain. "For twenty-two years I was privileged to serve our nation in the U.S. Navy, the way my father and grandfather did. And unlike many thousands of our young men who gave their lives in Vietnam for the cause of freedom, I was lucky to be given a second chance, a second chance to serve my country, a second chance to give something back to this nation which has given so much to me and to all of us. With your help I can be of even greater service to Arizona and America in the U.S. Senate."

The press called the debate a tie. McCain fumed when he saw himself perched on a footstool on the front page of the *Republic*. Jay Smith, convinced McCain had murdered Kimball, wondered if he should revise his prediction of McCain's vote total upward from his predebate figure of 57 percent. He decided he should, but kept it to himself. The election was more than two weeks away. With John McCain, anything could happen.

On election day, McCain followed the tradition he had established back in 1982 by going to the movies. He saw *"Crocodile" Dundee*. Jay Smith, mindful of the huge fund-raising advantage McCain enjoyed over Kimball— $2.6 million to $550,000—told his boss *The Color of Money* would have been more appropriate.

The polls had barely closed when the networks declared McCain the winner. The final margin was twenty percentage points, 60 percent to 40 percent. McCain headed to the downtown hotel where his supporters and the press had gathered. Earlier in the day, local TV producers told Smith that they had placed a riser at the spot where McCain was to deliver his anticipated victory speech. Make sure he stands on it, Jay, our cameras will never pick him up if he doesn't. Smith promised to do so, but in the flurry of election-day activities it slipped his mind.

Arriving at the hotel shortly after McCain, Smith saw reporters and well-wishers huddled together on the stage. From the midst of the throng he heard a familiar voice floating upward, thanking the voters for sending him to the Senate. Familiar but disembodied. McCain had seen the riser and kicked it aside. The White Tornado had become the Invisible Man.

The final days of the campaign were ripe with foreshadowing.

On November 2, two days before the election, R. W. Apple, Jr., of the *New York Times* all but conceded McCain the Senate seat, saying he "now seems poised to emerge as a significant figure in national politics."

The following day, November 3, the *Republic* carried a less flattering article on its lead local page. It said that McCain and six other congressmen who had received campaign contributions from Charles Keating had aided a Keating thrift—Lincoln Savings and Loan Association of Irvine, California—in a bitter battle with the Federal Home Loan Bank Board.

On election day, November 4, as the fifth man from the bottom in the Naval Academy Class of 1958 was being swept into the United

States Senate, the number-one man in that same class, national security adviser John Poindexter, was on the verge of ruin.

Poindexter was flying back to Washington aboard Air Force One with President Reagan on the final leg of the "last hurrah" campaign, Reagan's futile ten-day barnstorming mission to salvage the razor-thin Republican majority in the Senate.

Poindexter was seated up forward when Larry Speakes, Reagan's press spokesman, handed him a message pertaining to a bizarre tale drifting out of the Middle East. It seemed that the speaker of the Iranian parliament, Hashemi Rafsanjani, was saying that back in April the Reagan administration had sent Bud McFarlane on a secret mission to Tehran to trade arms for hostages. Betraying no emotion, Poindexter read the message and passed it back to Speakes, as if it were unworthy of comment. Speakes later called Poindexter's poker-faced response an Academy Award performance.

True to R. W. Apple, Jr.'s preelection prediction, McCain on moving to the Senate in January 1987 quickly established himself as an important new figure on the national political scene. The Senate had swung Democratic, but he had bucked the tide of GOP losses. By the following spring he was receiving serious mention as a running mate for George Bush, who had nailed down the Republican presidential nomination.

CHAPTER THIRTY-SEVEN

THE BIGGEST HAWK AND THE BIGGEST DOVE

On May 22, 1985, Ronald Reagan gave the commencement address to the Naval Academy graduating class at the Navy–Marine Corps Memorial Stadium. Among the dignitaries sharing the podium with the President were Bud McFarlane, the national security adviser, and the two brigade commanders from the Class of 1958, Vice

Admiral John Poindexter, McFarlane's deputy, and Rear Admiral Chuck Larson, the Academy superintendent.

Among the 1,042 graduating seniors waiting to shake the President's hand was Poindexter's son, Mark. The underclassmen in attendance included McFarlane's son, Scott, a sophomore destined to become brigade commander in the fall of 1986.

Reagan's speech was a mélange of patriotism, encouragement, and self-congratulation. He said the nation's military strength had declined over the decade of the 1970s as a result of "confusion stemming from the Vietnam War." By 1980, he said, the number of Navy ships had plunged to five hundred from nearly one thousand during the Southeast Asian conflict. But those days were over. "By the end of the decade," he boasted, "we'll realize our goal of a six-hundred-ship Navy, which will include fifteen deployable aircraft carriers."

The President singled out McFarlane and Poindexter by name, and said, "We've enlisted the talent of some Naval Academy graduates at the White House." He also tipped his hat to Jim Webb, sitting in a VIP section to the left of the podium, "the most decorated member of his class." Reagan then read a passage from *A Sense of Honor*, Webb's novel of Annapolis: "The President and the Congress may suffer bad news stories. The military man suffers the deaths of his friends, early and often."

Webb was thrilled. Also amazed. The President was reading from a book that had been loudly condemned by Academy officials and that had contributed mightily to his personal four-year exile from the Yard.

"Let me leave you with these thoughts," said Reagan. "Your countrymen have faith in you and expect you to make decisions. The issues will not be black and white; otherwise there would be no decision to make. Do not be afraid to admit and consider your doubts, but don't be paralyzed by them. Be brave. Make your judgment and then move forward with confidence, knowing that although there's never one hundred percent certainty, you have honestly chosen what you believe to be . . . the right course.

"Do this," he added, "and the American people will always back you up."

Listening to the President, McFarlane and Poindexter never for a moment thought that they would make what they considered honest decisions only to find that most Americans would not back them up, least of all the man speaking to their sons that day.

As for Webb, he remembered more of the President's speech than the flattering words directed at him. He never forgot what Reagan said about the six-hundred-ship Navy, from the first a high-profile goal of the administration. Soon it would be his to bring to fruition. Like McFarlane, Poindexter, and Ollie North, he would learn too late the perils of listening too closely to the strains of the Nightingale's Song.

Webb was there that day not solely as a novelist and Academy graduate. For the past year, he had been the assistant secretary of defense for reserve affairs, the first person to hold the post. He had been recruited by White House personnel director John Herrington, the ex-California DA who had first learned of Webb's existence driving across the San Francisco Bay Bridge five years earlier. Congress had created the position in recognition of the enormous reliance of the armed services on the National Guard and Reserves in the era of the all-volunteer army. On paper the Army had eighteen combat divisions. But several, by design, were understrength. In the event of a mobilization, the ranks were to be filled by National Guard and Reserve troops. To a lesser but still significant degree, the Navy, Marines, and Air Force were similarly dependent on the Guard and Reserves.

In short, if the nation went to war, it planned to do so with a combination of active-duty troops and the much-lampooned weekend warriors. Webb's job was to ensure that the plan was not a pipe dream, that the Guard and Reserves were well-trained, physically fit, and ready for integration into the combat forces at a moment's notice.

The job paid an added dividend. As an assistant secretary of defense, the civilian equivalent of a full admiral, he came in from the cold, inviting himself to the Academy—"often and with relish," according to *Newsweek*—to lecture midshipmen on honor and courage.

By then, Webb's career had taken on a pattern, public service interspersed with fiction writing and occasional forays into journalism. In late 1983, after completing his Emmy-winning report from Beirut for "MacNeil/Lehrer," he was getting the itch to return to the action.

For more than a year Herrington, who had become friends with Webb, had been trying to persuade him to join the administration. Each time Webb begged off. In December 1983, he finally called Herrington and said, "I think I'm ready to go to work."

His 1979 *Washingtonian* article on women in the military came back to haunt him. Following his nomination, Defense Secretary Weinberger demanded a written explication of his views. Webb supplied a detailed response, later described it derisively as a term paper. He did not back off on any of his points, but he maintained, as he had in the article, that women were qualified to hold virtually any job in the military that did not involve combat. As for females at the service academies, he called it a moot point. Wisely or not, Congress had spoken. Weinberger, in response to questions from journalists and advocacy groups, said Webb was going to be like a reformed smoker on women's issues. Webb felt demeaned by the process, both the request for the term paper and Weinberger's comment.

From that inauspicious beginning sprang a mutual admiration society. By late 1986, though, Webb was again feeling the literary urge. Preparing to write a novel about the Civil War, he submitted his resignation on January 2, 1987. He was offered other jobs in the administration, none attractive enough to change his mind. Putting five-year-old Jimmy to bed the night before his final leave-taking, he hugged his only son and said, "We're going to camp at Shiloh on the anniversary of the battle."

The next morning, while making a round of farewell courtesy visits, he was summoned to the phone. It was Weinberger.

"Jim, I know we've made you some offers, but I have one I don't think you can refuse. How would you like to be Secretary of the Navy?"

Said Webb, "I would be honored."

Reagan nominated him for the post on February 18. He had just turned forty-two.

May 1, 1987. Jim Webb stood at relaxed attention on the sun-drenched steps of Bancroft Hall, preparing to take the oath of office as the nation's sixty-sixth Secretary of the Navy. He was the first Academy graduate who had served on active duty to gain the post, an obscure nineteenth-century predecessor having been graduated but not commissioned.

Assembled below him on the weathered yellow bricks of Tecumseh Court were hundreds of well-wishers, a brigade honor guard, and most of his few close friends.

Blending pomp, color, and tradition, the scene had a timeless quality, the flapping of flags in the fresh spring breeze deepening the sense that some natural order was in the process of being fulfilled.

That same breeze carried an abundance of echoes, some pleasant, most of mixed timbre, others plainly discordant, nearly all embodied by the trim figure about to be sworn in as the civilian head of the Navy and Marine Corps.

Nearly two decades had passed since that June day in 1968 when a more innocent Jim Webb had triumphantly hurled his white midshipman's cap into the air to celebrate his graduation from Annapolis and his commissioning as a Marine second lieutenant.

That moment had coincided with the somber announcement a continent away in Los Angeles that an assassin's bullet had claimed the life of Robert Kennedy.

From even farther afield had come the distant rumblings of a war whose appetite for young men like Webb and his classmates remained ravenous despite the growing realization that it was already lost.

There were more personal echoes. Those familiar with Webb's turbulent relationship with Annapolis suspected that his choice of the Academy for the swearing-in ceremony had been guided by something more complex than the affection of an old grad for his alma mater.

Symbolic of that tangled association, dawn that day found the trees fronting Tecumseh Court in bloom with the undergarments of female midshipmen, a taunting declaration by the women of the brigade that they were at Annapolis to stay. Academy officials, publicly aghast, plucked the dangling skivvies from the trees long before the ceremony commenced.

The audience was remarkable, both for those who were there and those who weren't. In the first category were twenty-three members of Webb's old rifle platoon. In his remarks, he asked them to stand. Those who could, did. "While the rest of the country debated the war or ignored it, these twenty-three men picked up twenty-seven Purple Hearts," he said. "We owe them a lot more than our thanks, but I thank them today for their service."

The second category was smaller. Four men. Ollie North. Bud McFarlane. John Poindexter. John McCain. All lived in the Washington area, barely thirty miles away. Under normal circumstances they would have been in the audience saluting the new Navy Secretary. They had deep ties to the school. Like Webb, they had been touched in varying ways by the Vietnam War and its aftermath. And all four, again like Webb, had risen to prominence during the presidency of Ronald Reagan. None could be called Webb's friend because he bestowed that mantle warily, and only after a long testing period. But they were more than passing aquaintances.

That day, as on every day since the previous November, three of the missing men—North, McFarlane, and Poindexter—were busy dealing with the fallout from what had come to be known as the Iran-Contra scandal. As for McCain, earlier that morning, while the trees in Annapolis were being swept clean of panties and bras, he was flying to Tucson to preside at the opening of his newest senatorial office.

Webb invited his entire class, the Class of 1968, to the swearing-in, and some two hundred classmates came, from all across the country. Many wore buttons that read, " '68 Finally Did Something Right," a salty reference to Webb's promotion amid North's notoriety. A few days before the ceremony Webb received a letter from North. "Dear Mr. Secretary," it began. He congratulated Webb on his appointment, but said he would not be attending the ceremony. Given his current circumstances, he said, his presence would only be a distraction. Webb responded with a handwritten note that said, I appreciate your discretion, but you're a classmate, as welcome as any other classmate and fellow Marine, Semper Fi—Jim Webb. North stayed home.

At Webb's request, he was sworn in by Weinberger, who called him "a true American hero." The ceremony concluded in unorthodox fashion. Overruling objections from traditionalists, Webb had arranged for country-western star Lee Greenwood to serenade the assembly with his hit single of three years earlier, "God Bless the U.S.A." The catchy, patriotic ballad had been the campaign anthem of the 1984 Reagan reelection juggernaut, sung with gusto by the GOP faithful amid cascading red, white, and blue balloons from one end of the country to the other.

The post of Secretary of the Navy has traditionally been a stepping-stone to higher office. Webb's recent predecessors included two sitting U.S. senators, John Chafee of Rhode Island and John Warner of Virginia. Teddy Roosevelt had served as an assistant Navy secretary prior to the Spanish-American War. FDR held the same position under Woodrow Wilson during World War I. During those same years, across the Atlantic, the First Lord of the Admiralty was a budding British politician named Winston Churchill. For Jim Webb, on that triumphant day in 1987, all things seemed possible.

At the reception that followed the ceremony, Webb interrupted the festivities to perform his first official act. Calling for quiet, he asked "Big Mac" McDowell, his old forward observer, to step forward. As he did so, Webb pinned a medal on his chest, the Bronze Star he had put him in for eighteen years earlier. Like Dale Wilson's Silver Star, it had been lost in the bureaucracy for years until Webb shook it loose.

Webb admired much about his predecessor, John Lehman, notably his spirited and relentless advocacy of a six-hundred-ship Navy, but he had misgivings about some of Lehman's other policies. He was particularly troubled by arrangements Lehman had made with two outstanding Academy athletes, football running back Napoleon McCallum, a 1985 graduate, and basketball star David Robinson, a consensus All-American slated to graduate in June. Like other Annapolis men, both faced five-year military obligations. Lehman had ruled that McCallum could play for the Los Angeles Raiders as long as it did not interfere with his naval duties, then assigned him to a ship dry-docked in Long Beach, near the Raiders' practice field. As for Robinson, Lehman had agreed to let him serve just two years on active duty, with moonlighting privileges similar to McCallum's.

McCallum and Robinson had been model midshipmen, Robinson a high academic achiever as well. Lehman and the Navy brass explained the special treatment accorded the two men, both black, by saying that they had generated priceless publicity for the Academy and aided inestimably in recruiting, especially minority students.

John McCain questioned Webb about his intentions toward the two athletes during Senate confirmation hearings. "I would suggest a case can be made that Mr. McCallum and Midshipman Robinson have contributed enormously in raising the visibility of the service academies," said McCain. Webb's responses hinted that he was leaning the other way.

McCain's friend, Senator Bill Cohen, backed Webb: "I think that people like John McCain and Jim Webb are more important symbols to this country than they would be if they simply played a sport."

Other senators probed his views on women at the service academies. His response: "I believe that the service academies no longer exist purely to graduate combat leaders. That used to be true. But once the law was changed, the mission was changed. I accept that. It's history."

Al Gore, a Tennessee Democrat and Vietnam veteran, was not persuaded. He said Webb's responses seemed to imply that the changes at the academies, including the introduction of women, were not in the best interests of the schools or the nation.

"Am I wrong in getting that impression?" asked Gore.

"I would say no individual should feel very comfortable trying to read another individual's mind," replied Webb, glaring at Gore.

In office less than a week, he reversed Lehman's deals with McCallum and Robinson, forbidding them to play professional sports while on active duty. Being a naval officer is a full-time job, he said. He left intact Robinson's shortened military obligation on grounds that the arrangement had been made while he was still free to leave the Academy without penalty. *Newsweek* asked Webb about the argument that Robinson, at seven-foot-one, was too tall to serve on a Navy ship.

"Bullshit," replied Webb.

*   *   *

Jim Webb never learned to pull a punch. That quality defined him as a soldier, writer, and government official. It eventually accounted for the brevity of his tenure as Secretary of the Navy.

The day after being sworn in, he assembled every Navy admiral and Marine general in the Pentagon and gave them what Patrick A. McGuire of the *Baltimore Sun* called "a slightly more polished, but no less uncompromising version of the dead meat speech," a reference to Webb's warning to his platoon in 1970 about the consequences of lying to him.

Less than a month after taking over, he fired a broadside at the State Department, saying that the former ambassador to the Soviet Union, Arthur A. Hartman, bore part of the blame for the sex-for-secrets scandal involving Marine embassy guards in Moscow. Hartman, said Webb, had fostered a permissive atmosphere that allowed "extraordinary access to known KGB agents, dozens of them."

In September, speaking to the Brigade at Annapolis, Webb served notice on the Academy that he planned to impose exacting new policies. "Somewhere in the bitter confusion of the Vietnam era," he said, "when the military was being torn apart by vicious criticism, this institution apparently either lost its guts or its esteem."

He promised a more rigorous Plebe Year, longer cruises, and a return to a more stringent Honor Code. He revealed his position on honor offenses in a phrase—"No second chances." Alarmed by the poor showing of recent Academy graduates at the Marine Basic School, he instituted a special training and screening program for midshipmen planning to enter the Corps.

"Throughout your life, you will judge yourself against two harsh and often painful standards," he told the assembled midshipmen. "Did you get the job done? How many people did it cost?"

His first major personnel decision was to select a new commandant of the Marine Corps to succeed General P. X. Kelley. Kelley was President Reagan's favorite among the Joint Chiefs, but Webb did not think much of him, considered him a political general. Though popular within the officer corps, Kelley had his detractors there, too. Friends and critics alike were taken aback following the Beirut bombing when Kelley, testifying on Capitol Hill, declared, "I was not responsible." It was no less than the truth, as he was not in the operational chain of command. Even so, a Marine commandant denying responsibility when so many of his troops had been killed rankled many. It rankled even more when an Army general, Bernard Rogers, quickly asserted that he was responsible. That was also true in that as NATO commander Rogers was most assuredly in the command chain.

To Webb, Kelley represented a move away from the hard-charging commandants epitomized by the redoubtable Chesty Puller, patron saint of the Corps, more recently by Kelley's immediate predecessor, Robert Barrow, a battlefield hero in Korea and Vietnam. Searching for the right man, Webb conferred with Marine generals, both active and retired, including all former commandants. "Kelley has killed off all the gunfighters," one of his confreres told him. The remark reinforced Webb's suspicion that Kelley had thinned the ranks of top generals in the Puller-Barrow mold.

Narrowing his search, he sounded out his informal brain trust about Lieutenant General Al Gray, a gruff, tobacco-chewing ex-enlisted man on the edge of retirement. The first word from everyone's lips when Webb asked about Gray was warrior. Webb knew he had found his man.

In May 1987, responding to Iranian saber rattling in the Persian Gulf, President Reagan resorted to some diplomatic sleight of hand. Eleven Kuwaiti oil tankers changed their stripes, hoisted the U.S. flag, and became American oil tankers under international law. The Navy assumed responsibility for escorting the reflagged tankers in the Gulf and through the perilous Strait of Hormuz, which leads from the Gulf into the Arabian Sea.

Webb had no part in the decision, the roots of which predated his time in office. But he was troubled by it, vaguely at first, more deeply as his views crystallized.

The timing of the decision was enough to cause consternation. Two days earlier an Iraqi—not Iranian—warplane fired at least one missile at the frigate *Stark*, killing thirty-seven sailors and injuring twenty-one others. Weinberger, on ABC-TV's "Good Morning America," described the attack as "a single, horrible error on the part of the Iraqi pilot." Webb, who stood beside Reagan when the *Stark* limped home to Mayport, Florida, was not so sure.

In the weeks that followed, he sensed a tilt in U.S. policy toward Iraq that made him wary. Though he had no sympathy for Iran, he understood why the Iranians were harassing Kuwaiti ships. They carried Iraqi oil, the export of which was providing Saddam Hussein with the hard currency to bankroll the war. In addition, the port at Kuwait City was a transshipment point from which arms were trucked overland to Iraq.

There were also elements of this latest American military undertaking that reminded Webb of Lebanon, even more of Vietnam. The commitment of forces without congressional or popular mandate. A hazily defined mission. Restrictive rules of engagement. Taken together, they emitted a sucking sound, reminiscent of a quagmire.

Webb was not the only one to hear it. In June, John McCain, a freshman senator on the Armed Services Committee, sounded the alarm publicly, calling the reflaggings "a dangerous overreaction in perhaps the most violent and unpredictable region of the world." Like Webb, McCain was severely troubled by the pallid backing of friends and allies far more dependent on the Middle East oil trade than the United States. "Americans should not be placed in danger in the Gulf unless those nations that benefit—allied oil buyers and Arab sellers— provide some tangible support," he said.

On paper Webb was not a player. The Navy Secretary is not in the operational chain of command. His job is to see that ships and crews are ready for deployment, but he has no statutory authority over whether or not they should be deployed. For Webb, the role was an impossible one. The Navy, by virtue of the *Stark* attack, had already been blooded. Then the *Bridgeton*, the first tanker escorted through the Strait of Hormuz, hit an Iranian mine. He had a full-fledged armada—a battleship, cruisers, destroyers, and support vessels—sailing in harm's way. Yet the decisions were being made at a table to which he had not been invited. He decided he had to get to that table.

In early August, relying on what he called his "implicit role" as an adviser to the Secretary of Defense, he sent Weinberger a classifed memo stating his concerns, six pages of vintage Webb.

"I believe it is essential that our government lay out some clear long-term principles with respect to the use of U.S. forces in the Persian Gulf," he wrote. "The failure to do so will beyond doubt cause you to be criticized in the very near future, quite possibly from people who will read your own words back to you."

He went on to do just that, reprising for Weinberger his November 1984 National Press Club speech and questioning whether the Gulf deployment met three of the six standards the Defense Secretary had established in that address for the commitment of American military units.

He also raised an intriguing question: how do we know when we've won?

It is dramatically clear that we have offered up a myriad of ways to lose in this endeavor: any time a tanker is hit, any time we fail to be fully successful against an attack on one of our warships, any time a bomb goes off in an airport or a government official is assassinated, we will be perceived as having lost. There is no definitive action that will be accepted as evidence we have won, or when our commitment will be viewed as having been successfully completed.

Steeping in frustration, he searched for an opportunity to weigh in. In late August, thanks to a minor technical requirement, he saw his chance and battled his way to the table.

The Navy was negotiating the rental of two barges—essentially floating platforms—to serve as mother ships for a small contingent of Korean War minesweepers on their way to the Gulf, as well as for Navy SEAL teams, patrol boats, and helicopters. In all, the barges were to host more than 220 American servicemen.

The barges were needed because Kuwait had refused berthing privileges not merely to the minesweepers but to all their seagoing American protectors, as had other states on the Gulf littoral.

The Kuwaiti attitude—protect us, but don't come calling—outraged Webb. The barges were a more immediate concern. They looked like sitting ducks, more precisely like Marines huddled in a single barracks building.

As Navy Secretary, he was required to approve the contract by which the Navy agreed to indemnify the Kuwaiti owners of the barges for any damages they might incur. In August the contract was sent to him for his signature, a routine sign-off. Not so fast, said Webb.

On August 23 he fired off another memo to Weinberger, restating in even stronger terms his reservations about the mission, then impertinently questioning the use of the barges.

"What is the U.S. doing out in the middle of the Gulf, exposed to terrorist activities and sudden suicidal air attacks, when it is clear that the countries who seduced it into direct support don't have the courage to provide it support in return?"

He concluded the memo as follows:

I have not let the contracts on the floating platforms, and do not intend to do so unless one of two events occurs:
   a. I am convinced they are survivable in the sense that U.S. military vessels are survivable, and that their concept of use is militarily sensible, or
   b. I am directed to do so by you.

In a matter of days he was ushered into the Tank, the supersecret preserve of the Joint Chiefs in the Pentagon. He was seated at one side of the table. Across from him were Weinberger and one of the Defense

Secretary's closest advisers on the Gulf situation, Richard Armitage. The table was surrounded by officers assigned to the JCS. An Air Force general served as the briefing officer.

Weinberger made lengthy comments. Webb did a quick translation: Jim, you've got to get on board.

"Can I ask some questions?" said Webb. He proceeded to raise nearly all his concerns in a series of pointed queries.

Why are we sending a half dozen old minesweepers halfway around the world when we've just sold the Saudis nine brand-new ones? Answer: Their crews aren't good enough, they don't know how to use them yet. Webb: Then put American advisers on board and teach them. No direct answer; the unspoken response, according to Webb, was that the Saudis didn't want to confront the Iranians.

Webb kept rolling out the questions. What about the barges? You're going to have two hundred guys out there in the Gulf. Iran still has an air force. If I were the Iranians I'd try like hell to sink them. The response: There's no air threat. Webb: Just like I was told there was no mine threat?

The contractual issue eventually became moot. The Kuwaiti owners backed off on their demand for indemnification. But Webb felt he had accomplished something of value in the Tank, akin to peppering his seniors with discomfiting questions in Vietnam. *I wanted to make sure these people were thinking before they sent us off to do something weird.*

To Webb there was something weird about the whole American commitment in the Gulf, particularly the tilt toward Iraq. He remembered a weary Weinberger saying at one meeting, "I'm not very happy about this. We're supporting the second-worst regime in the world against the worst regime in the world." There were, Webb knew, global considerations, primarily the fear that the Soviet Union would move to exploit a power vacuum in the Gulf. Even that didn't explain it all, though.

He sensed that the United States was being manipulated by the Saudis and the Kuwaitis, neither of whom wanted to take on Iran, and by Japan, a nation dependent on Gulf oil. Somehow, it seemed, the Americans had been persuaded to do the dirty work for everyone else.

He also wondered if at some level the burgeoning Iran-Contra scandal was part of the equation, a chance for the administration to show it could get tough with Iran, that the covert sale of arms to Khomeini had been an anomaly, the responsibility of madmen McFarlane,

North, and Poindexter, having nothing to do with Ronald Reagan and steadier members of his administration.

Webb's doubts about the policy began to emerge publicly. In early September, the *Miami Herald* reported many of his concerns after obtaining a copy of the August "How do we know when we've won?" memo to Weinberger. With controversy bubbling around him, he reacted September 8 on "MacNeil/Lehrer." He said that some of his misgivings had eased in the month since he sent the memo. Not all of them, though. "What I would like to see is other countries who are benefiting from what we have done . . . living up to their responsibilities so we can downsize our naval presence." As to whether he supported the Gulf policy, he left the audience hanging. "I think it's the duty of any government official, if they cannot support the policy that is a central part of an administration program, they should leave. And I don't feel that I need to be doing that."

On October 19 four Navy destroyers shelled and burned two offshore oil drilling platforms that authorities said had been used as bases for Iranian gunboats. The action was said to be in retaliation for attacks on American-flagged vessels and other Persian Gulf shipping. Reagan called it "a prudent yet restrained response" to Iranian transgressions.

Webb had heard that song before, but never from Reagan. Two weeks later, at a luncheon interview with reporters and editors of the *Washington Times*, he stopped just short of saying the American action had been a joke.

In responding to Iranian attacks, he said, "the force used should be designed not simply to reciprocate for an action that has been conducted against you, but to preempt the next action. That's the only way you can gain the initiative in the military sense."

He fleshed out that statement in a 1990 interview. "You've got to say, Iran, laying a mine in international waters is an act of war. If you lay mines in international waters, we're going to destroy your minelaying capacity. And we could have done that. . . . We could have taken out the whole Iranian navy and not lost an aircraft."

He found himself in an increasingly untenable position. Iraq was not a friend, Iran was not an enemy, though it seemed intent on provoking the American armada.

"I was the biggest hawk and the biggest dove on this," he later said. "I kept saying, if you're going to do it, do it right, and if you're not going to do it, get our people out of there."

*　　*　　*

Weinberger completed nearly seven years as Defense Secretary on November 23, 1987. He was succeeded by national security adviser Frank Carlucci, who had replaced John Poindexter, fired when the Iran-Contra scandal erupted a year earlier. Webb would be gone less than three months after Weinberger's departure.

Webb had already had some run-ins with Carlucci. After the *Washington Times* article appeared, Carlucci had fired off a "Dear Cap" note to Weinberger, asking him to "instruct your secretary of the Navy" to keep such comments to himself. Earlier, Carlucci had called Webb at home one evening when it became known that he was questioning the party-line position that the naval activity in the Gulf would not increase Navy operating costs. Carlucci insisted there would be no additional costs. Webb felt his concurrence would buy him a seat at the table, but at a price he was unwilling to pay. After a pause, he told Carlucci, "I'll run the numbers and let you know." He did. In September the Pentagon placed the extra cost at $15 million to $20 million monthly for the foreseeable future.

Money—not millions, but billions—was becoming a problem. With the federal budget deficit out of control and Reagan reeling from Iran-Contra, Congress served notice that it intended to scale back defense spending. The White House and Hill leaders agreed to a $33 billion reduction in the Pentagon budget. Carlucci told the Navy to ante up $12 billion of the total cut. Webb came up with some ways to do it, none of which interfered with Reagan's seemingly sacred goal of a six-hundred-ship Navy. Each time he proposed a method to reach the $12 billion figure laid down by Carlucci, however, Carlucci's deputy, William Howard Taft IV, responded, "Frank wants ships." The Pentagon, in fact, had already sent a budget to the Hill calling for the scrapping of sixteen aging frigates, vessels similar to destroyers.

Webb wasn't serving up ships at his table. As recently as November, in accepting Weinberger's resignation, Reagan had paid homage to the goal of a six-hundred-ship Navy, which after seven years of rebuilding finally seemed within reach. Retiring the frigates meant that the target would not be achieved until well after Reagan left office, if ever. Webb was frustrated and angry. "The Reagan buildup did not reflect growth but a repair of the worst degradations of the 1970s when the fleet was severely cut back," he later said. "There was nothing magical about a 600-ship Navy except to remember it was once a 1000-ship Navy." Fewer ships meant longer sea tours, which stood to brutalize sailors and their families, a throwback to the seventies when the hollow joke among younger officers was, Make commander and get your divorce.

By the Navy's calculations, it would cost a total of $150 million annually to keep the frigates operating, peanuts in the context of the Pentagon's $300 billion budget. Webb reasoned that Carlucci, in the midst of the deficit angst, wanted to impress Congress with the Pentagon's determination to cut costs by having each of the services give up an eye-catching program or weapons system. For the Navy, that meant ships.

It didn't make sense to Webb. In peacetime, the Army and the Air Force conducted exercises; the Navy operated. The major international crises of the 1980s—Lebanon, Grenada, *Achille Lauro*, Libya, the Gulf—had all made extraordinary demands on the Navy. But that didn't seem to make any difference. It was all a matter of dollars and politics, as if the needs of the services depended on the money available, which was then divvied up according to some precooked formula, rather than on the missions each service was required to perform.

"I kept asking myself, 'Is there a strategy or is this like a balloon: When there's more money, the balloon gets larger, and when there's less money you let some air out of the balloon and it gets smaller?'" said Webb.

In early January, referring to the frigates, Webb told Will Taft that he would resign if he found he could not support scrapping the frigates. He also set about to devise a military strategy more in keeping with changes on the international scene.

As far back as 1984, he had written a memo to Weinberger suggesting that the administration rethink its commitment of forces to NATO, which he said was draining resources to such an extent that it endangered the ability of the military to respond elsewhere in the world. Like many members of Congress, he also believed the NATO allies, notably West Germany, as well as allies in the Far East—Japan and South Korea—should assume a greater burden of their own defense. He decided to go public with his views in hopes that his arguments would ignite what he considered a much-needed debate on American strategy for the next century. In the process, he hoped to save the frigates through a recognition that the United States was a maritime nation whose future relied on control of the world's sealanes.

On January 13 he startled official Washington with a speech to the National Press Club. Under the headline "Navy Chief Suggests Forces in Europe Be Cut," the *New York Times* reported that he had called for "a thorough review of the United States commitments to foreign nations and a re-examination of the deployment of

American forces around the world, especially in Europe." He also said more attention should be paid to Asia, Latin America, and Third World countries, urged greater reliance on seapower, and argued that the Army and the Air Force should absorb the bulk of the pending budget cuts.

The speech infuriated Shultz. Webb had not cleared it with him beforehand. It also sent shock waves through the NATO alliance, but did nothing to help salvage the frigates. For Webb, it was nearly over. In early February, the *Virginian-Pilot*, a Norfolk newspaper, reported that the Navy, led by Webb, was gamely trying to fend off Carlucci's demands to retire the frigates. "I think you will see the Navy hanging tough on this one," the paper quoted an unnamed Pentagon official as saying. "It won't agree to any force cuts and will be willing to fight it on the Hill."

The next day, Webb received a clipping of the article on which Carlucci had written, "I assume this is inaccurate and will be denied." Webb could hardly deny it since his subordinates, at his direction, had passed the information on to the *Pilot*. Carlucci's demand, in Webb's view, amounted to saying, "Not only are we going to do this to you, but you are going to say you did this to yourself."

On February 22, 1988, Webb sent a letter of resignation to President Reagan at the White House, then dropped a copy on the desk of a Carlucci aide. "I can only conclude that the decision to reduce the level of our fleet to a point that it may never reach the 600-ship goal was motivated by other than military and strategic reasoning," he said in the letter.

The story of his resignation was carried on the front page of most newspapers and played prominently in national newscasts. In the aftermath, the *Times* and the *Washington Post* editorialized against the manner of his departure. Both belittled the six-hundred-ship Navy as a meaningless goal, the *Times* calling it "a slogan, not a strategic concept," the *Post* saying the target was symbolic, not substantive, "and just a little bit of a game." No one, it seemed, had let Webb—let alone Reagan—in on the joke. Within a week, Webb was described as willful, bullheaded, petulant, and tantrum-prone by some of the nation's most influential newspapers. A Herblock cartoon in the *Post* pictured him in a child's sailor suit, pouting, trying to enter Carlucci's office. "He says he forgot his rubber ducky," the caption read.

In the weeks that followed, the officer corps of the Navy and Marine Corps seemed confused by the resignation. There was admiration for what was seen by many as an act of principle, but despair that he had left the Naval Service to the tender mercies of the politicians.

More than a few former colleagues felt he had made a decision to quit once Weinberger left and had simply been waiting for the chance to make a showy exit.

Of the many letters he received in the aftermath, perhaps the most fascinating came from Vice Admiral Leon "Bud" Edney. Six years earlier, Edney had been the Commandant of Midshipmen who informally banned Webb from the Naval Academy. When Webb was named Secretary, Edney, who had been working for John Lehman, offered his resignation. Webb kept him on, later promoted him to Chief of Naval Personnel.

In his letter to Webb, Edney wrote, "I have come to respect and admire your leadership, integrity and intellectual capacity more than any other individual I have been privileged to serve under in my 31 years."

On December 21, 1987, two months before he resigned, Webb nearly tripled, to fifteen thousand, the number of seagoing combat-support jobs open to women, moving the Navy into the forefront of the services in terms of expanding opportunities for females. Anticipating the Tailhook scandal by four years, he also ordered a Navy-wide crackdown on sexual harassment.

CHAPTER THIRTY-EIGHT

WHERE WAS AL KREKICH
WHEN WE NEEDED HIM?

And I said, "Hey, gunner man, that's quicksand, that's quicksand
  that ain't mud.
Have you thrown your senses to the war or did you lose them in
  the flood?"

—Bruce Springsteen, "Lost in the Flood"

Iran-Contra was the Watergate of the 1980s, complete with its
own colorful cast of characters and hastily contrived cover-up.
From the start, it had a kaleidoscopic quality, the pattern fracturing
and re-forming with each new wave of revelations. The lone constant
in those early days was the presence at the heart of the scandal of
North, McFarlane, and Poindexter, two Marines and an admiral, Annapolis men.

At first it seemed like something out of *Seven Days in May*, a right-
wing military cabal trying to take over the government. Even when it
became clear that it was not that at all, the military hue persisted as a
swarm of ex-soldiers emerged as key operatives—Dick Secord in particular, but others as well.

There were similarities between Watergate and Iran-Contra. Abuse
of authority. Bunker mentality. Cover-up. Oval Office tapes/NSC
PROFS messages. Televised hearings. World-class stupidity.

The analogy fell apart, though, when it came to the perps. Nixon
was smart, but paranoid. Reagan, not nearly so smart, was charming
and made a slicker getaway. The differences were just as striking when
it came to their subordinates.

The Watergate gang, many of them, cut their political teeth at the

University of Southern California, sabotaging student government elections through sleaze tactics called "ratfucking." McFarlane, North, and Poindexter came of age at Annapolis, dedicated their lives to public service, sailed in harm's way. Whatever else they were, they were not ratfuckers. The question was, were they just as dangerous?

Congressional investigators, among others, thought so. They concluded their probe of the scandal by asserting that North, McFarlane, and Poindexter were the ringleaders of a "cabal of zealots" headquartered in the NSC.

In North's case, they were right, and wrong. He was a zealot, but an ideological zealot only by happenstance. Mostly he was a zealot for the mission, whatever it was. At the time of Iran-Contra, he was still taking the message to Garcia, an Americanized version of Jerry Westerby, John le Carré's "honourable schoolboy." Reacting to the gloomy ruminations of the introspective, doubt-racked Smiley, Westerby says, "Sport . . . you point me and I'll march. Okay? You're the owl, not me. Tell me the shots, I'll play them."

As for the owls, McFarlane and Poindexter, they were anything but zealots. The right wing viewed McFarlane as irretrievably moderate, was dismayed when Reagan named him national security adviser. By then the New Right's Paul Weyrich had already pronounced him "created by God to disappear into crowds." Nor were conservative hearts set aflutter when Poindexter succeeded him. God forbid they should have found out he voted for Hubert Humphrey or that his wife had been arrested picketing the South African embassy.

All three were capable, hardworking, dedicated men who, it turns out, were in over their heads, at least in the drain field that was the Reagan administration. They were also flawed in ways that ultimately proved disastrous.

What follows in this chapter and the next is journalistic pointillism, an effort to fill in some gaps, to deepen the picture of North, McFarlane, and Poindexter in the Iran-Contra affair, Sunday in the Park with Ollie, Bud, and John, words and music by Ronald Reagan, apologies to Stephen Sondheim.

When the story of the secret arms sales to Iran came out, Reagan and others involved insisted that the overarching policy goal was to create a strategic opening to Iran. Critics insisted that it was an arms-for-hostages deal pure and simple, the larger policy considerations originally at play scraps on the cutting-room floor. As evidence, they trotted out various computer messages, usually from North, "1 747 w/50 HAWKS & w/400 TOWs = two AMCITs," shorthand missives that focused on arms and hostages but made scant mention of any grand scheme to improve U.S.-Iranian relations.

The debate raged, and still rages, but to what end? Clearly no improvement in relations between the two countries was possible until the hostages were released. North's job was to make that happen. As a fieldman, was he supposed to preface his every message with something to the effect that what he was doing was part of a broader initiative?

In fact, he made frequent mention of the big picture, though that seems to have been lost in the clutter of TOWs, AMCITs, and HAWKs. Both sides in the debate dug in. It was like the scene in the movie *Chinatown* where Jack Nicholson slaps around Faye Dunaway to force her to explain her relationship to the young girl she's hiding upstairs.

"She's my daughter." WHACK! "She's my sister." WHACK! "She's my daughter!" WHACK! "My sister!" WHACK! "Arms for hostages!" WHACK! "Strategic opening!" WHACK!

"She's my sister *and* my daughter!" said Dunaway, finally getting it right. The Iran-Contra crowd never did.

Iran-Contra needs no lengthy retelling. Its shape and most of the details are now familiar, though it retains the power to shock and befuddle. As Theodore Draper, its most erudite chronicler, has pointed out, the scandal grew out of two separate foreign policy initiatives that at a certain point were merged, with fatal consequences to both.

In August 1985 the United States secretly began a series of indirect (through Israel) and direct arms shipments to Iran. The shipments were not large, though they were far larger than Reagan said they were when the scandal broke. McFarlane, with Reagan's approval, set the operation in motion in hopes that it would pave the way for a reconciliation between the United States and Iran, the oil-rich, strategic gem of the Middle East that since 1979 had been ruled by the revolutionary regime of the Ayatollah Ruhollah Khomeini.

Each side insisted on something from the other to establish mutual credibility and seriousness of purpose. Iran, then engaged in a life-and-death struggle with its neighbor, Iraq, wanted weaponry. The United States wanted the release of its six hostages, held by Lebanese terrorists believed to be under the control or amenable to the influence of Tehran.

The Iranian arms sales story broke first, reaching the states on election day 1986. Poindexter's Oscar-caliber performance aboard Air Force One notwithstanding, it seemed McFarlane, North, and others had met secretly with Iranian officials in Tehran six months earlier. A furor ensued. The United States, it seemed, was taking secret actions at odds with its oft-enunciated public policy. The Reagan administration had stated on many occasions that it would not negotiate with terrorists. Ollie North, in fact, had written those words as guidance for the White House press office. Instead, for all the talk of attempting to achieve a rapprochement with Iran, it appeared that the administration was doing nothing less (and nothing more) than trading arms for hostages, if not with the hostage-holders themselves then with their patrons in Tehran.

Moreover, for the previous seven years, since 1979, the United States had maintained an arms embargo against Iran because of its support of terrorism. The administration also had a much-publicized diplomatic initiative under way known as Operation Staunch, aimed at discouraging other nations from selling arms to either belligerent in the Iran-Iraq War. The United States had taken a neutral stance in that war, calling on both sides to cease hostilities. Selling arms to Iran did not appear to meet any test of neutrality yet devised.

If nothing else, the administration seemingly had acted in a muddleheaded, thoroughly unprofessional manner. Keeping its actions secret from Congress and the American public, it left itself at the mercy of a shadowy crew of middlemen and an oddball group of Iranians, all of whom knew what was going on and any one of whom could blow the operation sky-high if it suited his purposes, as eventually, for one of them, it did.

There was also a senseless quality to the operation. If the Iranians needed weapons, ammunition, and spare parts for their war with Iraq, and the United States was willing to provide them in return for hostages, why wouldn't the Iranians direct their compatriots in Lebanon to take more hostages, if only to keep the barter shelves stocked? In fact, over the course of the fifteen months when the arms sales occurred, three of the six original hostages were released, but three other Americans were taken captive.

Thus in the days following the exposure of the Iranian arms sales, the Reagan administration stood accused of hypocrisy in the international arena and the court of public opinion. At a more mundane level, it seemed guilty of terminal witlessness.

Three weeks later, the other shoe dropped. At a hastily called press conference at the White House, Attorney General Edwin Meese reported that his investigation into the Iranian arms sales had turned up a new, potentially devastating element. Some of the profits from the arms deals—Meese estimated between $10 million and $30 million—

had been siphoned off and used to support the Nicaraguan Contras.

This became known as the diversion and it nearly brought down the Reagan administration. The President's men, spooked by the decade-old specter of Watergate, feared impeachment. The previous month, a plane flying supplies to the Contras had been shot down in Nicaragua. The lone survivor, an ex-Marine and former Air America operative named Eugene Hasenfus, said he was working for the CIA. Administration spokesmen denied any American involvement, but evidence that they were lying piled up quickly.

Taken together, the Hasenfus shoot-down and the diversion were seen as indisputable proof that the administration was engaged in Contra support activities that at best flew in the face of the Boland Amendment, a supposedly ironclad congressional ban on such support. At worst, those actions represented an unconstitutional effort to thwart the will of Congress.

McFarlane and Poindexter were major players in Iran-Contra. But North commanded center stage. In his hands he held the strings of the administration's two most sensitive foreign policy initiatives. Early in 1986 he looked from one to the other and tied their ends together, left over right and through, right over left and through, a perfect square knot, unslippable, or so he thought, though one wonders why.

Chuck Krulak, North's friend, knows why. "Scrape away all the veneer, he's a Marine infantry officer," said Krulak. He added, "He's not the smartest guy in the world."

Extracts from *Reef Points: The Annual Handbook of the Brigade of Midshipmen:*

THE ORDER
   Juniors are required to obey lawful orders of seniors smartly and without question. An expressed wish or request of a senior to a junior is tantamount to an order if the request or wish is lawful.

From "The Laws of the Navy," by Admiral R. A. Hopwood, R.N.

> Dost think in a moment of anger,
>   'Tis well with thy seniors to fight?
> They prosper who burn in the morning,
>   The letter they wrote overnight.

As the scandal unfolded, it became clear that the Academy training that had helped propel North, McFarlane, and Poindexter into the White House had played a powerful role in landing them in the dock.

At Annapolis and throughout their military careers they had been ingrained with the dictum that the wish of a superior officer was their command. Somewhere along the line, though, probably at the White House, a venue that has turned lesser men to fools, their common sense deserted them. They knew there were times when a subordinate must say no to a superior, but as the Iran-Contra affair makes clear, their threshold was appallingly high.

In the summer of 1984, for example, the most stringent of the Boland Amendments was awaiting final congressional passage. It promised to forbid Contra support activities by the CIA and other government agencies. One day Bud McFarlane met with Reagan, then told North that the President, the pending congressional ban notwithstanding, wanted the Contras held together "body and soul."

There were a number of possible responses to Reagan's words. North, on hearing them from McFarlane, might have said, "Bud, how does the President expect us to do that once the Boland Amendment is in place?" Or, "Bud, what precisely are you telling me to do, break the law?"

North, for his part, believed that the Boland Amendment, signed into law by Reagan as part of an omnibus defense spending bill on October 12, 1984, had a loophole. McFarlane is on record as saying he considered it airtight. That being so, he might have said to Reagan, "Mr. President, neither I nor any member of my staff can legally do that. I won't do it and I won't ask any of them to do it."

He said nothing of the sort. Instead, he walked out of the Oval Office and passed Reagan's message on to North. Later, he insisted that he told North the instructions meant nothing more than seeing that the Contras endured as a "credible political organization" until Congress came to its senses.

But whatever else he said, his lips emitted the phrase "body and soul," fateful words to a man of whom a fellow Marine, Fred Peck, once said, "Ollie North's commanding officer should never even think out loud."

A few years ago the militant environmental group Greenpeace had the Second Fleet steaming in circles. The Navy was trying to test-fire a new missile, but Greenpeace activists threatened to disrupt the launch by swarming all over an Atlantic test range in their high-powered Zodiac boats.

The Fleet's brain trust decided to use their own Zodiacs to sweep Greenpeace from the sea. Serious weapons were discussed. Rifles, shotguns, anything to persuade Greenpeace to clear the launch area or, failing that, to disable their boats.

The Fleet chief of staff, Captain Al Krekich, Annapolis '64, was disturbed by the direction the discussion was taking. Finally he weighed in.

"We're not going to do anything stupid here, are we?" he scowled through bushy black eyebrows. "Our mission is to launch a missile, not go to war with Greenpeace."

More benign and novel tactics soon surfaced. On launch day sailors threw fishing nets over the outboard motors of Greenpeace boats, fouling the propellers. They pelted other vessels with balloons and condoms filled with liquid detergent that burst on impact, making it difficult for crewmen to keep their feet and maneuver their craft. One balloon found the stack of the Greenpeace mother ship, the soap draining into the engine, killing the power plant. With Greenpeace immobilized, the missile was fired and no one was hurt.

In the wake of Iran-Contra, it was hard to avoid the judgment that the Reagan White House had too many Naval Academy guys running around in it. In fact, there was one too few. They needed Al Krekich, if only long enough to deliver the single line that might have changed history: We're not going to do anything stupid here, are we?

For McFarlane, it was never arms-for-hostages. He had been fretting about Iran as far back as 1981, two years before the first Americans were taken captive in Lebanon, four years before the Israelis came calling with an offer he couldn't refuse.

He was at State then, working for Haig: "I believed that a hostile Iran with Brezhnev in power (in the Soviet Union) and a weakened United States—weakened in the context of double-digit inflation, hollow army, all of the ills that afflicted us—was a very bad situation and that the Russians might well try to exploit our vulnerability to establish their own prevailing influence in Iran. In short, Iran was important."

He urged Haig to recommend to Reagan that Iran be made an early focus of the new administration's foreign policy. Haig agreed and a recommendation was forwarded to the White House.

Though few doubted Iran's strategic importance, nothing came of the recommendation at the time. At the NSC, however, McFarlane sustained his concern, forcing other agencies—State, Defense, and the CIA—to pay attention to Iran by ordering a series of policy reviews, hoping that eventually a diplomatic strategy would emerge for improving relations between the two old allies.

What he got, to his mind, was a justification for doing nothing, at least in the near term, a defensible position perhaps, but maybe not, considering the stakes.

In 1985, through Israeli and other intermediaries, an opportunity seemed to present itself. A faction in Iran—supposedly pragmatists or moderates, something other than Great Satanists—was said to be interested in warmer relations with the United States. Hashemi Rafsanjani, the speaker of the Iranian parliament and what passed for an up-and-comer in Tehran's murky political circles, was said to be the key figure, which turned out to be true. Both sides wanted a show of earnestness. The Iranians wanted arms, the Americans wanted the hostages freed.

The first arms shipment was sent in two stages, in August and September. Shortly thereafter a hostage, the Reverend Benjamin Weir, was released. The second shipment was in November. The Israelis, acting with the approval of the United States, provided the arms from their stockpiles on the condition that it could purchase replacements from the United States. Reagan, acting on the recommendation of McFarlane, approved both shipments. That was the sum total of arms transferred prior to McFarlane's leaving office at the end of 1985.

Throughout this period, there were promises and ploys from Manucher Ghorbanifar, the key Iranian middleman, but only a single hostage, Weir, was released. In addition, no high-level talks seemed in the offing, which was the point of the whole exercise, at least from McFarlane's perspective. By late November, the Geneva summit behind him, he began to smell a rat.

In early December, after submitting his resignation but before taking his final leave, McFarlane flew to London at Reagan's direction to meet with Ghorbanifar and others to survey the players personally.

He was revolted. Ghornbanifar tried to bully him, saying the Iranians were angry about receiving the wrong type of HAWK missiles the previous month. "Go pound sand," McFarlane replied, infuriated. Flying back to Washington, he told North and Dick Secord, who sat in on the meeting, that Ghorbanifar was "a borderline moron" and "one of the most despicable characters I have ever met." He did not mince words when he reported to Reagan, either. Ghorbanifar is devious, he lacks any semblance of integrity, we should not do business with him. Maybe someday we can try to open this channel again, but not now. Right now, McFarlane said, there is only one thing to do: shut this operation down. Then he left, hoping the President would do precisely that, but not fully convinced that he would. Before departing, McFarlane privately told Reagan that if the Iranian channel started showing promise for a true political dialogue, he would be glad to help in any way he could. "Thanks, Bud. I'll call on you," the President replied.

At first Reagan took McFarlane's advice, only to resurrect the operation before the month was out at the urging of Poindexter and North.

One of his biggest mistakes, McFarlane later said, was allowing arms to be introduced into the dialogue before obtaining concrete evidence of "the legitimacy, good faith, and competence" of the intermediaries with whom the Americans were dealing.

He had not exactly rushed into the deal. He knew nothing going in about Ghorbanifar, but the men who vouched for him had credibility—among them his friend David Kimche, director general of the Israeli Foreign Ministry.

He also remembered asking CIA director William Casey if he knew anything about Ghorbanifar at a meeting with Reagan in July 1985, before any arms had been shipped. In retrospect, Casey's response—"a blank stare," according to McFarlane—seemed singularly inappropriate. It was later revealed that the agency had put out a "burn notice" on Ghorbanifar in July 1984 after he twice failed polygraph exams. The notice described him as a fabricator whose information was not to be trusted.

Relying on Ghorbanifar, Reagan and McFarlane put their money on Rafsanjani, much as Nixon and Kissinger had played the China card a decade and a half earlier.

"That time we guessed right," said McFarlane. "Zhou Enlai and Mao delivered. Rafsanjani couldn't. But that's the mistake. We got behind a guy who couldn't deliver that soon. Two years later, he did deliver. He insisted with Khomeini on a cease-fire [in the Iran-Iraq War] and he got it. And he held sway ultimately to succeed Khomeini. So we bet on the right guy, but it was just too soon."

Rafsanjani was elected president of Iran in July 1989.

Vietnam bled all over Iran-Contra. It declared itself in the way McFarlane, North, and Poindexter dealt with colleagues in the Executive Branch and members of Congress. In whom they trusted, whom they didn't. Most of all, it could be seen in the relationship of McFarlane and North with the Contras, whom they saw through a lens tinged by Vietnam.

"I think Ollie came away from Vietnam saying you must never stop trying to support people that you've given your word to," said McFarlane.

That ideal soon collided with reality once North became involved with the Nicaraguan resistance. Lack of public and congressional support. The guerrillas' own inadequacies. The overwhelming discrepancy between Soviet aid to the Sandinistas and American assistance to the Contras.

North didn't care, at least insofar as his own commitment was concerned. Said McFarlane, "I think for him . . . it was again a circumstance in which we had made a commitment to people that he could see we were just about to break, and that the bottom-line consequence of that would be the death of a lot of people—Contras—and that he couldn't be party to that."

The more intellectual McFarlane shared those sentiments, but with the passage of time his lens acquired greater depth of field, as befitted his temperament and broader responsibilities as national security adviser. He looked back on Vietnam and saw not merely the humiliation of retreat, but the price in human terms to those left behind. Moreover, if a time came to advise the President to pull the plug on the Contras, it was his job to provide that counsel, not North's.

Explaining his thinking, he said, "As bad as it is to break a pledge to well-meaning people—specifically the Vietnamese or the Contras or Savimbi or the Afghans or any deserving, well-meaning cadre of people who aspire to democracy—as bad as it is to break a pledge to them, it is worse to encourage them to further loss of life when you know they cannot win, that they cannot win because you cannot deliver."

He also doubted that a covert policy could succeed for long, that eventually Reagan would have to expend large chunks of political capital in explaining and continuing to explain why the situation mattered, how the national interests of the United States were affected.

"For me, there were two glaring realities," he said. "One of them was that the Russians were putting $400 million a year into the Sandinista armed forces down there and we were never able to get more than $27 million while I was in government. That's damn near sixteen times our level of support. Even in guerrilla warfare, sixteen-to-one, those are not good odds.

"Secondly, the U.S. Congress sentiment toward this was not getting better; it was getting worse, I thought. And our ability to prevail in Congress I thought was getting worse."

A third reality was the resistance itself, with its suspect popular support and inability to produce any meaningful military victories. McFarlane, accompanied by North, tried to address those issues during a meeting with Contra leaders in Central America in January 1985.

"I said, 'Look, we've got a year tops. We've got to swing some voters and to do that two things have to happen. You've got to broaden your base and you've got to win on the battlefield. If you can't do those two things, we're not going to be able to carry this off and we'd better start understanding that right now.' "

He later said, "I don't think Ollie agreed with me."

He was right. Both men came out of the Vietnam era despairing of the broken promise, but ended up viewing it differently. For North, it was a pledge to himself never to break faith again, undergirded by the belief that sooner or later the United States would do the right thing. For McFarlane, the realist, it was a commitment never again to mislead people when, as Jim Webb once wrote, your nation seems intent on "fading again and again in the clutch."

> Midshipmen are persons of integrity: they do not lie, cheat or steal.

> —Honor Code, U.S. Naval Academy

> I think a reasonable amount of honesty is the best policy.

> —WILLIAM KRISTOL, Vice President Dan Quayle's chief of staff, quoted in the *Washington Post*, January 18, 1993

McFarlane tried to play a Washington power game for which he had neither the guile nor, in the end, the stomach. The rigid, unyielding rules of Annapolis by which he had lived his life fell victim to the situational ethics of the fetid swamp that Pierre L'Enfant transformed into the nation's capital nearly two centuries earlier.

He paid a steep price. The record of Iran-Contra reeks with examples of McFarlane lies, deceptions, misstatements, evasions, and half-truths, a display of dissembling so egregious as to be almost inexplicable. It was as if wires got crossed in his brain, short-circuiting his ability to speak the truth.

The first set of lies, in 1985, laid down the theme off which McFarlane, like a doped-up jazz musician, would improvise for the next two years, each jarring foray into the unfamiliar bebop world of prevarication further leaching his reputation for integrity.

In the summer of that year, congressional interest was pricked by press reports that identified North as the NSC's point man in a Contra support operation that appeared to violate the Boland Amendment.

On receiving inquiries from Indiana Democrat Lee Hamilton, the House Intelligence Committee chairman, and others, he conferred with North and reviewed pertinent documents. North had written numerous memos in which he imputed to himself a broad range of operational activities. But, as McFarlane well knew, North tended to exaggerate. How much was real and how much was typical Ollie bullshit? Probably a lot, he concluded. On their face, though, the memos were dynamite.

Responding to Hamilton on September 5, McFarlane wrote, "I can state with deep personal conviction that at no time did I or any member of the National Security Council staff violate the letter or spirit" of the law.

He would play the same tune with minor variations five more times during that period in an effort to deflect other congressional inquiries. He would later call the responses "too categorical," adding, "I did not give as full an answer as I should have." He would never live it down. But in an interview three years later he offered an explanation, not an altogether convincing one.

After sending the letter to Hamilton, he said, he called the congressman and offered a fuller oral accounting of North's activities. On September 10, he met privately with Hamilton and other committee members. As he understood it, he said, their concerns related to two questions: was North managing the war and was he raising money for the Contras?

McFarlane said he maintained that there was no way a lieutenant colonel in Washington could run a war in Central America. Yes, Ollie goes to Contra camps and gives them advice on various things—training, emplacement of mortars and other weapons, the kinds of things you'd expect a hard-charging Marine infantry officer to do—but he's not masterminding the war. That's just not possible. Nor is he raising funds for the Contras. He speaks to groups sympathetic to the guerrillas, but when members of the audience ask how they can contribute he tells them to get in touch with the Contra leaders in Miami.

In McFarlane's narrow depiction of North's role, North came across as a combination Basic School instructor, cheerleader, and tub-thumper for the cause. Panel members, he said, raised no strong objections. He himself considered it a reasonably honest assessment, certainly more candid than his written response, even though he suspected North had probably done somewhat more.

It was in this context, he said, a context of mutual recognition that what North was doing was no big deal, that his statement about not violating "the letter or spirit" of the law qualified as truthful. Not the spirit of the law as an outsider might construe it, he hastened to add, but as he understood it in the context of discussions of Boland with lawmakers prior to passage, at the meeting of September 10 and others during that period.

In other words, he misled Congress, at least on paper, but persuaded himself it was okay because he later gave members—insiders like himself—the true story, or a reasonable facsimile thereof, in person. He did not seem to regard the falsification of the written record as a serious matter. That was the way Washington worked.

North later called his superior's written response a lie, a description hard to contest, though it was not a gratuitous fabrication on McFarlane's part. Memos or no memos, he may not have known the extent of North's operational role. The Ollie bullshit factor was not a constant. It tended to fluctuate, making it difficult to compute on any given day.

He also knew that his answers could directly affect the fate of the Contras. Although the Boland Amendment was still in effect, Congress had already reconsidered the aid issue and approved a new $27 million package that would become available on October 1, the start of the new fiscal year. Revealing North's activities, especially as portrayed in North's own overheated memos, had the potential to foreclose future assistance.

Some of the documents were highly sensitive as well. One described North's meeting with a Chinese official in an effort to obtain anti-aircraft missiles for the Contras. Another discussed the covert aid provided the resistance by an unnamed Central American country. The president of that nation and the Chinese were relying on an American pledge of secrecy. If McFarlane gave the documents to Congress, they might leak, with international repercussions.

Far from plotting the overthrow of the Sandinistas, McFarlane was consumed that summer and fall with preparations for what he hoped would be the crowning achievement of his tenure as national security adviser, the rapidly approaching Geneva Summit, scheduled for November. For North, inquiries relating to the Contras struck at the heart of his White House duties. For McFarlane, they were a distraction. He wanted them off his screen. In replying to Congress, he faced a difficult choice between full disclosure and asking the President to invoke executive privilege. North argued for the latter. McFarlane said no. He had been in the White House during that heyday of executive privilege known as Watergate. He chose a third alternative. He tried to finesse the whole thing.

"I assert to you that there are accepted ways of dealing between the Congress and the Executive Branch which are time honored," he said years later. "I adhered to a higher standard than Henry Kissinger by a long way."

In the end, McFarlane dishonored himself. His personality, at least during the White House years, was a curious amalgam of soaring ambition, high competence, and a timidity that at times bordered on cravenness. He alone in the national security structure at the top echelon of the Reagan administration seemed to understand that covert support of the Contras was destined to fail. He voiced reservations here and there, but withheld the full depth of his misgivings from the President. "Where I went wrong," he told the congressional investigation committees, "was not having the guts to stand up and tell the President that. To tell you the truth, probably the reason I didn't is because if I'd done that, Bill Casey, Jeane Kirkpatrick, and Cap Weinberger would have said I was some kind of commie, you know." It was a pathetic admission, no less a window on the soul than James Watt's remark about the eclectic makeup of his commission. Somewhere along the line, the young Marine officer who stood his ground against William Westmoreland lost not just his judgment but his balls.

Once he started dissembling, it was as if someone had kicked out the chocks and sent a truckload of garbage hurtling downhill. In November 1986, with the Iranian arms sales exposed, he participated in falsifying a chronology of the initiative that sought, in his words, "to blur and leave ambiguous" the President's role. During the weeks that followed, he appeared before a number of congressional committees and the Tower Board, an investigative body established by Reagan, providing more misleading testimony. Finally, on February 21, he appeared before the Tower Board again and came clean on what drove the President.

"I have felt since last November—and that is where we started— that it has been, I think, misleading, at least, and wrong, at worst, for me to overly gild the President's motives for his decisions in this, to portray them as mostly directed toward political outcomes.

"The President acknowledged those and recognized that those were clearly important. However, by the tenor of his questioning, which was oriented toward the hostages and timing of the hostages, from his recurrent virtually daily questioning just about welfare and do we have anything new and so forth, it is very clear that his concerns here were for the return of the hostages."

Translated from Budspeak, he meant that Reagan's overriding concern was getting the hostages back, not a strategic opening to Iran. It was a concession to the obvious, but he was the first person in a position to know who said it. It was also an effort on his part to reclaim the reputation for honesty he had shredded with his own words over the previous year and a half.

McFarlane's woeful performance during that period defies any explanation that does not take into account his mental state. It seems safe to say that by the time Iran-Contra came to light, something had long since snapped in McFarlane; precisely what can only be guessed. He had been regularly whipsawed by Weinberger and Shultz, and, of course, Reagan. Other than in their opposition to the Iranian initiative, the two senior cabinet secretaries rarely agreed on anything. Reagan refused to impose discipline on them and would not give McFarlane the authority to do it for him. As one veteran of the Reagan White House put it, "The President didn't want to be Richard Nixon and he didn't want Bud to be Henry Kissinger." The pernicious indecision that resulted left him feeling helpless, not up to the job.

Other factors were at play. Did Don Regan's bullying, occasionally demeaning manner recall a painful childhood and a bullying, occasionally demeaning father? What about the infidelity rumors? Was there any truth to them? Assuming they were false, as they probably were, did they contribute to his emotional destabilization? There was also this: he was his own worst critic. Did he see something in himself that made him believe, accurately or not, that he didn't quite measure up? that he would always be second-rate?—perhaps the hardest fact a man can face, especially a man like McFarlane?

His emotional state did not improve after he resigned in December 1985. Distressed at being on the sidelines, he seemed to lose purpose. Ensconced at a prestigious downtown Washington think tank, sitting on corporate boards, he was making more money than he ever had in his life. But he had never cared much about money and took little joy from it. Reporters called from time to time to get his view on one issue or another, dropping his quote into the bottom half of the story, below the fold. He did have an encryption device at home linked to the NSC computer, which kept him in touch with North and Poindexter. But in his view at least, he was out of the action, a has-been, another K Street kibitzer.

The trigger for his emotional crisis is probably unknowable, the product of some dark night of the soul to which he and perhaps a few others are privy. What seems indisputable is that something happened, probably sometime in 1985, maybe as early as 1984. Despite the strain, he continued to perform extraordinarily well under pressure. He was cool and resourceful in the TWA hostage crisis and the *Achille Lauro* episode. He orchestrated a successful summit in Geneva. He set in motion the Iran initiative, saw it going sour, and tried to kill it. He functioned competently in Tehran, strictly following the guidelines set forth by the President and Poindexter, aborting the mission when it seemed appropriate to do so.

But for all that, during much of that period, Bud McFarlane was no longer the man he once was. He had surrendered too much of himself, cut too many corners, played too many Washington games, mortgaged his integrity to feed his ambition. And when that loan was finally called, he was damn near bankrupt.

By early February 1987, three months after the initial Iran-Contra revelations, McFarlane had plunged into an unremitting desolation. He alone of the major players had agreed to talk about the affair, North and Poindexter having taken the Fifth Amendment. He testified without immunity before four separate congressional committees. He appeared before the Tower Board. He responded to press inquiries and submitted to long television interviews. In the absence of other authoritative voices, his every sentence was scrutinized for inconsistencies, major and minor. Years later, in 1990 and after, Iran-Contra special prosecutor Lawrence Walsh would obtain previously undisclosed notes from Weinberger, Donald Regan, and Shultz aide Charles Hill that attested to the truthfulness of many of McFarlane's statements from that period, at least those relating to who knew about the early arms shipments. But that didn't come out until 1994, when Walsh issued his final report. Back in late 1986 and early 1987, it quickly became—in the words of his lawyer, Leonard Garment—McFarlane versus McFarlane.

Cut adrift, an administration obsessed with damage control treating him like a pariah, he seemed at a loss to know what he could reveal and what had to remain classified. He talked about the big picture, but hedged the details, sometimes with evasions, at other times with outright lies. For example, he told a congressional panel that North had divulged the diversion to him on the tarmac in Tel Aviv after the Tehran trip in May 1986, a major disclosure. But on December 1, he lied to the Senate intelligence committee on a far less significant matter. He said that after resigning as national security adviser he had no basis for knowing about North's pro-Contra activities other than through press reports. In fact, after his December 1985 resignation he regularly conferred with North about his Contra support efforts on the secure encryption device he kept at home.

His behavior grew more and more erratic. Appearing on ABC's

"Nightline" in December 1986, he seemed to deny the existence of an elusive chocolate cake rumored to have accompanied him, North, and the others on the Tehran mission, saying, "I don't do business like that." In a later "Nightline" appearance, under questioning from Ted Koppel, he clarified his nondenial denial, saying the cake was North's gambit, not his. "Simply put," he said, "there was a cake on the mission. I didn't buy it, bake it, cook it, eat it, present it, or otherwise get involved with it." To which he might have added: or tell the truth about it.

As his depression deepened, he tried to shake it. In December, with Iran-Contra shrapnel flying furiously, he hunkered down and composed an ambitious national security policy package that he hoped would impart fresh momentum to the foundering Reagan revolution and perhaps salvage some of his own reputation. He wrote night and day, his ideas sweeping across the full spectrum of foreign policy issues—arms control, the Middle East, Central America, defense spending. He passed it through an intermediary to George Shultz, who dropped him a note thanking him for his views, the classic Washington kiss-off. He held out hope that Reagan would incorporate some of his ideas into the January 27 State of the Union message. Not a word.

By early February he was suffocating in the reality of his new life. He was no longer a player and believed he could never hope to be a player again. He had set his nation on a course that, however well intended, had humiliated the President he had served for five years, the man who had given him the chance of a lifetime. His evasions, half-truths, and lies were swirling around in the malodorous Iran-Contra ether. It was only a matter of time until they reached critical mass and destroyed the good name he had carefully constructed over three decades of dedicated and distinguished public service.

By then, Jonny McFarlane was picking up frequent clues about her husband's state of mind, but they were not fully registering. At one point he said, "I'm depressed, and I'm going to be depressed for a long time." It was out of character for him. He rarely allowed himself to show uncertainty or weakness.

Jonny was normally quick to confront a problem, but she put off dealing with this one. She was getting ready to begin a leave of absence from her high school teaching job. All she had left to do was finish grading term papers and final exams. I really have to pay attention to what's going on with Bud, she told herself, taking comfort in the belief that she would soon have all the time she needed to devote to him. On February 8 she spent twelve hours working on student papers at home in Bethesda, assigning grades and writing comments well into the evening. Over the previous few days, her husband had been writing, too. He wrote a note to her, a note to an editor friend, and a note to a congressional committee admitting his role in obtaining a multimillion-dollar contribution for the Contras from the Saudis, through his old friend from Lebanon, Prince Bandar, by then the Saudi ambassador to the United States.

Exhausted, Jonny finally said she was going upstairs. McFarlane said he would just be another few minutes. Shortly after eleven, he went into the kitchen and propped the note to his wife against his briefcase. Then he unsealed a bottle of Valium and washed down about thirty pills with a glass of wine. After a few moments, he climbed the stairs to the second-floor bedroom and exchanged small talk with Jonny. "Good night," he murmured to his wife of thirty-three years as they lay together for what he thought would be the last time.

Days later, as he recovered from the failed suicide attempt at Bethesda Naval Hospital, he told his daughter, Laurie, that he felt as if he were lying in a giant pit and people were standing around the rim pelting him with garbage.

Mike Deaver came by to visit. "You've got nothing to be ashamed of," he told McFarlane. "Ronald Reagan used you." Later that day, Deaver said to his wife, Carolyn, "I wish Bud were an alcoholic. I could help him."

A number of Washington types called the suicide attempt a sham, designed to fail. They dismissed it as a transparent plea for sympathy, and clemency. Others viewed it as a cry for help on the part of a man who had depleted his emotional resources.

His closest friends saw it for what it was. Seppuku. Ritual suicide. The ultimate act of atonement.

"Go back to the Naval Academy, what we were all taught," said Brent Scowcroft, his old friend and mentor. "Even if you don't think you were completely responsible, it went wrong and you were there." Scowcroft was West Point, not Annapolis, but it was the same thing.

In March, home from the hospital, McFarlane was interviewed by Barbara Walters on ABC's "20/20." Speaking of Iran-Contra, he said, "I think, Barbara, that in a year's time, a curious and haunting factor that will come out in this episode is the Vietnam War."

In May, during a noon break in his four days of congressional testimony, he saw a television news spot that infuriated him. The reporter said the committee was dealing gingerly with him because of his suicide attempt and the likelihood that he was on medication.

After lunch, as House counsel John Nields resumed questioning, McFarlane was still fuming. He said he resented the implication that he was "a rather fragile flower" who had to be treated with kid gloves.

"That is nonsense," he told Nields, sounding like a Marine for the first time in months. "Shoot your best shot."

CHAPTER THIRTY-NINE

CHINATOWN

"Forget it, Jake, it's Chinatown."

—*Chinatown*, Paramount, 1974

An old Marine named Ben Frank likened Ronald Reagan's performance during Iran-Contra to the piano player in the whorehouse who tells the cops how shocked he was to learn what was going on upstairs.

Frank was right, but not completely. The White House, after all, was a class joint, not some run-of-the-mill brothel, and Reagan was not just a piano player.

He was the headliner, the crooner of the Nightingale's Song, though after a few years playing the White House his warble had gotten throatier. Midway through his second term, he seemed less Dennis Day, more Hoagy Carmichael, an aging tunesmith slouched over the keyboard, tickling the ivories, reprising old hits.

By then he had added some new verses to the Nightingale's Song and he sang them slightly off-key, but McFarlane, North, and Poindexter, soothed over the years by the original, were tone-deaf to the discordance in the updated version.

He had banged out a few new tunes, too, variations on the original, but still catchy, with hints of the old Reagan magic. The theme stayed the same, only this time the noble cause was not Vietnam or Lebanon but Nicaragua and the Contras. McFarlane, North, and Poindexter, always an appreciative audience, got the message, danced to the music, barely escaped the slammer.

Here is some of what they heard.

In a nationally televised speech from the Oval Office on May 9, 1984, Reagan said, "The Sandinista rule is a Communist reign of terror. . . . If the Soviet Union can aid and abet subversion in our hemisphere, then the United States has a legal right and a moral duty to help resist it. . . . This is not only in our strategic interest; it is morally right. It would be profoundly immoral to let peace-loving friends depending on our help be overwhelmed by brute force if we have any capacity to prevent it."

In October 1984, as the most restrictive version of the Boland Amendment was about to go into effect, he was asked how he felt about efforts by a group of southerners to provide private assistance "to stop Communism before it gets to our borders." Reagan replied, "Well, I have to say it's quite in line with what has been a pretty well-established tradition in our country."

In his State of the Union message on February 6, 1985, with Boland in full force, Reagan said, "We must not break faith with those who are risking their lives on every continent from Afghanistan to Nicaragua to defy Soviet-supported aggression and secure rights that have been ours since birth. . . . Support for freedom fighters is self-defense."

On March 1, 1985, at the Conservative Political Action Conference in Washington, he said, "They are our brothers, these freedom fighters, and we owe them our help. . . . They are the moral equal of our Founding Fathers and the brave men and women of the French Resistance. We cannot turn away from them."

Addressing elected officials at the White House on March 14, 1986, he said, "So, I guess in a way [the Nicaraguan rebels] are counterrevolutionary, and God bless them for being that way. And I guess that makes them Contras, and so it makes me a Contra, too."

A month and a half later, on May 2 aboard Air Force One, he expressed concern to Poindexter about a $100 million Contra aid bill tied up in the House. "Look, I don't want to pull out our support for the Contras for any reason," Poindexter quoted him as saying. "This would be an unacceptable option. . . . I am really serious. If we can't move the Contra package before June 9, I want to figure out a way to take action unilaterally to provide assistance."

A little over a year later, on May 15, 1987, speaking to a group of newspaper editors, he said, "As a matter of fact, I was very definitely involved in the decisions about support to the freedom fighters. It was my idea to begin with."

Of course no litany of Reagan's hits would be complete without that great old standard "Body and Soul," the signature tune of his later years, the one that Ollie North could never get out of his head.

Bill Haskell was medically retired after losing an eye in the same May 1969 battle in which his fellow Kilo Company platoon commander Oliver North won the Silver Star. Returning home to the Washington area, he completed his education at the University of Maryland and went to work for H&R Block as a tax preparer. In August 1985, a year before the Iran-Contra scandal broke, he came across a magazine article that provided an early glimpse of North's behind-the-scenes efforts on behalf of the Nicaraguan resistance. By then, Haskell owned the Block franchise in Upper Marlboro, Maryland, just outside the Capital Beltway.

Finishing the article, he picked up the phone, tracked down North, and volunteered to help.

"I have a lot of spare time," said Haskell. "You can have me all you want except during tax season."

"We can use you, but we can't pay you," said North.

"Fine," said Haskell. "I'm not looking for a job."

Overnight, Haskell became a key North operative. Before it all ended fifteen months later, he had overseen the construction of an airstrip in Costa Rica, negotiated the purchase of a Danish ship, the *Erria*, and handled a number of other sensitive missions for North. Other than expenses, he wouldn't accept a cent for his efforts. He regrets now that he didn't take a token sum in compensation. As an unpaid volunteer, he was ineligible for a $12,000 tax deduction, the amount he spent in legal fees after everything blew apart in November 1986. It is his only regret.

"I did it for the same reasons I joined the Marine Corps, adventure and duty, those two things," he said of his role in the Iran-Contra affair. "I thought I was providing some service to the country, just like Ollie was. And it certainly was an outstanding adventure."

Fresh from his effortless recruiting of Haskell, North phoned another old friend from Vietnam, Eric Bowen, who had taken over Haskell's platoon. North had decked Bowen in the ring back in 1969, but they were friends and had stayed in touch through the years. By 1985, when North called, Bowen was a successful, slightly manic real estate broker in the Buffalo, New York, area.

"Are you interested in working for me?" asked North.

"No," replied Bowen. "I'm happy doing what I'm doing in my life."

North sweetened the pot: "Bill's working for me."

Bowen thought it over, said he was going to pass anyway. He never relented, which made him one of the few men North tried to enlist who didn't wind up under klieg lights on Capitol Hill.

North had better luck with Rob Owen, who had missed Vietnam and never gotten over it. His older brother, Dwight, was killed there in 1967, when Rob was thirteen. Six years later, as a freshman at Stanford, he tried to join the Marines, but was rejected because of a lacrosse knee. After graduation, he applied to a half dozen California police organizations, but they all turned him down because of the knee injury. In 1980 he worked in refugee camps along the Thai-Cambodian border for the International Rescue Committee.

"If and when the test ever comes, I'm going to get my red badge of courage or die trying," he told journalist Christopher Buckley in 1983.

He met North in the summer of that same year, while working on Dan Quayle's senatorial staff. The following year North enlisted him into his Contra supply effort. Over the next two years Owen became the crucial middleman in North's Contra operation, a self-described secret agent, code-named The Courier. Lacking even a shred of training for the clandestine missions he undertook, he was nevertheless reasonably able. More to the point, he was eager to do the job.

North's most indispensable recruit—the man with the Ice-nine eyes, as Michael Kelly described him in the *Baltimore Sun*—was Bill Casey's idea. North sought the CIA director's help in the summer of 1984 when it was becoming depressingly clear to him what his duties entailed under the rubric of "body and soul."

"Do you know Dick Secord?" asked Casey.

North did, slightly. They had met during the AWACS battle in 1981, when Secord had been an Air Force major general and a deputy assistant secretary of defense.

Secord, Casey explained, was not just another military bureaucrat. He had flown nearly three hundred combat missions in Southeast Asia, advised the Shah's troops in northwest Iran in their efforts to quell a Kurdish insurrection, run much of America's secret air war in Laos, and helped plan the "Christmas bombing" of Hanoi.

More recently, following the abortive Desert One raid in April 1980, he had organized and trained a second, larger attack force to rescue the fifty-two American hostages in Iran. Though it had little obvious import at the time, Secord also knew a lot about Iran and its armed forces, having headed the Air Force military mission in Tehran during the mid-1970s.

"He's got the right experience for this sort of thing," said Casey. "He knows the right people, he gets things done, and he keeps his mouth shut. Why don't you call him?"

By then, Secord was no longer the Air Force water walker he had been since graduating from West Point in 1955. He was now, by default, a businessman. Reports of his association with Edwin P. Wilson, a renegade CIA contract employee who brokered arms to Libya, had torpedoed his career and convinced him to retire even though no charges were ever brought against him.

Secord was reluctant to get involved, but North recruited him through a combination of charm, enthusiasm, and manipulation. Within a matter of months, he was second only to North in running the matched set of covert operations that became Iran-Contra. By the summer of 1986, he had come to believe that his association with North, blessed by Bill Casey, might pave the way for a triumphant return to government service, perhaps as chief of the CIA's operations directorate. A few months after that, Secord was huddling with his lawyer, trying to figure a way to stay out of jail.

Albert Hakim, Secord's partner, came aboard as well. A globe-trotting Iranian-American businessman with an appetite for intrigue, Hakim became the banker for the Contra resupply operation and later the arms sales.

In the Shah's Iran, Hakim had become a successful broker of U.S.-made equipment by exploiting his relationships with high Iranian officials, for whom he served as briber and bagman.

He fled to the United States in 1979, just before the Shah's fall. Since then, his business interests had included security systems, satellite image processing, condominiums, and a chain of Oriental delicatessens.

As he later explained to Congress, he viewed his involvement in Iran-Contra as helping his adopted country, the United States, and his native land, Iran. He freely acknowledged that he stood to make a good deal of money in the process. It was, he seemed to be saying, the best of all possible worlds, a felicitous blend of patriotism and capitalism, the embodiment of the American dream.

Then there was Carl "Spitz" Channell, whose life and gaudy lifestyle would later be splashed across the television screen and the front pages of the nation's newspapers. A talented fund-raiser inspired by Ronald Reagan's pledge to help the Contras, he found his way to North and offered to help. Together they raised millions, mostly by playing on the fears of highly conservative and relatively obscure rich people, many of them elderly women. Though far to the right himself, Channell found the often uninformed conservatism of his targets alternately chilling and hilarious. They were, he said, paranoid, enthralled by secrecy. "They just loved to hide in closets and talk into cans with a string from one closet to the other." Channell considered himself a genius at raising money, until he saw Ollie North in action and realized he was a bush leaguer by comparison.

Check out the roster. A one-eyed tax preparer looking for adventure in the off-season. A haunted young man hoping to prove his manhood. A tarnished Air Force two-star. An ex-Iranian bagman. An outré fund-raiser who could persuade right-wing wahoos that by giving money they would stop hearing things that go bump in the night. The organization North was struggling to put together was like his high school track team back in Philmont. Whoever tried out made it.

In many ways, it was a hell of a team. North had been told, or so he thought, to create an organization that for a time could do for the Contras what until then had been done for them by the Central Intelligence Agency. This meant arranging for the purchase and shipment of weapons and ammunition. It meant airdropping supplies to rebels deep inside Nicaragua—arms, clothing, food, medicines, communications equipment. It meant training. It meant providing intelligence and tactical advice. It meant coming up with money to pay for all these things. It also meant persuading the Contras not to lose heart as the Congress went about deciding their fate.

The organization was always viewed—by North, Poindexter, and the others involved—as a stopgap measure, a way to keep the Contras in business until Congress revisited the issue, as it invariably did, and the CIA could take up where it left off prior to Boland. That point was often lost in the ambient noise of Iran-Contra. North was not running a secret war so much as he was managing a skin-of-the-teeth holding action.

He was, in his way, as unprepared for what he was being asked to do under his interpretation of body and soul as Rob Owen. Most revealing of his amateur status was his response early in the game when Casey told him to use a wire transfer to send money to the rebels. "What's a wire transfer?" asked North. Ignorant of the most rudimentary tradecraft of the covert world he was about to enter, he was akin to the man who, told by his wife to put something in the refrigerator, innocently asks, "Where's the refrigerator?"

Chuck Krulak, named Commandant of the Marine Corps in March 1995, described North best. He was a Marine infantry officer, a status that makes all things possible. The best Marine officers, no matter their rank, are second lieutenants at heart, ready to storm any beach, charge any hill, take out any pillbox. One wonders what it cost North in self-esteem in June 1986 when he finally sent a thinly veiled SOS to Poindexter, the first of several, declaring his exhaustion and confessing that the whole thing was becoming too much for "one slightly confused Marine LtCol."

All North was being asked to do was figure out how to arrange a wire transfer and, by the way, construct a miniaturized version of the Central Intelligence Agency to take care of the Contras for a year or so. Use anyone and anything you can scrape up. Oh, and while you're at it, take over this Iranian thing.

Against all odds, he did it. He roped in Secord and Hakim, signed up Spitz Channell and young Rob Owen, called on some old Vietnam buddies. Between them they bought a ship, secured some vintage planes, created a ragtag air force, built an airfield, established a communications network, raised money, purchased arms from China, from some Iron Curtain countries, and wherever else they could get them. Then they managed to deliver most of them. There were some blunders along the way, but two years later, when Congress again reversed itself and the CIA was allowed back in the action, the Contras were still alive.

Body and soul.

On Tuesday morning, July 7, 1987, the joint congressional committee investigating the Iran-Contra affair gathered in the Senate Caucus Room for the first day of North's testimony. The historic chamber, site of the Senate Watergate hearings fourteen years earlier, was charged with indignant bluster and delicious anticipation, as if a long-awaited public hanging were at hand. North had prepared an opening statement in which he hoped to put his actions in context, to explain why he had acted as he had. But the panel's cochairman, Senator Daniel Inouye, a Hawaii Democrat, declared that he would have to wait two full days to deliver it since he had not filed it forty-eight hours in advance, as required by the rules. The decision was a bully-boy tactic, designed to intimidate North, though Inouye described it as ensuring that the rule of law prevailed.

Had North been prone to intimidation, Inouye's ruling might have nudged him over the edge because the scene that first morning was not encouraging. Taking his place at the witness table, he looked up at twenty-six members of Congress—eleven senators and fifteen representatives—arrayed in two semicircular tiers above him. In the days preceding his testimony, when he was still little more than a name and a face to the public, several had said they expected nothing but lies from him. Aides hovered behind the members, a scant fraction of the 181 congressional staffers assigned to the probe. Unseen but omnipresent was a special prosecutor named seven months earlier, in his pocket a commissioning letter that contained but a single name: Oliver L. North.

But North was not intimidated. He had learned some hard lessons in the previous seven months as he watched Ronald Reagan beat a hasty retreat from Iran-Contra, leaving his wounded strewn on the battlefield. Now, the terrain at last to his liking, North was taking no prisoners. He rose from his seat to be sworn, Bud McFarlane's old silver oak leaves tacked to his shoulders, Annapolis ring gleaming from his finger, Vietnam War medals covering his chest like body armor. At that moment, he seemed to embody his generation, the portion to which he belonged; to the others, the bright people of that same generation, unblooded, faking egg allergies, he must have seemed an avenging angel, their worst nightmare come true. At least, as Hemingway said, how pretty to think so. As for North's congressional inquisitors, they were left for dead when he completed his testimony eight days later.

When North finally made his opening statement, he put Congress on trial.

"The Congress," he began, "must accept at least some of the blame in the Nicaraguan freedom fighters' matter. Plain and simple, the Congress is to blame because of the fickle, vacillating, unpredictable, on-again, off-again policy toward the Nicaraguan democratic resistance, the so-called Contras. I do not believe that the support of the Nicaraguan freedom fighters can be treated as the passage of a budget. I suppose that if the budget doesn't get passed on time again this year, it will be inevitably another extension of another month or two.

"But the Contras, the Nicaraguan freedom fighters, are people—living, breathing young men and women who have had to suffer a desperate struggle for liberty with sporadic and confusing support from the United States of America.

"Armies need food and consistent help. They need a flow of money, of arms, clothing, and medical supplies. The Congress of the United States allowed the Executive to encourage them to do battle and then abandoned them. The Congress of the United States left soldiers in the field unsupported and vulnerable to their Communist enemies."

During questioning, a committee lawyer probed the Vietnam factor, suggesting that the loss of the war may have influenced North's actions. North snapped: "The war wasn't lost on the battlefield. It was lost right here, in this city." Later the same day, Don Moore, a fellow Kilo Company platoon commander, said, "I feel like he's taken his battle right to the source."

North and Poindexter believed that the Boland Amendment around which the allegations of wrongdoing against themselves and others pivoted, contained a loophole that sanctioned their actions. Their position was not indefensible.

Boland II, as it was known, was not a stand-alone measure, but rather one paragraph in a four-inch-thick appropriations resolution that included nine of the thirteen spending bills needed to fund the government for fiscal year 1985. Signed into law by the President on October 12, 1984, nearly two weeks after the new fiscal year had begun, Boland II read in full as follows:

> During fiscal year 1985, no funds available to the Central Intelligence Agency, the Department of Defense, or any other agency or entity involved in intelligence activities may be obligated or expended for the purpose or which would have the effect of supporting, directly or indirectly, military or paramilitary operations in Nicaragua by any nation, group, movement or individual.

In floor debate prior to passage, the sponsor, House intelligence committee chairman Edward P. Boland, said, "There are no exceptions to the prohibition." The Massachusetts Democrat's successor as intelligence committee chair, Indiana Democrat Lee H. Hamilton, in damning testimony at the 1990 Poindexter trial, left no doubt as to the "entity" at which the measure was aimed: "We drafted the Boland Amendment broadly for precisely the reason that we wanted to cover the National Security Council."

All of which begged a question: why not say so instead of resorting to the murky "any other agency or entity involved in intelligence activities"?

In truth, the Boland Amendment was a slim reed upon which to allege a violation of the law, as the minority report of the Iran-Contra congressional investigating committees made clear.

The minority report was in many ways a partisan Republican effort to insulate Reagan from the actions of his underlings. Even so, it contained several perceptive passages, not least its contention that the NSC staff was covered by neither the letter nor the spirit of Boland II, despite claims to the contrary from Boland, Hamilton, and others.

The minority insisted that Boland II was a product of compromise, not the result of a single spirit animating Congress, an assertion borne out by the record. Even with that caveat, the minority maintained that the legal issue turned not on the question of what Congress meant, but on what it said and, more important, what it failed to say.

A sweeping, all-inclusive prohibition would not have been unprecedented or difficult to draft. As evidence, the minority cited a number of previous measures, notably the landmark Clark Amendment of 1976, similar in intent to Boland in that it cut off aid to a guerrilla force, in that instance Angolan rebels. The Clark language read as follows:

> Notwithstanding any other provisions of law, *no assistance of any kind* may be provided for the purpose, or which would have the effect, of promoting or augmenting, directly or indirectly, the capacity of any nation, group, organization, movement or individual to conduct military or paramilitary operations in Angola [author's italics].

Why didn't Congress simply insert "Nicaragua" in place of "Angola," thus removing any element of ambiguity and depriving the NSC of the loophole subsequently exploited by North and Poindexter? In choosing not to include the NSC staff by name or to cover it with a flat government-wide ban, what signal was it sending? As the minority asserted in its report, "Congress obviously knows how to write an airtight prohibition when it wants to."

Congress did more than confuse the issue with fuzzy language. Boland was not a statute that remained in force unless repealed. As a rider to an appropriations bill, it had limited duration, in this case the twelve-month period ending September 30, 1985. Said Theodore Draper, "The one-year span of the amendment was an invitation to seek ways of evading it until the next appropriation bill came around."

Having passed Boland in a fit of pique following public disclosure of the CIA's role in the mining of Nicaraguan harbors, Congress tipped its willingness to reconsider the prohibition once its ire had cooled. The same appropriations bill contained language promising the administration an expedited vote on a new $14 million Contra aid package anytime after February 28, 1985.

In other words, angry at Bill Casey, Congress retaliated against the Contras, sentencing them to a term of twelve months without American aid while holding open the possibility of parole after five months.

That action was typical of a Congress in which the balance of power was shifting to Vietnam-era members, the chronological peers of Mc-

Farlane, North, and Poindexter, notably the congressional class of 1974, men who had never seen service in Vietnam or anywhere else. In their defense it can be said that having never set foot on a battlefield, they may not have fully appreciated what it meant to be bloody, hungry, and out of ammunition. If they did understand, as North and McFarlane most certainly did, then their fitful support of the Contras lacked any semblance of morality, integrity, or humanity.

Though sharing the belief that press coverage had undercut the Vietnam war effort, McFarlane and Poindexter as national security advisers dealt differently with reporters.

McFarlane had the more mature view of the press, seeing it as more sinned against than sinning during Vietnam. He also took as an article of faith from Vietnam a belief that high-risk policies rarely succeed without popular support. As a result, he cultivated reporters in hopes that administration policies would get a fair hearing.

Poindexter, reflecting the standard post-Vietnam military view of the press, considered most reporters biased or stupid, without redeeming social value. He had little time for them, which led to one of his biggest blunders, the failure to prepare in advance a press strategy in the event the Iranian arms sales were exposed.

The China opening offers an object lesson. In 1971, during the waning days of direct American involvement in Vietnam, Henry Kissinger secretly traveled to China, the nation whose allegedly predatory designs on Indochina and the rest of Southeast Asia had led the United States to sacrifice nearly sixty thousand men.

He did not go empty-handed. According to McFarlane, the gifts Kissinger bestowed on the Chinese included highly sensitive intelligence information regarding their primary adversary, the Soviet Union, just as the United States, on Poindexter's watch, passed along intelligence on Iraq to the Iranians.

When Kissinger's trip became public knowledge, he was not indicted; he was hailed as a hero and genius, even though Americans were still fighting and dying in Vietnam and several hundred others, John McCain among them, were rotting away in various POW camps.

Why did the China and Iran initiatives play so differently with the American public? In the case of the former, the administration told the story in its own way, in its own time, presenting it as a triumph, the Henryman, playin' the China card.

No doubt Kissinger, with his knack for public relations and self-promotion, also had a press strategy worked out in case the China initiative came to light prematurely. Not Poindexter. For all his talent as a manager, his hostility toward the press blinded him to one of the most obvious needs of the high-stakes Iranian venture, a plan for telling the people why its government had acted as it had. The Tower Board blamed this failure on Don Regan, but Poindexter later conceded in an interview that the fault lay with him.

In those early days, the initial furor notwithstanding, many people still had an open mind. Harvard presidential scholar Richard Neustadt, a lifelong Democrat, was one of them. He lamented the arms sales and wondered how the administration could have mortgaged its credibility to such an erratic regime. But he also raised a provocative question: "When was the last time we impeached a President for trying to bring American boys home?"

It wasn't enough to be willing to listen, though. There had to be something to hear, a full explanation and a coherent statement of policy, not just unconvincing denials and people running around saying it was all McFarlane's fault—the administration's, though not Poindexter's, first line of defense.

Even when explanations and policy statements were offered, however, administration spokesmen, operating in crisis conditions, were inadequately briefed on what had transpired. As a result, each new revelation rocked them back on their heels, further eroding their credibility.

Poindexter's glaring oversight led to the fiasco that followed the election day exposure of the operation, first the denials, then the grudging, limited confirmations, finally the low point of those early days, the Reagan press conference on November 19.

Three times in the course of that session Reagan denied that Israel had been a participant in the arms deals even though Poindexter and Don Regan had confirmed the Israeli role at earlier press briefings. "I'll have to talk to him about that," said the befuddled Reagan when a reporter told him what Regan had said. Less than thirty minutes after the news conference ended, the White House put out a terse statement that said, indeed, there had been third-country involvement, meaning Israel.

The way the administration was falling all over itself, it was hard to avoid the feeling that someone was guilty of something. And that was more than a week before anybody had heard of the diversion.

The public spectacle that attended the dramatic exposure of the diversion by Edwin Meese in the White House press room on November 25, 1986, riveted the nation. Moments before, President Reagan had announced that North had been fired and Poindexter had resigned. Then the President turned the mike over to Meese and took cover, like Don Pardo announcing the players at the start of a "Saturday Night Live" broadcast, a disembodied voice bearing no responsibility for the hijinks to follow.

For the next hour or so, Meese did all that Reagan could have asked of him. He singled out North as the mastermind of the diversion, implicated Poindexter and, to a lesser extent, McFarlane. Most critically, he insulated and exculpated the President. "The President knew nothing about it until I reported it to him," said the Attorney General when asked the inevitable Watergate question, What did the President know and when did he know it? Meese was on safe ground in his response. Number one, the President had told him he was unaware of the diversion. Number two, you could say Reagan didn't know about a lot of things and the odds that you were right would be pretty heavily in your favor.

Before Meese finished doing the President's job for him, he said that the Justice Department was looking into the legality of the diversion to determine whether there was "any criminality involved" on North's part.

Reagan phoned North later that afternoon. He was huddled in a hotel room with Secord and Secord's lawyer, Thomas Green, when the call came through. He had raced over there after the news conference.

North stood at attention as the President's voice came on the line. "Ollie," he said, "you have to understand, I just didn't know."

And then Reagan, whose Attorney General had just raised the prospect of criminal charges against North, called North "a national hero."

Poindexter watched the press conference on television from the West Wing office he was about to vacate. Linda, a seminarian about to be ordained an Episcopal priest, was with him. Neither said much as the President, then Meese, held forth. Poindexter did not feel angry. If anything, he had a sense of frustration, of missed opportunities. Right to the end he and North had been working feverishly to spring one last hostage. More than anything else, he felt tired. He had been in the White House five and a half years. When Meese finished, he picked up his briefcase, and he and Linda went home.

Earlier in the day, he had reported to the President in the Oval Office and tendered his resignation. Reagan said something to the effect that Poindexter was acting in the grand tradition of the ship's captain taking blame for any disaster that befalls his vessel. Other than one Christmas card, he did not hear from Reagan again for the next six years.

A day later, the NSC staff said good-bye to Poindexter in the Indian Treaty Room. They presented him with his cabinet chair. George Bush stopped in to say so long. Ronald Reagan did not, having already flown off to Santa Barbara for the Thanksgiving holidays.

Admiral Jim Holloway took Poindexter to lunch at the Metropolitan Club within a day or so of his departure.

"John, who's your lawyer?" asked Holloway.

Poindexter was startled. "I don't follow you," he replied. "I haven't done anything wrong. Why do I need a lawyer?"

At first North thought the diversion was "a neat idea," a phrase that seemed to put it into the same category as a Coke date, cruising Main Street, or kidnapping the Army mule. Later, when it had taken on a more sinister cast, he called it the deepest, darkest secret of the Reagan administration, "the secret within a secret."

Whatever it was, it brought the Reagan administration to its knees. Nearly everyone developed amnesia or ran for the hills, presumably to get a better view of North, McFarlane, and Poindexter twisting, à la Watergate, slowly, slowly in the wind.

What was the diversion?

By early 1986, arms from U.S. arsenals were being shipped to Iran through various middlemen. The Department of Defense, which supplied the weaponry, was setting the price paid by the intermediaries, who then sold the arms to Iran at a higher price, the difference their profit. No one tried to bargain with the Pentagon. In a seller's market, DOD got what it asked. Had it demanded more, no doubt it would have gotten more.

The diversion, or the "residuals," as North persisted in calling them, came not from the Pentagon's pockets but from the pockets of the middlemen, who were making healthy profits and offered little complaint. In a way, it was a form of tithing. North, at least, appears to have seen it that way. As a result, the Contras got a few million bucks.

There were problems, as even North has acknowledged. The Iranians, who supported the regime in Managua, might well have gone berserk when they found out that their money was being skimmed to aid the Contras. Berserk Iranians were not in anyone's interest, especially American hostages.

There were a host of legal and accounting problems as well. The diverted profits were deposited in Swiss bank accounts maintained by

Secord and Hakim, who in turn transferred a portion, an estimated $3.8 million, to the Contras. But was the money theirs to transfer, as they and North maintained? Or did the funds belong to the United States, as the Democratic majority on the joint congressional panel insisted? If so, a whole host of legal issues came into play.

Years later, in his autobiography, North had another neat idea. He wondered if Meese's dramatic exposure of the diversion might have actually been a switch on the switch.

The administration chose to focus almost exclusively on the "diversion," and there was certainly a lot to be gained by presenting it that way. This particular detail was so dramatic, so sexy, that it might actually—well, *divert* public attention from other, even more important aspects of the story, such as what *else* the President and his top advisers had known about and approved. And if it could be insinuated that this supposedly terrible deed was the exclusive responsibility of one mid-level staff assistant at the National Security Council (and perhaps his immediate superior, the national security adviser), and that this staffer had acted on his own (however unlikely *that* might be), and that, now that you mention it, his activities might even be *criminal*—if the public and press focused on that, then maybe you didn't have another Watergate on your hands after all. Especially if you insisted that the President knew nothing about it [North's italics].

McFarlane and Poindexter were like hotshot young reporters who perform brilliantly running down a high-profile scandal but have problems with the more mundane aspects of their job, explaining the impact of the new master water-and-sewer plan or handling a breaking story on deadline. In a word, they lacked seasoning when they were elevated to the position of national security adviser. Seasoning cannot be taught, nor is it a function of talent or capacity for hard work, both of which McFarlane and Poindexter had in abundance. It is a function of experience, time in grade.

Both men also had individual failings. If McFarlane had personality flaws, Poindexter had blind spots.

He placed too much trust in the system. Though North troubled him at times, Poindexter believed that he wouldn't have been at the NSC if he couldn't do the job. In effect, he saw him much as he saw his old executive officer, Will King, back when Poindexter took command of the *England* in 1974.

It was a case of mistaken identity. King was cool and capable, but he knew his limits and did not overreach. Until the end, the notion of limits, particularly personal ones, limits that might apply to *him*, was not on North's disk.

Then there was the nature of the duties and responsibilities heaped on North. One suspects that had King been asked, as North was, to handle the Contra and Iranian accounts, in addition to the antiterrorism portfolio, he would have said, Skipper, we've got to talk about this. By contrast, North saluted, executed a smart about-face, and galloped off in search of the ever-elusive Garcia.

Because it simplified his life, Poindexter also allowed Shultz and Weinberger to avert their eyes from Iran. After venting his objections to the Iranian initiative, Shultz told Poindexter that he wanted to know only what he needed to know. Poindexter complied, interpreting Shultz's words narrowly. Thus, when everything fell apart, Shultz complained that he had been cut out of the loop. Weinberger took a walk as well. The Tower Board saw the actions of the two senior cabinet members for what they were:

> . . . Secretary Shultz and Secretary Weinberger in particular distanced themselves from the march of events. Secretary Shultz specifically requested to be informed only as necessary to do his job. Secretary Weinberger had access through intelligence to details about the operation. Their obligation was to give the President their full support or, if they could not in conscience do that, to so inform the President. Instead, they simply distanced themselves from the program. They protected the record as to their own positions on this issue. They were not energetic in attempting to protect the President from the consequences of his personal commitment to freeing the hostages.

Theodore Draper, in *A Very Thin Line,* makes a similar point. He suggests that the two cabinet secretaries, their advice rejected, should have taken their cue from Cyrus Vance, President Carter's Secretary of State, who resigned to protest the ill-fated 1980 Iranian hostage rescue mission.

"This precedent was not followed by Shultz and Weinberger," says Draper, "with the result that they permitted months to go by without doing much of anything to prevent or protest against what they knew to be wrong. Weinberger merely sulked in self-imposed silence. Shultz at least woke up in the last days of November 1986 and . . . compelled President Reagan and Attorney General Meese to face the issue."

Having assiduously "protected the record" of their involvement, Shultz and, to a lesser extent, Weinberger emerged at the congressional hearings as heroes. Thanks in no small measure to Poindexter.

For one thing, he allowed them to give the Iran initiative a wide berth because it dovetailed with his desire to carry out the President's wishes without constantly being challenged and second-guessed. In addition, it corresponded with his belief that the operation needed to be kept secret since State and Defense were almost as prone to leaks as the Hill. As statutory members of the cabinet, moreover, Shultz and Weinberger could be compelled to testify by Congress, so the less they knew the better.

Had he even the mildest instinct for self-preservation, Poindexter would not have permitted Shultz and Weinberger to steal away so easily, if only to ensure that the blame was spread around should the operation fail.

There was a more crucial reason for keeping Shultz and Weinberger in the lineup. They were the President's senior foreign policy advisers. He needed to hear their counsel even if it cut against the grain of his policies. And he needed to keep hearing it whether he liked it or not, not because they were right, which they were, but because a President, any President, must consistently battle the isolation of the White House by aggressively exposing himself to strong conflicting views.

In Poindexter's defense, the last time Ronald Reagan had heard strong conflicting views on a major national security issue, it led to policy drift, immobilization, uncertain execution, and 241 dead Americans.

(Years later, when many more facts were in, it became clear that Ronald Reagan's top aides had not been kept as much in the dark as they claimed in 1986 and 1987. Lawrence Walsh, the Iran-Contra special prosecutor, went so far as to gain an indictment of Weinberger in 1992 on charges of perjury and making false statements. Walsh stopped just short of doing the same to Shultz. George Bush pardoned Weinberger prior to his trial.)

Poindexter can be faulted in another way. He had no real understanding of or appreciation for the way the American political system worked. He was neither a martinet nor a zealot. He had no agenda of his own, either. But he had an idealized view of how Congress was supposed to operate that had barely progressed beyond high school civics. The real Congress did not work that way at all. He saw it as cumbersome, unresponsive, preening, sycophantic, self-serving, at times corrupt, which fit neatly with his experience working for Jim Holloway and the Vietnam-era biases of his own generation of military men. Interestingly, his experiences in the service did not mirror those of his fellow soldiers who served in Vietnam. At the same time, their hostility infected him, entering his system without his knowing it, like a germ.

He did not try to fight it off. As smart as he was, he did not have an aggressive, challenging intelligence, especially on matters that were of marginal interest to him. Congress is corrupt. The press has no redeeming social value. Had he probed these supposed verities with one-tenth the vigor with which he studied gamma rays and thulium compounds, he might have discerned, as McFarlane had, that Congress and the press were not so easily pigeonholed. Congress could be an ally. The press might give you a fair shake, especially if you took time to explain what you were doing and why.

But Poindexter did not question his preconceptions. He gave in to them without a fight, let them color his attitudes and his actions. So programmed, he said, Fine, someone other than me can deal with Congress. I'll get someone else to handle the press. As he once said, I don't do things I don't do well.

Nor did it ever occur to him, as it had to McFarlane, that the ultimate safeguard of American democracy might be the messiness and ponderous pace by which Congress goes about its constitutionally mandated duties. As McFarlane later put it, "How in the dickens do you get to graduate from the Naval Academy first in your class and not understand the separation of powers?"

Having picked up the Vietnam virus from others, Poindexter nevertheless failed to heed the most important lesson of the American tragedy in Indochina. If you can't persuade Congress and the people that your policy makes sense, you'd better take another look at the policy.

If Poindexter's trust in the system caused him to mistake Ollie North for Will King, that same mind-set led him into an even more disastrous blunder. He confused Reagan with a President who knew what he was doing. It became a false syllogism. Presidents understand the issues, formulate plans of action, make clear-cut decisions, issue unambiguous orders. Ronald Reagan is President. Therefore, therefore, therefore. Q.E.D.

In Poindexter's area of responsibility, national security, Reagan rarely did any of those things. Beirut was a stark example of presidential dithering, setting the table for Iran-Contra, national policy falling victim to diverse interpretations of what the President said, didn't say, or seemed to say. Poindexter's mistake was thinking Reagan meant what he said.

"As NSC adviser, Poindexter made his agenda the implementation of what he felt was in the mind of Ronald Reagan," writes Roy Gutman in *Banana Diplomacy*.

If that was the case, and there seems little doubt that it was, Poindexter was just doing what came naturally. Though he had been a successful commanding officer, he was best known for his talents as a senior staff officer—to three Secretaries of the Navy, to Jim Holloway, Bill Clark, and McFarlane. His value to them was not simply that he was well-organized, but that he often knew before they did what they wanted—Radar O'Reilly with an Annapolis sheen. The problem was, even Henry Blake was less ditzy than Ronald Reagan.

Of course, Poindexter had lots of clues to Reagan's thinking, at least when it came to the Contras and the hostages. He then took Reagan at his word because Poindexter had an almost childlike belief that the system worked, that the American form of government was no more capable of depositing a dolt in the Oval Office than the Navy was in assigning him an executive officer who couldn't run a ship. (Somehow the Congress escaped inclusion in this act of faith, which may say as much about the Congress as it does about Poindexter.) The incongruity of Poindexter's high-handedness is that he alone among the President's most senior aides managed to ignore the evidence of his own eyes and cling to the notion that Reagan was a man to be taken seriously, not manipulated for his own good. Before he learned better, Don Regan explained his M.O. as White House chief of staff as letting Reagan be Reagan. Only Poindexter, the last pilgrim, adhered to that dictum to the bitter end.

The question that set loose the impeachment demons and threatened to raise Iran-Contra to Watergate proportions was whether the President knew about the diversion. The investigators never got closer than Poindexter, everyone's number-two man suddenly making like Harry Truman. "The buck stops here, with me," he told the congressional committees.

If there is more to tell, he will probably take it to the grave, which leaves plenty of room for speculation. First, there's the question of whether he recognized just how explosive the diversion was likely to be if it ever got out. He said he did, which was precisely why he said he kept it secret from the President. But that is debatable. Up to then he had displayed little sensitivity to political realities. Equally plausible is that he viewed using the Ayatollah's money to help the Contras as a magnificently conceived sting operation, not something that threatened the very existence of the Reagan presidency.

Assuming he comprehended the gravity of the diversion, he may well have assumed that Bill Casey, who enjoyed a closer relationship to Reagan, had told the President about it. Or maybe Poindexter told the President and Reagan simply forgot. North and McFarlane consider that a likely explanation. North, in his autobiography, says the

President "didn't always know what he knew." Said McFarlane, less gingerly, "John was in a terribly awkward position if he told him, because it is very likely that Reagan would have taken that knowledge and would have said, 'Great! Gee, that's terrific.' And with the attention span of a fruit fly, it would have been out of his mind in about thirty seconds."

That may be as close to the answer as anyone will ever come.

As Secretary of the Navy, Jim Webb knew he was in a no-win situation. Poindexter, a man he liked and respected, had been his boss during the tenures of his predecessors John Chafee and John Warner. North, whom he disliked, was widely reputed to be an old rival, the press early on having picked up on their boxing match of twenty years earlier. Webb also realized that a number of matters relating to Poindexter and North could find their way to his desk—mostly relating to pay and retirement. He already felt himself under pressure from high-ranking naval officers at the Pentagon to return to Poindexter the third star he had lost when Reagan fired him. That would allow Poindexter to retire as a vice admiral rather than as a rear admiral. The difference in pension benefits was not much, but the status three stars conferred within the naval community was considerably greater than two stars. A few weeks after Webb took office, Poindexter requested a meeting, saying he wanted to explain his role in the naming of Carl Trost as CNO over Frank Kelso. Webb expected the issue of retirement rank to come up, but it didn't. Instead, Poindexter said his piece about Trost and Kelso, then the two men reminisced about old times. Afterward, Webb said, "Poindexter's a good guy," but he declined to step into the retirement debate. It was, he reasoned, too soon. The full dimensions of Poindexter's Iran-Contra role had yet to take shape. Plus, there was no way Congress at that early date was going to approve Poindexter for three stars even if Webb pushed it.

North was a different story. Once Webb became Secretary of the Navy, press inquiries about North expanded geometrically. Webb refused to say anything about their relationship or his negative feelings about his classmate. His standard answer to reporters was that North had been a brave and resourceful Marine officer in Vietnam, a truthful if narrow response.

But several things troubled Webb. Reviewing North's official Marine Corps biography, which is routinely written by the subject himself, Webb felt that it was seriously inflated. It said, for example, that North had served as a company commander in combat, which was not true. The bio also said that he had participated in both "conventional and unconventional warfare operations" in Vietnam. There were no instances of unconventional warfare activities in North's record. However perilous, the duties of a rifle platoon commander do not fall into the unconventional category.

The most serious matter arose when Webb read press reports that said North had failed to list his hospitalization at Bethesda Naval Hospital on an FBI questionnaire that was part of his background check prior to reporting to the White House in 1981. The questionnaire specifically asked about psychiatric treatment, which Webb had reason to believe North had received. Moreover, as Webb well knew, lying on the form or withholding pertinent information was a felony under both civilian and military law. It occurred to Webb that he could, perhaps should, formally ask the Marine Corps to explain the apparent omission, an action that might well trigger court-martial proceedings against North on that point alone. He decided against it. A select House-Senate congressional panel and a special prosecutor were already investigating North. Gang tackling was not Webb's style. Whatever North had done would come out sooner or later. The decision made, Webb informed his staff that any matters relating to North should be directed to the deputy secretary.

A few days after the diversion was exposed, Poindexter was called to testify before the House Armed Services Committee. It was the lame-duck period and John McCain was still a member of the panel, his swearing in as a senator still a month away.

Having heard that Poindexter planned to take the Fifth Amendment, he invited him to stop by his office prior to appearing before the committee. Poindexter showed up with his attorney, Richard Beckler, one of the city's premier criminal lawyers, Jim Holloway having explained the facts of life to his friend and former aide.

After his guests had been seated and served coffee, McCain said, "John, you can't become the first admiral in the history of the United States Navy to plead the Fifth."

Beckler responded for Poindexter, explaining that the admiral would explain everything in detail at the right time, but not that day.

McCain, unappeased, pressed his case: "John, you can't do it."

Poindexter said little, impassively sipped his coffee. The scene had an Alice-in-Wonderland quality, the Annapolis screw-off preaching to the model midshipman. A few minutes later, Poindexter walked into the hearing room, was sworn in, and asked a question. He refused to answer on the grounds that it might incriminate him.

Several months later, during a break in Poindexter's testimony at the congressional Iran-Contra hearings, NBC's Tom Brokaw asked McCain to explain his classmate's self-proclaimed decision not to tell Reagan about the diversion.

"I know John to be a man of the highest integrity," said McCain. "At the same time it is difficult to comprehend why he would not inform the President of activities of that magnitude. . . . I think he made a terrible mistake."

Afterward, an infuriated Mark Hill, by then cochairman of the Poindexter legal defense fund, called McCain in his Senate office and demanded to know how he could make such a statement.

Didn't you do the same kind of thing, working behind the President's back, when we were trying to get Congress to fund the carrier? asked the retired rear admiral.

McCain called Hill an old goat.

Question: What does Bud McFarlane have in common with Spam? As well as with nylon stockings? and Bill Cosby? and Curious George? and even the Golden Gate Bridge?

Answer: They are all observing their fiftieth birthday!

So read the invitation sent out by Jonny McFarlane for her husband's surprise birthday party on Sunday evening, July 9, 1987, at The Barns at Wolf Trap, an indoor-outdoor concert hall outside Washington. The suggested dress was denim.

The timing was auspicious. North had just completed four days of testimony on Friday, but would return to the witness table on Monday, the day after the party. McFarlane had testified in May, taking blame, trying to protect North, but still delivering damning testimony against him. Unknown to all but a few at the party, McFarlane had asked to testify a second time when North finished in order to challenge a number of his statements.

The 150 or so celebrants that night resembled a gathering of the Illuminati at a dude ranch, priestly vestments chucked aside in favor of Levi's, plaid shirts, and Weejuns, socks optional. They feasted on barbecued beef, corn on the cob, and other bunkhouse delicacies, washing it all down with icy bottles of yuppie beer, Heineken or Dos Equis.

Vice President Bush was the surprise celebrity guest. As his limousine and Secret Service entourage waited outside, he leaned against the bar, chatting easily with a parade of courtiers. Ex–rodeo cowboy Malcolm Baldrige, the Secretary of Commerce, and John Block, the guitar-strumming Agriculture Secretary, represented the cabinet, as did Susan Baker, the wife of Treasury Secretary Jim Baker. The administration's arms control elite turned out in force—Paul Nitze, Max Kampelman, Ed Rowny, and Bob Linhardt. Guests included two former national security advisers, Zbigniew Brzezinski and Brent Scowcroft, the latter destined to assume the position again in the Bush administration a year and a half later. Ken Duberstein and Craig Fuller of the White House staff were there, as was Mike Deaver, then awaiting trial on perjury charges; John Lehman, Jim Webb's predecessor as Secretary of the Navy; Wilma Hall, McFarlane's longtime secretary, and her daughter, Fawn, Heeder of a Higher Law, Siren of the Shredder. The McFarlane kids, Laurie, Melissa, and Scott, were there, as was old friend John Grinalds. The lobbying community was represented by Tom Korologos, of the powerhouse firm of Timmons and Company, a friend of McFarlane's since their days together in the Nixon White House. Representative Dick Cheney, a Wyoming Republican and an old McFarlane friend turned inquisitor by virtue of his membership on the congressional investigating committee, was accompanied by his wife, Lynn, head of the National Endowment for the Humanities. Tacked prominently to a notice board in the reception area were congratulatory telegrams from Richard Nixon, Gerald Ford, and Henry Kissinger.

The Capitol Steps, a comedy troupe of with-it Hill staffers whose musical parodies were all the rage in Washington that summer, provided customized entertainment, much of it poking fun at the Reagan administration, the guest of honor, and his embattled cronies. McFarlane loved it, as did Bush, who guffawed and slapped his thighs throughout the performance. The Capitol Steps broke out a new song for the occasion, sung to the tune of "Hooray for Hollywood," and with the refrain, "We'd do what Ollie would . . ." Their repertoire also included "Thank God I'm a Contra Boy" and "Bomb Tehran, Tehran," to the melody of "Qué Será, Será."

When his turn came to speak, McFarlane, surprised and touched, explained that Jonny had lured him to the party by telling him they were going to a Mexican restaurant. He was amazed, he said, that such a large assemblage managed to keep the party secret. Then he said:

"What I want to know is, where was all this conspiratorial talent when Ollie and I needed you?"

It brought down the house—no one laughed louder than Bush—but you half expected Lawrence Walsh, the Iran-Contra special prosecutor, to burst through the door, a star pinned to his chest, and haul the whole crowd off to the pokey.

*   *   *

When North tried to defend his Iran-Contra activities by insisting that he was only following orders, critics hurled his words back at him. He was, they said, seeking refuge in the so-called Nuremberg Defense, after the manner of German war criminals. The more literate of his detractors regularly trotted out Hannah Arendt's book on the trial of Adolf Eichmann, pointing to the passage in which she writes of the "banality of evil," as if the phrase epitomized North, as if all that kept him from being a Nazi butcher was the absence of orders or the right opportunity.

On hearing North make that defense, those more generously disposed to him were set to musing. Reagan had told him to hold the Contras together body and soul. What if Reagan had said something else. "Ollie, cure poverty." Or, "Ollie, I want to know, once and for all, is there or isn't there a God? You've got two months. I want a definitive answer." Can there be any doubt North would have attacked those projects with the same vigor and enthusiasm with which he pursued the Iranian and Central American initiatives?

What's important, of course, is what he did, or tried to do.

Oliver North tried to bring home six Americans who had been held hostage in Lebanon for periods ranging from several months to several years. At times he showed great resourcefulness, at other times he stumbled badly. Wearing his other hat, he attempted to keep a guerrilla army that was largely a creation of the United States in the field, which meant ensuring that they had beans, boots, Band-Aids, and bullets. Along the way he lied to Congress and may well have defied it, depending on how Boland II is interpreted. He also shredded documents, purportedly to protect the operation and those he felt would be in mortal danger if their involvement became known publicly. One suspects there was an element of self-protection involved as well.

Equally important is what he did not do. He did not gas Jews. Not even close. Anyone who does not understand the distinction is a fool. As for those who know the difference and persist in comparing North to a Nazi, one wonders what lies beneath such bluster and rhetorical overkill. Many, one suspects, are running scared, hoping to avoid a long overdue showdown with a part of themselves purposely and deservedly obscured for decades.

Something about which they would just as soon not have to answer tasteless questions.

EPILOGUE

I went down to the sacred store
Where I heard the music years before
But the man there said the music wouldn't play
In the streets the children screamed
The lovers cried and the poets dreamed
But not a word was spoken
The church bells all were broken
And the three men I admire most
The Father, Son and the Holy Ghost
They caught the last train for the coast
The day the music died.

—DON McLEAN, "American Pie"

At noon on January 20, 1989, George Bush was sworn in as the nation's forty-first President. An hour later, at Andrews Air Force Base, Ronald Reagan climbed the steps of a military transport bearing the Stars and Stripes of the nation over which he had presided for the previous eight years. At the top, he paused to wave to a somber crowd of military families gathered to bid him a final farewell. Engines roared. Within minutes he was flying home to California, leaving behind a mixed legacy. A robust if suspect economy. A strengthened national defense. Grenada. Beirut. Libya. Improved U.S.-Soviet relations. Tax reform. Iran-Contra. A song.

After resigning as Secretary of the Navy in February 1988, Jim Webb occupied himself with a number of projects—screenplays, an occasional speaking engagement, a new book. In March 1989 he was invited to give the keynote address at an international conference of journalists in Washington sponsored by an arm of the Reverend Sun Myung Moon's Unification Church. The other speakers included Ollie North. Webb, asked his speaking fee, replied, "Five dollars more than Ollie." The man on the other end of the line gulped. The next day, though, he called back. "Okay," he said, "$18,005." Webb, flabbergasted, spent the better part of a day mentally squandering the windfall. He saw a fishing boat, small but not too small, in his future.

Finally he called back, apologized, said he realized he had a previous engagement.

Not long after his resignation, he bought a condominium apartment to use as a writing office in a high-rise in Rosslyn, across the Potomac from Georgetown. The workspace was bright and spacious. He turned the lone bedroom into a weight room, but did not transfer the speed bag or the heavy bag that had hung from the ceiling of his old office. The best thing about the new place was the view. From his wide balcony, he could look across the Potomac at the stately granite structures of official Washington. Directly below, almost near enough to touch, stood the Marine Memorial, depicting five men raising the flag on a small Pacific island called Iwo Jima.

Webb, alone among the five principals in this book, opposed American military involvement in the Persian Gulf. In newspaper articles, television appearances, and testimony before Congress, he expressed his opposition early, often, and fiercely. One must go back to the Mexican War, he wrote in the *Wall Street Journal*, "to find a President so avidly desirous of putting the nation at risk when it has not been attacked."

On January 12, 1991, the day the Senate debated whether or not to authorize the use of force in the Gulf, he addressed a small antiwar gathering of military families, reducing abstractions to flesh and blood. "You don't use force, you send people," he declared. "You send young people who have dreams, who want a future."

The President "has been maneuvering the nation toward war for several months," he said. Bush fought with distinction in World War II, said Webb, "but with all due respect none of his children served in Vietnam."

After the speech, he led a token protest march on the Capitol, effectively severing what few ties he still had to the Republican Party establishment. He displayed neither concern nor remorse.

"I'm comfortable saying what I said," he insisted as he and about sixty other nonbelievers trudged through the cold, gray Washington morning. "The rest will take care of itself."

His opposition to the U.S. buildup in the Gulf was rooted in the Lebanon experience and the central lesson he had drawn from it: never get involved in a five-sided argument. He also insisted that U.S. involvement could set loose forces that might haunt American policy in the region for decades to come.

He did not say so directly, but he hinted strongly that the manipulation toward war he discerned on Bush's part was driven in large measure by domestic political considerations, that is, a desire for re-election.

This put Webb in an uncomfortable position. His latest novel, *Something to Die For*, was reaching bookstores as war was breaking out. The plot concerned the efforts of an ambitious Secretary of Defense to maneuver the nation into a military conflict on the Horn of Africa, along the Red Sea, a few hundred miles from the Persian Gulf.

Webb had completed the manuscript more than a year earlier, months before Saddam Hussein invaded Kuwait, but that point was conveniently overlooked during his book tour by interviewers eager to elicit his antiwar views. The internal tension was irresistible. A decorated Marine whose novel seemed to mirror current events and who just happened to be the Navy Secretary in the administration in which George Bush served as Vice President.

The book tour was unpleasant. He made it clear that whatever his prewar sentiments, he supported the troops now that hostilities were under way and that he would say nothing to undermine the war effort or the morale of the men and women on the ground in the Gulf. But that was rarely good enough.

The call-in shows were the worst. He stuck to his pledge not to challenge the war for the duration, but his earlier opposition followed him. He was called unpatriotic, a sissy, and a wimp. A caller in New York said he'd lost his guts. "I don't need some guy hiding behind a telephone in New York City willing to bleed to the last drop of somebody else's blood to talk to me about guts," an angry Webb responded.

A few months later, he returned to Vietnam for the first time since the war. He went with Senator Bob Kerrey, who left part of his leg there in the process of winning the Medal of Honor. Other than Vietnam, Webb and Kerrey, a moderate Democrat, had little obvious in common. They became friends when Webb offered his support after Republicans questioned the Nebraska senator's patriotism for opposing troop commitments in the Gulf.

Webb had long since gravitated toward the large Vietnamese community in the Washington area, many of them men and women who had arrived in the United States penniless but through hard work and entrepreneurial spirit moved into the middle class. Through them, he developed an abiding interest in the plight of the hundreds of thousands of Vietnamese suffering at the hands of the Hanoi regime because they had fought on the other side in the war or worked for the Americans.

He and Kerrey spent two days in Hanoi and a third in Ho Chi Minh City, formerly Saigon, before Kerrey headed home. During that time, they met with the prime minister and other senior government officials, Kerrey the heavyweight, Webb the inconspicuous corner man.

Webb stayed on for another four days by himself. Though certain he was being watched, he was shorn of his official escort once Kerrey left, which allowed him to poke around on his own.

Ho Chi Minh City, he found, was still a vibrant, exhilarating metropolis. But journalistic instinct and a novelist's eye took him below the surface where he discovered a depth of suffering that confirmed the grisly tales told by his Vietnamese-American friends. On a midnight visit to the old Saigon railroad station, he saw hundreds of destitute former South Vietnamese soldiers, sleeping on the sidewalks, denied jobs and medical care, preyed on by youth gangs. It was, he thought, a place without hope. He concluded, despite official disclaimers, that the government was practicing a form of blood guilt, disfranchising not just the men but their families through two and three generations.

One day he toured a museum devoted to American wartime atrocities. When he had seen enough, he sauntered over to a guard. "*Suc my*," he said, meaning "Never happened." He added, in English, "It's bullshit."

He walked the streets or traveled by cyclo, an updated rickshaw powered by a driver pedaling in back. He wore his old bush hat just as NVA veterans wore their pith helmets, as a badge of honor, and rolled his shirt sleeve up over the shoulder so his USMC tattoo was visible. "Hey, Marine, America number one," a passing cyclist shouted. People on street corners, old allies, some with makeshift artificial limbs, smiled and raised their hands in cautious little waves that resembled salutes. He smiled and waved back, began to think of the excursion as a kind of victory parade.

"Why did you come back?" asked his cyclo driver, a man about forty.

"Because I love Vietnam, because I feel so badly for the people who were my friends," he answered.

He felt a hand on his shoulder, turned, saw tears in the driver's eyes. "I knew you would come back," the man said.

Back home, he intensified his efforts on behalf of the disfranchised Vietnamese, writing and speaking about them, arranging demonstrations of solidarity, studying the language.

Since then, he has returned to Vietnam several more times. In 1992, he went back with Mac McGarvey, covering some of the same ground as before, Hanoi and Ho Chi Minh City, and other places he'd never seen during the war.

His visit in February 1993 was different. This time he traversed territory he knew well. An Hoa, Go Noi Island, the Arizona Valley. Squatting in hooches, he made friends with former enemies, debated old battles, told them about his latest project. He had turned *Fields of Fire* into a screenplay. He wanted to shoot it there, on hallowed ground, ground that had tasted holy blood. Snake's. McGarvey's. Tom Martin's. Dale Wilson's. By late 1994 he had obtained seed financing, assembled much of the cast, and was looking to begin filming in a matter of months.

Carlton Sherwood, a Pulitzer Prize–winning reporter friend of Webb, said in 1987 that Webb had taken the job as Secretary of the Navy because he felt an obligation to "walk the point" one last time. "He's on watch," said Sherwood, "for those who served and died with him."

Webb said something akin to that in a Memorial Day speech at Arlington National Cemetery the same year. "The first duty is to remember," he said. "Those of us who have seen war's ugliness know that a battlefield does not honor its dead. It devours them without ceremony. Nor does a battlefield honor heroes. It mocks their sacrifice with continuing misery and terror. It is for those who survived to remember sacrifice, and to honor our heroes."

Webb, it is said, can be mean, vindictive, self-important, and overbearing. Such criticism is not confined solely to critics. In truth, there are bothersome facets to his personality. His self-assurance is formidable, possibly rendering him less capable of even short forays into uncertainty such as he made at Georgetown Law years ago and which, however painful, led to explosive creative and personal growth. A classmate who knows Webb well, admires him, but harbors some of the standard ambivalence about him, put it this way: "No one can be as good as what's written about Jim, but he's almost that good."

A naval officer who worked with Webb at the Pentagon later said of him, "Webb was frozen in time as a Marine in Vietnam and he saw the whole world through those glasses." Others had recognized something of that same quality. Many others thought Webb had greater vision than his Pentagon colleague perceived, but his seeming fixation with Vietnam troubled even his friends, made them wonder if he would ever be able to move beyond it. After a while, though, still unsure he would ever be able to deepen his depth of field, they decided it didn't matter. If Webb never accomplished another thing, it was enough that he was their generation's Doctor T. J. Eckleburg, the oculist on the billboard in *The Great Gatsby* whose eyes looked down through enormous yellow spectacles on a valley of powdery gray ash and into the fractured soul of a nation. As far as these men were concerned, Webb's glasses had been ground just right, and they did not want the prescription changed anytime soon.

*   *   *

John McCain did not become the Republican vice presidential nominee in 1988, but as the Bush years began he continued to gain political momentum. He led the fight to win confirmation of his old mentor, John Tower, as Secretary of Defense, losing the battle, but earning new stature in the Senate.

In early October 1989, he won a grueling and notable legislative victory, defying both the Republican and Democratic leadership and forcing the repeal of a catastrophic health insurance law passed the previous year.

The final vote came in the early-morning hours of Saturday, October 7. Torie Clarke, his press secretary, had a freshly butchered 110-pound pig in the bathtub of her first-floor flat in Georgetown, shipped in from Iowa for a backyard barbecue that afternoon. Planned as a gathering of friends, it would now do double duty as a victory celebration. But McCain never showed up. Something bad was in the air.

Sunday, October 8, 1989, marked the zenith of McCain's astounding rise and the start of his even more rapid descent. That morning he was on CBS's "Face the Nation" discussing events in Panama. The *Washington Post* and the *Los Angeles Times* both ran op-ed pieces written by him on the health insurance issue. But back in Phoenix, the *Arizona Republic* led the paper with a story tying him to Charles Keating, the embattled savings-and-loan kingpin. Keating, his family, and associates had contributed $112,000 to McCain's House and Senate campaigns. Keating had also been McCain's friend. The main story was accompanied by two sidebars fleshing out the details of the relationship. The Keating story had been exploding around McCain for months, bracketing him like mortar fire. Now the gunners were firing for effect.

"I'm really sorry I didn't come to your party," said McCain as he met a hung-over Clarke outside the CBS News bureau that morning. "I was too depressed. I thought I would be a wet blanket."

"John, you couldn't be a wet blanket if you tried," laughed Clarke.

She was wrong. The next three years were among the most dispiriting of his life as he struggled to clear his name. He alternated between anger and depression, the resilience his Vietnamese captors failed to beat out of him only fitfully evident. What had been perhaps the most happy-go-lucky of senatorial offices was soon gripped by paranoia and an ever-deepening despondence. Everyone down to the lowliest intern still called him by his first name, but the excitement and joy of working for a senator with seemingly boundless prospects was gone, replaced by the aroma of impending political death.

He talked about not running again when he came up for reelection in 1992. By then his three younger children would be old enough to understand the vicious attack ads he had every reason to believe the opposition would mount. He did not know if he was up for the fight. Having survived five and a half years in prison, he seemed totally unprepared for the horror to arise and come at him again in a different form.

"This is the worst thing, the absolute worst thing that ever happened to me," he said at one point early on as aides gathered in his office.

"It can't be the worst thing," said one of those present, amazed at his use of the superlative.

"No," he said, "this is worse."

Carelessly choosing his friends, as he had in the case of publisher Duke Tully, he had stumbled into a scandal of immense proportions. Keating, it turned out, had built his financial empire on the life savings of elderly retirees, men and women who watched helplessly as their dreams were snuffed out along with the assets of Keating's Lincoln Savings and Loan, an Irvine, California, thrift.

The story was complicated, but the press found a tagline that simplified it. McCain and four other senators with ties to Keating were dubbed "the Keating Five." The label stuck, imputing to all the same degree of guilt even though it soon became evident that at least two, McCain and former astronaut John Glenn of Ohio, were far less culpable, if they were culpable at all.

The major allegation was that the five senators improperly pressured officials of the Federal Home Loan Bank Board to make concessions that might help Keating save his ailing savings and loan. The result was a delay in action against Lincoln that drained the accounts of depositors.

Stripped of the veneer of sleaze that coated the affair, McCain's defense of his actions was solid and credible. It didn't matter. The Keating Five label endured, shabby journalistic shorthand that made up in simplemindedness what it lacked in precision, five faces symbolizing a scandal that stood to cost taxpayers untold billions as a result of rampant thrift failures, $2.6 billion because of Lincoln alone, the costliest bailout ever. Stories routinely carried head shots of the five senators, adorned with boldface dollar figures showing the amount Keating had raised and contributed to their political organizations. News reports invariably referred to five "powerful" senators. At the time of the meetings that lay at the heart of the charges, McCain had been a senator for less than four months.

Eight weeks of public hearings before a joint House-Senate ethics committee ended in January 1991. On February 27, after six weeks of deliberations, the panel handed down its judgment. The interim had been filled with reports of political gamesmanship aimed mainly at keeping McCain, the lone Republican among the five, from getting off scot-free. Democrat Alan Cranston was hammered, the lawmakers concluding that he had engaged in "an impermissible pattern of conduct in which fund raising and official activities were substantially linked." McCain, at the other end of the culpability spectrum, received a mild rebuke for exercising "poor judgment." He pronounced himself vindicated and put aside lingering thoughts of retirement.

Later, Cindy McCain, normally cool and composed, burst into tears when asked how much the process had changed her husband. "I watched John just crumble," she said. Overnight, it seemed, he had gone from a youthful, dynamic senator to an anxious, distracted figure, slumped in a chair, finally looking his age, staring bleakly into space.

On paper, McCain had everything going against him as he hit the campaign trail for the 1992 election. A firestorm of antiincumbent sentiment was sweeping the nation, fueled by the savings-and-loan scandal. In a year dubbed by pundits "The Year of the Woman," his Democratic opponent was Phoenix community activist Claire Sargent. Former right-wing Republican governor Evan Mecham was running as an independent, his candidacy seemingly a vehicle to take vengeance on McCain for calling on him to resign from office in January 1988 following his indictment on six felony counts.

The Gulf War helped restore McCain's image. His military background made him much in demand as a television commentator, nationally and in Arizona, even as his integrity was being questioned daily in hearings televised gavel to gavel on C-SPAN. Now, the hearings behind him, he picked up the pace of his campaign. Soon White Tornado sightings were being reported all across the state. By early 1992, his poll standing had improved and his campaign coffers were filling up steadily.

As the campaign neared its end, Bush was plummeting everywhere, even in Arizona. McCain, according to election-eve polls, was expected to crush Sargent and Mecham. Taking nothing for granted, McCain spent the day before the election driving himself hundreds of miles, gorging on Whattaburgers, shaking every hand in sight.

On election night, friends and campaign workers gathered in his north Phoenix home. Four television sets were mounted side by side in the living room. The polls closed at 7:00 P.M. At 7:01 CBS declared him the winner. By 7:05 ABC and NBC had followed suit. CNN waited till 7:15. He had received a whopping 58 percent of the vote in a three-way race, but he seemed subdued. By then the dimensions of Bush's defeat had become clear.

About an hour later, he headed downtown to the GOP's election night headquarters at the Hyatt Regency. He waited until Bush made his concession speech, then entered the packed ballroom to chants of "six more years." In deference to Bush's loss, he kept his remarks brief. He thanked everyone who had helped him in the campaign and promised to work to break the gridlock in Washington. As he concluded, the "six more years" chant resumed. From deep in the crowd a lone voice shouted, "McCain for President."

A few weeks later, Cindy said, "He's doing a lot better now, but, no, he's not all the way back. I don't think he ever will be." Men and women he barely knew had rallied around him during the bad times, but he had been wounded by the silence of old friends. In Washington he began his second term working as feverishly as ever, seemingly content to be a good senator, his national ambitions dulled by the ordeal of the previous three years.

"I've seen a glow go out of him," said Cindy. "This is a guy that could reach for the stars and now he can't—or he won't."

In July 1994, he spoke at the commissioning ceremony in Bath, Maine, for the USS *John S. McCain*, an Aegis-class destroyer named after his father and grandfather. "They were my first heroes," he said, "and their respect for me has been the most lasting ambition of my life." The principal speaker that day was former President George Bush.

By mid-1994 McCain had gained fresh stature by challenging President Clinton's policies in Somalia, loudly warning against committing troops to the Balkans, and sounding the alert on North Korea's nuclear ambitions. To some he seemed the near-perfect candidate to challenge the President in 1996, but he brushed aside all approaches, even after a Republican tide swept the nation in November, giving the GOP control of both houses of Congress for the first time in forty years. Instead he left the field to a collection of retreads and wannabes, along with one fresh new face, retired Army General Colin Powell, former chairman of the Joint Chiefs of Staff.

Presidential prospects aside, McCain had become the GOP's unofficial spokesman on national security issues. In the fall he took the lead in opposing American intervention in Haiti, appearing almost daily on radio and television or in the newspaper. The notion that he might someday be Secretary of State or Defense in a Republican administration was beginning to take root. And there was renewed talk about Vice President.

Orson Swindle had urged him when he first took office as a congressman not to forget where he came from. He never did, as evidenced by the commencement address he gave in June 1994 to the Marine Corps Command and Staff College at Quantico.

He told the graduates that they faced new, uncharted dangers in the post–Cold War era, and that the old bipolar world, "where our enemy was indeed evil, but not irrational," was gone. "If I am nostalgic for it at all, it is only a middle-aged man's nostalgia for the time where his youth was spent," he said. "My world, after all, had its moments of cruelty and terror, some of which it was my fate to witness personally."

It was a moving speech, touching chords of honor, patriotism, and the historic gallantry of the Corps, but he delivered it in a businesslike manner. As he neared the end, though, his voice caught in his throat, and for a moment it seemed as if he might not be able to continue.

I have memories of a place so far removed from the comforts of this blessed country that I have learned to forget some of the anguish it once brought me. But my happiness these last twenty years has not let me forget the friends who did not return with me to the country we loved so dearly. The memory of them, of what they bore for honor and country, causes me to look in every prospective conflict for the shadow of Vietnam.

I do not let that shadow hold me in fear from my duty as I have been given light to see that duty. Yet it no longer falls to me to bear arms in my country's defense. It falls to you. I pray that if the time comes for you to answer the call to arms, the battle will be necessary and the field well chosen. But that is not your responsibility. Your honor is in your answer, not your summons.

In August 1994 his life was rocked again, once more clouding his future. Cindy narrowly escaped criminal indictment for siphoning off prescription drugs from a medical assistance team she had set up in 1989 to work in Third World countries. Her addiction dated back to the early days of the Keating Five scandal. The *Arizona Republic*, always among the harshest of McCain's critics, ran an editorial cartoon showing Cindy holding an emaciated black child upside down and shaking him over what appeared to be a field of corpses. "Quit your crying and give me the drugs," read the caption.

Bud McFarlane, Ollie North, and John Poindexter have spent much of the past few years in the federal courthouse in Washington. McFarlane testified in North's trial, North testified in Poindexter's, Poindexter testified in no one's, not even his own. All three were called numerous times for closed-door testimony by independent counsel Lawrence Walsh.

For a time following McFarlane's suicide attempt, reports of erratic behavior persisted. There was also the occasional ugly scene. One of the worst occurred at the MacArthur Theater in northwest Washington as he and his party—which included Jonny, his lawyer, Len Garment, and Garment's wife, Suzanne—were leaving after the movie. As they passed the candy counter a tall blond man threw a cup of 7-Up in McFarlane's face, momentarily blinding him. He thought at first it might be acid. Shouted his attacker, "The Contras are cutthroats and you're a murderer!" McFarlane lunged at him, but Garment restrained his client.

Friends continued to worry about him, especially as he kept giving mea culpa interviews. "Why does he keep doing this to himself?" asked Mike Deaver. After a small fire in the kitchen of McFarlane's new home in Georgetown, one of his former associates had to be assured that it was not, as the associate put it, "a self-immolation thing."

By then McFarlane had begun reweaving his life, dropping a stitch here and there, gradually mending the fabric. He opened a small consulting firm to advise clients on overseas investment opportunities. For a time he fretted about charging for his services. Entrepreneurship did not come naturally to him. Eventually he overcame his qualms and was still in business six years later, a globe-trotting broker of mutually advantageous marriages between underdeveloped nations and U.S. corporations. He refused to take payment from any of the governments he advised, viewing it as a conflict of interest to promote to them a project that might well be built by one of his corporate clients. In August 1994, he spoke with pride of a six-hundred-megawatt power plant about to be built in Baluchistan, a Pakistani province, by a consortium of American firms that he had put together. Similar projects were in the offing in Thailand, Malaysia, and a second site in Pakistan.

An improbable Capitol Hill press conference in February 1989 demonstrated the extent to which the Washington community had closed ranks around him. The occasion was the release of a study prepared by an ad hoc arms control commission that McFarlane had assembled two years earlier, at the height of his Iran-Contra troubles.

The fascinating aspect was not the report but the commission members, all major players in the national security community. The chairman was Harold Brown, Jimmy Carter's Defense Secretary. Members included Sam Nunn, the Georgia Democrat who chaired the Senate

Armed Services Committee; John Warner of Virginia, the committee's senior Republican; Democrat Les Aspin of Wisconsin, the House Armed Services chairman, later Clinton's Secretary of Defense; former Undersecretary of the Navy R. James Woolsey, later Clinton's CIA director; and Amos Jordan, from the Center for Strategic and International Studies, the high-powered Washington think tank that sponsored the study. Brent Scowcroft had been the cochairman but withdrew a couple of months earlier after being named George Bush's national security adviser.

There were obvious questions, none relating to arms control. What was Bud McFarlane doing with all those heavy hitters? Wasn't this the same Bud McFarlane who the previous March had walked into a courtroom a few blocks away and pleaded guilty to four misdemeanor charges of unlawfully withholding material from Congress? The Bud McFarlane who was slated to be the key prosecution witness at the trial of Oliver North in that same courthouse where he had copped his plea, where at that very moment the process of empaneling North jurors was under way?

On closer examination, it became clear that all the panel members were, to varying degrees, friends of McFarlane. At a teary farewell party after leaving the NSC in December 1985 he had described Nunn as the man most qualified to be President. He had worked closely over the years with Aspin. Warner was an old colleague from his days on the Hill. And on and on.

As the press conference commenced, Nunn and Warner, seated on either side of McFarlane, resembled a Praetorian guard, poised to hurl themselves across his body should the press raise the not entirely boorish question of why someone who had admitted misleading Congress was sitting in the very midst of some of its most august members. Everyone on the panel, in fact, seemed protective of him, even as they took turns lauding him as the driving force behind the study. No indelicate questions were asked, raising suspicions that the panel and the press were colluding in what might be called the reclamation of Bud McFarlane.

But why? There could be little doubt about McFarlane's motivations in assembling the group, what with his desire to remain a player and leave his imprint on foreign policy. The others, however, had nothing to gain, and arguably something to lose, by throwing in with him, given his post–Iran-Contra circumstances. As friends, they had already shown their concern in private ways. They did not need to be seen publicly embracing him. In a city where the first reaction to a runner stumbling is to pile on and knee him in the groin, it was enough that they had shunned efforts to ruin him.

As the press conference concluded, McFarlane drifted off to the side as commission members posed for photographers. "Come on in here, come on in here, Bud," said Aspin, his arm sweeping McFarlane into the picture, not just to the edge of the group, but into its very center. Standing there, McFarlane broke into a grin, a big grin, one that made the normally impossible journey from mouth to eyes.

Afterward, McFarlane greeted old friends in the press, elaborating on the report. As he departed, he was collared by NBC's agressive, at times abrasive, but always well-informed Andrea Mitchell. It wasn't the same as being ambushed by her at the White House, but it was something. It beat oblivion.

The press conference lent fresh perspective to McFarlane's birthday party at Wolf Trap two years earlier. At the time, it seemed almost sinister, a gathering of some of Washington's most powerful men and women, including a sitting Vice President, whooping it up and seemingly thumbing their noses at a nation then convulsed by scandal.

Looking back, it seems that something much different was going on that evening, something more personal, something real in a city whose touch with reality can never be taken for granted. It was as if all those luminaries, knowing full well that the story of the party would leak, as it did, had individually decided that Bud McFarlane, a man who had made grave mistakes, was worth saving even at some cost to themselves. By their presence they were saying, We don't know why he did what he did, and we don't excuse or condone it, but this is a decent man, someone we care about, not a ratfucker.

During his naval career John Poindexter had rarely returned to Odon, especially after his parents moved to nearby Mitchell in the early 1970s. In August 1987, though, a few weeks after testifying before the Iran-Contra congressional committees, he went back as grand marshal of the Old Settlers' Day parade, an annual event in the tiny southwestern Indiana town. Perched with Linda on the back of a baby-blue Ford Fairlane convertible, he seemed happy to be home. As fezzed Shriners darted about in miniature jalopies, he pulled out the bulky old Zippo lighter that had become a familiar prop at the hearings, raised it as if toasting wartime comrades, then fired his pipe. As smoke engulfed his features, the crowd cheered, which seemed to please him. For a day, at least, he could feel like a hero making a triumphant homecoming, rather than what he was, a man in need of old friends who remembered who he used to be.

As Poindexter was testifying about shredding and the destruction of documents, a local Washington television station inadvertently gave one of his old friends some free publicity. The station found a local firm that specialized in such work, filmed the company's industrial-strength shredder in action, and interviewed the owner, Bob Caldwell, never suspecting that Caldwell had been Poindexter's Academy roommate. That evening Poindexter and Caldwell took separate turns on the six o'clock news.

Throughout the long legal saga, Poindexter kept his own counsel, remained a private person. Other than at the courthouse, Poindexter sightings were rare. He grew a mustache. The press churlishly speculated that he was cultivating a new look for his trial. He did nothing to disabuse them of the notion. In fact, doctors at Bethesda Naval Hospital had discovered a golf-ball-sized tumor in a sinus cavity behind his left eye. To remove it, they had to cut from his lower eyelid, along the crease of his nose and through his upper lip and lay open half his face. The mustache started out as a temporary measure to cover the wound on his lip. But Linda liked it, so he kept it. The tumor was not malignant.

Poindexter never backed off on his assertion that he did not tell Reagan about the diversion, but in an October 1994 interview he added two fascinating pieces to the Iran-Contra puzzle.

The first had to do with North's admission during the 1987 congressional hearings that he lied to the House Intelligence Committee the previous summer about the extent of his activities in support of the Contras. At the time, Poindexter received a report from North on what he had told the panel. In response, Poindexter sent North a computer message that said, "Bravo Zulu," Navy parlance for "Well done." Poindexter's understanding of what North had said, however, did not include lying.

"There is a difference between withholding information from Congress and out-and-out lying," said Poindexter. "The intent was that he would answer their questions by talking around the issues and not out-and-out lie to the committee. And I think that's what he did," meaning bob-and-weave, not lie.

Poindexter was thus shocked in July 1987 when North testified during the congressional hearings that he had in fact lied to the committee the year before. Poindexter decided that for tactical reasons North's lawyer, Brendan Sullivan, had put him up to saying he had lied when he hadn't, "figuring that coming out and admitting that was a better defense."

Sometime after, Poindexter learned that Sullivan was not the culprit, that it was all Ollie. Poindexter said he asked North about his testimony, saying he assumed Sullivan had orchestrated it.

"He said, 'No, that's not the case. In fact, when I said that, Brendan kicked me under the table so hard I almost yelled,' " recalled Poindexter. "But then he was stuck with that."

Poindexter, shaking his head, added, "Ollie did it on his own, as he is sometimes prone to do, I think a sort of macho kind of thing."

North lied about lying? "Essentially," said Poindexter.

On its face, the second new element sounds preposterous, but it dovetails so neatly with Poindexter's style of management that there can be little doubt that it's true. At its heart lies the infamous McFarlane letters of September 1985 in which he told Lee Hamilton and others that he could state "with deep personal conviction" that neither he nor any member of the NSC staff had violated "the letter or spirit" of the Boland Amendment.

The letters plagued not only McFarlane but Poindexter as well, since he had referenced them—and thus effectively repeated McFarlane's overblown denials—in his written responses to renewed congressional queries about North a year later. Poindexter's apparent endorsement of the McFarlane letters, in fact, was cited in one of the charges on which he was later convicted. According to Poindexter, however, he had not even read the letters when he referenced them to Hamilton; he simply assumed them to be truthful, if artfully crafted, responses to the questions put to McFarlane.

Poindexter did not get around to reading the letters until the following year when he was preparing for his August 1987 congressional testimony. He was flabbergasted.

"I could not in my wildest imagination imagine that Bud had written what he did in '85," he said. "I could not imagine why Bud was being so specific about things that clearly were not true. . . . They were absolutely incredible letters."

In June 1988, while Poindexter was under indictment and awaiting trial, his son Tom entered Annapolis. Late in the afternoon, after most reporters covering Induction Day had left, the new class was sworn in on Tecumseh Court. As he administered the oath, Rear Admiral Ronald Marriott, the superintendent, was surrounded by a small group of senior Navy and Marine officers whose sons or daughters were entering that day. Poindexter, resplendent in his dress whites, was among them. After the public ceremony, he and the other ranking officers administered the oath privately to their offspring in the commandant's office. Tom looked young and wary as he kissed his parents good-bye and disappeared into Bancroft Hall. Poindexter looked proud. Tom was the second of his five sons to enter the Academy, the third to become an officer in the Navy. Alan had gone to Georgia Tech and been commissioned through the naval ROTC program.

There was a bizarre quality to Poindexter's participation that day. From his vantage point, and that of his family, he had dedicated his life to service to his country and paid a fearsome price. Yet he was dispatching his son along the same road he had taken three decades earlier. If he felt any bitterness, sensed the incongruity, it was not evident. He would later say that he had never felt anger toward the Navy, that the Navy had treated him well. If anything, watching Tom climb the ladder into Mother Bancroft, there was a sense of continuity, even, when he thought about it, renewal.

In April 1990 he was found guilty on five Iran-Contra charges and sentenced to six months in prison, the only figure in the scandal to pull jail time. He never served it. A series of appeals followed, which dragged on for the next two and one-half years. In May 1992 Tom graduated from Annapolis, taking his commission in the Marine Corps. President Bush spoke at commencement. There was a brief exchange as the Chief Executive handed Tom his diploma. Bush seemed momentarily taken aback. Later that day, a handwritten note bearing the gold presidential seal was delivered by White House courier to the Poindexter home in Rockville, Maryland.

> Just back from Annapolis
> May 27, 1992
>
> Dear John
>
> When that great looking son of yours, as he walked across the stage, proudly told me "I'm John Poindexter's son," I didn't have a chance to tell him this: "Ensign, you have a wonderful Dad."
>
> Please tell him that for me and tell him, too, that I'm so glad he told me who he is—I wish him all the best.
>
> Sincerely,
> George Bush

For years Poindexter held out hope that Reagan, and later Bush, would pardon him. Not because he believed he was guilty, but just to end the financial drain and let him get on with his life. Through it all, the trial and the appeals that followed, he maintained his dignity, never became a handwringer. Working out of his home, he started a small software company. He wrote the programs; a partner handled the marketing. Linda became associate pastor of a church in Chevy Chase, Maryland. Life went on.

In November 1991 his conviction was reversed by a federal appeals court that split two to one in its ruling. A year later, in October 1992, special prosecutor Walsh asked the Supreme Court to review the case and reinstate the conviction. In December the High Court, without comment, declined to do so. Poindexter's ordeal was over. He celebrated at the offices of his legal team on Pennsylvania Avenue, overlooking the new Navy Memorial. By chance, Bush was there that day, dedicating the site. Watching the proceedings from an upstairs window, Poindexter and the lawyers joked about hanging out a sign for Bush's benefit: "We Didn't Need You After All." Afterward, Poindexter went home. He and Linda did not bother to celebrate. The whole thing had an anticlimactic quality and they were played out. Linda had a church cookie swap to attend that night. Poindexter spent the evening at the computer.

In December 1992 Bush issued Christmas Eve pardons to McFarlane and five other Iran-Contra figures, including Weinberger, who was awaiting trial on perjury and false-statement charges brought by special prosecutor Walsh. Less than a month later Poindexter returned to the White House for the first time since November 1986. Bush was to present Reagan with the Medal of Freedom, the nation's highest civilian award. Reagan, Poindexter believed, had put him on the guest list.

The ceremony was a gathering of the clan, many of whom had not been back to the White House since Reagan left office. Former cabinet members and top aides like Cap Weinberger, George Shultz, Don Regan, Bud McFarlane. Old congressional allies like Barry Goldwater, Jack Kemp, John McCain. Not Ollie North.

Poindexter thought Reagan looked terrible—stooped, shrunken, his walk shuffling. On the podium, he seemed confused, until he got to his prepared remarks. "The script sort of ignited him," said Poindexter.

On the receiving line, he told Bush, "I think you did the right thing in pardoning Cap and the others. I'm glad I won on my own."

Greeting Reagan, he said, "Good morning, Mr. President, I'm John Poindexter." Reagan seemed remote, detached, uncertain to whom he was talking.

McFarlane departed immediately after the ceremony, so Poindexter had no chance to say hello. They had not talked at any length in years, though they occasionally ran into each other at Washington gatherings. Poindexter chatted with Weinberger and Regan, had a brief, perfunctory exchange with Shultz.

John and Cindy McCain joined him and Linda. They talked about the bad times both families had survived. McCain said something about how the Keating Five experience had given him a new perspective on a lot of things. Poindexter took the remark as a concession by McCain that perhaps he had been too harsh in his comments to Tom Brokaw during the Iran-Contra hearings. The commiseration was brief. Looking to the future, they spoke expectantly of the thirty-fifth reunion of the Class of 1958, coming up in the fall.

Only one member of the class remained on active duty. Chuck Larson. McCain's old friend, Poindexter's old rival. By then Larson was CINCPAC, Jack McCain's last job, and looked like a future CNO. That did not materialize, but in 1994 he was recalled to the Academy for an unprecedented second stint as superintendent to pick up the pieces after the worst cheating scandal in the history of the school. Seven years earlier, as Secretary of the Navy, Jim Webb had taken an uncompromising stand on honor offenses. No second chances. He wasn't around long enough to make it stick and no one else, it seemed, took him seriously. Now the soul of the Academy was up for grabs.

In the wake of Oliver North's congressional testimony, a wave of Olliemania swept the nation. His words had tapped a vein in the collective American consciousness. Everything from kids to sandwiches, heavy on the bologna, was named after him. Around that time an old Washington hand named Joe Barrett was showing his son, David, around the Capitol. David had just completed Marine boot camp but was wearing civvies. A group of young congressional staffers stopped to compliment him on his terrific "Ollie North haircut." Where'd you get it? they asked. Parris Island, David replied. The name didn't mean anything to them. Where's that, they asked, some place in Georgetown?

Headquarters Marine Corps resembled an Ollie North petting zoo as officers clustered around television sets during his six days of testimony. The reaction recalled his Patton performance at Annapolis a decade and a half earlier, the younger men enthralled by him, grayer heads wary of his impact. His classmate, John McKay, with whom he had an up-and-down relationship for years, remembered another officer telling North, "It's too bad you're getting out of the Marine Corps, Ollie, because you won't have people like John and me to keep you honest and you'll go out and bullshit everybody."

That view was confined to some of those who knew him. Millions more, of course, condemned his actions. But through it all, including his May 1989 court conviction on three felony counts, millions of other Americans continued to respond to him enthusiastically, not because of what he had done in Iran-Contra but because of what he seemed to stand for. America at its best, strong, heroic, unafraid. Many Vietnam veterans found themselves caught in the middle. Appalled by his actions, they were reluctant to turn on him. Reason enough that he had been where they had been when so many others had not. In many ways, that was the key to North's appeal. Ollie North didn't just happen; he was made possible by events long ago and far away.

To meet staggering legal costs, North retired from the Marine Corps and began speaking around the country, soon commanding upwards of $20,000 a speech. He started a company, Guardian Technologies, which made body armor and was able to turn a profit within two years. He also established an organization called Freedom Alliance, which gave him a platform for his increasingly conservative views, as well as a political action committee that raised money for like-minded candidates.

In January 1994, to the surprise of no one, he announced that he was running as a Republican for the Senate seat in Virginia held by Democrat Chuck Robb, a decorated Vietnam-era Marine married to Lyndon Johnson's daughter Lynda. The reaction to North's candidacy was predictable: first he lies to Congress, now he wants to be a senator. James Miller, who succeeded David Stockman as Reagan's budget director, entered the race as the candidate of politically correct Virginia Republicans. Ronald Reagan wrote, or at least signed, a letter released by the Miller campaign attacking North. In the days leading up to the state GOP convention in June, John Warner, Virginia's senior senator, threatened to bolt the party if North was nominated. A few months earlier, Warner and others had approached Jim Webb about running against North. Webb gave the proposal serious thought, but declined the rematch. Getting *Fields of Fire* on film had become his top priority. The fourteen thousand delegates to the state convention on Saturday, June 4, nominated North over Miller 55 percent to 45 percent.

The next day, John McCain said on the CBS program "Face the Nation" that North's nomination would make it difficult for Republicans to take the Senate seat in Virginia. After that, he kept his distance from the race, no easy matter, as he was making public appearances all over the country for GOP candidates in his capacity as vice chairman of the Republican Senatorial Campaign Committee. Senator Phil Gramm, the chairman and one of McCain's best friends, urged him to go to Virginia and campaign for North. McCain, quietly and without fanfare, refused.

Others were not so reluctant. Six possible 1996 GOP presidential candidates—Gramm, Senator Bob Dole, former Vice President Dan Quayle, former Secretary of State James Baker, former Defense Secretary Dick Cheney, and former Housing Secretary Jack Kemp—all embraced North on the stump.

Bud McFarlane, one of those who knew North best, denounced him in his 1994 autobiography as "deceitful, mendacious, and traitorous," as well as "devious, self-serving, self-aggrandizing and true first and foremost to himself." In September McFarlane said much the same thing on a heavily promoted, season-opening segment of "60 Minutes," the CBS news magazine. The North campaign responded by questioning McFarlane's emotional stability and distributing portions of the North trial transcript in which the judge questioned McFarlane's veracity.

Someone who knew North equally well, John Poindexter, joined North's campaign committee and made a few public appearances on his behalf. In Norfolk he tried to deflect McFarlane's criticism. McFarlane, said Poindexter, was singing a different tune from the one he sang at North's trial in 1989.

Poindexter was infuriated by news stories that persistently employed words such as "architect" to describe North's role in the Iran-Contra scandal. Whatever North had done, he had been the fieldman, not the architect. The job description for architect fitted McFarlane and Poindexter himself, perhaps even Reagan, better than it did North. Poindexter did what he could to change perceptions. The only stand-up guy in the whole tangled mess, he reaffirmed his 1987 congressional testimony at the same Norfolk appearance: "I told Ollie North to use the proceeds from the Iranian arms sales for the Contras."

In October Jim Webb weighed in. He had been hearing on the grapevine that North had recently elevated his claims concerning his role in Webb's Annapolis novel, A Sense of Honor. In the past, North had supposedly maintained that he was the model for Cervanek, the character who defeats the protagonist Fogarty in the boxing match sequence. Now North was asserting that he was Fogarty himself. Or so Webb had come to believe. When the connection was made in print by a Virginia newspaper, Webb was outraged, since North figured in his conception of neither character.

Around that time, following a speaking engagement, a woman came up to Webb and said, "We were just talking about your friend."

"Excuse me?" said Webb.

"You know, Oliver North," said the woman. "Your friend, Ollie."

"Look," said Webb, "Oliver North's not my friend."

"Well, you wrote a book about him," insisted the woman.

In truth, Webb had never written a word about North, either in his fiction or his journalistic work. Still, Webb said nothing. Few strictures hold as much sway over Annapolis men as the unwritten rule from Academy days: never bilge a classmate.

Then North crossed the line. In late September he disparaged Robb's Vietnam service, calling him an "Eighth and I Marine," referring to the Marine barracks in Washington that serves as the backdrop for ceremonial occasions and dress parades. The implication was that Robb had been a REMF.

That was too much for Webb. He knew that Robb had fought ferociously to win command of an infantry company in combat against a protective Marine hierarchy that had no interest in seeing the President's son-in-law on the weekly casualty list. As he had when Bob Kerrey's service was questioned during debate over the Persian Gulf in 1991, Webb called Robb and offered to help.

On October 7, Webb and five other Vietnam veterans—among them Kerrey, classmate John McKay, and retired Marine Lieutenant Colonel Bill Cowan, Annapolis '66—held a press conference in front of the Iwo Jima Memorial to denounce North and endorse Robb.

In what the *Washington Post* described as "often emotional tones," the six men took turns accusing North of habitual lying and sullying his oath of office by misleading Congress. Webb, without naming names, questioned the motives and integrity of fellow Republicans who had flocked to North's standard.

"There is no greater example of how corrupt the process is than to watch people who still privately condemn Mr. North at the same time publicly endorse him for the Senate. The message they are sending is that conduct which betrays the public trust can be excused if political expediency is at stake."

Webb then spoke of the Brigade of Midshipmen, young men and women struggling to regain the honor of an institution engulfed in shame because of the previous year's cheating scandal.

"What message are we sending them by this sort of equivalence? That you don't lie, cheat, or steal, or tolerate among you anyone who does—unless you need to gain control of the Senate?"

North spokesman Mark Merritt called Webb's remarks "petty and juvenile," a transparent attempt to settle an old score. "Jim Webb is trying to win in the political arena what he wasn't able to win in the boxing arena thirty years ago," said Merritt.

John McCain, meanwhile, felt the press was ganging up on North, but thought North had gone too far in demeaning Robb's war record. "I did not think that was a fair shot," he told Robb. "If anybody asks me, I'll tell them you served your country honorably in Vietnam, as Ollie North did."

Robb was carrying baggage, too, the result of highly publicized personal indiscretions dating back several years. With North and Robb both viewed as damaged goods, two independents entered the race—ex-governor Douglas Wilder, a Democrat who dropped out late in the campaign, and former state attorney general Marshall Coleman, a Republican supported by Warner, and himself a Vietnam-era Marine.

The campaign was one of the nastiest in the country in 1994, the two major candidates outdoing themselves in the ugliness of their television commercials. North, who raised a staggering $20 million from a network of conservatives, Christian fundamentalists, and veterans, ran a positive ad late in the campaign that put a human face to his involvement in the Iran-Contra affair. The commercial might have had more impact had it not been lost in the clutter of electronic viciousness.

The ad simply showed former Lebanon hostage David Jacobsen speaking into the camera. "I know politicians like to point their fingers at Oliver North about Iran-Contra," said Jacobsen. "They weren't there. I was. If it wasn't for Ollie North I would never have seen my family again. I'm making this ad because I want you to know, Oliver North is one of the finest men I've ever known."

A week before the election, John Poindexter also tried to lend perspective to North's Iran-Contra activities. "I know all the facts," he told a crowd of North supporters in Richmond. "Ollie did what he was told to do in support of the President's policies and he did it very effectively with a dedication, courage, innovation, and patriotism that I have seldom witnessed in other officers who have worked for me."

The favorite going into the final two weeks of the campaign, North came under blistering criticism as it drew to a close. Perhaps most damaging was a public scolding administered by Nancy Reagan, who said in an appearance in New York that North had "lied to my husband and lied about my husband." Many took her remarks as a signal that Ronald Reagan was reaffirming his concerns about North of several months earlier. If so, it seemed no less than political infanticide—the Nightingale strangling its young in the nest.

Three days before the election, in a handwritten letter addressed to "My fellow Americans," Reagan said he had been informed by his doctors that he was in the early stages of Alzheimer's, an incurable disease of the brain.

The November election coincided with North's abrupt departure from the White House eight years before. Coleman drained votes from North, and Robb beat him 46 percent to 43 percent. In his concession speech, North recalled his boxing career at the Naval Academy. The first year, he said, he made it to the quarterfinals, then lost. The second year he got as far as the semifinals before being beaten.

"But the third time I won," he said, igniting cheers, applause, and chants of "Ollie! Ollie!" and "Ninety-six! Ninety-six!"

To many, North was history. His endorsement and fund-raising ability might help conservative candidates in the future but he seemed destined to roam the political fringe. He could challenge John Warner for his Senate seat in 1996, perhaps even gain the GOP nomination again. But Warner, no doubt, would run and possibly win as an independent. More likely, Warner and North would split the conservative vote and clear the way for a Democrat like former governor Gerald Baliles. At least that was the conventional wisdom in the aftermath of the election.

Those who had followed North's career closely were not so quick to dismiss him. They sensed that his appeal went well beyond the zealots of the religious right who had been his most conspicuous supporters. Like John McCain, a more worthy heir to the Reagan legacy, North had proven himself a natural politician, although a terribly polarizing one. That might change and he could turn out to be a responsible and enduring public figure. But in a time of uncertainty at home and instability abroad, he also had chilling potential for demagoguery. Reagan was gone, but the music played on. And Oliver North, testing his wings, perfecting his song, had become the Nightingale.

A NOTE ON RESEARCH METHODS

The reader is rightly wary of a book about five Naval Academy graduates written by a sixth. In particular, the reader reasonably wants to know the relationship between the principals and the author. The question of what agreements, if any, existed between principals and author is equally pertinent.

First, let me emphasize that I have no personal relationship with any of the principals. I graduated from Annapolis in June 1964, between John McCain, John Poindexter, and Bud McFarlane on one end and Oliver North and Jim Webb on the other. I overlapped only with North. He was originally in the Class of 1967, thus a freshman during my senior year, though he later moved to the Class of 1968. In any event, our paths never crossed at Annapolis.

I did not meet any of the principals, nor any of their friends as far as I know, until the 1980s. Before then I had heard of McCain and Webb, but was not aware the others existed.

I met Webb in the spring of 1981, interviewing him with another reporter for a series about the VA, the extent of my participation in the project because I changed papers shortly thereafter, from the *Baltimore Evening Sun* to the *Baltimore* (morning) *Sun*. I next encountered Webb in 1987 when I was commissioned by *Esquire* magazine to write an article about him and North. I interviewed Webb for the piece, which appeared in the March 1988 issue under the title "The

Secret War of Ollie and Jim." North, then embroiled in Iran-Contra notoriety, refused to be interviewed for the article.

From March 1983 to June 1988 I was the *Sun*'s White House correspondent. During that five-year period I encountered McFarlane frequently, always on a professional basis. He was deputy national security adviser when I took over the White House beat, then national security adviser from October 1983 to December 1985—in short, an important figure in the administration I was covering. Eleven months later he resurfaced as a major player in Iran-Contra, by then the focus of my reporting.

During my time covering the Reagan White House I met Oliver North once, interviewing him for a profile I was doing on McFarlane. I met Poindexter and interviewed him once after he became national security adviser. McFarlane and North were confidential sources for a number of reporters. I was not one of them. Poindexter, so far as I know, was nobody's source.

I met John McCain in 1987, a few months after he was elected to the Senate. I was among a group of White House reporters who questioned him as he left a West Wing meeting with President Reagan. I interviewed him a month or so later for the *Esquire* piece on North and Webb.

I began work on this book with the intention of completing it with or without the cooperation of the principals. Obviously, I wanted their cooperation and requested it. However, either directly, in writing, through their lawyers or aides, or some combination thereof, I made it clear that this was an independent project and that all judgments would be mine alone. I promised nothing more than an honest effort to write their stories—"the good, the bad, and the ugly," as Ollie North promised the congressional Iran-Contra investigating committees.

That was it. I did not offer—and none of the principals asked—to see any of my work prior to publication. They are seeing it for the first time in this book.

McCain, Webb, and McFarlane agreed at the outset to what became a long series of interviews with each. Poindexter politely rebuffed my efforts for three years, until the fall of 1991, then talked to me at length over the next year. North ignored me until New Year's Day 1992, when he called and said he could spare some time. I interviewed him four times for a total of about ten hours, far less than the other principals.

A few unrelated points. There are passages in the book in which thoughts or emotions are described. In each instance, those descriptions are supported by direct statements by the individuals involved, almost exclusively in statements to me during interviews.

On a very few occasions, I have relied on the recollections of individuals who spoke to me on the condition that they not be identified or who asked that a portion of their comments not be attributed to them by name.

As for quotations, they are used here only when at least one participant in a conversation provided them, either in interviews with me, in their own writings, or, on a few occasions, in other published material. To the extent possible, the quotations were checked against the recollections of other participants.

NOTES

PROLOGUE

The quotes from Ronald Reagan about the Vietnam War are from *President Reagan: The Role of a Lifetime*, by Lou Cannon. Barbara Feldon told the tale of the nightingale on March 30, 1987, to a U.S. Labor Department conference on Work and Family.

BOOK I. IHTFP

INTRODUCTION

The quote from Rear Admiral Habermeyer is from a December 1988 interview. The history of the Academy is drawn from Jack Sweetman's *The U.S. Naval Academy: An Illustrated History*. The description of Plebe Year is based on conversations with Fred Fagan and other Annapolis men, Jim Webb's *A Sense of Honor*, James Calvert's *The Naval Profession*, David Poyer's *The Return of Philo T. McGiffin*, augmented by the personal experiences of the author. The letter from Ronald Benigo was written to the author in 1990. Also, *Reef Points, 1993–1994: The Annual Handbook of the Brigade of Midshipmen, 88th Edition*.

Chapter 1. HALOS AND HORNS

The description of John McCain as a youth is based on interviews with him; his mother, Roberta McCain; and his brother, Joseph P. McCain. Accounts of McCain at Episcopal were provided by schoolmates Sandy Ainslie, the current headmaster; Rives Richey; Angus McBryde; Malcolm Matheson; Bentley Orrick; and masters Riley Deeble, Allen Phillips, and Patrick Henry Callaway. The flavor of the institution was rendered by an alumnus, Ken Ringle, in "The School with a Southern Accent," which appeared in the *Washington Post* on November 11, 1989, on the occasion of Episcopal's 150th anniversary. Also, Richard Pardee Williams's book about the school, *The High School: A History of the Episcopal High School in Virginia at Alexandria*.

McCain's account of his time at Annapolis was supplemented by interviews with Roberta McCain, Carol McCain, Frank Gamboa, Charles Larson, John Dittrick, Ron Fisher, William Hemingway, and Nils (Ron) Thunman.

John Poindexter's youth in Odon, the flavor of the town, and the history of the family were described by Poindexter; his mother, Ellen Poindexter; his sister, Candace Treibic; his aunt Nancy Hardy; and his cousin the late Richard (Dickie Ray) Poindexter; as well as Frank Dixon, Kenneth Hudson, Kenneth Jensen, Richard Laughlin, John and Sue Ann Myers, Leila (Core) McElravy, William McGovren, Lela Pate, Carval Stotts, Laura (Russell) Strain, and Freida Tarvin. David Reed, of the Hudson Institute in Indianapolis, told me about Indiana, its history, economics, and demography. *Hoosiers: The Fabulous Basketball Life of Indiana*, by Phillip M. Hoose, provided a backdrop against which to view the nonathletic Poindexter.

Roger Ailes's description of the young Richard Nixon is contained in *The Selling of the President, 1968*, by Joe McGinniss (New York: Trident Press, 1969).

The portrait of Poindexter at Annapolis was drawn from interviews with Poindexter, Linda Poindexter, Laura (Russell) Strain, William Bauer, Robert Caldwell, Frank Gamboa, William Hemingway, Harry McConnell, Charles Larson, and Whitmel Swain.

Poindexter provided a copy of his essay "A Portrait of the Naval Officer as a Young Midshipman."

The description of John S. (Slew) McCain is based on accounts in various publications, notably *Bull Halsey*, by E. B. Potter, and *Admiral Halsey's Story*, by William F. Halsey and J. Bryan 3rd. John S. (Jack) McCain, Jr., was described in interviews by his wife, Roberta McCain; sons John and Joseph; Nicholas Brown; Herb Hetu; Isaac Kidd, Jr.; and others, as well as in numerous publications.

Chapter 2. IMAGINATION IS FUNNY

Bud McFarlane's youth and Annapolis years were recalled in interviews with his sisters, Barbara Staton and Mary Pitcock; his brother, William McFarlane; Mary Jane (Choate) Bardos; Jonda McFarlane; Florence Reiling; Richard Ellinger; Robert Drozd; and McFarlane himself. FDR's whistlestop at Wichita Falls and the 1938 congressional election in Texas are described in contemporary newspaper accounts, notably in the *Graham* (Texas) *Leader* and the *Graham Daily Reporter*. Frank Ikard shared his recollections of the senior McFarlane, as did Horace Busby.

Chapter 3. SHOWDOWN

North's pre-Annapolis years, primarily his youth and life in Philmont, were recalled in interviews with North, Robert Bowes, Jean Carl, Lynore (White) Carnes, Thomas Gibbons, James Grasso, Joseph and Irma Haag, DeLores Hermance, Peter Hermance, Mildred Johnson, Margaret Montague, Florence Mossman, Philip Mossman, Gladys Oles, Peter Reiss, Howard Rhodes, William Richards, Russell Robertson, Dale Rowe, Vivian Rowe, Eric Van Deusen, Glenn Warner, Jr., and Annette (Shutts) Wells.

Webb recalled his youth and pre-Annapolis years in interviews, as did his father,

James Webb, Sr., and his brother, Gary Webb, along with Hal Foster and Oleg Jenkovic. Webb provided a copy of the untitled poem written the night before his high school graduation.

In addition to North and Webb themselves, their years at Annapolis were described by Roger Charles, William Corson, Helmuts Feifs, Chris Glutting, James Gehrdes, Keith Haines, Thomas Hayes, Jack Holly, the late Father Laboon, John McKay, John and Tamma McKee, Terrence Murray, Reid Olson, Thomas Parker, Gary Pease, Kendell Pease, Fred Peck, Victor Reston, Ray Roberts, Jack Rose, Barbara (DuCote) Samorajczyk, Frank Simmons, John Sinclair, Emerson Smith, William Stensland, Walter Teichgraber, Mark Treanor, Gary Webb, George Webb, and Glenn Warner, Sr..

Various published accounts augmented the interviews, notably *Guts and Glory: The Rise and Fall of Oliver North*, by Ben Bradlee, Jr.; North's autobiography, *Under Fire: An American Story*; and Webb's novel of Annapolis, *A Sense of Honor*.

William Corson's book *The Betrayal* provides an unsparing analysis of the Vietnam War while revealing much about the author. Shelby Coffey III, writing in *Potomac*, as the *Washington Post*'s Sunday magazine was then called, filled in many of the blanks in a May 18, 1969, article entitled "Marine with Revolution on His Mind." The quotes from Corson in this chapter are drawn from Coffey's piece.

North denied ever lording his boxing championship over Webb, but Barbara DuCote, then Webb's fiancée, later his wife, and now Barbara Samorajczyk, recalled the incident at the pep rally.

Richard A. Petrino wrote about North allegedly trying to purge his medical records on the op-ed page of the *Los Angeles Times*, December 30, 1986.

BOOK II. FIELDS OF FIRE

INTRODUCTION

No source was more important to the writing of this section than *Chance and Circumstance: The Draft, the War and the Vietnam Generation*, by Lawrence M. Baskir and William A. Strauss. Equally valuable were *The Best and the Brightest*, by David Halberstam, and *Vietnam: A History*, by Stanley Karnow.

James Fallows's "What Did You Do in the Class War, Daddy?" which appeared in the October 1975 issue of the *Washington Monthly*, was one of the most perceptive and powerful articles written about the Vietnam era.

The comment about Vietnam veterans going to ground is from Harold G. Moore and Joseph L. Galloway, *We Were Soldier Once . . . and Young: Ia Drang, the Battle That Changed the War in Vietnam*.

The anger reflected in this section came out in scores of interviews with Vietnam veterans. Paul Goodwin, Robert Bedingfield, and Milton Copulos are quoted directly.

Chapter 4. FIRE AT SEA

This chapter is based primarily on interviews with John McCain, Carol McCain, Charles Larson, and Ron Fisher.

McCain vividly recalled his experiences in the July 29, 1967, fire aboard the *Forrestal*. Fisher provided an extraordinary video of the tragedy, *Trial by Fire: A Carrier Fights for Its Life*, produced in 1973 by the Naval Photographic Center. The video, relying on manned and unmanned cameras, recorded the sights and sounds of the conflagration.

Chapter 5. MUSIC BINGO, DUMMY MATH, AND GAMMA RAYS

Those interviewed included John Poindexter, Linda Poindexter, and, from Poindexter's days at the California Institute of Technology, Rudolf Mössbauer, Felix Boehm, and Herb Henrikson.

Chapter 6. WELCOME TO THE GALLANT MARINES

This account is based primarily on McFarlane's recollections. Samuel Holt, who was at Fort Sill with McFarlane, was also interviewed. In addition, McFarlane provided his service record, which included the class standings and fitness reports quoted. Stanley Karnow's *Vietnam: A History* provided historical context, as did contemporary newspaper and magazine accounts.

Chapter 7. THE CROWN PRINCE

Throughout discussions of his imprisonment, John McCain was a reluctant witness and a difficult interviewee, at least when discussing his own experiences. For the most part, he confirmed incidents described by prisonmates or discussed in published accounts. He did tell funny prison stories and often recalled the heroism of others, never his own.

Those interviewed for this and other chapters on McCain's imprisonment were Carol McCain, Roberta McCain, Joseph McCain, George (Bud) Day and Doris Day, Isaac Kidd, Jr., William Lawrence, Charlie Plumb, Ned Shuman, James Stockdale, Orson Swindle, Konrad Trautman, Jack Van Loan, and James Warner.

Dealing at length with McCain in prison, and indispensable to re-creating prison life, was *P.O.W.: A Definitive History of the American Prisoner-of-War Experience in Vietnam, 1964–1973*, by John G. Hubbell, in association with Andrew Jones and Kenneth Y. Tomlinson. See also John Dramesi, *Code of Honor*; Stephen A. Rowan, *They Wouldn't Let Us Die*; James and Sybil Stockdale, *In Love and War*; Jeremiah Denton, *When Hell Was in Session*; Ernest C. Brace, *A Code to Keep: The True Story of America's Longest-Held Civilian Prisoner of War in Vietnam*; and George E. Day, *Return with Honor*.

McCain told part of his tale in "Inside Story: How the POWs Fought Back," *U.S. News & World Report*, May 14, 1973.

Over the Beach: The Air War over Vietnam, by Zalin Grant, vividly re-created the lives of Navy pilots on Yankee Station.

Chapter 8. THE BLOODY FILTER

This chapter drew largely on McFarlane's recollections. Karnow's *Vietnam: A History*, provided historical context. *Big Story*, by Peter Braestrup, raised serious questions about press coverage of the Tet Offensive of 1968.

General Westmoreland, in a September 12, 1994, interview, said he had "absolutely no recollection" of the encounter with McFarlane. Westmoreland insisted that upbraiding a junior officer in the presence of his commanding officer "was not compatible with my command style." He added, "If that took place, it was an aberration."

Chapter 9. DO YOU WANT TO GO HOME?

See Notes to Chapter 7.

McCain's refusal to accept early release is memorialized in a secret cable, now declassified, dated September 13, 1968. W. Averell Harriman, at the time chief U.S. negotiator to the Paris Peace Talks, relates a discussion with his North Vietnamese counterpart, Le Duc Tho: "At tea break Le Duc Tho mentioned that DRV had intended to release Admiral McCain's son as one of the three pilots freed recently, but he had refused."

Chapter 10. THE CHERRY BOY

Interviewed for this chapter were Oliver North, Paul Goodwin, Charles Krulak, Lloyd Banta, Robert Bedingfield, Eric Bowen, Roger Charles, William Corson, John Dolaghan, John (Mike) Flynn, Helmuts Feifs, William Haskell, Randy Herrod, Jake Laboon, John McKay, Don Moore, and Ernest Tuten.

Betsy North recalled her courtship and marriage in an interview that accompanied David Friend's article, "A Man of Many Faces: Oliver North May Go to Jail, but Iranscam's Central Player Shows Another Side—as a Suburban Father," published in the August 1987 issue of *Life*.

North wrote about his experiences in Vietnam in his autobiography, *Under Fire: An American Story*, and in *One More Mission: Oliver North Returns to Vietnam*. Ben Bradlee, Jr.'s *Guts and Glory: The Rise and Fall of Oliver North*, contains a fine chapter on North in Vietnam. Also helpful, though occasionally taking liberties with the facts (see Notes to Chapter 15), was *Blue's Bastards: A True Story of Valor Under Fire*, by Randy Herrod.

The Lance Morrow passage is from his essay "1968," which appeared as part of *Time*'s commemorative cover story, "1968: The Year That Shaped a Generation," published January 11, 1988.

Betsy North never responded to a written request for an interview or verbal requests conveyed through her husband.

John Irving calls Chuck Krulak "my hero" on the Acknowledgments page of his novel *A Prayer for Owen Meany* (New York: William Morrow, 1989).

Chapter 11. THE NATURAL

This chapter is based on the recollections of Jim Webb, Glenn Boggs, Gino Castignetti, Jake Laboon, Robert (Big Mac) McDowell, Mac (Little Mac) McGarvey, Barbara (DuCote) Samorajczyk, John Van Scholten, Dale Wilson, and Michael Wyly.

Many of Webb's experiences and emotions in Vietnam are mirrored in his novels, *Fields of Fire*, *A Sense of Honor*, *A Country Such As This*, and *Something to Die For*.

The tale of Big Mac McDowell and the boot lieutenant was first related in print by Patrick A. McGuire in his fine piece "From Vietnam to the Pentagon: The Fields of Fire of Navy Secretary James Webb," *Baltimore Sun Magazine*, June 28, 1987.

Chapter 12. TRUSTING THE SYSTEM

The section about the Whiz Kids is based on interviews with John and Linda Poindexter, Clarence (Mark) Hill, Harvey Safeer, and Daniel Rathbun. Useful books included two by David Halberstam, *The Best and the Brightest* and *The Reckoning*, as well as *McNamara: His Ordeal in the Pentagon*, by Henry L. Trewhitt, and *How Much Is Enough: Shaping the Defense Program, 1961–1969*, by Alain C. Enthoven and K. Wayne Smith.

In a July 28, 1965, radio and television address to the nation on the Vietnam buildup, President Johnson said, "After this past week of deliberations, I have concluded that it is not essential to order reserve units into service now. If that necessity should later be indicated, I will give the matter most careful consideration and I will give the country due and adequate notice before taking such action, but only after full preparations."

Daniel Costello and Richard Murphy, both skippers of the *Lawrence*, discussed in interviews Poindexter's performance as the ship's executive officer.

Poindexter's time in the Secretary of the Navy's office was recalled in interviews with two men who held the post while he was there, John Chafee and John Warner, as well as Jim Webb, Herb Hetu, Robert Caldwell, Thor Hanson, and Charles Larson.

William King and Poindexter provided details of the latter's duty aboard the *England*.

Chapter 13. 'TIS THE SEASON TO BE JOLLY

See Notes to Chapter 7.

Chapter 14. STRANGER IN A STRANGE LAND

According to Department of Defense manpower statistics, 343,300 men were drafted in fiscal year 1968, running from July 1967 through June 1968, more than during any similar period in the Vietnam era.

Interviews for the section on Webb in the Secretary of the Navy's office included Senators John Chafee and John Warner; Jim Webb; John Poindexter; and William Holmberg.

Biographical material on the late Howard Westwood was drawn from a chapter on the law firm of Covington and Burling in *The Superlawyers*, by Joseph C. Goulden (New York: Weybright and Talley, 1972), and from a similar chapter in *The Other Government: The Unseen Power of Washington Lawyers*, by Mark J. Green (New York: Grossman Publishers, 1975).

Webb discussed his time at Georgetown in interviews. Heathcote Wales, in a 1987 interview, confirmed giving the exam that included the question about a fictional sergeant named Webb. He said it was not intended to give offense or upset Jim Webb. In a letter dated August 26, 1973, Webb expressed his anger to the dean of the Georgetown Law Center. "To approach such a situation with levity defiles the sanctity of human sacrifice, regardless of one's metaphysical opinion as to the value of that sacrifice," Webb wrote.

Webb first wrote about Micronesia in "Turmoil in Paradise: Micronesia at the Crossroads," *U.S. Naval Institute Proceedings*, July 1972. The book that followed his 1973 trip there was entitled *Micronesia and the U.S. Pacific Strategy* (New York: Praeger, 1974). He wrote about his impressions in a May 25, 1981, *Washington Post* op-ed piece entitled "The Power of Remembering." It is quoted at length in the chapter.

The battles for Guam, Saipan, and Tinian, including statistics on battlefield casualties, are discussed in J. Robert Moskin's *The U.S. Marine Corps Story,* Second Revised and Updated Edition.

Chapter 15. THE REASONABLE AND HONEST WAR CRIMINAL

Jim Webb, Oliver North, Randy Herrod, Harry Palmer, Jr., and Denzil Garrison were interviewed for this chapter.

The investigation of the Son Thang (4) killings and the trials of Sam Green and Randy Herrod are treated at length in *Marines and Military Law in Vietnam: Trial by Fire,* written by Lieutenant Colonel Gary D. Solis, USMC, and published in 1989 by the History and Museums Division, Headquarters, U.S. Marine Corps.

North, with William Novak, wrote about Herrod's trial in his 1991 autobiography, *Under Fire: An American Story.* Herrod provided his version in a 1989 memoir, *Blue's Bastards: A True Story of Valor Under Fire.* Webb wrote about Sam Green's trial in "The Sad Conviction of Sam Green: The Case for the Reasonable and Honest War Criminal," published in the winter 1974 issue of *Res Ipsa Loquitar: Georgetown Review of Law and Public Interest.*

Court documents were also perused. Webb provided a copy of the telegram from James Chiara following Green's death, his letter to Roberta Green, and her Christmas reply.

There was an intriguing postscript to the story. Herrod devotes half of *Blue's Bastards* to his court-martial, an intense tale made all the more vivid by his recounting of the terror that gripped him as he faced a possible death sentence.

"I had one more ordeal to live through—the moment when I would hear myself pronounced guilty and then sentenced to death by firing squad," he writes of his state of mind as the court retired to deliberate on a verdict.

The life-and-death stakes are hammered home on the dust jacket, which carries a photo of North and Herrod and a blurb: "In Vietnam Randy Herrod saved Oliver North's life. Then Oliver North came back to save his."

It's just not true. The authorities declared Herrod's case noncapital, ruling out the death penalty, when it was referred to trial in May, three months before the August court-martial, according to the official Marine history of the affair and contemporary press reports.

North contributed two fat paragraphs of praise for the book that were printed on the back of the dust jacket. He said in a 1992 interview that he knew at the time of the court-martial that Herrod was not on trial for his life and was unaware that Herrod had misrepresented the situation in his book until this author brought it to his attention.

"When you're as intense about getting things done as I am, you speed-read something like that," he said. He expressed concern that Herrod might be hurt on learning that he had not read *Blue's Bastards* more closely, said nothing about the purposeful distortion Herrod had perpetrated on those who bought and read his book or that he, North, had fostered with his strong dust jacket endorsement.

Chapter 16. LONG TALL SALLY

See Notes to Chapter 7.

An Associated Press photograph of John McCain limping from a plane at Clark Air Base ran on page 1 of the *New York Times*, March 15, 1973.

Chapter 17. THE WATER WALKER

Interviewees for this chapter included Oliver North, Charles Krulak, Paul Goodwin, Edward Bronars, Donald Price, Lee Johnson, John Sattler, Sally Schulze, Jim Webb, James Jones, David Haughey, Roy Carter, Charles Hester, Robert Bedingfield, Stanley Ostazewski, Richmond O'Neill, and Ross Perot.

The chapter also draws on Ben Bradlee, Jr.'s *Guts and Glory* and North's autobiography, *Under Fire*. The review of North's book by Roger Charles appeared November 3, 1991, in the *Chicago Tribune*.

Betsy North declined to be interviewed for this book. On whether or not she had found someone else in his absence, North said in a December 1993 interview, "We have now been married twenty-five years and have raised four lovely children who have grown in strength and grace and wisdom. And I'm grateful for that."

Chapter 18. ADULT EDUCATION

McFarlane was the primary source for this chapter. Stanley Karnow's *Vietnam: A History* provided context. McFarlane wrote about this period himself in *Crisis Resolution: Presidential Decision Making in the "Mayaguez" and Korean Confrontations,* coauthored by Richard G. Head and Frisco W. Short, and in his 1994 autobiography, *Special Trust*.

Chapter 19. A TUTORIAL WITH THE GREATS

Webb was the primary source for this chapter. He also provided copies of his correspondence with Ted Purdy and John Kirk. John Herrington, in an interview, told of hearing Webb promoting his book on the radio.

In *A Moveable Feast* (New York: Charles Scribner's Sons, 1964), Hemingway writes, "I was learning something from the painting of Cezanne that made writing simple true sentences far from enough to make the stories have the dimensions that I was trying to put in them. I was learning very much from him but I was not articulate enough to explain it to anyone."

Reviews of *Fields of Fire* appeared in *The New Republic*, the *Washington Post*, *West Coast Review of Books*, *Publishers Weekly*, *Time*, *Choice*, *Naval War College Review*, *Newsweek*, the *Houston Chronicle*, and the *Houston Post*. Jimmy Breslin's comment appeared in an article entitled "It's a Fine Mess, Ollie," in the *New York Daily News*, December 4, 1986.

Perspective on *Fields of Fire* was provided by Kathleen M. Puhr's "Four Fictional Faces of the Vietnam War," in *Modern Fiction Studies*, Spring 1984.

Brad Lemley first told the story of Webb's visits to the National Gallery of Art in a December 8, 1985, *Washington Post Magazine* piece entitled "Never Give an Inch: James Webb's Struggles with Pen and Sword."

George Christian first told the tale of the hat in the *Houston Chronicle*, October 30, 1983. His article was entitled "Throw Your Hat Across the Fence."

Chapter 20. REENTRY

Interviewed for this chapter were John McCain, Carol McCain, Roberta McCain, Michael Deaver, Nancy Reynolds, Diane Lawrence (formerly Diane Rauch), William Lawrence, James Lake, Arnold Isaacs, Edwin (Ned) Shuman, and Carl Smith.

The picture of McCain shaking hands with Richard Nixon was taken by United Press International. It ran in the *Washington Post* on May 25, 1973, and in other publications.

McCain's article "Inside Story: How the POWs Fought Back" appeared in the May 14, 1973, issue of *U.S. News & World Report*.

Chapter 21. A CHANGE OF HEART

Interviewed for this chapter were John Poindexter, Linda Poindexter, James Holloway, Staser Holcomb, William King, Harold Lewis, Nicholas Brown, Richard McKenna, and Frank Gamboa.

The description of Admiral Raymond A. Spruance is from John B. Lundstrom's introduction to Thomas B. Buell's biography of the admiral, *The Quiet Warrior*.

Chapter 22. PUG HENRY

The primary interviews for this chapter were with Bud McFarlane, Brent Scowcroft, and Andrew Dougherty.

The book McFarlane wrote at the National War College with Richard G. Head and Frisco W. Short was entitled *Crisis Resolution: Presidential Decision Making in the "Mayaguez" and Korean Confrontations*. It was published in Boulder, Colorado, by Westview Press in 1978.

The article he wrote on U.S.-Soviet relations at the War College was entitled "The Political Potential of Parity," published in the *U.S. Naval Institute Proceedings,* February 1979.

Chapter 23. WOMEN CAN'T FIGHT

Primary interviews for this chapter were with Jim Webb, John Holden, Dale Wilson, William Lawrence, and Carlton Sherwood.

Robert Burns, '79, passed on the information about the debate over the inscription on the class ring and its resolution.

Webb's remarks at the Vietnam Veteran of the Year awards ceremony were reprinted as "The Invisible Vietnam Veteran" on the op-ed page of the *Washington Post,* August 4, 1976.

"Women Can't Fight" appeared in the November 1979 issue of *Washingtonian*.

Webb's view of the sexual tension at the Academy that followed the introduction of women in 1976 was ratified in a striking April 1981 series on the Academy by Sherwood, a Pulitzer Prize–winning reporter, at the time a Washington correspondent for the Gannett News Service. The *Wilmington Evening Journal*, one of the newspapers that carried the series, entitled it "Academy at Sea," and ran it April 19 to April 22.

Sherwood reported that as of the fall of 1981 Academy personnel records showed that twenty-nine midshipmen had been prosecuted for sexual misconduct since 1977, with the males suffering much harsher punishment. He also reported that a far greater number of sexual offenses—over one hundred since 1977—had been handled informally.

Sherwood's series featured an account of a November 22, 1980, "sexathon" in which five males were charged with having sexual intercourse with a female midshipman, who admitted instigating the encounters. Sixteen seconds of one were filmed by a male participant. Mary Lamble, the woman, told Sherwood that during her final three months at the Academy, during which she was seeking a discharge because of an injured knee, she had sex "with about twenty" midshipmen. "Not really a lot for some women in the dormitory," she said. Lamble also said, "It goes on all the time, but usually the officers look the other way. One woman kept count of the guys she slept with—fifty-seven in one year. She got caught several times, but nothing much happened, some demerits. To get caught you've got to be awful unlucky or have a bad attitude. It's not the type of thing the Academy wants to deal with."

Lamble was permitted to resign without any duty obligation and awarded a medical discharge. Two of the men, both seniors, were expelled and ordered to serve three years as enlisted men. The other three were put on probation and received demerits.

Sherwood also reported that a woman staff officer and fifteen female midshipmen engaged in homosexual activities at the officer's off-base residence.

Mary Lord of *Newsweek* followed up on Sherwood's series, which also reported on drug use at the Academy, in an April 27, 1981, piece. Lord reported that the five male midshipmen had intercourse with Lamble "to the glee of comrades assembled in the hall outside" the room.

Various sources associated with the Academy told this author in interviews that as a result of the incident the Twenty-ninth Company, the unit to which the midshipmen involved belonged, acquired a raunchy, inside-the-Yard nickname: "Stand in line, Twenty-nine."

A Sense of Honor was widely reviewed following publication. Reviews quoted in the chapter were by David Shribman, *Washington Star*, March 3, 1981; Carey Winfrey, *New York Times Book Review*, April 5, 1981; and R. James Woolsey, *Washington Post*, July 7, 1981. Other reviews, most of which appeared between March and May 1981, are listed in the Bibliography.

Retired Admiral Leon A. (Bud) Edney confirmed in a December 1993 interview that upon becoming Commandant of Midshipmen in 1981 he unofficially prohibited Webb from speaking or appearing at the Academy. Edney, a widely respected and highly decorated combat pilot who served four tours in Vietnam, said he tended to agree with much of what Webb had written over the years. But by virtue of his authorship of *A Sense of Honor* and "Women Can't Fight," Edney said, Webb had become a "cult hero" to male midshipmen and his appearance at the Academy stood to be disruptive as the school was still struggling to make the transition from all-male to co-ed.

Efforts by Academy officials to dampen demand for the book were reported by Stephen Hunter in the *Baltimore Sun* of April 19, 1981; Edwin McDowell in the *New York Times* of February 28, 1981; by David Shribman in the *Washington Star* of March 3, 1981; and by Gene Bisbie in the *Annapolis Evening Capital* of March 4, 1981. A cartoon by Eric Smith in the *Evening Capital* of March 9, 1981, showed an admiral, apparently the Superintendent, demanding of a worried English professor, "Get me the faculty list. I want to court-martial James Webb's writing teacher."

Chapter 24. GUERRILLA WARFARE

Primary sources for this chapter were John McCain, Cindy McCain, Carol McCain, William Cohen, James Holloway, William Bader, Albert (Pete) Lakeland, James Jones, James McGovern, and Clarence (Mark) Hill.

John Poindexter was Admiral Holloway's executive assistant in 1977 when the CNO tapped his classmate John McCain for the Senate liaison post, but Poindexter played no role in the selection.

Chapter 25. GARLIC IN A CROWDED ELEVATOR

Interviewed for this chapter were Oliver North, Charles Krulak, Edward Bronars, Jerome Hagen, Fred Peck, Jim Jones, Donald Price, John McKay, Michael Lundblad, Roy Carter, Nathaniel Davis, Victor Taylor, and Harry Jenkins.

This chapter drew from North's 1991 autobiography, *Under Fire*, written with William Novak, and Ben Bradlee, Jr.'s biography of North, *Guts and Glory*.

Jerry Hagen, a retired Marine brigadier general, recalled his experiences with North in a letter to the author dated January 8, 1991.

Fred Peck's letter was written to the author on December 17, 1988.

BOOK III. THE NIGHTINGALE'S SONG

INTRODUCTION

Those interviewed included Michael Deaver, Peggy Noonan, Larry Speakes, Bud McFarlane, and John Poindexter.

Two fine books by Lou Cannon were drawn on for the introduction: *President Reagan: The Role of a Lifetime*, published in 1991, and *Reagan*, published in 1982. Several other books were most useful in the writing of the introduction, including Donald T. Regan's *For the Record: From Wall Street to Washington* (1988); Michael K. Deaver's *Behind the Scenes*, written with Mickey Herskowitz (1987); Peggy Noonan's *What I Saw at the Revolution: A Political Life in the Reagan Era* (1990); and Larry Speakes's *Speaking Out: The Reagan Presidency from Inside the White House*, written with Robert Pack (1988).

Francis Clines drew his comparison between Kennedy and Reagan during a casual conversation with the author while both were covering Reagan's trip to the demilitarized zone between North and South Korea in 1984.

The author also relied on numerous articles written and interviews conducted during his five years covering the Reagan White House from 1983 to 1988, as well as his own observations during that period.

Chapter 26. OLLIE, BUD, AND JOHN

This chapter was based on interviews with Bud McFarlane, John Poindexter, Oliver North, Geoffrey Kemp, Roger Fontaine, Victor Taylor, Jeremiah O'Leary, and Howard Teicher.

North's penchant for expanding his bureaucratic turf has been attested to in various publications and documents, including Constantine C. Menges's *Inside the National Security Council: The True Story of the Making and Unmaking of Reagan's Foreign Policy* (1988) and NSC staff member Jacqueline Tillman's April 2, 1987, deposition by the staff of the Senate Select Committee on Military Assistance to Iran and the Nicaraguan Opposition.

North's autobiography, *Under Fire* (1991), Ben Bradlee, Jr.'s biography of North, *Guts and Glory* (1988), and McFarlane's autobiography, *Special Trust* (1994), were especially helpful in writing this chapter.

See also three *Baltimore Sun* articles by the author: "Ex-Marine Nobody Knows Becomes National Security 'Mover, Shaker' " (June 13, 1983), "Guilt-Ridden Mc-Farlane Was Never a 'Member of the Club' " (May 10, 1987), and "Reagans Keep Life in the White House Simple" (January 29, 1984).

The saddest song of 1968 was "Abraham, Martin and John," by Dion.

Chapter 27. THE CANDIDATE FROM HANOI

Those interviewed included John McCain, Cindy McCain, Carol McCain, J. Brian (Jay) Smith, John Kolbe, Sam Stanton, Michael Murphy, and Orson Swindle.

Jay Smith provided a videotape compilation of McCain's television ads.

The First District race was covered closely by the *Arizona Republic* and the *Phoenix Gazette*. Articles from both papers, and others, were utilized as background for this chapter. Several key pieces are listed in the bibliography. Kolbe, of the *Gazette*, first reported (May 20, 1982) Jim Mack's unsuccessful effort to elicit damaging personal information about McCain from ex-wife Carol.

Chapter 28. SCORPIONS IN A JAR

Interviewees for this chapter included Jim Webb, John Wheeler, Jan Scruggs, Robert Doubek, William Jayne, Milton Copulos, and Carlton Sherwood.

The controversy over the Vietnam Veterans Memorial is chronicled most completely and evenhandedly by Christopher Buckley in his September 1985 *Esquire* piece, "The Wall," and by Rick Atkinson in his 1989 book, *The Long Gray Line: The American Journey of West Point's Class of 1966*. This author takes exception to some elements in both publications.

Jan Scruggs, with an assist from Joel L. Swerdlow, told the story of the Memorial from his vantage point in *To Heal a Nation: The Vietnam Veterans Memorial*, published in 1985.

Innumerable articles have been written about the Memorial, many listed in the Bibliography. Jim Webb expressed his misgivings in "Reassessing the Vietnam Veterans Memorial," the *Wall Street Journal*, December 18, 1981. Other articles of special interest include the following: "Art Disputes War: The Battle of the Vietnam Memorial," by Tom Wolfe in the *Washington Post*, October 13, 1982; Robert W. Doubek's "The Story of the Vietnam Veterans Memorial," *The Retired Officer*, November 1983; Tom Carhart's "Insulting Vietnam Veterans" in the *New York Times*, October 24, 1981; "Memorials," by Charles Krauthammer, writing as C.K., in *The New Republic*, May 23, 1981.

Ned Martel's short but compelling portrait of Wheeler appeared in the October 1990 issue of *Dossier*.

Philosophy professor Charles L. Griswold, in the summer 1986 issue of *Critical Inquiry*, provided a provocative, learned, and often lyrical essay on the Memorial.

Chapter 29. NOBLE CAUSE REDUX

Interviewees included Bud McFarlane, John Poindexter, Robert Dillon, Geoffrey Kemp, John Lehman, Les Janka, Philip Dur, Howard Teicher, Caspar Weinberger, Jim Webb, William Cowan, Bernard Trainor, and Pat Collins.

Several books were most valuable in the writing of this chapter, notably *Best Laid Plans: The Inside Story of America's War Against Terrorism*, by David C. Martin and John Walcott; *President Reagan: The Role of a Lifetime*, by Lou Cannon; *Secret Warriors: Inside the Covert Military Operations of the Reagan Era*, by Steven Emerson; *U.S. Marines in Lebanon 1982–1984*, by Benis M. Frank; *The U.S. Marine Corps Story*, Second Revised and Updated Edition, by J. Robert Moskin; *From Beirut to Jerusalem*, by Thomas L. Friedman; *Twin Pillars to Desert Storm: America's Flawed Vision in the Middle East from Nixon to Bush*, by Howard Teicher and Gayle Radley Teicher; *Command of the Seas: Building the 600-Ship Navy*, by John F. Lehman, Jr.; *Fighting for Peace: Seven Critical Years in the Pentagon*, by Caspar W. Weinberger; *Turmoil and Triumph: My Years as Secretary of State*, by George P. Shultz; *An American Life*, by Ronald Reagan; and *Special Trust*, by Robert C. McFarlane with Zofia Smardz.

Also invaluable was the *Report of the DOD Commission on Beirut International Airport Terrorist Act, October 23, 1983*. Dated December 20, 1983, the report became known as the Long Commission Report after the panel's chairman, Admiral Robert L. J. Long, USN (Ret.), Annapolis '44.

Numerous newspaper and magazine articles relating to the U.S. involvement in Lebanon were perused, many of them listed in the Bibliography. Former NSC aide Geoffrey Kemp provided a valuable inside account of McFarlane's view of the situation in Lebanon in "Lessons of Lebanon: A Guide for Future U.S. Policy," in the summer 1988 issue of *Middle East Insight*.

Chapter 30. THE DOUBTERS

John McCain's remarks on Lebanon on the House floor are printed in the *Congressional Record* of September 28, 1983. Both McCain and Jim Webb were interviewed.

William Greider's "Profiles in Cowardice," about the House debate on Lebanon, was published in the November 24, 1983, issue of *Rolling Stone*.

The September 28 House vote on Lebanon was reported in the *New York Times* and elsewhere the following day.

Interviewees included McCain, Webb, and Lisa Boepple, a McCain aide.

Chapter 31. THE PRESBYTERIAN CLIMAX

Bud McFarlane, Michael Deaver, and James Baker were interviewed. The failed Baker-Deaver coup is discussed in detail in *The Power Game: How Washington Works*, by Hedrick Smith, and *President Reagan: The Role of a Lifetime*, by Lou Cannon.

The bombing of the Marine barracks is discussed in the Long Commission Report and in Martin and Walcott's *Best Laid Plans*, both cited in Notes to Chapter 29.

Chapter 32. PUT 'EM UP, PUT 'EM UP

See Notes to Chapter 29.

In addition to the books listed there, George Wilson's *Supercarrier: An Inside Account of Life Aboard the World's Most Powerful Ship, the U.S.S. John F. Kennedy* provided useful insight into the December 1983 raid on Syrian positions in Lebanon. Both *The Power Game: How Washington Works*, by Hedrick Smith, and *Best Laid Plans: The Inside Story of America's War Against Terrorism*, by David C. Martin and John Walcott, provide similar accounts of the joint raid.

Chapter 33. REMEMBER YAMAMOTO

Interviewees included Oliver North, John Poindexter, Bud McFarlane, James Stark, Clarence (Mark) Hill, Richard Armitage, William Corson, Jack Holly, Larry Speakes, and Constantine Menges. A number of others spoke on the condition that they not be identified by name.

Books consulted included *Best Laid Plans: The Inside Story of America's War Against Terrorism*, by David C. Martin and John Walcott; *Special Trust*, by Robert C. McFarlane with Zofia Smardz; *Under Fire: An American Story*, by Oliver L. North and William Novak; *Guts and Glory: The Rise and Fall of Oliver North*, by Ben Bradlee, Jr.; *Landslide: The Unmaking of the President 1984–1988*, by Jane Mayer and Doyle McManus; *Speaking Out: The Reagan Presidency from Inside the White House*, by Larry Speakes with Robert Pack; *Inside the National Security Council: The True Story of the Making and Unmaking of Reagan's Foreign Policy*, by Constantine C. Menges; *What I Saw at the Revolution: A Political Life in the Reagan Era*, by Peggy Noonan; *Turmoil and Triumph: My Years as Secretary of State*, by George P. Shultz; and *Perilous Statecraft: An Insider's Account of the Iran-Contra Affair*, by Michael A. Ledeen.

Newsweek's inside story on the *Achille Lauro* intercept was contained in a cover story entitled "Special Report: Getting Even" in the October 21, 1985, issue. The issue included six separate stories related to the episode. North was identified as the man conceiving the idea of the intercept in " 'You Can Run but You Can't Hide,' " by John Walcott and others.

Newsweek identified North as the source for its account of the intercept in the July 27, 1987, issue.

North, in a December 1993 interview, was far less certain about who came up with the idea for the intercept. "Look," he said, "if you're sitting in a meeting with twelve guys or whatever it was and an idea comes up—I don't think—I didn't claim credit for the idea in *Under Fire*." Informed that he had, he said, "No. That came out of the crisis management team and the way I wrote it up in *Under Fire* is exactly the way I remember it. And I know Jim Stark feels he didn't get credit for it, okay, and I'm not here to deny Jim credit for anything. He's a fine guy."

So the idea came out of a crisis management team? "Yes. We'd been meeting nonstop for days."

Asked who said "Remember Yamamoto?" North replied, "I think I did, but I understand that others think they said it, too."

The tale of North's confrontation with Admiral Crowe was reported by Seymour Hersh in "Target Qaddafi," which appeared in the *New York Times Magazine* of February 22, 1987.

Jacqueline Tillman's comments are contained in her deposition of April 2, 1987, to staff members of the Senate Iran-Contra investigating committee. A transcript appears in Volume 26 of Appendix B, Depositions, to the *Report of the Congressional Committees Investigating the Iran-Contra Affair.*

Chapter 34. AN ALIEN PRESENCE

Interviewees included Donald Regan, Bud McFarlane, Paul Thompson, Michael Deaver, James Baker, John Poindexter, Karna Small, Ed Rollins, James Lake, Robert Sims, James Stark, James Rentschler, Bernard Weinraub, Mitch Daniels, George Keyworth, Larry Speakes, Geoffrey Kemp, Constantine Menges, Clarence (Mark) Hill, Nancy Reynolds, Dennis Thomas, and Howard Teicher.

Books consulted included *Special Trust*, by Robert C. McFarlane with Zofia Smardz; *President Reagan: The Role of a Lifetime*, by Lou Cannon; *Guts and Glory: The Rise and Fall of Oliver North*, by Ben Bradlee, Jr.; *Landslide: The Unmaking of the President 1984–1988*, by Jane Mayer and Doyle McManus; *For the Record: From Wall Street to Washington*, by Donald T. Regan; *Deadly Gambits: The Reagan Administration and the Stalemate in Nuclear Arms Control*, by Strobe Talbott; *The Master of the Game: Paul Nitze and the Nuclear Peace*, by Strobe Talbott; *The Turn: From the Cold War to a New Era—The United States and the Soviet Union 1983–1990*, by Don Oberdorfer; *Twin Pillars to Desert Storm: America's Flawed Vision in the Middle East from Nixon to Bush*, by Howard Teicher and Gayle Radley Teicher; *Inside the National Security Council: The True Story of the Making and Unmaking of Reagan's Foreign Policy*, by Constantine C. Menges; *Speaking Out: The Reagan Presidency from Inside the White House*, by Larry Speakes with Robert Pack; *Under Fire: An American Story*, by Oliver L. North and William Novak; *From Hiroshima to Glasnost: At the Center of Decision—A Memoir*, by Paul H. Nitze, with Ann M. Smith and Steven L. Rearden; *What I Saw at the Revolution: A Political Life in the Reagan Era*, by Peggy Noonan; and *Perilous Statecraft: An Insider's Account of the Iran-Contra Affair*, by Michael A. Ledeen.

Donald Regan, in a December 1994 interview, did not deny making essentially the comments attributed to him regarding McFarlane and the White House reporter. But he pointed out that the rumors had been rampant for weeks, if not longer, and he was not giving them new currency on those few occasions when he alluded to them in response to questions. The author, as a White House correspondent during that period, can attest to the pervasiveness of the rumors, which he heard from other reporters, not from Regan or any member of Regan's staff. Regan did question the quote attributed to him in *Landslide* pertaining to the *Newsweek* meeting. In particular, he denied saying he had "counsel[ed]" McFarlane. He said he told the journalists, in response to a question, that he had discussed the matter over lunch with McFarlane in California and McFarlane had assured him it was not true.

As for the encounter with McFarlane following the death of Major Nicholson, Regan said the description in the text—drawn from interviews with McFarlane and accounts in McFarlane's book and elsewhere—was "reasonably accurate." Said Regan, "Did I chew him out? Yeah, I chewed him out . . . and his feelings got hurt."

Chapter 35. I DON'T HAVE ANY LIFE

Interviewees included John and Linda Poindexter, Carol McCain, Thor Hanson, John McCain, Oliver North, Laura (Russell) Strain, James Holloway, Paul Thompson,

James Stark, Peggy Noonan, Constantine Menges, Richard Armitage, Clarence (Mark) Hill, Larry Speakes, and Dennis Thomas.

Books consulted included *Special Trust*, by Robert C. McFarlane with Zofia Smardz; *Guts and Glory: The Rise and Fall of Oliver North*, by Ben Bradlee, Jr.; *Landslide: The Unmaking of the President 1984–1988*, by Jane Mayer and Doyle McManus; *President Reagan: The Role of a Lifetime*, by Lou Cannon; *Under Fire: An American Story*, by Oliver L. North and William Novak; *For the Record: From Wall Street to Washington*, by Donald T. Regan; *The Turn: From the Cold War to a New Era—The United States and the Soviet Union 1983–1990*, by Don Oberdorfer; *The Master of the Game: Paul Nitze and the Nuclear Peace*, by Strobe Talbott; *Inside the National Security Council: The True Story of the Making and Unmaking of Reagan's Foreign Policy*, by Constantine C. Menges; *What I Saw at the Revolution: A Political Life in the Reagan Era*, by Peggy Noonan; *Speaking Out: The Reagan Presidency from Inside the White House*, by Larry Speakes with Robert Pack; *Twin Pillars to Desert Storm: America's Flawed Vision in the Middle East from Nixon to Bush*, by Howard Teicher and Gayle Radley Teicher; *From Hiroshima to Glasnost: At the Center of Decision—A Memoir*, by Paul H. Nitze, with Ann M. Smith and Steven L. Rearden; and *Perilous Statecraft: An Insider's Account of the Iran-Contra Affair*, by Michael A. Ledeen.

Also useful was Seymour Hersh's "Target Qaddafi," which appeared in the *New York Times Magazine* of February 22, 1987; however, this author's research does not support Hersh's central contention that killing Qaddafi was a primary goal of the raid on Libya.

Chapter 36. THE WHITE TORNADO

Interviewees included John McCain, Cindy McCain, J. Brian (Jay) Smith, Victoria (Torie) Clarke, John Kolbe, Wes Gullett, Sam Stanton, Michael Murphy, William Cohen, John Warner, and Thomas Ridge.

The *Washington Times* article, "From Hanoi to the House," was written by George Archibald and appeared on February 3, 1983.

McCain's trip to Vietnam and the political benefits were well chronicled by the Arizona press. See especially "Coming Home: Political Bonanza Is Seen in McCain's Mission to Vietnam," by Joel Nilsson in the *Arizona Republic*, January 27, 1985.

"Honor, Duty and a War Called Vietnam," ran on CBS on April 10, 1985.

Once they got on to the story that the man who had been their publisher since 1980 had made up his war record, the *Arizona Republic* and the *Phoenix Gazette* covered the sad tale of Darrow (Duke) Tully vigorously and completely. Charles Kelly, based on his reporting and the reporting of other *Republic* staff members, wrote a gripping account of Tully's life entitled "A Hero That Never Was," published January 26, 1986.

The 1986 U.S. Senate campaign in Arizona was covered closely by the state's major newspapers, including the *Arizona Republic*, the *Phoenix Gazette*, the (Tucson) *Arizona Daily Star*, and the *Mesa Tribune*. Selected articles are listed in the Bibliography.

Phoenix Gazette political columnist John Kolbe wrote about McCain's temper on January 23, 1986. The article was entitled "Golden Boy McCain Has Unsettling Flaw—His Temper." Kolbe did so again on July 30, 1986, in an article entitled "Angry McCain Could Turn Senate Race into Contest After All."

Political columnist Pat Murphy, of the *Arizona Republic*, poked fun at Richard

Kimball's campaign document in a February 20, 1986, article entitled "Mr. Kimball Tries to Go to Washington by Utilizing 'Progressivity.' "

McCain's growing national stature was noted during the 1986 Senate campaign by several syndicated columnists and national publications, including the following: Jack Germond and Jules Witcover in "A New Arizona Institution," *Phoenix Gazette*, April 7, 1986; George S. Will in "Hanoi to Phoenix to Washington," published February 20, 1986, in the *Washington Post* and elsewhere; and R. W. Apple, Jr., in "National Role Is Seen for Arizona Politician," the *New York Times*, November 2, 1986.

Richard Kimball attacked McCain for the political action committees contributing to his campaign in a July 18, 1986, press release entitled "Kimball: 'McCain Is Being Bought and Paid For.' "

The picture of McCain standing on a riser during the debate was taken by Suzanne Starr of the *Arizona Republic*. It ran with an October 18, 1986, article on the debate by Don Harris entitled "McCain, Kimball Clash on Arms, 'Contra' Aid." The cutline read: "John McCain, several inches shorter than Richard Kimball, stands on a box, making it easier for TV cameras to pan from one candidate to the other."

Anne Q. Hoy, of the *Arizona Republic*, provided a thorough and provocative postelection profile of McCain. The article, published November 9, 1986, was entitled "Meteoric Climb: McCain's Rise to the Senate Caps Ambitious Career Path."

The election eve (November 3, 1986) article linking McCain to Charles Keating was entitled "McCain, Kolbe Tied to Lobby: Given Contributions; Aided Keating Firm in Battle over S&Ls." It was written by United Press International and the staff of the *Arizona Republic*.

The exchange between John Poindexter and Larry Speakes aboard Air Force One was based on an interview with Speakes and on Speakes's book (written with Robert Pack), *Speaking Out: The Reagan Presidency from Inside the White House.*

In addition to their three natural children, Meghan, Jack, and Jimmy, the McCains have adopted two others, Cari and Bridget.

Chapter 37. THE BIGGEST HAWK AND THE BIGGEST DOVE

Interviewees included Jim Webb, Thomas Daly, Richard Armitage, Caspar Weinberger, Frank Carlucci, Victor Reston, Kendell Pease, Thomas Hayes, Harlan Ullman, and Mark Treanor.

General P. X. Kelley, USMC (Ret.), declined to comment for this chapter.

Webb provided declassified versions of his memos to Weinberger.

John McCain voiced his reservations on the reflaggings on various occasions during this period, including a June 21, 1987, article he authored for the *Arizona Republic*, entitled "Sailing into Harm's Way, Administration Overreacts in Plan to Reflag Tankers, McCain Says," and in an interview with Jack Germond and Jules Witcover of the *Baltimore Evening Sun*, published May 28, 1987.

President Reagan, in a letter dated November 5, 1987, accepting Caspar Weinberger's resignation, said: "You've been indispensable in upgrading our military preparedness by promoting the B-1 bomber, overseeing expansion of our Navy to 600 ships, and eloquently advocating the Strategic Defense Initiative. . . ."

Secretary Weinberger, in an August 1994 interview, reaffirmed his support for the six-hundred-ship Navy. Asked if he shared Webb's position, Weinberger replied, "Yes. I never had the slightest doubt about it. We had the carrier groups that were to make it up. It wasn't just a number plucked out of the sky. And it was essential."

Asked if Webb was "deluded" in thinking the six-hundred-ship Navy was important, Weinberger said, "Oh, no. No, no. Not in any way."

Secretary Carlucci, in an October 1994 interview, said he understood why an individual might feel compelled to resign in protest, but questioned whether Webb had acted peremptorily since Webb had never discussed the issue of the frigates directly with him and, so far as he knew, had not sought a private meeting to argue his case. Carlucci agreed, however, that Webb was making his arguments to the right man in Deputy Secretary William Taft in that budget matters had been delegated to Taft.

"On the subject that precipitated his resignation, I don't think we ever had a conversation," said Carlucci. "I had clearly given Will Taft responsibility for the budget. On the other hand, if a subject is important enough to precipitate somebody's resignation, obviously there is an appeal channel to me which would have been highly appropriate to use." As for Webb's manner of resigning, Carlucci said, "Obviously I respect somebody who resigns over a matter of conscience. He disagreed with my decision, he had every right to resign in protest. I obviously would have preferred that he come and tell me to my face, rather than sending me a copy of a letter he sent to the White House."

As for calling Webb at home to assure him there would be no additional operating costs as a result of the Gulf deployment, Carlucci said he did not recall the conversation. He also said that as national security adviser he typically dealt with the service secretaries such as Webb through Defense Secretary Weinberger.

Chapter 38. WHERE WAS AL KREKICH WHEN WE NEEDED HIM?

Interviewees for this chapter and the next included Bud McFarlane, Jonda McFarlane, John Poindexter, Linda Poindexter, Richard Poindexter, Jim Webb, John McCain, Oliver North, Leonard Garment, Samuel Holt, Paul Thompson, Thomas Korologos, Lauren McFarlane, Melissa McFarlane, Robert Sims, Brent Scowcroft, Les Janka, Alexander Krekich, Shlomo Gazit, Carl (Spitz) Channell, Clarence (Mark) Hill, James Holloway, Eric Bowman, William Haskell, Charles Krulak, Michael Deaver, Rodney McDaniel, Will King, and Keith Haines.

Books relied on most heavily for this chapter and the next included the following: *A Very Thin Line: The Iran-Contra Affairs*, by Theodore Draper; *President Reagan: The Role of a Lifetime*, by Lou Cannon; *Landslide: The Unmaking of the President 1984–1988*, by Jane Mayer and Doyle McManus; *Best Laid Plans: The Inside Story of America's War Against Terrorism*, by David C. Martin and John Walcott; *Banana Diplomacy: The Making of American Policy in Nicaragua 1981–1987*, by Roy Gutman; *Secret Warriors: Inside the Covert Military Operations of the Reagan Era*, by Steven Emerson; *Guts and Glory: The Rise and Fall of Oliver North*, by Ben Bradlee, Jr.; *Men of Zeal*, by William S. Cohen and George J. Mitchell; *Scandal: The Culture of Mistrust in American Politics*, by Suzanne Garment; *Perilous Statecraft: An Insider's Account of the Iran-Contra Affair*, by Michael A. Ledeen; *Special Trust*, by Robert C. McFarlane with Zofia Smardz; *Inside the National Security Council: The True Story of the Making and Unmaking of Reagan's Foreign Policy*, by Constantine C. Menges; *Under Fire: An American Story*, by Oliver L. North and William Novak; *For the Record: From Wall Street to Washington*, by Donald T. Regan; *Honored and Betrayed: Irangate, Covert Affairs, and the Secret War in Laos*, by Richard Secord with Jay Wurts; *Turmoil and Triumph: My Years as Secretary of State*, by George P. Shultz; *The Power Game: How Washington Works*, by Hedrick Smith; *Speaking*

Out: The Reagan Presidency from Inside the White House, by Larry Speakes with Robert Pack; *Twin Pillars to Desert Storm: America's Flawed Vision in the Middle East from Nixon to Bush*, by Howard Teicher and Gayle Radley Teicher; *Fighting for Peace: Seven Critical Years in the Pentagon*, by Caspar W. Weinberger; *Veil: The Secret Wars of the CIA 1981–1987*, by Bob Woodward; and *An American Life*, by Ronald Reagan.

In addition, critical to this chapter and the next were the following documents: *Report of the President's Special Review Board*, also known as the Tower Commission Report; *Report of the Congressional Committees Investigating the Iran-Contra Affair* (with Appendices); and *Iran-Contra: The Final Report*, by Lawrence E. Walsh, independent counsel.

Beyond independent research for this book, the author also relied in part on his own reporting on the Iran-Contra affair as White House correspondent for the *Baltimore Sun*.

Chapter 39. CHINATOWN

See Notes to Chapter 38 for interviews conducted and books consulted.

Regarding the comparison of Iran-Contra and the playing of the China card by Henry Kissinger: On July 28, 1965, in a radio and television address to the nation, President Johnson spoke of China's role in the Vietnam conflict. He said that Vietnam was "a different kind of war," then added: "But we must not let this mask the central fact that this is really war. It is guided by North Vietnam and it is spurred by Communist China. Its goal is to conquer the South, to defeat American power, and to extend the Asiatic dominion of Communism. And there are great stakes in the balance. Most of the non-Communist nations of Asia cannot, by themselves and alone, resist the growing might and grasping ambition of Asian Communism."

The author, after conferring with his editors, attended Bud McFarlane's birthday party at Wolf Trap. An account of the party by Donnie Radcliffe appeared in the *Washington Post* of July 14, 1987, "For McFarlane, a Golden Boy Serenade."

William Kristol's comment about honesty in Washington appeared in a January 18, 1993, *Washington Post* article, "Feint Dams for Those High-Level Leaks," by Joel Achenbach. Achenbach notes that Kristol's comment was delivered "wryly."

Every major newspaper covered the Iran-Contra affair in detail. The author relied heavily, though not exclusively by any means, on accounts in the *Baltimore Sun*, the *New York Times*, the *Washington Post*, the *Boston Globe*, the *Wall Street Journal*, and the *Los Angeles Times*.

The *Washington Post* published an intriguing op-ed piece by Bud McFarlane shortly after the story of the Iranian arms sales broke in which he compared the initiative to the secret diplomacy that led to the China opening under Richard Nixon. The article, entitled "McFarlane on Why," ran November 13, 1986.

In his final report, issued in January 1994, independent counsel Lawrence Walsh asserted that there had been a cover-up in which senior members of the administration had participated. He won an indictment of Caspar Weinberger in 1992 on charges of perjury and making false statements. Weinberger, wrote Walsh, "lied to investigators to conceal his knowledge of the Iranian arms sales." Weinberger denied the charge.

Walsh stopped just short of indicting George Shultz as well. Noting that Shultz and other State Department officials were "the emerging heroes of the Iran/Contra story and seemed to have nothing to hide" back in 1987, Walsh said that new evidence in the form of handwritten notes discovered in 1990 and 1991 gravely undercut the protestations of outrage by Shultz and others.

"Independent Counsel concluded that Shultz's testimony was incorrect, if not false, in significant respects and misleading," wrote Walsh. He went on to say that he declined to prosecute the former Secretary of State because the evidence did not establish beyond a reasonable doubt that Shultz's testimony had been "willfully false . . . [h]owever difficult it may be to believe that Shultz could forget events that troubled him so deeply."

Walsh's investigation of George Bush belied the assertion of the Vice President (and later President) that he was "out of the loop" on Iran-Contra matters, but no prosecution resulted. In December 1992, twelve days before Weinberger was to go on trial, Bush pardoned the former Secretary of Defense along with Bud McFarlane, former Assistant Secretary of State Elliott Abrams, and three other Iran-Contra figures.

EPILOGUE

Interviewees included John Poindexter, John McCain, Bud McFarlane, Jim Webb, and Oliver North.

Laurie Kellman, of the *Washington Times*, reported on John Warner's efforts to persuade Jim Webb to run against Oliver North in "Webb Not Jumping into Race," published April 1, 1994.

John McCain, in his 1992 reelection race, again raised far more money than his opponents. According to the Federal Election Commission, he raised $3.3 million during the 1991–92 election cycle, compared to $288,000 for Claire Sargent and $90,000 for Evan Mecham.

The editorial cartoon of Cindy McCain shaking the child was by Benson. It ran in the *Arizona Republic* on August 23, 1994.

The cheating scandal at the Naval Academy was chronicled exhaustively and aggressively by Tom Bowman and JoAnna Daemmrich of the *Baltimore Sun*. Absent their aggressive reporting, the magnitude of the scandal might never have come to light.

Oliver North's campaign for the U.S. Senate in Virginia was aggressively chronicled by Kent Jenkins, Jr., and Donald P. Baker of the *Washington Post*.

BIBLIOGRAPHY

Books Read or Consulted

Several of the books listed here deserve special mention for their pertinence, insight, or both. Jack Sweetman's *The U.S. Naval Academy: An Illustrated History* was a fine guide. The Vietnam War era is rendered superbly by David Halberstam in *The Best and the Brightest*; by Stanley Karnow in *Vietnam: A History*; by Rick Atkinson in *The Long Gray Line: The American Journey of West Point's Class of 1966*; by Neil Sheehan in *A Bright Shining Lie: John Paul Vann and America in Vietnam*; and by Lawrence M. Baskir and William A. Strauss in *Chance and Circumstance: The Draft, the War and the Vietnam Generation*, the last a truly invaluable resource. Out of print and difficult to find, John G. Hubbell's *P.O.W.: A Definitive History of the American Prisoner-of-War Experience* is a stunning chronicle. Anyone writing about the modern presidency should start with Richard E. Neustadt's classic, *Presidential Power*, first published in 1960 and updated twice, now including a look at the Reagan years and the Iran-Contra affair. The 1990 update is *Presidential Power and the Modern Presidents: The Politics of Leadership from Roosevelt to Reagan*. Lou Cannon's *President Reagan: The Role of a Lifetime* provided a clear sight line into the operation of the Reagan White House and the nature of Mr. Reagan himself. *Landslide: The Unmaking of the President 1984–1988*, by Jane Mayer and Doyle McManus, did the same, but narrowed the focus to Reagan's second term and the Iran-Contra affair. Peggy Noonan's engaging and provocative memoir, *What I Saw at the Revolution: A Political Life in the Reagan Era*, demonstrated anew the value of peripheral vision. *Best Laid Plans: The Inside Story of America's War Against Terrorism* by David C. Martin and John Walcott more than lived up to its title. So did Roy Gutman's *Banana Diplomacy: The Making of American Diplomacy in Nicaragua 1981–1987* and Steven Emerson's *Secret Warriors: Inside the Covert Military Operations of the Rea-*

gan Era. Ben Bradlee, Jr.'s *Guts and Glory: The Rise and Fall of Oliver North* provided a road map into the life of his subject and one of mine. Theodore Draper, in *A Very Thin Line: The Iran-Contra Affairs,* produced a remarkably lucid work of scholarship based solely on a perusal of the written record—documents, published materials, testimony, trial transcripts—at least as it existed to 1990.

Three governmental reports were invaluable in assessing Iran-Contra—the report of the Tower Commission, the report of the joint congressional committee that investigated the Iran-Contra affair, and the *Final Report* of Iran-Contra special prosecutor Lawrence Walsh.

I didn't agree with everything I read, but each of the books, documents, and other published materials in the list that follows helped move me along.

Atkinson, Rick. *The Long Gray Line: The American Journey of West Point's Class of 1966.* Boston: Houghton Mifflin, 1989.

Barrett, Laurence I. *Gambling with History: Reagan in the White House.* Garden City, N.Y.: Doubleday, 1983.

Baskir, Lawrence M., and William A. Strauss. *Chance and Circumstance: The Draft, the War and the Vietnam Generation.* New York: Vintage Books, 1978.

Brace, Ernest C. *A Code to Keep: The True Story of America's Longest-Held Civilian Prisoner of War in Vietnam.* New York: St. Martin's, 1988.

Bradlee, Ben, Jr. *Guts and Glory: The Rise and Fall of Oliver North.* New York: Donald I. Fine, 1988.

Braestrup, Peter. *Big Story.* 2 vols. Boulder, Col.: Westview Press, 1987.

Broughton, Jack. *Thud Ridge.* New York: Bantam Books, 1985.

Buell, Thomas B. *The Quiet Warrior: A Biography of Admiral Raymond A. Spruance.* Boston: Little, Brown, 1974.

Calvert, James. *The Naval Profession.* New York: McGraw-Hill, 1965.

Cannon, Lou. *Reagan.* New York: G. P. Putnam's Sons, 1982.

———. *President Reagan: The Role of a Lifetime.* New York: Simon & Schuster, 1991.

Cohen, William S. *Roll Call: One Year in the United States Senate.* New York: Simon & Schuster, 1981.

———. *One-Eyed Kings.* New York: Doubleday, 1991.

———, and George J. Mitchell, *Men of Zeal.* New York: Viking Penguin, 1988.

Corson, William R. *The Betrayal.* New York: W.W. Norton, 1968.

Cruz, Arturo, Jr. *Memoirs of a Counter-Revolutionary: Life with the Contras, the Sandinistas, and the CIA.* New York: Doubleday, 1989.

Day, George E. *Return with Honor.* Mesa, Ariz.: Champlin Museum Press, 1990.

Deaver, Michael K., with Mickey Herskowitz. *Behind the Scenes.* New York: William Morrow, 1987.

Denton, Jeremiah A., Jr., with Ed Brandt. *When Hell Was in Session.* Clover, S.C.: Commission Press, 1976.

Downs, Frederick, Jr. *The Killing Zone: My Life in the Vietnam War.* New York: W.W. Norton, 1978.

———. *Aftermath: A Soldier's Return from Vietnam.* New York: W.W. Norton, 1984.

Draper, Theodore. *A Very Thin Line: The Iran-Contra Affairs.* New York: Hill and Wang, 1991.

Emerson, Steven. *Secret Warriors: Inside the Covert Military Operations of the Reagan Era*. New York: G.P. Putnam's Sons, 1988.

Enthoven, Alain C., and Wayne K. Smith. *How Much Is Enough?: Shaping the Defense Program, 1961–1969*. New York: Harper & Row, 1971.

Frank, Benis M. *U.S. Marines in Lebanon 1982–1984*. Washington, D.C.: History and Museums Division, Headquarters, U.S. Marine Corps, 1987.

Friedman, Thomas L. *From Beirut to Jerusalem*. New York: Farrar Straus Giroux, 1989.

Gaither, Ralph. *With God in a P.O.W. Camp*. Nashville: Broadman Press, 1973.

Garment, Suzanne. *Scandal: The Culture of Mistrust in American Politics*. New York: Anchor Books, 1992.

Grant, Zalin. *Over the Beach: The Air War in Vietnam*. New York: W.W. Norton, 1986.

Greene, Bob. *Homecoming: When the Soldiers Returned from Vietnam*. New York: G.P. Putnam's Sons, 1989.

Grey, Anthony. *Saigon*. Boston: Little, Brown, 1982.

Gutman, Roy. *Banana Diplomacy: The Making of American Policy in Nicaragua 1981–1987*. New York: Simon & Schuster, 1988.

Haig, Alexander M., Jr. *Caveat*. New York: Macmillan, 1984.

Halberstam, David. *The Best and the Brightest*. New York: Random House, 1972.

Halsey, William F., and J. Bryan III. *Admiral Halsey's Story*. New York: Whittlesey House, 1947.

Hartmann, Frederick H. *Naval Renaissance: The U.S. Navy in the 1980s*. Annapolis, Md.: Naval Institute Press, 1990.

Head, Richard G., Frisco W. Short, and Robert C. McFarlane. *Crisis Resolution: Presidential Decision Making in the "Mayaguez" and Korean Confrontations*. Boulder, Col.: Westview Press, 1978.

Herrod, Randy. *Blue's Bastards: A True Story of Valor Under Fire*. Washington, D.C.: Regnery Gateway, 1989.

Hersh, Seymour M. *The Price of Power: Kissinger in the Nixon White House*. New York: Summit Books, 1983.

Hoose, Phillip M. *Hoosiers: The Fabulous Basketball Life of Indiana*. New York: Vintage Books, 1986.

Hubbell, John G., in association with Andrew Jones and Kenneth Y. Tomlinson. *P.O.W.: A Definitive History of the American Prisoner-of-War Experience in Vietnam, 1964–1973*. New York: Reader's Digest Press, 1976.

Karnow, Stanley. *Vietnam: A History*. New York: Penguin Books, 1984.

Ledeen, Michael A. *Perilous Statecraft: An Insider's Account of the Iran-Contra Affair*. New York: Charles Scribner's Sons, 1988.

Lehman, John F., Jr. *Command of the Seas: Building the 600-Ship Navy*. New York: Charles Scribner's Sons, 1988.

Lovell, John P. *Neither Athens Nor Sparta: The American Service Academies in Transition*. Bloomington: Indiana University Press, 1979.

Mackey, Sandra. *Lebanon: Death of a Nation*. New York: Congdon & Weed, 1989.

Martin, David C., and John Walcott. *Best Laid Plans: The Inside Story of America's War Against Terrorism*. New York: Harper & Row, 1988.

Mayer, Jane, and Doyle McManus. *Landslide: The Unmaking of the President 1984–1988*. Boston: Houghton Mifflin Company, 1988.

McFarlane, Robert C., with Zofia Smardz. *Special Trust*. New York: Cadell & Davies, 1994.

Menges, Constantine C. *Inside the National Security Council: The True Story of the Making and Unmaking of Reagan's Foreign Policy*. New York: Simon & Schuster, 1988.

Moore, Harold G., and Joseph L. Galloway, *We Were Soldiers Once . . . and Young: Ia Drang, the Battle That Changed the War in Vietnam*. New York: Random House, 1992.

Moskin, J. Robert. *The U.S. Marine Corps Story*. Second revised and updated edition. New York: McGraw-Hill, 1987.

Moyers, Bill. *The Secret Government: The Constitution in Crisis*. Cabin John, Md./Washington, D.C.: Seven Locks Press, 1988.

Mulligan, James A. *The Hanoi Commitment*. Virginia Beach, Va.: RIF Marketing, 1981.

Myrer, Anton. *Once an Eagle*. New York: Holt, Rinehart & Winston, 1968.

Neustadt, Richard E. *Presidential Power: The Politics of Leadership from FDR to Carter*. New York: John Wiley & Sons, 1980.

———. *Presidential Power and the Modern Presidents: The Politics of Leadership from Roosevelt to Reagan*. New York: Free Press; London: Macmillan, 1990.

———, and Ernest R. May. *Thinking in Time: The Uses of History for Decision Makers*. New York: The Free Press, 1986.

Nitze, Paul H., with Ann M. Smith and Steven L. Rearden. *From Hiroshima to Glasnost: At the Center of Decision—A Memoir*. New York: Grove Weidenfeld, 1989.

Noonan, Peggy. *What I Saw at the Revolution: A Political Life in the Reagan Era*. New York: Random House, 1990.

North, Oliver L., and William Novak. *Under Fire: An American Story*. New York: HarperCollins and Zondervan, 1991.

North, Oliver L., and David Roth. *One More Mission: Oliver North Returns to Vietnam*. Grand Rapids, Mich., and New York: Zondervan and HarperCollins, 1993.

Oberdorfer, Don. *The Turn: From the Cold War to a New Era—The United States and the Soviet Union 1983-1990*. New York: Poseidon Press, 1991.

Plumb, Charlie. *I'm No Hero: A POW Story as Told to Glen DeWerff*. Independence, Mo.: Independence Press, 1973.

Potter, E. B. *Bull Halsey*. Annapolis, Md.: Naval Institute Press, 1985.

Poyer, David. *The Return of Philo T. McGiffin*. New York: St. Martin's, 1983.

Reagan, Ronald. *An American Life*. New York: Simon & Schuster, 1990.

Reef Points, 1993-1994: The Annual Handbook of the Brigade of Midshipmen, 88th Edition. Annapolis, Md.: United States Naval Academy (no publication date).

Regan, Donald T. *For the Record: From Wall Street to Washington*. San Diego, New York, London: Harcourt Brace Jovanovich, 1988.

Report of the President's Special Review Board. Washington, D.C.: U.S. Government Printing Office, 1987 (known as the Tower Commission Report after its chairman, former U.S. Senator John G. Tower).

Santoli, Al. *New Americans: An Oral History*. New York: Viking, 1988.

Schemmer, Benjamin F. *The Raid*. New York: Harper & Row, 1976.

Schulze, Richard C. *Leatherneck Square: A Professional Marine's Personal Perspective of the Vietnam Era*. The Huckleberry Press, 1989.

Scruggs, Jan C., and Joel L. Swerdlow. *To Heal a Nation: The Vietnam Veterans Memorial.* New York: Harper & Row, 1985.

Secord, Richard, with Jay Wurts. *Honored and Betrayed: Irangate, Covert Affairs, and the Secret War in Laos.* New York: John Wiley & Sons, 1992.

Sheehan, Neil. *A Bright Shining Lie: John Paul Vann and America in Vietnam.* New York: Random House, 1988.

Shultz, George P. *Turmoil and Triumph: My Years as Secretary of State.* New York: Charles Scribner's Sons, 1993.

Smith, Hedrick. *The Power Game: How Washington Works.* New York: Random House, 1988.

Solis, Gary D. *Marines and Military Law in Vietnam: Trial by Fire.* Washington, D.C.: History and Museums Division, Headquarters, U.S. Marine Corps, 1989.

Speakes, Larry, with Robert Pack. *Speaking Out: The Reagan Presidency from Inside the White House.* New York: Charles Scribner's Sons, 1988.

Stockdale, Vice Admiral James B. *A Vietnam Experience: Ten Years of Reflections.* Stanford, Cal.: Hoover Institution, 1984.

Stockdale, Jim, and Sybil Stockdale. *In Love and War.* New York: Harper & Row, 1984.

Sweetman, Jack. *The U.S. Naval Academy: An Illustrated History.* Annapolis, Md.: Naval Institute Press, 1979.

Taking the Stand: The Testimony of Lieutenant Colonel Oliver L. North. New York: Pocket Books, 1987.

Talbott, Strobe. *Deadly Gambits: The Reagan Administration and the Stalemate in Nuclear Arms Control.* New York: Alfred A. Knopf, 1984.

———. *The Master of the Game: Paul Nitze and the Nuclear Peace.* New York: Alfred A. Knopf, 1988.

Teicher, Howard, and Gayle Radley Teicher. *Twin Pillars to Desert Storm: America's Flawed Vision in the Middle East from Nixon to Bush.* New York: William Morrow, 1993.

Tower, John G. *Consequences: A Personal and Political Memoir.* Boston: Little, Brown, 1991.

Trewhitt, Henry L. *McNamara: His Ordeal in the Pentagon.* New York: Harper & Row, 1971.

U.S. Senate Select Committee on Secret Military Assistance to Iran and the Nicaraguan Opposition and U.S. House of Representatives Select Committee to Investigate Covert Arms Transactions with Iran. *Report of the Congressional Committees Investigating the Iran-Contra Affair* (with Appendices). Washington, D.C.: U.S. Government Printing Office, 1987.

Walsh, Lawrence E. *Iran-Contra: The Final Report.* New York: Times Books, 1994.

Webb, James H., Jr. *Micronesia and the U. S. Pacific Strategy,* New York: Praeger, 1974.

Webb, James. *Fields of Fire.* New York: Prentice-Hall, 1978.

———. *A Sense of Honor.* New York: Prentice-Hall, 1981.

———. *A Country Such As This.* New York: Doubleday, 1983.

———. *Something to Die For.* New York: William Morrow, 1991.

Weinberger, Caspar W. *Fighting for Peace: Seven Critical Years in the Pentagon.* New York: Warner Books, 1990.

Wheeler, John. *Touched with Fire: The Future of the Vietnam Generation.* New York: Franklin Watts, 1984.

Williams, Richard Pardee. *The High School: The History of the Episcopal High School in Virginia at Alexandria.* Boston: Vincent-Curtis, 1964.

Wilson, George. *Supercarrier: An Inside Account of Life Aboard the World's Most Powerful Ship, the U.S.S. John F. Kennedy.* New York: Macmillan, 1988.

Woodward, Bob. *Veil: The Secret Wars of the CIA 1981–1987.* New York: Simon & Schuster, 1987.

Wright, Robin. *Sacred Rage: The Wrath of Militant Islam.* New York: Touchstone/Simon & Schuster, 1986.

Articles and Documents

Agence France-Presse. "Hanoi Says McCain's Son Terms U.S. 'Isolated,'" *New York Times*, November 11, 1967.

Allen, Henry. "Vietnam: Hazy Images and Searing Memories—The Drama of the Absolutely Ordinary Soldier," *Washington Post*, November 11, 1992.

Alvarez, Everett, Jr. "Sound: A POW's Weapon," *U.S. Naval Institute Proceedings*, August 1976.

Andersen, Kurt, reported by Jay Branegan/Washington. "A Homecoming at Last," *Time*, November 22, 1982.

Apple, R. W., Jr. "Adm. McCain's Son, *Forrestal* Survivor, Is Missing in Raid," *New York Times*, October 28, 1967.

———. "National Role Is Seen for Arizona Politician," *New York Times*, November 2, 1986.

Archibald, George. "From Hanoi to the House," *Washington Times*, February 3, 1983.

Arizona Republic. "Those Key Races," September 5, 1982 (endorsement editorial).

———. "McCain Challenges Vietnam on POWs," February 24, 1985.

———. "U.S. Senate: John McCain Recommended," October 26, 1986 (endorsement editorial).

Arnebeck, Bob. "Monumental Folly," *The Progressive*, July 1982.

Atkins, Norman. "Oliver's Twists," *Rolling Stone*, July 16–30, 1987.

Babington, Charles. "Vietnam War Looms Over Veterans Day," *Washington Post*, November 12, 1992.

Baer, Susan. "When Fiction Nears Truth, Webb's War Novel Poses Predicament," *Baltimore Sun*, February 13, 1991.

Bauer, Paul F. "'A Sense of Honor' Another Excellent Book by James Webb," *Cecil Whig*, March 25, 1981.

Beck, Melinda, with Mary Lord. "Refighting the Vietnam War," *Newsweek*, October 25, 1982.

Bennett, Ralph Kinney. "Grenada: Anatomy of a 'Go' Decision," *Reader's Digest*, February 1984.

Bisbie, Gene. "A Nuclear Prep School," *Annapolis Evening Capital*, March 4, 1981.

Boeth, Richard. "Fields of Fire," *Newsweek*, October 9, 1978.

Breslin, Jimmy. "It's a Fine Mess, Ollie," *New York Daily News,* December 4, 1986.

Brisbane, Arthur S. "President Leads Tribute to Vietnam Veterans: Reconciliation Theme Voiced in Mall Ceremony," *Washington Post*, November 12, 1984.

Brock, David. "The Consummate Staff Man: John M. Poindexter at NSC," *Insight* (*Washington Times* magazine), February 10, 1986.

Broder, David S. "Some Questions for the Secretary," *Washington Post*, December 23, 1984.

———. "McCain: Strong-Man Weinberger Finds Defense-Minded Arizonan Is Equally Tough Critic," *Arizona Republic*, January 3, 1985.

———. "Beaches and Peoples: A Matter of Time," *Washington Post*, July 19, 1987.

Brower, Brock. "Bud McFarlane, Semper Fi," *New York Times Magazine*, February 22, 1989.

Brown, L. T. " 'Honor' Has Questions for U.S. Fighters" (review of *A Sense of Honor*, by James Webb), *Indianapolis News*, April 4, 1981.

Broyles, William, Jr. "Remembering a War We Want to Forget," *Newsweek*, November 22, 1983.

———. "A Ritual for Saying Goodbye," *U.S. News & World Report*, November 10, 1986.

Buckley, Christopher. "Viet Guilt," *Esquire*, September 1983.

———. "The Wall," *Esquire*, September 1985.

Buckley, Tom. "Anyone for War?" (review of *The Long Gray Line*, by Rick Atkinson), *New York Times Book Review*, October 22, 1989.

Bunting, Josiah, III. "The Launching of a Midshipman" (review of *A Sense of Honor*, by James Webb), *Washington Post Book World*, March 29, 1981.

Burchell, Joe. "McCain, Kimball Start with Opposing Styles," *Arizona Daily Star* (Tucson), February 2, 1986.

———. "McCain Denies Letter's Charge He Is Insensitive to Senior Citizens," *Arizona Daily Star* (Tucson), June 21, 1986.

Cannella, David. "Kimball Seizes on Foe's Faux Pas, Will Chisel at 'Insensitive' McCain," *Arizona Republic*, July 13, 1986.

Cannon, Lou. "Of Arms and the Man," *Washington Post Book World*, December 8, 1991.

Carhart, Tom. "Insulting Vietnam Veterans," *New York Times*, October 24, 1981.

———. "A Better Way to Honor Viet Vets," *Washington Post*, November 15, 1981.

———. "Coming Out of the Shadows of Vietnam," *Washington Times*, September 20, 1982.

———. "Poll Shows Most Viet-Vets Against Memorial Design," *Washington Times*, October 12, 1982.

Carter, Hodding, III. "A Confederacy of Liars, Guarded by a Yawning Watchdog," *Wall Street Journal*, January 25, 1990.

Charles, Roger. "Oliver North's Version," *Chicago Tribune*, November 3, 1991.

Choice. Review of *Fields of Fire*, by James Webb, December 1978.

Christian, George. "Throw Your Hat Across the Fence," *Houston Chronicle*, October 30, 1983.

Coffey, Shelby, III. "Marine with Revolution on His Mind," *Potomac*, May 18, 1969. (*Potomac* was the name of *Washington Post* Sunday magazine at the time.)

Copulos, Milt. "Background to Betrayal: Viet Vets Want Their Memorial Back," *Soldier of Fortune*, May 1983.

Crovitz, L. Gordon. "Ollie's Story: Iran-Contra Hostage Crisis, Day 1,769," *Wall Street Journal*, October 23, 1991.

Cullen, Robert B., with Rod Nordland, Theodore Stanger et al. "Cruising on a Murderous Course," *Newsweek*, October 21, 1985.

Davis, Bob. "A Simple Black Wall Embraces the Rituals of Saying Goodbye," *Wall Street Journal*, November 4, 1992.

Davis, Nathaniel. "On Teaching North: Far Too Many Grays," *Los Angeles Times*, December 21, 1986.

Deckard, Rob. "Annapolis in Transition" (review of *A Sense of Honor*, by James Webb), *Louisville Times*, March 28, 1981.

Deming, Angus, with Ruth Marshall and Milan J. Kubic. "Arafat vs. Himself," *Newsweek*, October 21, 1985.

Dolan, Maura. "Clues to Poindexter Found in Early Life," *Los Angeles Times*, May 3, 1987.

———, and Richard E. Meyer. "Friends Recall Fired Aide: North Tended from Start to Go Too Far," *Los Angeles Times*, March 1, 1987.

Doubek, Robert. W. "The Story of the Vietnam Veterans Memorial," *The Retired Officer*, November 1983.

Dunn, Si. "Annapolis and 'Honor': True or Not, It's a Good Story" (review of *A Sense of Honor*, by James Webb), *Dallas Morning News*, May 3, 1981.

Everett, Bart. "No One Triumphs from This Tough Training" (review of *A Sense of Honor*, by James Webb), *Los Angeles Times*, April 26, 1981.

Fagan, Fred T., Jr. Review of *Fields of Fire*, *Naval War College Review*, February 1979.

Fallows, James. "What Did You Do in the Class War, Daddy?," *Washington Monthly*, October 1975.

Feldman, Trude. "Three Thanksgivings: The Saga of Robert McFarlane," *McCall's*, November 1987.

Foreign Service of the United States of America. Telegram. W. Averell Harriman to Secretary of State, September 13, 1968.

Forgey, Benjamin. "The Memorial's Moment of Truce: A Solution with Pride, Harmony and Vision," *Washington Post*, February 9, 1983.

"Former Marine in Line to Be Chosen as Head of Veterans' Agency," *Washington Post*, April 2, 1981.

Franklin, Ben A. "President Accepts Vietnam Memorial," *New York Times*, November 12, 1984.

———. "On the Phenomenon That Was the Vietnam Era," *New York Times*, June 8, 1986.

Friend, David. "A Man of Many Faces: Oliver North May Go to Jail, but Iranscam's Central Player Shows Another Side—as a Suburban Father," *Life*, August 1987. (Includes interview with Betsy North.)

Gelb, Leslie H. "Security Council's 'Mr. Indispensable,' " *New York Times*, October 18, 1982.

Germond, Jack W., and Jules Witcover. "A New Arizona Institution," *Phoenix Gazette*, April 7, 1986.

———. "Moves in Gulf Becoming Risky," *Baltimore Evening Sun*, May 28, 1987.

Geyelin, Philip. "Echoes of Vietnam," *Washington Post*, May 10, 1987.

Glaser, Vera. "People to Watch: John McCain," *The Washingtonian*, April 1986.

Greider, William. "Profiles in Cowardice," *Rolling Stone*, November 24, 1983.

Griffin, Sean. "McCain Settles in at Senate, Hopes to Be There 'Long Time,' " *Phoenix Gazette*, April 20, 1987.

Griswold, Charles L. "The Vietnam Veterans Memorial and the Washington Mall:

Philosophical Thoughts on Political Iconography," *Critical Inquiry*, Summer 1986.

Grove, Lloyd. "At the Bosnia Crossroads—No: The Senator, Wary of the Perils of Failure," *Washington Post*, May 5, 1993.

Harris, Art. "The Abiding Riddle of Oliver North," *Washington Post*, December 23, 1986.

Harris, Don. "Former Prisoner of War Declares Candidacy for 1st District," *Arizona Republic*, March 25, 1982.

———. "GOP 1st District Quartet Singing Familiar Medley on Issues," *Arizona Republic*, June 13, 1982.

———. "Discord Sharpens Among Republicans as District 1 Contenders Trade Barbs," *Arizona Republic*, June 28, 1982.

———. "Newcomer Touts His Knowledge of Capitol Hill," *Arizona Republic*, July 11, 1982.

———. "GOP Primary in 1st District Termed Close," *Arizona Republic*, August 29, 1982.

———. "GOP Hopefuls Highlight Races for Congress," *Arizona Republic*, September 5, 1982.

———. "McCain Takes District 1 Primary," *Arizona Republic*, September 8, 1982.

———. "The Walking and Knocking Begins Again," *Arizona Republic*, September 9, 1982.

———. "McCain's Campaign Spending Leads in Congressional Races," *Arizona Republic*, October 21, 1982.

———. "Tully's Lies Rang True to Combat Flier McCain," *Arizona Republic*, January 4, 1986.

———. "Kimball Levels Conflict Charges Against McCain, Consultant," *Arizona Republic*, May 21, 1986.

———. "McCain, Kimball Clash on Arms, 'Contra' Aid," *Arizona Republic*, October 18, 1986.

———. "Kimball Says McCain Is Pushing U.S. Toward Latin America War," *Arizona Republic*, October 20, 1986.

———. "McCain, Kimball Spar in Second of 3 Senate-Race Debates," *Arizona Republic*, October 23, 1986.

———. "McCain Is Battling Label of 'Bought and Paid For,' " *Arizona Republic*, November 1, 1986.

———. "McCain Beats Kimball in Senate Race," *Arizona Republic*, November 5, 1986.

Hersh, Seymour M. "P.O.W.'s Maintained Discipline but Had Some Quarrels," *New York Times*, February 23, 1973.

———. "Target Qaddafi," *New York Times Magazine*, February 22, 1987.

———. "The Iran-Contra Committees: Did They Protect Reagan?," *New York Times Magazine*, April 29, 1990.

Hoffman, David, and Lou Cannon. "President Overruled Advisers on Announcing Defense Plan," *Washington Post*, March 26, 1983.

Horowitz, Rick. "Maya Lin's Angry Objections," *Washington Post*, July 7, 1982.

Horrock, Nicholas M. "Gen. Al Gray Taking Professional Style, Teamwork to the Top," *Daily News* (Jacksonville, N.C.), June 28, 1987 (reprinted from *Chicago Tribune*).

Howard, Margo. "Lunch on the Left Bank: Jim Webb," *Boston Magazine*, March 1993.

Hoy, Anne Q. "McCain Collects 13 Times Sum Raised by Kimball in Senate Bid," *Arizona Republic*, February 2, 1986.

———. "McCain Romping Ahead of Kimball in Raising, Spending Money," *Arizona Republic*, July 18, 1986.

———. "Meteoric Climb: McCain's Rise to the Senate Caps Ambitious Career Path," *Arizona Republic*, November 9, 1986.

Hull, Robert L., Jr. "Author's Talent Mixes Realism with Fiction" (review of *A Sense of Honor*, by James Webb), *State Journal-Register* (Springfield, Ill.), March 29, 1981.

Hunter, Stephen. "Naval Academy, Author Far Apart on Modern-Day 'Rite of Manhood,' " *Baltimore Sun*, April 19, 1981.

Jenkins, Kent, Jr. "Six Veterans Bash North, Push Robb for Senate," *Washington Post*, October 8, 1994.

———. "North's Agenda Would Make Him 'Lightning Rod' as Senator," *Washington Post*, October 10, 1994.

———. "North Has Raised $15 Million, May Set Record for Senate Race," *Washington Post*, October 15, 1994.

———. "North Says U.S. Military Unable to Stop Saddam," *Washington Post*, October 10, 1994.

———. "Dole Accuses Gore of Taking 'Cheap Shot,' " *Washington Post*, October 13, 1994.

———. "After a Summer of Cool Restraint, North, Robb Start Slinging the Mud," *Washington Post*, October 8, 1994.

———, and Donald P. Baker. "Virginia GOP Nominates North for Senate: Miller's Strong Showing Highlights Vulnerability of Party's Choice," *Washington Post*, June 5, 1994.

Jennings, Max. "Kimball Peddling Foolishness: Demo Keeps McCain Misstep Before Voters," *Mesa Tribune*, July 13, 1986.

Johnson, Haynes, and David S. Broder. "Voting from a Vietnam Veteran's Perspective," *Washington Post*, January 13, 1991.

Johnston, David. "North Says Reagan Knew of Deal," *New York Times*, October 20, 1991.

———. "North Says Bush Knew Shape of His Efforts to Aid Contras," *New York Times*, October 23, 1991.

Jordan, Mary. "Hundreds Bring Anti-War Message to D.C.," *Washington Post*, January 13, 1991.

Katz, Lee Michael. "North's Book Sheds No Light, Just 'Suspicion,' " *USA Today*, October 21, 1991.

Kelley, Charles, with Carol Sowers, Jacquee G. Petchel, Art Thomason, and Earl Zarbin. "A Hero That Never Was: Ex-Publisher's 'Mittylike' Fantasy a Life of Grief, Deceit," *Arizona Republic*, January 26, 1986.

Kellman, Laurie. "Webb Not Jumping into Race," *Washington Times*, April 1, 1994.

Kelly, Michael. "Two Men Who Helped North Still Support the Cause," *Baltimore Sun*, August 9, 1987.

———, and Liz Bowie. "Enigma of Colonel North Stands at Scandal's Center," *Baltimore Sun*, December 14, 1986.

————, and Robert Timberg. "Owen Is Called a Key Link in Contra Supply Efforts," *Baltimore Sun*, December 18, 1986.

Kemp, Geoffrey. "Lessons of Lebanon: A Guide for Future U.S. Policy," *Middle East Insight*, Summer 1988.

————. "As the World Turns," *The New Republic*, November 21, 1988.

Kemper, Vicki. "The Making of a Candidate," *Common Cause Magazine*, Winter 1993.

Kimball, Richard, for U.S. Senate Committee. "Kimball: 'McCain Is Being Bought and Paid For,' " July 18, 1986 (press release from Kimball for U.S. Senate Committee).

Kirkus Reviews. Review of *A Sense of Honor*, by James Webb, February 15, 1981.

Kirschten, Dick. "Clark Emerges as a Tough Manager, Not a Rival to Secretary of State," *National Journal*, July 17, 1982.

Klassen, Teri. "McCain 'Seizure World' Crack Protested," *Arizona Republic*, July 9, 1986.

Klein, Phillip D. "The Naval Academy—Blemishes and All" (review of *A Sense of Honor*, by James Webb), *Virginian-Pilot and the Ledger-Star*, April 12, 1981.

Kolbe, John. "Time, Circumstance Thin Ranks of Hopeful Rhodes Successors," *Phoenix Gazette*, February 15, 1982.

————. "John McCain, Surprise Leader in House Race, Target of Mudslinging," *Phoenix Gazette*, May 20, 1982.

————. "GOP Race for Rhodes' Seat Too Close to Call—Almost," *Phoenix Gazette*, August 26, 1982.

————. "Golden Boy McCain Has Unsettling Flaw—His Temper," *Phoenix Gazette*, January 23, 1986.

————. "Angry McCain Could Turn Senate Race into Contest After All," *Phoenix Gazette*, July 30, 1986.

————. "Traveling Burt and Johnny Show Not Politics as Usual," *Phoenix Gazette*, August 22, 1986.

————. "Enough! Senate Candidates Should Finish Kindergarten," *Phoenix Gazette*, October 1, 1986.

————. "Goldwater: A 'Prophet' with 'Real Ideas,' " *Phoenix Gazette*, December 3, 1986.

————. "McCain's Return to Grace Capped on Convention Dais," *Phoenix Gazette*, August 20, 1992.

Krauthammer, Charles (writing as C.K.). "Memorials," *The New Republic*, May 23, 1981.

Laake, Deborah. "A Hero's Image," *New Times*, May 28, 1986.

LaFraniere, Sharon, and Priscilla Painton. "President Leads Tribute to Vietnam Veterans: Ex-Soldiers Search for Familiar Faces," *Washington Post*, November 12, 1984.

Lardner, George, Jr. "North: Reagan 'Knew Everything,' " *Washington Post*, October 20, 1991.

Lavin, Cheryl. "The Puzzle of Oliver North," *Chicago Tribune*, March 8, 1987.

Leavy, Jane. "McFarlane and the Taunting Glare of Truth," *Washington Post*, May 7, 1987.

Leber, Michele M. Review of *A Sense of Honor*, by James Webb, *Library Journal*, April 15, 1981.

Lemley, Brad. "Never Give an Inch: James Webb's Struggles with Pen and Sword," *Washington Post Magazine*, December 8, 1985.

Leonard, Susan. "Publisher Tully Quits; Made Up War Record," *Arizona Republic*, December 27, 1985.

Lopez, Larry (Associated Press). "McCain Remodeling Phoenix Home, Planning to Move from 1st District," *Arizona Republic*, October 29, 1986.

Lord, Mary. "Scandals at Annapolis," *Newsweek*, April 27, 1981.

MacEachern, Doug. "Who Is John McCain Really? And What's He Up to in Congress?," *New Times*, January 18–24, 1984.

Maddex, Diane. "Strategist Says U.S. Micronesia Land Needs Not Fully Explained," *Pacific Daily News* (Guam), June 5, 1974.

Mano, D. Keith. "James Webb," *People*, May 5, 1986.

"Marianas and Military," *Pacific Daily News* (Guam), June 28, 1974.

Martel, Ned. "Out on a Limb," *Dossier*, October 1990.

Matthews, Mark, and Robert Timberg. "Iranian Arms Middleman Reportedly Left McFarlane Suspicious," *Baltimore Sun*, January 21, 1987.

McCain, John S., III. "Inside Story: How the POWs Fought Back," *U.S. News & World Report*, May 14, 1973.

———. "Inside Vietnam: What a Former POW Found," *U.S. News & World Report*, March 11, 1985.

———. "Not in Vain: The Painful Lessons of the War Have to Be Faced," *Arizona Republic*, April 28, 1985.

———. "Where Is Their Alternative Policy?" *Washington Times*, March 25, 1987.

———. "Sailing into Harm's Way, Administration Overreacts in Plan to Reflag Tankers, McCain Says," *Arizona Republic*, June 21, 1987.

"McCain, Kolbe Tied to Lobby: Given Contributions; Aided Keating Firm in Battle over S&Ls," *Arizona Republic*, November 3, 1986.

McCombs, Phil. "Maya Lin and the Great Call of China," *Washington Post*, January 3, 1982.

———. "Watt's Memorial Turnabout," *Washington Post*, February 2, 1983.

———. "The Memorial's Moment of Truce: Flag, Statue Approved for 'Front Door' of Lin's Vietnam Design," *Washington Post*, February 9, 1983.

———. "No Medals for Memorial," *Washington Post*, June 12, 1986.

———. "Vietnam: Hazy Images and Searing Memories—The Two Wars of Duong Nguyen," *Washington Post*, November 11, 1992.

McDowell, Edwin. "Unflattering Book Unwelcome in Navy," *New York Times*, February 28, 1981.

McFarlane, Robert C. "At Sea—Where We Belong," *U.S. Naval Institute Proceedings*, November 1971.

———. "The Political Potential of Parity," *U.S. Naval Institute Proceedings*, February 1979.

———. "Out of Africa—by Default," *Washington Post*, August 3, 1986.

———. "Let's Get on with the Opportunity from Iceland," *Washington Post*, October 15, 1986.

———. "McFarlane on Why," *Washington Post*, November 13, 1986.

———. "Give Top Billing to Strategic Arms," *New York Times*, June 23, 1987.

———. "The Contras Are What We've Got," *Los Angeles Times*, September 21, 1987.

———. "Don't Scrap the Midgetman in Haste," *Los Angeles Times*, December 17, 1987.

———. "Time Out on Defense: Without a New Strategic Consensus, Budget Cuts Will Only Bring Chaos," *Washington Post*, January 3, 1988.

———. "Why Does the Electorate Give Us Incompetents at the Helm of State?" *Los Angeles Times*, April 7, 1988.

———. "Risking Double Defeat: No Arms Treaty and Bad Arms," *New York Times*, July 1, 1988.

———. "A Crusade Stalled, a Risk Averted," *Los Angeles Times*, July 27, 1988.

———. "To Soviets, Reagan Made 'Devil's Leverage' Real," *Los Angeles Times*, September 1, 1988.

———. "Consider What Star Wars Accomplished," *New York Times*, August 24, 1993.

McGuire, Patrick A. "Academy Cool to 'Controversial' Graduate," *Baltimore Sun*, May 17, 1983.

———. "From Vietnam to the Pentagon: The Fields of Fire of Navy Secretary James Webb," *Baltimore Sun Magazine*, June 28, 1987.

McManus, Doyle. "North Says Reagan Knew of Funds Diversion," *Los Angeles Times*, October 20, 1991.

———. "Ollie North, Semper Fi," *Los Angeles Times*, October 24, 1991.

Mesa Tribune, "McCain Bashing" (editorial), February 9, 1988.

Morganthau, Tom, with Mary Lord. "Honoring Vietnam Veterans—at Last," *Newsweek*, November 22, 1982.

Morris, Donald R. "Annapolis: A Rapid Development of Unpromising Material" (review of *A Sense of Honor*, by James Webb), *Houston Post*, March 22, 1981.

Morrow, Lance. "1968," *Time*, January 11, 1988.

Murphy, Pat. "Give 'Em Hell, John? McCain Whistles While He Works," *Arizona Republic*, February 4, 1986.

———. "Mr. Kimball Tries to Go to Washington by Utilizing 'Progressivity,' " *Arizona Republic*, February 20, 1986.

Nilsson, Joel. "Rhodes Will Leave House When Term Ends This Year," *Arizona Republic*, January 22, 1982.

———. "Cash Stirs Rancor in GOP Race," *Arizona Republic*, July 25, 1982.

———. "3 Perspectives on District 1 Race," *Arizona Republic*, October 11, 1982.

———. "Ex-POW McCain May Return to Hanoi," *Arizona Republic*, December 21, 1984.

———. "McCain, CBS News Crew Ready for Trip to Vietnam," *Arizona Republic*, January 18, 1985.

———. "McCain Barred by Vietnam, Heads Home," *Arizona Republic*, January 23, 1985.

———. "Return by McCain to State Follows Failure in Attempt to Enter Vietnam," *Arizona Republic*, January 24, 1985.

———. "Coming Home: Political Bonanza Is Seen in McCain's Mission to Vietnam," *Arizona Republic*, January 27, 1985.

———. "Kimball and His Campaign Move to the High Road," *Arizona Republic*, February 4, 1986.

"1968: The Year That Shaped a Generation," *Time*, January 11, 1988.

O'Malley, William J. Review of *A Sense of Honor*, by James Webb, *Best Sellers*, June 1981.

Pacific Daily News (Guam). "On Guam and Pacific Defense," October 9, 1972 (editorial).

Perl, Peter. " 'A Mass Obscenity,' Demonstrations Set Near Vietnam Memorial Anger Vets," *Washington Post*, June 24, 1983.

Peterson, Cass. "Webb Bows Out as Candidate to Head Veterans Agency," *Washington Post*, April 26, 1981.

Petrino, Richard A. "Ollie North, the Misdirected Midshipman," *Los Angeles Times*, December 30, 1986.

Powell, Jody. "McFarlane Bolts the Pack with Arms-Policy Dissent," *Los Angeles Times*, January 19, 1985.

Powell, Stewart. "A Sacred Place on the Potomac," *U.S. News & World Report*, November 10, 1986.

Prendergast, Alan. "Disciplined Sensitivity Unfolds in 'Sense of Honor,' " *Denver Post*, April 12, 1981.

Press, Aric, with Debbie Seward, Ann MacDaniel, et al. "Italy and the Law: Will Justice Be Done?," *Newsweek*, October 21, 1985.

Pressley, Sue Anne. "Catching Up with Life: The Return of Everett Alvarez," *Washington Post*, November 12, 1989.

"Prospective V.A. Chief Withdraws over Cutbacks," *New York Times*, April 29, 1981.

Publishers Weekly. Review of *Fields of Fire*, by James Webb, July 17, 1978.

———. Review of *A Sense of Honor*, by James Webb, February 27, 1981.

Puhr, Kathleen M. "Four Fictional Faces of the Vietnam War," *Modern Fiction Studies*, Spring 1984.

Radcliffe, Donnie. "Washington Ways: For McFarlane, a Golden Boy Serenade," *Washington Post*, July 14, 1987.

Reed, Kit. Review of *A Sense of Honor*, by James Webb, *Middletown Press* (Conn.), March 31, 1981.

Report of the DOD Commission on Beirut International Airport Terrorist Act, October 23, 1983. Dated December 20, 1983 (known as the Long Commission Report after the chairman, Admiral Robert L. J. Long, USN [Ret.]).

Ringle, Ken. "The School with a Southern Accent," *Washington Post*, November 11, 1989.

Robbins, William. "Ex-P.O.W.'s Charge Hanoi with Torture," *New York Times*, September 3, 1969.

Roberts, Steven V. "House, 270 to 161, Votes to Invoke War Powers Act," *New York Times*, September 29, 1983.

"The Roosevelt Memorial: A Set of Bookends," *Newsweek*, January 16, 1961.

Sagalyn, Raphael. Review of *Fields of Fire*, by James Webb, *The New Republic*, October 21, 1978.

Scarlett, Harold. "A War Novel at the Killing and Dying Level," *Houston Post*, September 17, 1978.

Schwartz, John. "Kimball Knocks on Doors, Raps Drug Use," *Arizona Republic*, September 7, 1986.

Scruggs, Jan Craig. "Forgotten Veterans of 'That Peculiar War,' " *Washington Post*, May 25, 1977.

Seib, Gerald F. "North's Book Asserts Reagan Knew of Scheme," *Wall Street Journal*, October 21, 1991.

Sherwood, Carlton, Gannett News Service. "Sexual Bias Shakes Naval Academy," *Sunday News Journal* (Wilmington, Del.), April 19, 1981.

———. "The Official Asexual Attitude Turns '(Un)Steady as She Goes,' " *Evening Journal* (Wilmington, Del.), April 20, 1981.

———. "Did Drug Probe at Annapolis Become a Witch Hunt?," *Evening Journal* (Wilmington, Del.), April 21, 1981.

———. "Did Women Middies Torpedo Annapolis Training?," *Evening Journal* (Wilmington, Del.), April 22, 1981.

Shribman, David. "James Webb: Making Waves at Annapolis" (review of *A Sense of Honor*, by James Webb), *Washington Star*, March 3, 1981.

Smith, J. Brian. "Train Tour Traumas: The Anatomy of a Successful Media Event," *Campaigns & Elections*, July–August 1986.

Sowers, Carol. "Goldwater's Message Used Against McCain," *Arizona Republic*, September 7, 1982.

"Special Report: Getting Even," *Newsweek*, October 21, 1985.

Stanley, Alessandra, and Bruce Van Voorst. "Healing Viet Nam's Wounds," *Time*, November 26, 1984.

Stanton, Sam. "McCain, 3 in GOP Tell Mecham to Quit," *Arizona Republic*, January 17, 1988.

Stengel, Richard, Jeanne McDowell, and Alessandra Stanley. "True Belief Unhampered by Doubt," *Time*, July 13, 1987.

Sterba, James P. "U.S. Planes Pick Up 108 Freed Prisoners from Hanoi," *New York Times*, March 14, 1973.

———. "P.O.W. Commander Among 108 Freed," *New York Times*, March 15, 1973.

"Stop That Monument," *National Review*, September 18, 1981.

Swerdlow, Joel L. "To Heal a Nation" (adapted from the book *To Heal a Nation*, by Jan C. Scruggs and Joel L. Swerdlow), *National Geographic*, May 1985.

Thomas, Evan. "New Navy Boss: Poet and Warrior," *Newsweek*, May 4, 1987.

Timberg, Robert. "Cynicism over Iran Finally Leveled Carter," *Baltimore Evening Sun*, November 6, 1980.

———. "Reagan Was Last of High Command to Be Told of Dogfight with Libyans," *Baltimore Sun*, August 20, 1981.

———. "Ex-Marine Nobody Knows Becomes National Security 'Mover, Shaker,' " *Baltimore Sun*, June 13, 1983.

———. " '79 McFarlane Article Holds Clues to Man Today," *Baltimore Sun*, December 20, 1983.

———. "Reagans Keep Life in White House Simple," *Baltimore Sun*, January 29, 1984.

———. "Eight Years: Outsider to Incumbent," *Baltimore Sun*, August 23, 1984.

———. "Staff Shifts Usher in Uncertainty," *Baltimore Sun*, January 20, 1985.

———. "McFarlane Tightens Foreign Policy Grip," *Baltimore Sun*, February 6, 1985.

———. "U.S. Security Adviser Formulating Strategy," *Baltimore Sun*, June 18, 1985.

———. "Trek Toward Summit Started in 1984," *Baltimore Sun*, November 17, 1985.

———. "Reagan Says Arms Control Was Advanced," *Baltimore Sun*, November 22, 1985.

————. "The Shaping of Ollie North," *Baltimore Sun*, December 7, 1986.

————. "Guilt-Ridden McFarlane Was Never a 'Member of the Club,' " *Baltimore Sun*, May 10, 1987.

————. "McFarlane Suggests North Initiated Contra Aid Efforts," *Baltimore Sun*, May 12, 1987.

————. "In Washington's Long Passion Play, Characters Often Lived Up to Their Billing," *Baltimore Sun*, August 9, 1987.

————. "The Private War of Ollie and Jim," *Esquire*, March 1988.

Time. Review of *Fields of Fire*, by James Webb, October 30, 1978.

Toobin, Jeffrey. "Ollie's Next Mission," *The New Yorker*, December 27, 1993.

"Tracking Oliver North," *Life*, May 1987.

Truehart, Charles. "Ollie North's Covert Memoir," *Washington Post*, October 17, 1991.

"Two Leaks, but by Whom?," *Newsweek*, July 27, 1987.

Walcott, John, et al. " 'You Can Run but You Can't Hide,' " *Newsweek*, October 21, 1985.

Warmbold, Ted. "Is the Real War Inside the Naval Academy?," *Los Angeles Herald Examiner*, April 12, 1981.

Washington Times. "An Inappropriate Award" (editorial), June 11, 1986.

Webb, James H. "Roles and Missions: Time for a Change," *Marine Corps Gazette*, March 1972.

————. "Where Do You Fall?," *Quantico Sentry*, July 10, 1970.

————. "Turmoil in Paradise: Micronesia at the Crossroads," *U.S. Naval Institute Proceedings*, July 1972.

————. Letter to Dean Greenhalgh, August 26, 1973, "Re: Our conversation of 20 August regarding Professor Wales's Exam."

————. "The Sad Conviction of Sam Green: The Case for the Reasonable and Honest War Criminal," *Res Ipsa Loquitar: Georgetown Review of Law and Public Interest*, Winter 1974.

————. "The Invisible Vietnam Veteran," *Washington Post*, August 4, 1976.

————. "Muzzling Generals: An 'Arrogant' Act, a Waste of Lives," *Washington Post*, June 11, 1977.

————. "What Viet Vet Needs," *Dallas Morning News*, June 1, 1979.

————. "Women Can't Fight," *The Washingtonian*, November 1979.

————. "The Power of Remembering," *Washington Post*, May 25, 1981.

————. "Reassessing the Vietnam Veterans Memorial," *Wall Street Journal*, December 18, 1981.

————. "When a One-Armed Man Is Not a Loser," *Parade*, November 21, 1982.

————. "What We Can Learn from Japan's Prisons," *Parade*, January 15, 1984.

————. "Viet Vets Didn't Kill Babies and They Aren't Suicidal," *Washington Post*, April 6, 1986.

————. "A Legacy for My Daughter," *Newsweek*, November 7, 1988.

————. "Can He Come Home Again?," *Parade*, April 2, 1989.

————. "Don't Call on the Guard," *Washington Post*, April 13, 1989.

————. "For a Defense That Makes Sense," *New York Times Magazine*, May 21, 1989.

————. "Battlefield Success Doesn't Guarantee Victory," *Wall Street Journal*, January 1, 1991.

————. "Don't Abandon America's Forgotten Allies," *VFW*, September 1991.

————. "Not All the Wounds Have Healed," *Parade*, August 23, 1992.

———. "Lift the Embargo Against Vietnam—Help Old Allies," *Wall Street Journal*, February 2, 1994.

———. "Back to Vietnam," *San Diego Tribune*, February 13, 1994.

———. "The Military Is Not a Social Program," *New York Times*, August 18, 1993.

Weinraub, Bernard. "Carter Hails Veterans of Vietnam in Signing Bill for a War Memorial," *New York Times*, July 2, 1980.

Weisman, Steven R. "A Haig Confidant Gets Post at White House," *New York Times*, January 21, 1982.

———. "Man in the News: New Man on Reagan's Mideast Team: Robert Carl McFarlane," *New York Times*, July 23, 1983.

Weiss, Philip. "Oliver North's Next War," *New York Times Magazine*, July 4, 1993.

West Coast Review of Books. Review of *Fields of Fire*, by James Webb, November 1978.

West, Woodie. "For Honor, Rough Sailing" (review of *A Sense of Honor*, by James Webb), *Washington Star*, March 29, 1981.

Wheeler, John. "Offerings at the Wall," *Washington Post*, September 13, 1992.

Whitaker, Mark. "Confronting the Risks Ahead," *Newsweek*, October 21, 1985.

Wildavsky, Rachel. "Does Oliver North Tell the Truth?," *Reader's Digest*, June 1993.

Will, George F. "Hanoi to Phoenix to Washington," *Washington Post*, February 20, 1986.

Willey, Keven Ann. "Kimball Invades McCain Broadcast: Host Denies Debate Offered; Republican Declines Exchange," *Arizona Republic*, August 20, 1986.

Winfrey, Carey. "Trouble at the Academy" (review of *A Sense of Honor*, by James Webb), *New York Times Book Review*, April 5, 1981.

Wolfe, Tom. "Art Disputes War: The Battle of the Vietnam Memorial," *Washington Post*, October 13, 1982.

Woolsey, R. James. "Honor and Good Sense," *Washington Post*, July 7, 1981.

Wynn, Bernie. "McCain Is Holding Edge in District 1 Campaign; Voter Turnout Will Determine Outcome," *Arizona Republic*, September 4, 1982.

———. "John McCain Showing Savvy Early in Game," *Arizona Republic*, November 28, 1982.

Yardley, Jonathan. "Oliver North's October Surprise," *Washington Post*, October 21, 1991.

INTERVIEWS

At the Woodrow Wilson International Center for Scholars in Washington, D.C., where I spent twenty-two months of the seven years I worked on this book, one of the Fellows recalled an assertion by Lord Acton that any writer who relies heavily on face-to-face discussions with his subjects should continually bear in mind: "The living," Lord Acton said, "do not give up their secrets with the candor of the dead."

Having offered up that caveat, I affirm the obvious. Books, other published materials, and documents were indispensable, but *The Nightingale's Song* is primarily the product of hundreds of hours of interviewing, with the principals as well as with men and women who have known them or were in a position to provide insight into their lives or the events in which they participated. In some cases, those interviews found their way directly into the text of the book. Some interviews provided context and texture, informing the book in important ways even though they are not specifically cited in the text.

By way of apology, I must concede that I took up the time of many people researching the childhoods and growing-up periods, essentially the pre-Annapolis years, of the five principals. This apology is especially directed at the residents of Odon, Indiana, and Philmont, New York, the childhood homes of John Poindexter and Oliver North, respectively. I spent several days in both towns, where men and women who knew or remembered the principals gave generously of their time to assist me. Until the final draft, this book contained individual chapters on each of the principals, based in large measure on those interviews. Deep into the process, my editor told me something that was becoming increasingly clear to me, but which I didn't want to accept. This book, he said, should begin at Annapolis. He was right. He also said that my time had not been wasted, that what I had learned about those early years would inform this book in important ways. I believe he was right about that, too. I hope my friends in Odon and Philmont agree.

As this book was taking shape in my mind, I wrote an article about Jim Webb and Oliver North for the March 1988 *Esquire*, entitled "The Private War of Ollie and Jim." The interviews conducted for that piece played directly into *The Nightingale's Song* and so are listed here. During that same period, I wrote a long profile of Bud McFarlane, who, having survived his suicide attempt, was about to testify before the congressional Iran-Contra investigating committees. Some of those interviews are also cited here. (A few persons to whom I spoke asked not to be identified by name. They had their reasons and I have respected them.)

#Denotes multiple interviews.
*Denotes U.S. Naval Academy graduate.

Lee S. (Sandy) Ainslie, Jr.
*Amb. Richard L. Armitage
Jules Baalog
William B. Bader
The Hon. James A. Baker III
Sgt. Maj. Lloyd R. Banta, USMC (Ret.)
Mary Jane (Choate) Bardos
*Col. William D. Bauer, USMC (Ret.)
*Cdr. Stephen E. Becker, USN (Ret.)
Robert Bedingfield
*Ronald Benigo
*#Rear Adm. Dennis C. Blair, USN
Felix Boehm
Lisa Boepple
*H. Glenn Boggs
Eric H. Bowen
Robert Bowes
*#Lt. Gen Edward J. Bronars, USMC (Ret.)
*Capt. Nicholas Brown, USN (Ret.)
*Lt. Cdr. Robert A. Burns, USNR
Horace Busby
*Cdr. Robert K. Caldwell, USN (Ret.)
Patrick Henry Callaway
*Vice Adm. James F. Calvert, USN (Ret.)
Jean Carl
The Hon. Frank C. Carlucci
#Lynore (White) Carnes
Thomas Carothers
*Col. Roy L. Carter, USMC (Ret.)
*Lt. Cdr. Michael S. Case, USNRR
Col. Gino Castignetti, USMC (Ret.)
Scott Celley
U.S. Sen. John H. Chafee
#Carl R. (Spitz) Channell
*Col. Roger G. Charles, USMC (Ret.)
#Victoria (Torie) Clarke

U.S. Sen. William S. Cohen
Col. Pat Collins, USMC (Ret.)
#Milton Copulos
#Lt. Col. William R. Corson, USMC (Ret.)
Cdr. Daniel J. Costello, USN (Ret.)
*Lt. Col. William V. Cowan III, USMC (Ret.)
Charles Crane
The Hon. Lorne Craner
Lt. Col Robert J. Dalton, USMC (Ret.)
*Capt. Thomas M. Daly, USN (Ret.)
Mitchell E. Daniels, Jr.
Amb. Nathaniel Davis
Col. George E. (Bud) Day, USAF (Ret.) and Doris Day
#Michael K. Deaver
William Riley Deeble III
#Amb. Robert S. Dillon
*Capt. John James Dittrick, Jr., USN (Ret.)
Frank Dixon
Capt. John Dolaghan, USN-Chaplains Corps (Ret.)
Robert Doubek
Col. Andrew Dougherty, USAF (Ret.)
#First Lt. Frederick L. Downs, Jr., USA (Ret.)
*Robert H. Drozd
#Rear Adm. Philip A. Dur, USN
*Adm. Leon A. Edney, USN (Ret.)
Richard P. Ellinger
Capt. Kent W. Ewing, USN
*Col. Fred T. Fagan Jr., USMC (Ret.)
James Fallows
*Dr. Helmuts A. Feifs
Rear Adm. Jimmie B. Finkelstein, USN (Ret.)

*#Capt. James R. (Ron) Fisher, USN (Ret.)

Lt. Col. John G. (Mike) Flynn, USMC (Ret.)

Roger W. Fontaine

Hal Foster

*#Capt. Frank Gamboa, USN (Ret.)

State Sen. Denzil Garrison

Maj. Gen. Shlomo Gazit, Israeli Defense Forces (Ret.)

James Gehrdes

Thomas Gibbons

*Cdr. Joseph Christopher Glutting, USN

#Col. Paul B. Goodwin, USMC (Ret.)

James Grasso

Donald Greene

*Col. John E. Greenwood, USMC (Ret.)

Wes A. Gullett

Joseph and Irma Haag

*Rear Adm. Howard W. Habermeyer, Jr., USN (Ret.)

Brig. Gen. Jerome T. Hagen, USMC (Ret.)

*H. Keith Haines II

*Vice Adm. C. Thor Hanson, USN (Ret.)

Nancy Hardy

First Lt. William C. Haskell, USMC (Ret.)

Col. David Haughey, USMC (Ret.)

*Cdr. Thomas Hayes, USN (Ret.)

*Col. John W. (Bill) Hemingway, USMC (Ret.)

Herb Henrikson

DeLores Hermance

Dr. Peter Hermance

The Hon. John S. Herrington

Randy Herrod

Lt. Col. Charles Hester, USMC (Ret.)

#Capt. Herb Hetu, USN (Ret.)

*#Rear Adm. Clarence A. (Mark) Hill Jr., USN (Ret.)

*#Vice Adm. M. Staser Holcomb, USN (Ret.)

John R. Holden

*#Adm. James L. Holloway III, USN (Ret.)

*Col. John J. (Jack) Holly, USMC

*Lt. Col. William C. Holmberg, USMC (Ret.)

Samuel C. O. Holt

Cdr. Phillip G. Hough, USNRR

Kenneth Hudson

The Hon. Frank N. Ikard

Arnold Isaacs

Les Janka

#William Jayne

Brig. Gen. Harry W. Jenkins, Jr., USMC

Capt. Oleg Jenkovic, USN (Ret.)

Kenneth (Nip) Jensen

*Cdr. Jacob Lee Johnson, Jr., USN (Ret.)

Mildred Johnson

Maj. Gen. James L. Jones, USMC

Gen. P. X. Kelley, USMC (Ret.)

Geoffrey Kemp

George A. Keyworth II

*Adm. Isaac C. Kidd, Jr., USN (Ret.)

Capt. Will King, USN (Ret.)

John Kolbe

Thomas Korologos

*Rear Adm. Alexander J. Krekich, USN

*#Gen. Charles C. Krulak, USMC

*Capt. John Francis (Jake) Laboon, Jr., S.J. USN-CHC (Ret.)

James Lake

Albert A. (Pete) Lakeland, Jr.

*Adm. Charles R. Larson, USN

Richard Laughlin

Diane (Rauch) Lawrence

*Vice Adm. William P. Lawrence, USN (Ret.)

The Hon. John F. Lehman, Jr.

*Capt. Harold S. Lewis, USN (Ret.)

*Maj. Michael T. Lundblad, USMC (Ret.)

Maj. Gil A. Macklin, USMC (Ret.)

Col. Robert MacPherson, USMC

Angus McBryde

#Carol McCain

Cindy McCain

*#U.S. Sen. John S. McCain III

Joseph P. McCain

Roberta McCain

*Cdr. Harry E. McConnell, USN (Ret.)

Capt. Rodney B. McDaniel, USN (Ret.)

C. Robert (Big Mac) McDowell

Lela (Core) McElravy

Jonda McFarlane

Laurie McFarlane

Melissa McFarlane
*#Lt. Col. Robert C. McFarlane, USMC (Ret.)
Capt. William D. McFarlane, Jr., USNR
Mac (Little Mac) McGarvey
*The Hon. James F. McGovern
William McGovren
Col. Fred McGrath, USMC (Ret.)
*#Col. John C. McKay, USMC
*John R. McKee, Jr.
Tamma (Webb) McKee
*Capt. Richard B. McKenna, USN
Donald E. Mathes
Gail and Malcolm Matheson III
Constantine C. Menges
F. Andrew Messing, Jr.
Margaret (Peggy) Montague
Don Moore
Rudolf L. Mössbauer
Florence Mossman
#Mayor Philip (Po) Mossman
Daniel H. Mudd
Michael Murphy
*Capt. Richard G. Murphy, USN (Ret.)
*Brig. Gen. Terrence P. Murray, USMC
John L. Myers
Sue Ann Myers
Richard E. Neustadt
Amb. Paul H. Nitze
Peggy Noonan
*#Lt. Col. Oliver L. North, USMC (Ret.)
Jeremiah O'Leary
Gladys Oles
*Col. Reid H. Olson, USMC
Richmond O'Neill
Bentley Orrick
Stanley Ostazewski
Harry R. Palmer, Jr.
*Lt. Cdr. Thomas L. Parker, USNR
Fulvia Partridge
Lela Pate
*George M. Pease
*Rear Adm. Kendell M. Pease, Jr., USN
*#Col. Frederick C. Peck, USMC
*H. Ross Perot
Allen Carleton Phillips, Jr.
Mary (McFarlane) Pitcock

*Capt. Joseph Charles Plumb, Jr., USNRR
Ellen Poindexter
*#Rear Adm. John M. Poindexter, USN (Ret.)
#The Rev. Linda Poindexter
#Richard R. (Dickie Ray) Poindexter
#Col. Donald L. Price, USMC (Ret.)
Daniel B. Rathbun
David Reed
The Hon. Donald T. Regan
Florence Reiling
Peter Reiss
Amb. James M. Rentschler
*Lt. Col. Victor F. Reston, USMC (Ret.)
Nancy Reynolds
Howard Rhodes
William Richards
F. Rives Richey
Gov. Tom Ridge
*Ray A. Roberts
Russell Robertson
Peter Rodman
Edward J. Rollins
Lt. Col. Ralph Rosaker, USMC (Ret.)
*Capt. John M. (Jack) Rose, USN
Dale Rowe
Vivian Rowe
Harvey B. Safeer
Barbara (DuCote) Samorajczyk
*Col. John F. Sattler, USMC
Col. John C. Scharfen, USMC (Ret.)
Sally S. Schulze
The Hon. Brent Scowcroft
Jan C. Scruggs
#Carlton Sherwood
*Capt. Edwin A. (Ned) Shuman III, USN (Ret.)
*Cdr. David F. (Frank) Simmons, USN (Ret.)
The Hon. Robert B. Sims, also Capt. USN (Ret.)
*John R. Sinclair
Karna Small
Carl M. Smith
#Coach Emerson Smith
#J. Brian (Jay) Smith
Larry M. Speakes

Sam Stanton
*Rear Adm. James R. Stark, USN
Barbara (McFarlane) Staton
Col. Peter Stenner, USMC
Maj. William C. Stensland, USMC (Ret.)
Vice Adm. James B. Stockdale, USN (Ret.)
Carval J. Stotts
Laura (Russell) Strain
*Col. Whitmel B. Swain, USAF (Ret.)
Joel L. Swerdlow
#Col. Orson G. Swindle, USMC (Ret.)
Freida Tarvin
Lt. Col. Victor Taylor, USMC (Ret.)
#Howard Teicher
*Lt. Cdr. Walter M. Teichgraber, USN (Ret.)
W. Dennis Thomas
Cdr. Paul B. Thompson, USN
*Vice Adm. Nils R. Thunman, USN (Ret.)
Lt. Gen. Bernard E. Trainor, USMC (Ret.)
Col. Konrad Trautman, USAF (Ret.)
*Mark C. Treanor

Candace (Poindexter) Treibic
Ernest Tuten
*Cdr. Harlan K. Ullman, USN (Ret.)
Eric Van Deusen
Col. Jack Van Loan, USAF (Ret.)
John Van Scholten
Heathcote Wales
Glenn Warner, Jr.
Glenn Warner, Sr.
James H. Warner
U.S. Sen. John W. Warner
Gary Webb
*Capt. George J. Webb, Jr., USN
*#Capt. James H. Webb, Jr., USMC (Ret.)
Col. James H. Webb, Sr., USAF (Ret.)
The Hon. Caspar W. Weinberger
Bernard Weinraub
Annette Shutts Wells
Gen. William C. Westmoreland, USA (Ret.)
John P. Wheeler III
Craig Whitney
Dale Wilson
#Col. Michael Wyly, USMC (Ret.)

ACKNOWLEDGMENTS

I began thinking about this book almost from the moment the Iran-Contra affair erupted. At first, I thought I wanted to write about the scandal itself, but I soon realized that the involvement of Bud McFarlane, John Poindexter, and Oliver North was what interested me most—and not just because of our common Naval Academy roots, but also because of the Vietnam War and what it had meant to a generation.

As I tried to puzzle out what I might have to say, *Esquire* commissioned an article about North at Annapolis. The piece was quickly expanded to include North's classmate Jim Webb, who had just become Secretary of the Navy. "The Private War of Ollie and Jim," published in March 1988, helped to clarify my thinking about the book. Much of that clarity, as well as fine editing, was provided by my editor at *Esquire*, David Hirshey.

Full-time work on the book began in June 1988, when I took a one-year leave of absence from the Washington bureau of the *Baltimore Sun*, my professional home since 1973. I returned to the *Sun* more than five years later, in October 1993, still not finished. No amount of thanks can repay my bosses and colleagues for their forbearance during that period. In particular, my thanks to John S. Carroll, editor; James Houck, former managing editor; Kathryn Christensen, former managing editor; William K. Marimow, associate managing editor; Paul West, Washington bureau chief; Frank Starr, former Washington bureau chief; Edwin Goodpaster, national editor; Gilbert Watson, metropolitan editor; and Eileen Canzian, state editor.

Eventually it came down to my wife's salary and a home equity credit line, but I had substantial financial assistance for a long time. For twenty-two months, from June 1989 through March 1991, my work was supported by a fellowship at the Woodrow Wilson International Center for Scholars in Washington, D.C. There can be no finer place to research and write a book. Thanks for help and encouragement to Charles Blitzer, Sam Wells, Jon Yellin, Phil Cook, Mike Lacey, Robert Litwak, Zed David, Lawrence Lichdy, Jeff Paine, Jay Tolson, Anne Sheffield, Fran Hunter, and many others. The Wilson Center also provided me with a string of bright, engaging, and energetic research assistants—Josh Lauring, Wayne Safro, Malia Adler, Will Culver, and David Stearns. The community of Fellows and Guest Scholars served as consistent intellectual stimulation. Special thanks to Shlomo Gazit, Charles Griswold, Bob Donovan, Ray Scherer, Martin Kramer, Menahem Milson, Ron Crocombe, Martin Schramm, Joel Swerdlow, and Frances Gouda.

Helping enormously to underwrite my work at the Wilson Center was the Florence and John Schumann Foundation, headed by Bill Moyers. Peter Kovler also arranged a most helpful grant from the Marjorie Kovler Fund.

The Wilson Center fellowship and support from the Schumann Foundation were forthcoming in large measure because of the caliber of men who supported my application—author David Halberstam and Harvard professors Richard E. Neustadt and Ernest R. May.

The Naval Academy provided valuable assistance through its public affairs office, particularly PAOs Steve Becker and Mike John. Noel Milan, an assistant PAO, helped as well. The assistance of Jane Price at the Academy Archives was invaluable.

Thanks also to Caroline Scullin, Bud McFarlane's executive assistant; Mark Salter, Scott Celley, and Didi Blackwood in John McCain's senatorial office; and Marsha Fishbaugh in Oliver North's office.

Mary Drake and her crack team of stenographers provided accurate and timely transcribing of hundreds of interviews, many quite sensitive. Anne Q. Hoy, then with the *Arizona Gazette*, now of *Congressional Quarterly*, shared with me pertinent portions of her files on John McCain. The late Richard (Dickie Ray) Poindexter showed me around Odon, in the process providing his idiosyncratic view of the town and his more straitlaced cousin. Philip (Po) Mossman, the mayor of Philmont, New York, pointed me in all the right directions in Oliver North's hometown and in the evenings served up much-welcomed cold beer at his tavern on Main Street.

Every writer who undertakes a project of the scope of *The Nightingale's Song* remembers with special gratitude and affection a handful of people who were always there when it mattered most—scrambling, facilitating, encouraging. In my case, they were Torie Clarke, whom I met when she was John McCain's press secretary, and Colonel Fred Peck, first encountered as the press spokesman at Headquarters, Marine Corps. On the eve of his departure for Somalia in 1992 he broke off packing to run down some elusive telephone numbers for me. I didn't ask him to do it. He did it, I'm convinced, just to show me he could. Encouragement when it counted also came from my agent, Philippa Brophy. She can walk point for me anytime.

My friend and onetime rival at the *Baltimore Sun*, Richard Ben Cramer, encouraged this project from start to finish. Ernest (Pat) Furgurson, the *Sun*'s distinguished former Washington bureau chief and the most fluid writer I know, read the manuscript and offered scores of valuable suggestions. Dominick Anfuso, my editor at Simon & Schuster, edited with a light touch until it came time to weigh in. Then he did, powerfully. Thanks to special friends Tommy Wall, Minor Carter, Wayne Safro, Cy Avara, and Sid DeSantis for their kindness and generosity of spirit.

Michael Himowitz, a fine reporter and editor at the *Baltimore Sun*, sent me to the store with a letter that began, "This man is a computer idiot. Please give him the following. . . ." He than drove 100 miles to set me up with whatever it is they gave me, and generously fielded many frantic late-night phone calls when, despite his best efforts, I screwed things up anyway.

In addition to my researchers at the Wilson Center, valuable freelance research assistance was provided by my son Craig Timberg and my daughter, Amanda Timberg, and Robert Fahs, who at this writing is about to receive his doctorate from the University of Hawaii. My oldest son, Scott Timberg, read the penultimate manuscript and offered extraordinarily detailed and cogent criticism. Fred Monyak, Nelson Schwartz, Kristin Kimball, and Casandra Jones pitched in at the end, when their help was much needed. My youngest son, Sam, now ten, let me help coach his baseball team for four years, thus affording me a grip, however tenuous, on a better world than the one I was exploring, and typed the last word of the manuscript.

This book would never have been written had it not been for Jane Benson Timberg and Dr. Lynn Ketcham.

My wife, Kelley Andrews, kept me going throughout this long, at times trying period. She served as organizer, facilitator, and editor, reading every word of every chapter in all their incarnations, invariably offering perceptive advice, all the while running the house, attending to Sam, and working a full-time job. She had many reasons to complain, but she never did, not once. That qualifies her for sainthood. Thank God she's no saint.

All five principals gave greatly of their time to this project with no assurances that the final product would be to their liking, as I'm certain many parts of it are not. To all five, and the hundreds of other men and women who found time for me, my sincere thanks and deep appreciation. If this book matters, they are a large part of the reason. Any errors or omissions are mine.

Finally, undying gratitude to my true friends, defined as those who quickly and mercifully learned to avoid greeting me with the words "How's the book going?"

INDEX

ABOUT THE AUTHOR

Robert Timberg graduated from the United States Naval Academy in 1964 and was commissioned a second lieutenant in the Marine Corps. He served with the First Marine Division in South Vietnam from March 1966 to February 1967.

Timberg has been a newspaper reporter for the past twenty-five years. From 1973 to 1981 he worked for the *Baltimore Evening Sun*. In 1981 he joined the Washington bureau of the *Baltimore Sun*. From 1983 to 1988 he was the *Sun*'s White House correspondent. In 1986 he was awarded the Aldo Beckman Award, given annually by the White House Correspondents Association for excellence in covering the White House. He is currently deputy chief of the *Sun*'s Washington bureau.

Timberg holds a master's degree in journalism from Stanford. He was a Nieman Fellow at Harvard and a Fellow at the Woodrow Wilson International Center for Scholars in Washington, D.C.

In addition to daily reporting, Timberg has contributed articles to *Esquire*, the *Washington Journalism Review*, and *Nieman Reports*.

He lives with his wife, Kelley Andrews, a federal government official, and youngest son, Sam, in Bethesda, Maryland. He has three older children, Scott and Craig, both newspaper reporters, and Amanda, a senior in college.